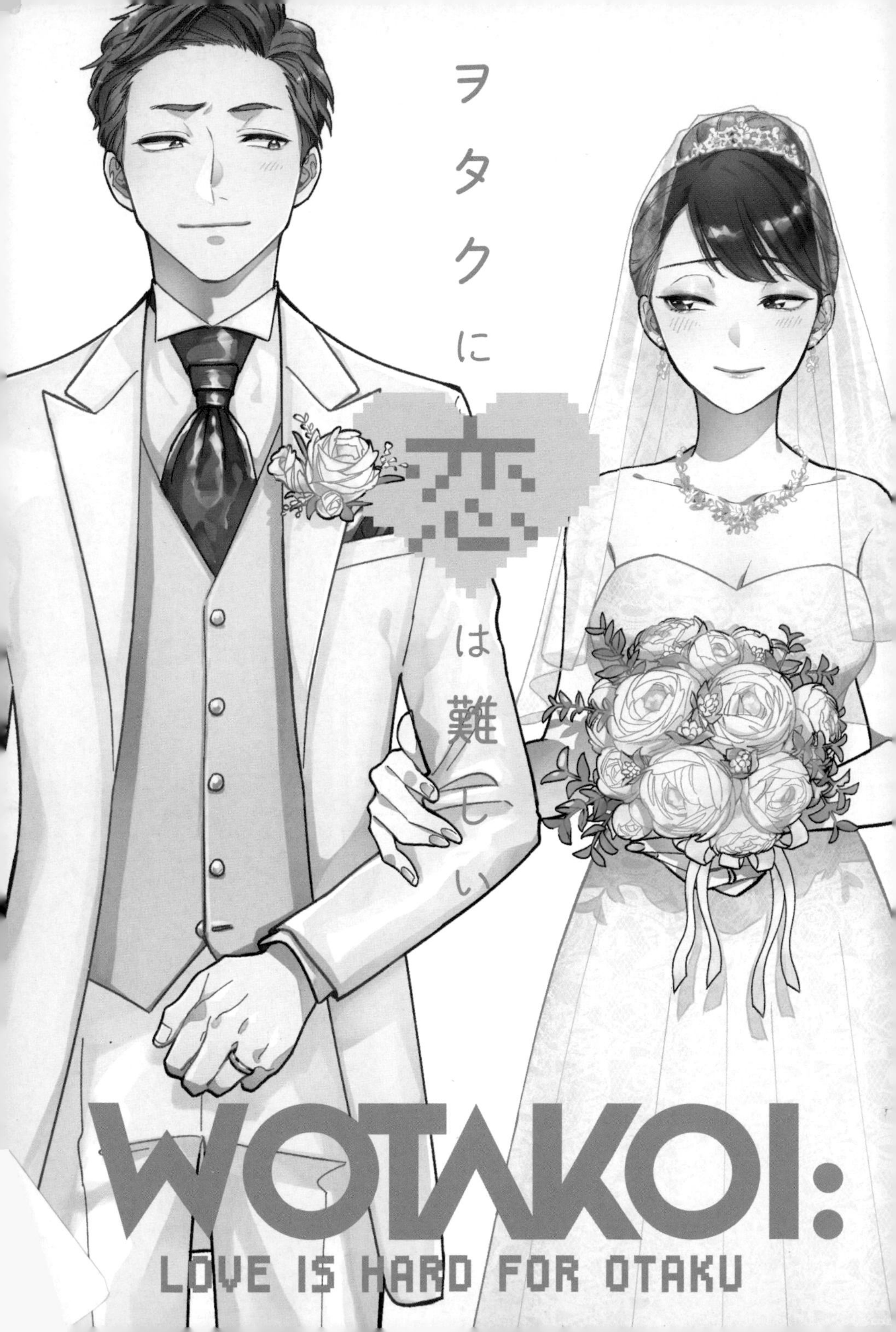
ヲタクに恋は難しい
WOTAKOI:
LOVE IS HARD FOR OTAKU

WOTAKOI:
LOVE IS HARD FOR OTAKU

FUJITA

Episode....62

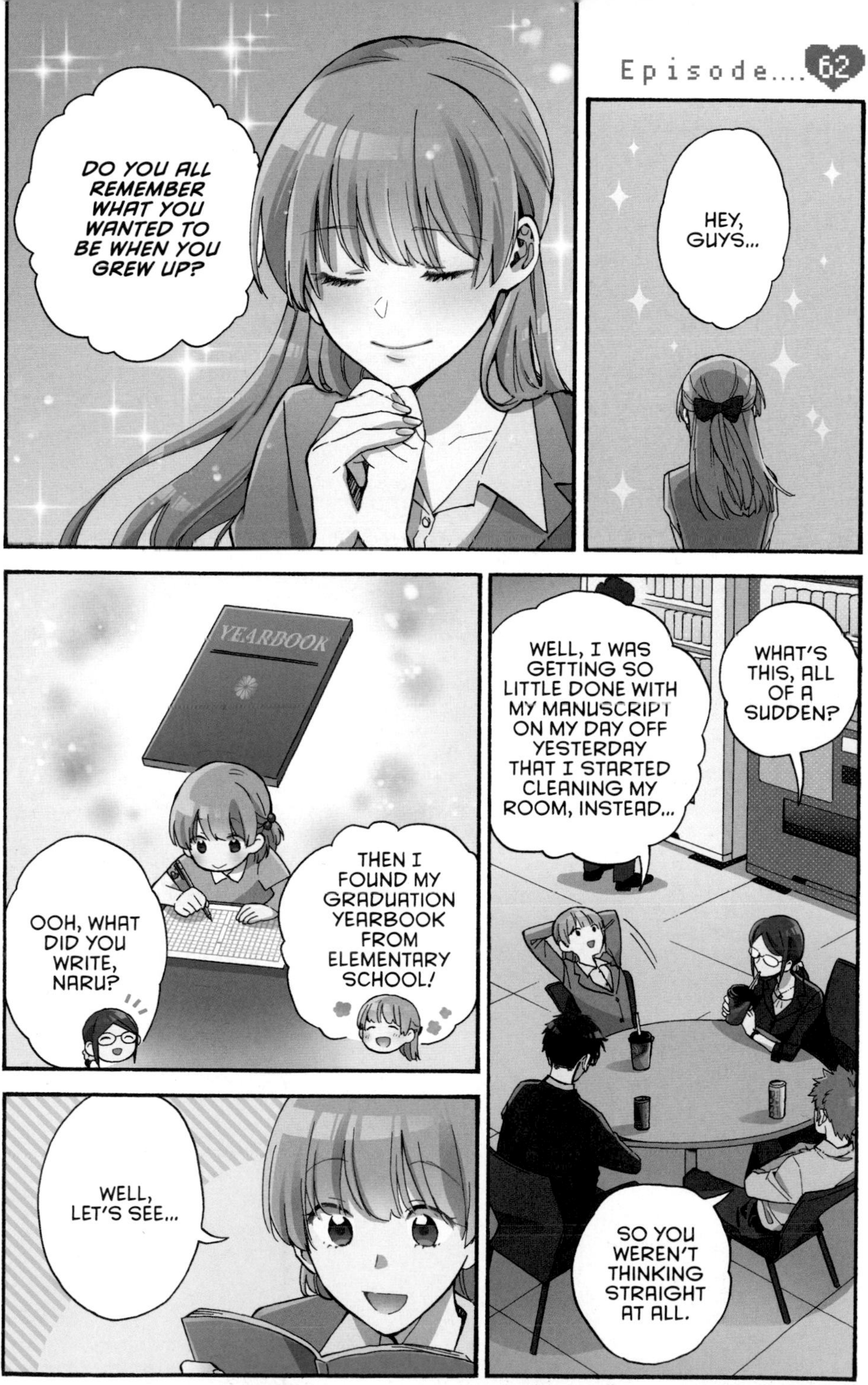
HEY, GUYS...
DO YOU ALL REMEMBER WHAT YOU WANTED TO BE WHEN YOU GREW UP?
WHAT'S THIS, ALL OF A SUDDEN?
WELL, I WAS GETTING SO LITTLE DONE WITH MY MANUSCRIPT ON MY DAY OFF YESTERDAY THAT I STARTED CLEANING MY ROOM, INSTEAD...
SO YOU WEREN'T THINKING STRAIGHT AT ALL.
YEARBOOK
THEN I FOUND MY GRADUATION YEARBOOK FROM ELEMENTARY SCHOOL!
OOH, WHAT DID YOU WRITE, NARU?
WELL, LET'S SEE...

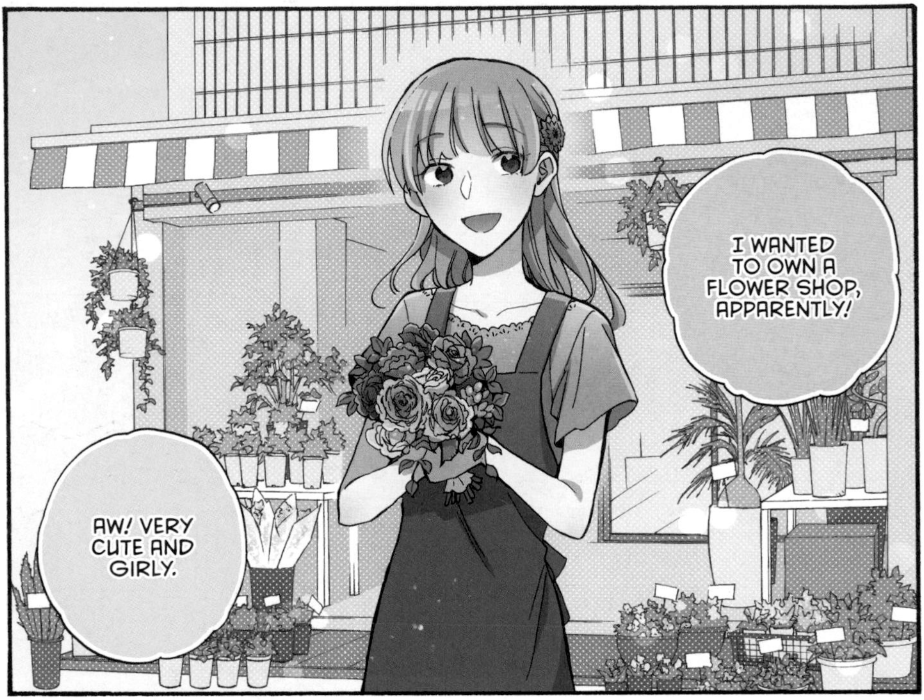
I WANTED TO OWN A FLOWER SHOP, APPARENTLY!
AW! VERY CUTE AND GIRLY.

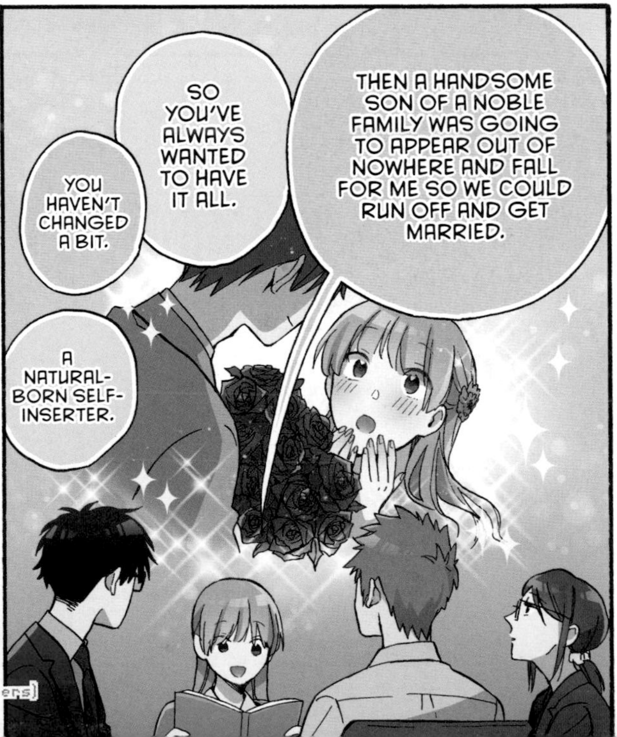
THEN A HANDSOME SON OF A NOBLE FAMILY WAS GOING TO APPEAR OUT OF NOWHERE AND FALL FOR ME SO WE COULD RUN OFF AND GET MARRIED.
SO YOU'VE ALWAYS WANTED TO HAVE IT ALL.
YOU HAVEN'T CHANGED A BIT.
A NATURAL-BORN SELF-INSERTER.

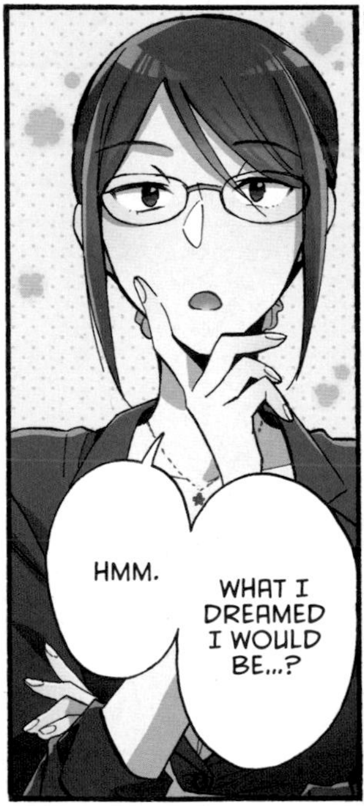
WHAT I DREAMED I WOULD BE...?
HMM.

 (A staunch head full of flowers)

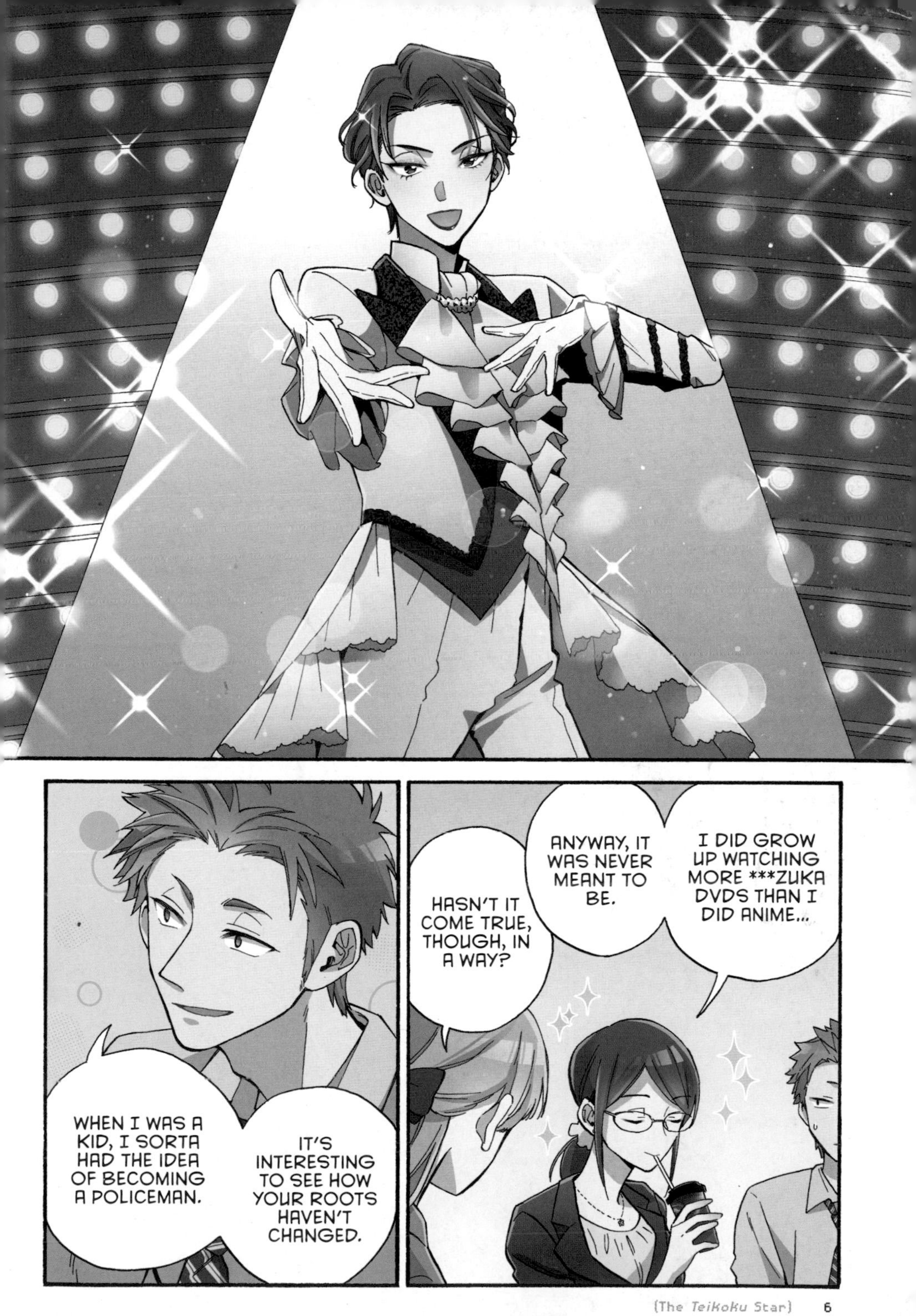
I DID GROW UP WATCHING MORE ***ZUKA DVDS THAN I DID ANIME...
ANYWAY, IT WAS NEVER MEANT TO BE.
HASN'T IT COME TRUE, THOUGH, IN A WAY?
IT'S INTERESTING TO SEE HOW YOUR ROOTS HAVEN'T CHANGED.
WHEN I WAS A KID, I SORTA HAD THE IDEA OF BECOMING A POLICEMAN.

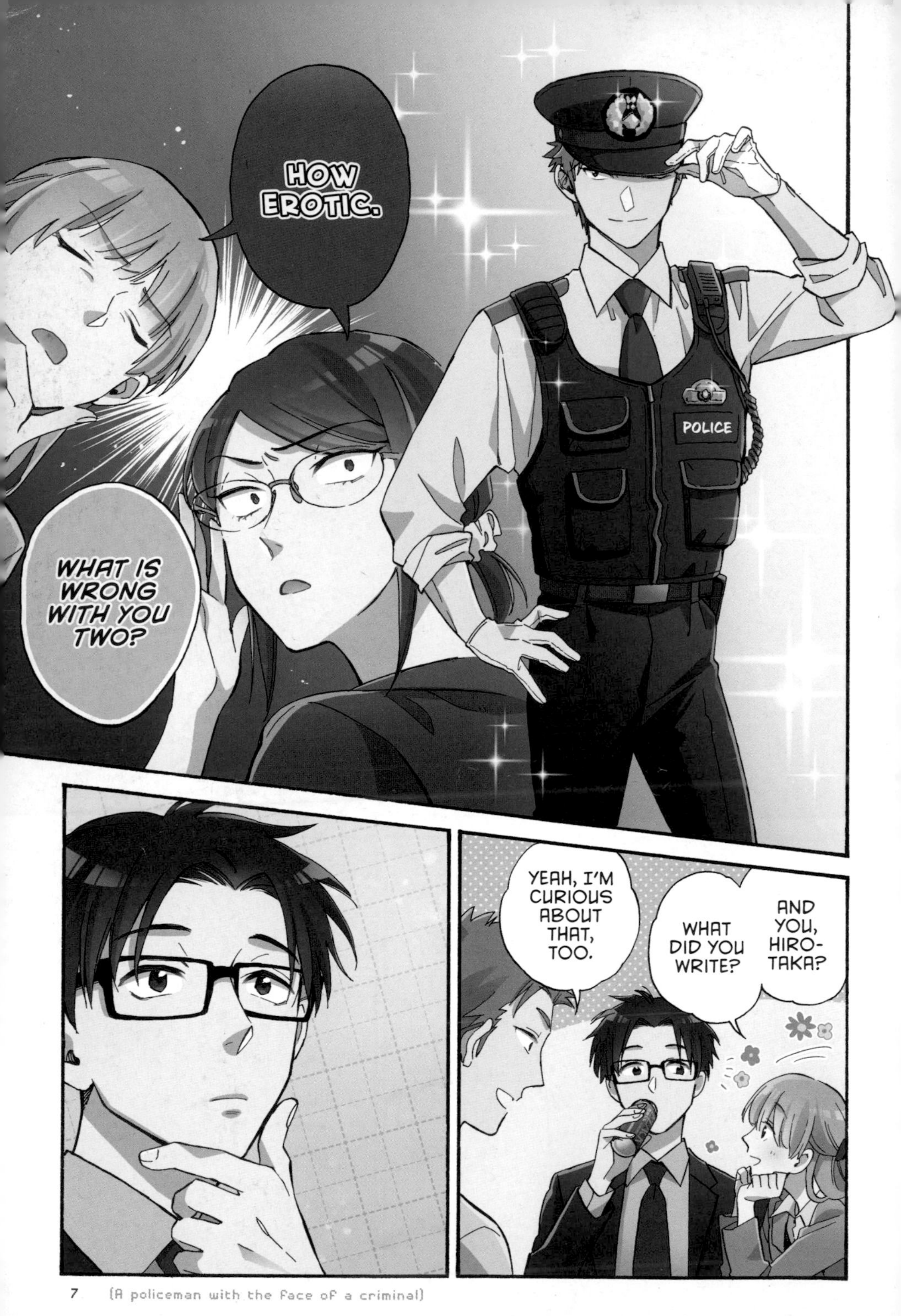
HOW EROTIC.
POLICE
WHAT IS WRONG WITH YOU TWO?
AND YOU, HIRO-TAKA?
WHAT DID YOU WRITE?
YEAH, I'M CURIOUS ABOUT THAT, TOO.

(A policeman with the face of a criminal)

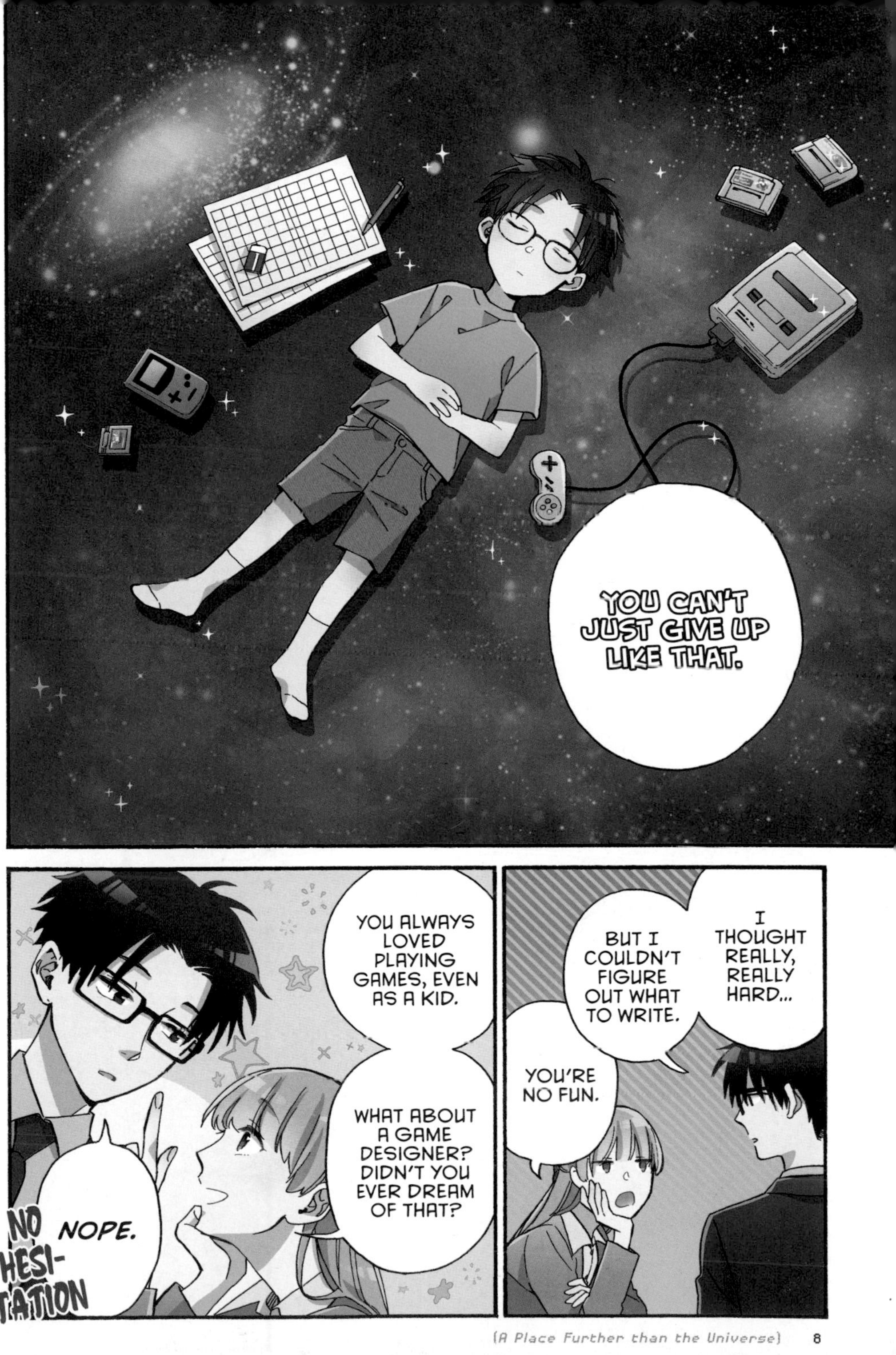
YOU CAN'T JUST GIVE UP LIKE THAT.
I THOUGHT REALLY, REALLY HARD...
BUT I COULDN'T FIGURE OUT WHAT TO WRITE.
YOU'RE NO FUN.
YOU ALWAYS LOVED PLAYING GAMES, EVEN AS A KID.
WHAT ABOUT A GAME DESIGNER? DIDN'T YOU EVER DREAM OF THAT?
NOPE.
NO HESI-TATION

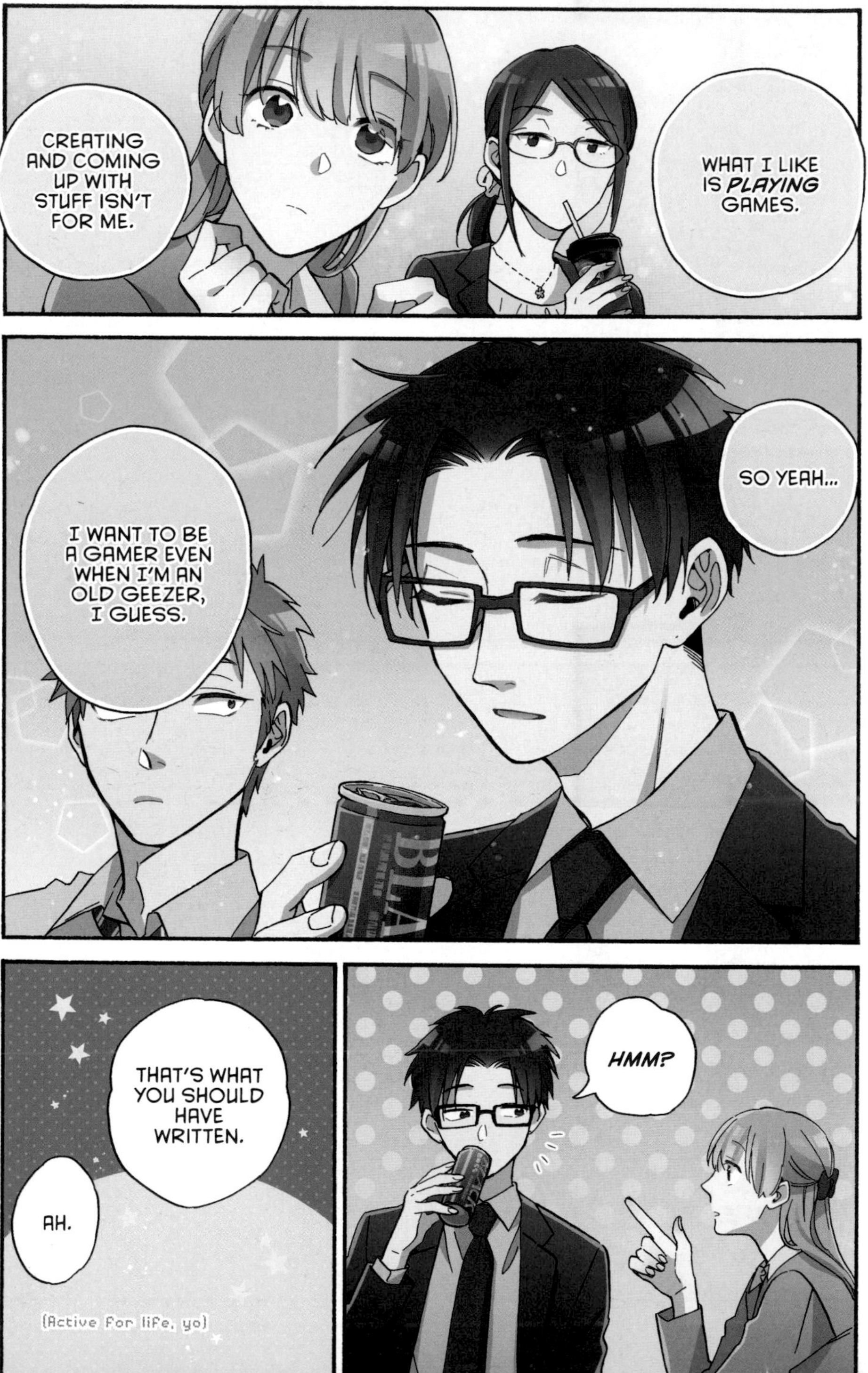
WHAT I LIKE IS *PLAYING* GAMES.
CREATING AND COMING UP WITH STUFF ISN'T FOR ME.
SO YEAH...
I WANT TO BE A GAMER EVEN WHEN I'M AN OLD GEEZER, I GUESS.
HMM?
THAT'S WHAT YOU SHOULD HAVE WRITTEN.
AH.
(Active for life, yo)

BONUS CONTENT

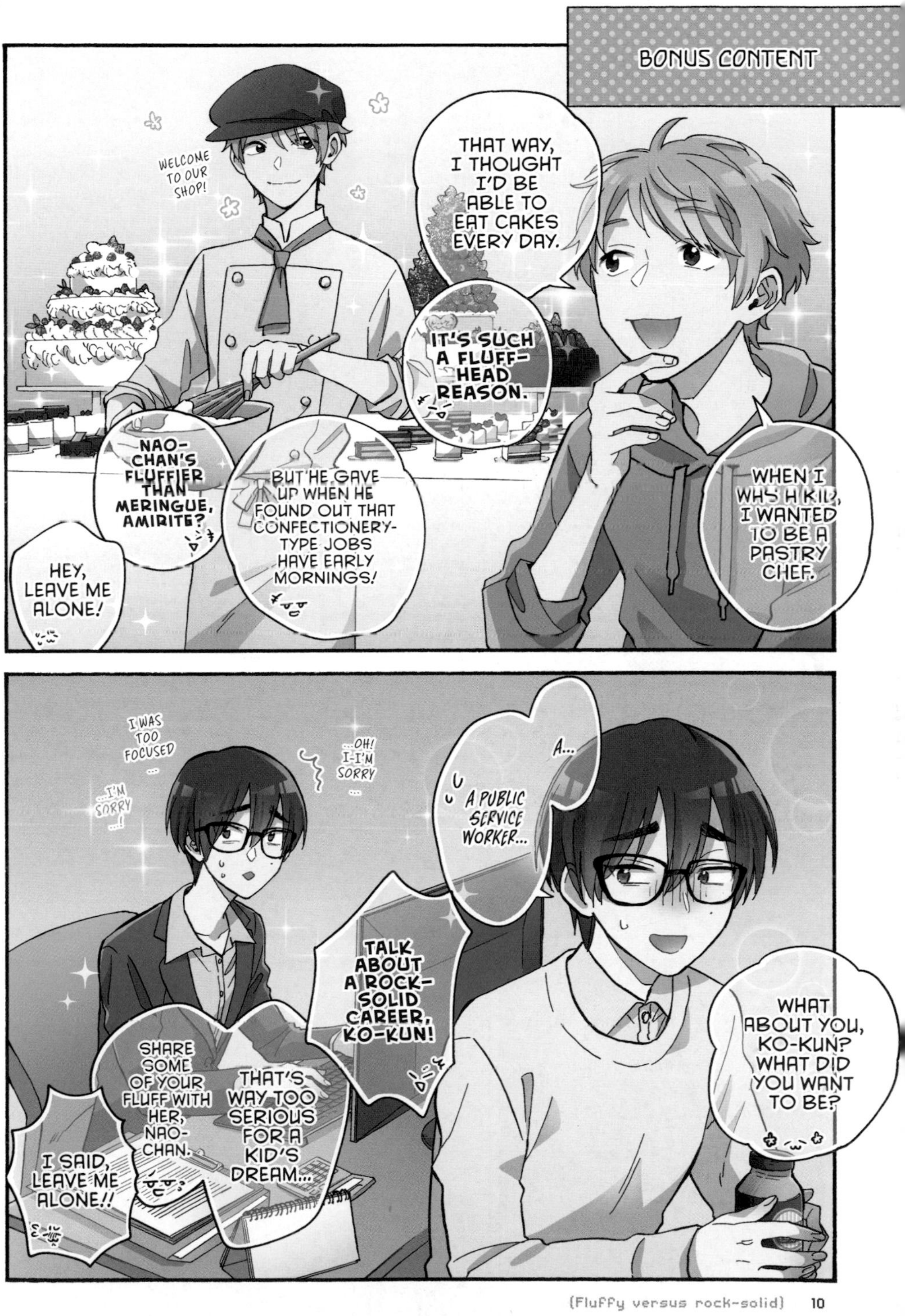
WHEN I WAS A KID, I WANTED TO BE A PASTRY CHEF.
THAT WAY, I THOUGHT I'D BE ABLE TO EAT CAKES EVERY DAY.
IT'S SUCH A FLUFF-HEAD REASON.
WELCOME TO OUR SHOP!
BUT HE GAVE UP WHEN HE FOUND OUT THAT CONFECTIONERY-TYPE JOBS HAVE EARLY MORNINGS!
NAO-CHAN'S FLUFFIER THAN MERINGUE, AMIRITE?
HEY, LEAVE ME ALONE!
WHAT ABOUT YOU, KO-KUN? WHAT DID YOU WANT TO BE?
A...
A PUBLIC SERVICE WORKER...
TALK ABOUT A ROCK-SOLID CAREER, KO-KUN!
...OH! I-I'M SORRY...
I WAS TOO FOCUSED...
...I'M SORRY...!
THAT'S WAY TOO SERIOUS FOR A KID'S DREAM...
SHARE SOME OF YOUR FLUFF WITH HER, NAO-CHAN.
I SAID, LEAVE ME ALONE!!

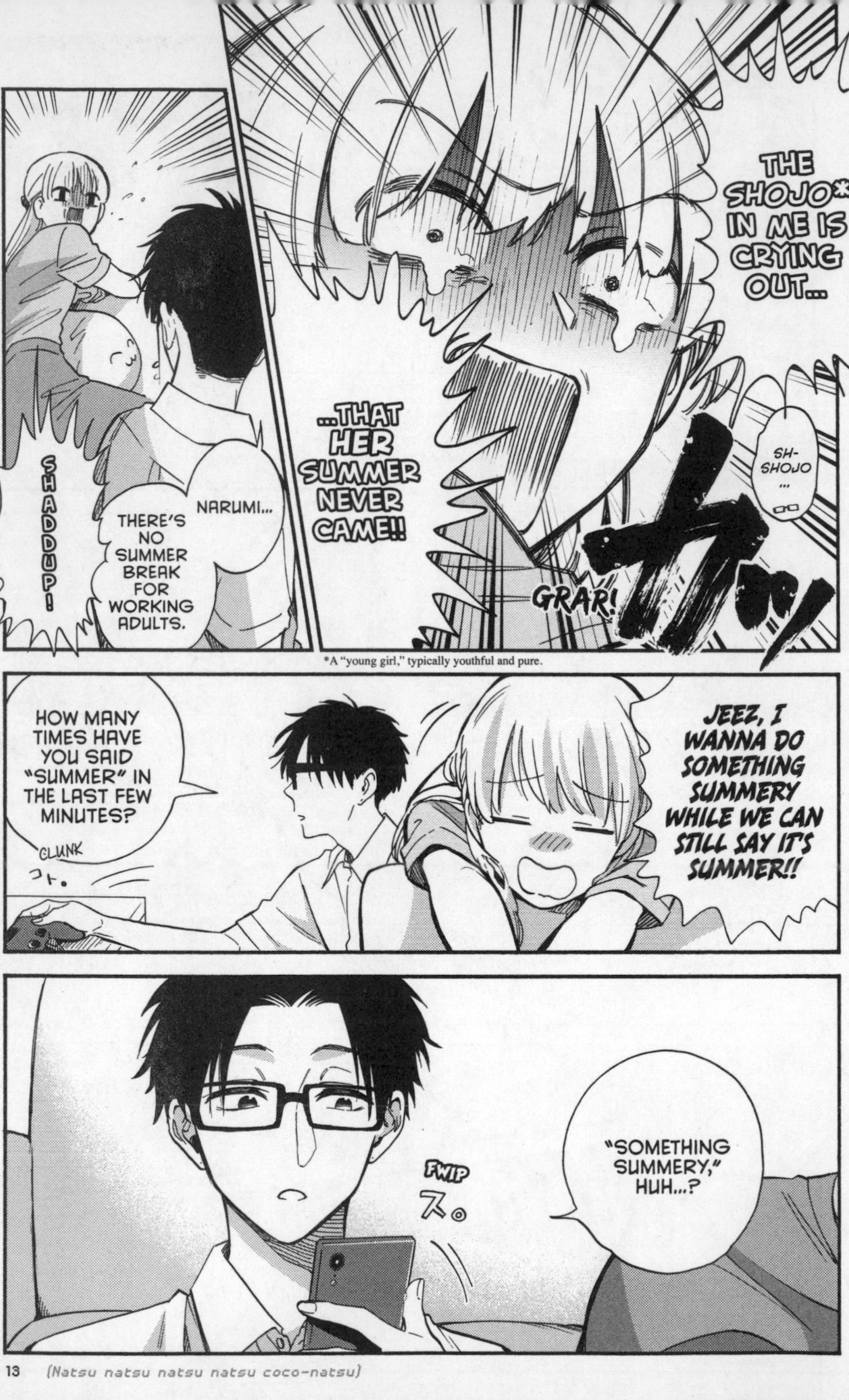
THE SHOJO* IN ME IS CRYING OUT...
...THAT HER SUMMER NEVER CAME!!
SH-SHOJO...
GRAR!
NARUMI... THERE'S NO SUMMER BREAK FOR WORKING ADULTS.
SHADDUP!
JEEZ, I WANNA DO SOMETHING SUMMERY WHILE WE CAN STILL SAY IT'S SUMMER!!
HOW MANY TIMES HAVE YOU SAID "SUMMER" IN THE LAST FEW MINUTES?
CLUNK
"SOMETHING SUMMERY," HUH...?
FWIP

*A "young girl," typically youthful and pure.

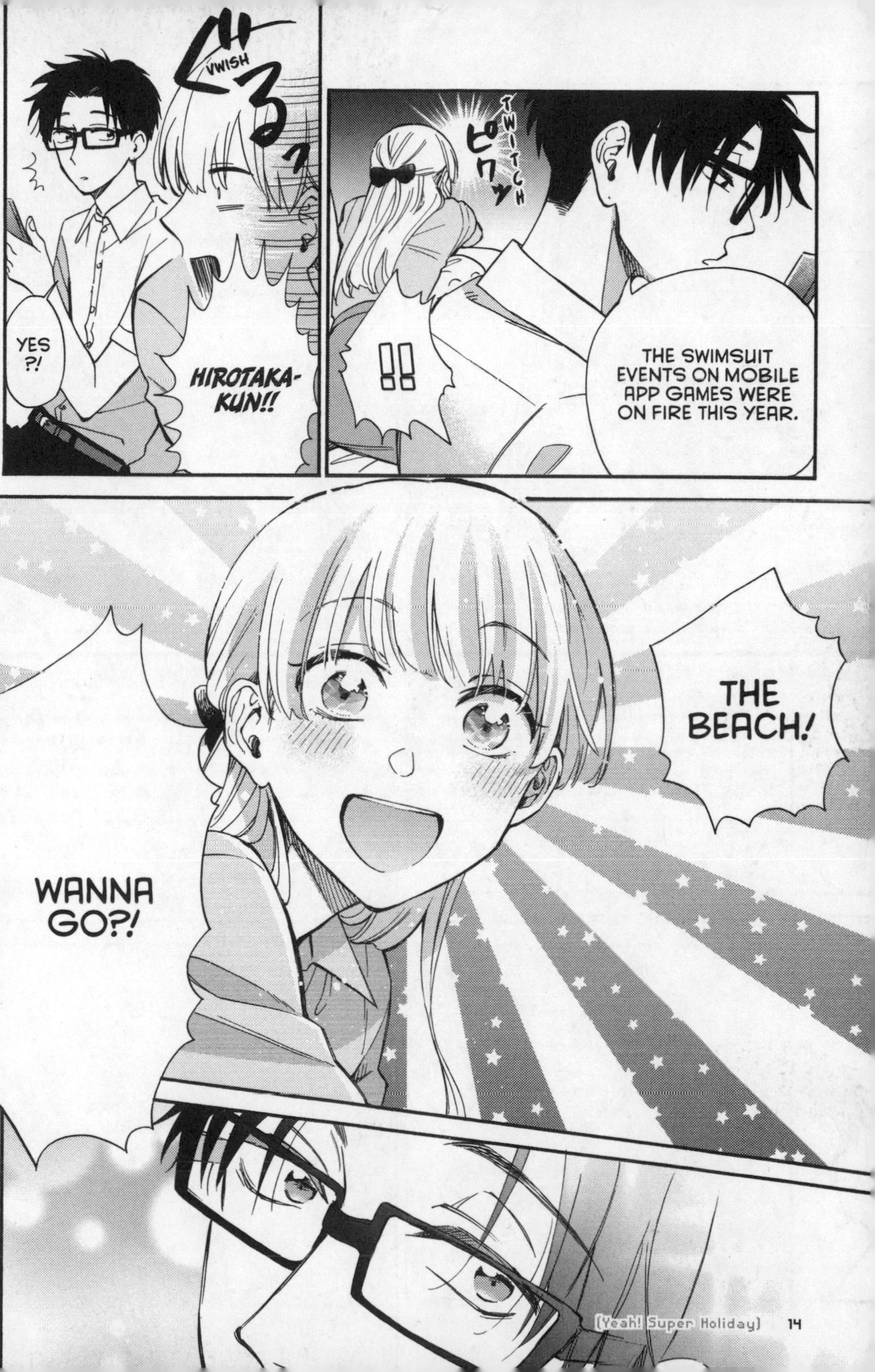
THE SWIMSUIT EVENTS ON MOBILE APP GAMES WERE ON FIRE THIS YEAR.
ピクッ
TWITCH
!!
ぐるっ
VWISH
HIROTAKA-KUN!!
YES?!
THE BEACH!
WANNA GO?!

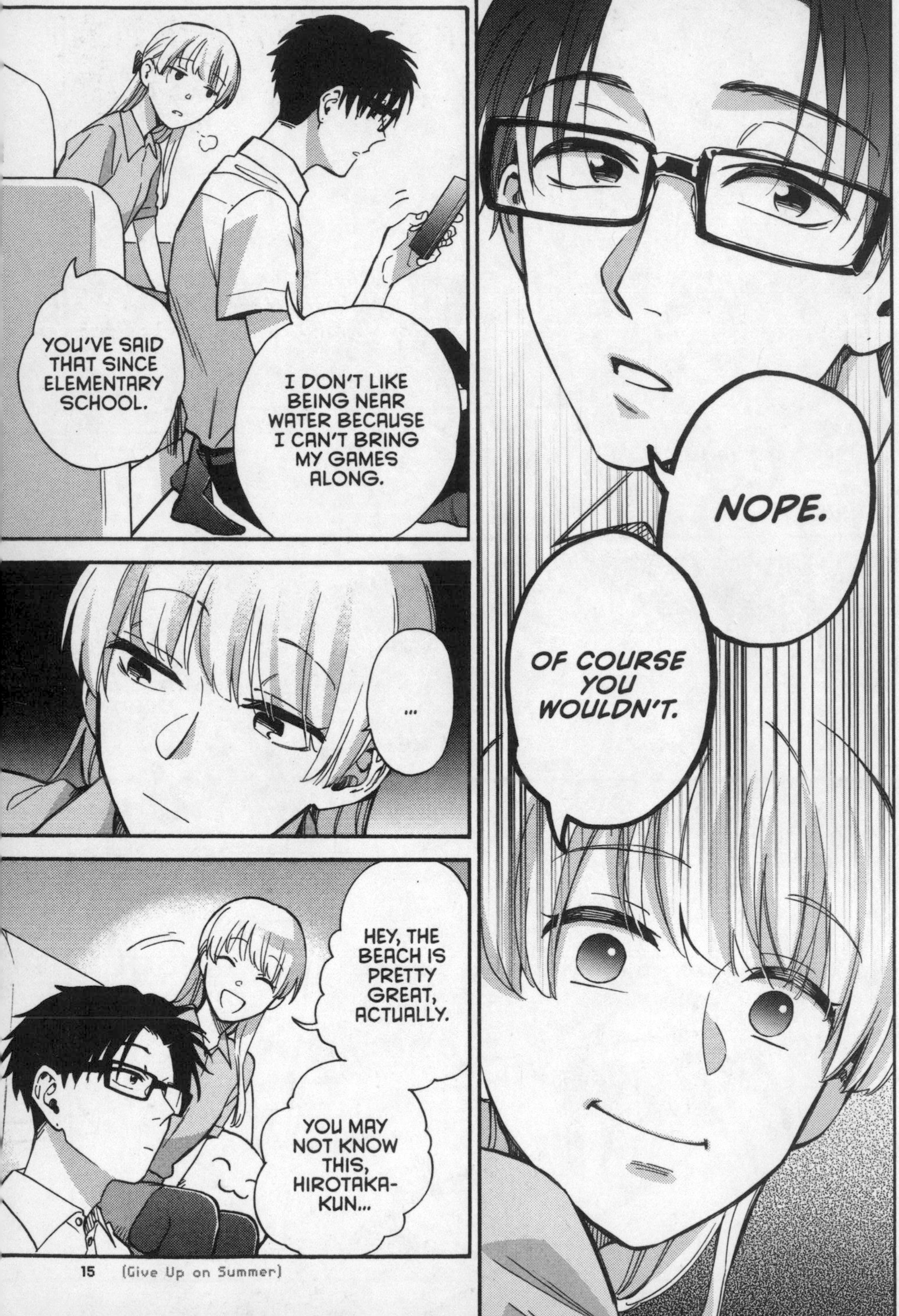
NOPE.
OF COURSE YOU WOULDN'T.
I DON'T LIKE BEING NEAR WATER BECAUSE I CAN'T BRING MY GAMES ALONG.
YOU'VE SAID THAT SINCE ELEMENTARY SCHOOL.
...
HEY, THE BEACH IS PRETTY GREAT, ACTUALLY.
YOU MAY NOT KNOW THIS, HIROTAKA-KUN...

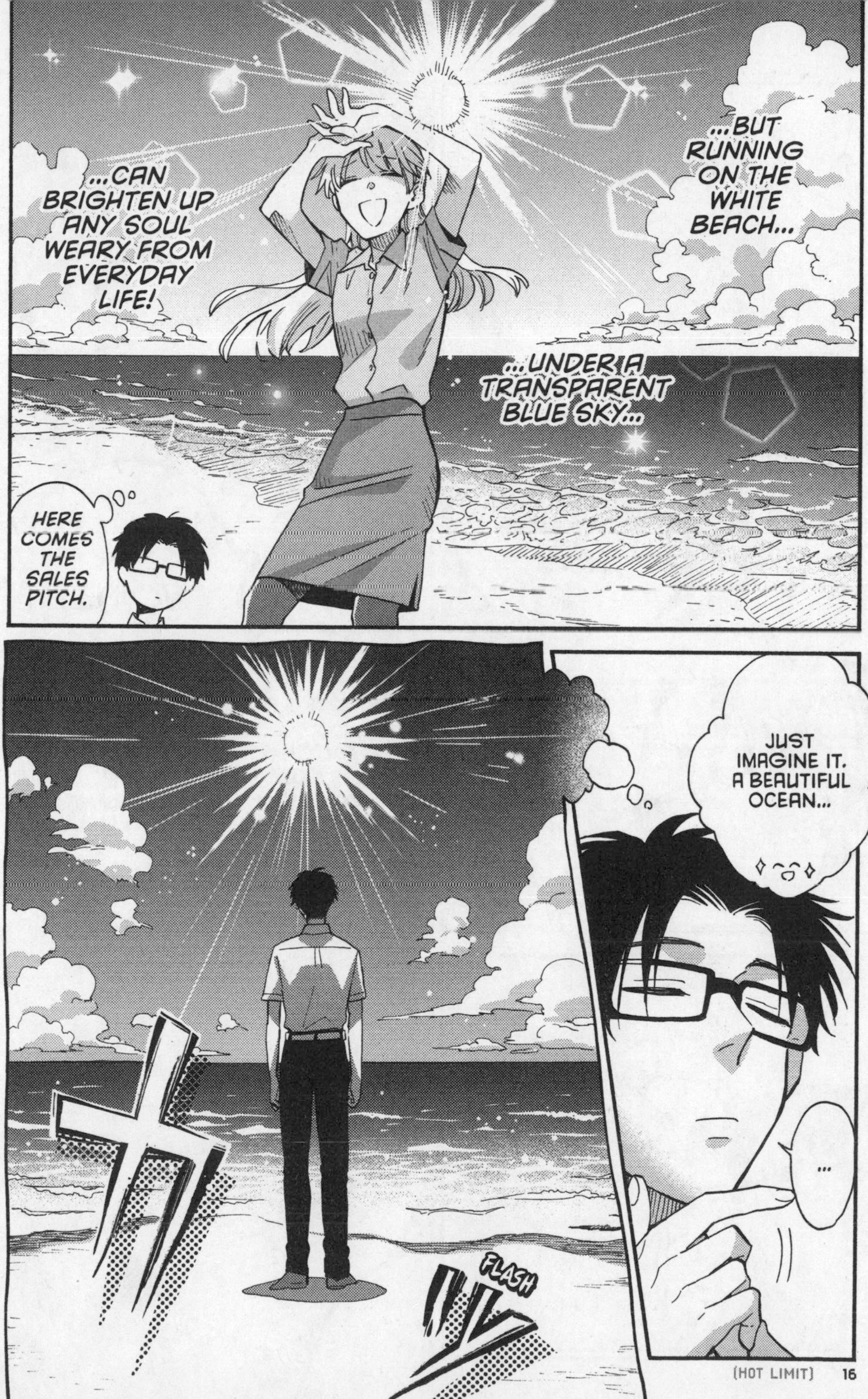
...BUT RUNNING ON THE WHITE BEACH...
...UNDER A TRANSPARENT BLUE SKY...
...CAN BRIGHTEN UP ANY SOUL WEARY FROM EVERYDAY LIFE!
HERE COMES THE SALES PITCH.
JUST IMAGINE IT. A BEAUTIFUL OCEAN...
...
FLASH

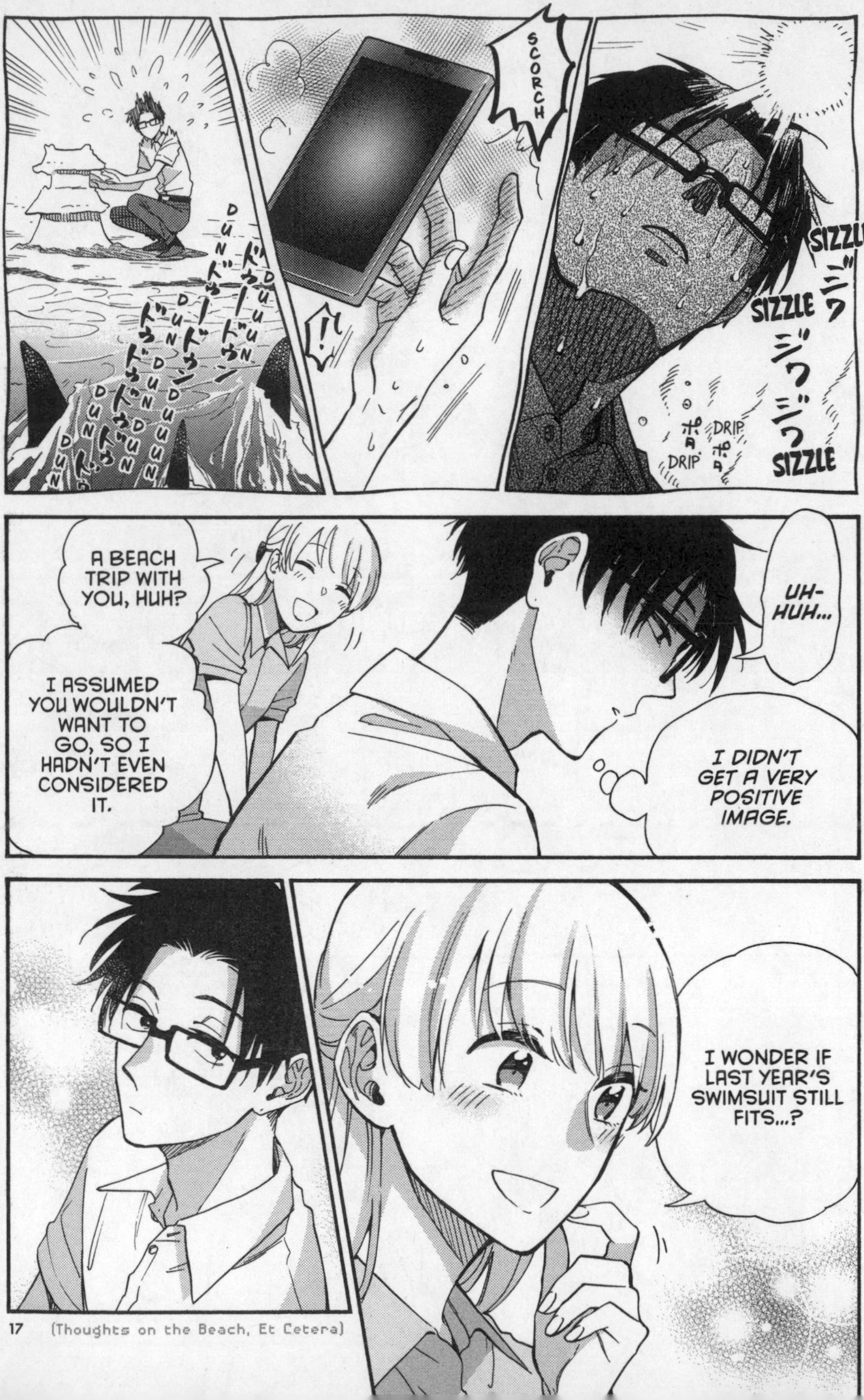
SIZZLE
SIZZLE
SIZZLE
DRIP
DRIP
SCORCH
!!
DUN DUN DUN DUN DUN DUN DUN DUUUN DUUUN
UH-HUH...
A BEACH TRIP WITH YOU, HUH?
I DIDN'T GET A VERY POSITIVE IMAGE.
I ASSUMED YOU WOULDN'T WANT TO GO, SO I HADN'T EVEN CONSIDERED IT.
I WONDER IF LAST YEAR'S SWIMSUIT STILL FITS...?

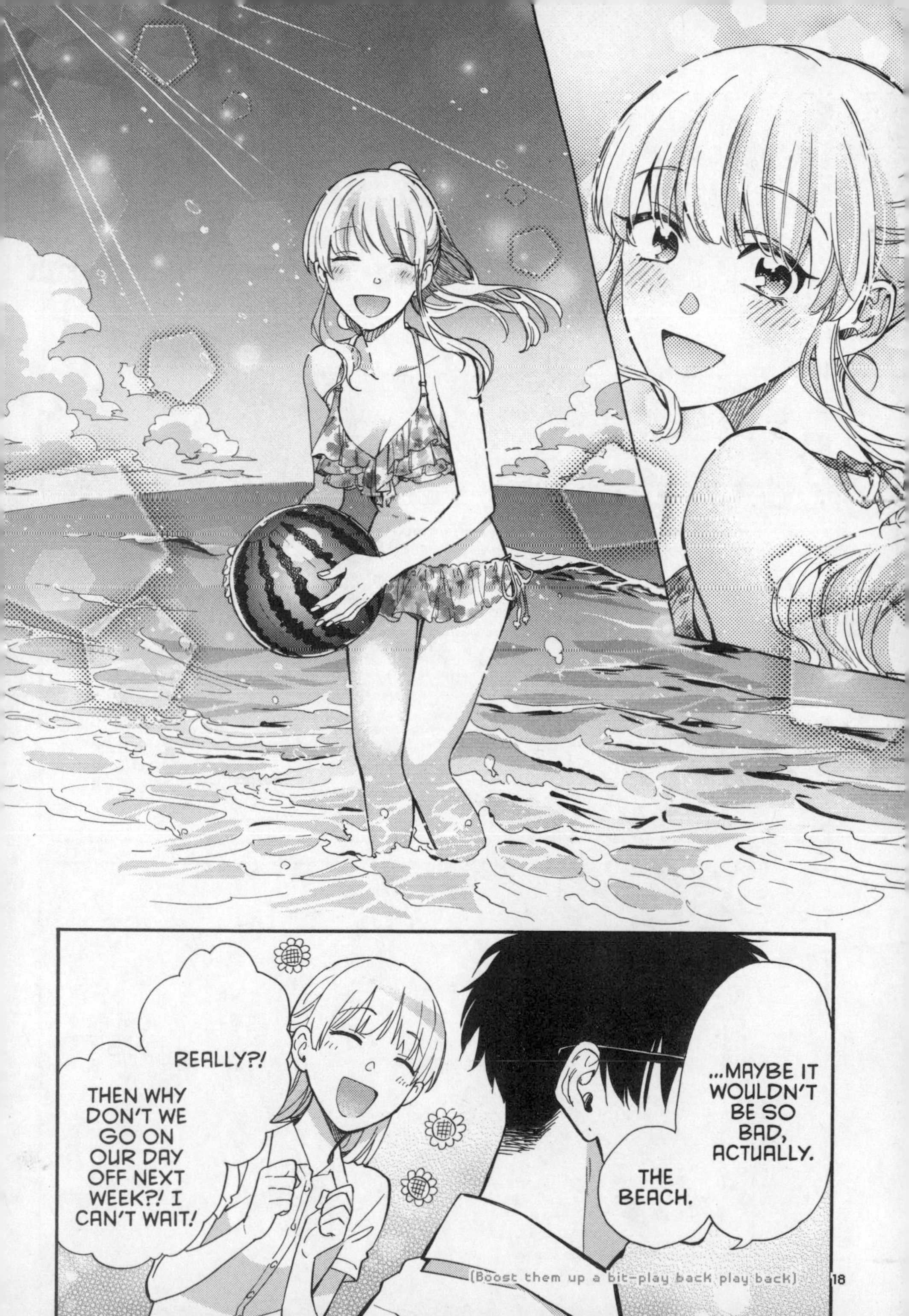
...MAYBE IT WOULDN'T BE SO BAD, ACTUALLY.
THE BEACH.
REALLY?!
THEN WHY DON'T WE GO ON OUR DAY OFF NEXT WEEK?! I CAN'T WAIT!

(Boost them up a bit—play back play back)

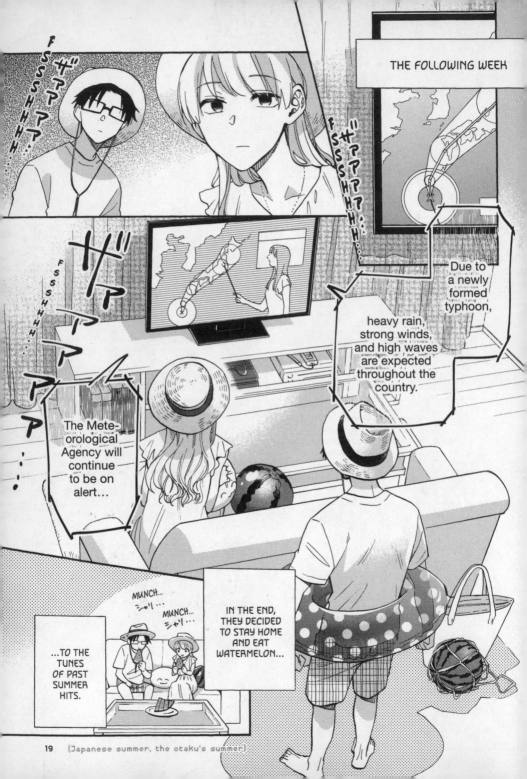

THE FOLLOWING WEEK

FSSSHPPPPHHH...

FSSSHHHPPPPHH...

FSSSHHHPP...

Due to a newly formed typhoon, heavy rain, strong winds, and high waves are expected throughout the country.

The Meteorological Agency will continue to be on alert...

MUNCH... ムシャ...

MUNCH... ムシャ...

IN THE END, THEY DECIDED TO STAY HOME AND EAT WATERMELON...

...TO THE TUNES OF PAST SUMMER HITS.

(Japanese summer, the otaku's summer)

CHARACTERS 01

Narumi Momose

. . .

Birthday
May 3rd

Age
26

Height
154 cm

Blood type
A

Constellation
Taurus

Narumi Momose's fashion

| **Hirotaka Nifuji** | Everyday clothes |

Hirotaka Nifuji's fashion

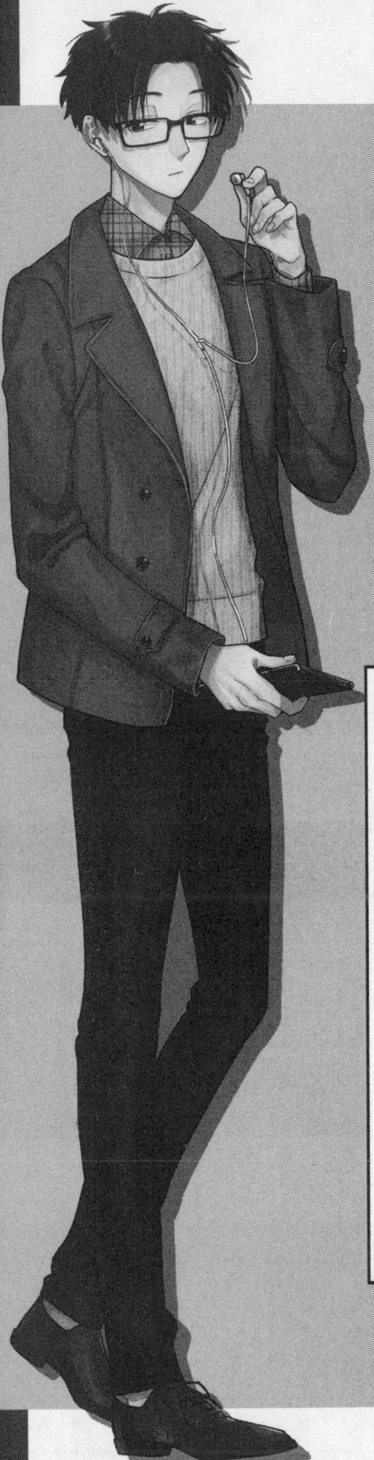

Hirotaka Nifuji

• • •

Birthday
Mar 20th

Age
26

Height
184 cm

Blood type
B

Constellation
Pisces

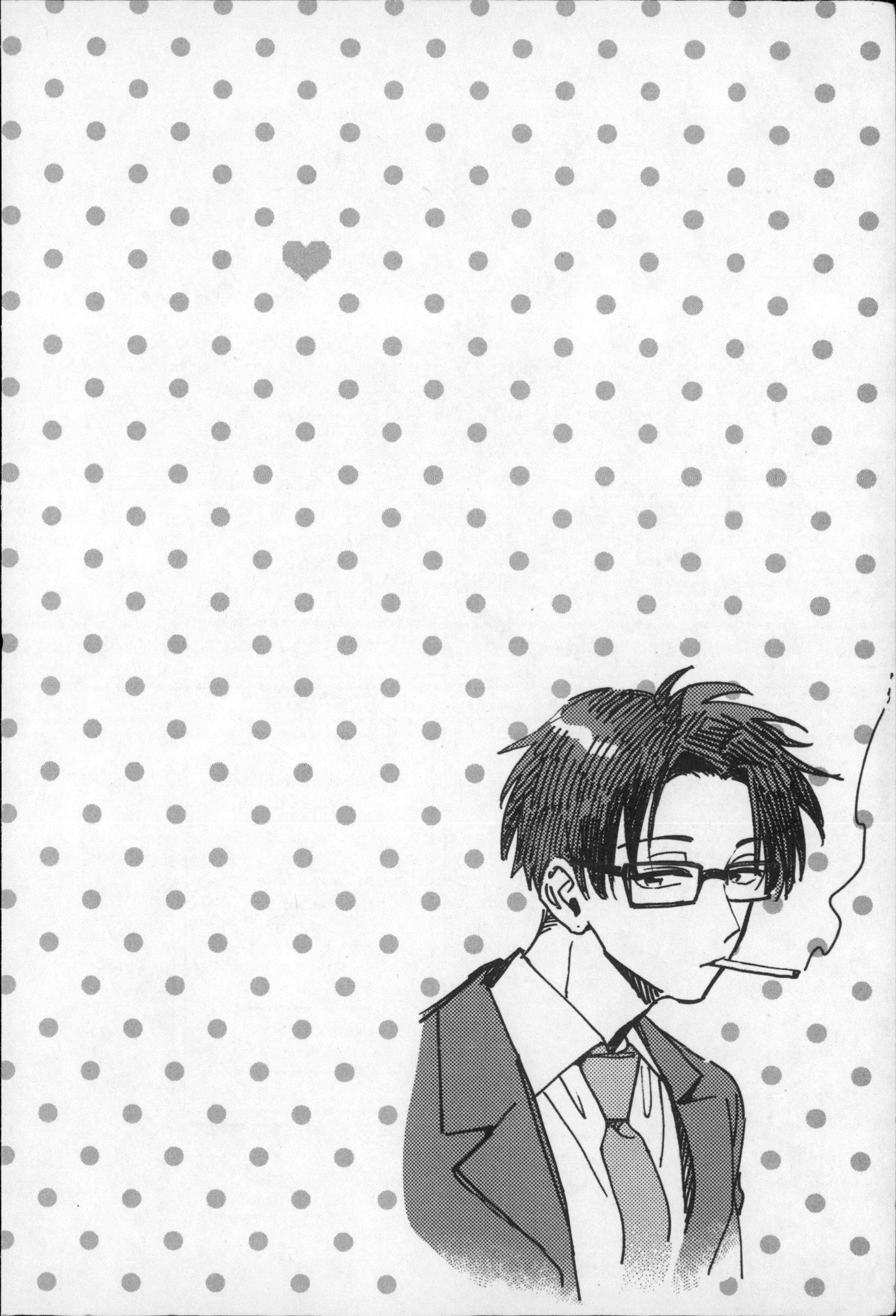

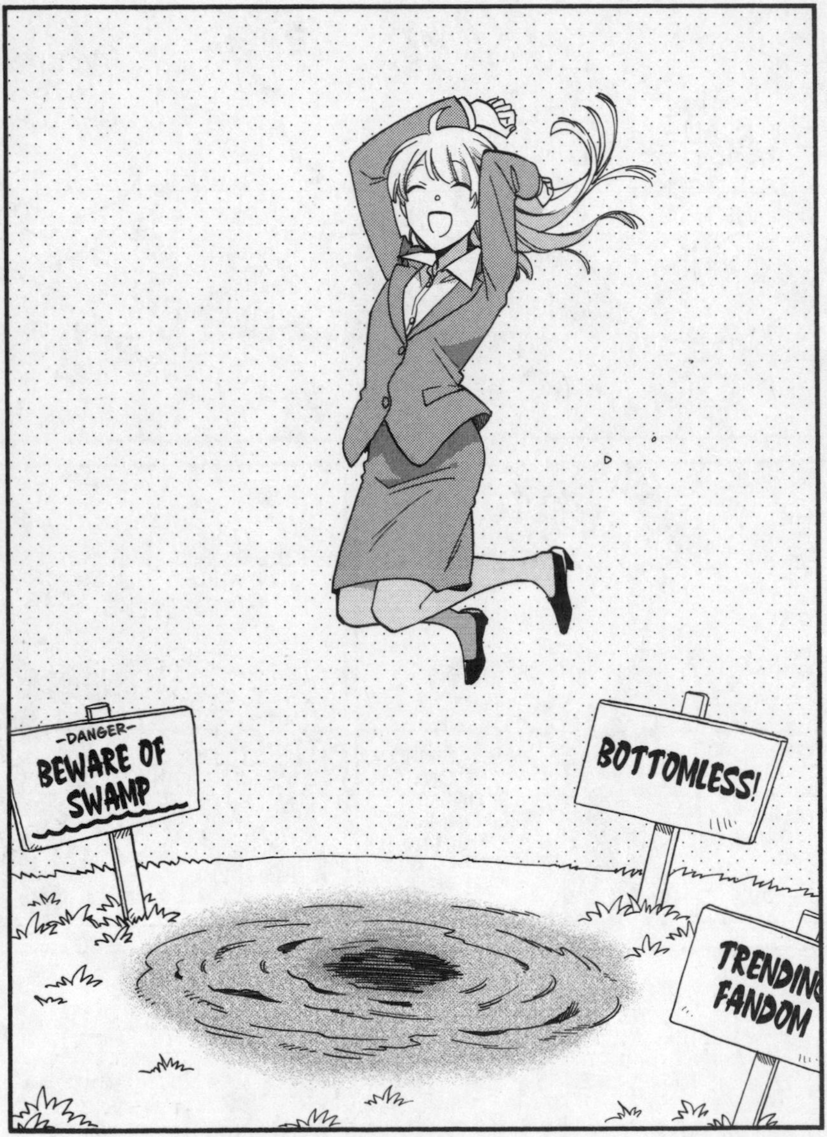

-DANGER-
BEWARE OF SWAMP
BOTTOMLESS!
TRENDING FANDOM

Episode.... 64

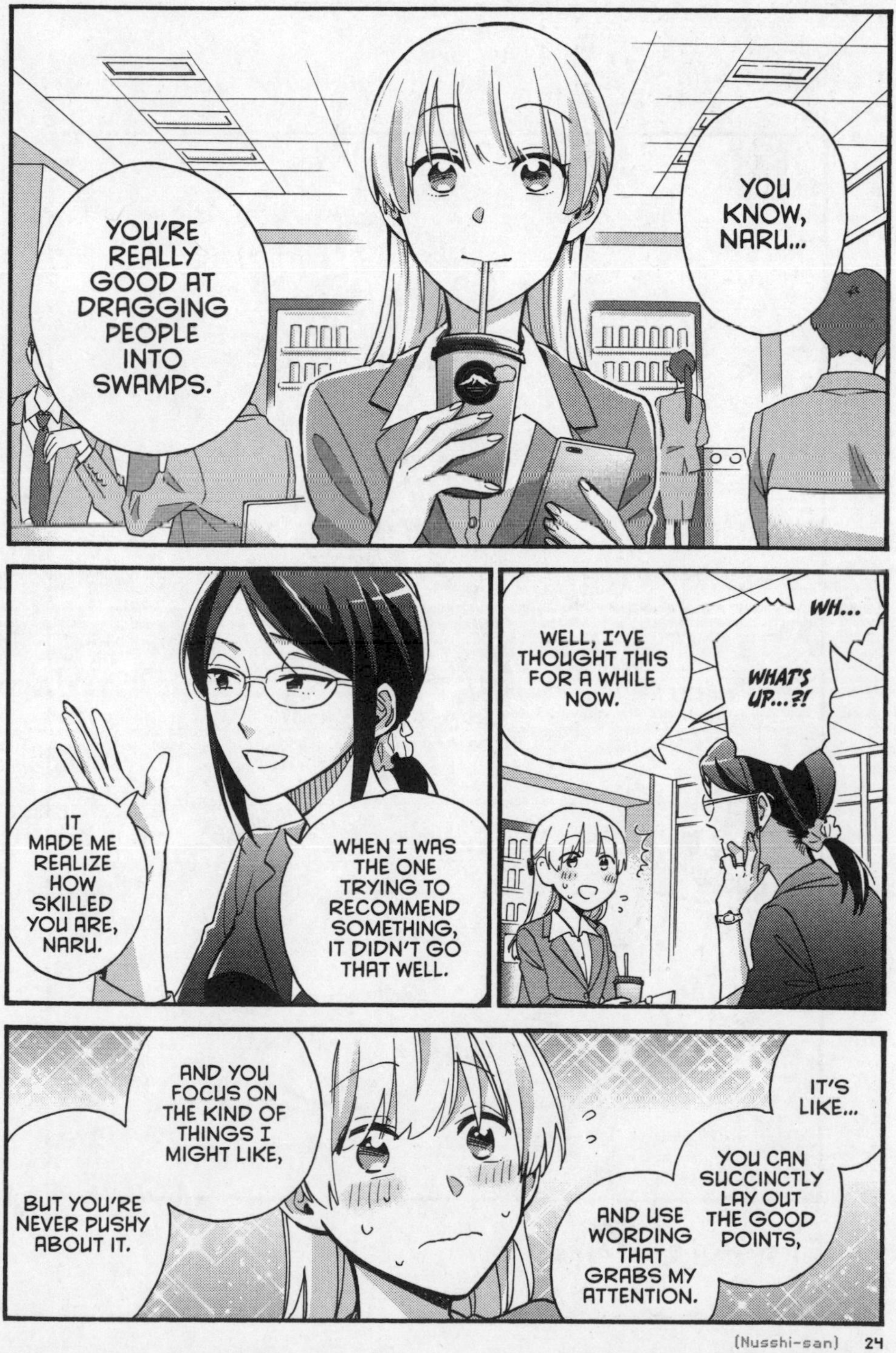
YOU KNOW, NARU...
YOU'RE REALLY GOOD AT DRAGGING PEOPLE INTO SWAMPS.
WH...
WHAT'S UP...?!
WELL, I'VE THOUGHT THIS FOR A WHILE NOW.
WHEN I WAS THE ONE TRYING TO RECOMMEND SOMETHING, IT DIDN'T GO THAT WELL.
IT MADE ME REALIZE HOW SKILLED YOU ARE, NARU.
IT'S LIKE...
YOU CAN SUCCINCTLY LAY OUT THE GOOD POINTS,
AND USE WORDING THAT GRABS MY ATTENTION.
AND YOU FOCUS ON THE KIND OF THINGS I MIGHT LIKE,
BUT YOU'RE NEVER PUSHY ABOUT IT.

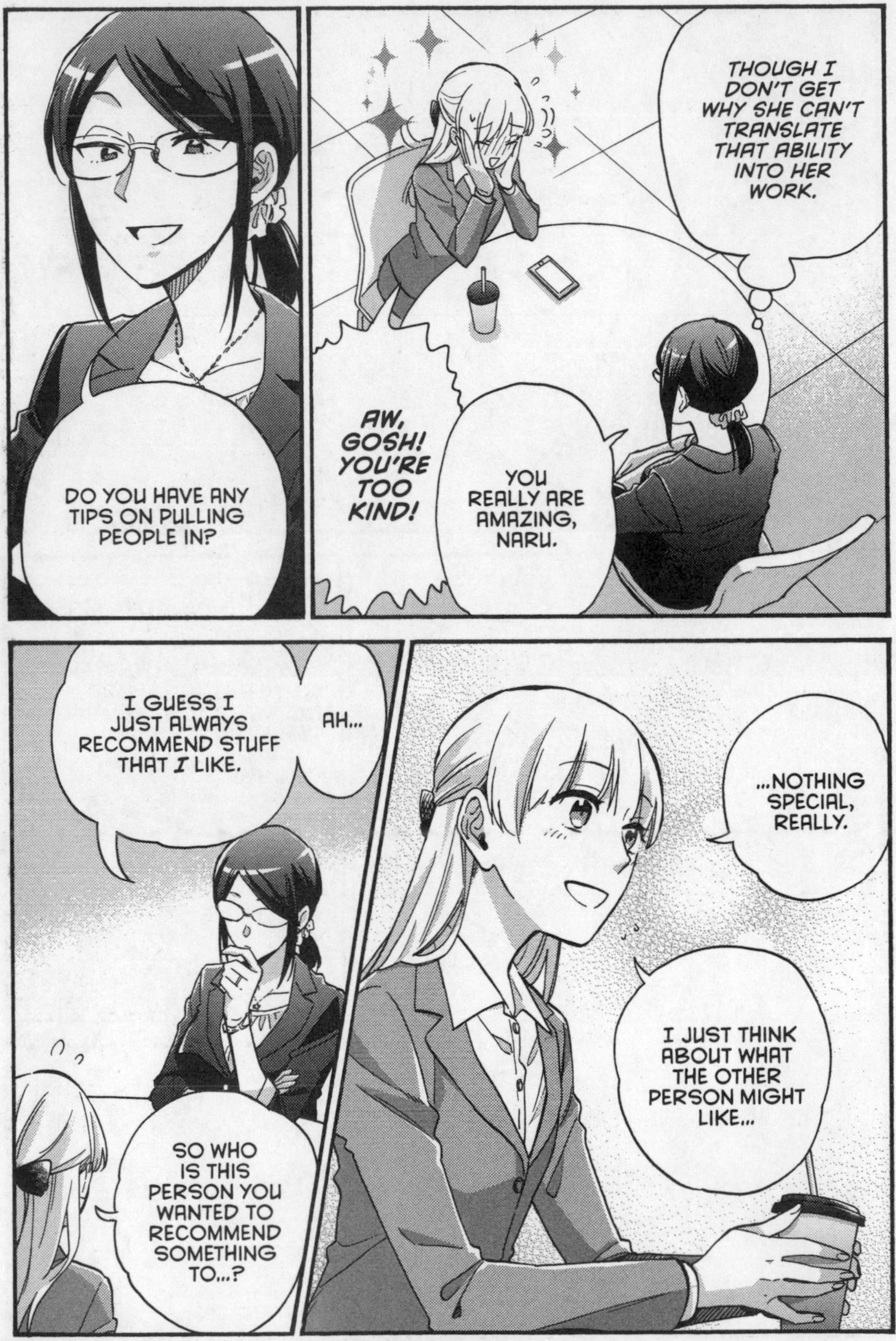
THOUGH I DON'T GET WHY SHE CAN'T TRANSLATE THAT ABILITY INTO HER WORK.
YOU REALLY ARE AMAZING, NARU.
AW, GOSH! YOU'RE TOO KIND!
DO YOU HAVE ANY TIPS ON PULLING PEOPLE IN?
...NOTHING SPECIAL, REALLY.
I JUST THINK ABOUT WHAT THE OTHER PERSON MIGHT LIKE...
AH...
I GUESS I JUST ALWAYS RECOMMEND STUFF THAT *I* LIKE.
SO WHO IS THIS PERSON YOU WANTED TO RECOMMEND SOMETHING TO...?

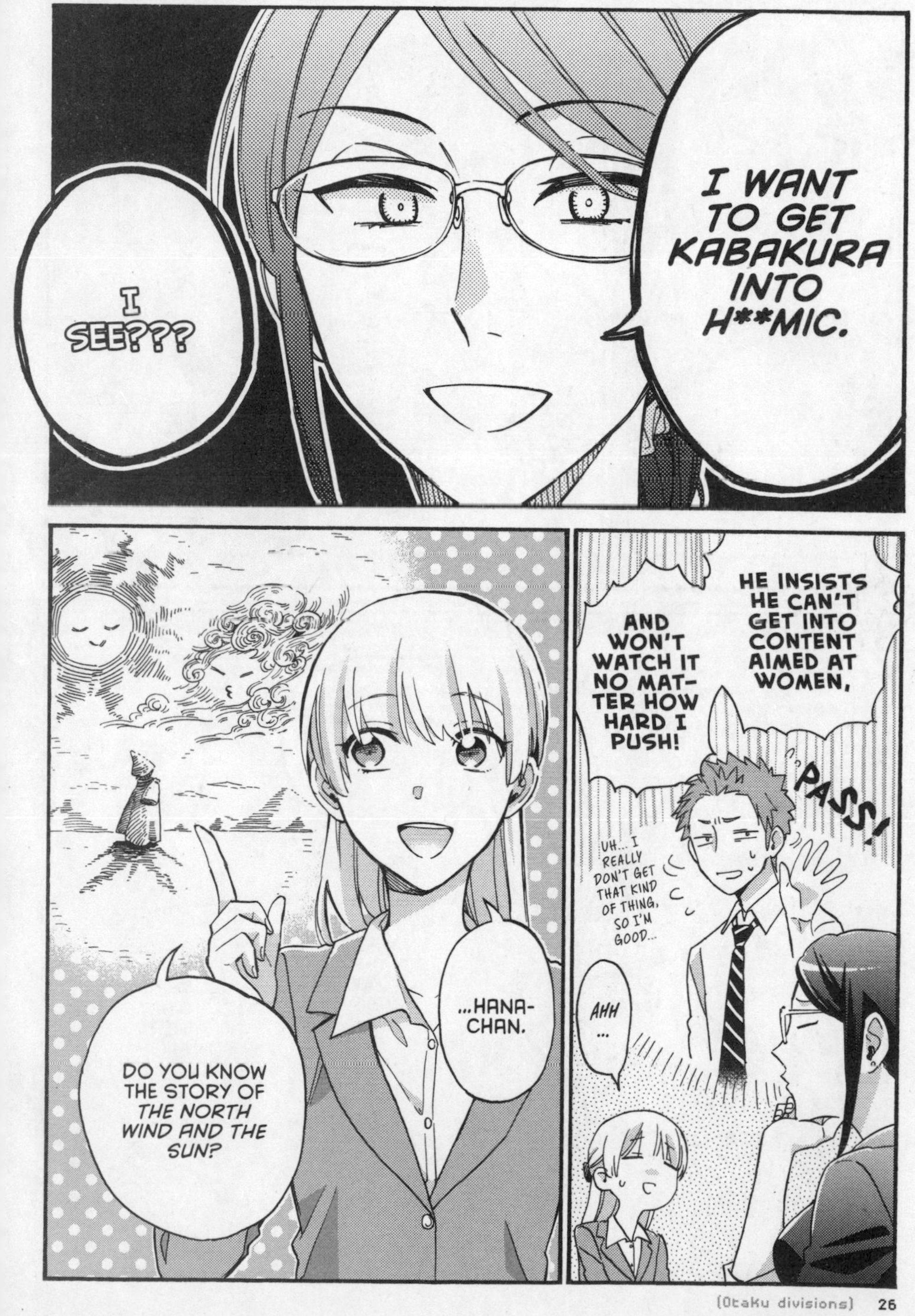
I WANT TO GET KABAKURA INTO H**MIC.
I SEE???
HE INSISTS HE CAN'T GET INTO CONTENT AIMED AT WOMEN,
AND WON'T WATCH IT NO MATTER HOW HARD I PUSH!
PASS!
UH... I REALLY DON'T GET THAT KIND OF THING, SO I'M GOOD...
AHH ...
...HANA-CHAN.
DO YOU KNOW THE STORY OF *THE NORTH WIND AND THE SUN*?

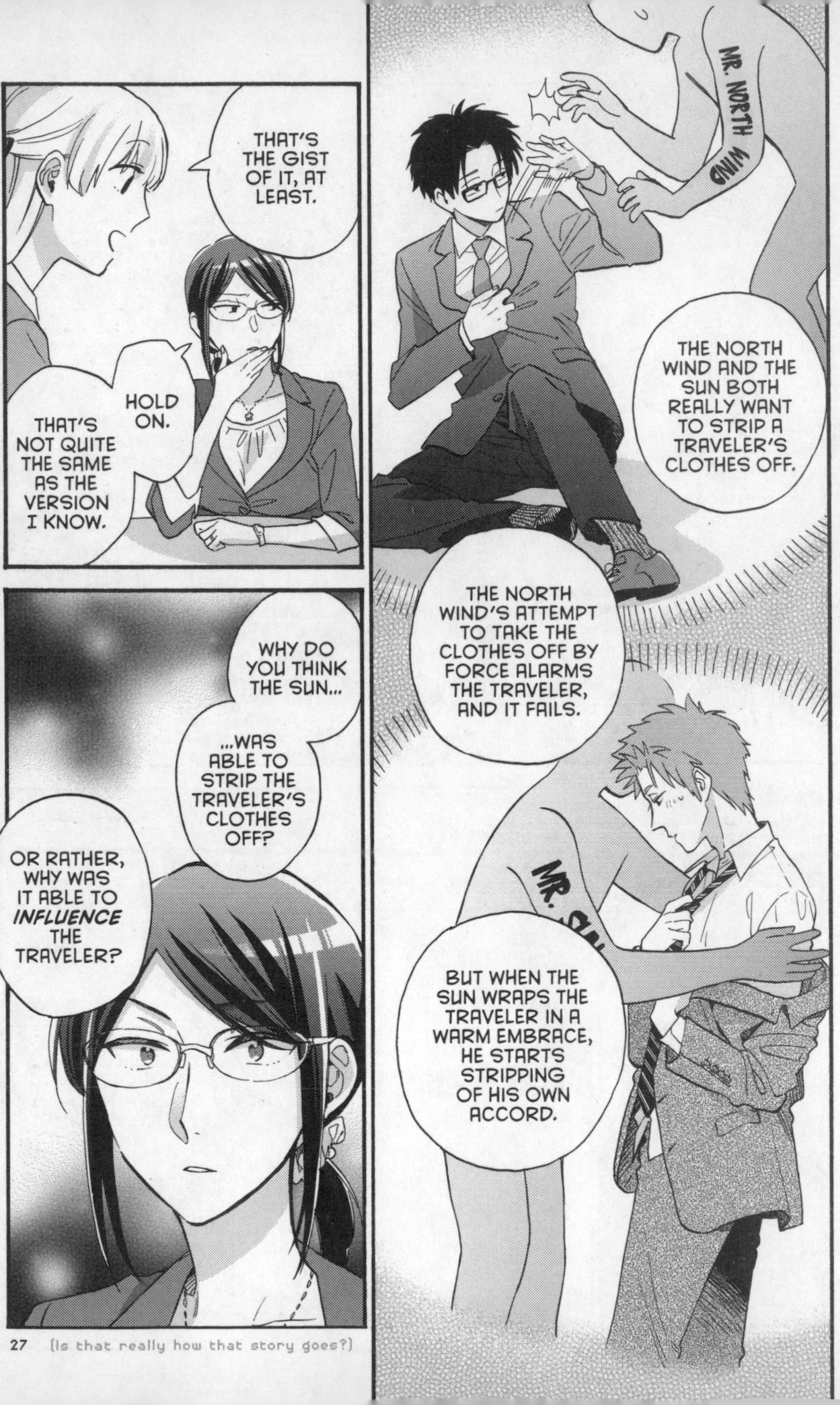
MR. NORTH WIND
THE NORTH WIND AND THE SUN BOTH REALLY WANT TO STRIP A TRAVELER'S CLOTHES OFF.
THE NORTH WIND'S ATTEMPT TO TAKE THE CLOTHES OFF BY FORCE ALARMS THE TRAVELER, AND IT FAILS.
BUT WHEN THE SUN WRAPS THE TRAVELER IN A WARM EMBRACE, HE STARTS STRIPPING OF HIS OWN ACCORD.
THAT'S THE GIST OF IT, AT LEAST.
HOLD ON.
THAT'S NOT QUITE THE SAME AS THE VERSION I KNOW.
WHY DO YOU THINK THE SUN...
...WAS ABLE TO STRIP THE TRAVELER'S CLOTHES OFF?
OR RATHER, WHY WAS IT ABLE TO *INFLUENCE* THE TRAVELER?

[Is that really how that story goes?]

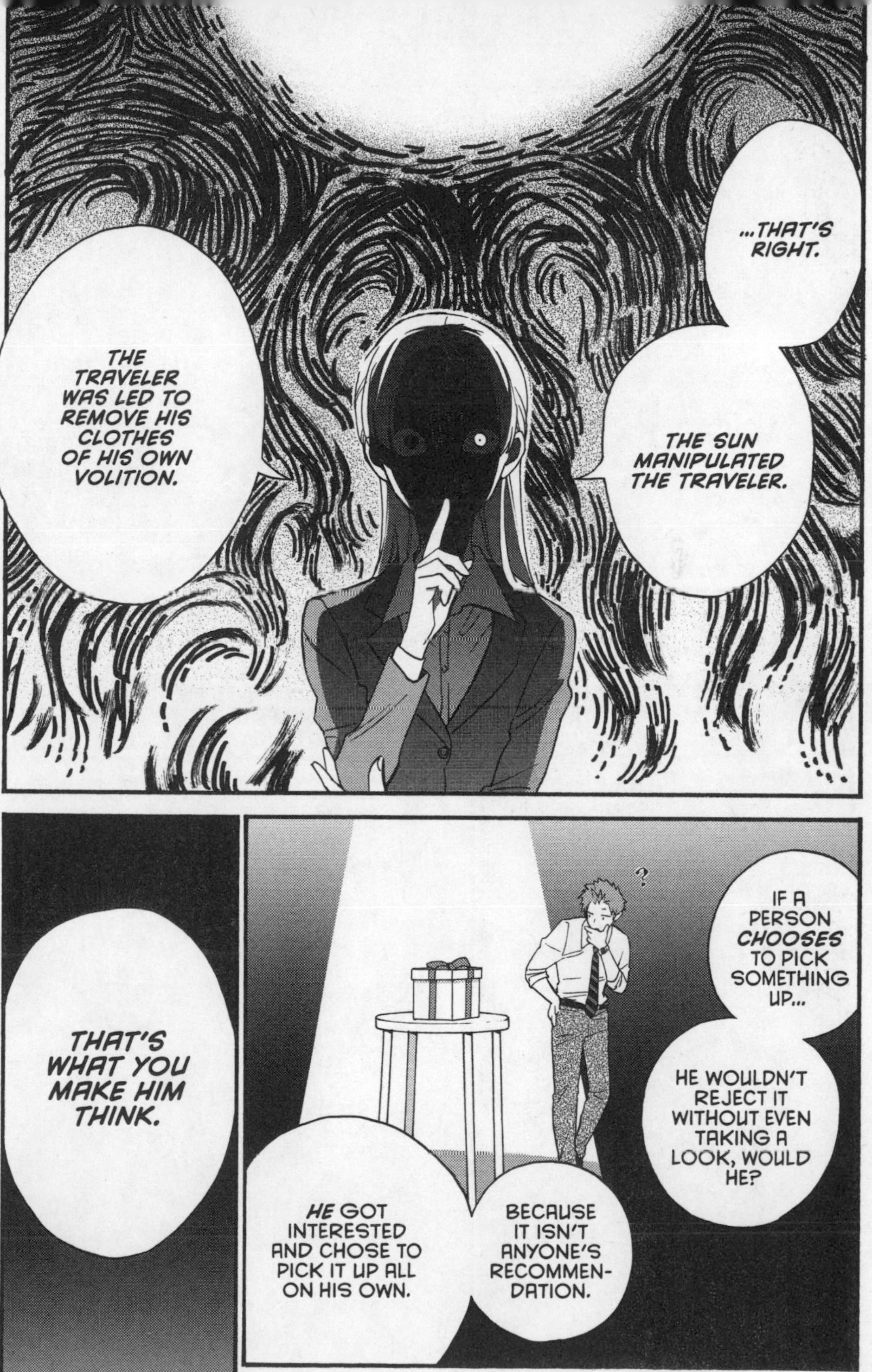
...THAT'S RIGHT.
THE SUN MANIPULATED THE TRAVELER.
THE TRAVELER WAS LED TO REMOVE HIS CLOTHES OF HIS OWN VOLITION.
?
IF A PERSON *CHOOSES* TO PICK SOMETHING UP...
HE WOULDN'T REJECT IT WITHOUT EVEN TAKING A LOOK, WOULD HE?
BECAUSE IT ISN'T ANYONE'S RECOMMEN-DATION.
HE GOT INTERESTED AND CHOSE TO PICK IT UP ALL ON HIS OWN.
THAT'S WHAT YOU MAKE HIM THINK.

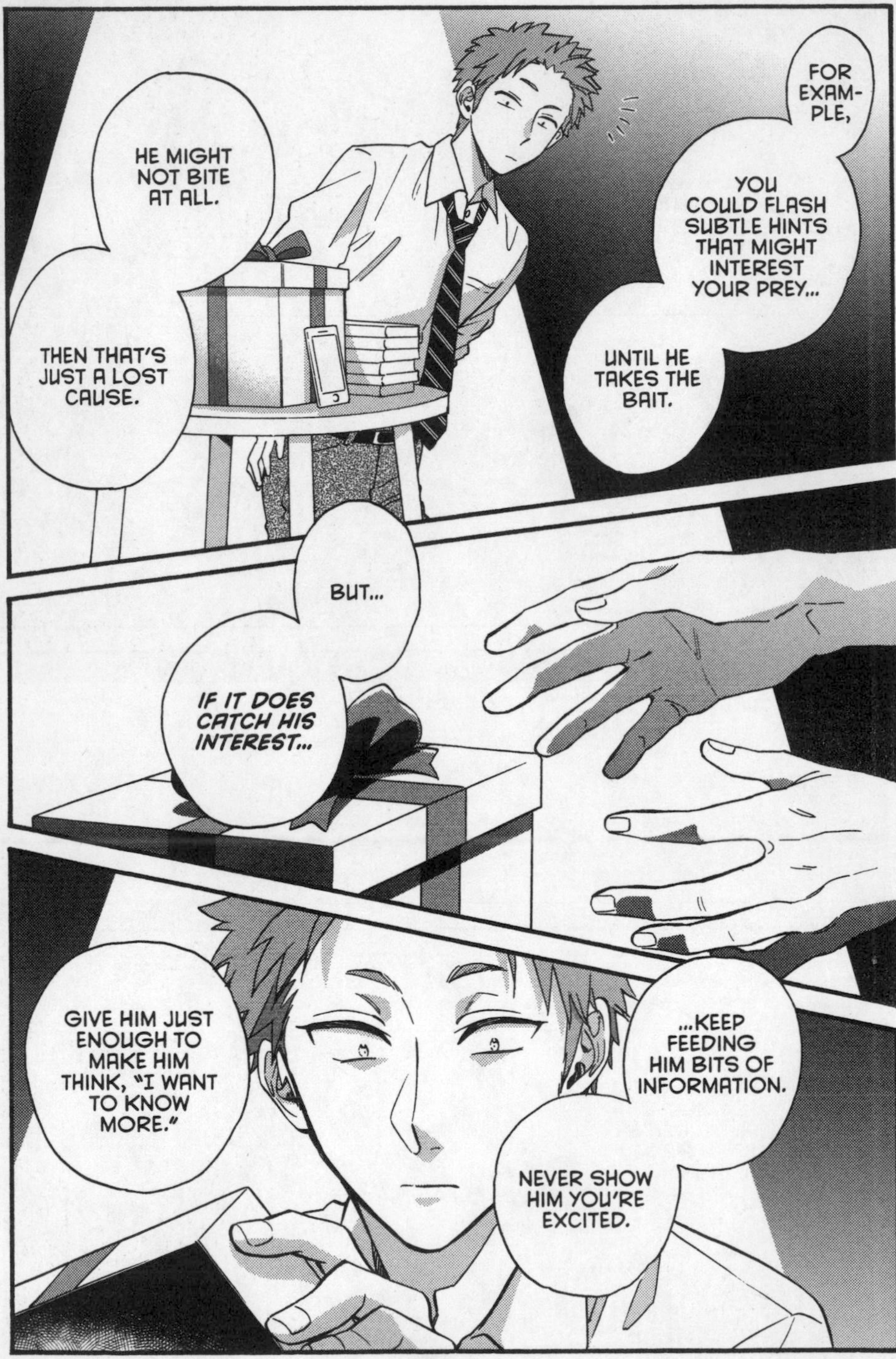
FOR EXAMPLE,
YOU COULD FLASH SUBTLE HINTS THAT MIGHT INTEREST YOUR PREY...
UNTIL HE TAKES THE BAIT.
HE MIGHT NOT BITE AT ALL.
THEN THAT'S JUST A LOST CAUSE.
BUT...
IF IT DOES CATCH HIS INTEREST...
...KEEP FEEDING HIM BITS OF INFORMATION.
GIVE HIM JUST ENOUGH TO MAKE HIM THINK, "I WANT TO KNOW MORE."
NEVER SHOW HIM YOU'RE EXCITED.

 (Come on... Come on...)

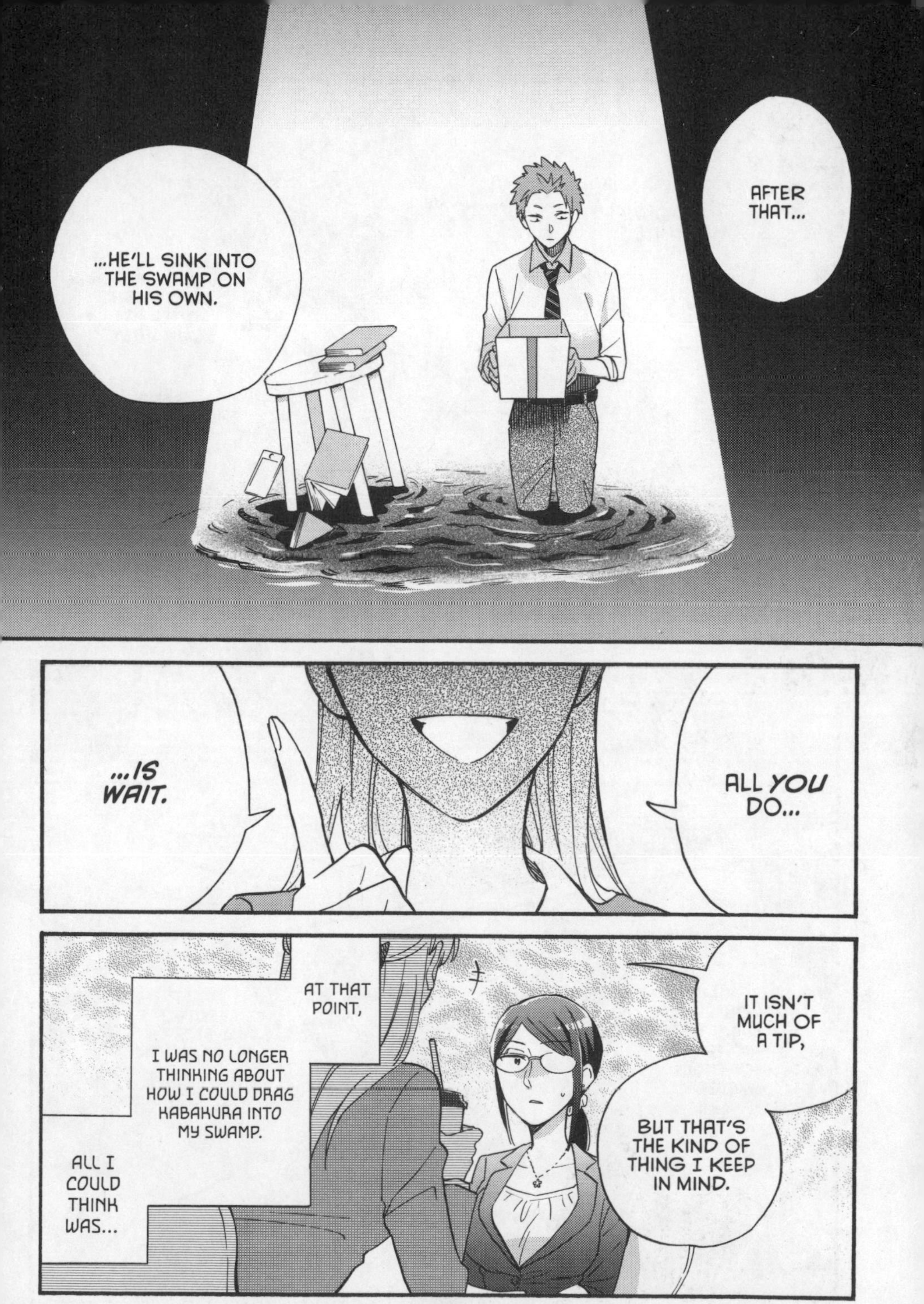
AFTER THAT...
...HE'LL SINK INTO THE SWAMP ON HIS OWN.
ALL *YOU* DO...
...IS *WAIT.*
IT ISN'T MUCH OF A TIP,
BUT THAT'S THE KIND OF THING I KEEP IN MIND.
AT THAT POINT,
I WAS NO LONGER THINKING ABOUT HOW I COULD DRAG KABAKURA INTO MY SWAMP.
ALL I COULD THINK WAS...

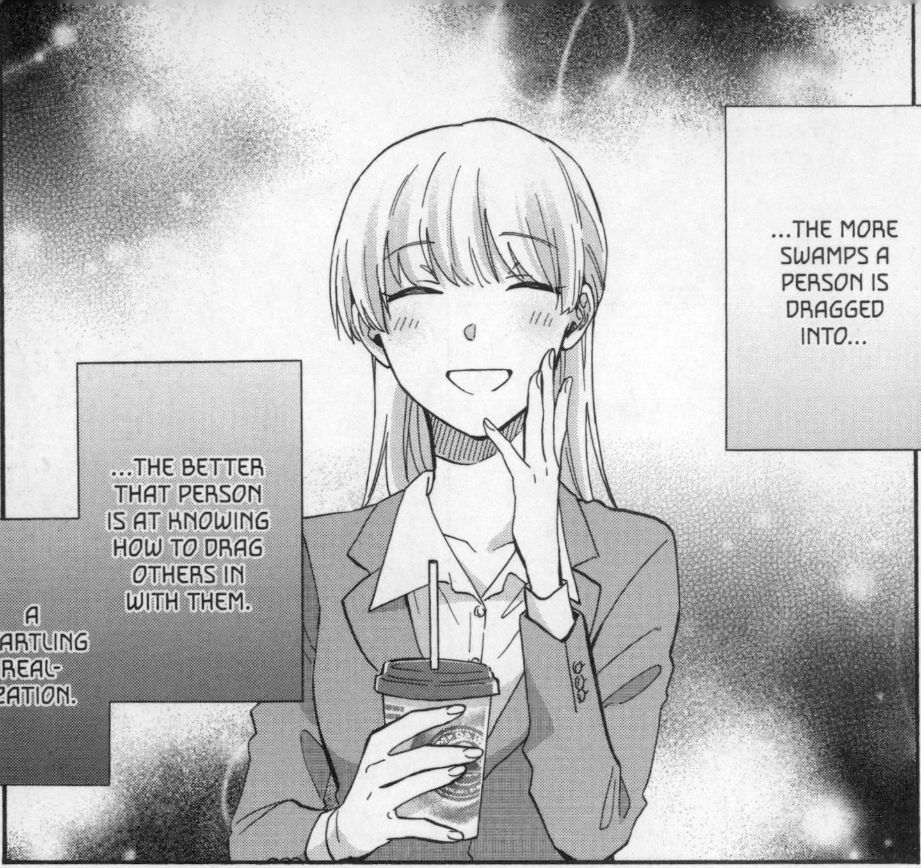
...THE MORE SWAMPS A PERSON IS DRAGGED INTO...
...THE BETTER THAT PERSON IS AT KNOWING HOW TO DRAG OTHERS IN WITH THEM.
A STARTLING REAL-IZATION.

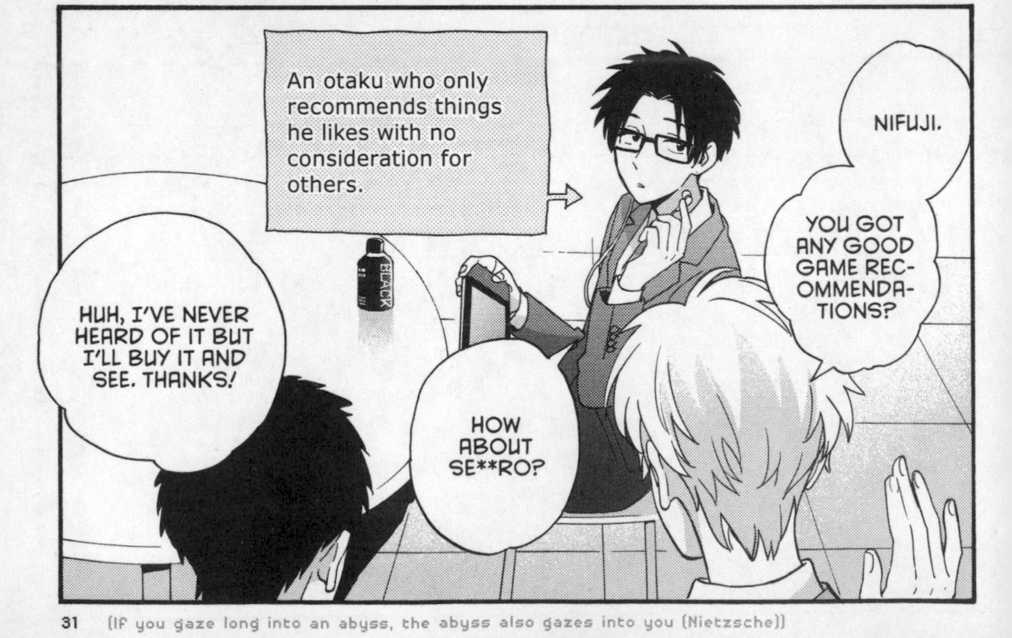
NIFUJI.
YOU GOT ANY GOOD GAME REC-OMMENDA-TIONS?
An otaku who only recommends things he likes with no consideration for others.
HOW ABOUT SE**RO?
HUH, I'VE NEVER HEARD OF IT BUT I'LL BUY IT AND SEE. THANKS!

(If you gaze long into an abyss, the abyss also gazes into you (Nietzsche))

Hanako Koyanagi

· · ·

Birthday
Aug 28th

Age
27

Height
167 cm

Blood type
AB

Constellation
Virgo

Hanako Koyanagi's fashion

CHARACTERS 03

CHARACTERS 04

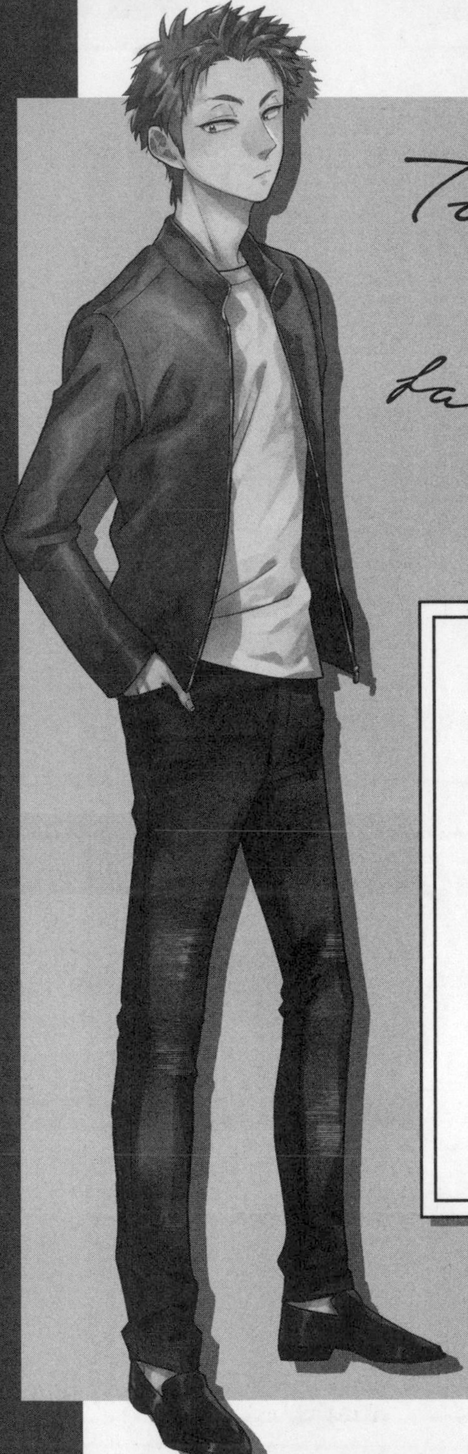

Taro Kabakura's fashion

Taro Kabakura

• • •

Birthday
Nov 9th

Age
28

Height
180 cm

Blood type
O

Constellation
Scorpio

Episode....65 marriage...1

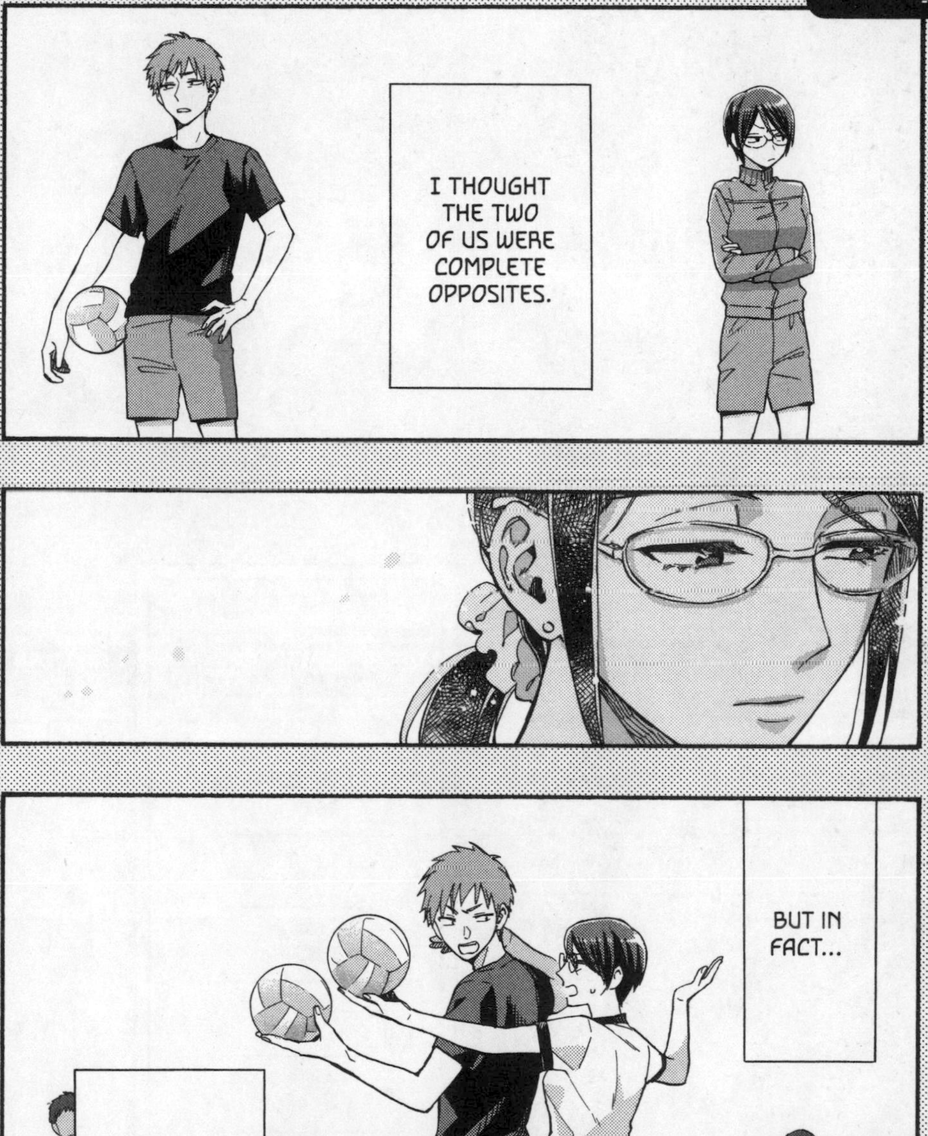
I THOUGHT THE TWO OF US WERE COMPLETE OPPOSITES.
BUT IN FACT...
...WE WEREN'T, REALLY.

(Completely opposite but pretty similar)

I THINK WE'RE GONNA DISBAND OVER MUSICAL DIFFERENCES.

I THINK WE'RE GONNA BREAK UP OVER DIFFERENT IDEAS ABOUT THE WEDDING,

I MEAN.

SIGH...

?

FAN SERVICE, PLZ

HANA-CHA

...AND, MAKE IT A SPECIAL, ONE-OF-A-KIND CEREMONY, RIGHT?!

YOU WANT TO BE PARTICULAR ABOUT THE THINGS THAT MATTER...

A WEDDING IS A ONCE-IN-A-LIFETIME THING...

A BIG MOMENT WHERE THE SPOTLIGHT IS ON YOU.

YES!

THAT'S RIGHT!

OF COURSE YOU DO, NO QUESTION ABOUT IT!

[He always screws up the rhythm!]

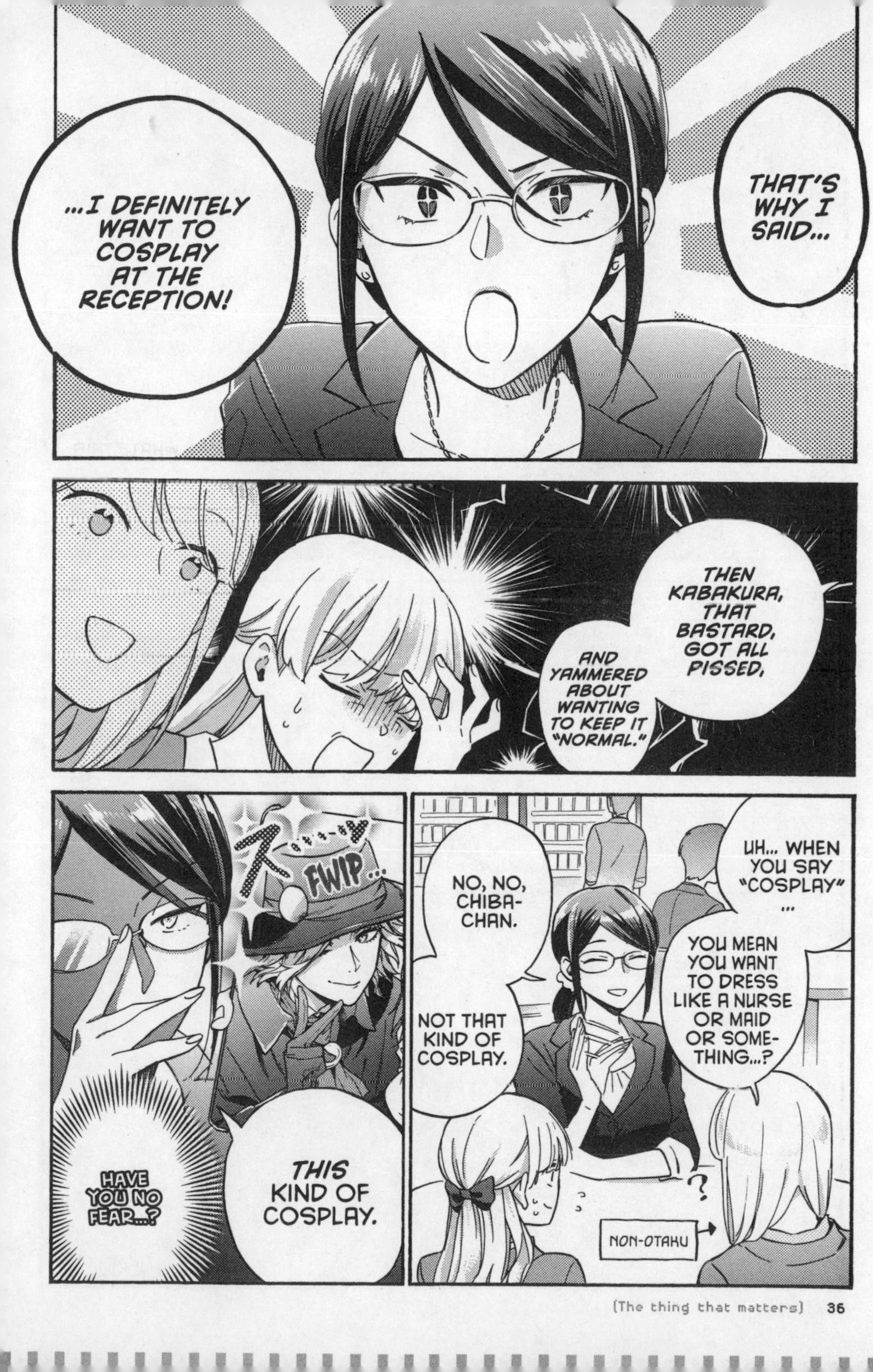
THAT'S WHY I SAID...
...I DEFINITELY WANT TO COSPLAY AT THE RECEPTION!
THEN KABAKURA, THAT BASTARD, GOT ALL PISSED,
AND YAMMERED ABOUT WANTING TO KEEP IT "NORMAL."
UH... WHEN YOU SAY "COSPLAY" ...
YOU MEAN YOU WANT TO DRESS LIKE A NURSE OR MAID OR SOME-THING...?
NON-OTAKU
NO, NO, CHIBA-CHAN.
NOT THAT KIND OF COSPLAY.
FWIP...
THIS KIND OF COSPLAY.
HAVE YOU NO FEAR...?

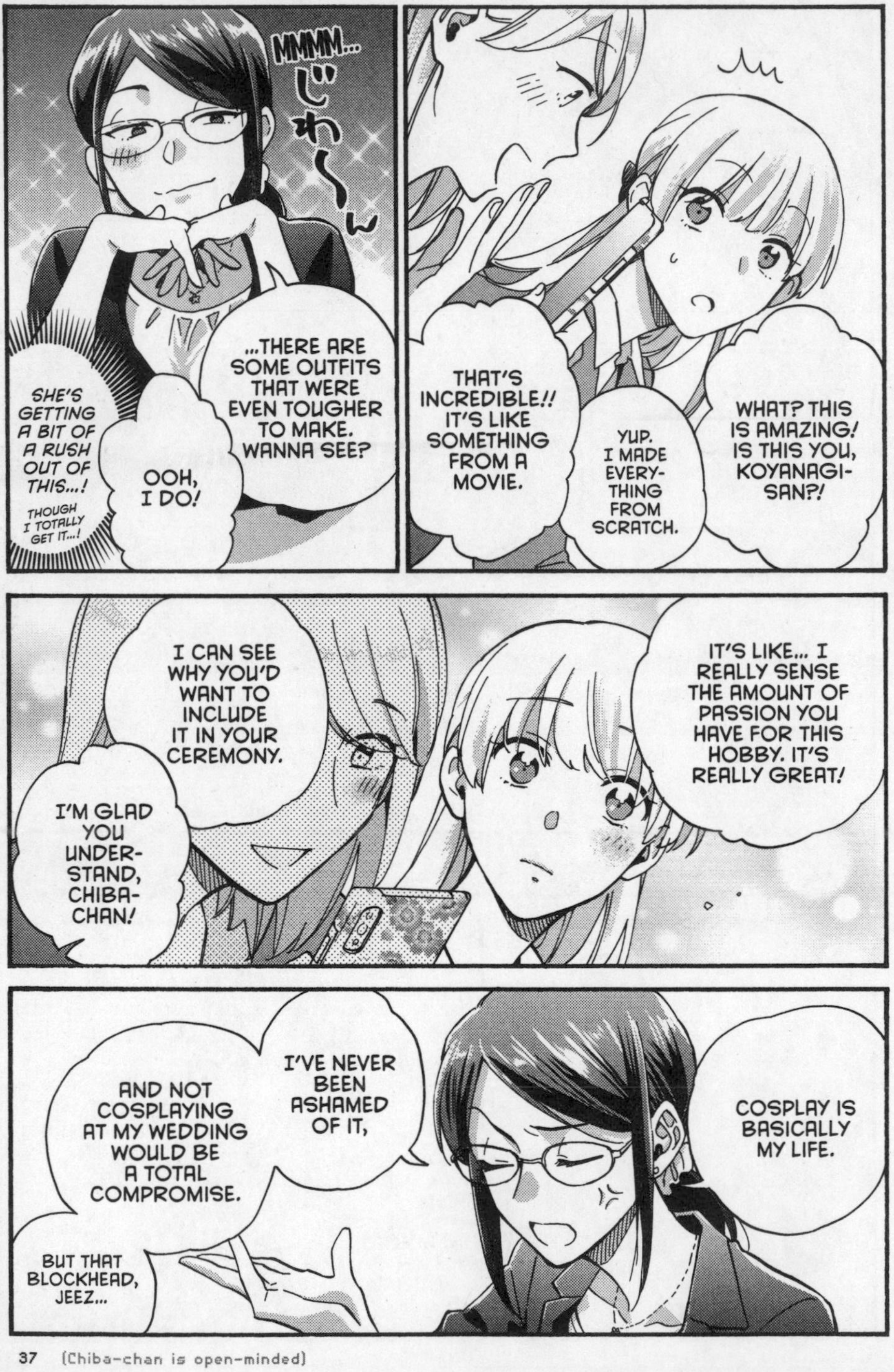
WHAT? THIS IS AMAZING! IS THIS YOU, KOYANAGI-SAN?!
YUP. I MADE EVERYTHING FROM SCRATCH.
THAT'S INCREDIBLE!! IT'S LIKE SOMETHING FROM A MOVIE.
MMMM...
じわ〜ん
...THERE ARE SOME OUTFITS THAT WERE EVEN TOUGHER TO MAKE. WANNA SEE?
OOH, I DO!
SHE'S GETTING A BIT OF A RUSH OUT OF THIS...!
THOUGH I TOTALLY GET IT...!
IT'S LIKE... I REALLY SENSE THE AMOUNT OF PASSION YOU HAVE FOR THIS HOBBY. IT'S REALLY GREAT!
I CAN SEE WHY YOU'D WANT TO INCLUDE IT IN YOUR CEREMONY.
I'M GLAD YOU UNDERSTAND, CHIBA-CHAN!
COSPLAY IS BASICALLY MY LIFE.
I'VE NEVER BEEN ASHAMED OF IT,
AND NOT COSPLAYING AT MY WEDDING WOULD BE A TOTAL COMPROMISE.
BUT THAT BLOCKHEAD, JEEZ...

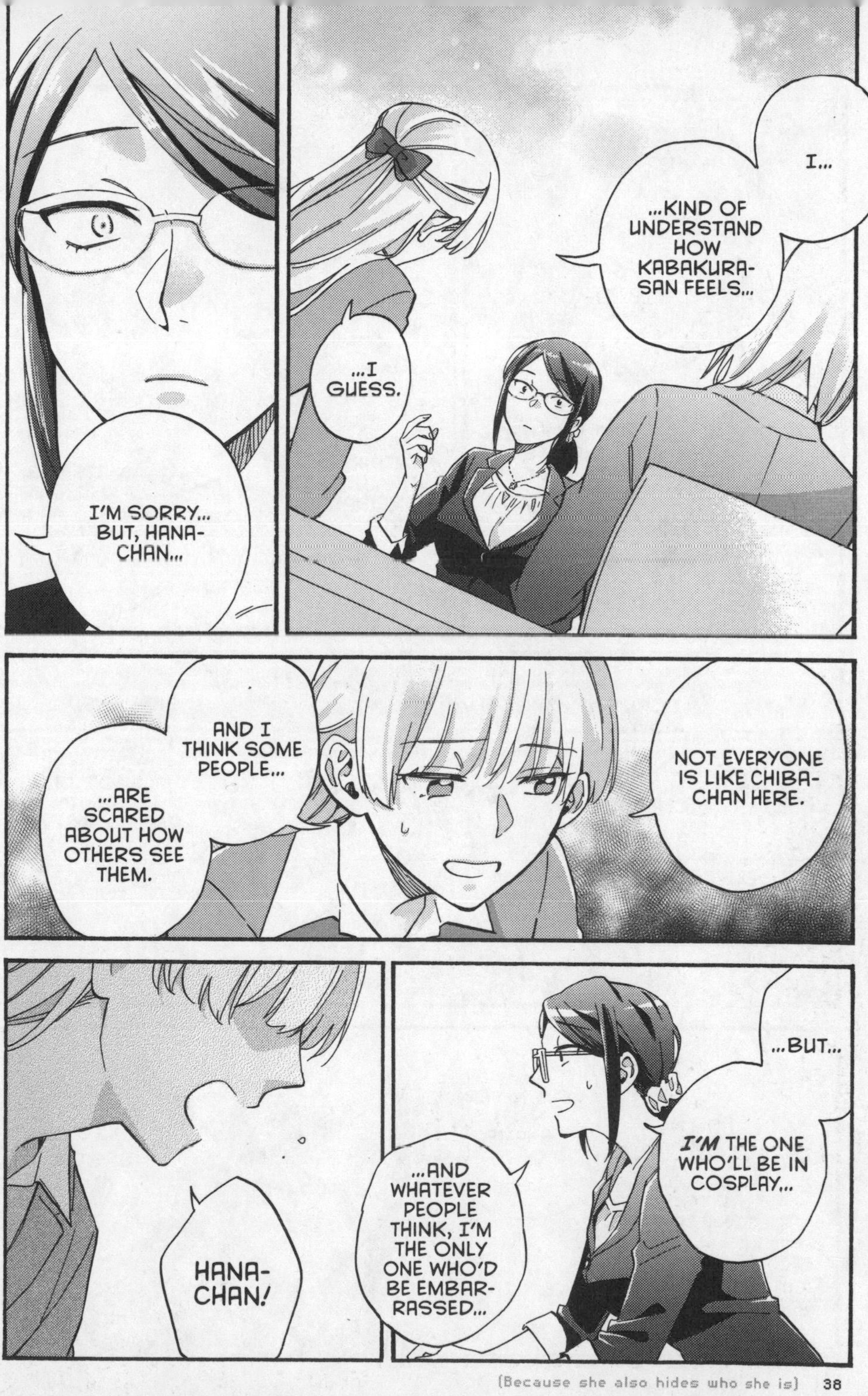
I...
...KIND OF UNDERSTAND HOW KABAKURA-SAN FEELS...
...I GUESS.
I'M SORRY... BUT, HANA-CHAN...
NOT EVERYONE IS LIKE CHIBA-CHAN HERE.
AND I THINK SOME PEOPLE...
...ARE SCARED ABOUT HOW OTHERS SEE THEM.
...BUT...
I'M THE ONE WHO'LL BE IN COSPLAY...
...AND WHATEVER PEOPLE THINK, I'M THE ONLY ONE WHO'D BE EMBARRASSED...
HANA-CHAN!

(Because she also hides who she is)

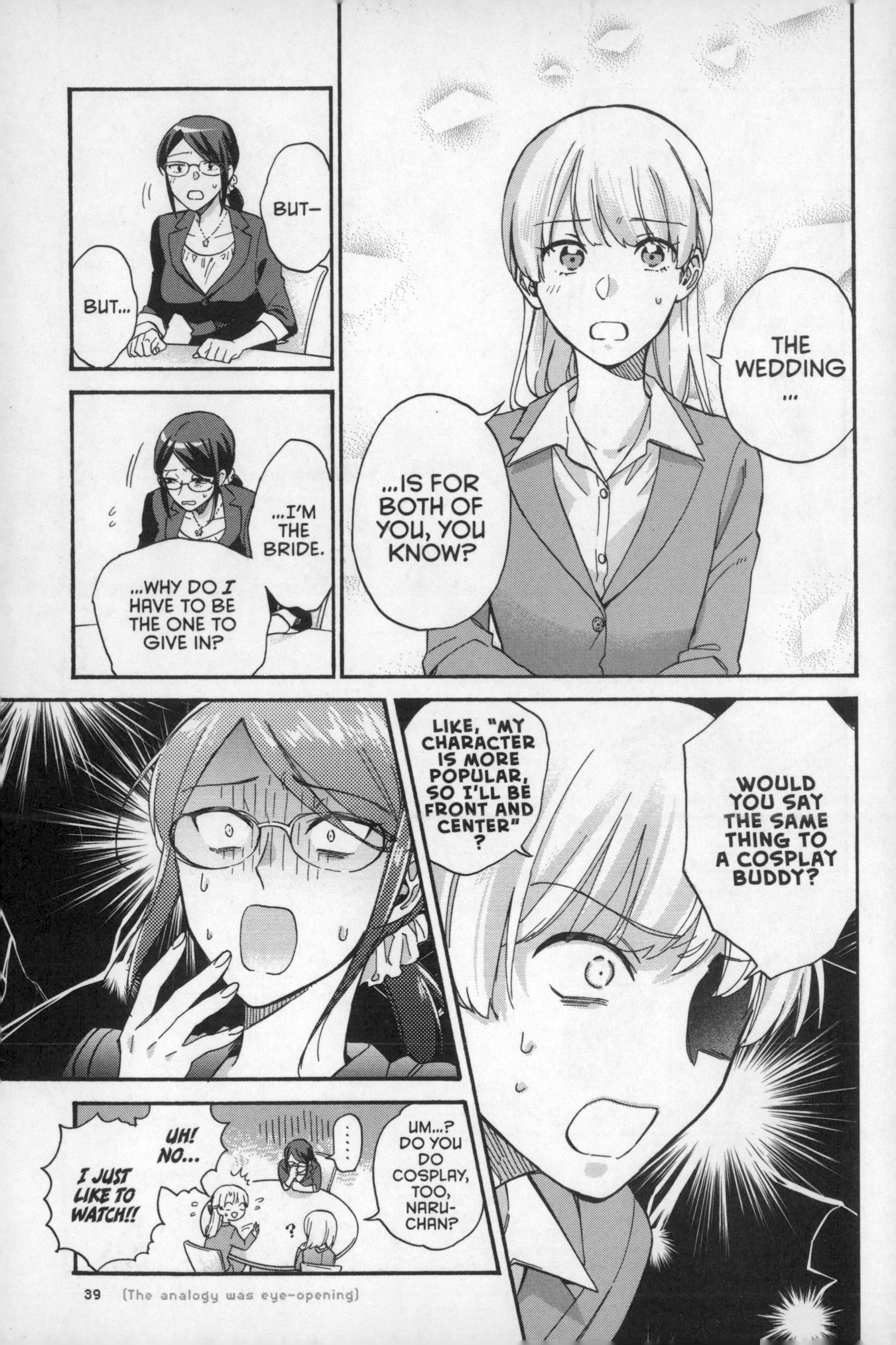
THE WEDDING ...
...IS FOR BOTH OF YOU, YOU KNOW?
BUT–
BUT...
...I'M THE BRIDE.
...WHY DO I HAVE TO BE THE ONE TO GIVE IN?
WOULD YOU SAY THE SAME THING TO A COSPLAY BUDDY?
LIKE, "MY CHARACTER IS MORE POPULAR, SO I'LL BE FRONT AND CENTER" ?
.....
UM...? DO YOU DO COSPLAY, TOO, NARU-CHAN?
UH! NO...
I JUST LIKE TO WATCH!!

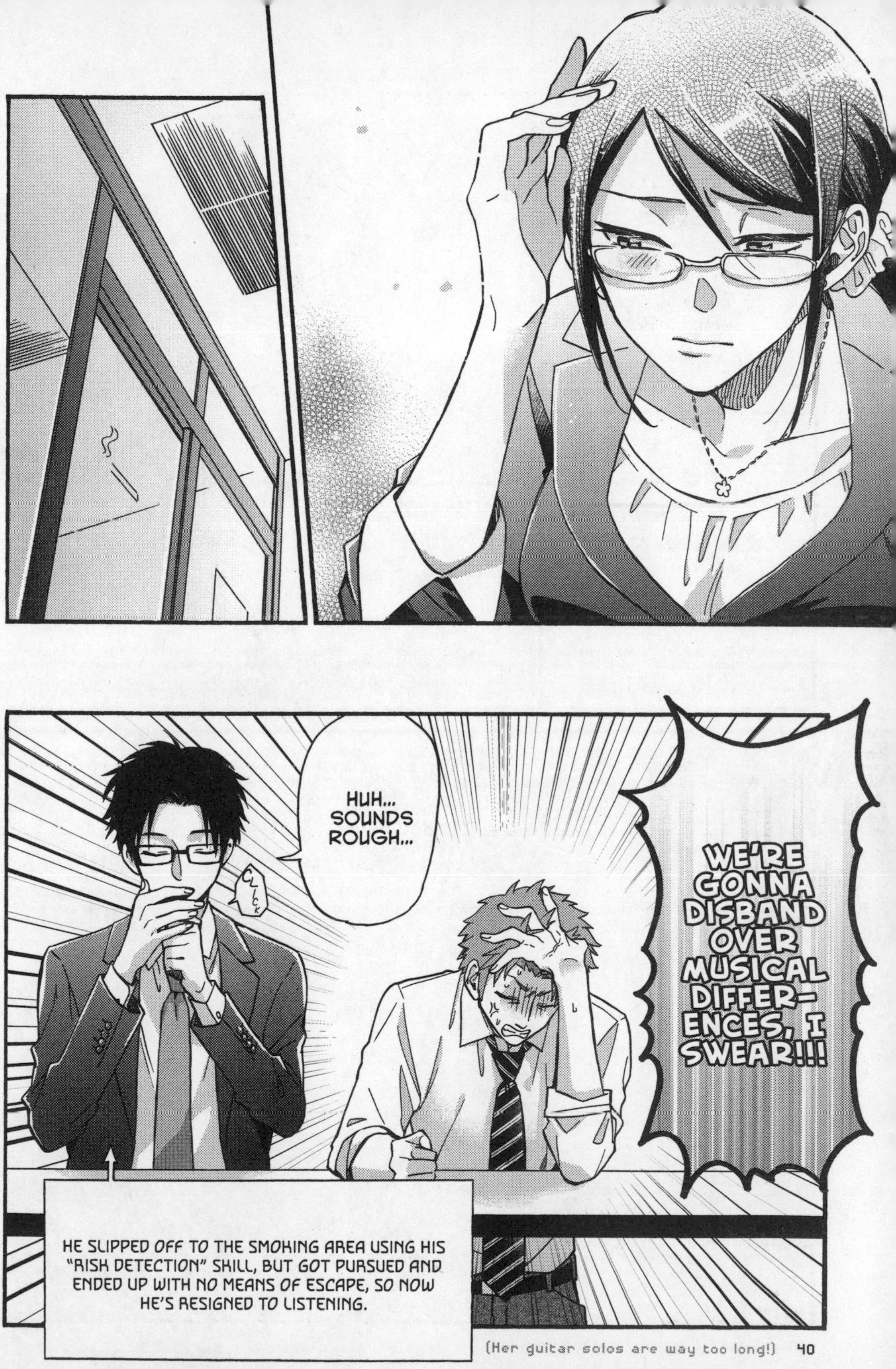
WE'RE GONNA DISBAND OVER MUSICAL DIFFER-ENCES, I SWEAR!!!
HUH... SOUNDS ROUGH...
CLICK
HE SLIPPED OFF TO THE SMOKING AREA USING HIS "RISK DETECTION" SKILL, BUT GOT PURSUED AND ENDED UP WITH NO MEANS OF ESCAPE, SO NOW HE'S RESIGNED TO LISTENING.

(Her guitar solos are way too long!)

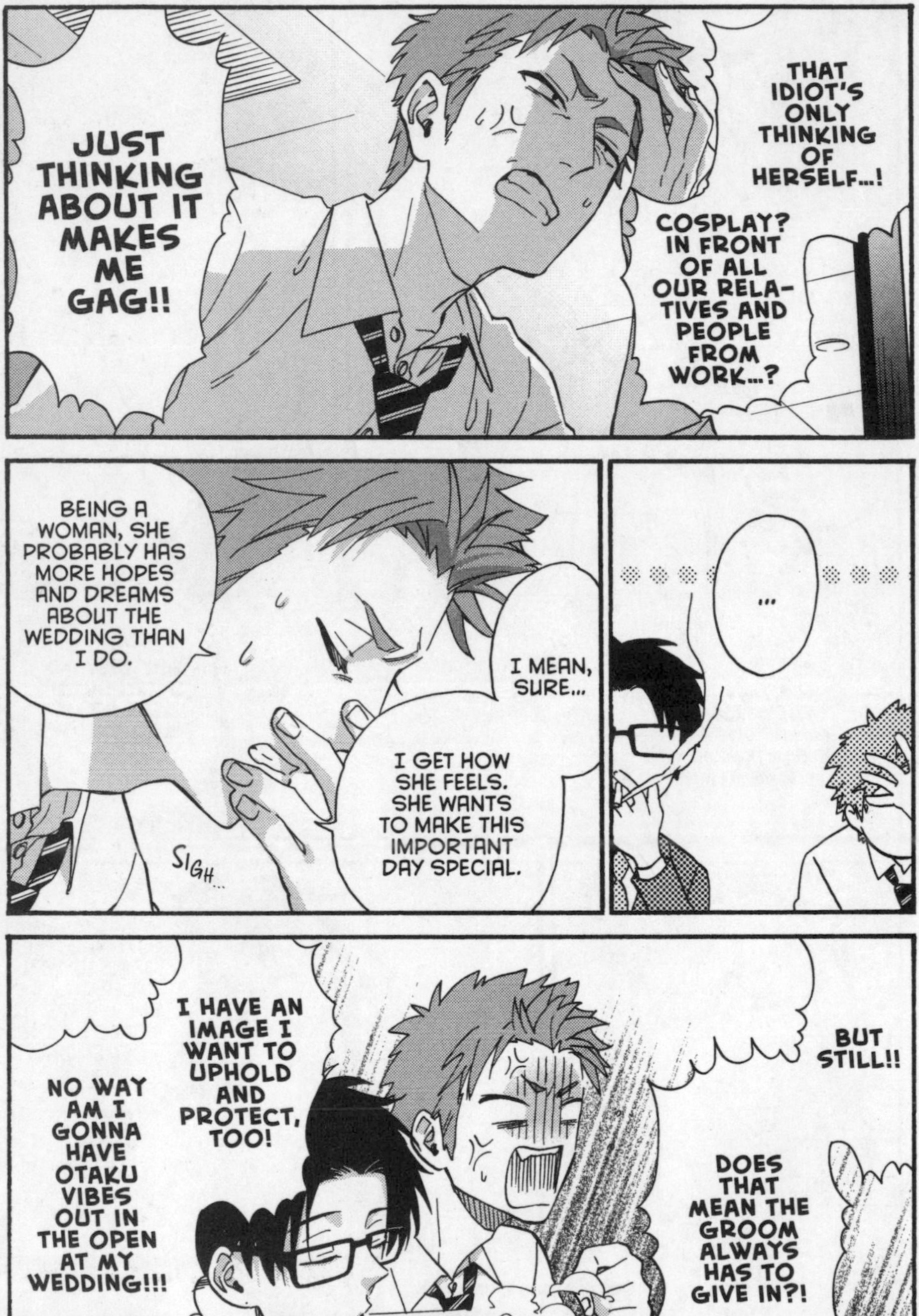
THAT IDIOT'S ONLY THINKING OF HERSELF...!
COSPLAY? IN FRONT OF ALL OUR RELA-TIVES AND PEOPLE FROM WORK...?
JUST THINKING ABOUT IT MAKES ME GAG!!
...
I MEAN, SURE...
I GET HOW SHE FEELS. SHE WANTS TO MAKE THIS IMPORTANT DAY SPECIAL.
BEING A WOMAN, SHE PROBABLY HAS MORE HOPES AND DREAMS ABOUT THE WEDDING THAN I DO.
SIGH...
BUT STILL!!
DOES THAT MEAN THE GROOM ALWAYS HAS TO GIVE IN?!
I HAVE AN IMAGE I WANT TO UPHOLD AND PROTECT, TOO!
NO WAY AM I GONNA HAVE OTAKU VIBES OUT IN THE OPEN AT MY WEDDING!!!

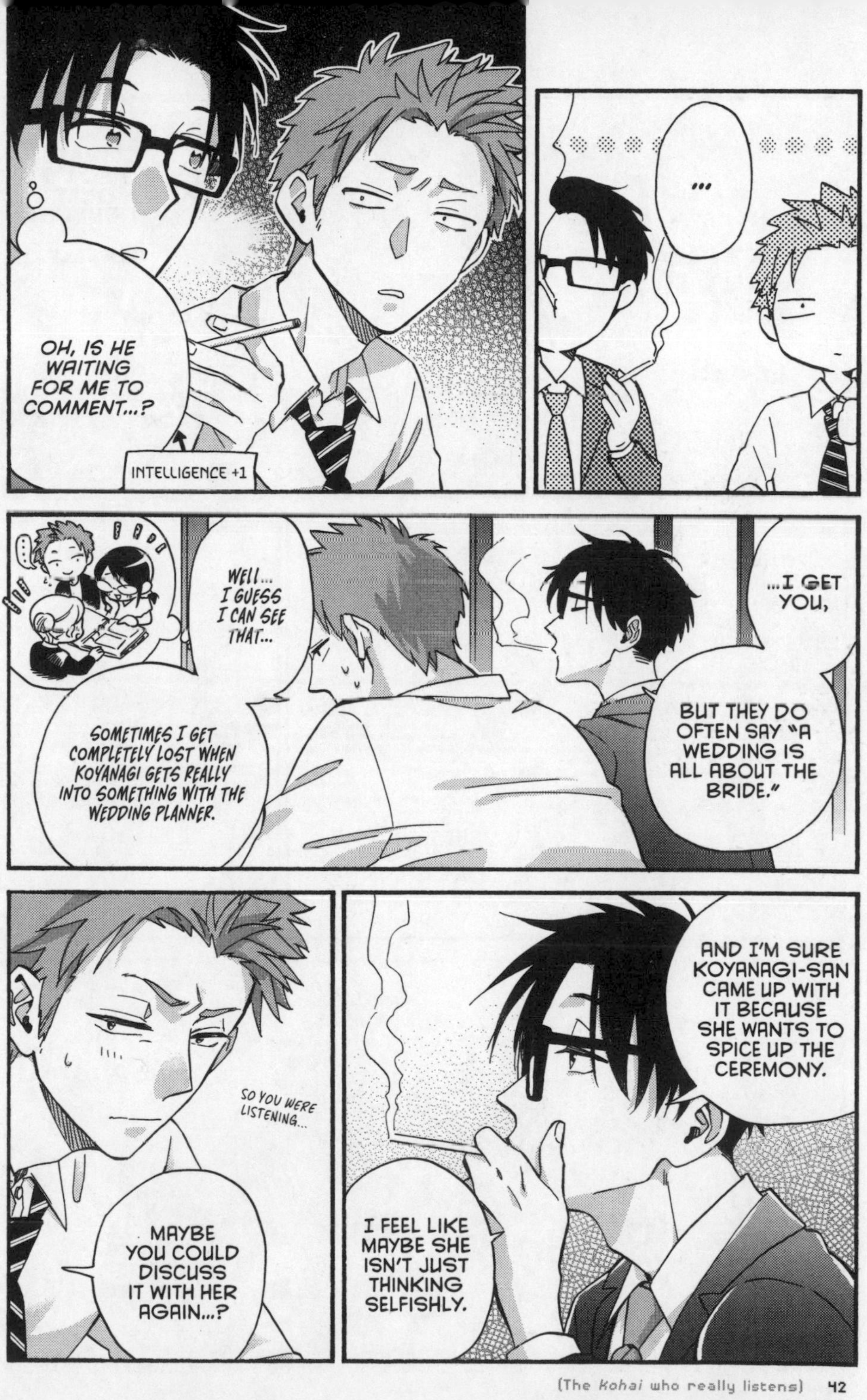
...
OH, IS HE WAITING FOR ME TO COMMENT...?
INTELLIGENCE +1
...I GET YOU,
BUT THEY DO OFTEN SAY "A WEDDING IS ALL ABOUT THE BRIDE."
WELL... I GUESS I CAN SEE THAT...
SOMETIMES I GET COMPLETELY LOST WHEN KOYANAGI GETS REALLY INTO SOMETHING WITH THE WEDDING PLANNER.
AND I'M SURE KOYANAGI-SAN CAME UP WITH IT BECAUSE SHE WANTS TO SPICE UP THE CEREMONY.
I FEEL LIKE MAYBE SHE ISN'T JUST THINKING SELFISHLY.
SO YOU WERE LISTENING...
MAYBE YOU COULD DISCUSS IT WITH HER AGAIN...?

(The *kohai* who really listens)

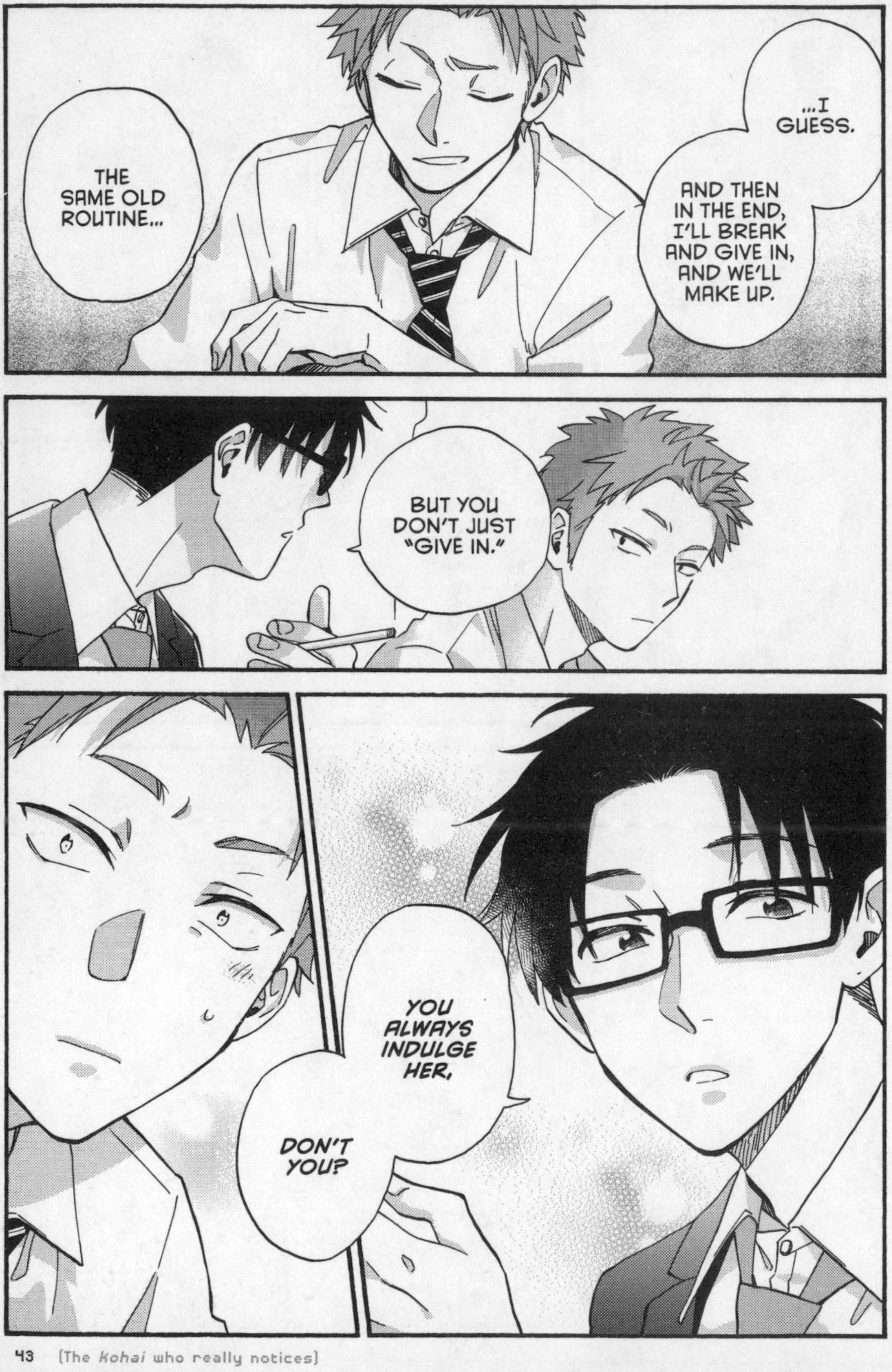
...I GUESS.
AND THEN IN THE END, I'LL BREAK AND GIVE IN, AND WE'LL MAKE UP.
THE SAME OLD ROUTINE...
BUT YOU DON'T JUST "GIVE IN."
YOU ALWAYS INDULGE HER,
DON'T YOU?

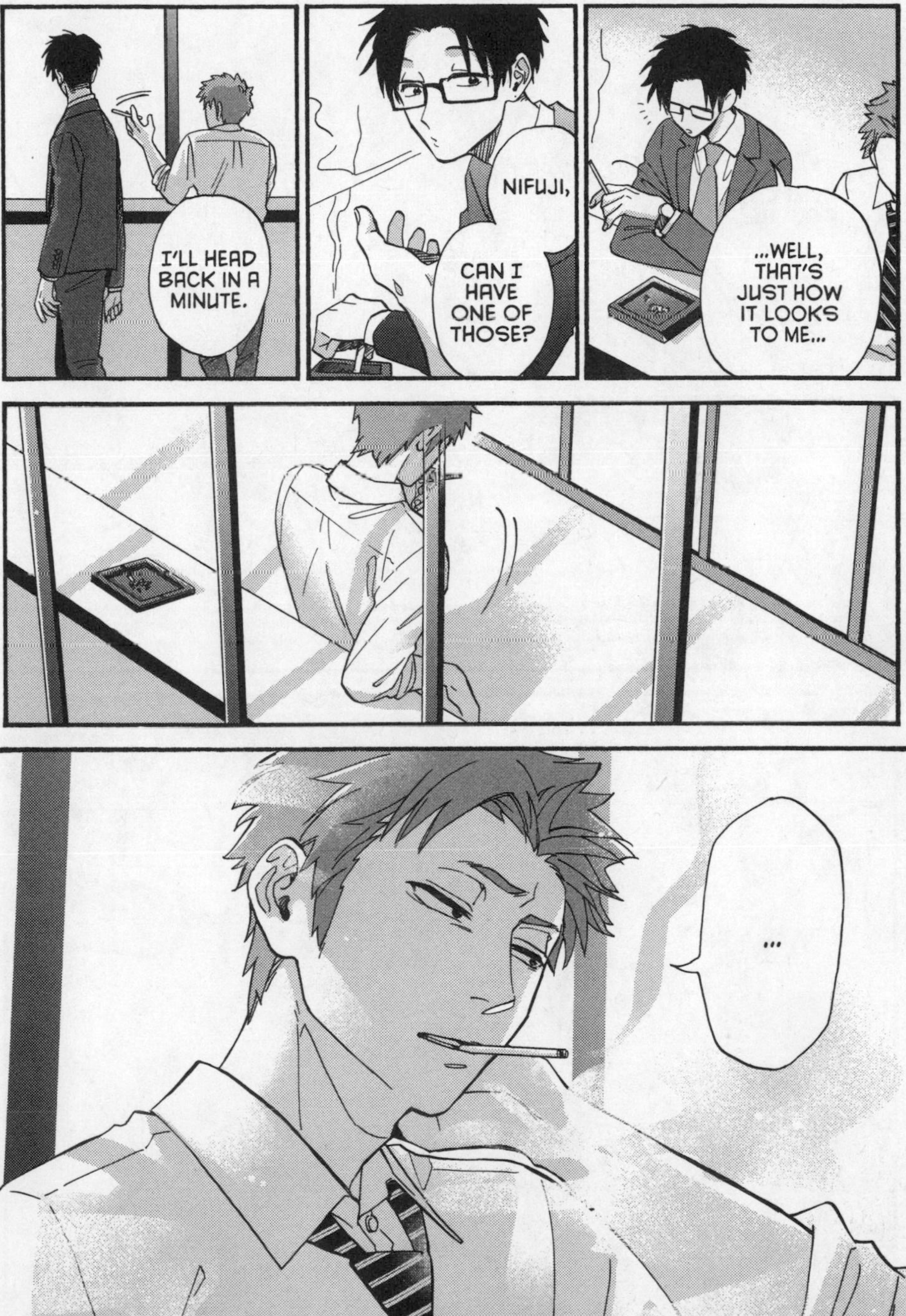
...WELL, THAT'S JUST HOW IT LOOKS TO ME...
NIFUJI,
CAN I HAVE ONE OF THOSE?
I'LL HEAD BACK IN A MINUTE.
...

← To be continued...

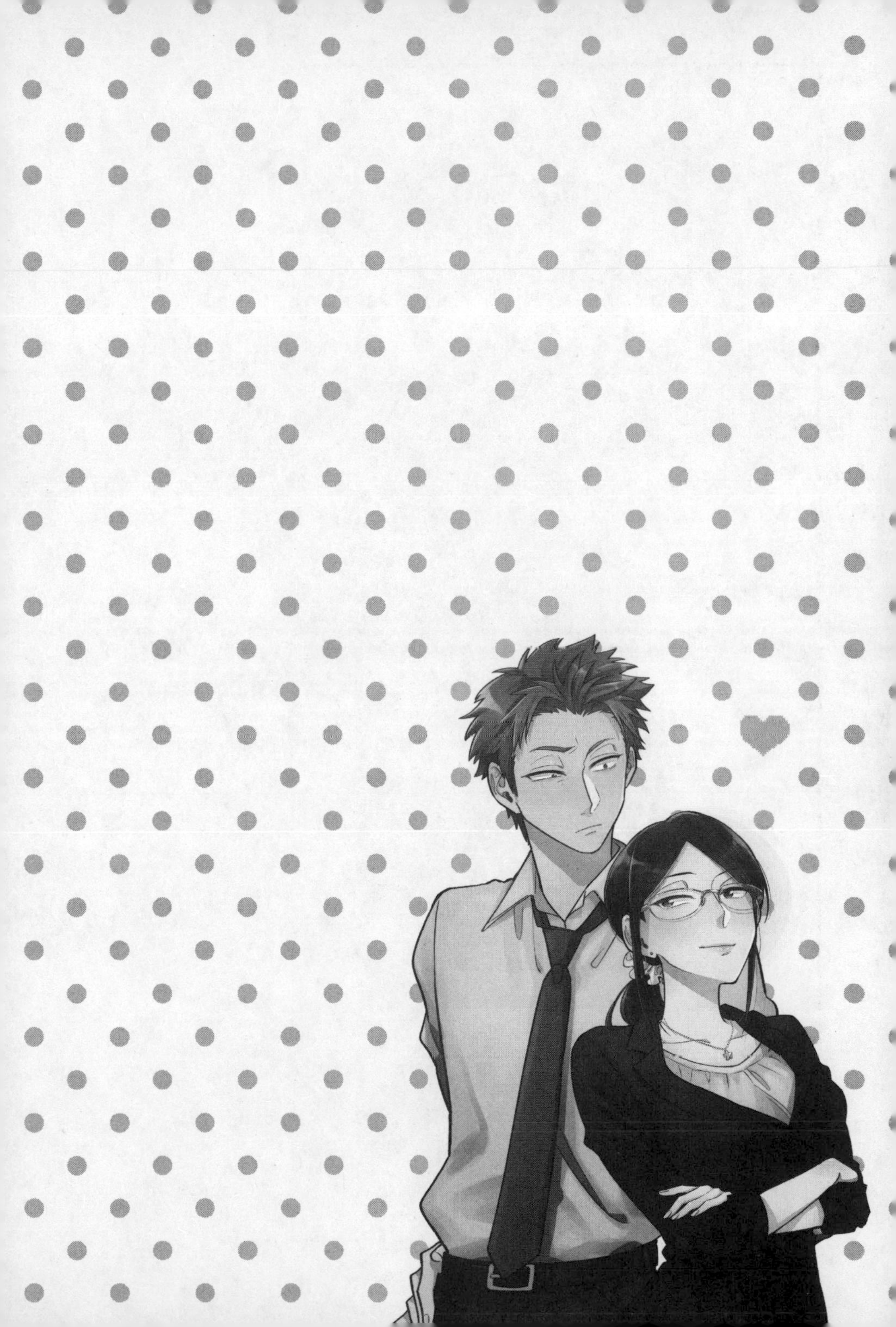

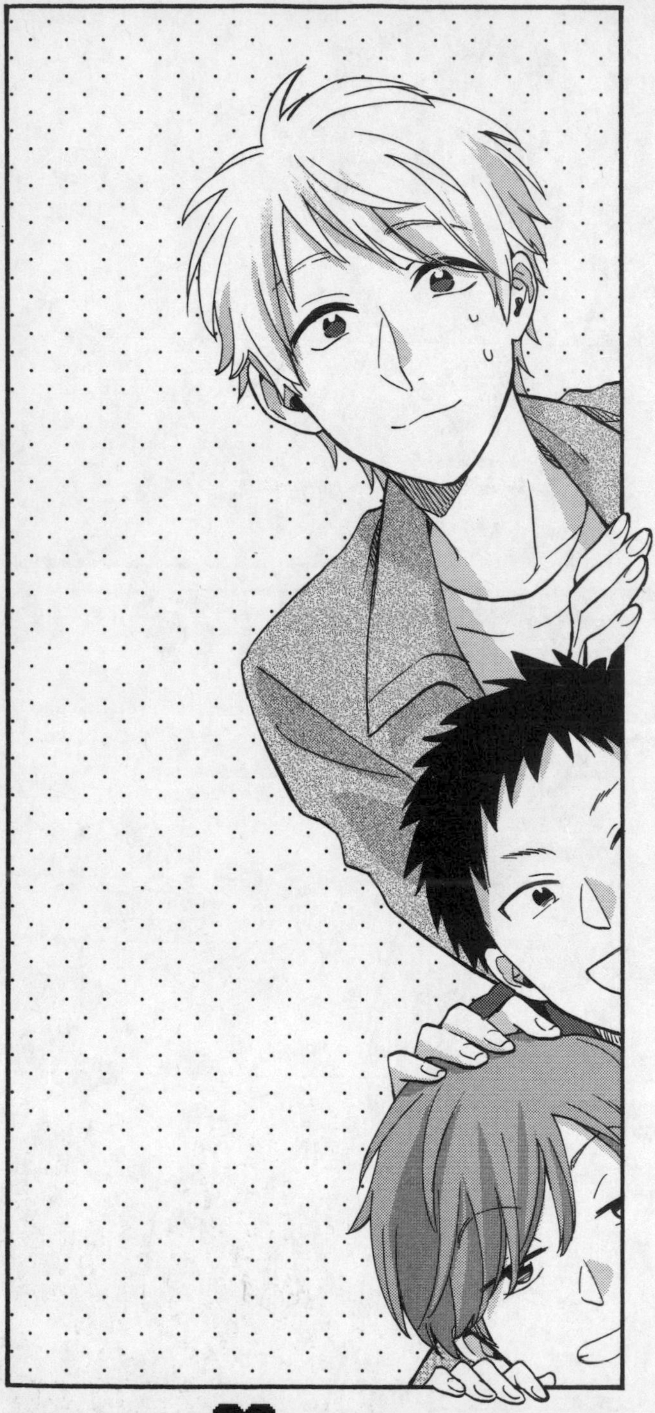

Episode....66

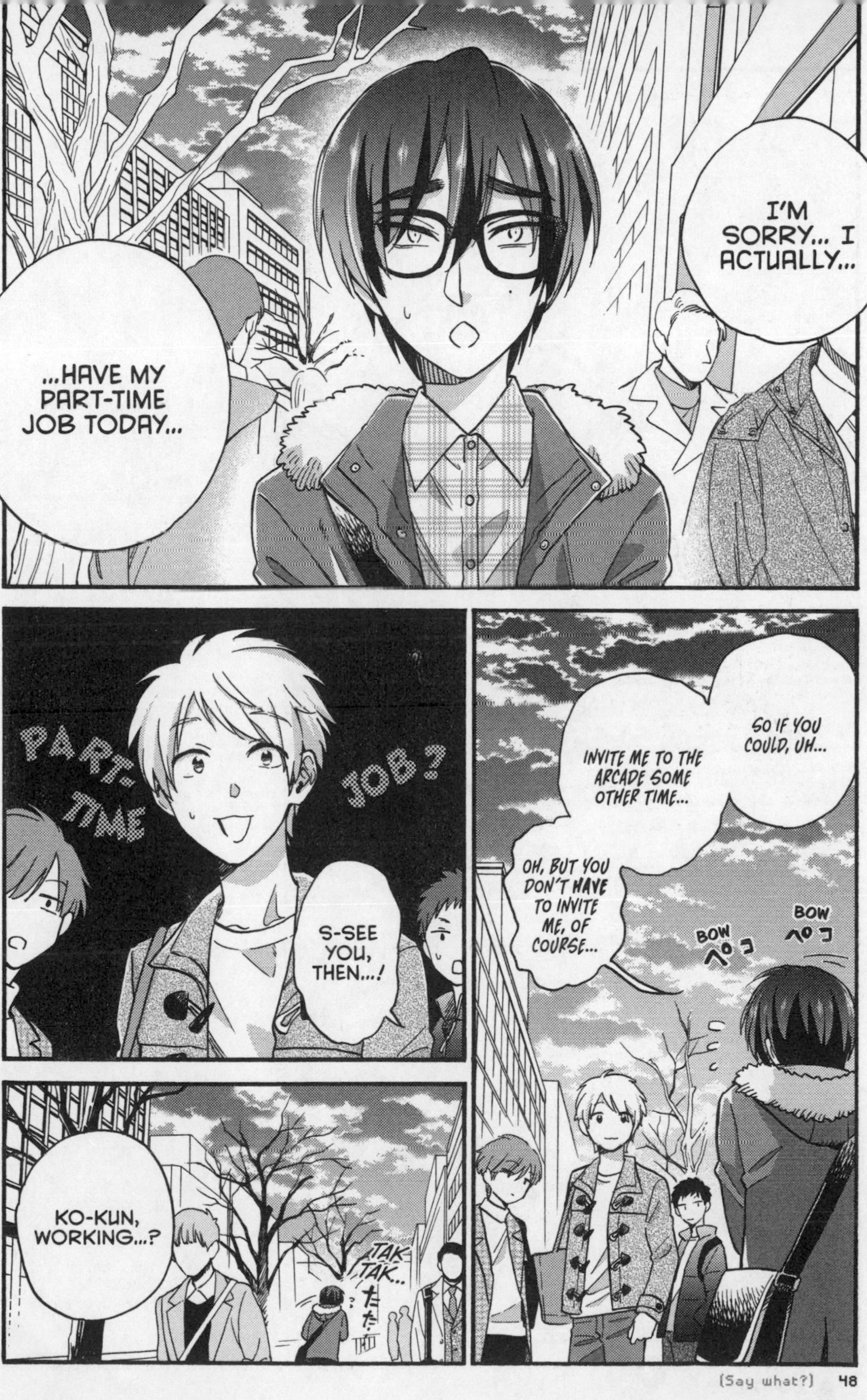
I'M SORRY... I ACTUALLY...
...HAVE MY PART-TIME JOB TODAY...
SO IF YOU COULD, UH...
INVITE ME TO THE ARCADE SOME OTHER TIME...
OH, BUT YOU DON'T HAVE TO INVITE ME, OF COURSE...
BOW ぺこ
BOW ぺこ
PART-TIME JOB?
S-SEE YOU, THEN...!
KO-KUN, WORKING...?
TAK TAK... たた

(Say what?)

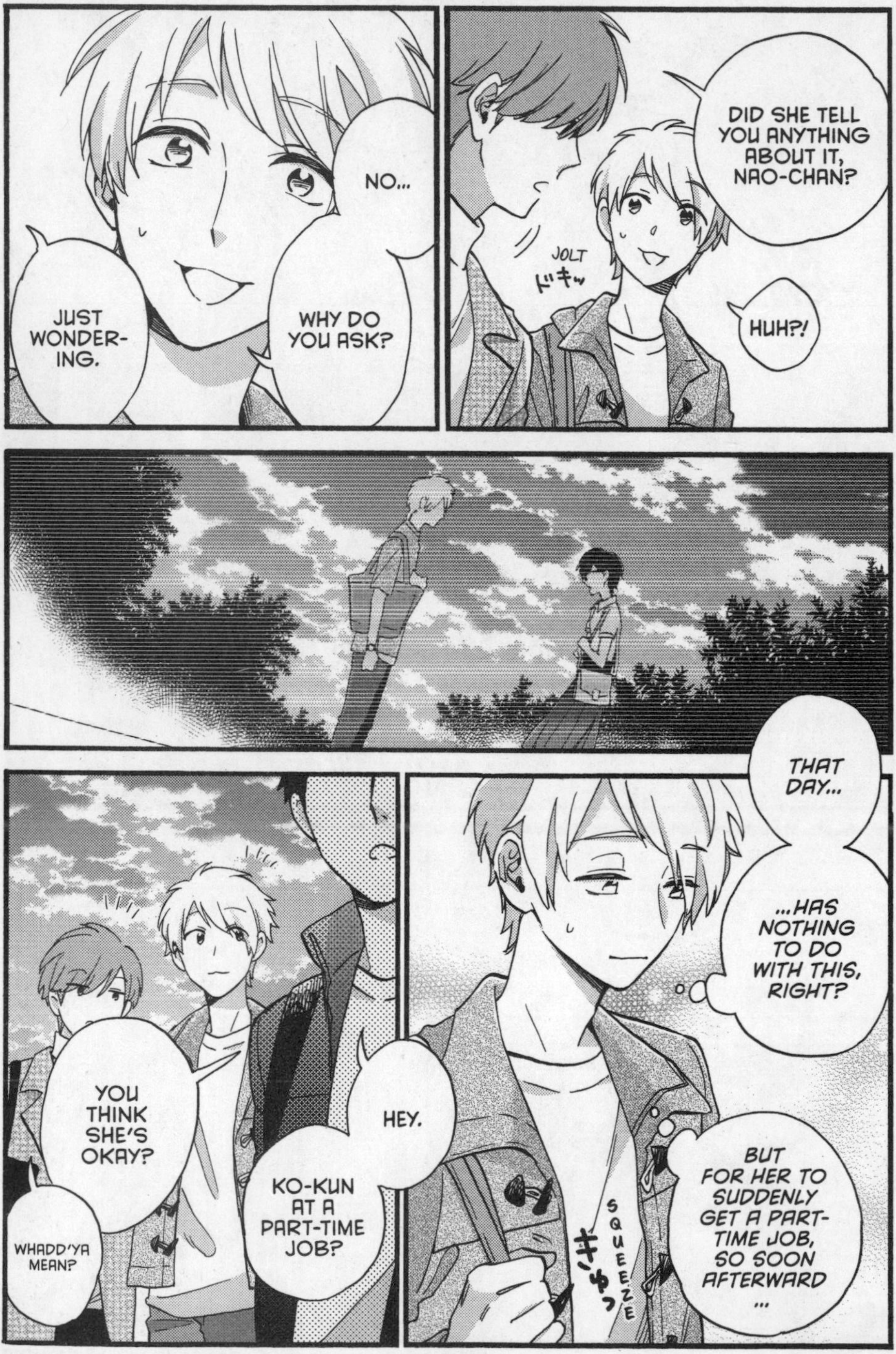
DID SHE TELL YOU ANYTHING ABOUT IT, NAO-CHAN?
JOLT ドキッ
HUH?!
NO...
WHY DO YOU ASK?
JUST WONDER-ING.
THAT DAY...
...HAS NOTHING TO DO WITH THIS, RIGHT?
BUT FOR HER TO SUDDENLY GET A PART-TIME JOB, SO SOON AFTERWARD ...
SQUEEZE きゅっ
HEY.
KO-KUN AT A PART-TIME JOB?
YOU THINK SHE'S OKAY?
WHADD'YA MEAN?

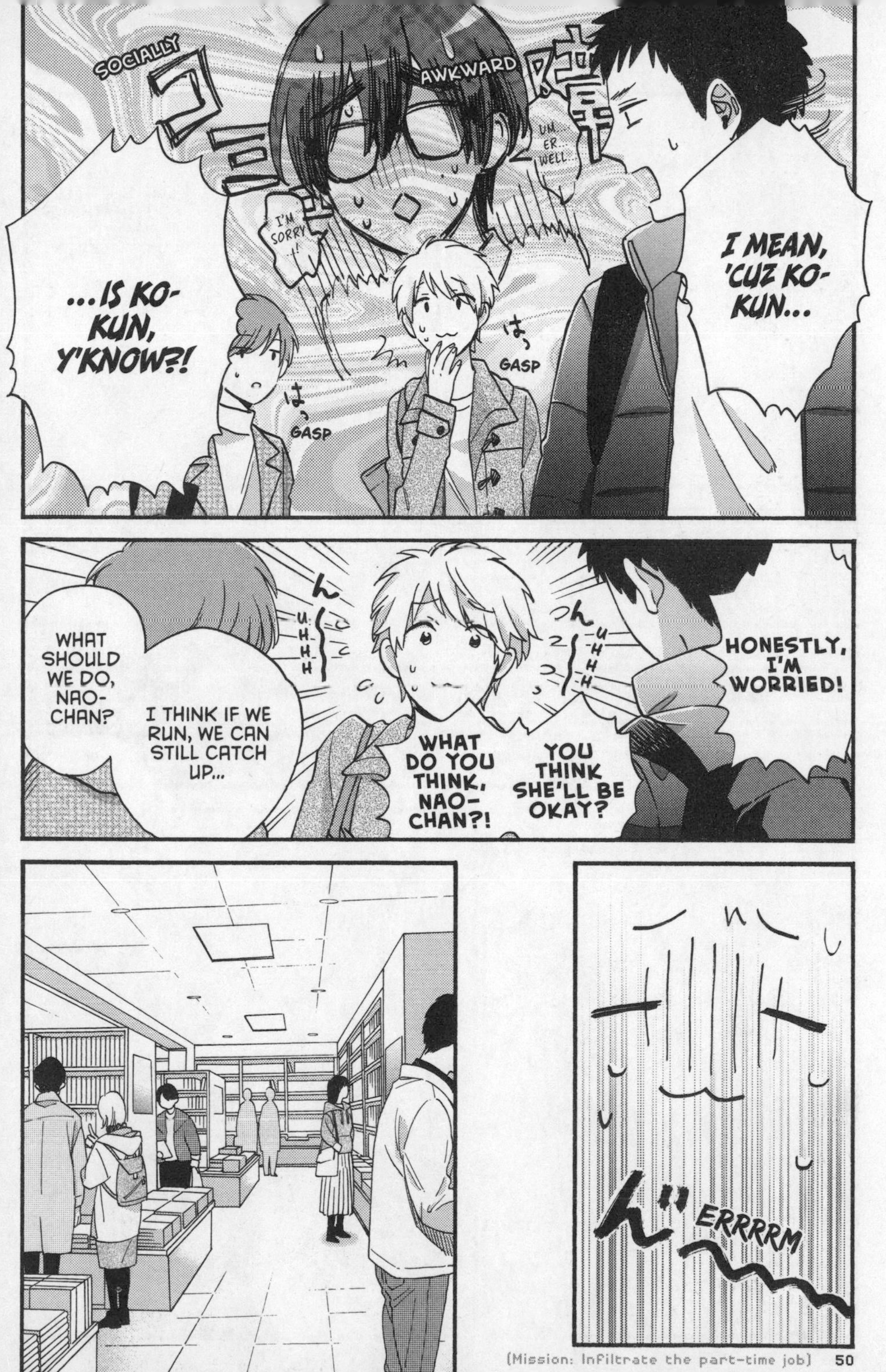
I MEAN, 'CUZ KO-KUN...
UM... ER... WELL...
AWKWARD
SOCIALLY
I'M SORRY!
GASP
GASP
...IS KO-KUN, Y'KNOW?!
HONESTLY, I'M WORRIED!
UHHH
YOU THINK SHE'LL BE OKAY?
WHAT DO YOU THINK, NAO-CHAN?!
UHHH
I THINK IF WE RUN, WE CAN STILL CATCH UP...
WHAT SHOULD WE DO, NAO-CHAN?
ERRRRM

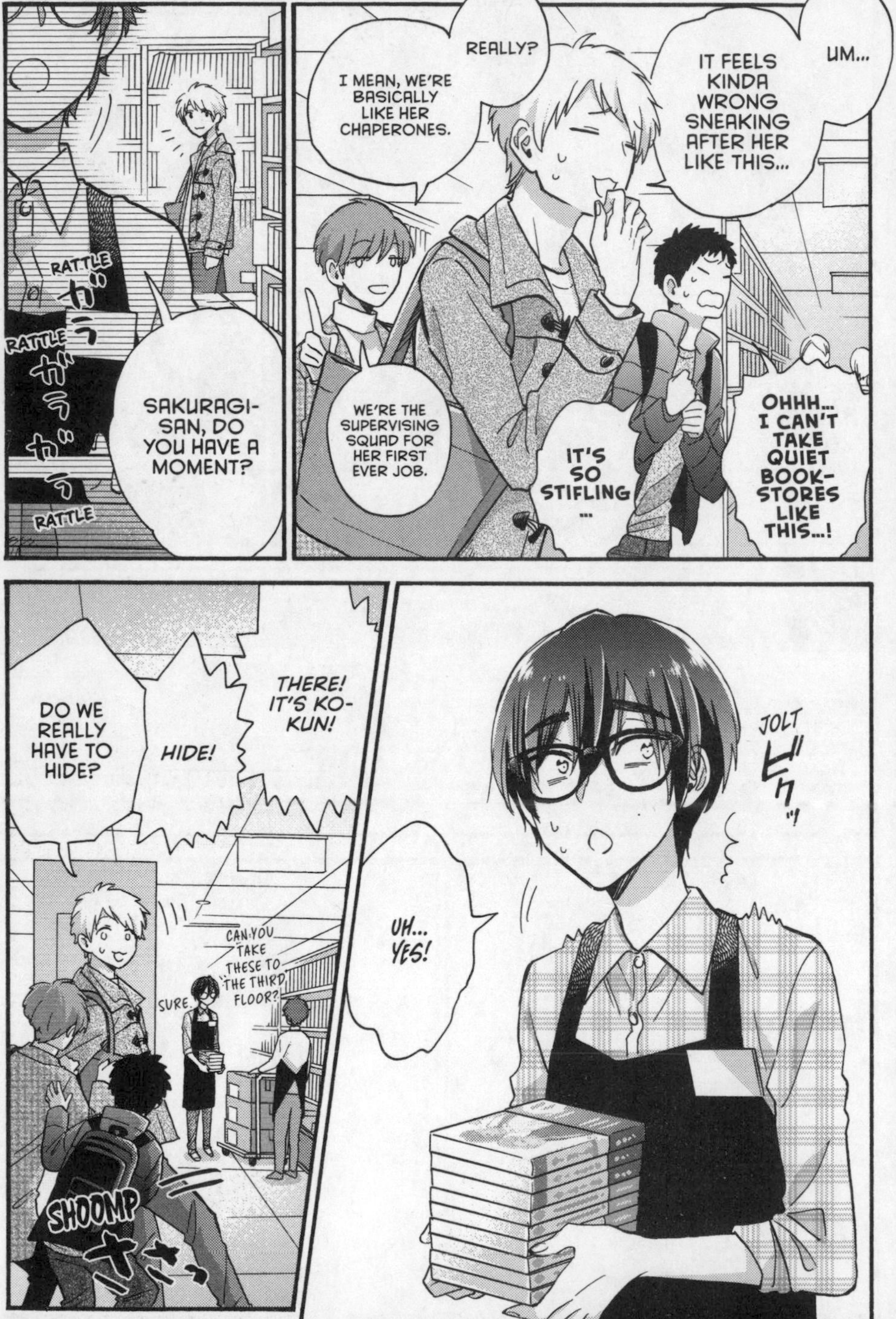
UM...
IT FEELS KINDA WRONG SNEAKING AFTER HER LIKE THIS...
REALLY?
I MEAN, WE'RE BASICALLY LIKE HER CHAPERONES.
OHHH... I CAN'T TAKE QUIET BOOK-STORES LIKE THIS...!
IT'S SO STIFLING...
WE'RE THE SUPERVISING SQUAD FOR HER FIRST EVER JOB.
RATTLE
RATTLE
RATTLE
SAKURAGI-SAN, DO YOU HAVE A MOMENT?
JOLT
UH... YES!
THERE! IT'S KO-KUN!
HIDE!
DO WE REALLY HAVE TO HIDE?
CAN YOU TAKE THESE TO THE THIRD FLOOR?
SURE.
SHOOMP

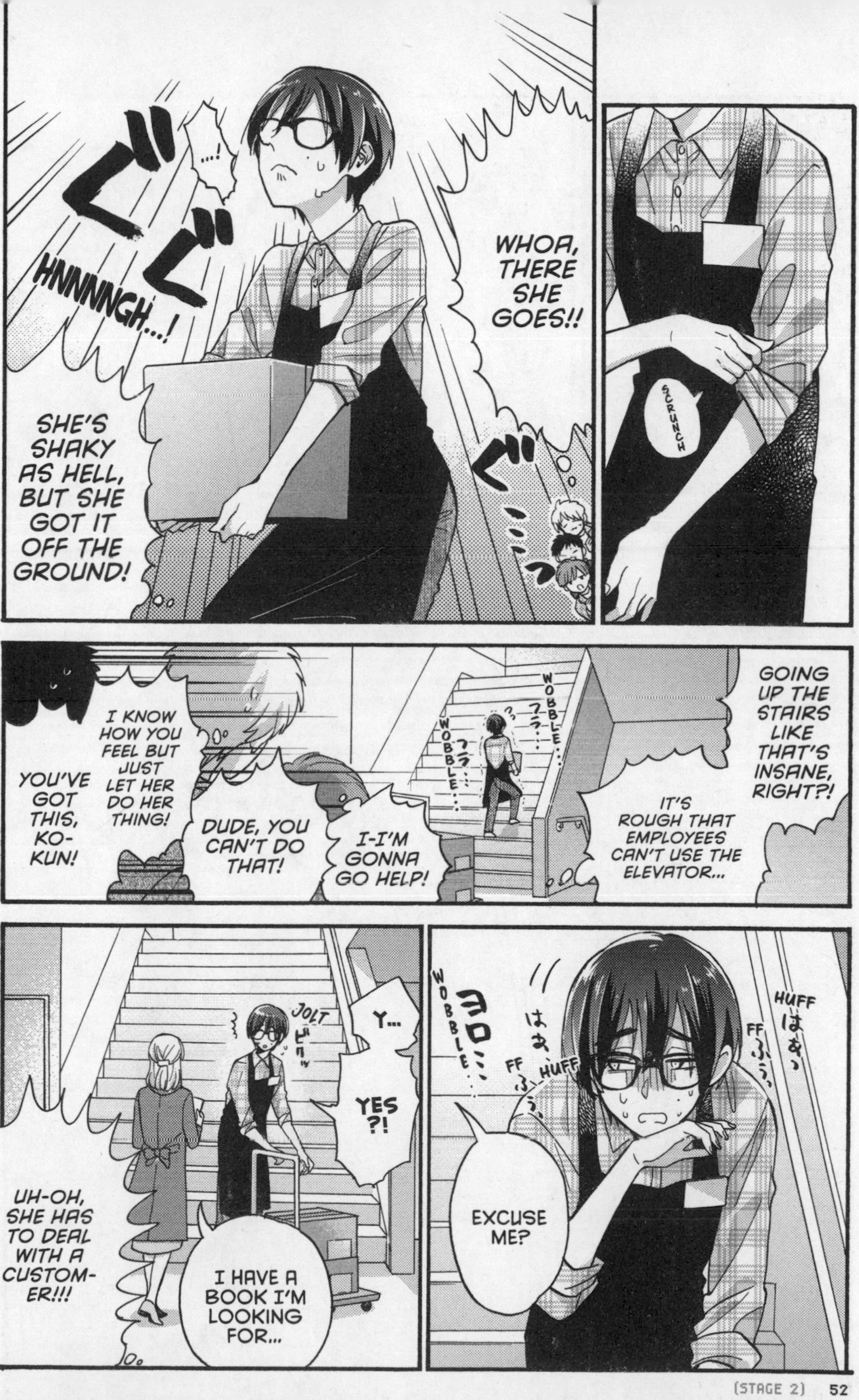
SCRUNCH
WHOA, THERE SHE GOES!!
...!
HNNNNGH...!
SHE'S SHAKY AS HELL, BUT SHE GOT IT OFF THE GROUND!
GOING UP THE STAIRS LIKE THAT'S INSANE, RIGHT?!
IT'S ROUGH THAT EMPLOYEES CAN'T USE THE ELEVATOR...
WOBBLE... フラ...
WOBBLE... フラ...
I-I'M GONNA GO HELP!
DUDE, YOU CAN'T DO THAT!
I KNOW HOW YOU FEEL BUT JUST LET HER DO HER THING!
YOU'VE GOT THIS, KO-KUN!
HUFF はぁっ
FF ふぅ
HUFF はぁ
FF ふぅ
WOBBLE... ヨロ...
EXCUSE ME?
Y...
JOLT ビクッ
YES?!
UH-OH, SHE HAS TO DEAL WITH A CUSTOMER!!!
I HAVE A BOOK I'M LOOKING FOR...

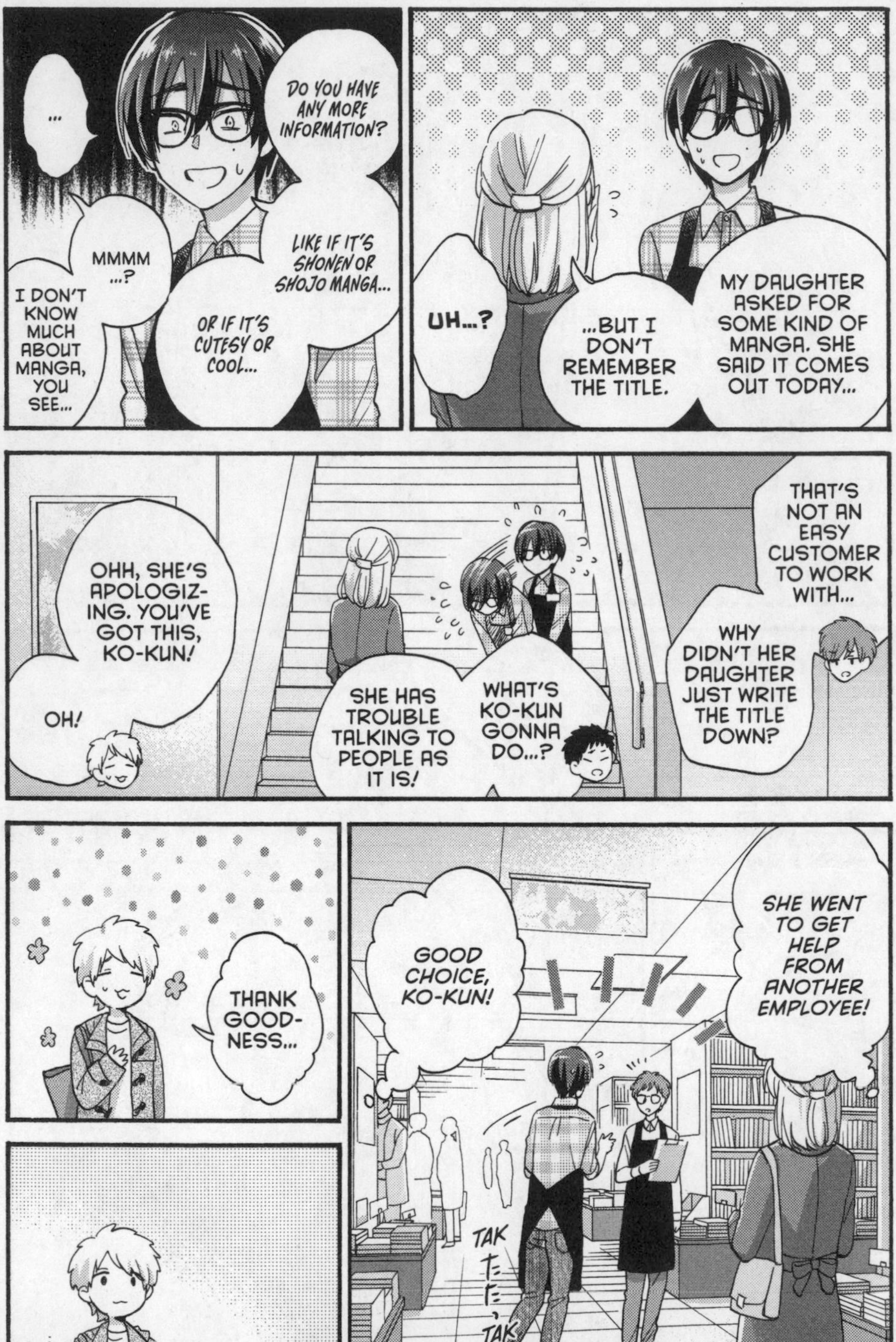
MY DAUGHTER ASKED FOR SOME KIND OF MANGA. SHE SAID IT COMES OUT TODAY...
...BUT I DON'T REMEMBER THE TITLE.
UH...?
DO YOU HAVE ANY MORE INFORMATION?
...
LIKE IF IT'S SHONEN OR SHOJO MANGA...
OR IF IT'S CUTESY OR COOL...
MMMM ...?
I DON'T KNOW MUCH ABOUT MANGA, YOU SEE...
THAT'S NOT AN EASY CUSTOMER TO WORK WITH...
WHY DIDN'T HER DAUGHTER JUST WRITE THE TITLE DOWN?
WHAT'S KO-KUN GONNA DO...?
SHE HAS TROUBLE TALKING TO PEOPLE AS IT IS!
OHH, SHE'S APOLOGIZING. YOU'VE GOT THIS, KO-KUN!
OH!
SHE WENT TO GET HELP FROM ANOTHER EMPLOYEE!
GOOD CHOICE, KO-KUN!
TAK
TAK
THANK GOODNESS...

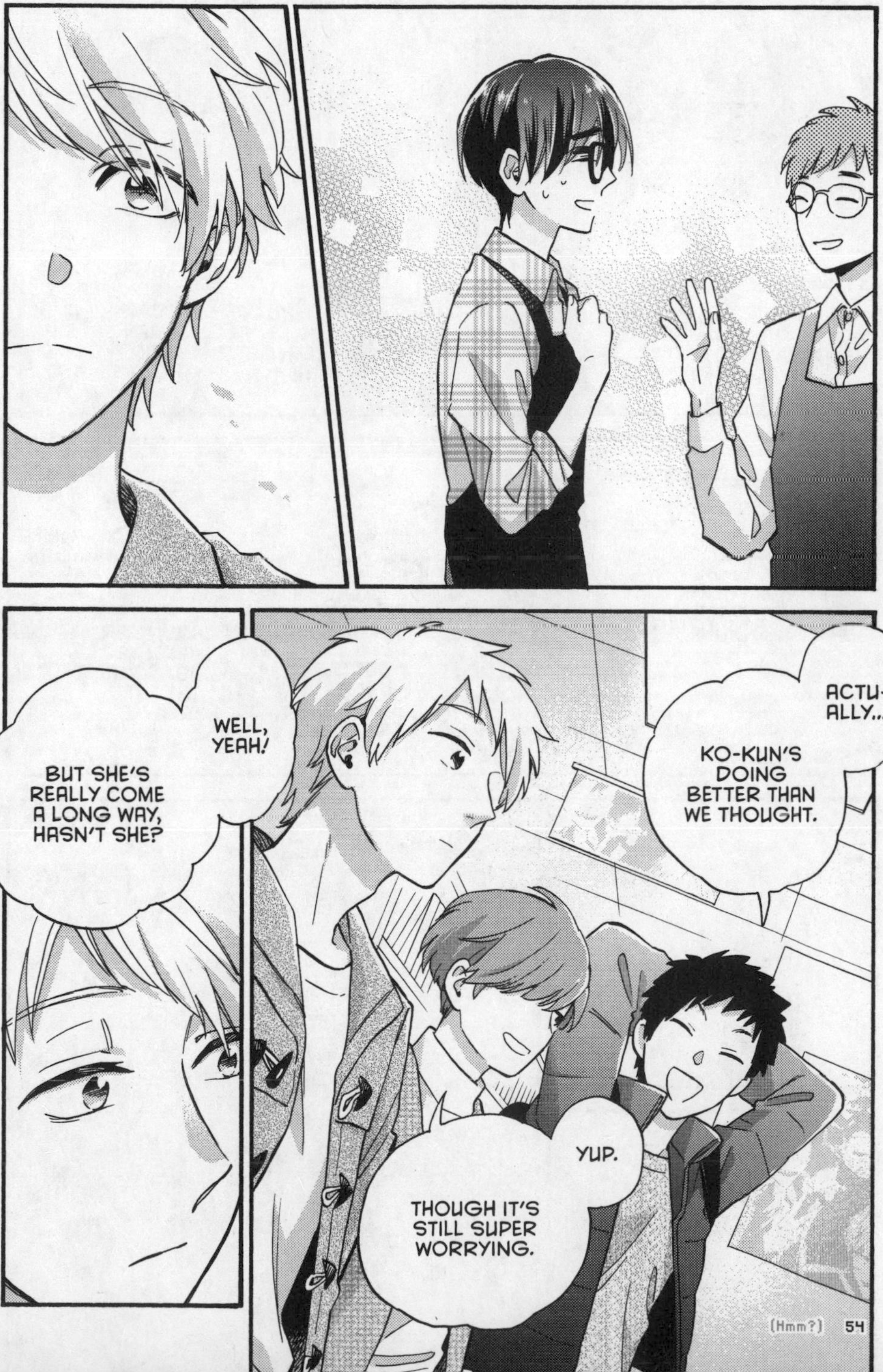
ACTU-ALLY...
KO-KUN'S DOING BETTER THAN WE THOUGHT.
YUP.
THOUGH IT'S STILL SUPER WORRYING.
WELL, YEAH!
BUT SHE'S REALLY COME A LONG WAY, HASN'T SHE?
[Hmm?]

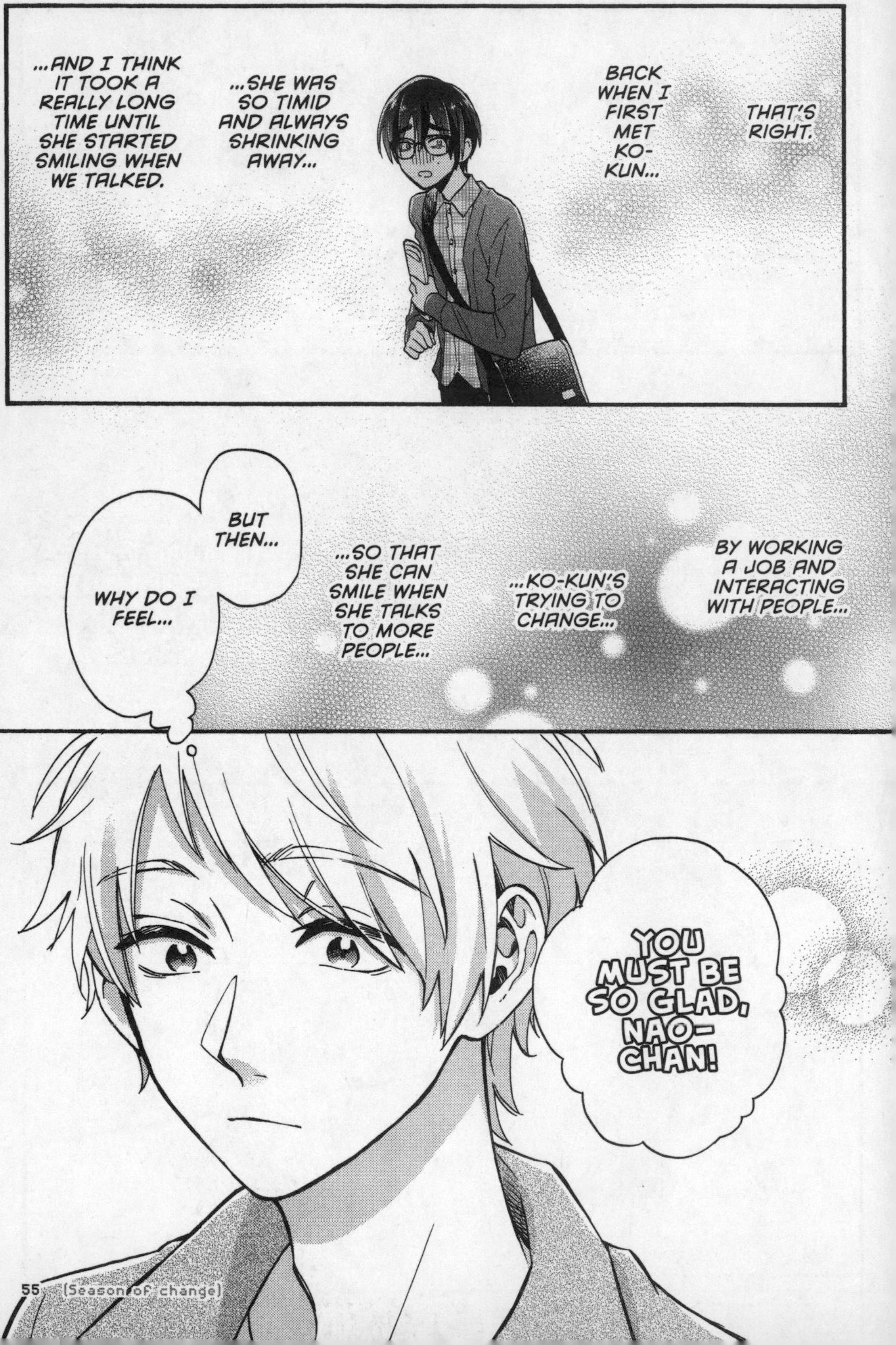
THAT'S RIGHT.
BACK WHEN I FIRST MET KO-KUN...
...SHE WAS SO TIMID AND ALWAYS SHRINKING AWAY...
...AND I THINK IT TOOK A REALLY LONG TIME UNTIL SHE STARTED SMILING WHEN WE TALKED.
BY WORKING A JOB AND INTERACTING WITH PEOPLE...
...KO-KUN'S TRYING TO CHANGE...
...SO THAT SHE CAN SMILE WHEN SHE TALKS TO MORE PEOPLE...
BUT THEN...
WHY DO I FEEL...
YOU MUST BE SO GLAD, NAO-CHAN!

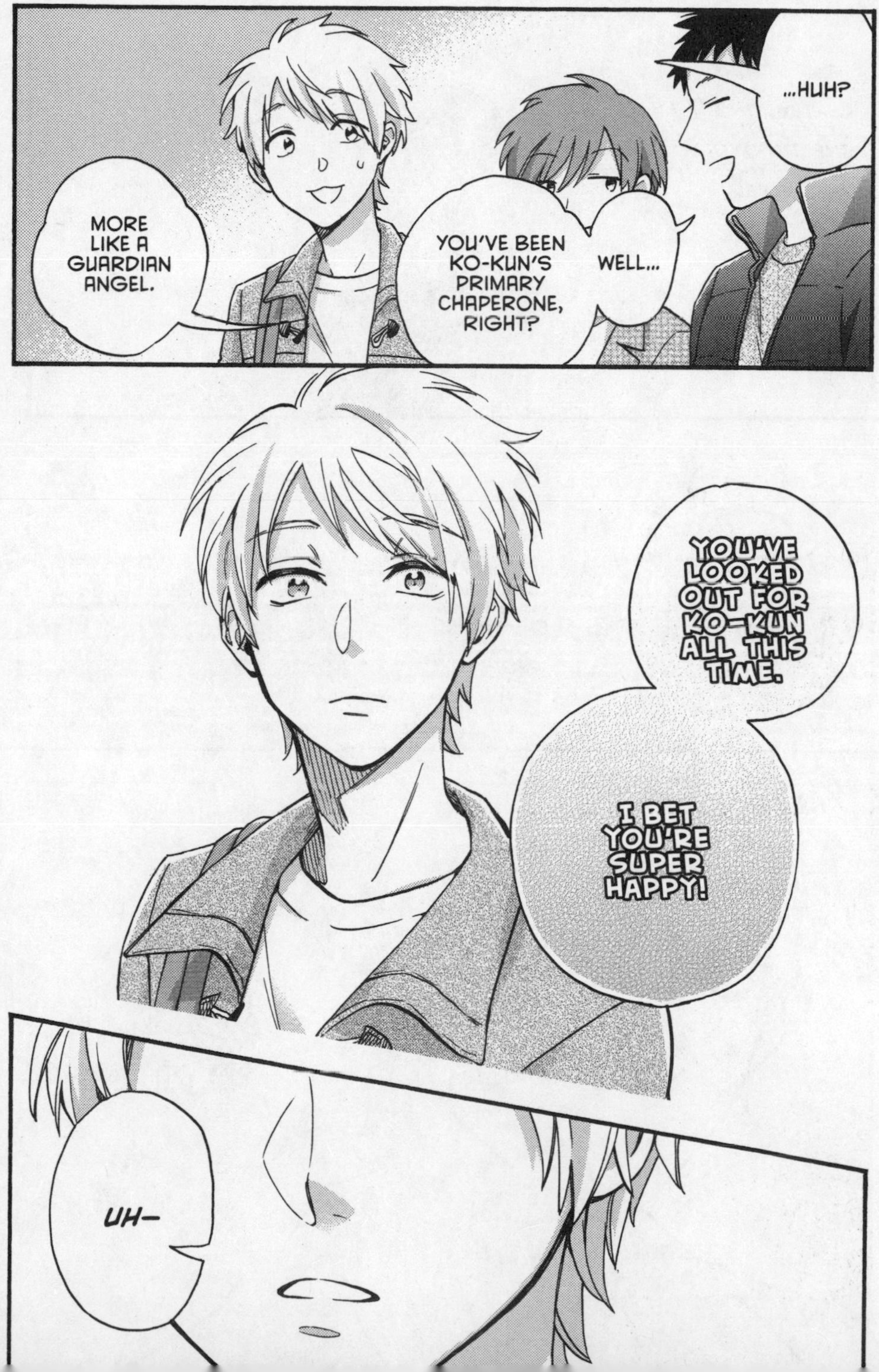
...HUH?
WELL...
YOU'VE BEEN KO-KUN'S PRIMARY CHAPERONE, RIGHT?
MORE LIKE A GUARDIAN ANGEL.
YOU'VE LOOKED OUT FOR KO-KUN ALL THIS TIME.
I BET YOU'RE SUPER HAPPY!
UH-

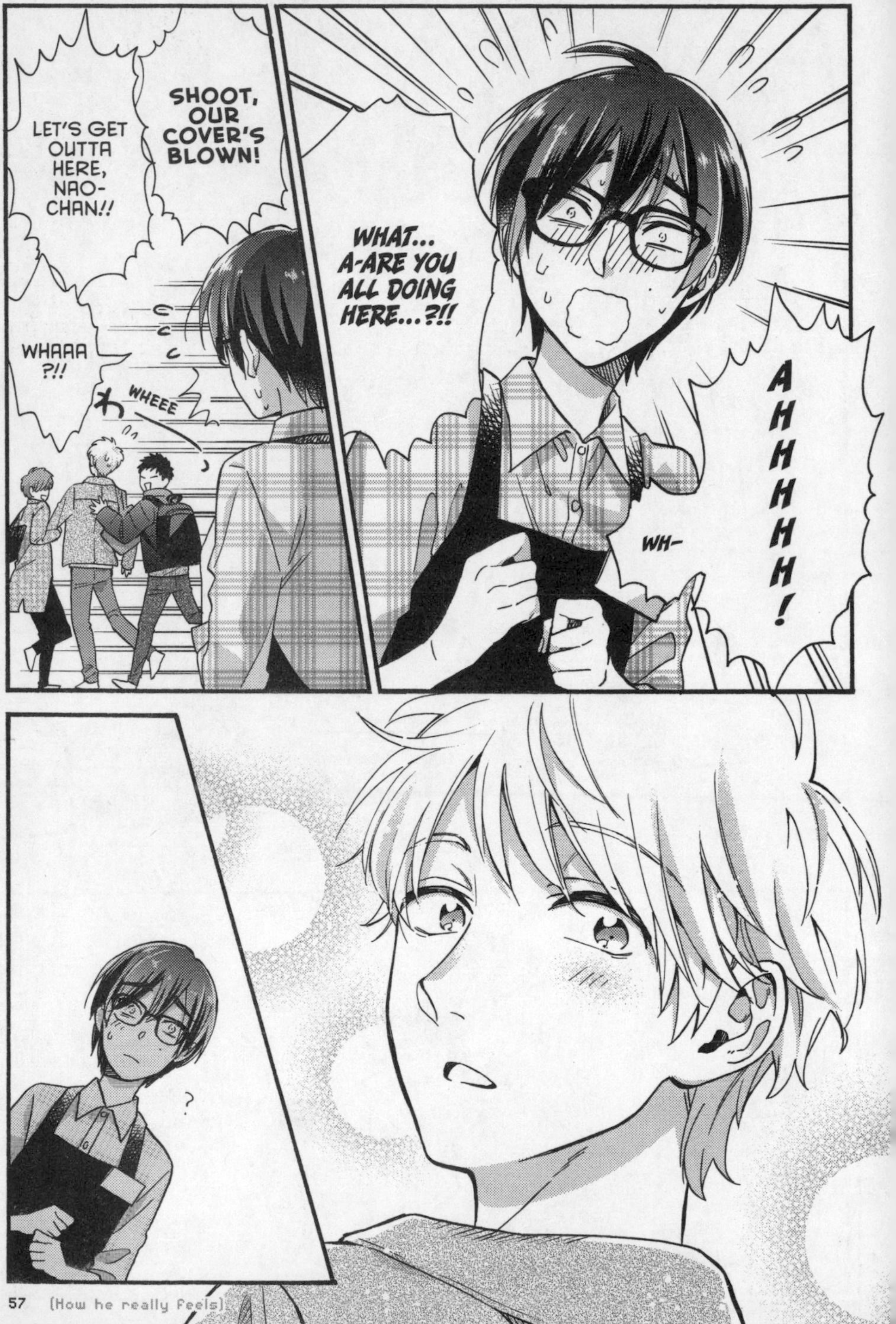
WHAT... A-ARE YOU ALL DOING HERE...?!!
AHHHHHH!
WH-
SHOOT, OUR COVER'S BLOWN!
LET'S GET OUTTA HERE, NAO-CHAN!!
WHAAA ?!!
WHEEE
わ
?

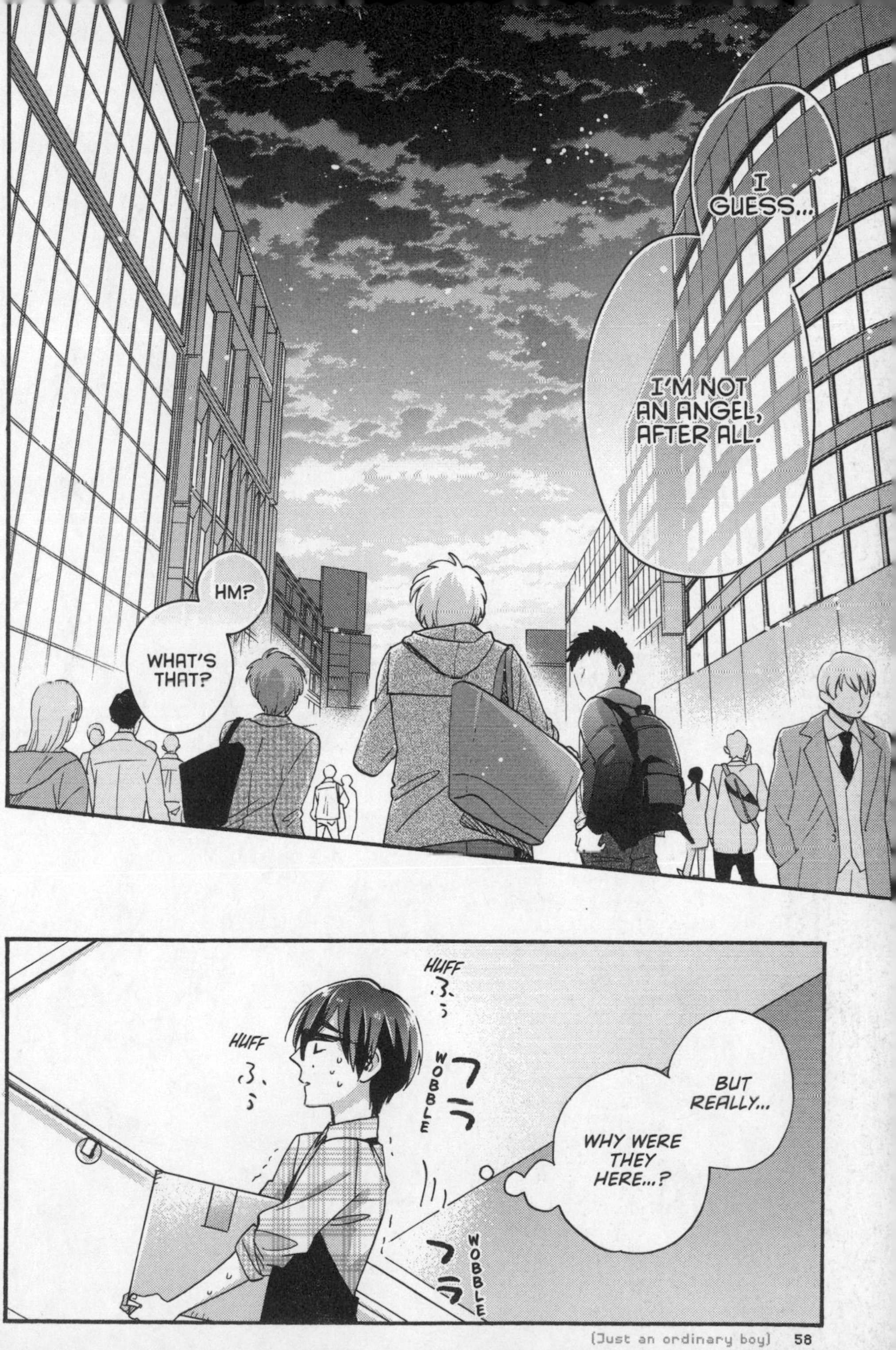
I GUESS...
I'M NOT AN ANGEL, AFTER ALL.
HM?
WHAT'S THAT?
BUT REALLY...
WHY WERE THEY HERE...?
HUFF ふぅ
HUFF ふぅ
WOBBLE フラ
WOBBLE フラ

CHARACTERS 05

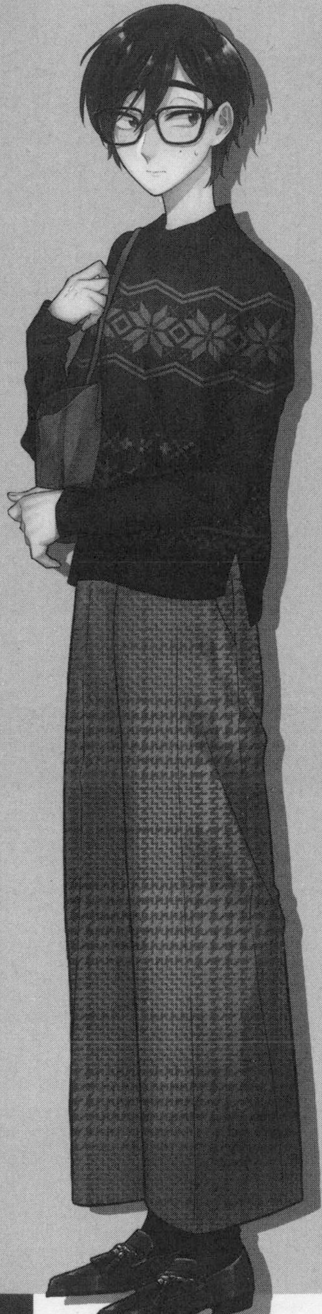

Ko Sakuragi's fashion

Ko Sakuragi

...

Birthday
Oct 15th

Age
19

Height
170 cm

Blood type
A

Constellation
Libra

Naoya Nifuji

• • •

Birthday
Apr 21

Age
19

Height
177 cm

Blood type
AB

Constellation
Taurus

Naoya Nifuji's fashion

CHARACTERS **06**

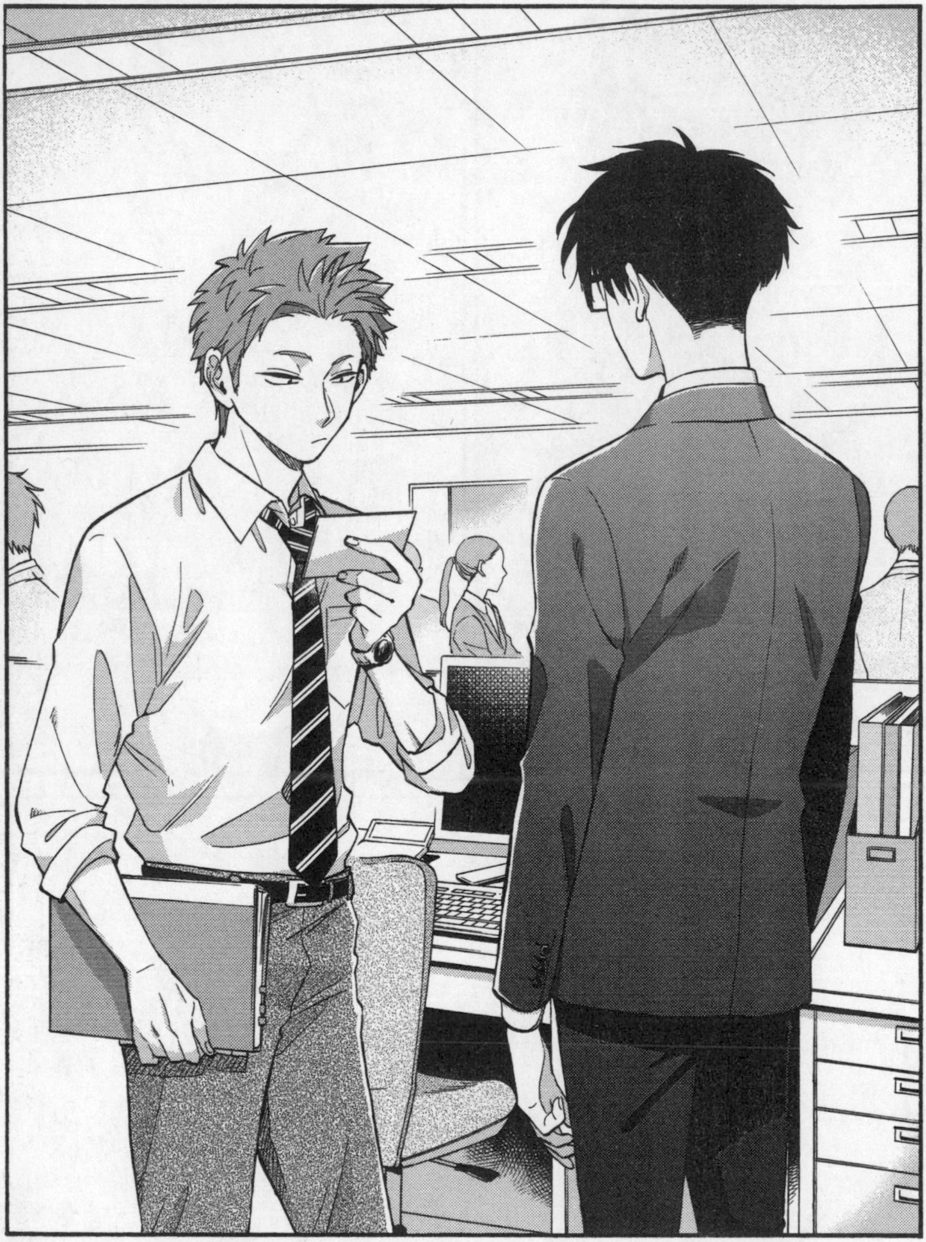

Episode.... 67

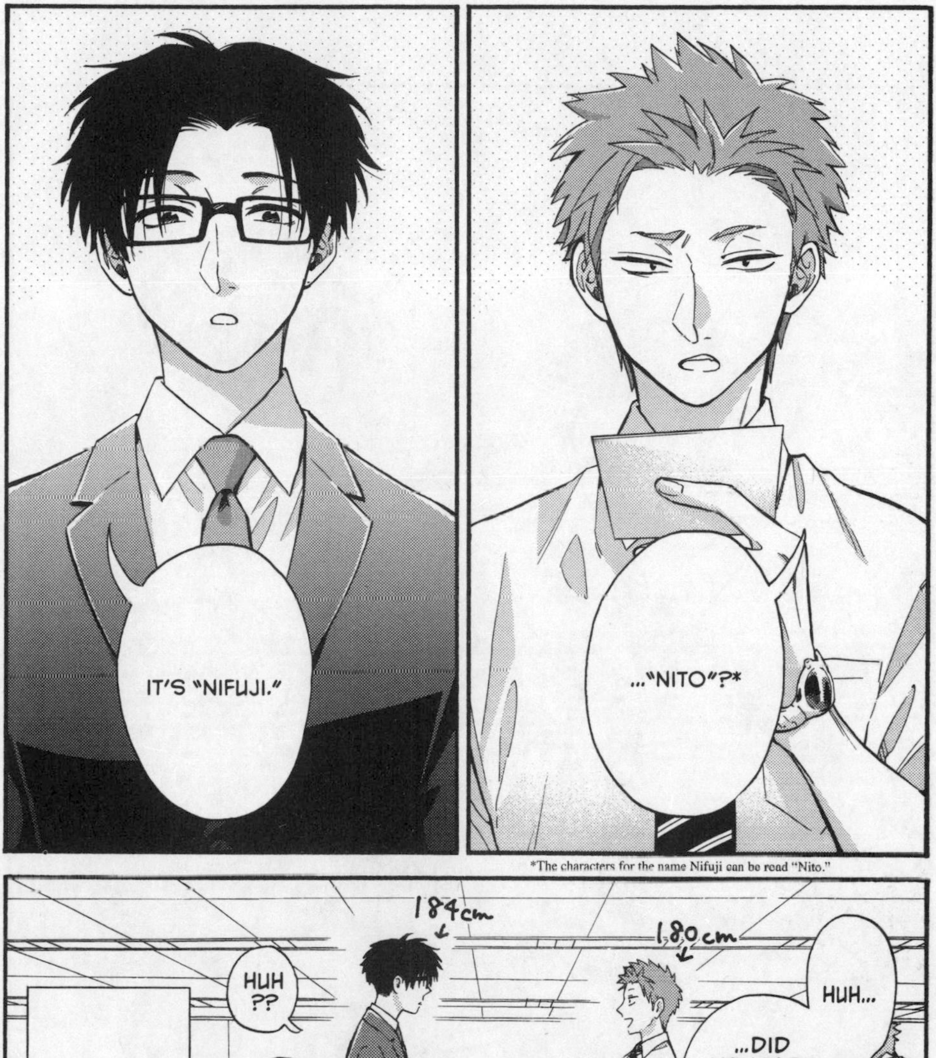
..."NITO"?*
IT'S "NIFUJI."

*The characters for the name Nifuji can be read "Nito."

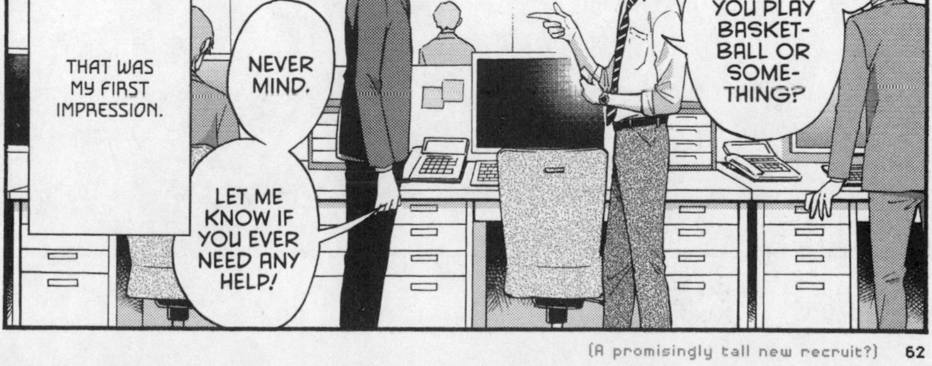
HUH...
...DID YOU PLAY BASKET-BALL OR SOME-THING?
180 cm
184 cm
HUH ??
NEVER MIND.
LET ME KNOW IF YOU EVER NEED ANY HELP!
THAT WAS MY FIRST IMPRESSION.

(A promisingly tall new recruit?)

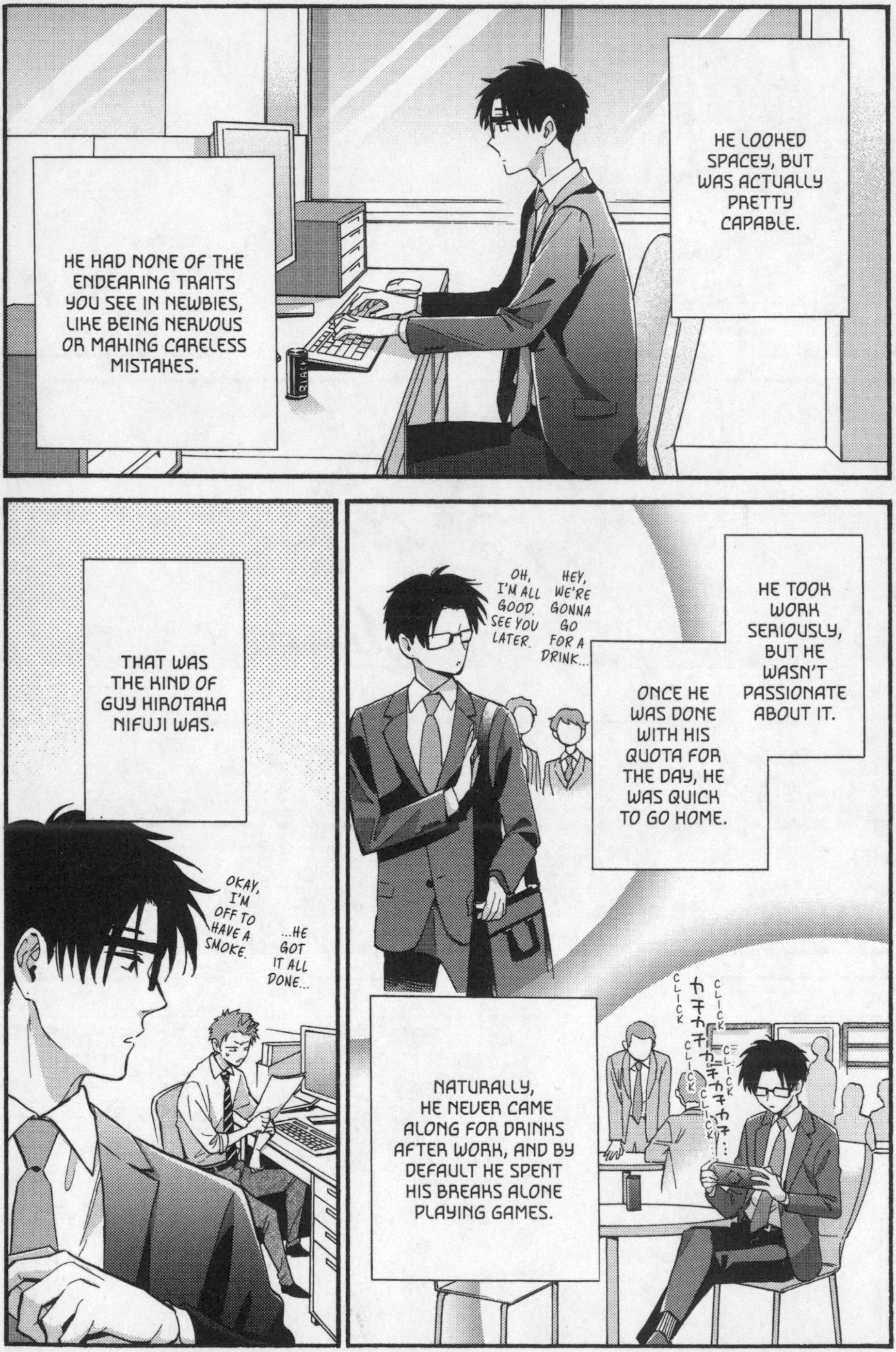
HE LOOKED SPACEY, BUT WAS ACTUALLY PRETTY CAPABLE.
HE HAD NONE OF THE ENDEARING TRAITS YOU SEE IN NEWBIES, LIKE BEING NERVOUS OR MAKING CARELESS MISTAKES.
BLACK
HE TOOK WORK SERIOUSLY, BUT HE WASN'T PASSIONATE ABOUT IT.
ONCE HE WAS DONE WITH HIS QUOTA FOR THE DAY, HE WAS QUICK TO GO HOME.
HEY, WE'RE GONNA GO FOR A DRINK...
OH, I'M ALL GOOD. SEE YOU LATER.
カチカチ CLICK CLICK
カチカチ... CLICK CLICK
NATURALLY, HE NEVER CAME ALONG FOR DRINKS AFTER WORK, AND BY DEFAULT HE SPENT HIS BREAKS ALONE PLAYING GAMES.
THAT WAS THE KIND OF GUY HIROTAKA NIFUJI WAS.
OKAY, I'M OFF TO HAVE A SMOKE.
...HE GOT IT ALL DONE...

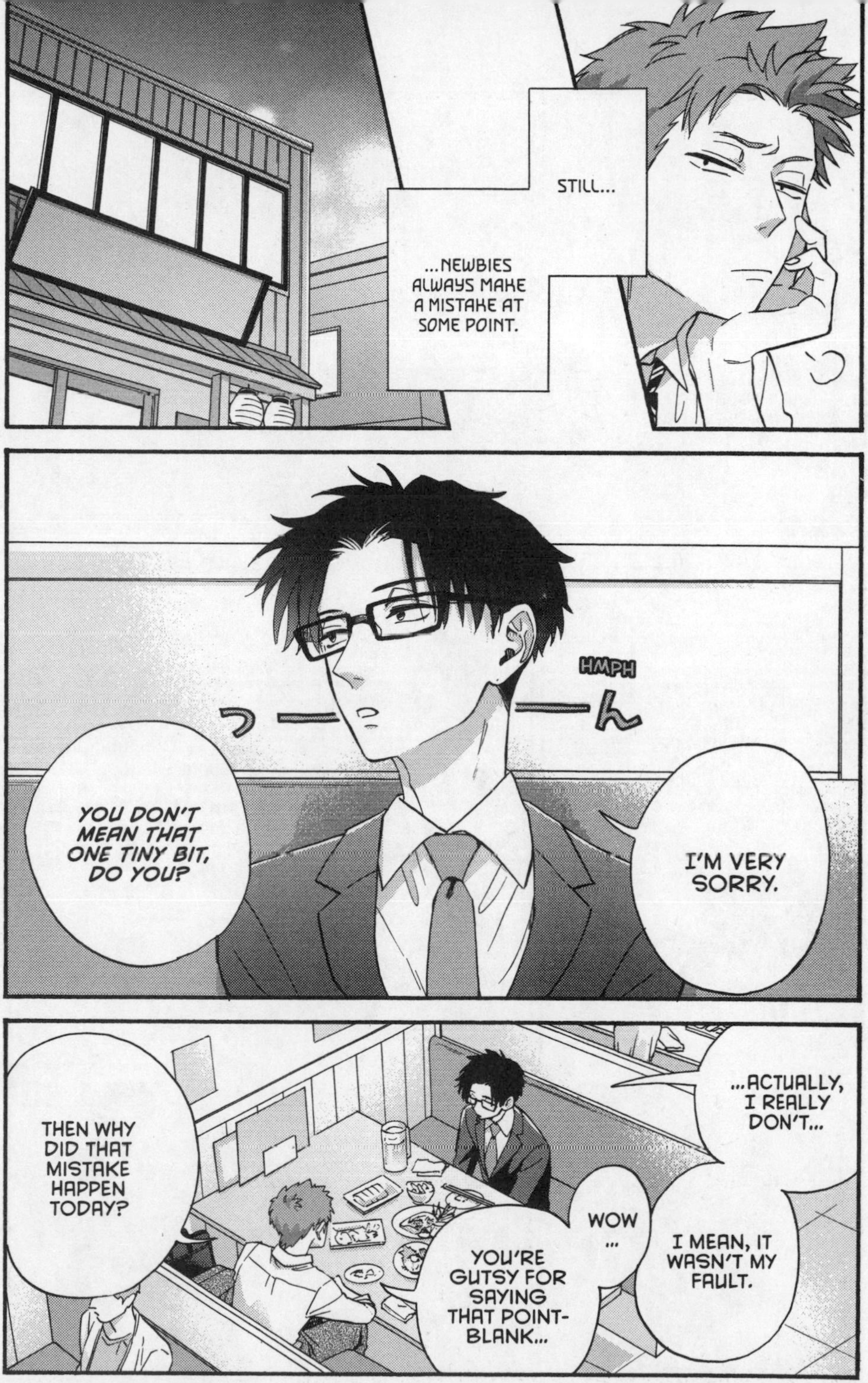
STILL...
...NEWBIES ALWAYS MAKE A MISTAKE AT SOME POINT.
HMPH
つーーーん
I'M VERY SORRY.
YOU DON'T MEAN THAT ONE TINY BIT, DO YOU?
...ACTUALLY, I REALLY DON'T...
I MEAN, IT WASN'T MY FAULT.
WOW...
YOU'RE GUTSY FOR SAYING THAT POINT-BLANK...
THEN WHY DID THAT MISTAKE HAPPEN TODAY?

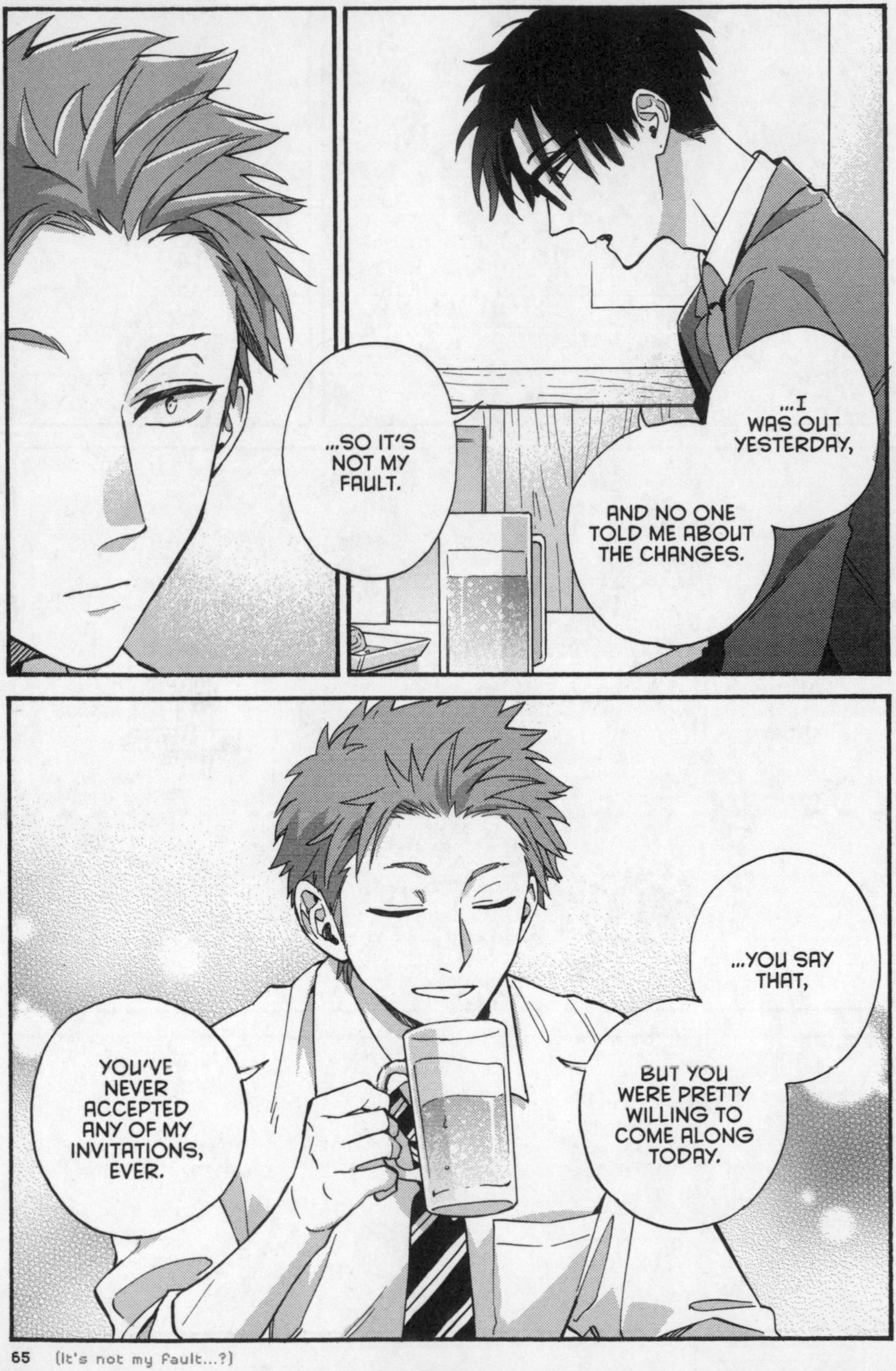
...I WAS OUT YESTERDAY,
AND NO ONE TOLD ME ABOUT THE CHANGES.
...SO IT'S NOT MY FAULT.
...YOU SAY THAT,
BUT YOU WERE PRETTY WILLING TO COME ALONG TODAY.
YOU'VE NEVER ACCEPTED ANY OF MY INVITATIONS, EVER.

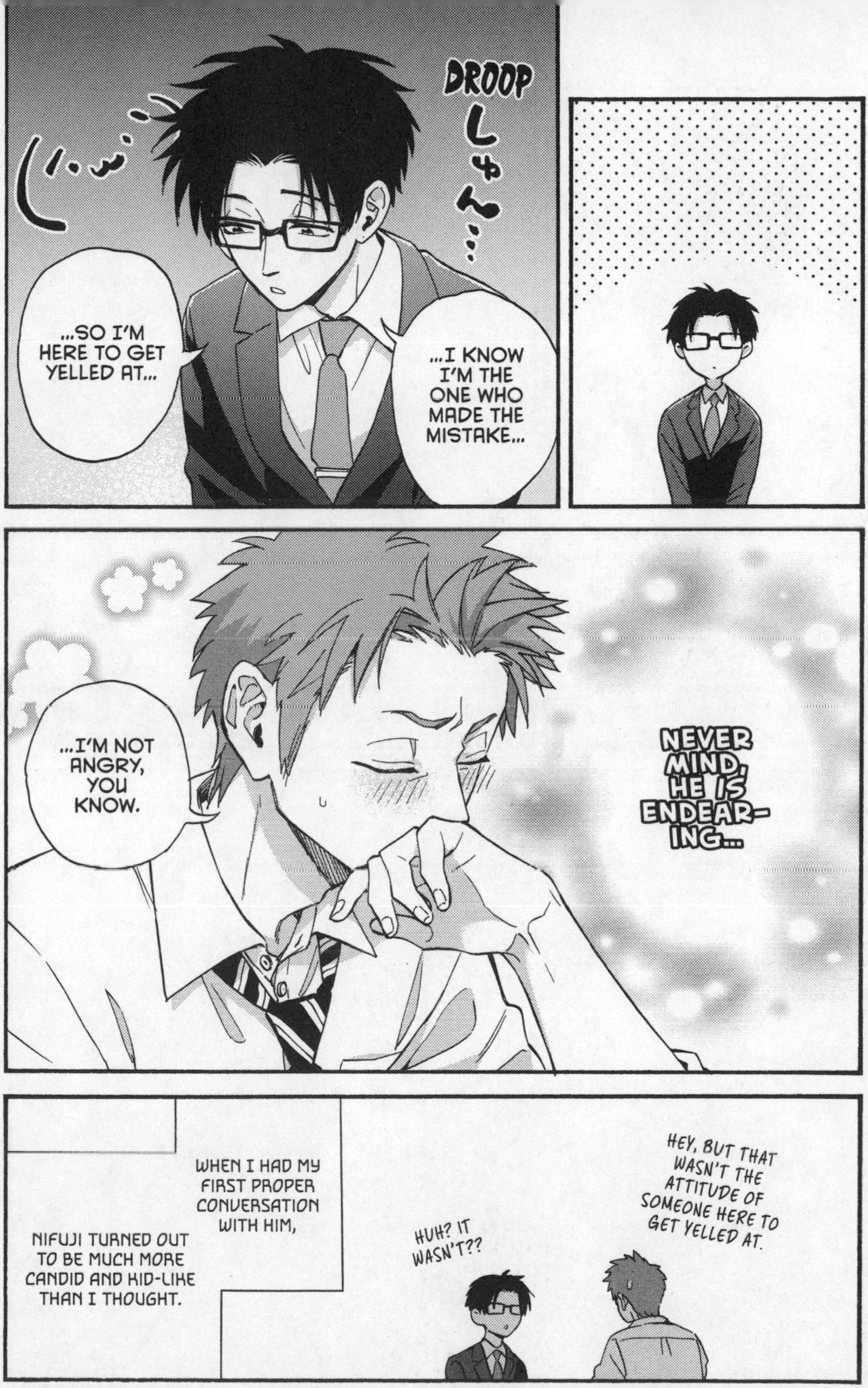
DROOP
しゅん…
...I KNOW I'M THE ONE WHO MADE THE MISTAKE...
...SO I'M HERE TO GET YELLED AT...
じ…
NEVER MIND, HE IS ENDEARING...
...I'M NOT ANGRY, YOU KNOW.
HEY, BUT THAT WASN'T THE ATTITUDE OF SOMEONE HERE TO GET YELLED AT.
HUH? IT WASN'T??
WHEN I HAD MY FIRST PROPER CONVERSATION WITH HIM,
NIFUJI TURNED OUT TO BE MUCH MORE CANDID AND KID-LIKE THAN I THOUGHT.

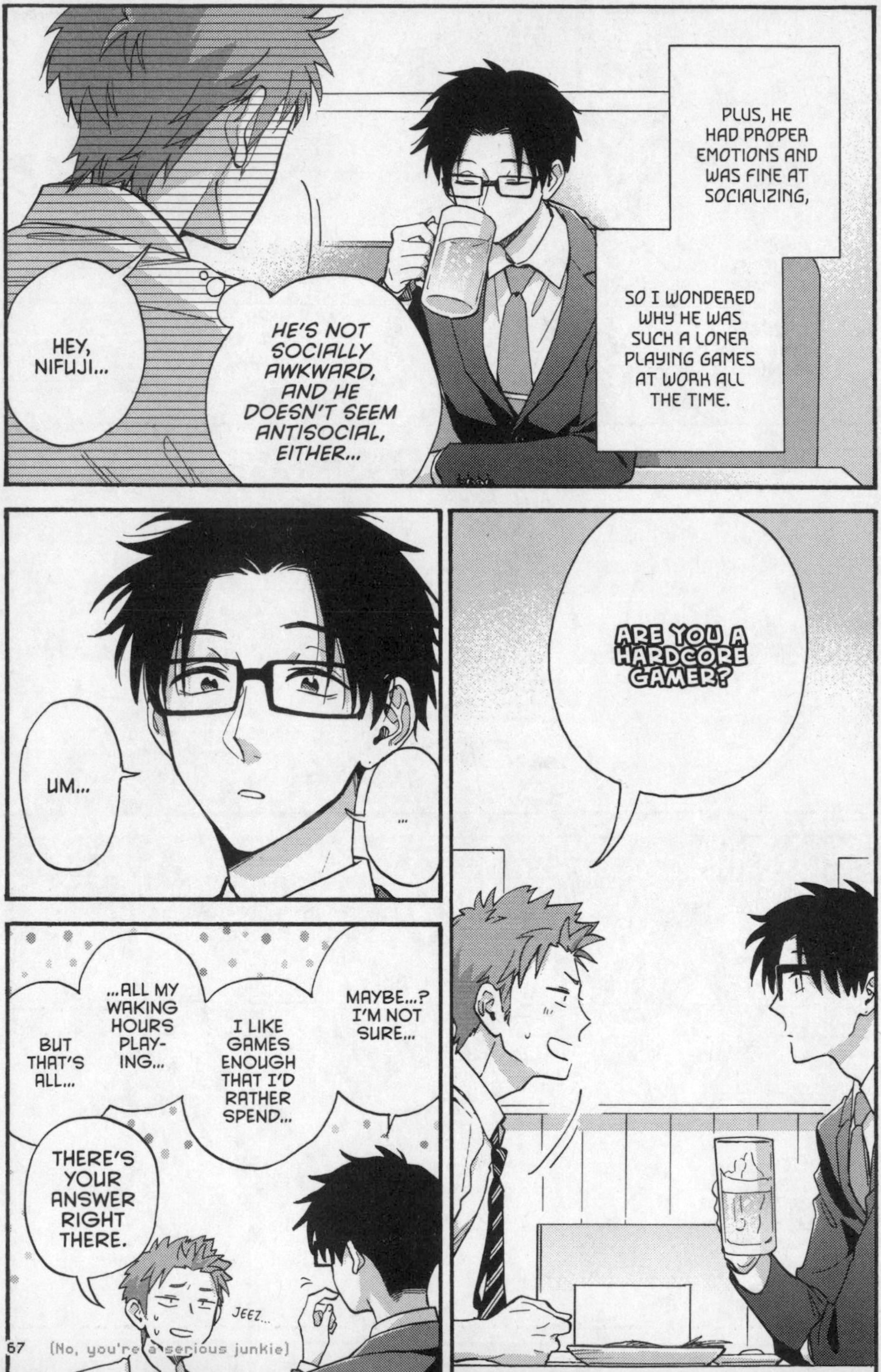
PLUS, HE HAD PROPER EMOTIONS AND WAS FINE AT SOCIALIZING,
SO I WONDERED WHY HE WAS SUCH A LONER PLAYING GAMES AT WORK ALL THE TIME.
HE'S NOT SOCIALLY AWKWARD, AND HE DOESN'T SEEM ANTISOCIAL, EITHER...
HEY, NIFUJI...
ARE YOU A HARDCORE GAMER?
...
UM...
MAYBE...? I'M NOT SURE...
I LIKE GAMES ENOUGH THAT I'D RATHER SPEND...
...ALL MY WAKING HOURS PLAYING...
BUT THAT'S ALL...
THERE'S YOUR ANSWER RIGHT THERE.
JEEZ...
(No, you're a serious junkie)

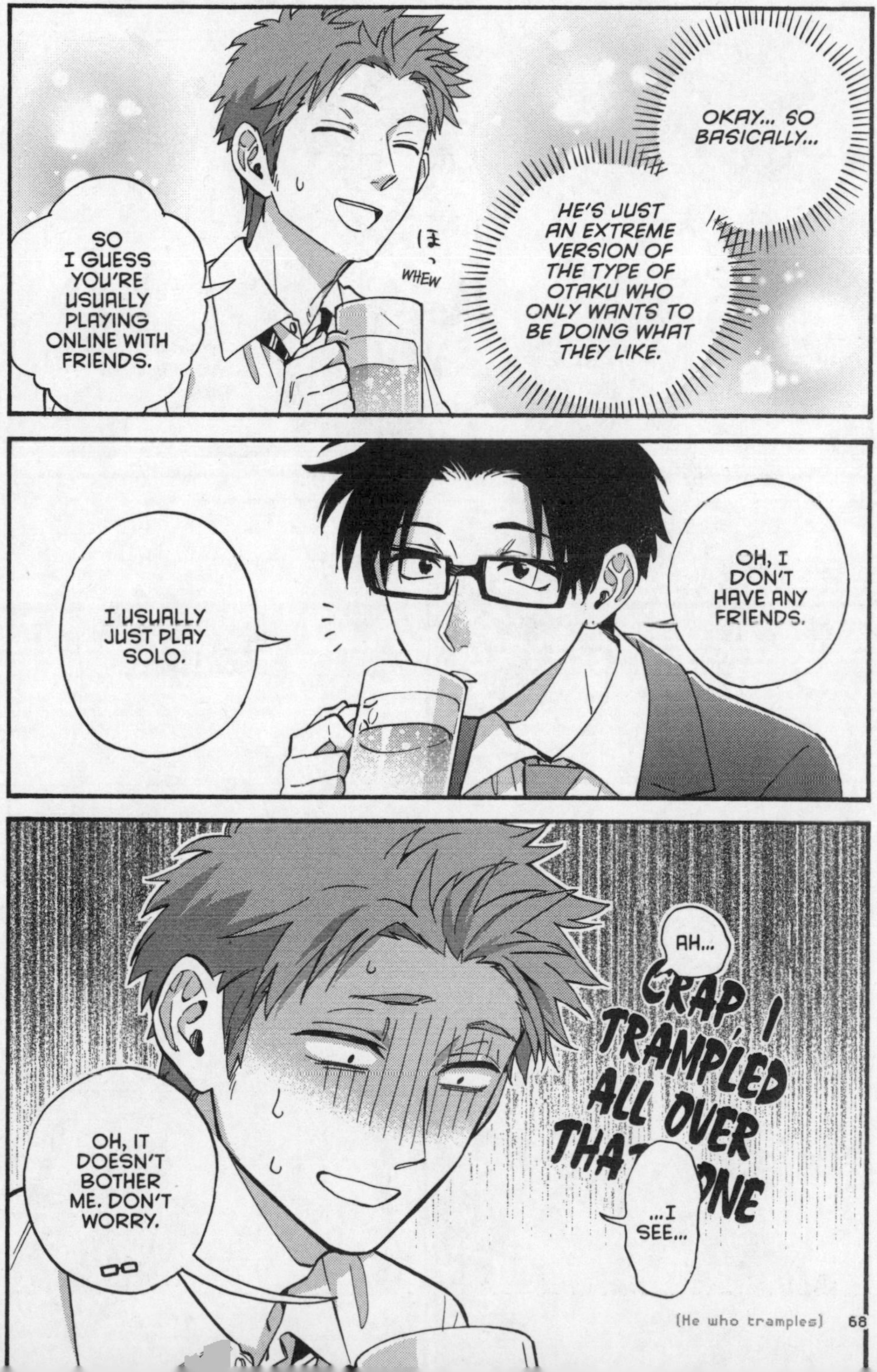
OKAY... SO BASICALLY...
HE'S JUST AN EXTREME VERSION OF THE TYPE OF OTAKU WHO ONLY WANTS TO BE DOING WHAT THEY LIKE.
ほっ
WHEW
SO I GUESS YOU'RE USUALLY PLAYING ONLINE WITH FRIENDS.
OH, I DON'T HAVE ANY FRIENDS.
I USUALLY JUST PLAY SOLO.
AH...
CRAP, I TRAMPLED ALL OVER THA ONE
...I SEE...
OH, IT DOESN'T BOTHER ME. DON'T WORRY.

WELL, THE BEST GAMES ARE FUN PLAYED SOLO, TOO.
FIRST-PERSON SHOOTERS AND STUFF AREN'T GREAT WITH JUST A.I., THOUGH.
HE REALLY DOESN'T SEEM TO CARE ABOUT WHAT OTHERS THINK...
SO IT PROBABLY DOESN'T BOTHER HIM, FOR REAL.
BUT...
IT BOTHERS ME.
...HEY.
YOU KNOW HOW IF YOU GET REALLY DEEP INTO A DATING SIM, YOU EVENTUALLY WIN OVER ALL THE CHARACTERS?
AND SOMETIMES YOU END UP LIKING SOMEONE WHO WASN'T YOUR TYPE AT ALL AS HER STORY PROGRESSES?
WOW, I LIKE THIS ONE! SO CUTE!
DONE
HUH?
SHE'S ACTUALLY PRETTY CUTE!
...OKAY...
WHAT I MEAN IS...

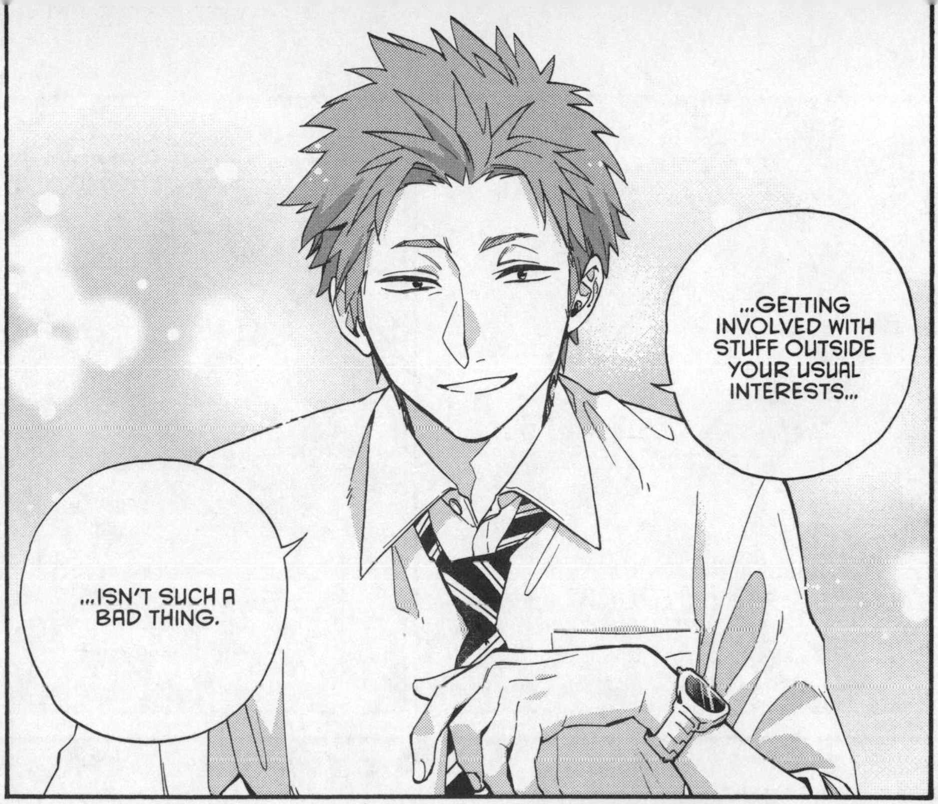
...GETTING INVOLVED WITH STUFF OUTSIDE YOUR USUAL INTERESTS...
...ISN'T SUCH A BAD THING.
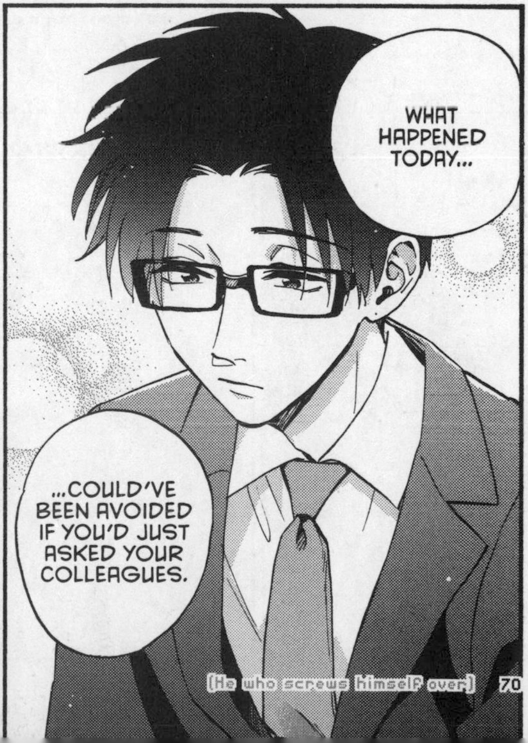
WHAT HAPPENED TODAY...
...COULD'VE BEEN AVOIDED IF YOU'D JUST ASKED YOUR COLLEAGUES.
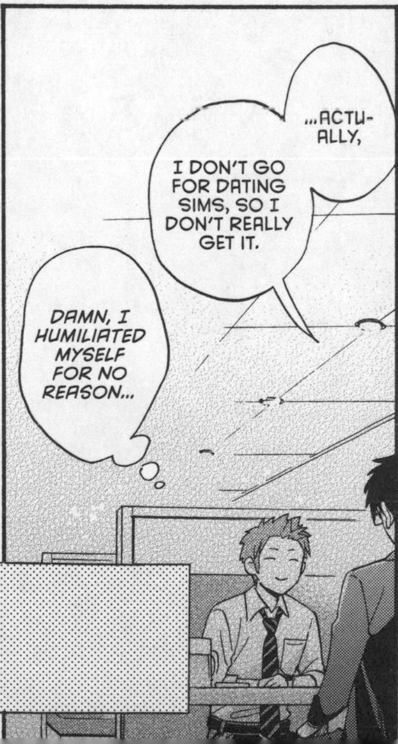
...ACTU-ALLY,
I DON'T GO FOR DATING SIMS, SO I DON'T REALLY GET IT.
DAMN, I HUMILIATED MYSELF FOR NO REASON...

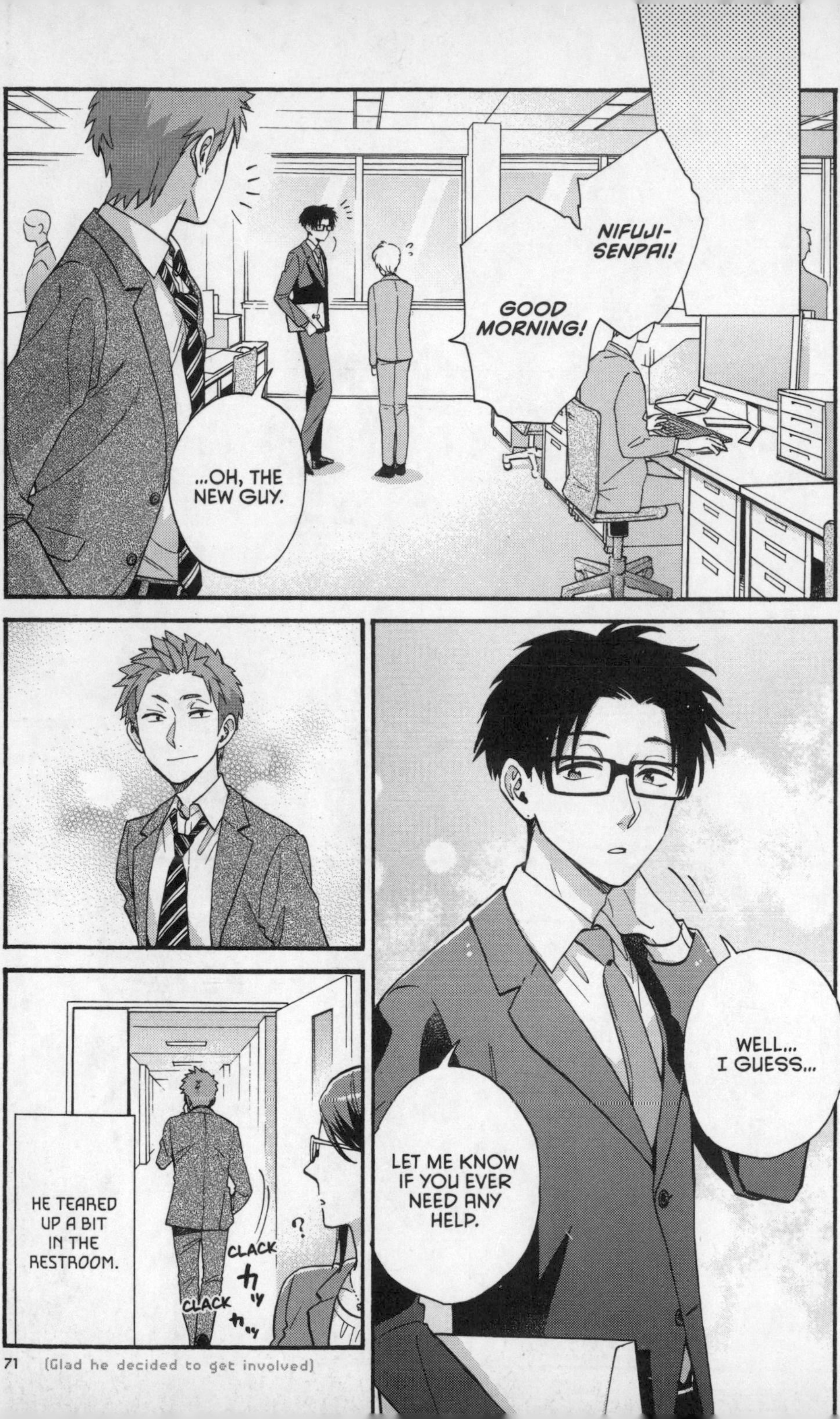
NIFUJI-SENPAI!
GOOD MORNING!
...OH, THE NEW GUY.
WELL... I GUESS...
LET ME KNOW IF YOU EVER NEED ANY HELP.
HE TEARED UP A BIT IN THE RESTROOM.
CLACK
CLACK

 (Glad he decided to get involved)

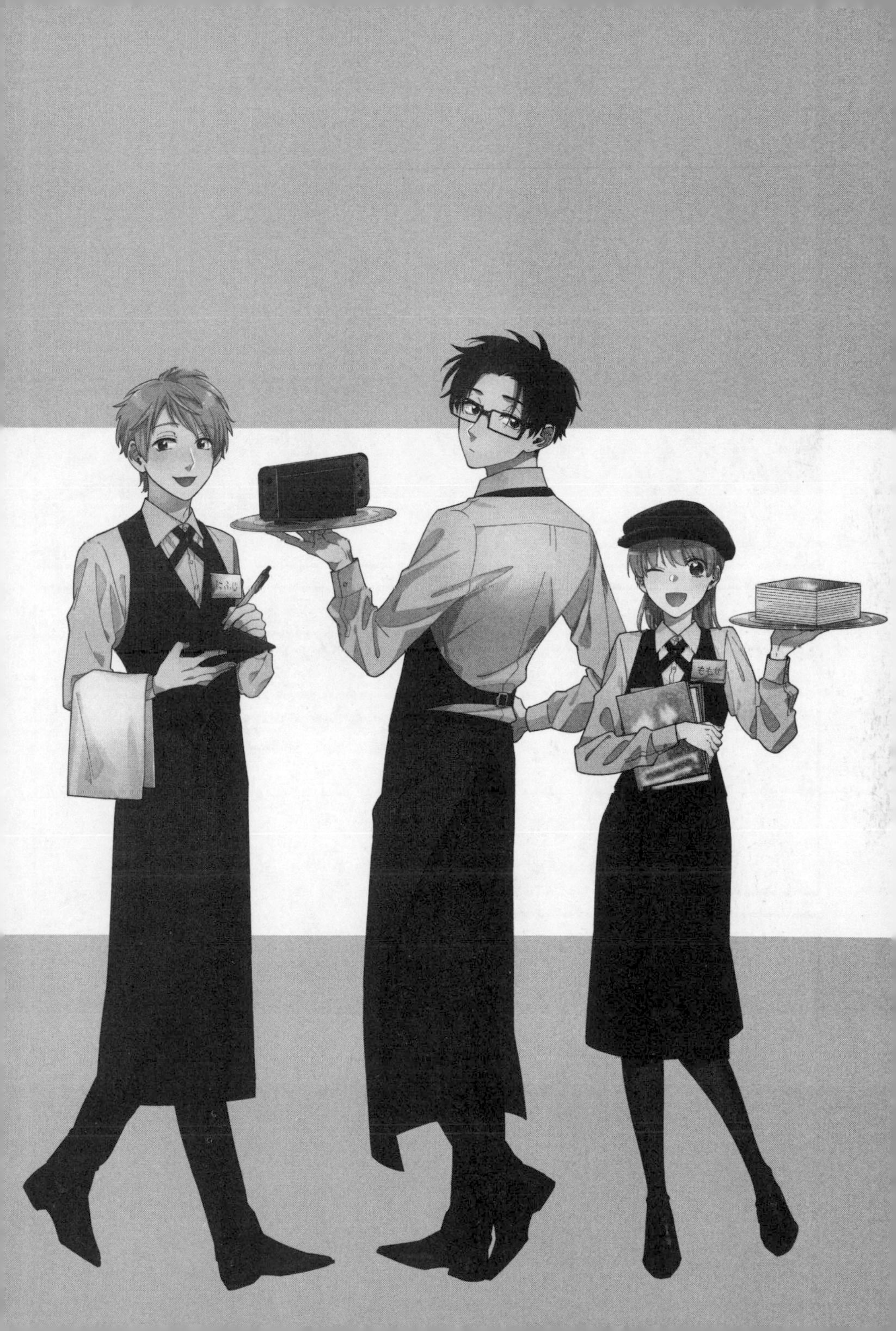

Wotakoi: Love is Hard for Otaku

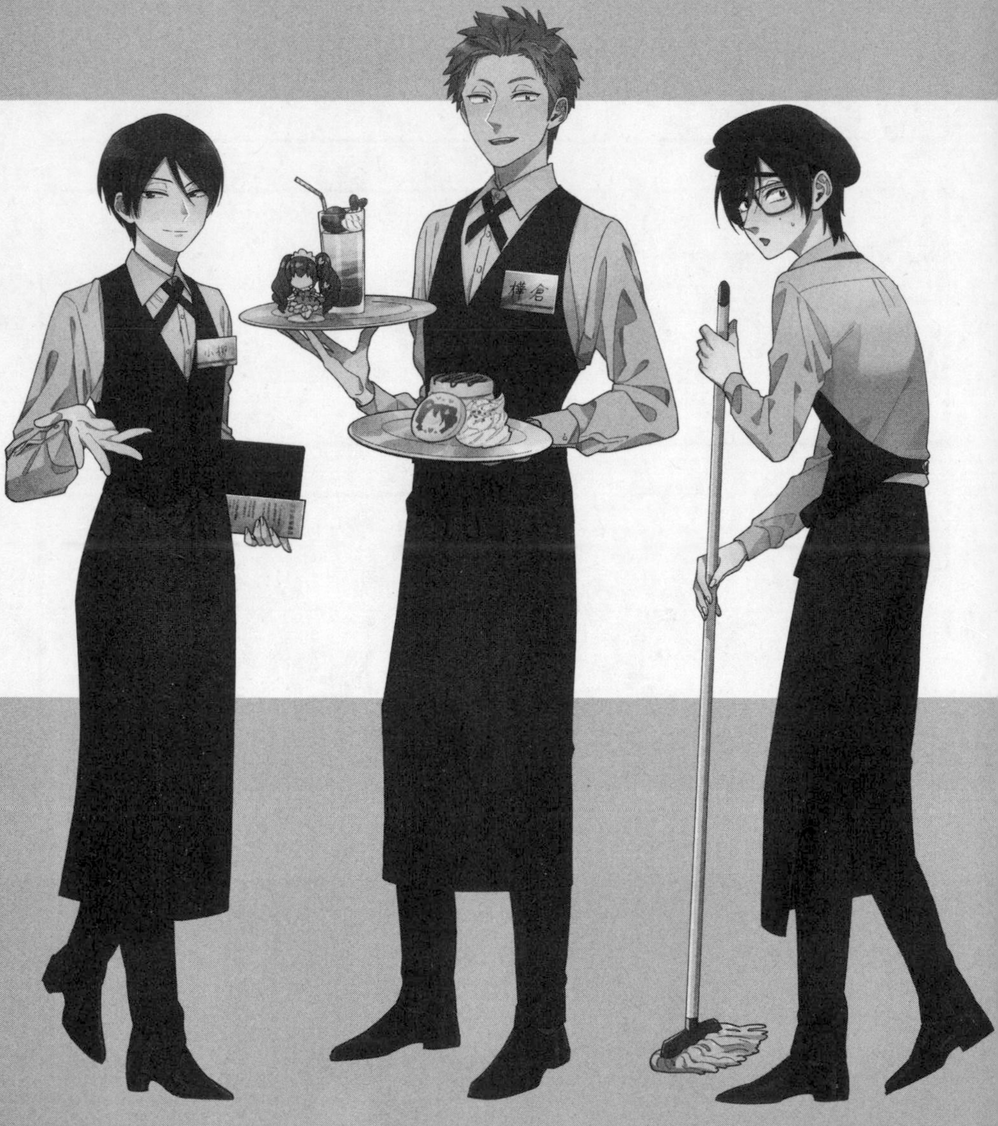
樺倉
小柳

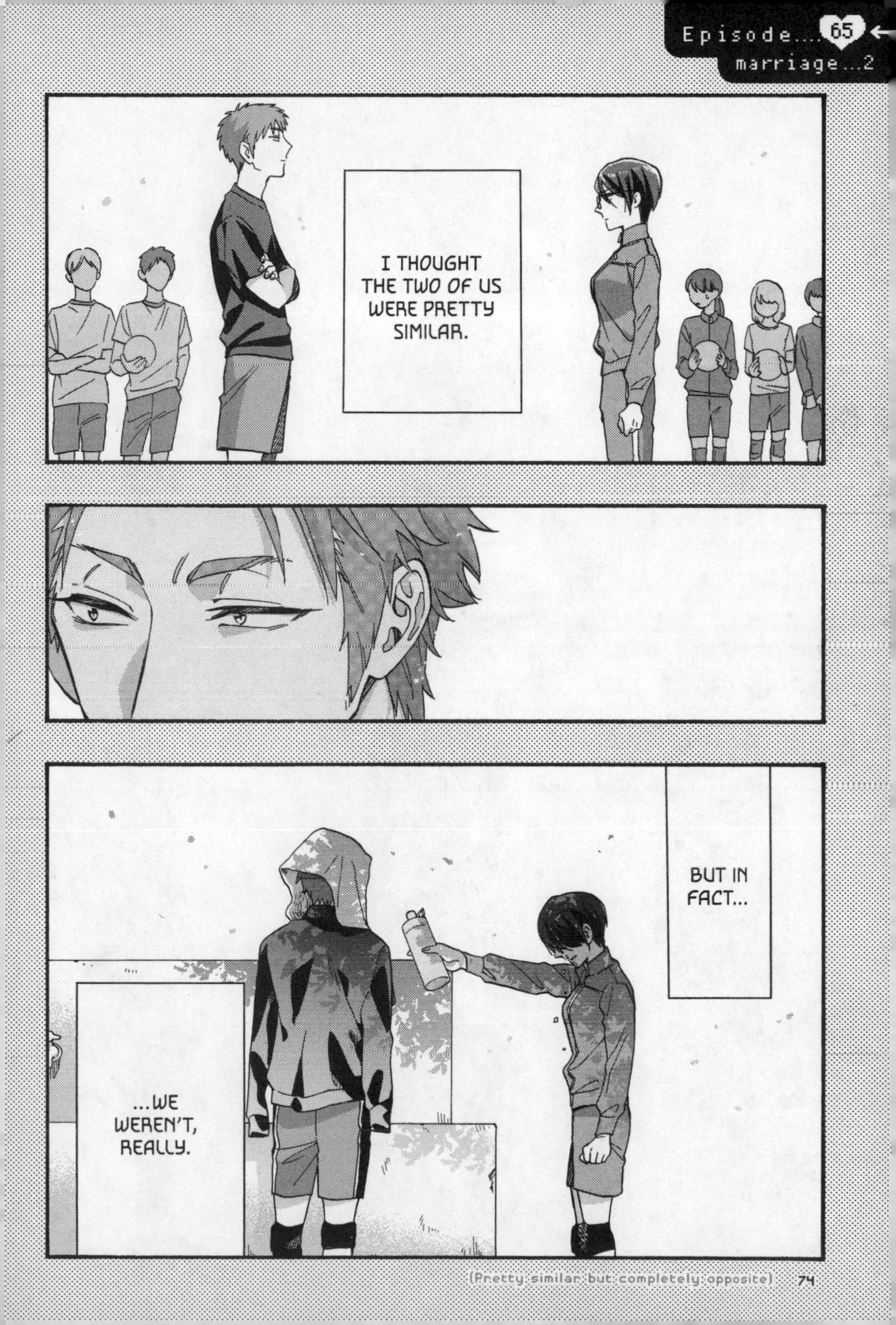
I THOUGHT THE TWO OF US WERE PRETTY SIMILAR.
BUT IN FACT...
...WE WEREN'T, REALLY.

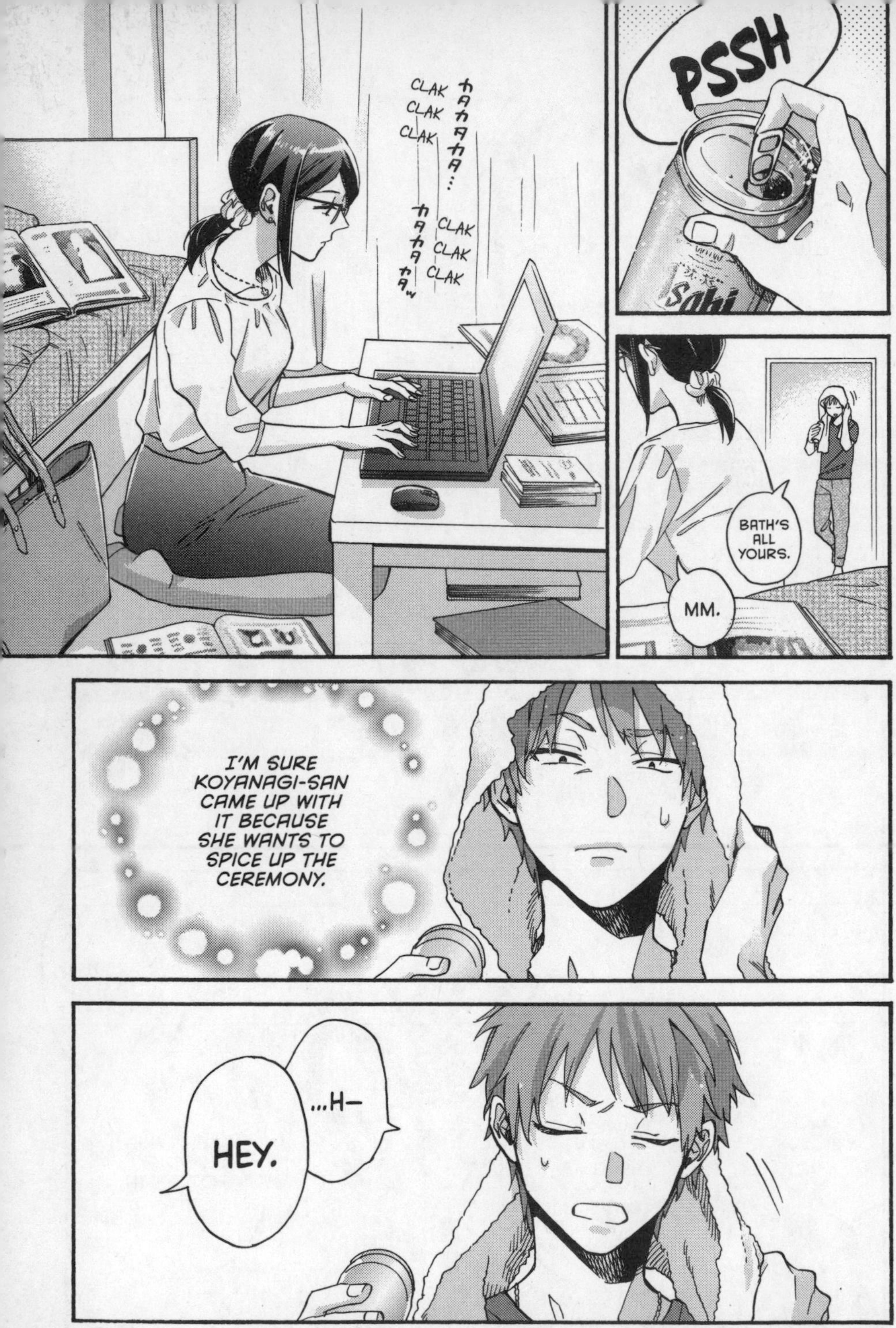
PSSH
BATH'S ALL YOURS.
MM.
CLAK CLAK CLAK
カタカタカタ…
CLAK CLAK CLAK
I'M SURE KOYANAGI-SAN CAME UP WITH IT BECAUSE SHE WANTS TO SPICE UP THE CEREMONY.
...H-
HEY.

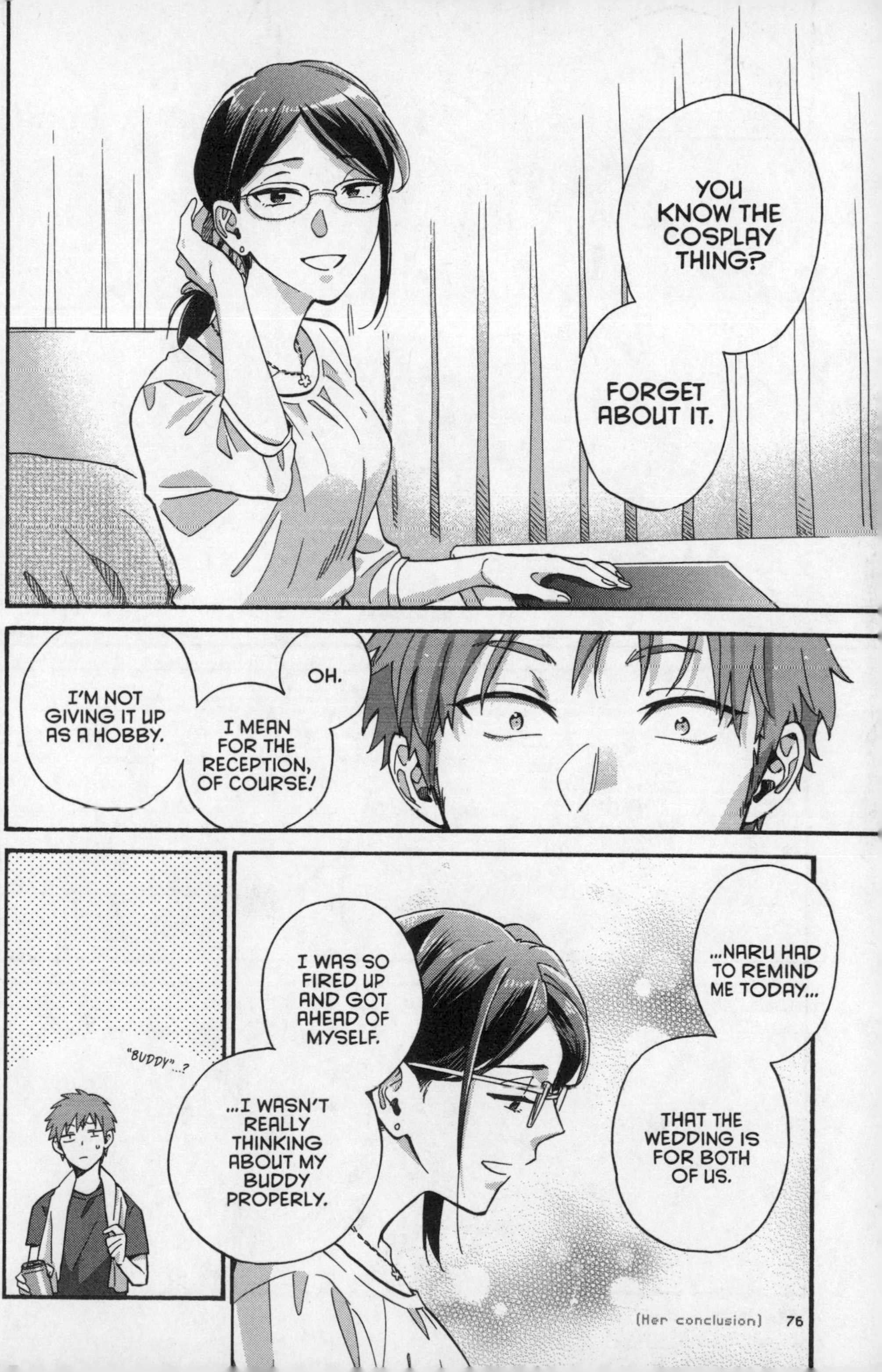
YOU KNOW THE COSPLAY THING?
FORGET ABOUT IT.
OH.
I MEAN FOR THE RECEPTION, OF COURSE!
I'M NOT GIVING IT UP AS A HOBBY.
...NARU HAD TO REMIND ME TODAY...
THAT THE WEDDING IS FOR BOTH OF US.
I WAS SO FIRED UP AND GOT AHEAD OF MYSELF.
...I WASN'T REALLY THINKING ABOUT MY BUDDY PROPERLY.
"BUDDY"...?

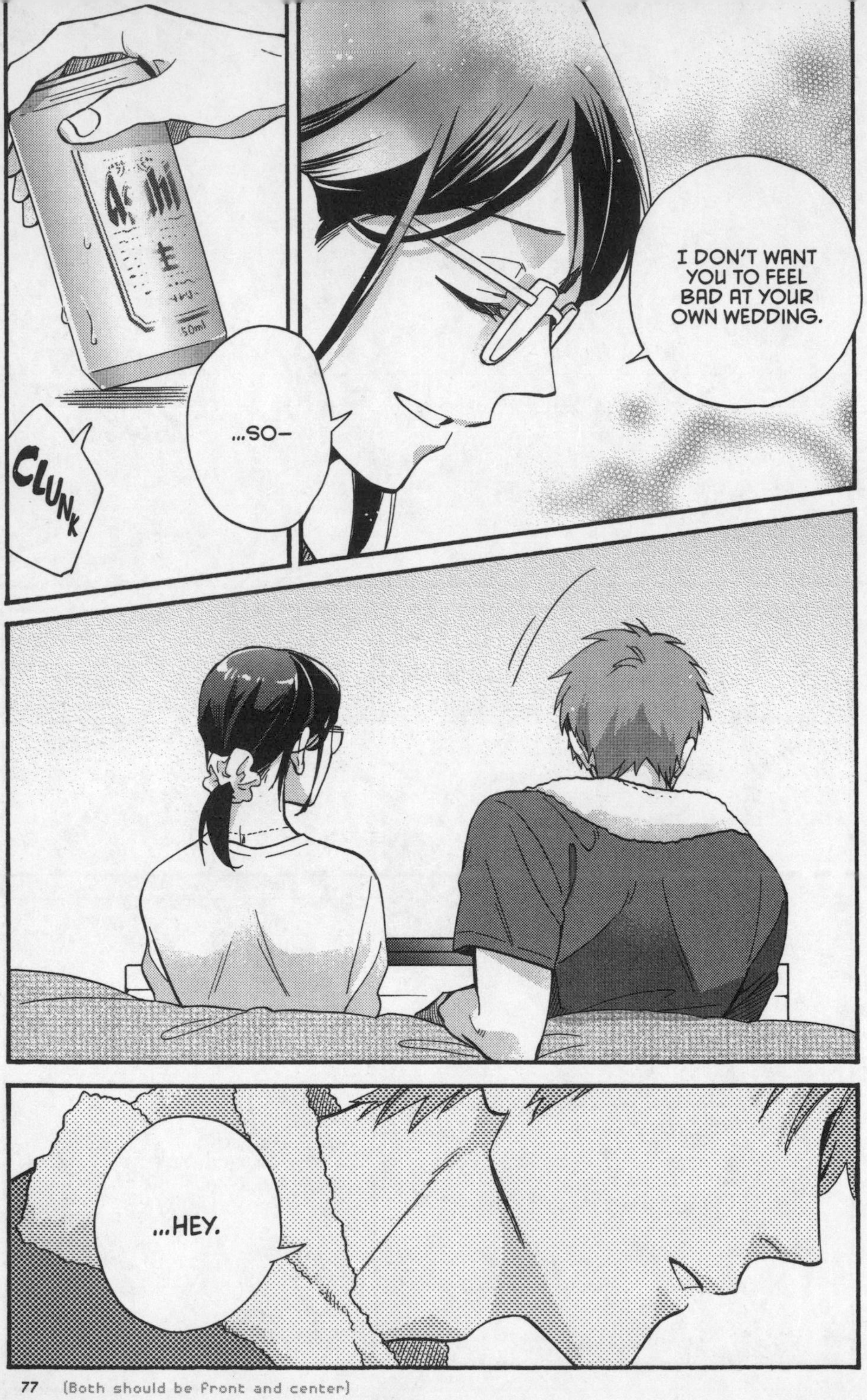
I DON'T WANT YOU TO FEEL BAD AT YOUR OWN WEDDING.
...SO–
CLUNK
...HEY.

 [Both should be front and center]

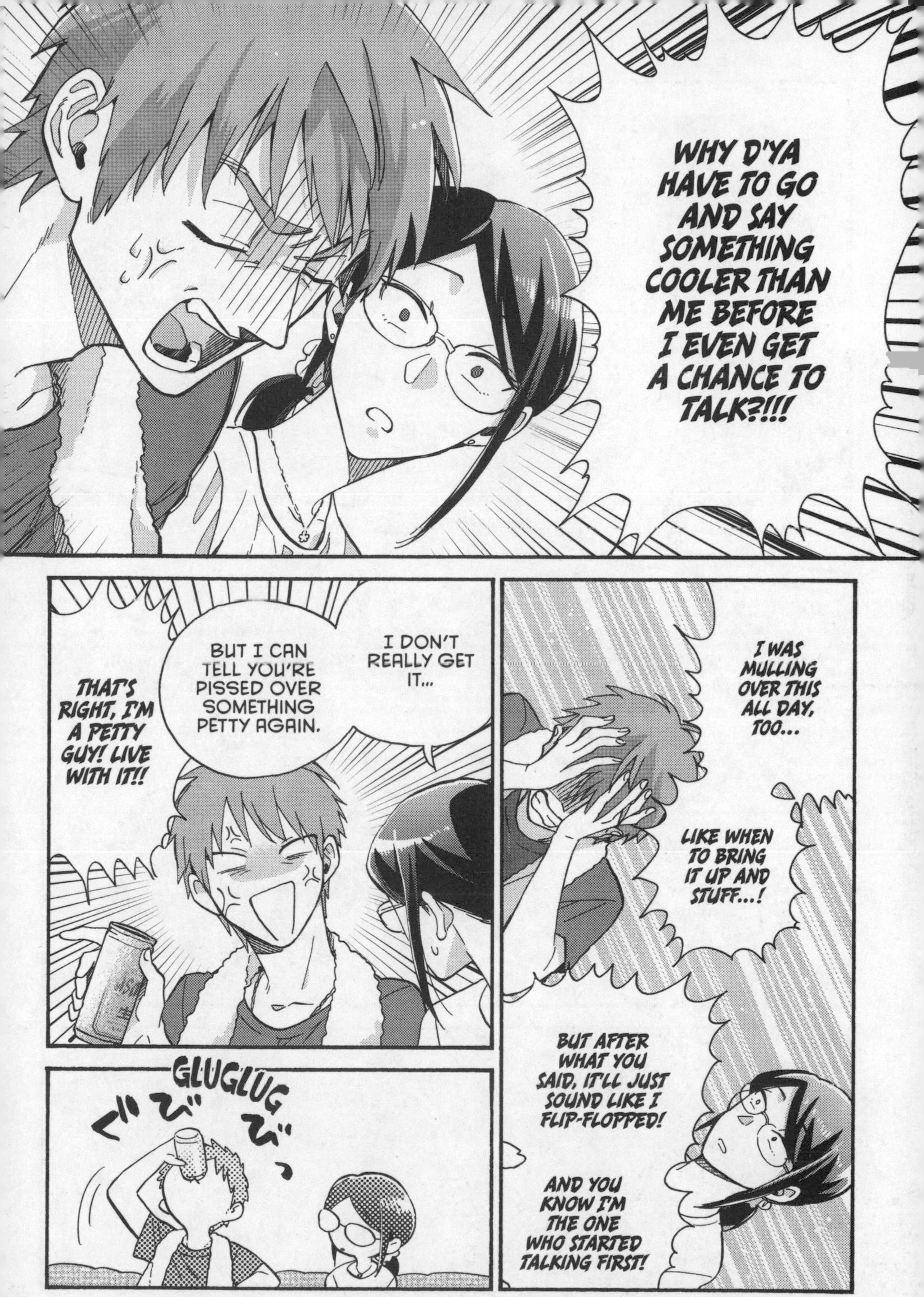
WHY D'YA HAVE TO GO AND SAY SOMETHING COOLER THAN ME BEFORE I EVEN GET A CHANCE TO TALK?!!!
I WAS MULLING OVER THIS ALL DAY, TOO...
LIKE WHEN TO BRING IT UP AND STUFF...!
BUT AFTER WHAT YOU SAID, IT'LL JUST SOUND LIKE I FLIP-FLOPPED!
AND YOU KNOW I'M THE ONE WHO STARTED TALKING FIRST!
I DON'T REALLY GET IT...
BUT I CAN TELL YOU'RE PISSED OVER SOMETHING PETTY AGAIN.
THAT'S RIGHT, I'M A PETTY GUY! LIVE WITH IT!!
GLUGLUG
ぐびびっ

(Don't go and say it first!)

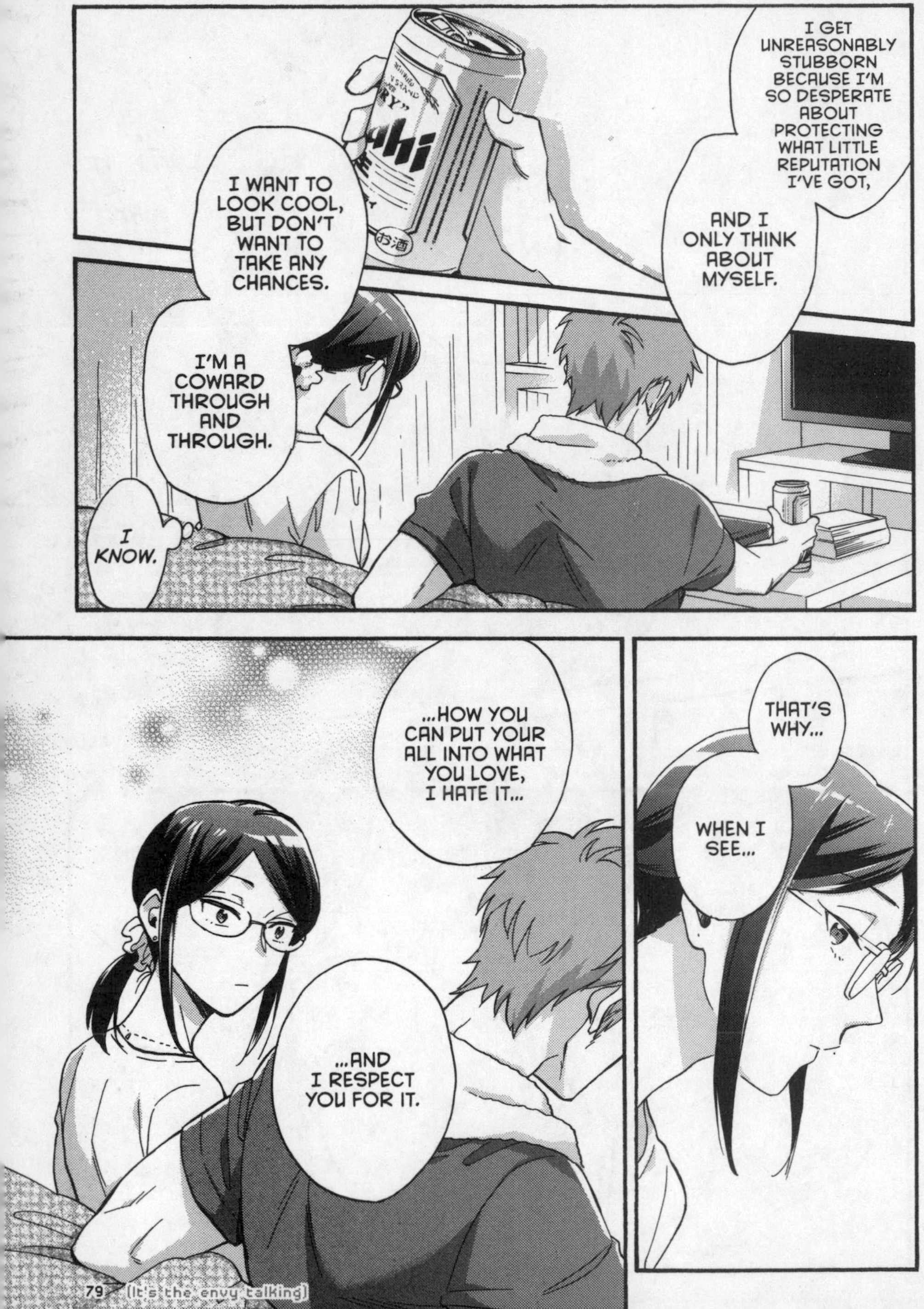
I GET UNREASONABLY STUBBORN BECAUSE I'M SO DESPERATE ABOUT PROTECTING WHAT LITTLE REPUTATION I'VE GOT,
AND I ONLY THINK ABOUT MYSELF.
I WANT TO LOOK COOL, BUT DON'T WANT TO TAKE ANY CHANCES.
I'M A COWARD THROUGH AND THROUGH.
I KNOW.
THAT'S WHY...
WHEN I SEE...
...HOW YOU CAN PUT YOUR ALL INTO WHAT YOU LOVE, I HATE IT...
...AND I RESPECT YOU FOR IT.

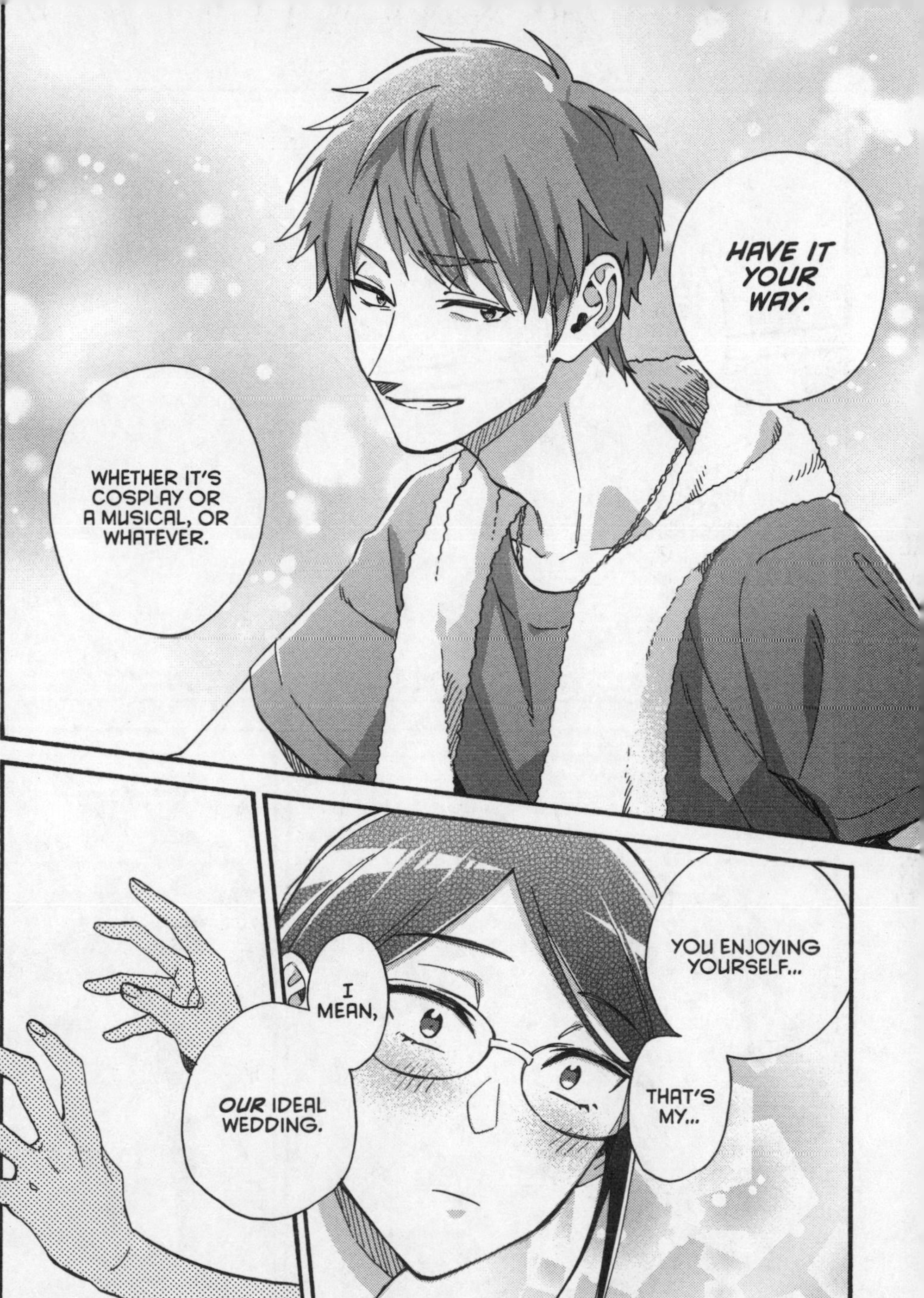
HAVE IT YOUR WAY.
WHETHER IT'S COSPLAY OR A MUSICAL, OR WHATEVER.
YOU ENJOYING YOURSELF...
THAT'S MY...
I MEAN,
OUR IDEAL WEDDING.

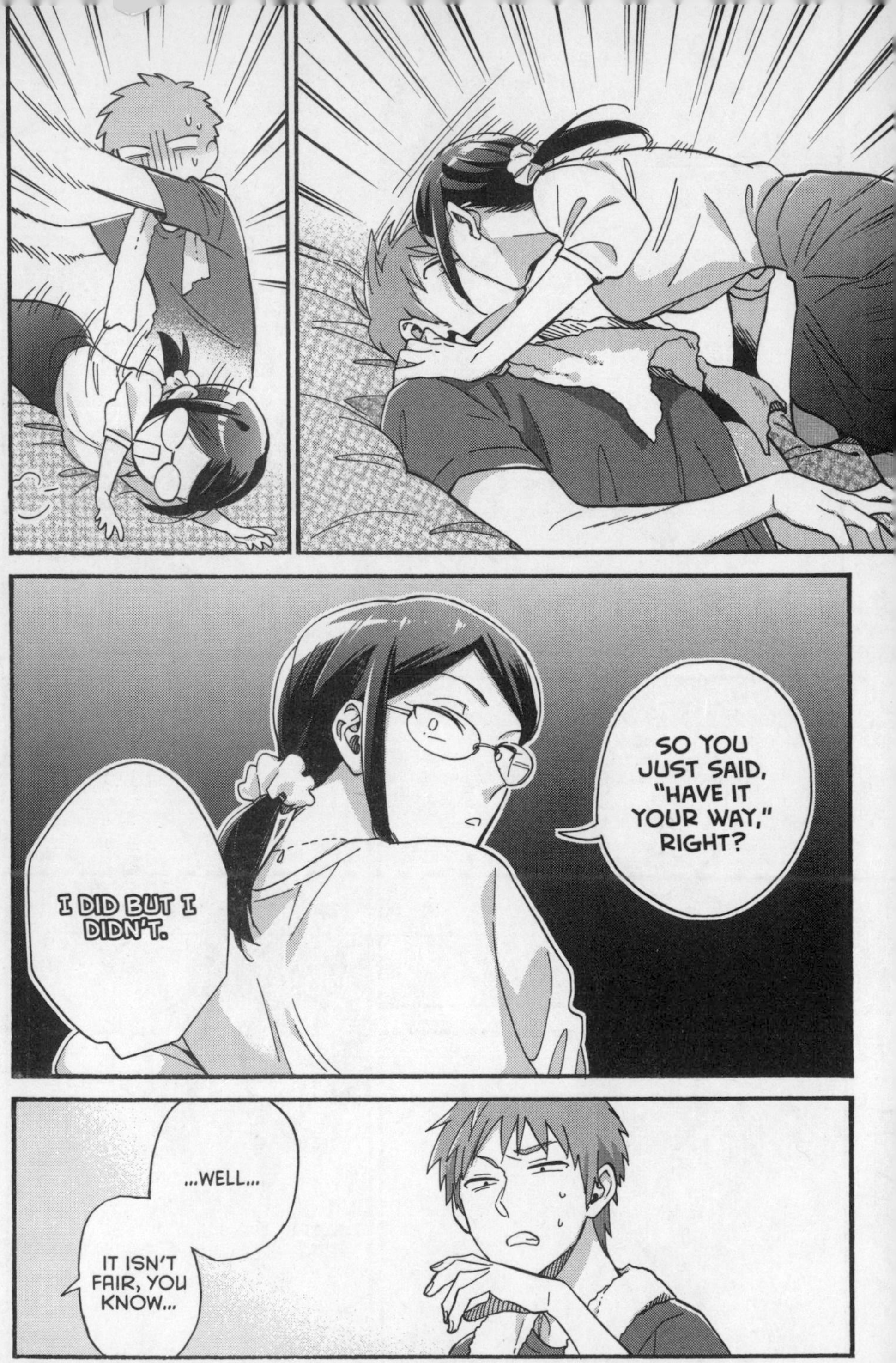
SO YOU JUST SAID, "HAVE IT YOUR WAY," RIGHT?
I DID BUT I DIDN'T.
...WELL...
IT ISN'T FAIR, YOU KNOW...

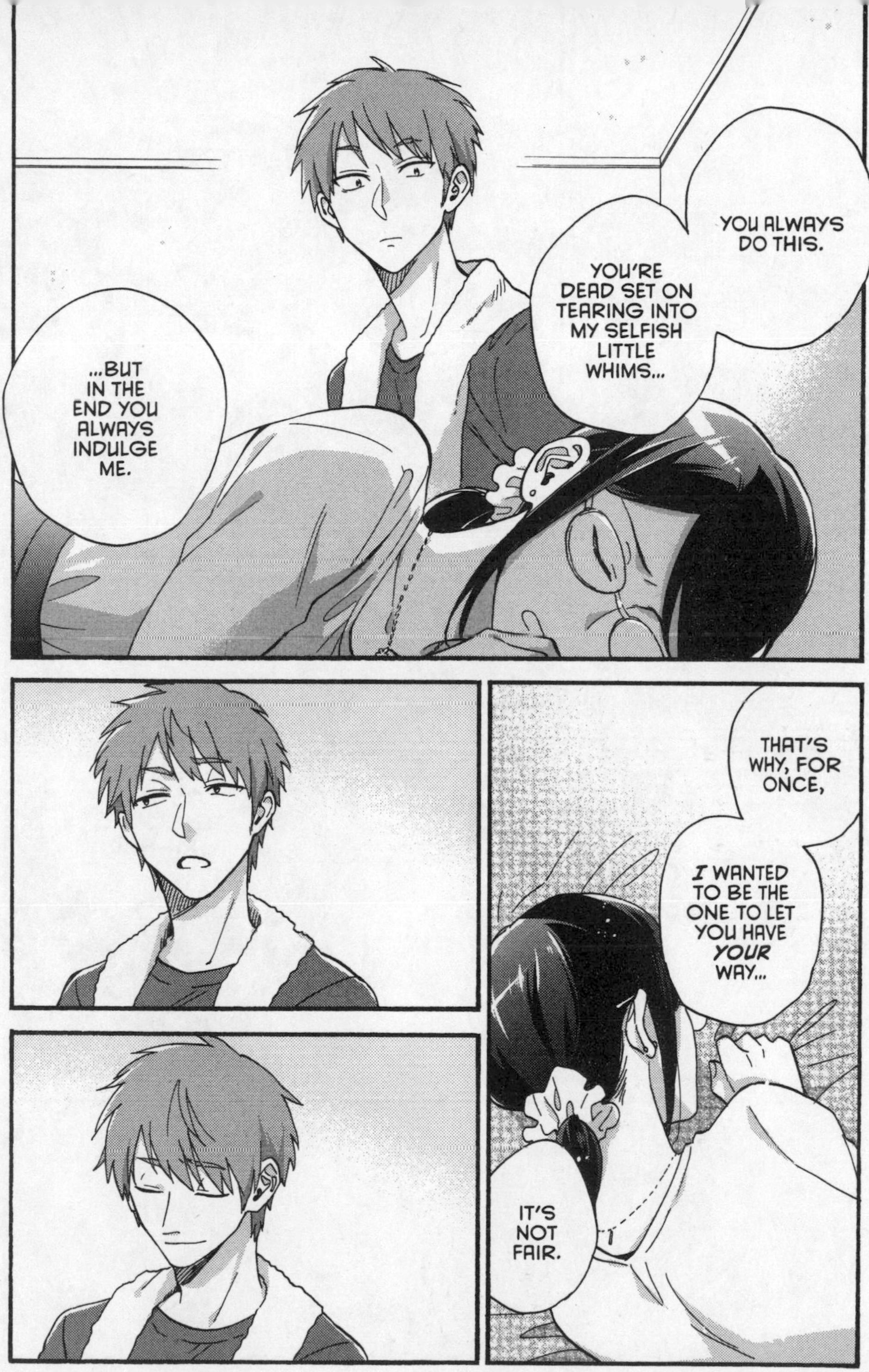
YOU ALWAYS DO THIS.
YOU'RE DEAD SET ON TEARING INTO MY SELFISH LITTLE WHIMS...
...BUT IN THE END YOU ALWAYS INDULGE ME.
THAT'S WHY, FOR ONCE,
I WANTED TO BE THE ONE TO LET YOU HAVE *YOUR* WAY...
IT'S NOT FAIR.

(She realizes he's been indulging her)

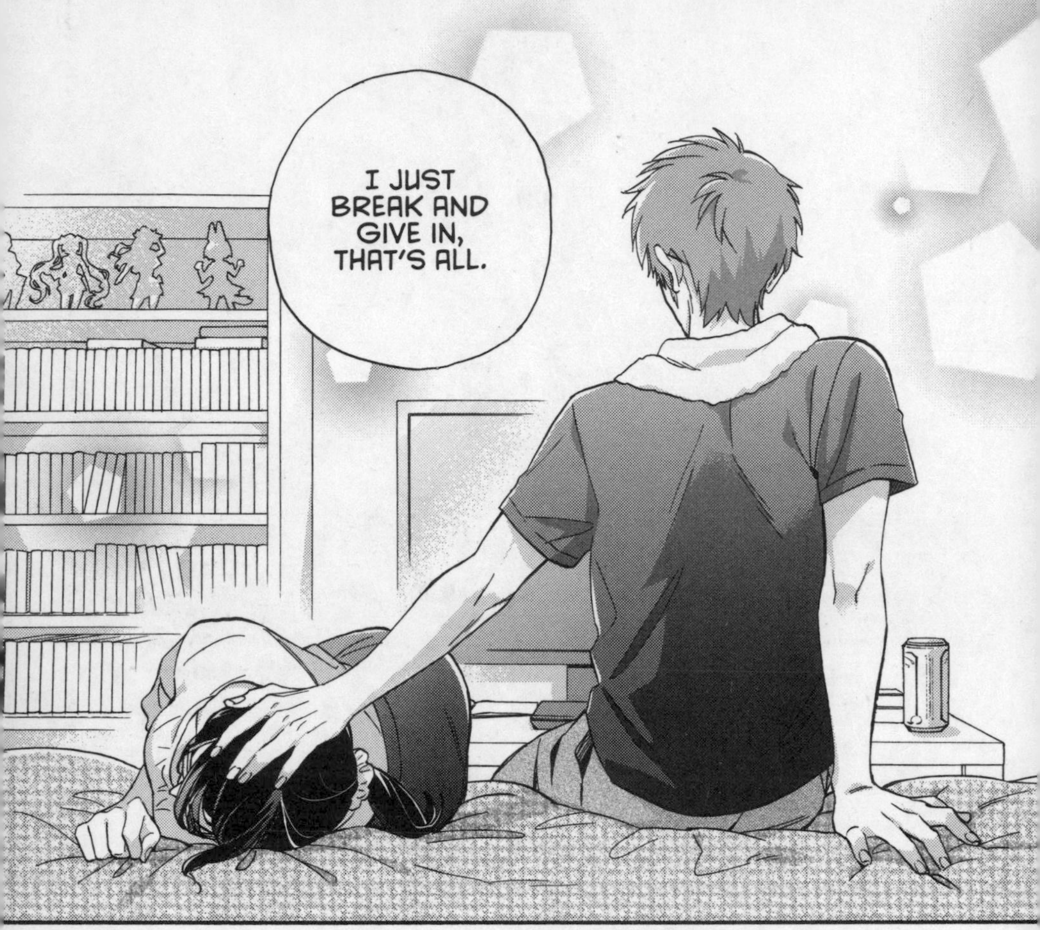
I JUST BREAK AND GIVE IN, THAT'S ALL.

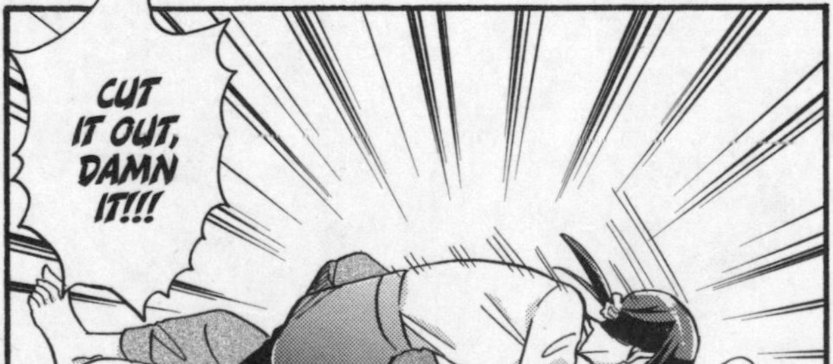
CUT IT OUT, DAMN IT!!!

 (You have until tomorrow to think about why you lost)

← To be continued...

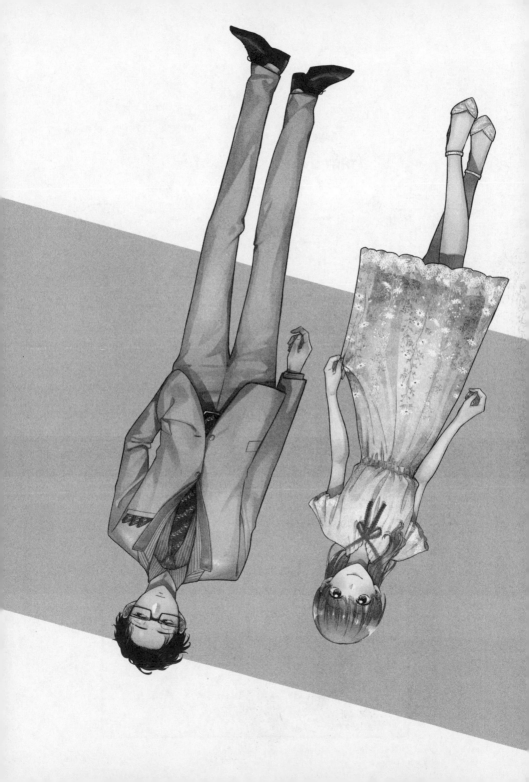

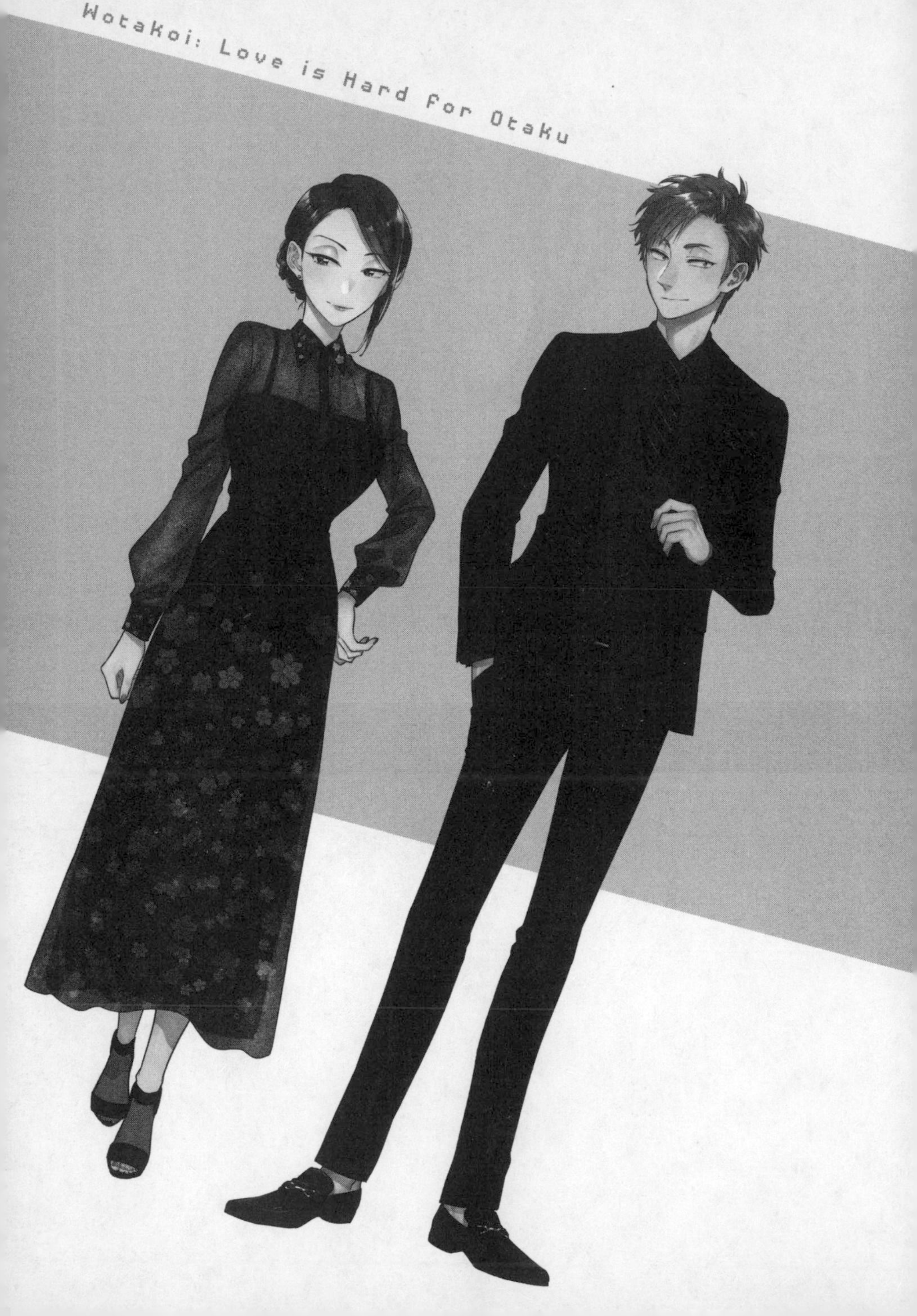
Wotakoi: Love is Hard for Otaku

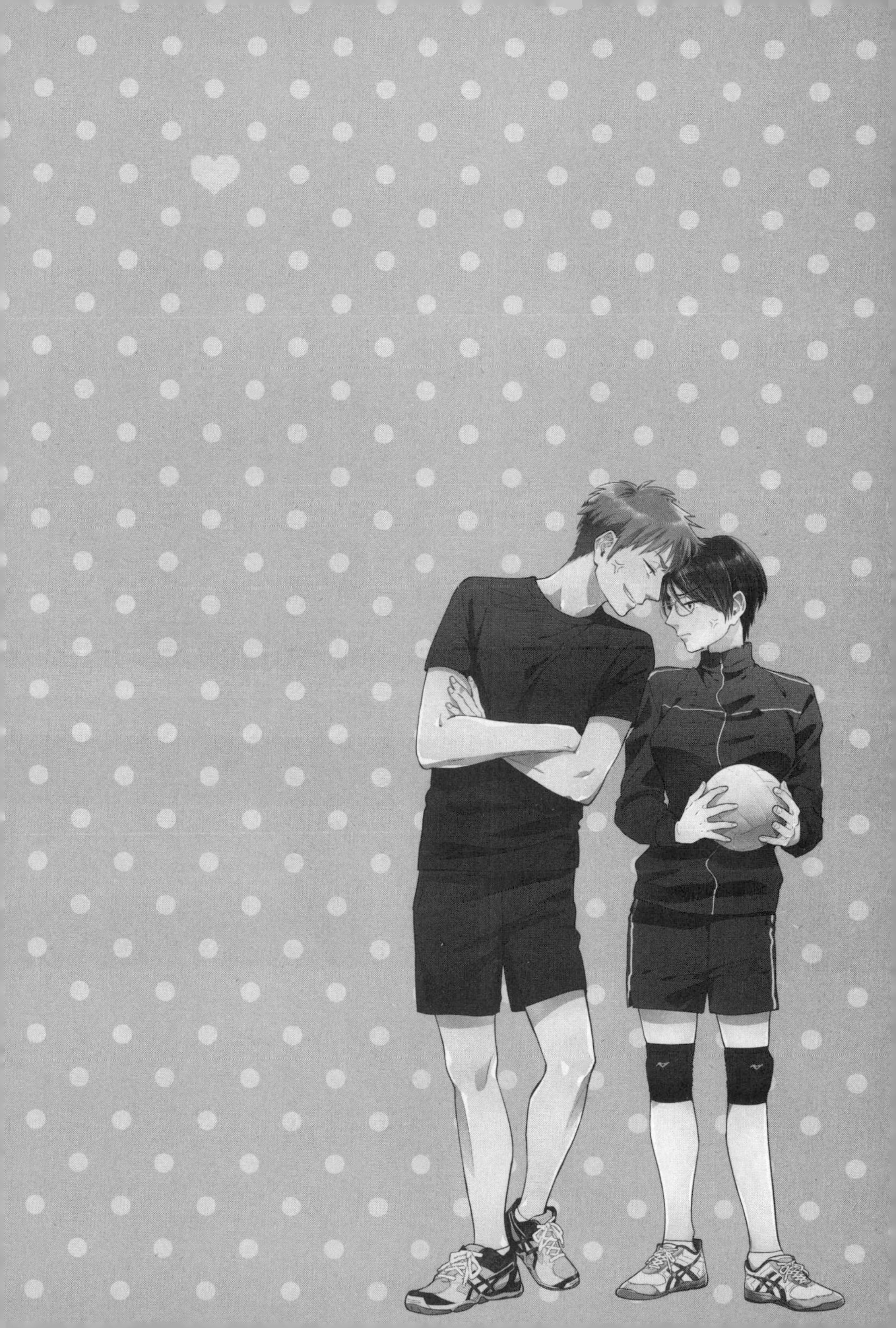

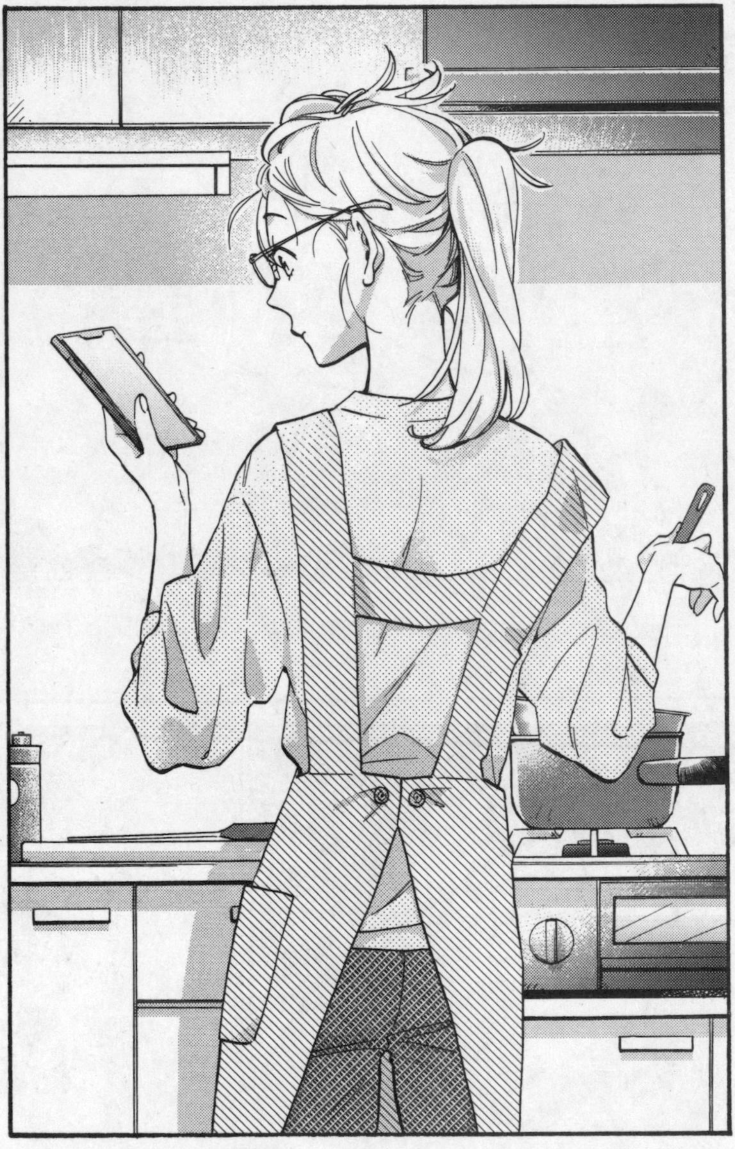

Episode.... 68

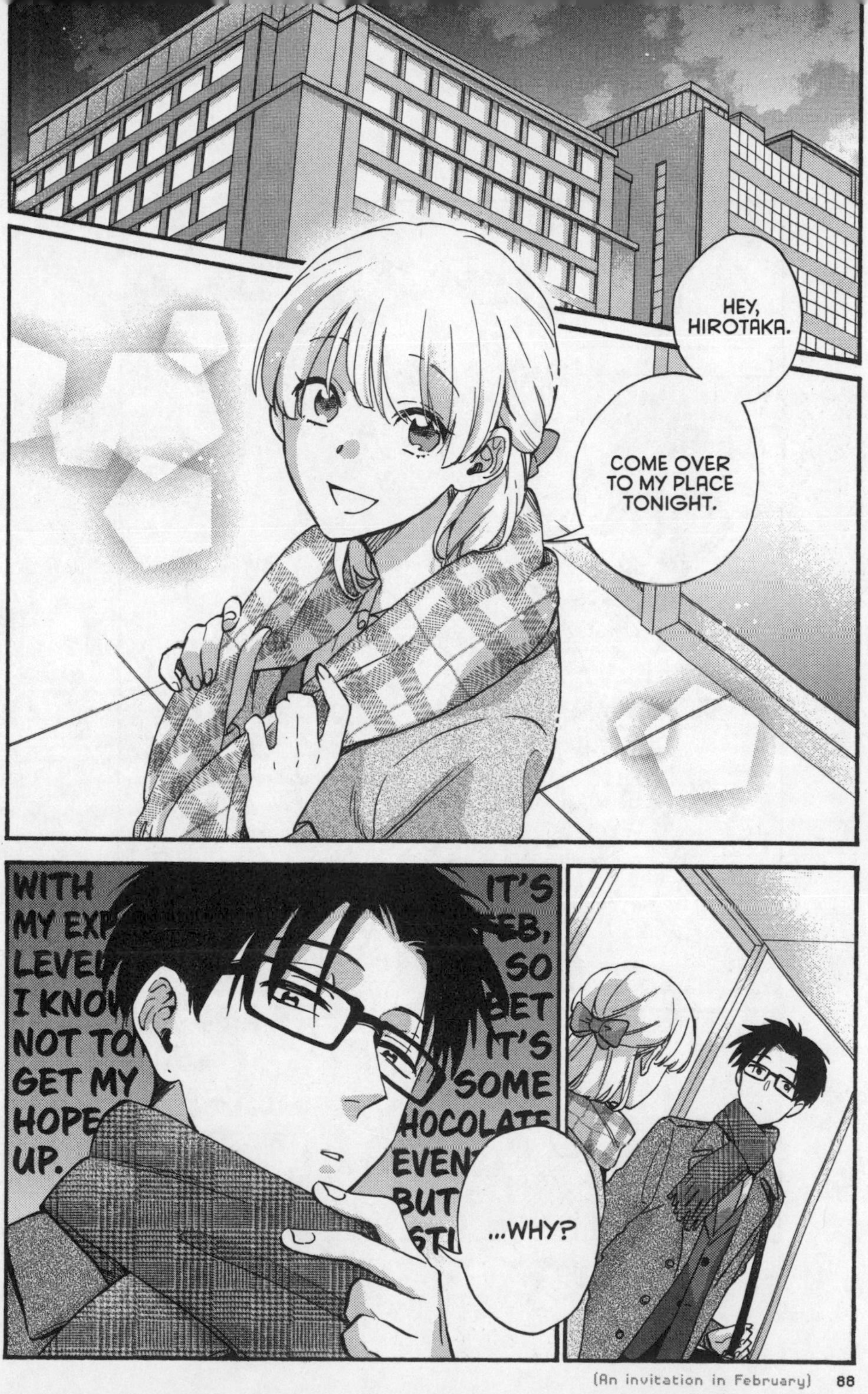
HEY, HIROTAKA.
COME OVER TO MY PLACE TONIGHT.
IT'S FEB, SO BET IT'S SOME HOCOLATE EVEN BUT STI
WITH MY EXP LEVE I KNOW NOT TO GET MY HOPE UP.
...WHY?

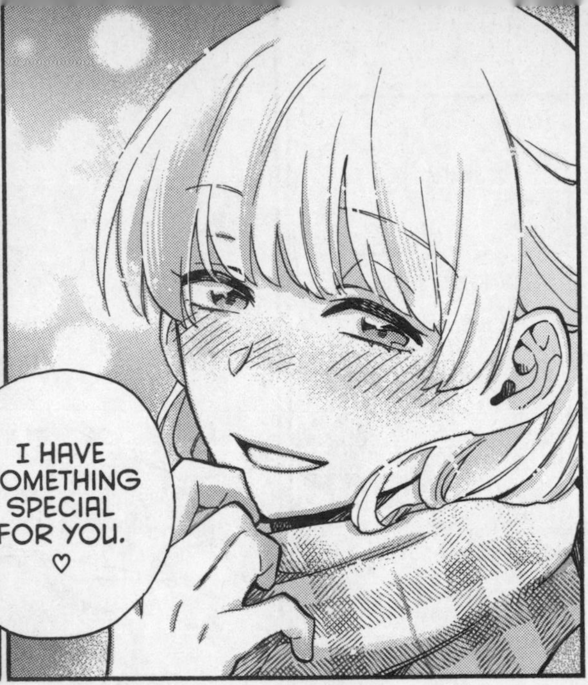
I HAVE SOMETHING SPECIAL FOR YOU. ♡

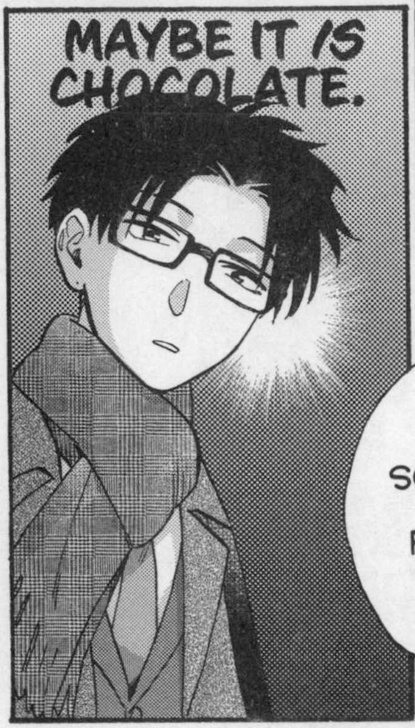
MAYBE IT IS CHOCOLATE.

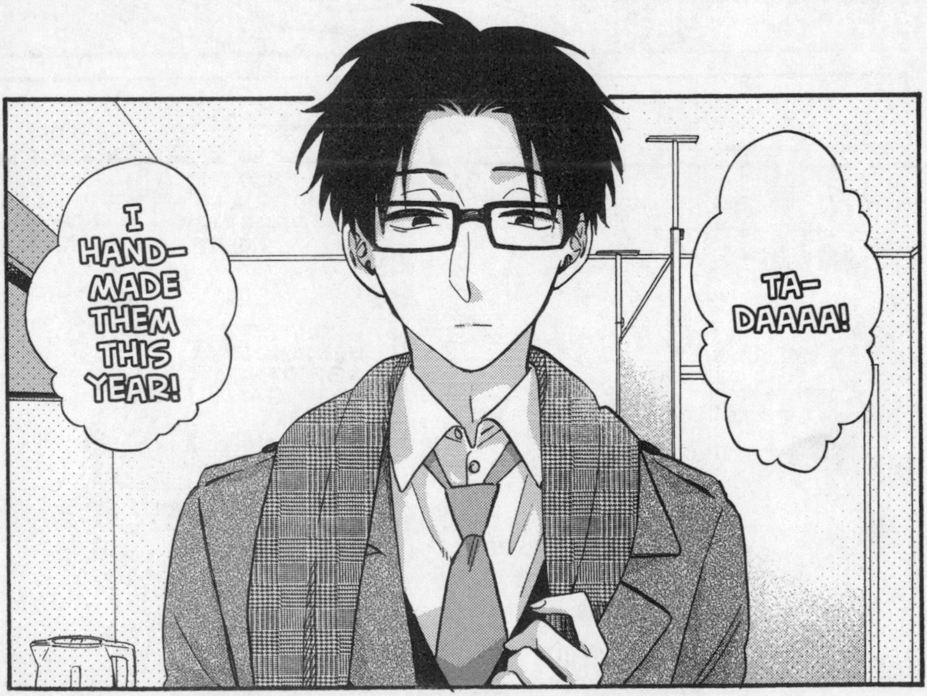
TA-DAAAA!
I HAND-MADE THEM THIS YEAR!

*Holiday marking start of spring on lunar calendar

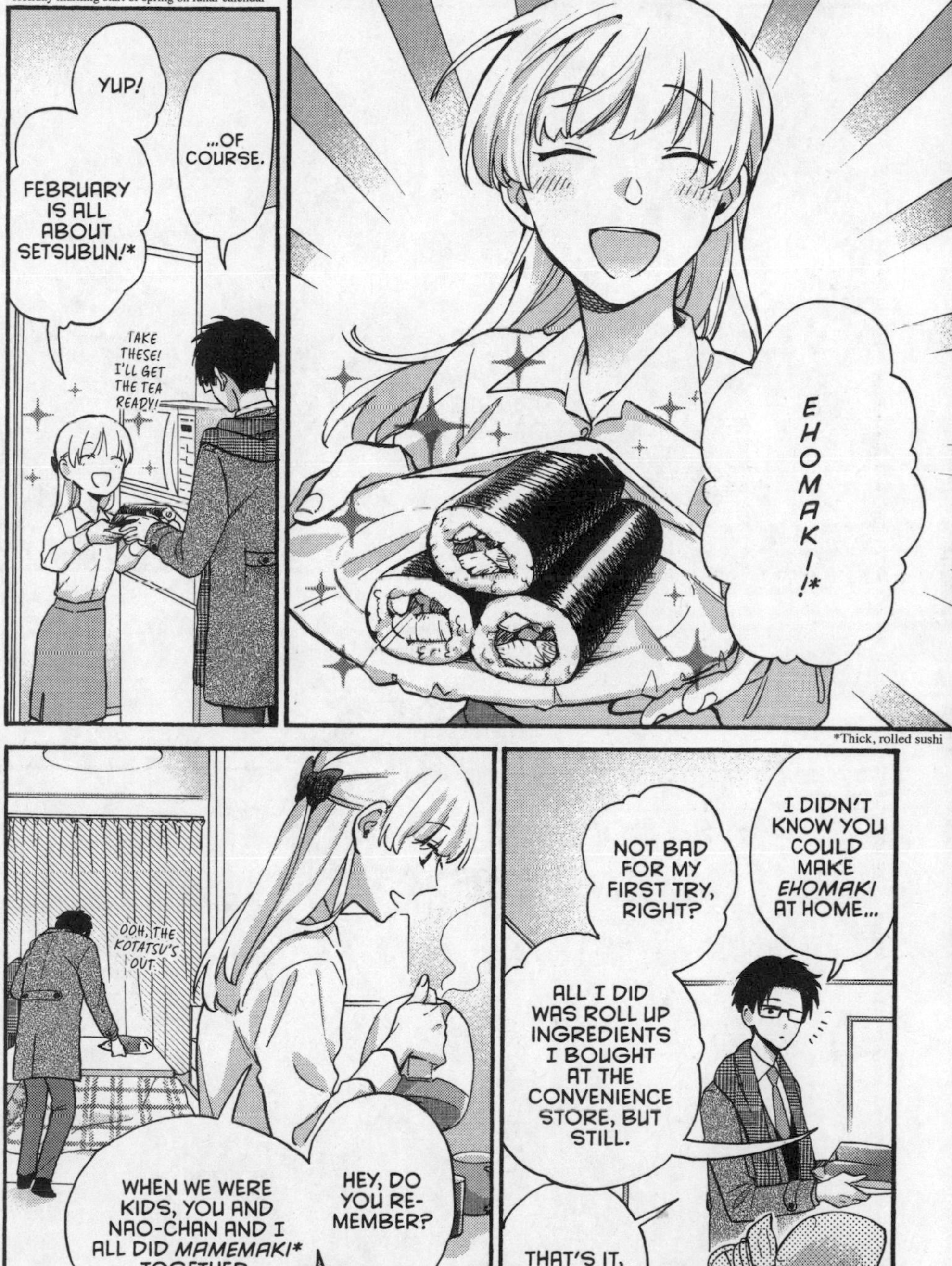
EHOMAKI!*
...OF COURSE.
YUP!
FEBRUARY IS ALL ABOUT SETSUBUN!*
TAKE THESE! I'LL GET THE TEA READY!
I DIDN'T KNOW YOU COULD MAKE *EHOMAKI* AT HOME...
NOT BAD FOR MY FIRST TRY, RIGHT?
ALL I DID WAS ROLL UP INGREDIENTS I BOUGHT AT THE CONVENIENCE STORE, BUT STILL.
THAT'S IT, HUH...?
OOH, THE KOTATSU'S OUT.
HEY, DO YOU REMEMBER?
WHEN WE WERE KIDS, YOU AND NAO-CHAN AND I ALL DID *MAMEMAKI** TOGETHER.

*Thick, rolled sushi

*Ritual for chasing away evil spirits

[Sour* outcome]

*Because sushi rice has vinegar in it

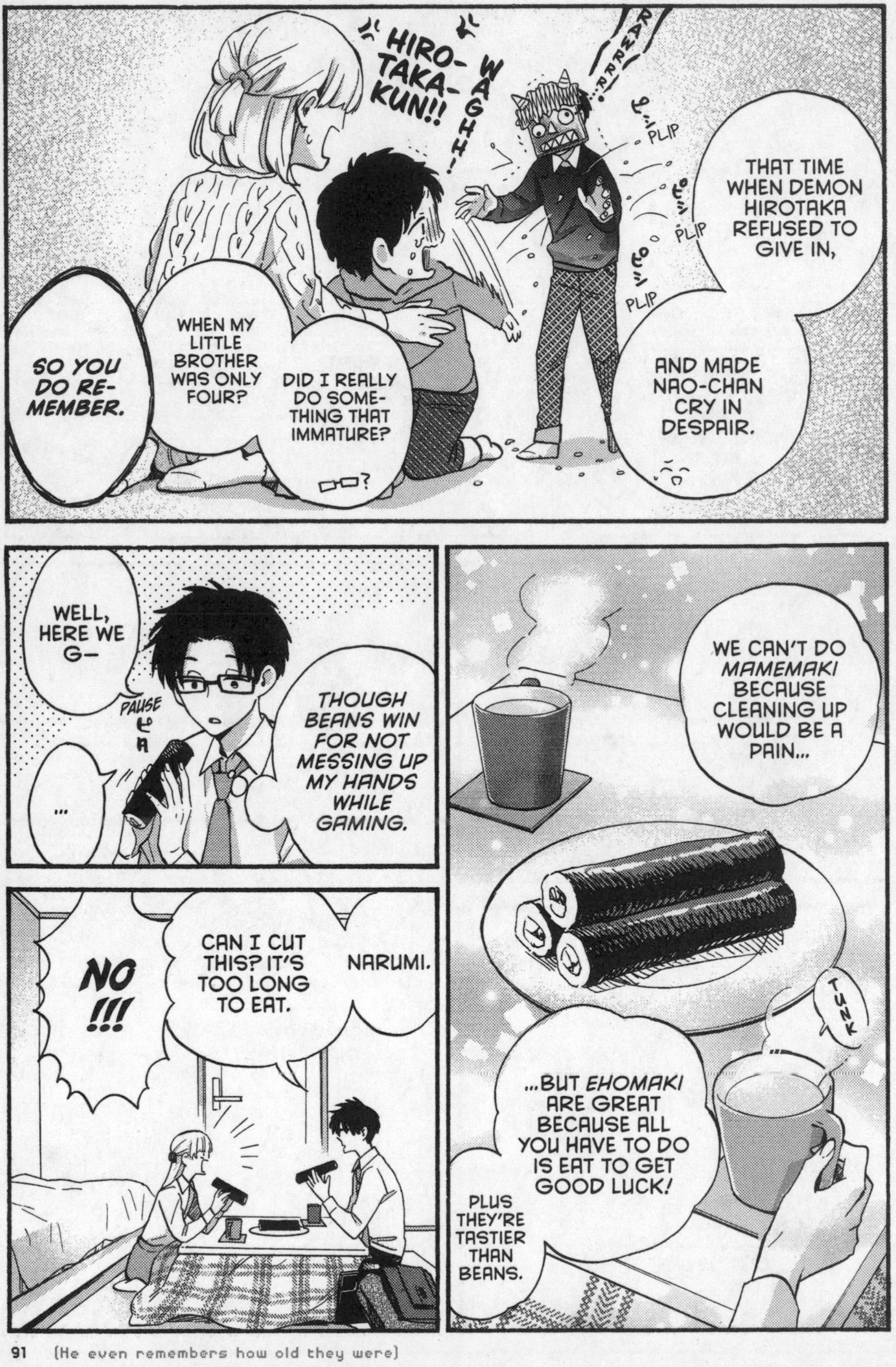
RAWRRR
THAT TIME WHEN DEMON HIROTAKA REFUSED TO GIVE IN,
PLIP
PLIP
PLIP
AND MADE NAO-CHAN CRY IN DESPAIR.
WAGHH!
HIRO-TAKA-KUN!!
DID I REALLY DO SOME-THING THAT IMMATURE?
WHEN MY LITTLE BROTHER WAS ONLY FOUR?
SO YOU DO RE-MEMBER.
WE CAN'T DO *MAMEMAKI* BECAUSE CLEANING UP WOULD BE A PAIN...
TUNK
...BUT *EHOMAKI* ARE GREAT BECAUSE ALL YOU HAVE TO DO IS EAT TO GET GOOD LUCK!
PLUS THEY'RE TASTIER THAN BEANS.
THOUGH BEANS WIN FOR NOT MESSING UP MY HANDS WHILE GAMING.
WELL, HERE WE G—
PAUSE
...
NARUMI.
CAN I CUT THIS? IT'S TOO LONG TO EAT.
NO !!!

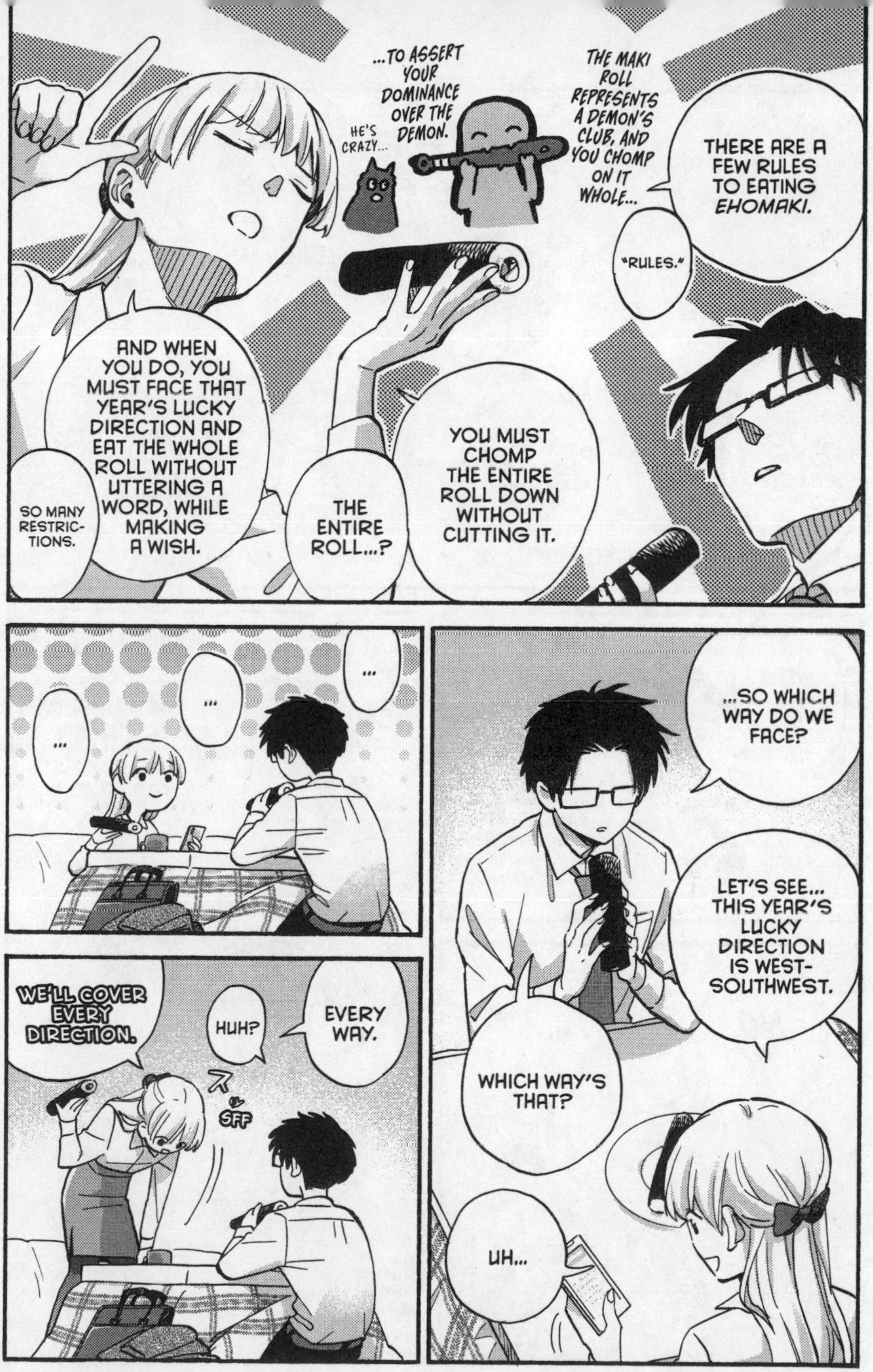
THERE ARE A FEW RULES TO EATING EHOMAKI.
THE MAKI ROLL REPRESENTS A DEMON'S CLUB, AND YOU CHOMP ON IT WHOLE...
...TO ASSERT YOUR DOMINANCE OVER THE DEMON.
HE'S CRAZY...
"RULES."
YOU MUST CHOMP THE ENTIRE ROLL DOWN WITHOUT CUTTING IT.
THE ENTIRE ROLL...?
AND WHEN YOU DO, YOU MUST FACE THAT YEAR'S LUCKY DIRECTION AND EAT THE WHOLE ROLL WITHOUT UTTERING A WORD, WHILE MAKING A WISH.
SO MANY RESTRIC-TIONS.
...SO WHICH WAY DO WE FACE?
LET'S SEE... THIS YEAR'S LUCKY DIRECTION IS WEST-SOUTHWEST.
WHICH WAY'S THAT?
UH...
...
...
...
EVERY WAY.
HUH?
WE'LL COVER EVERY DIRECTION.
SFF

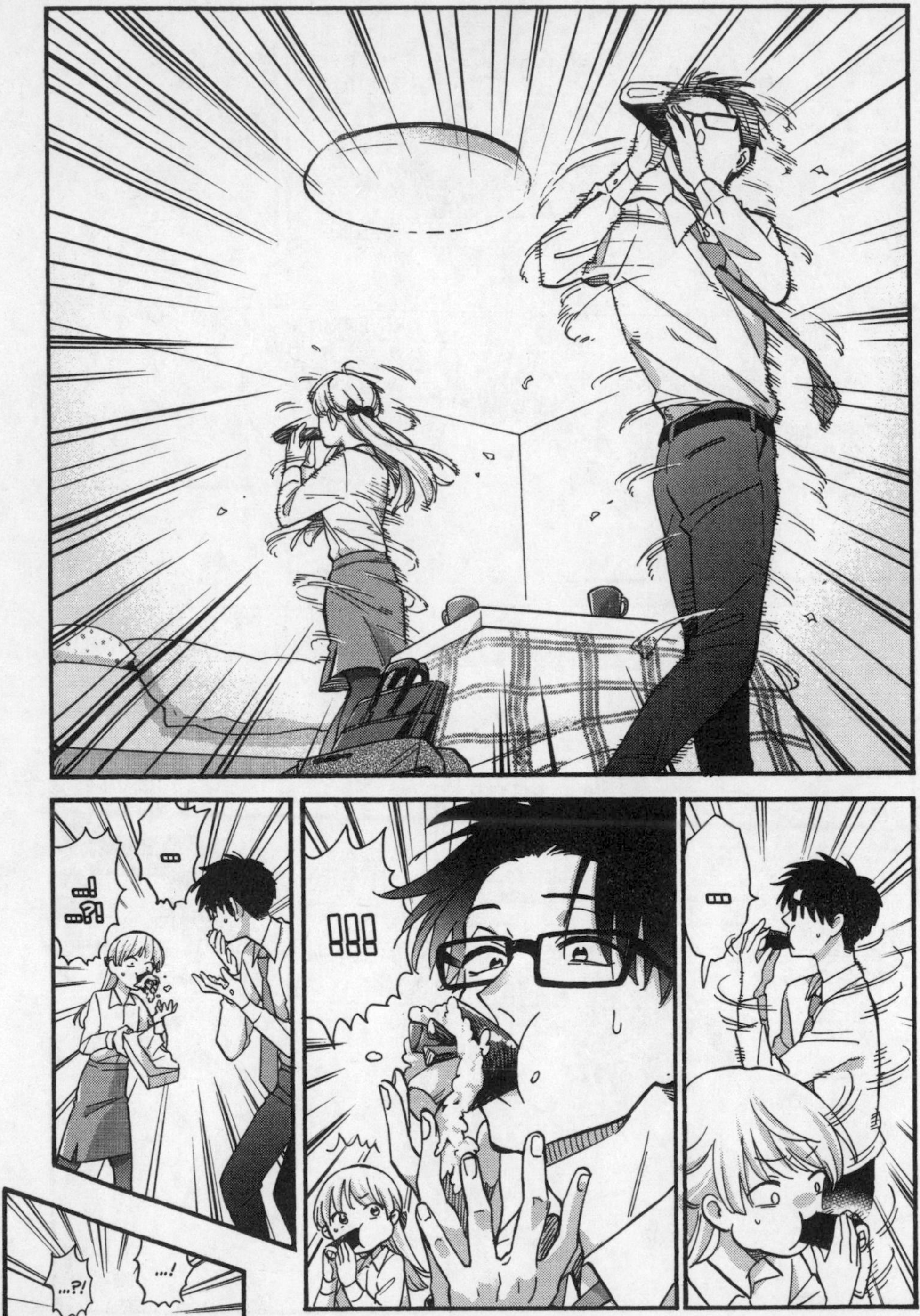

...
!!!
...
...!
...?!
...!
...?!

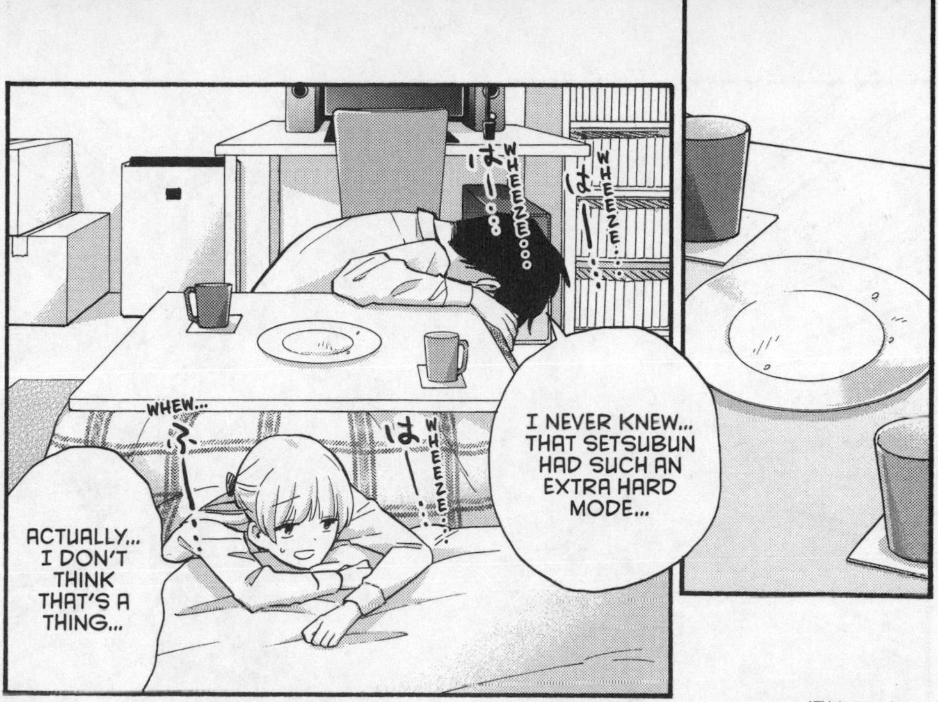
WHEEZE...
WHEEZE...
I NEVER KNEW... THAT SETSUBUN HAD SUCH AN EXTRA HARD MODE...
WHEEZE...
WHEW...
ACTUALLY... I DON'T THINK THAT'S A THING...

*Third-person shooter

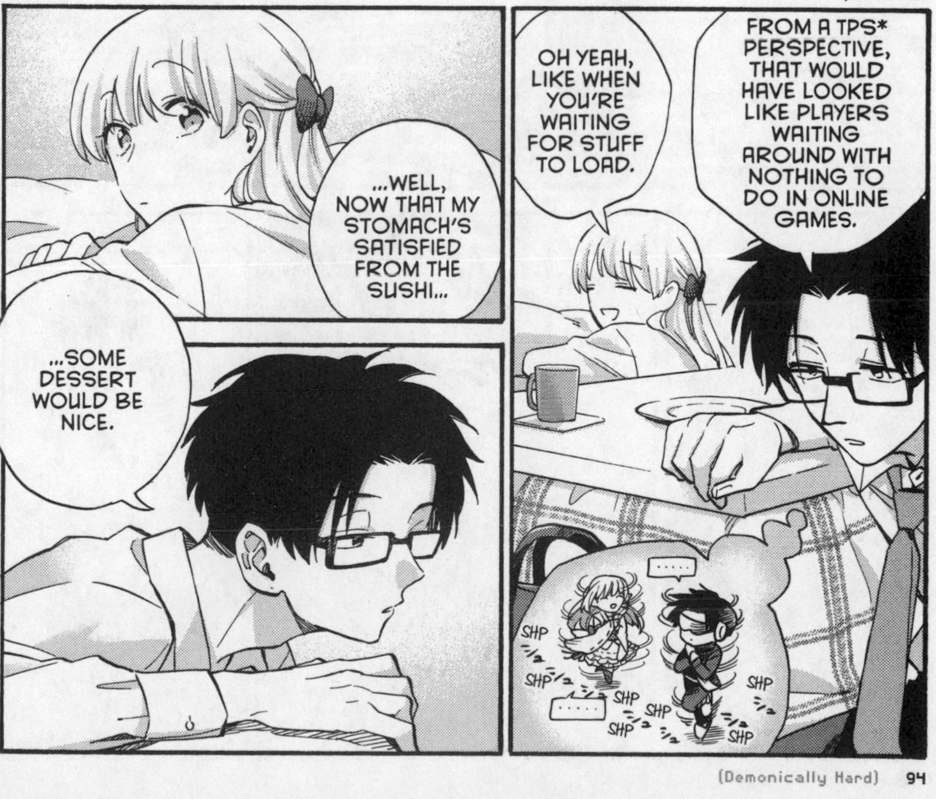
FROM A TPS* PERSPECTIVE, THAT WOULD HAVE LOOKED LIKE PLAYERS WAITING AROUND WITH NOTHING TO DO IN ONLINE GAMES.
OH YEAH, LIKE WHEN YOU'RE WAITING FOR STUFF TO LOAD.
.....
SHP
SHP
SHP
SHP
.....
SHP
SHP
SHP
...WELL, NOW THAT MY STOMACH'S SATISFIED FROM THE SUSHI...
...SOME DESSERT WOULD BE NICE.

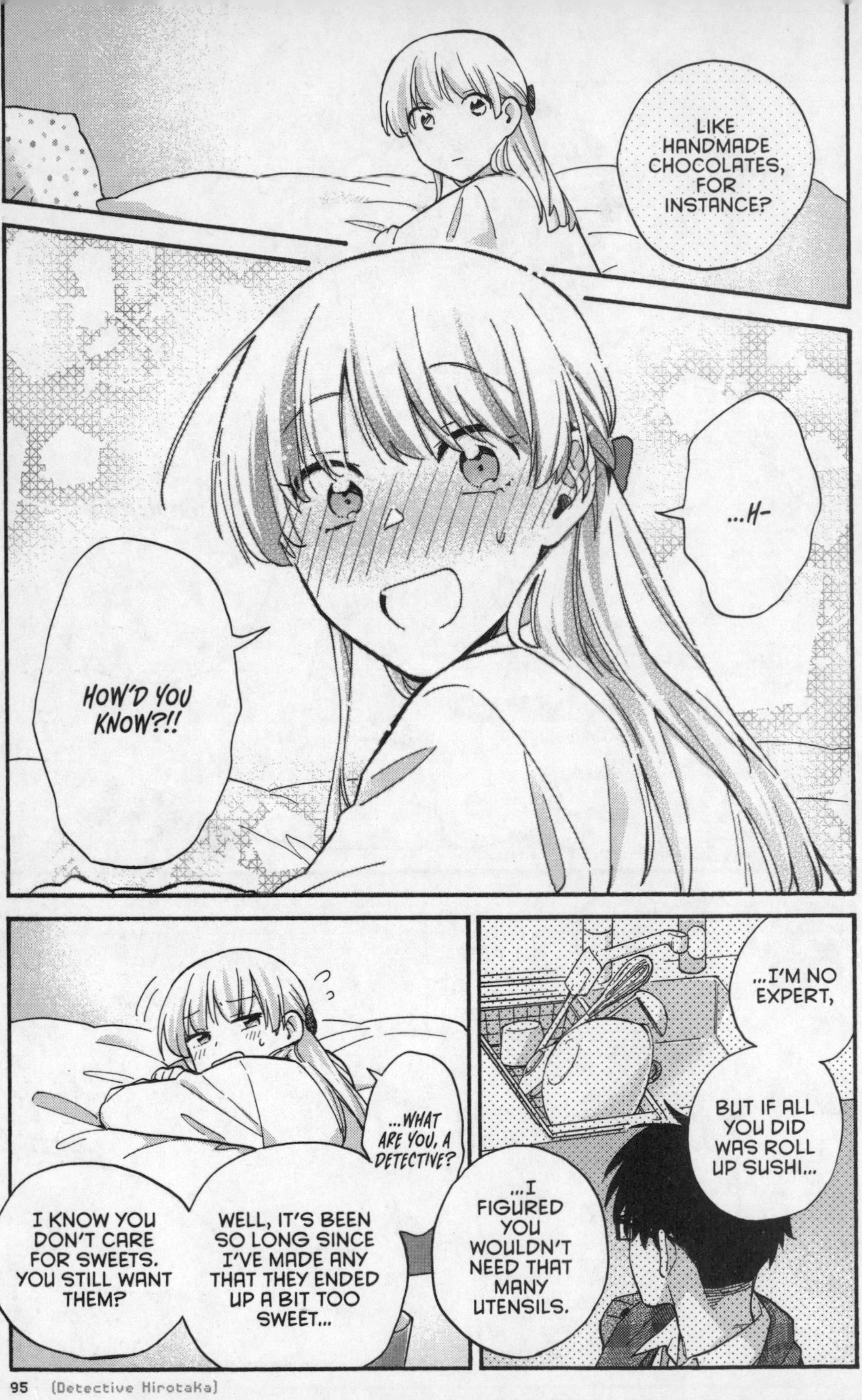
LIKE HANDMADE CHOCOLATES, FOR INSTANCE?
...H-
HOW'D YOU KNOW?!!
...I'M NO EXPERT,
BUT IF ALL YOU DID WAS ROLL UP SUSHI...
...I FIGURED YOU WOULDN'T NEED THAT MANY UTENSILS.
...WHAT ARE YOU, A DETECTIVE?
WELL, IT'S BEEN SO LONG SINCE I'VE MADE ANY THAT THEY ENDED UP A BIT TOO SWEET...
I KNOW YOU DON'T CARE FOR SWEETS. YOU STILL WANT THEM?

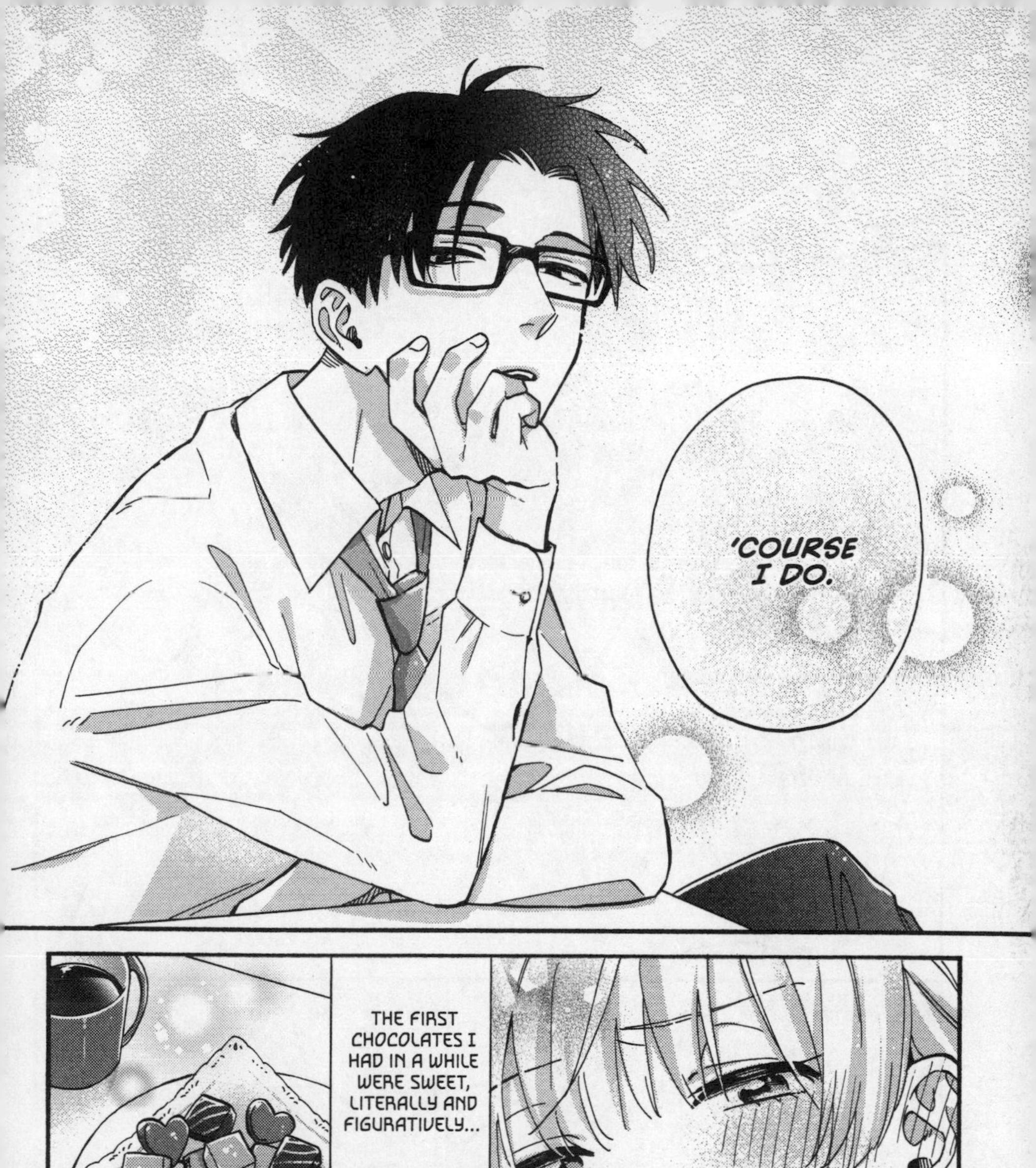
'COURSE I DO.
THE FIRST CHOCOLATES I HAD IN A WHILE WERE SWEET, LITERALLY AND FIGURATIVELY...
...AND THEY ALSO HAD A HINT OF SUSHI VINEGAR, SOMEHOW.

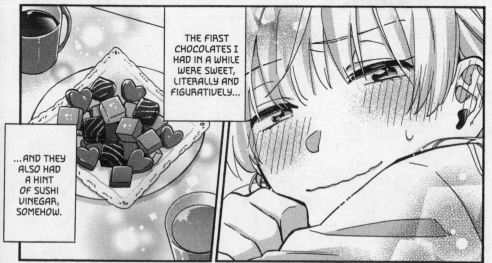

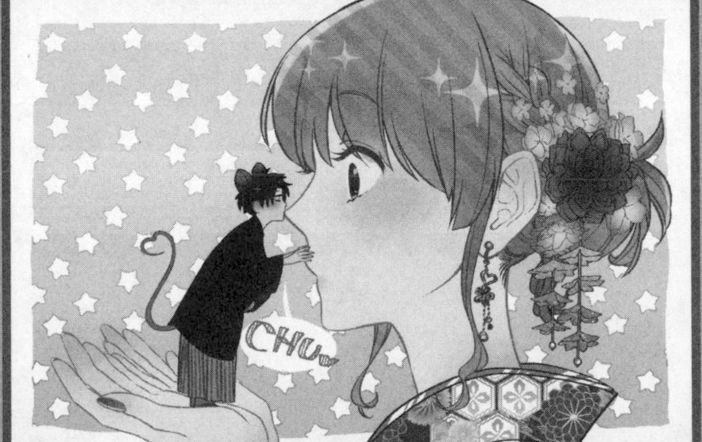
CHU

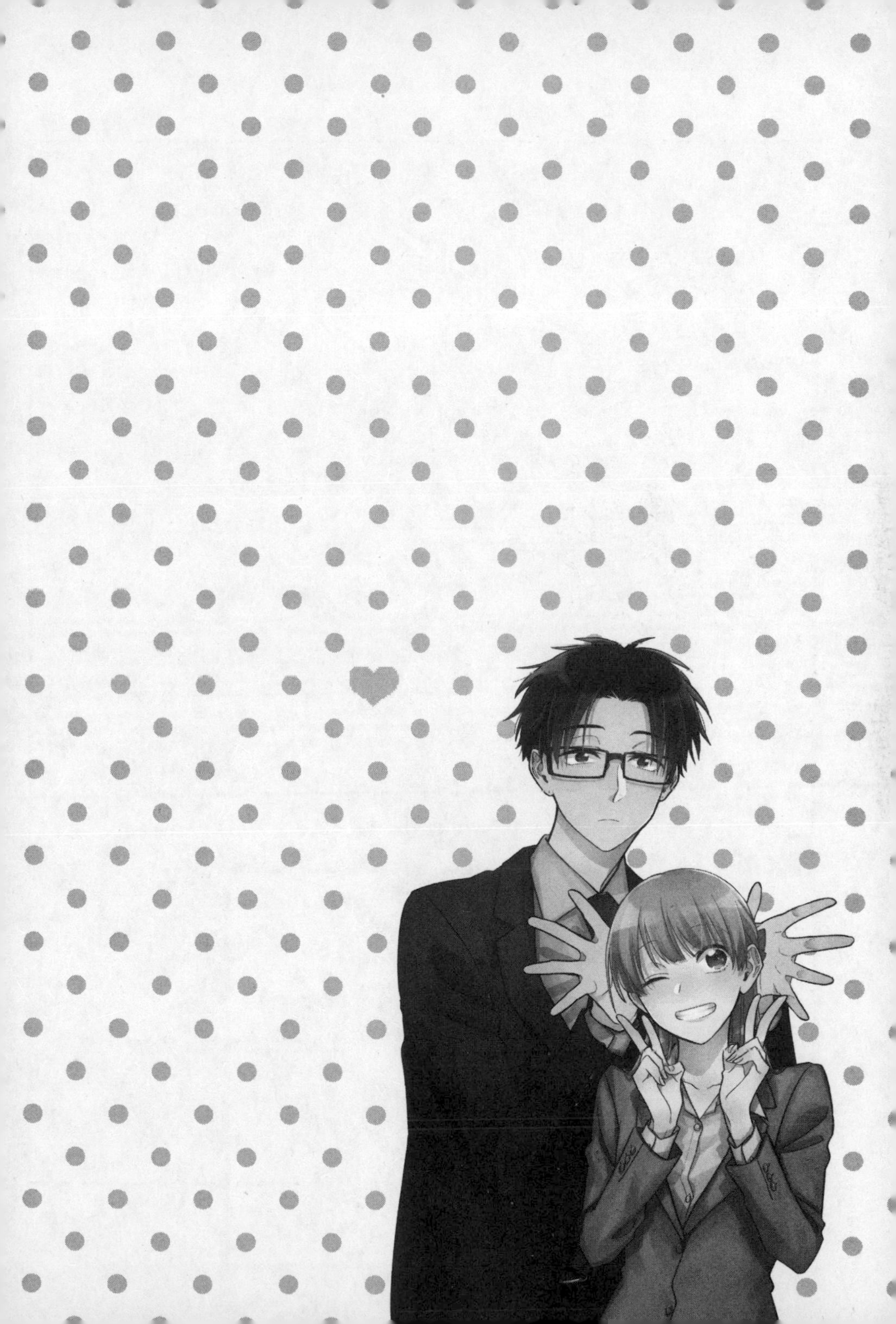

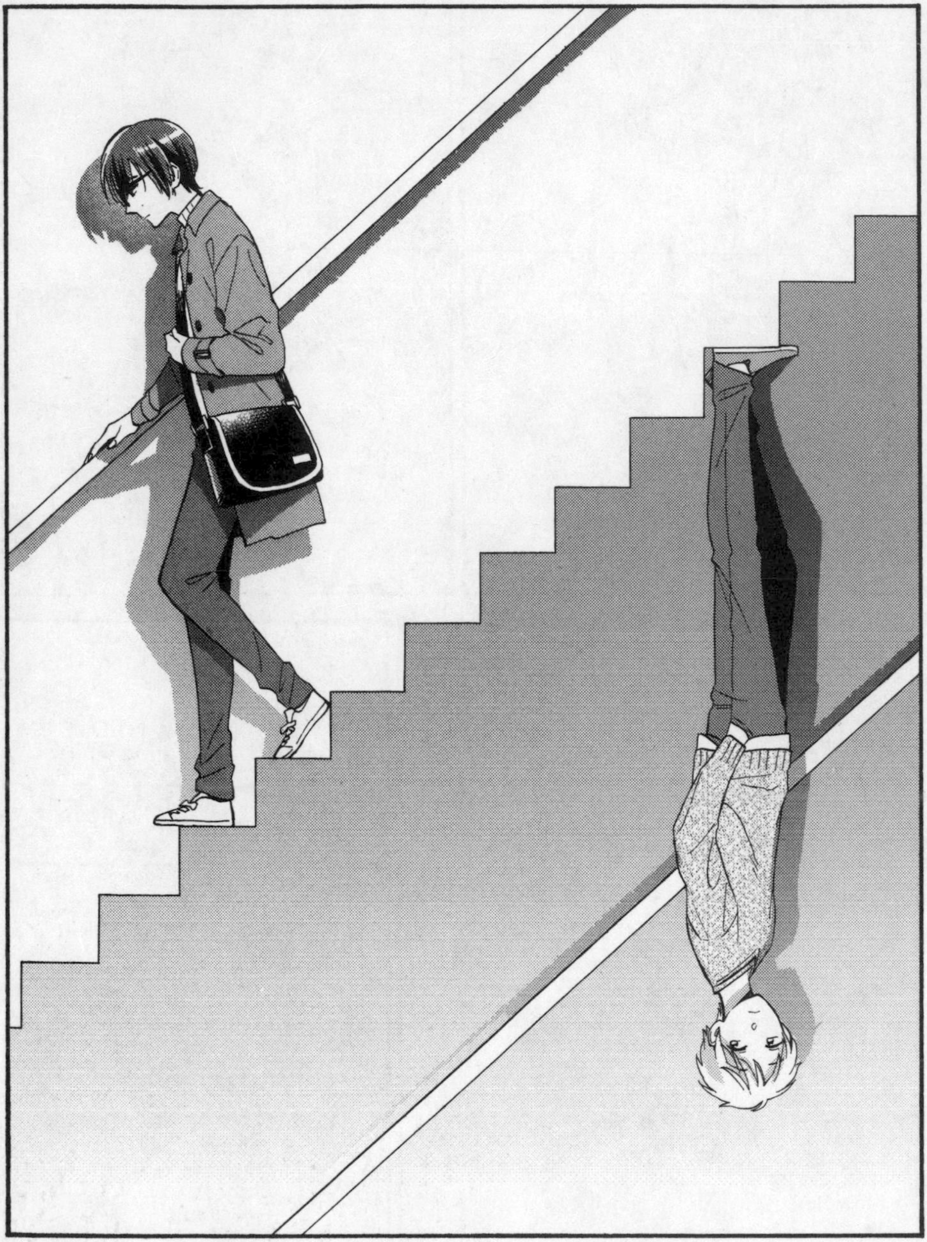

Episode....69

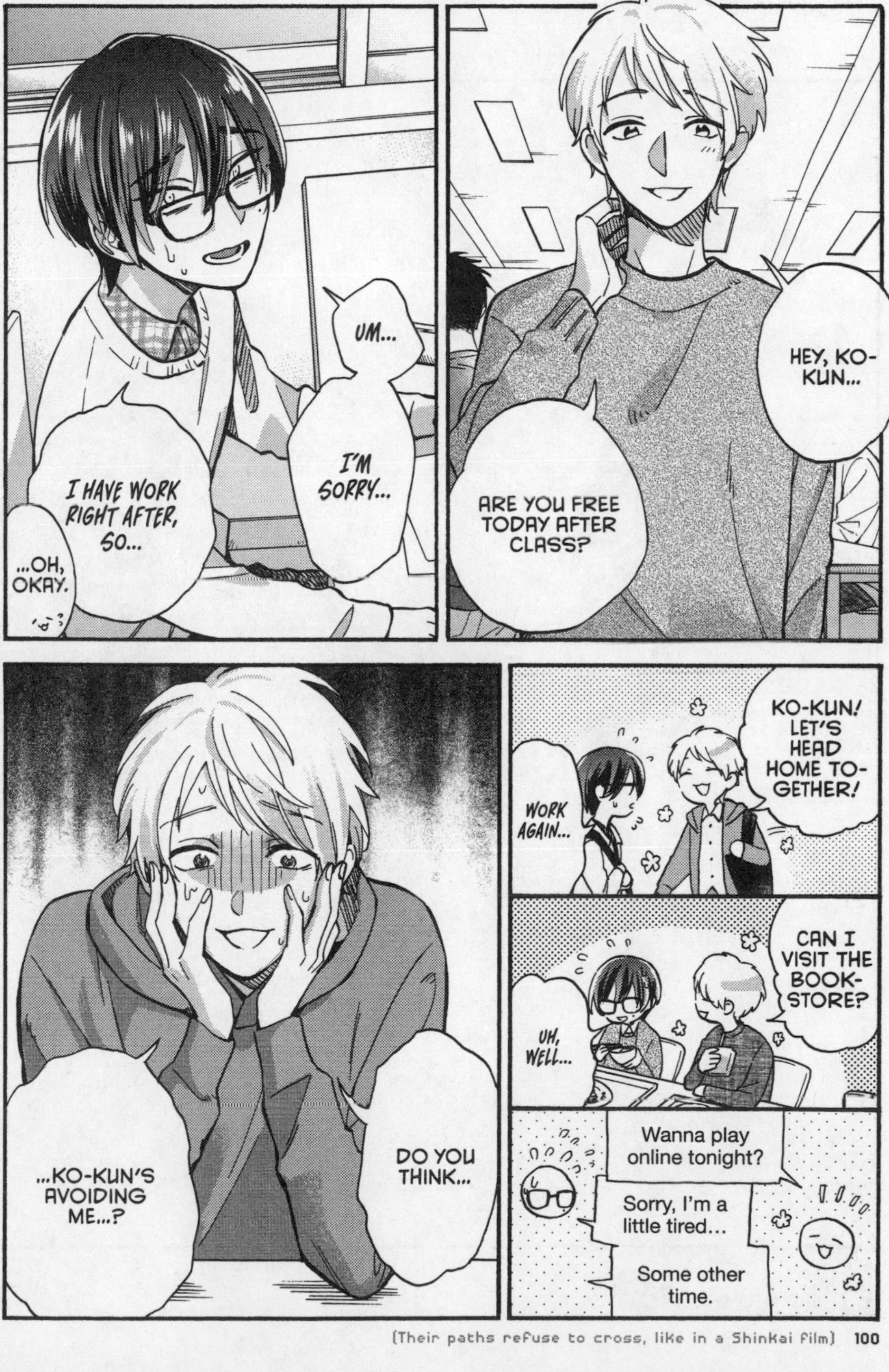
HEY, KO-KUN...
ARE YOU FREE TODAY AFTER CLASS?
UM...
I'M SORRY...
I HAVE WORK RIGHT AFTER, SO...
...OH, OKAY.
KO-KUN! LET'S HEAD HOME TOGETHER!
WORK AGAIN...
CAN I VISIT THE BOOKSTORE?
UH, WELL...
Wanna play online tonight?
Sorry, I'm a little tired...
Some other time.
DO YOU THINK...
...KO-KUN'S AVOIDING ME...?

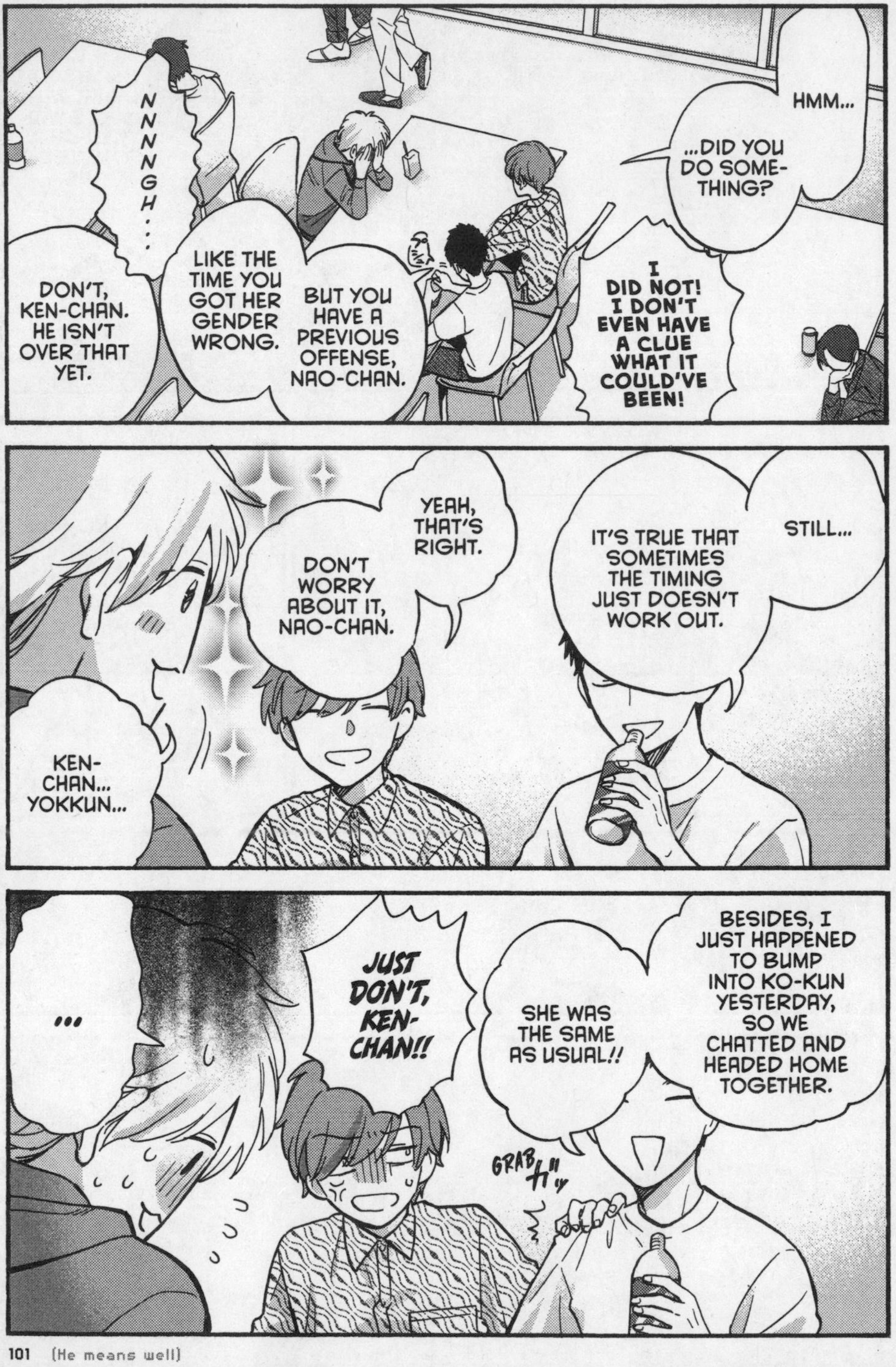
HMM...
...DID YOU DO SOME-THING?
I DID NOT! I DON'T EVEN HAVE A CLUE WHAT IT COULD'VE BEEN!
BUT YOU HAVE A PREVIOUS OFFENSE, NAO-CHAN.
LIKE THE TIME YOU GOT HER GENDER WRONG.
NNNNGH...
DON'T, KEN-CHAN. HE ISN'T OVER THAT YET.
STILL...
IT'S TRUE THAT SOMETIMES THE TIMING JUST DOESN'T WORK OUT.
YEAH, THAT'S RIGHT.
DON'T WORRY ABOUT IT, NAO-CHAN.
KEN-CHAN... YOKKUN...
BESIDES, I JUST HAPPENED TO BUMP INTO KO-KUN YESTERDAY, SO WE CHATTED AND HEADED HOME TOGETHER.
SHE WAS THE SAME AS USUAL!!
GRAB
JUST DON'T, KEN-CHAN!!
...

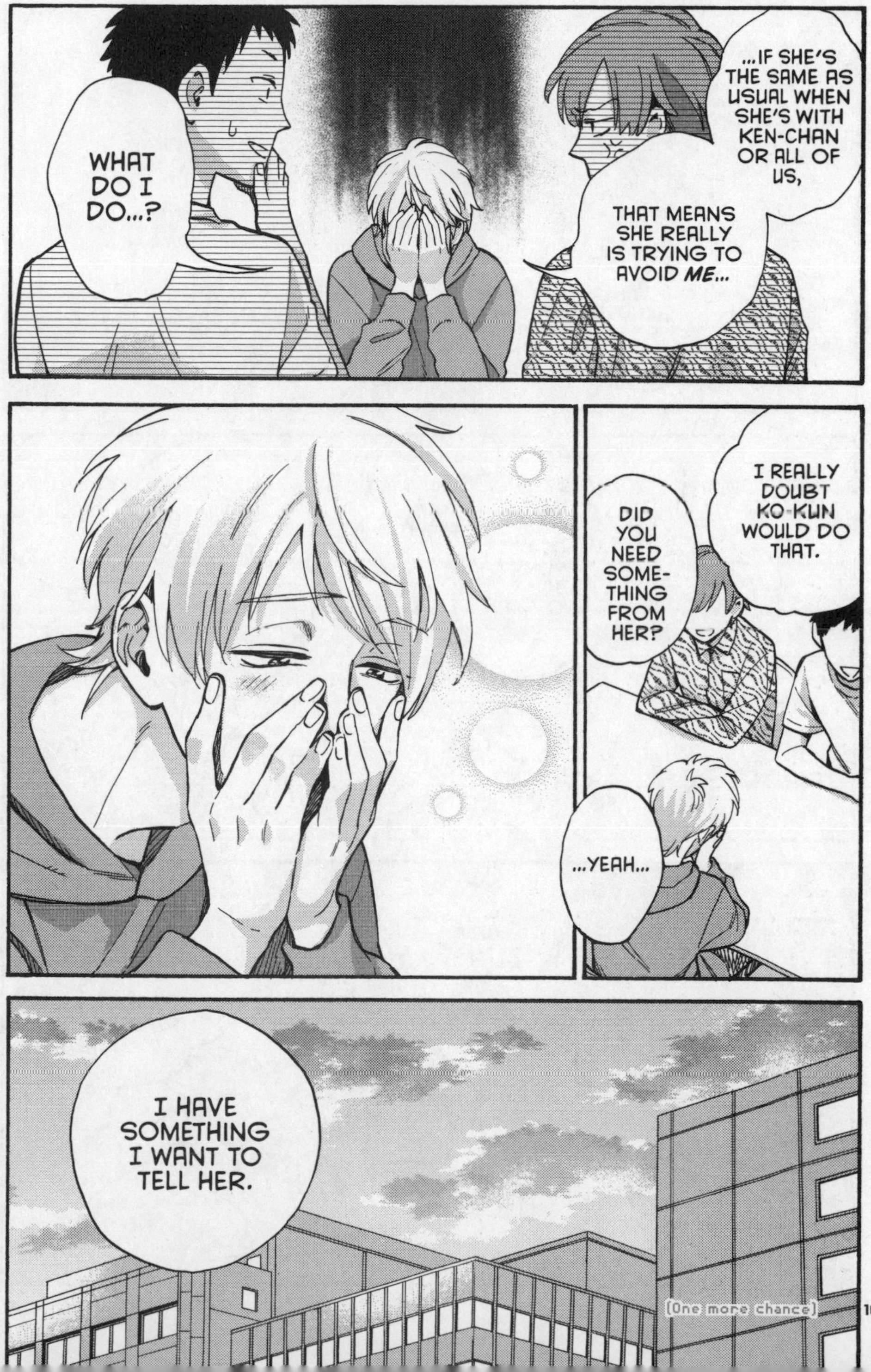
...IF SHE'S THE SAME AS USUAL WHEN SHE'S WITH KEN-CHAN OR ALL OF US,
THAT MEANS SHE REALLY IS TRYING TO AVOID *ME*...
WHAT DO I DO...?
I REALLY DOUBT KO-KUN WOULD DO THAT.
DID YOU NEED SOME-THING FROM HER?
...YEAH...
I HAVE SOMETHING I WANT TO TELL HER.

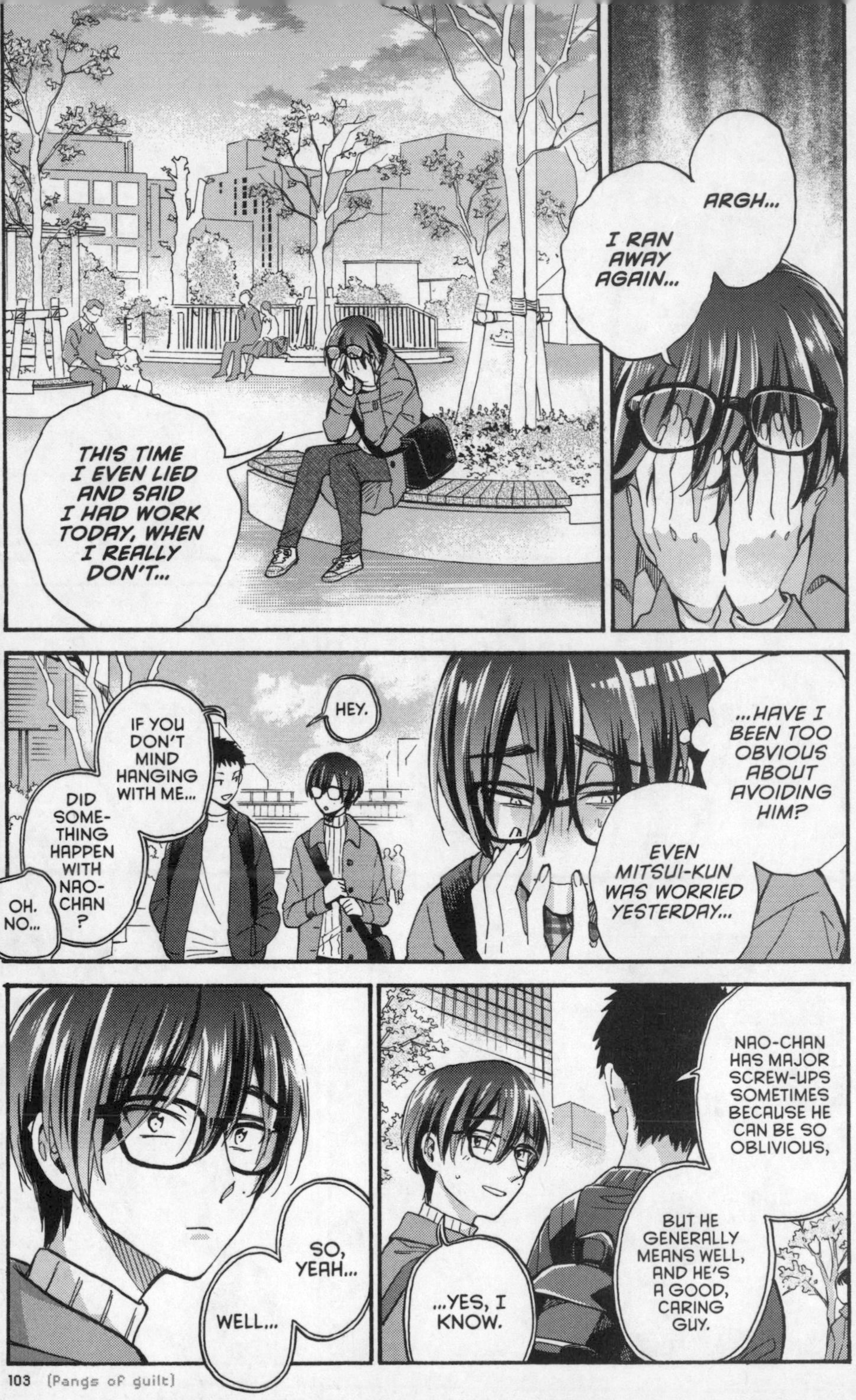
ARGH...
I RAN AWAY AGAIN...
THIS TIME I EVEN LIED AND SAID I HAD WORK TODAY, WHEN I REALLY DON'T...
...HAVE I BEEN TOO OBVIOUS ABOUT AVOIDING HIM?
EVEN MITSUI-KUN WAS WORRIED YESTERDAY...
HEY.
IF YOU DON'T MIND HANGING WITH ME...
DID SOME-THING HAPPEN WITH NAO-CHAN?
OH. NO...
NAO-CHAN HAS MAJOR SCREW-UPS SOMETIMES BECAUSE HE CAN BE SO OBLIVIOUS,
BUT HE GENERALLY MEANS WELL, AND HE'S A GOOD, CARING GUY.
...YES, I KNOW.
SO, YEAH...
WELL...

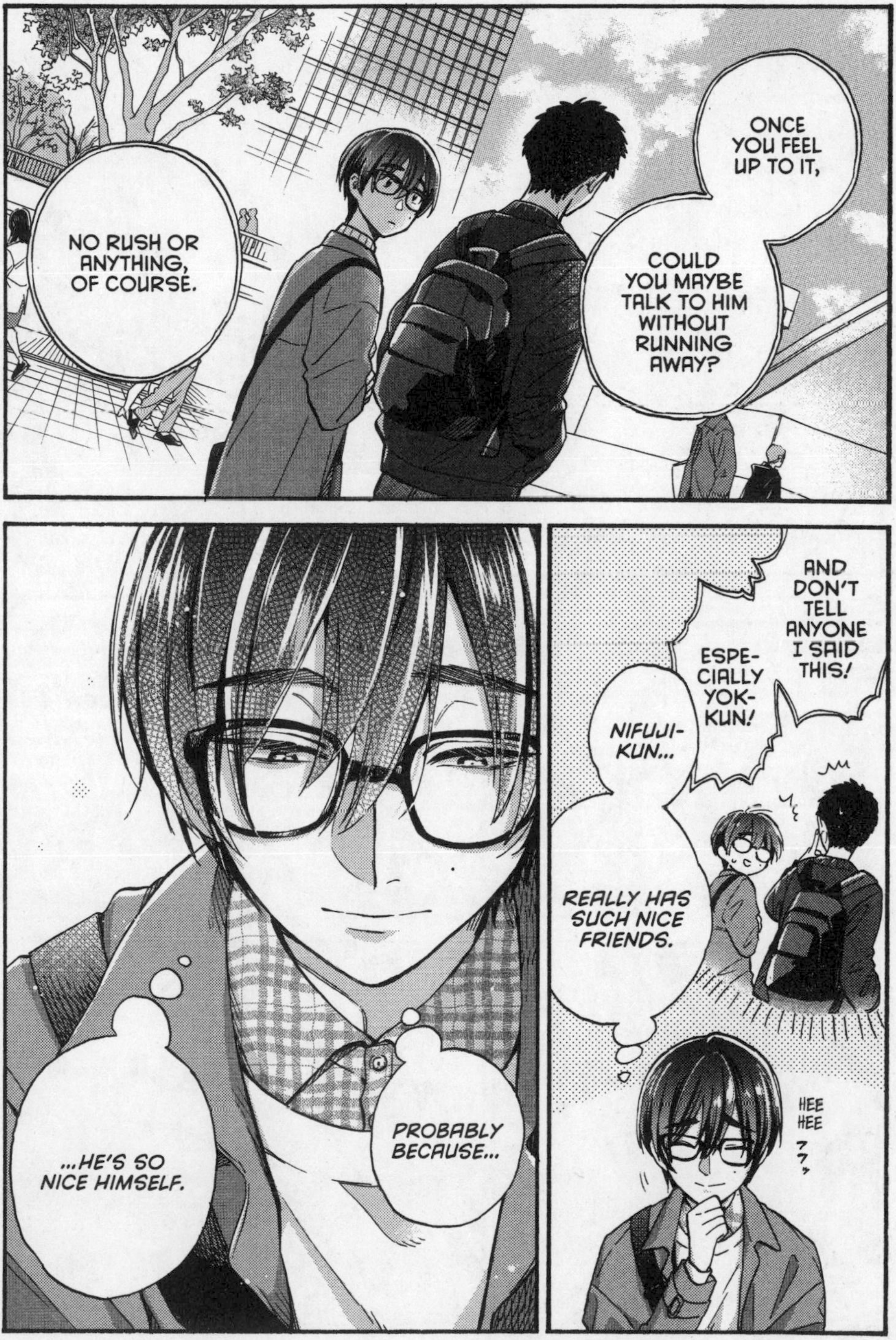
ONCE YOU FEEL UP TO IT,
COULD YOU MAYBE TALK TO HIM WITHOUT RUNNING AWAY?
NO RUSH OR ANYTHING, OF COURSE.
AND DON'T TELL ANYONE I SAID THIS!
ESPE-CIALLY YOK-KUN!
NIFUJI-KUN...
REALLY HAS SUCH NICE FRIENDS.
HEE HEE
PROBABLY BECAUSE...
...HE'S SO NICE HIMSELF.

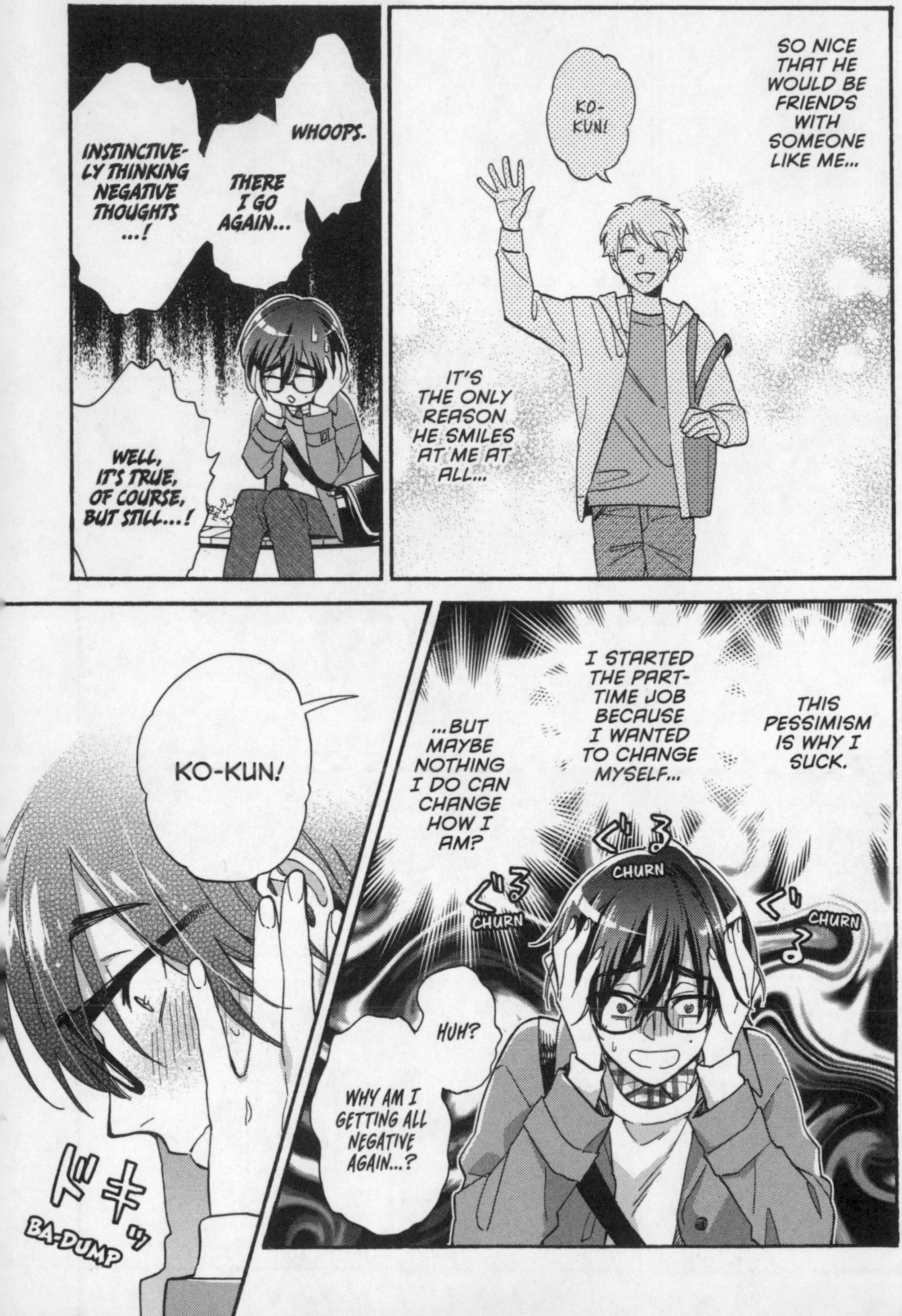
SO NICE THAT HE WOULD BE FRIENDS WITH SOMEONE LIKE ME...
KO-KUN!
IT'S THE ONLY REASON HE SMILES AT ME AT ALL...
WHOOPS.
THERE I GO AGAIN...
INSTINCTIVE-LY THINKING NEGATIVE THOUGHTS ...!
WELL, IT'S TRUE, OF COURSE, BUT STILL...!
THIS PESSIMISM IS WHY I SUCK.
I STARTED THE PART-TIME JOB BECAUSE I WANTED TO CHANGE MYSELF...
...BUT MAYBE NOTHING I DO CAN CHANGE HOW I AM?
ぐる
CHURN
ぐる
CHURN
ぐる
CHURN
HUH?
WHY AM I GETTING ALL NEGATIVE AGAIN...?
KO-KUN!
ドキッ
BA-DUMP

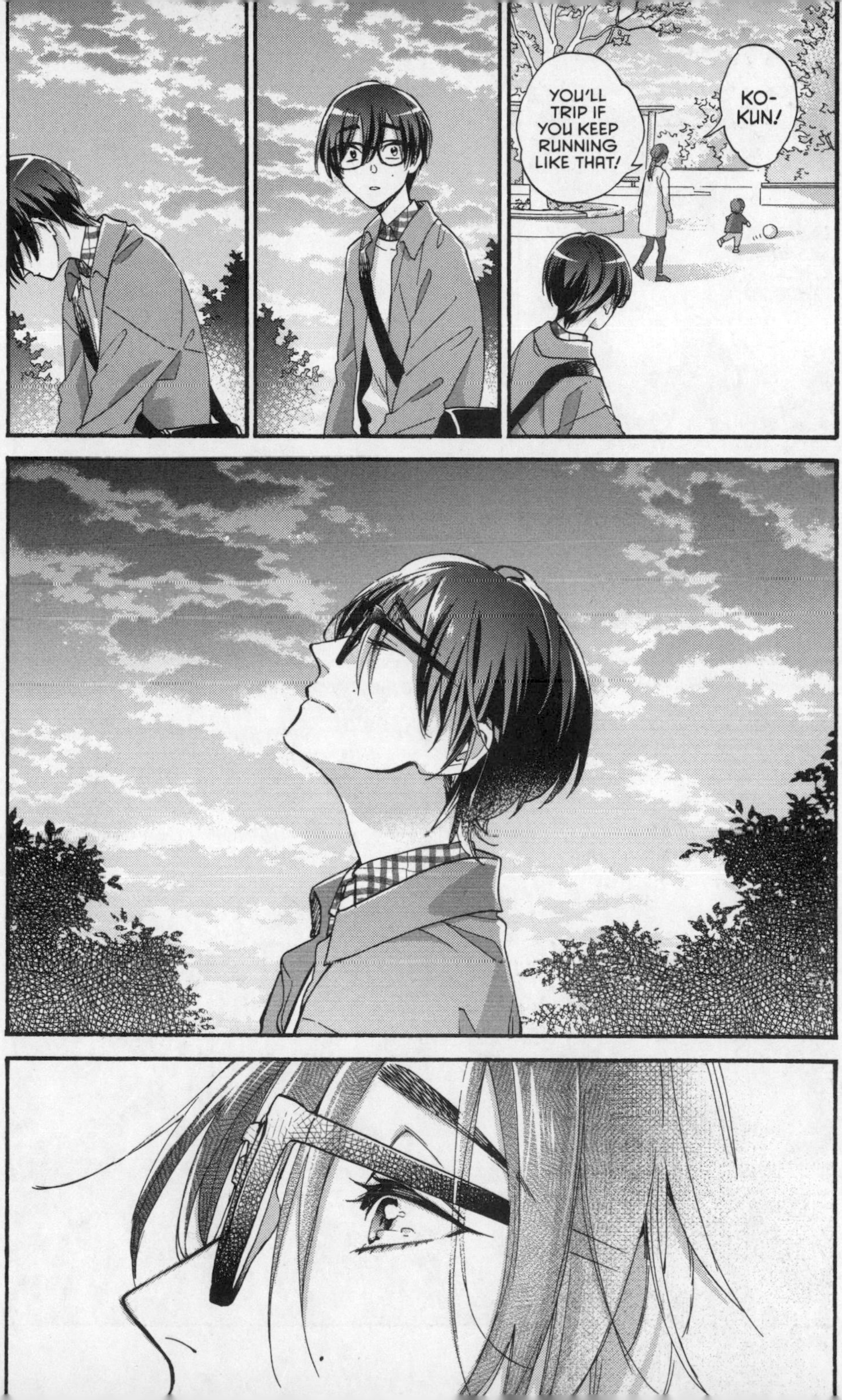
KO-KUN!
YOU'LL TRIP IF YOU KEEP RUNNING LIKE THAT!

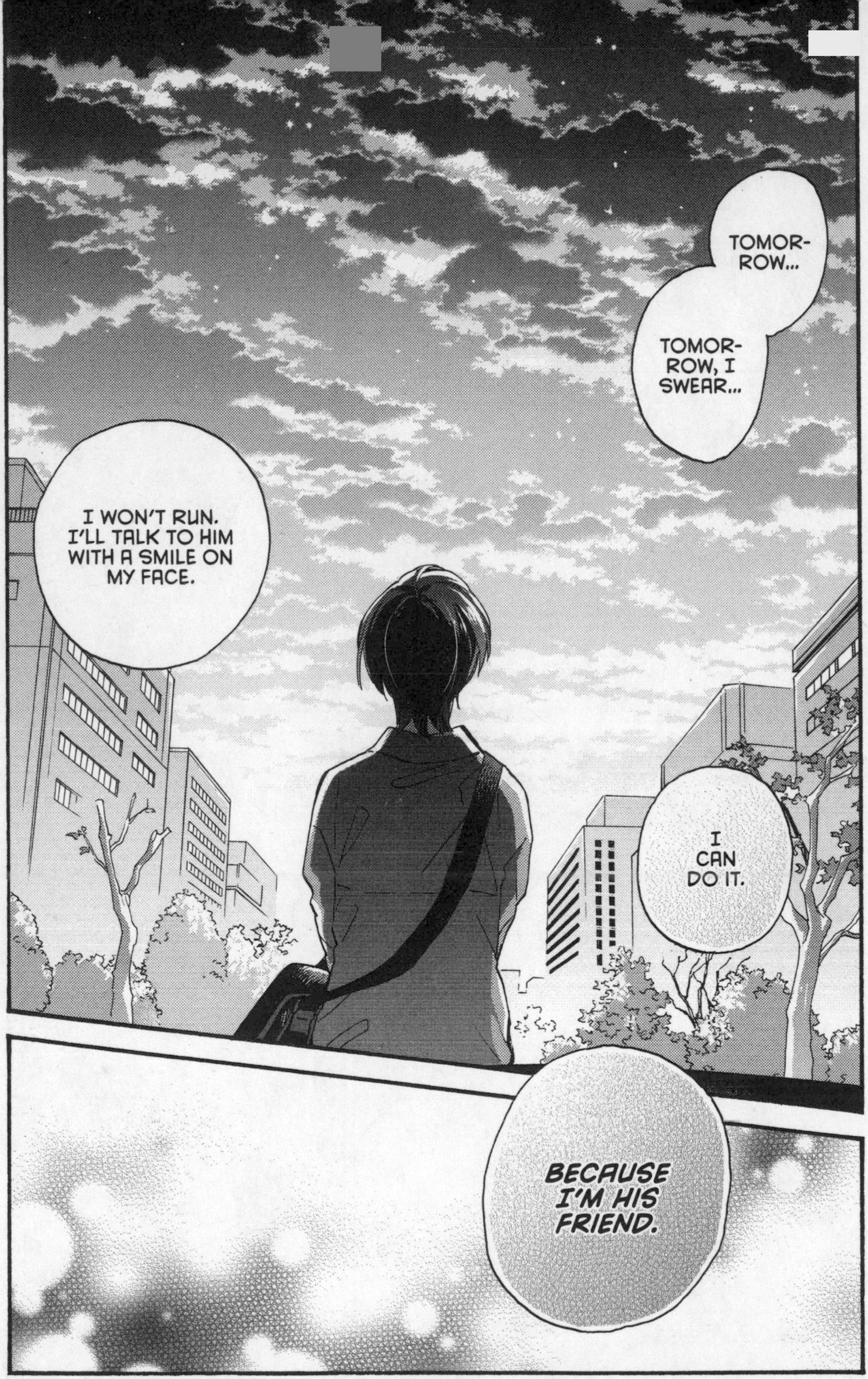
TOMOR-ROW...
TOMOR-ROW, I SWEAR...
I WON'T RUN. I'LL TALK TO HIM WITH A SMILE ON MY FACE.
I CAN DO IT.
BECAUSE I'M HIS FRIEND.

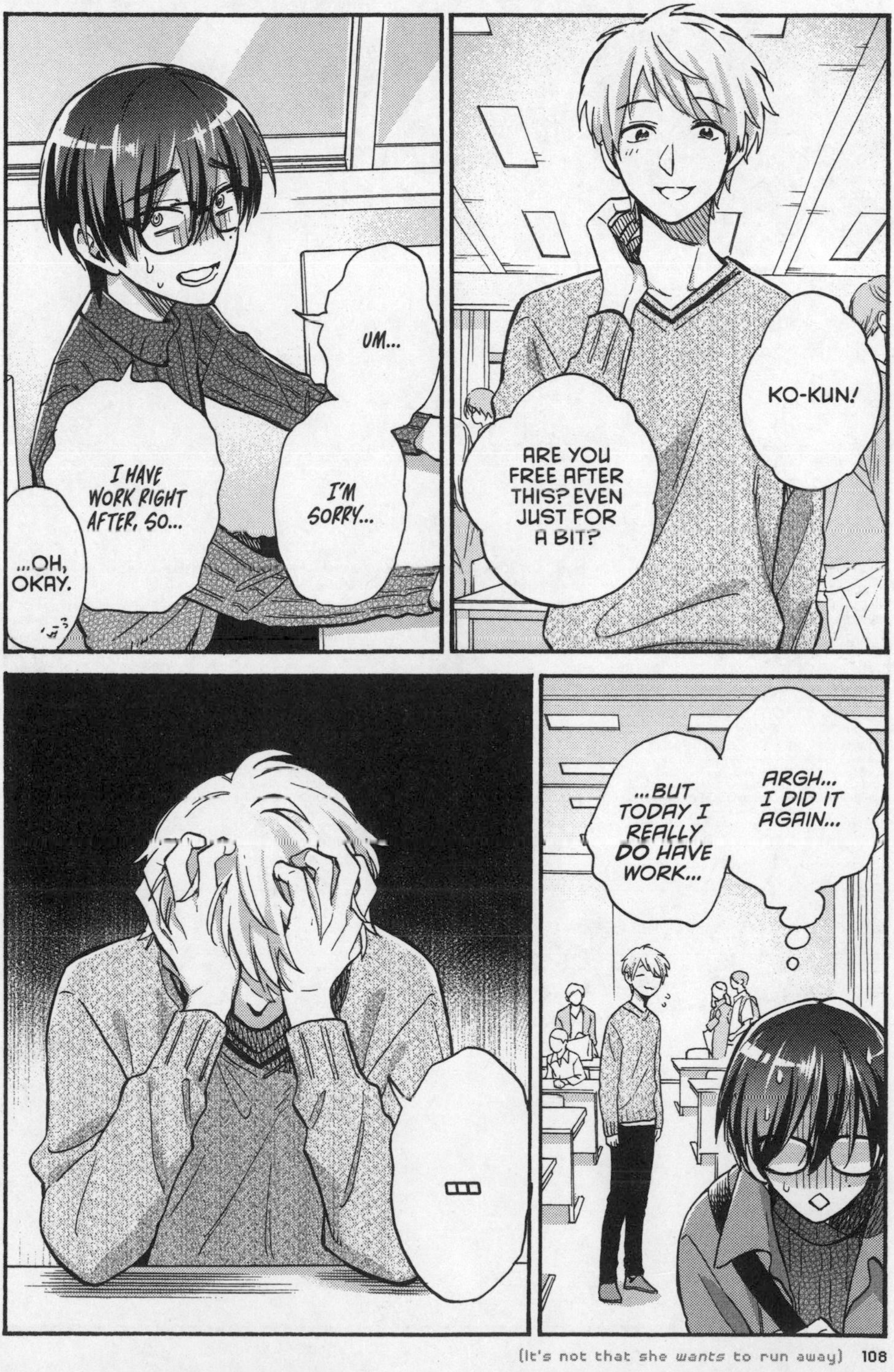
KO-KUN!
ARE YOU FREE AFTER THIS? EVEN JUST FOR A BIT?
UM...
I'M SORRY...
I HAVE WORK RIGHT AFTER, SO...
...OH, OKAY.
ARGH... I DID IT AGAIN...
...BUT TODAY I REALLY DO HAVE WORK...
...

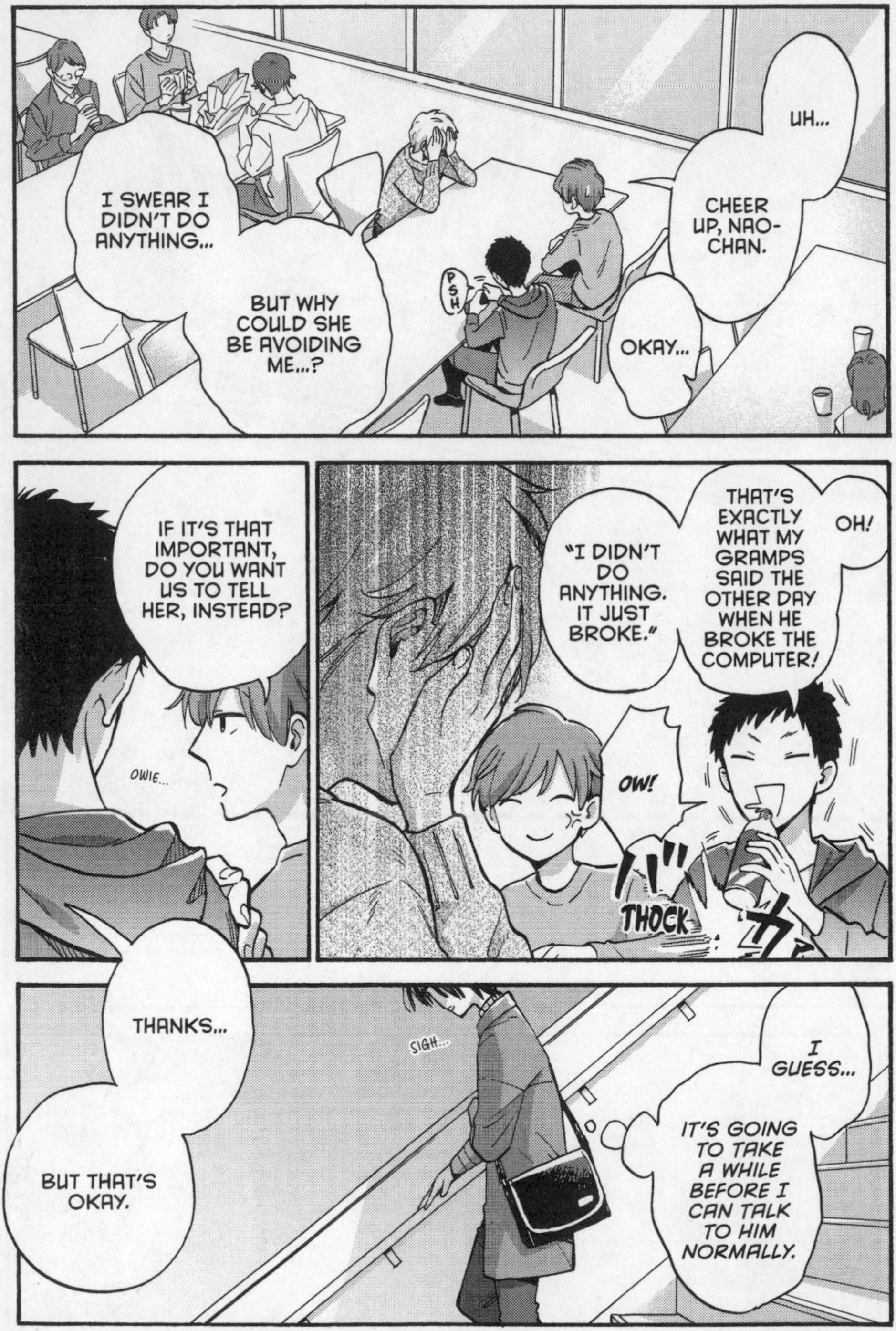
UH...
CHEER UP, NAO-CHAN.
OKAY...
PSH
I SWEAR I DIDN'T DO ANYTHING...
BUT WHY COULD SHE BE AVOIDING ME...?
OH!
THAT'S EXACTLY WHAT MY GRAMPS SAID THE OTHER DAY WHEN HE BROKE THE COMPUTER!
"I DIDN'T DO ANYTHING. IT JUST BROKE."
OW!
THOCK
IF IT'S THAT IMPORTANT, DO YOU WANT US TO TELL HER, INSTEAD?
OWIE...
I GUESS...
IT'S GOING TO TAKE A WHILE BEFORE I CAN TALK TO HIM NORMALLY.
SIGH...
THANKS...
BUT THAT'S OKAY.

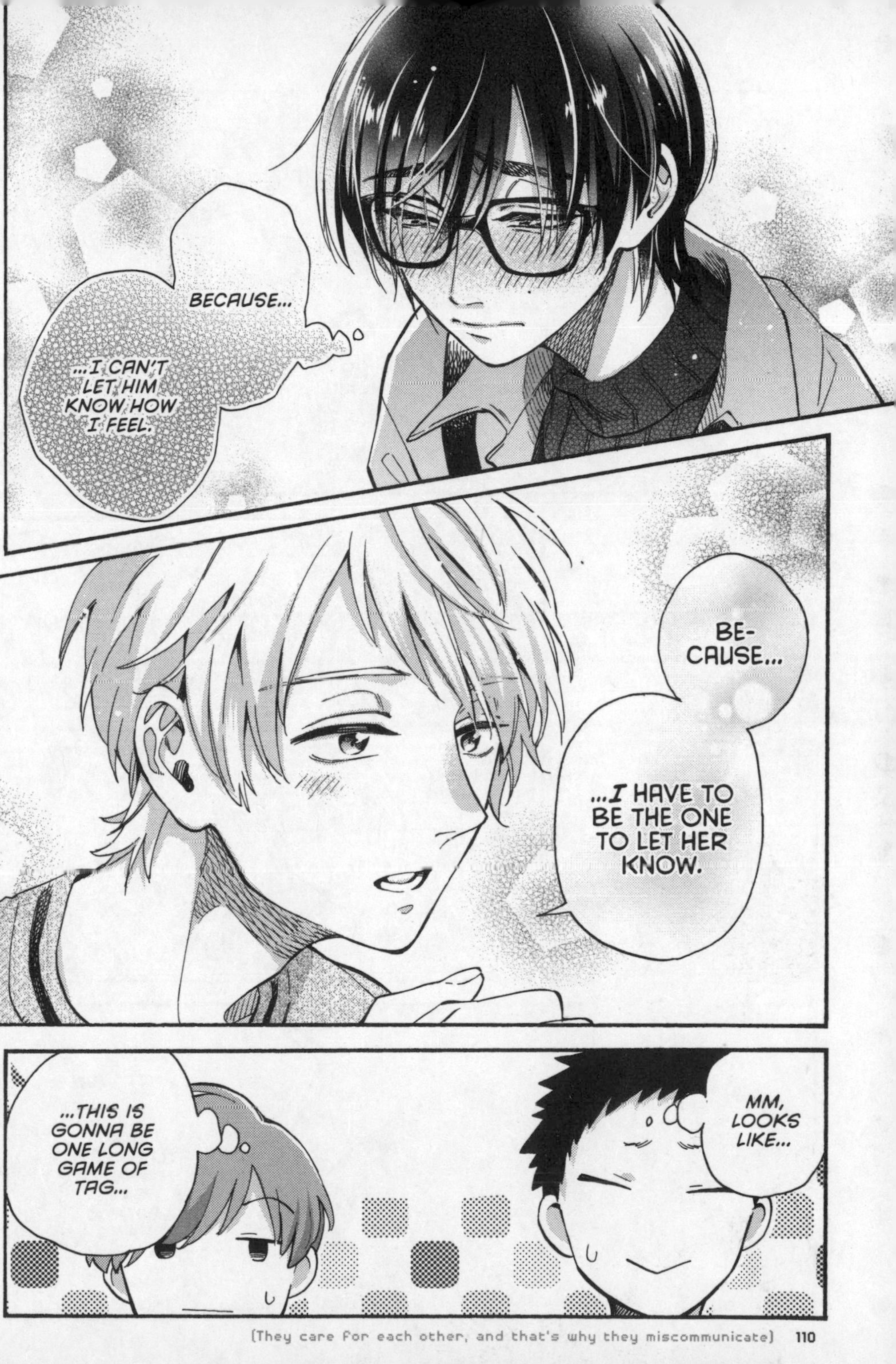
BECAUSE...
...I CAN'T LET HIM KNOW HOW I FEEL.
BE-CAUSE...
...I HAVE TO BE THE ONE TO LET HER KNOW.
MM, LOOKS LIKE...
...THIS IS GONNA BE ONE LONG GAME OF TAG...

(They care for each other, and that's why they miscommunicate)

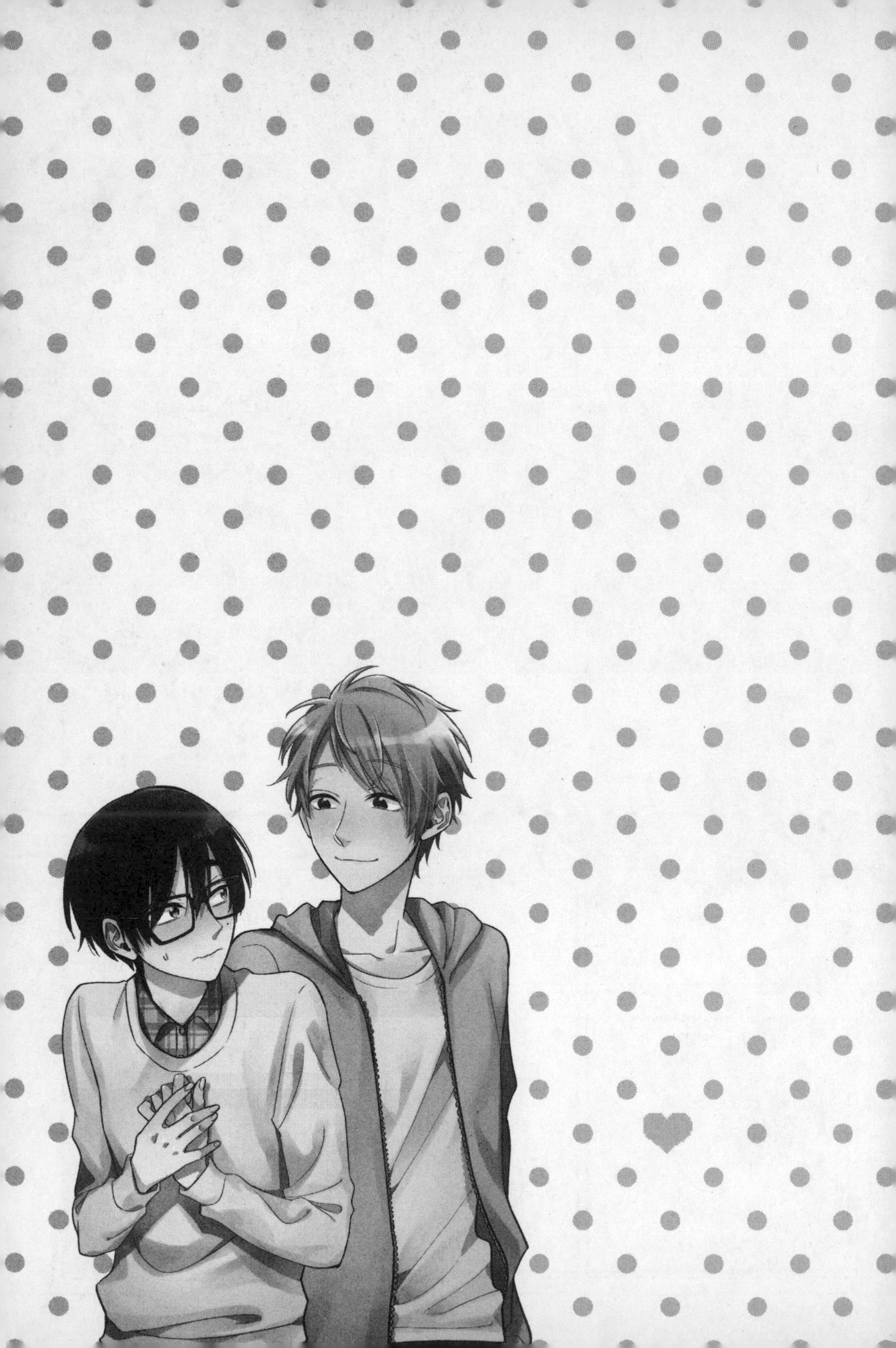

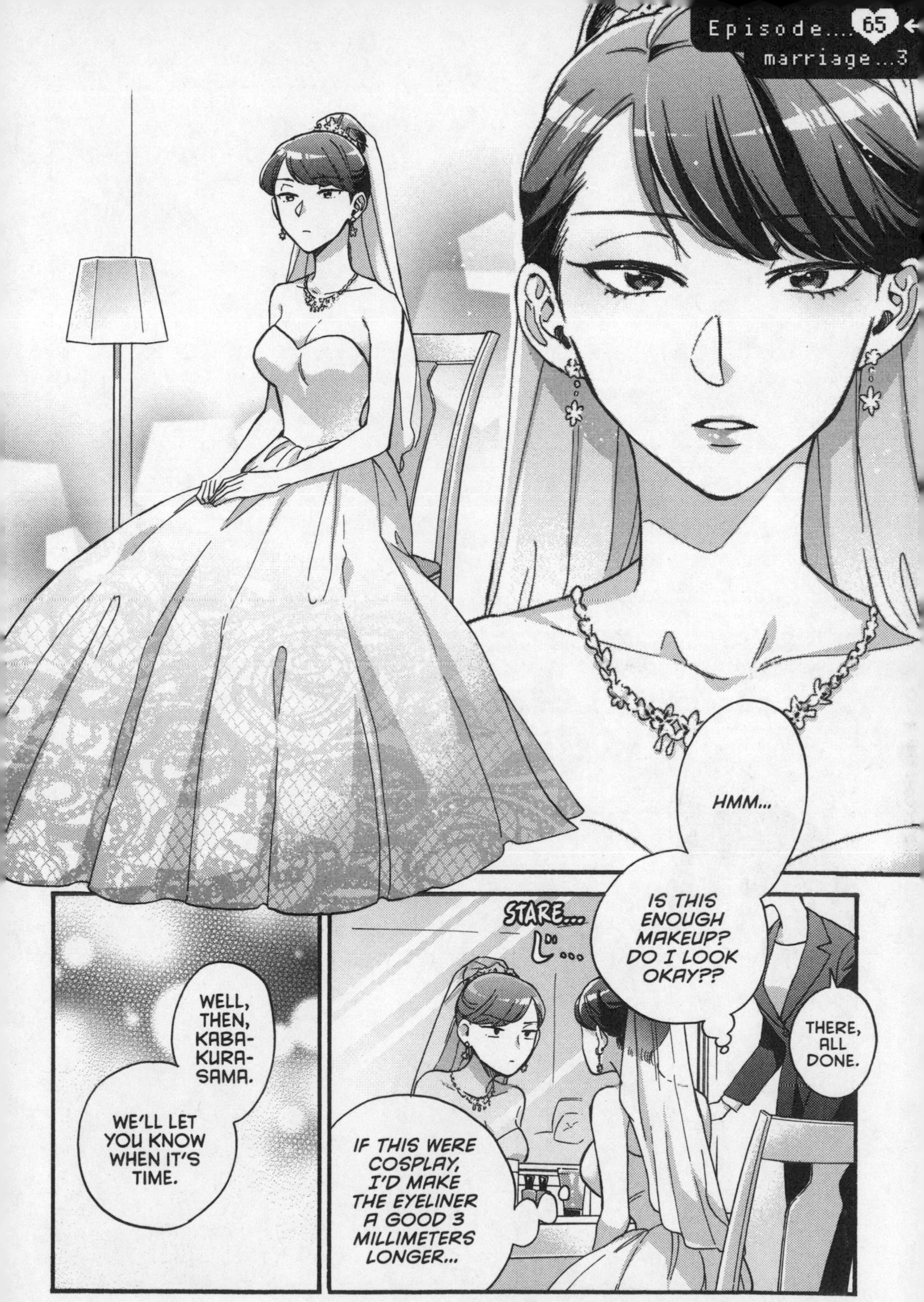
Episode... 65
marriage...3
HMM...
STARE...
IS THIS ENOUGH MAKEUP? DO I LOOK OKAY??
THERE, ALL DONE.
IF THIS WERE COSPLAY, I'D MAKE THE EYELINER A GOOD 3 MILLIMETERS LONGER...
WELL, THEN, KABAKURA-SAMA.
WE'LL LET YOU KNOW WHEN IT'S TIME.

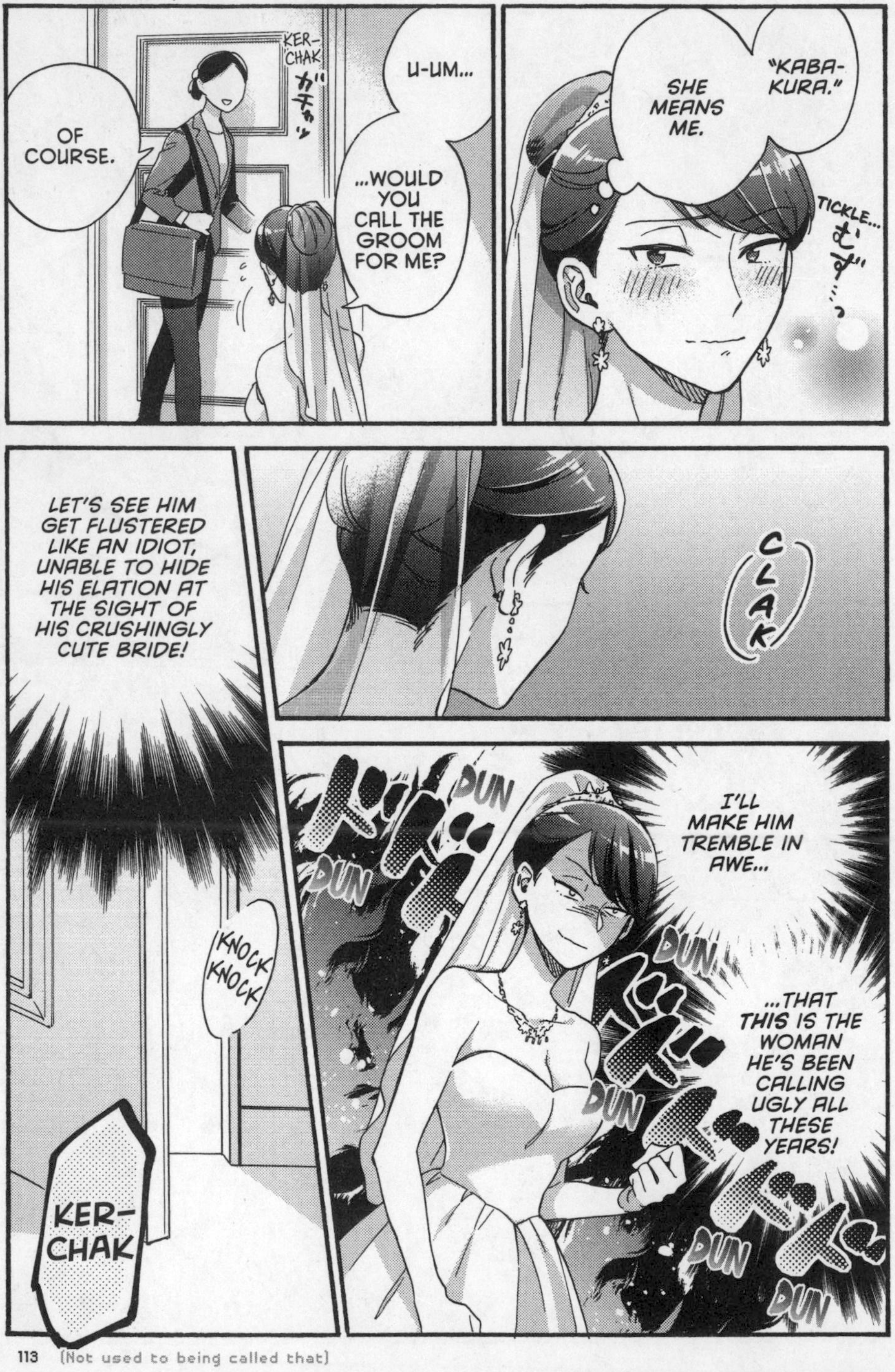
"KABA-KURA."
SHE MEANS ME.
TICKLE...
U-UM...
...WOULD YOU CALL THE GROOM FOR ME?
KER-CHAK
OF COURSE.
CLAK
DUN
DUN
I'LL MAKE HIM TREMBLE IN AWE...
DUN
...THAT THIS IS THE WOMAN HE'S BEEN CALLING UGLY ALL THESE YEARS!
DUN
DUN
DUN
DUN
LET'S SEE HIM GET FLUSTERED LIKE AN IDIOT, UNABLE TO HIDE HIS ELATION AT THE SIGHT OF HIS CRUSHINGLY CUTE BRIDE!
KNOCK KNOCK
KER-CHAK

 (Not used to being called that)

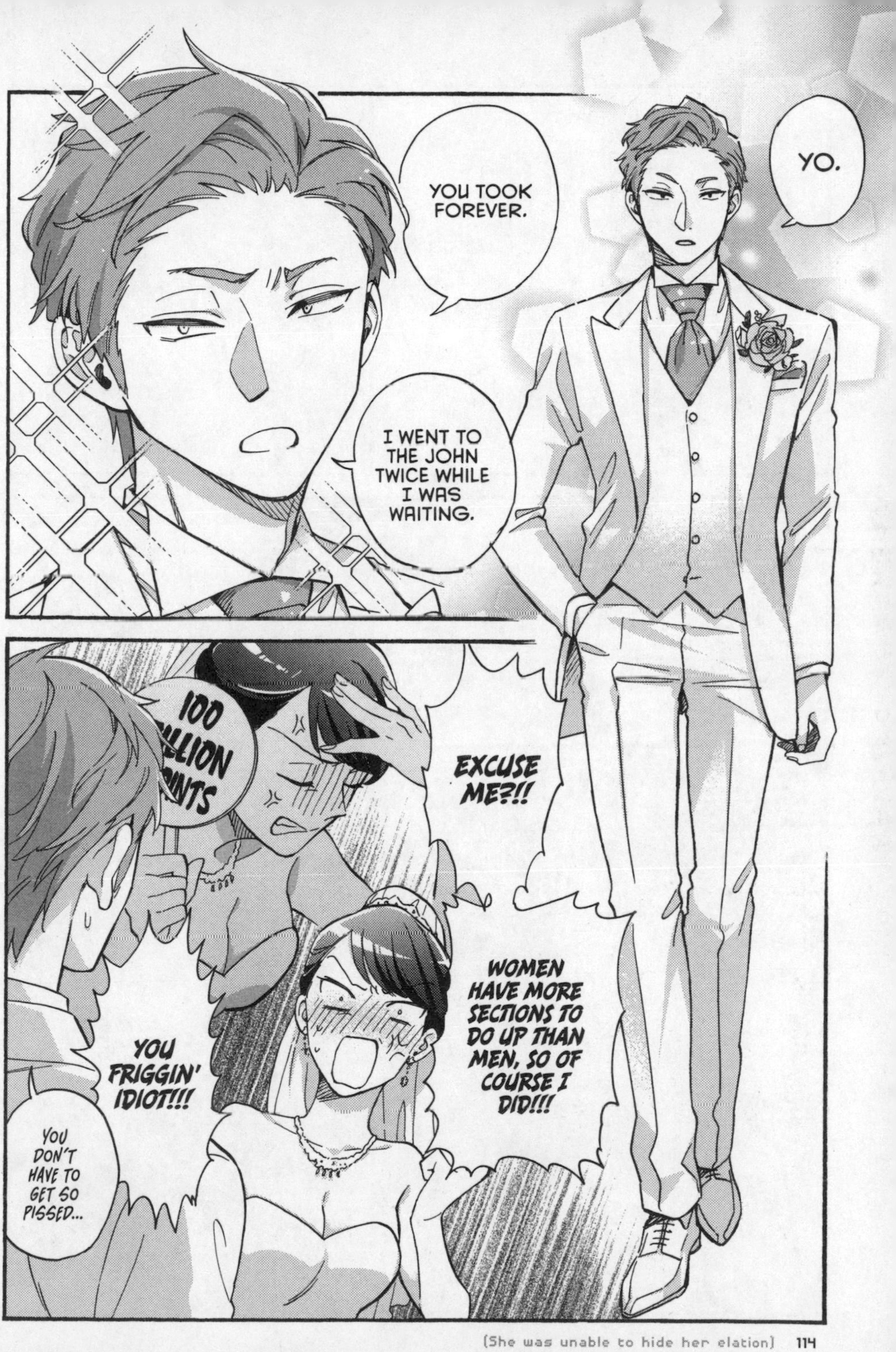
YO.
YOU TOOK FOREVER.
I WENT TO THE JOHN TWICE WHILE I WAS WAITING.
EXCUSE ME?!!
100
WOMEN HAVE MORE SECTIONS TO DO UP THAN MEN, SO OF COURSE I DID!!!
YOU FRIGGIN' IDIOT!!!
YOU DON'T HAVE TO GET SO PISSED...

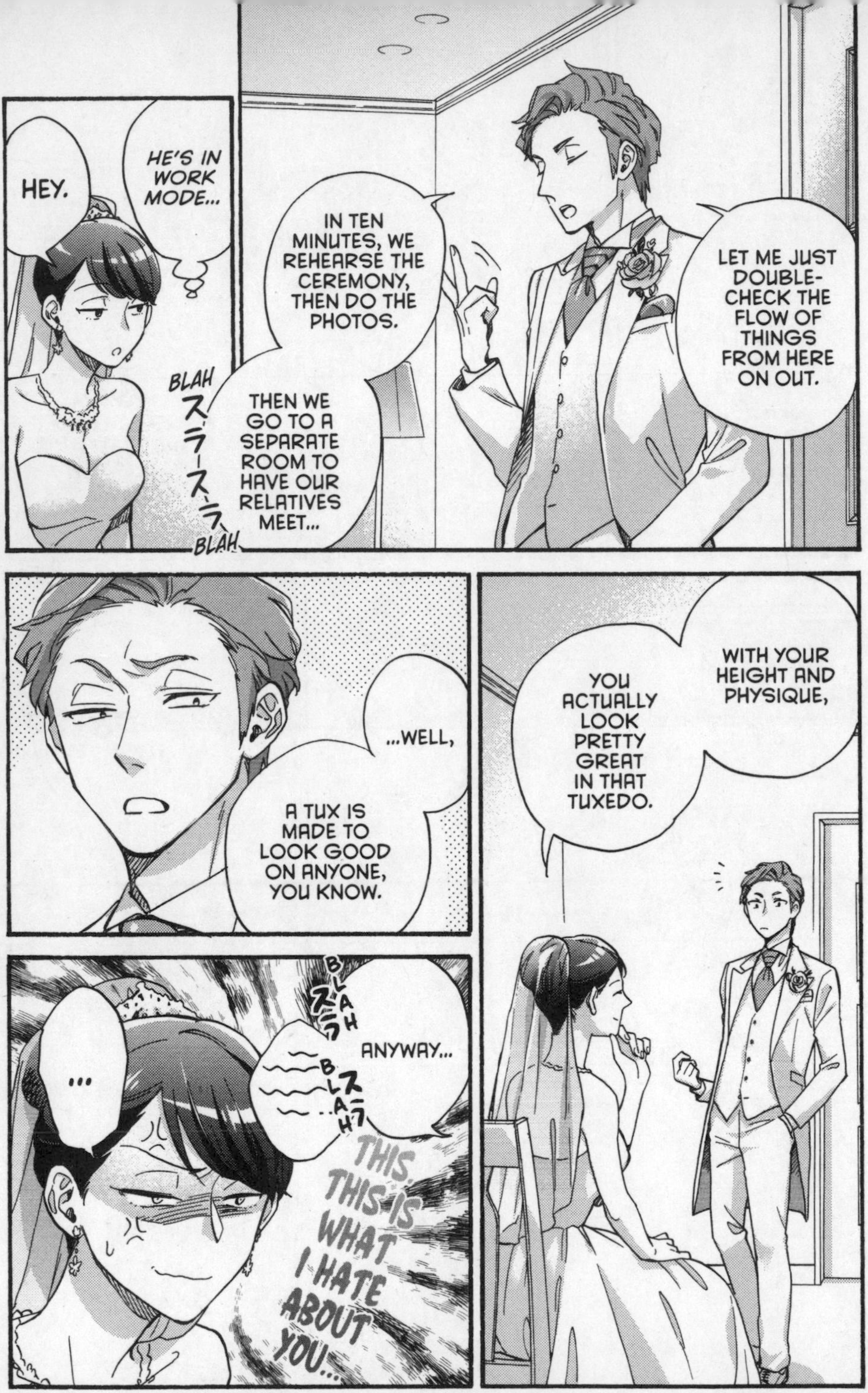
LET ME JUST DOUBLE-CHECK THE FLOW OF THINGS FROM HERE ON OUT.
IN TEN MINUTES, WE REHEARSE THE CEREMONY, THEN DO THE PHOTOS.
THEN WE GO TO A SEPARATE ROOM TO HAVE OUR RELATIVES MEET...
BLAH スラースーラ BLAH
HE'S IN WORK MODE...
HEY.
WITH YOUR HEIGHT AND PHYSIQUE,
YOU ACTUALLY LOOK PRETTY GREAT IN THAT TUXEDO.
...WELL,
A TUX IS MADE TO LOOK GOOD ON ANYONE, YOU KNOW.
BLAH スラ
ANYWAY...
BLAH スーラ
...
THIS. THIS IS WHAT I HATE ABOUT YOU...

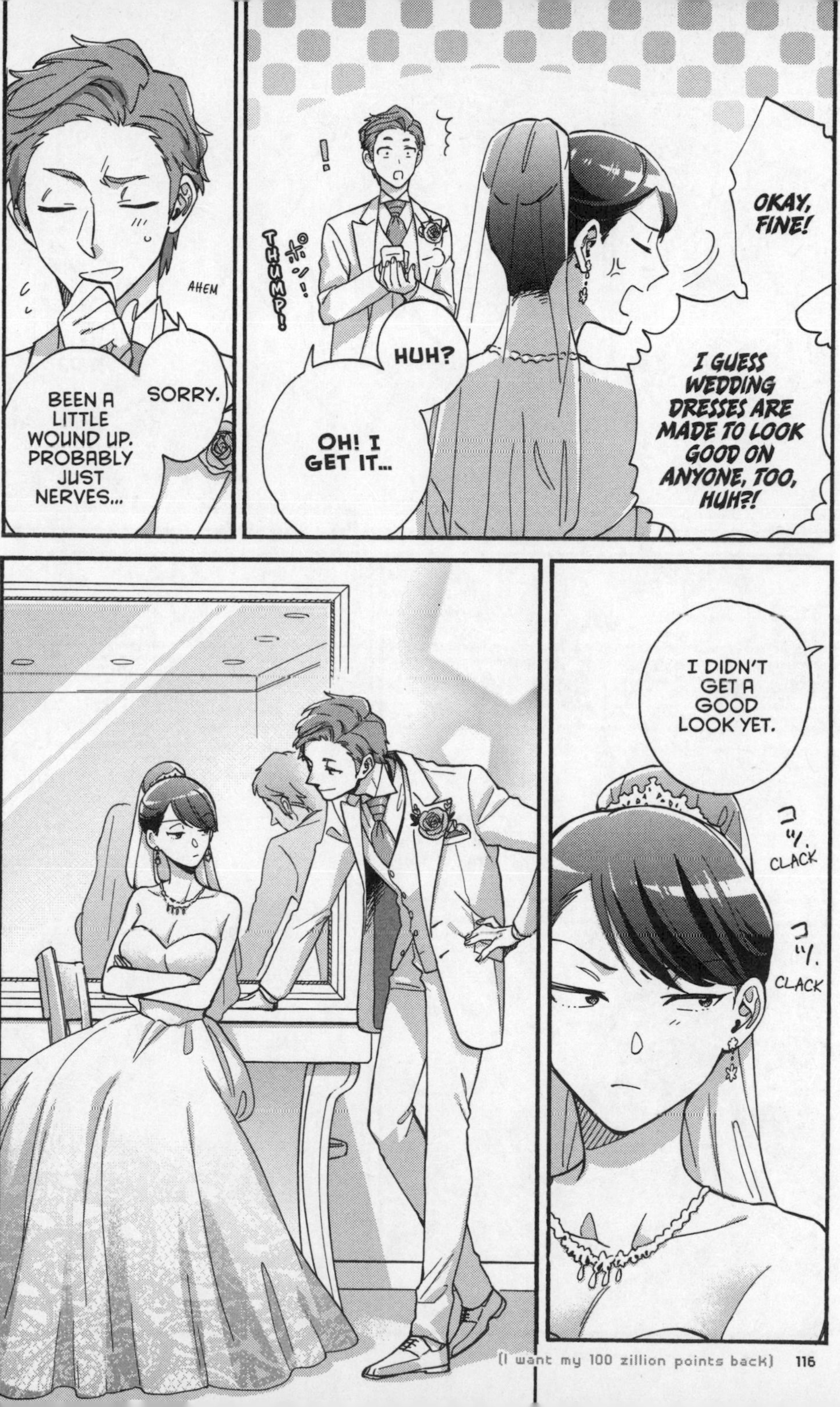
OKAY, FINE!
I GUESS WEDDING DRESSES ARE MADE TO LOOK GOOD ON ANYONE, TOO, HUH?!
HUH?
THUMP!
OH! I GET IT...
AHEM
SORRY.
BEEN A LITTLE WOUND UP. PROBABLY JUST NERVES...
I DIDN'T GET A GOOD LOOK YET.
CLACK
CLACK

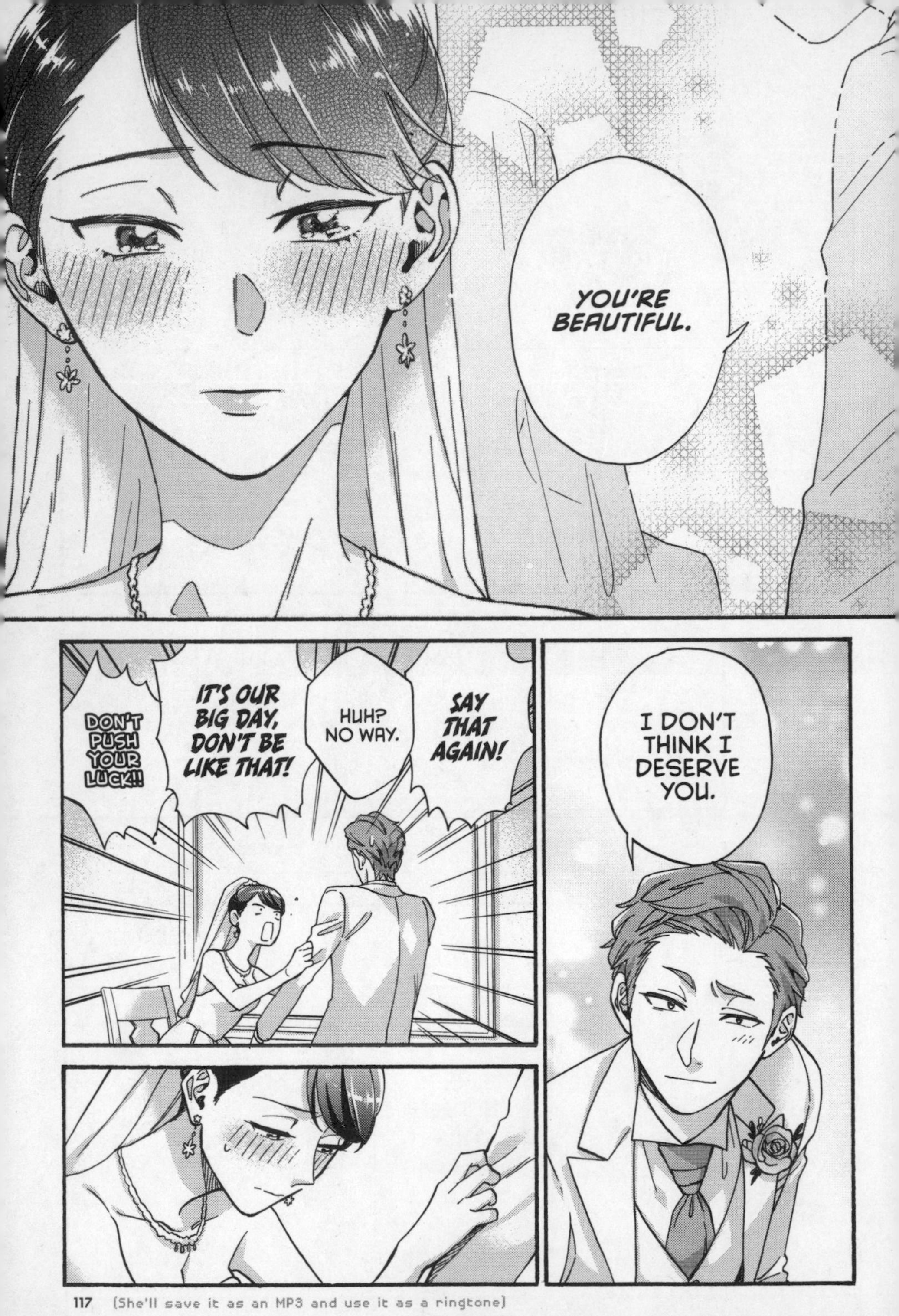
YOU'RE BEAUTIFUL.
I DON'T THINK I DESERVE YOU.
SAY THAT AGAIN!
HUH? NO WAY.
IT'S OUR BIG DAY, DON'T BE LIKE THAT!
DON'T PUSH YOUR LUCK!!

 (She'll save it as an MP3 and use it as a ringtone)

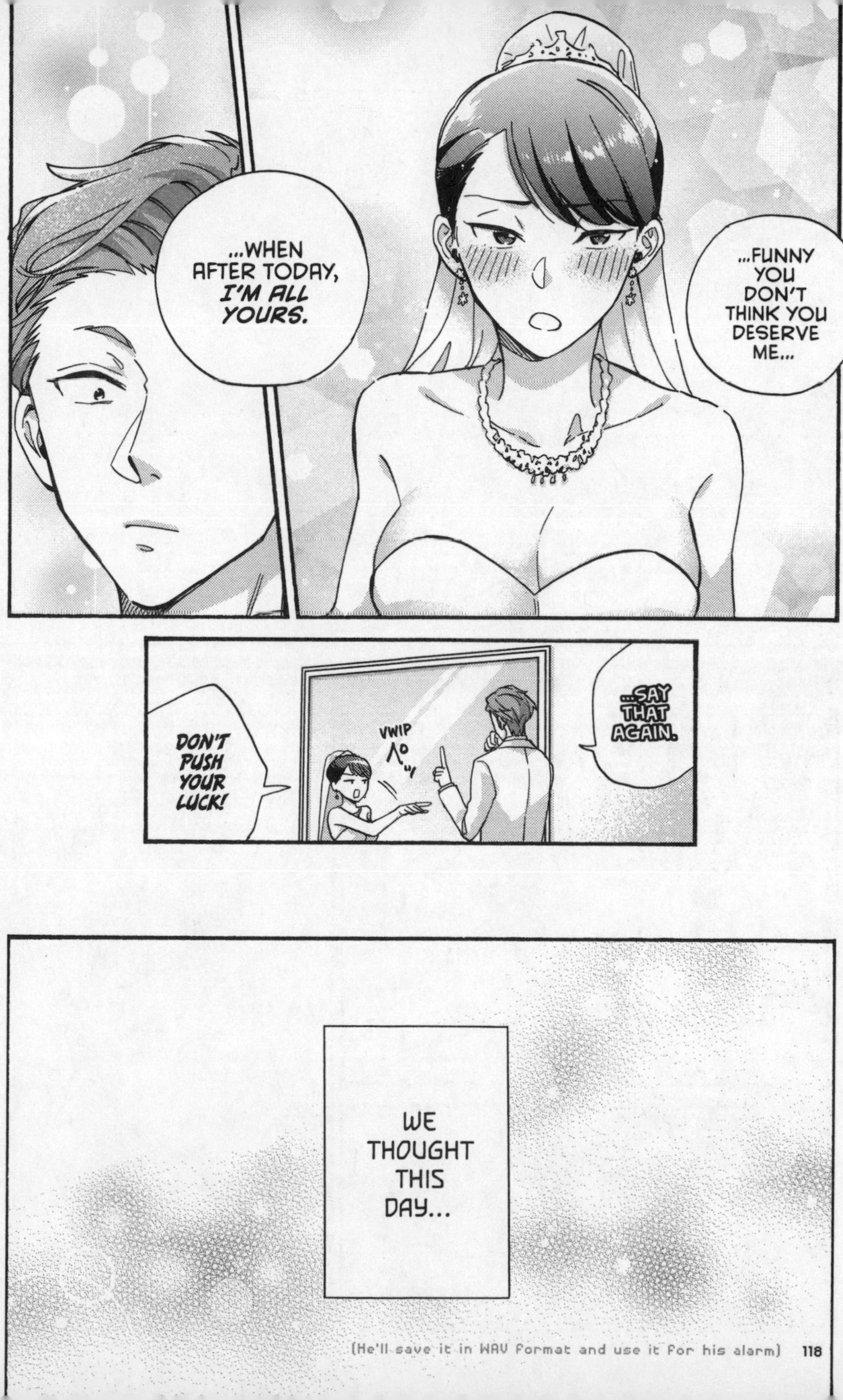
...FUNNY YOU DON'T THINK YOU DESERVE ME...
...WHEN AFTER TODAY, *I'M ALL YOURS.*
...SAY THAT AGAIN.
VWIP
DON'T PUSH YOUR LUCK!
WE THOUGHT THIS DAY...
(He'll save it in WAV format and use it for his alarm)

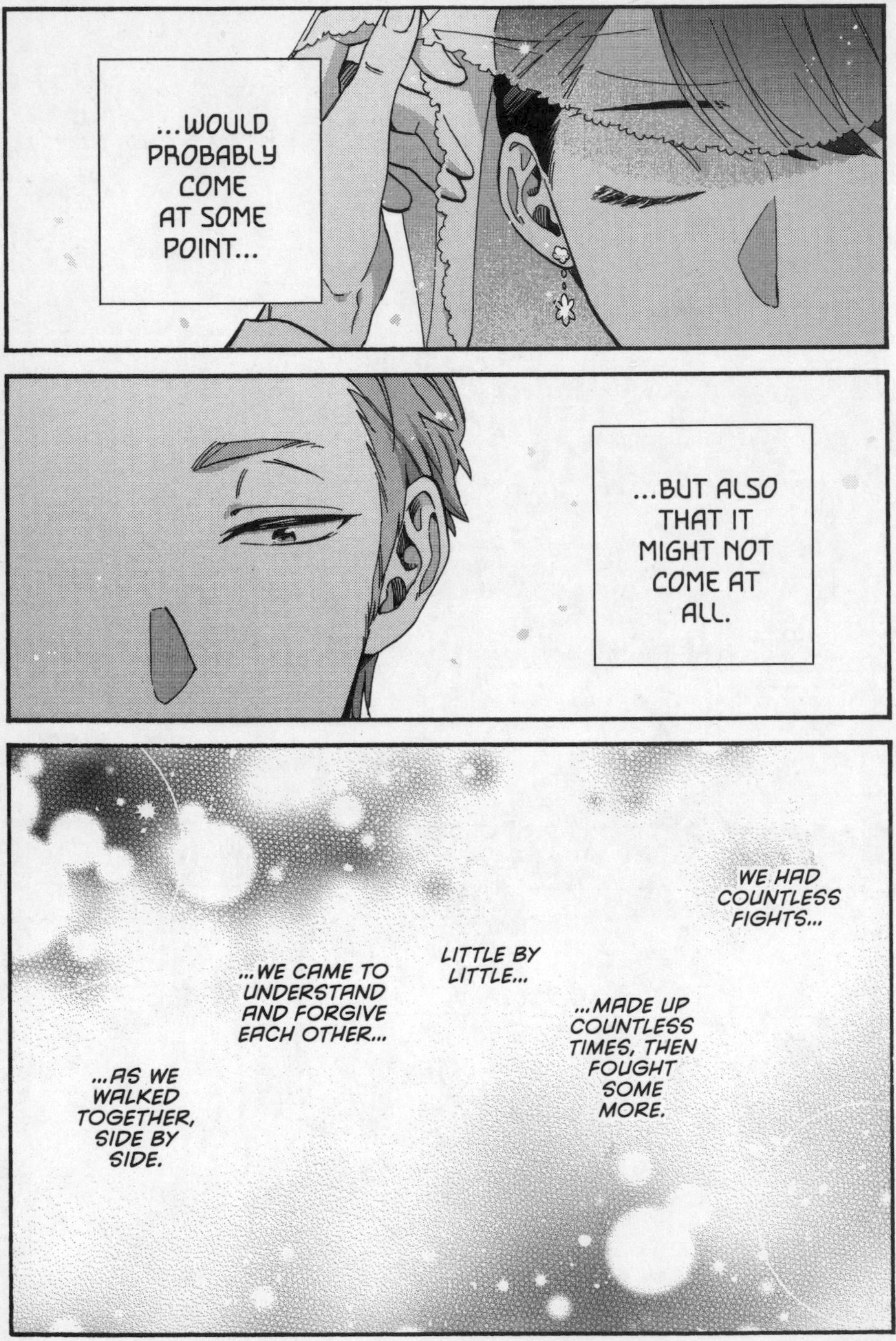
...WOULD PROBABLY COME AT SOME POINT...
...BUT ALSO THAT IT MIGHT NOT COME AT ALL.
WE HAD COUNTLESS FIGHTS...
...MADE UP COUNTLESS TIMES, THEN FOUGHT SOME MORE.
LITTLE BY LITTLE...
...WE CAME TO UNDERSTAND AND FORGIVE EACH OTHER...
...AS WE WALKED TOGETHER, SIDE BY SIDE.

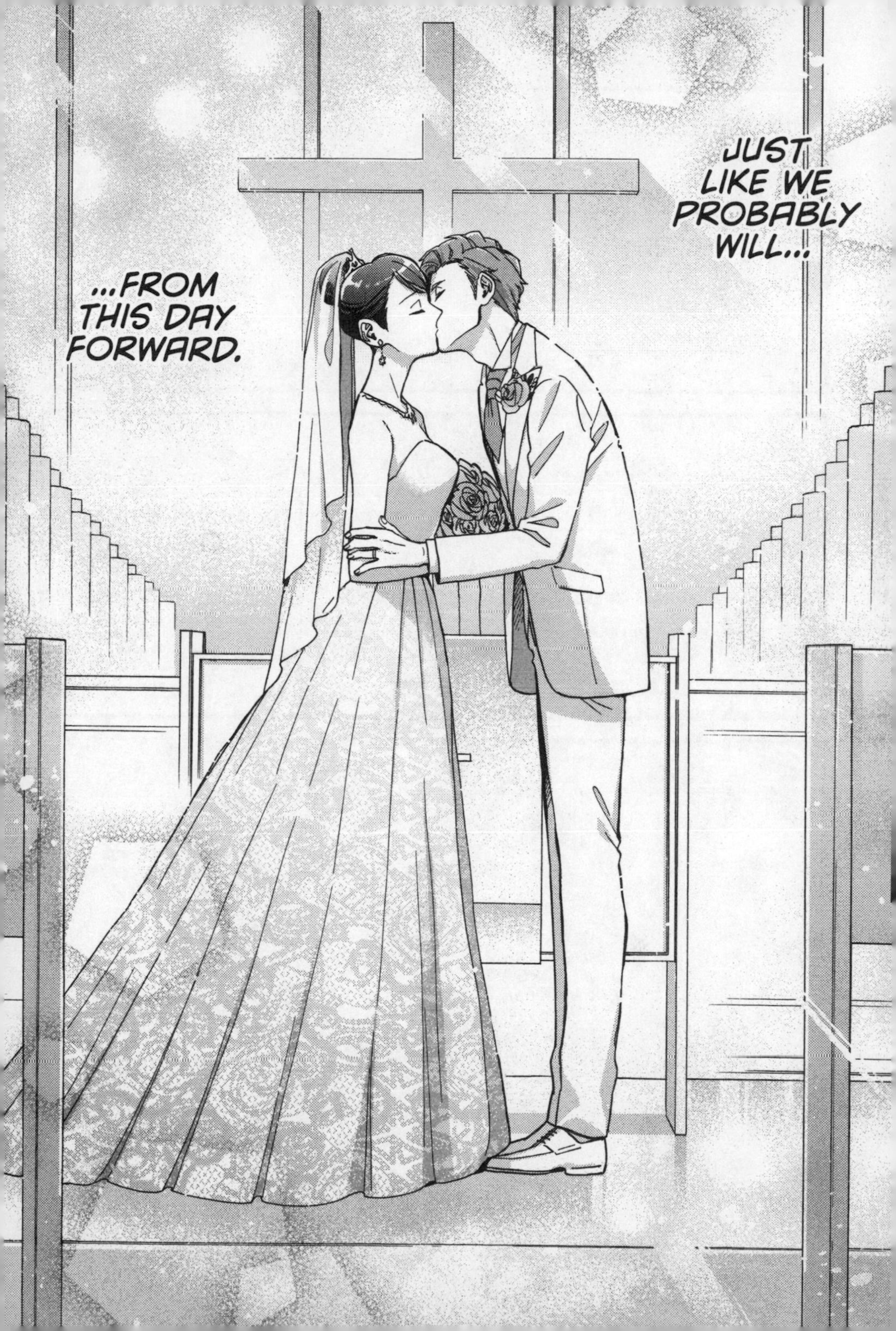
JUST LIKE WE PROBABLY WILL...
...FROM THIS DAY FORWARD.

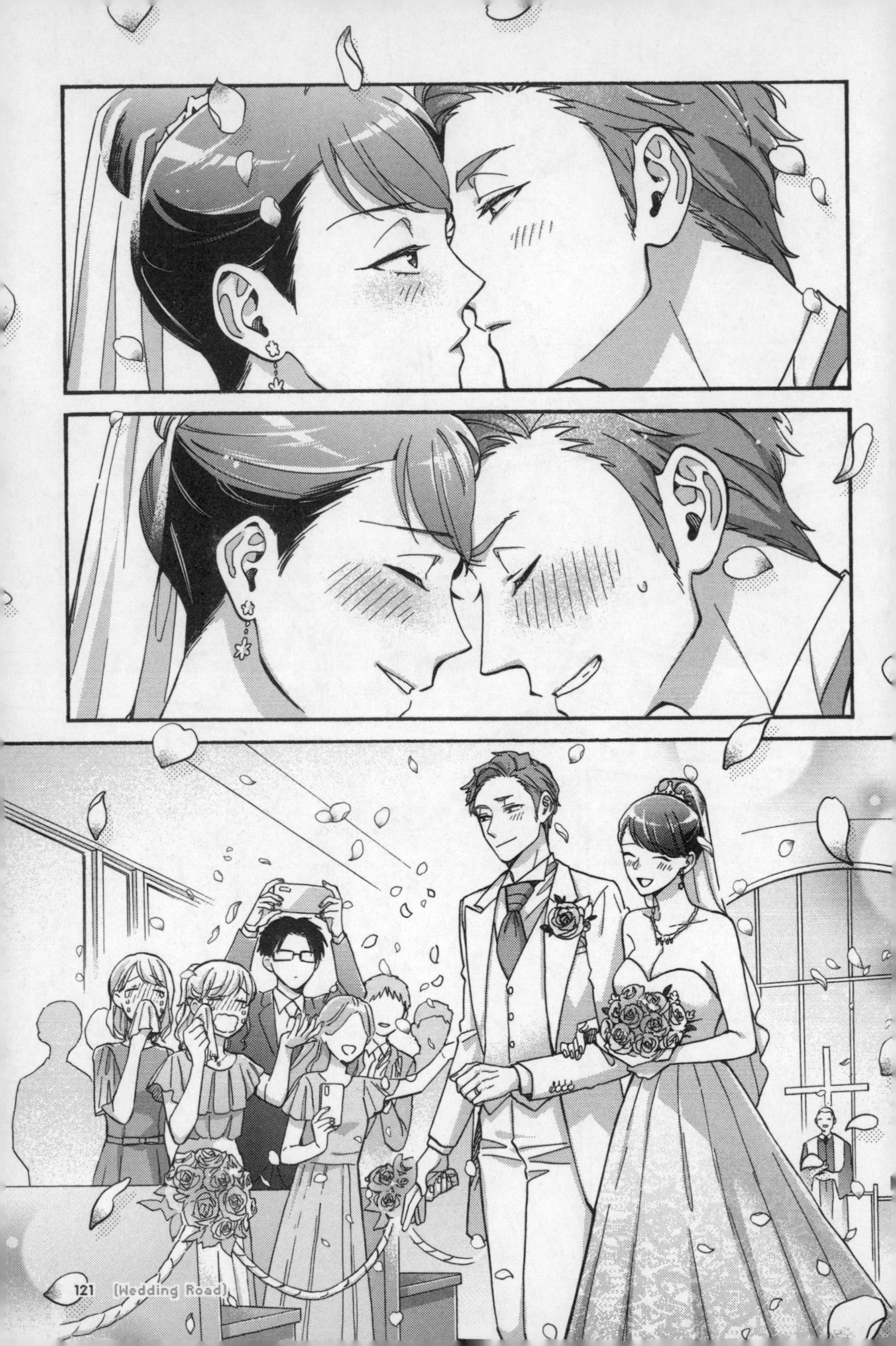

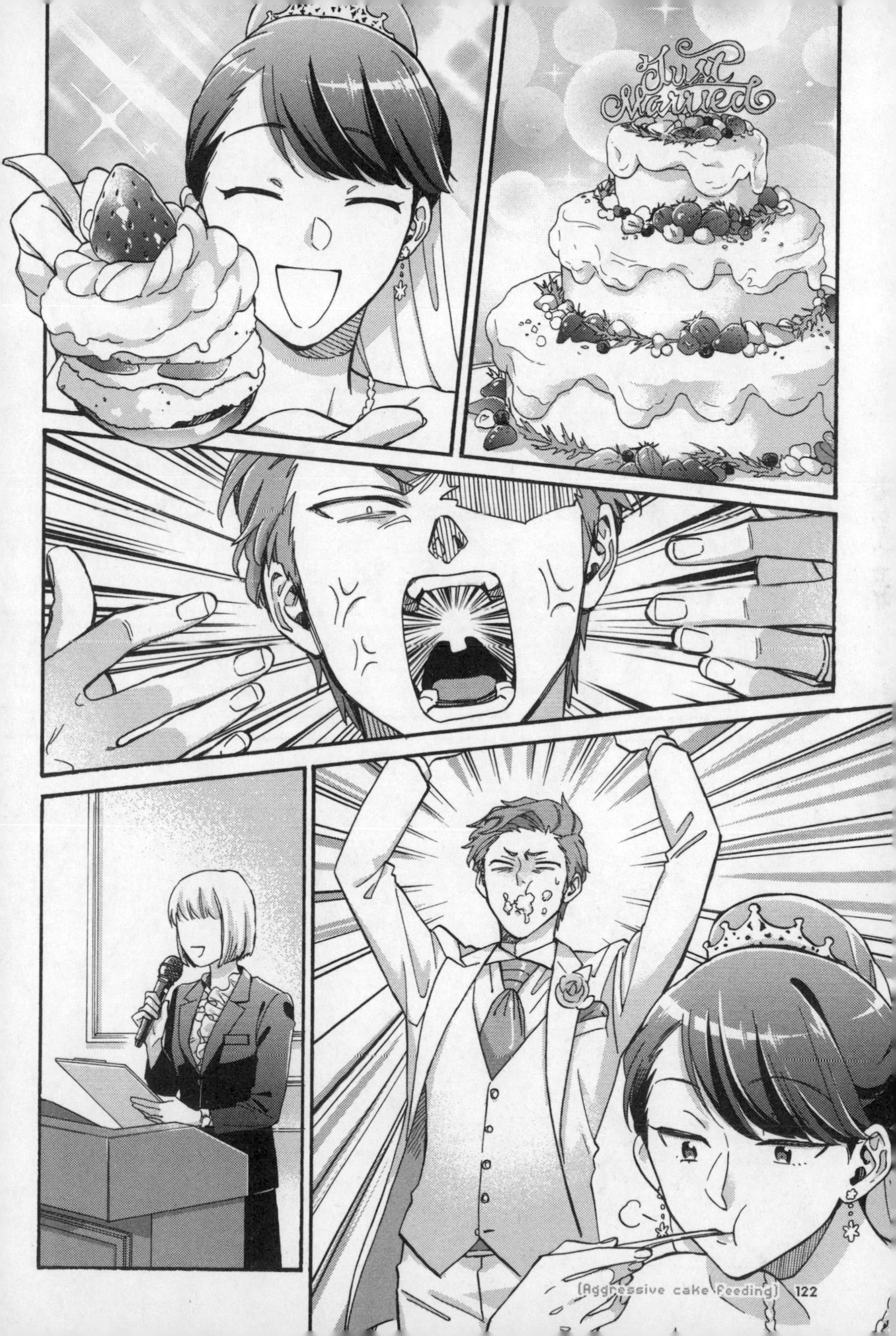

Just Married

[Aggressive cake feeding] 122

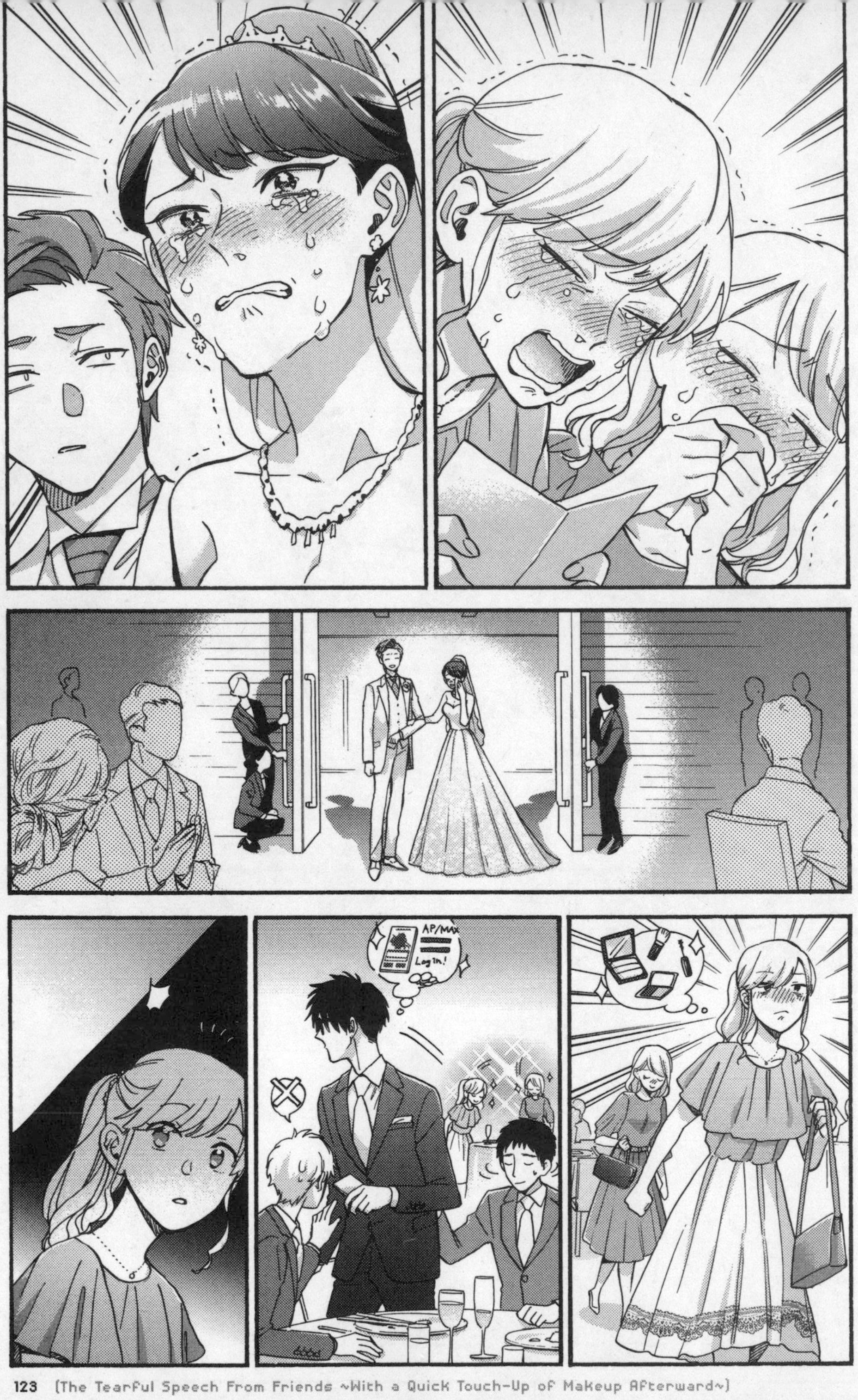
AP/MAX
Log in!

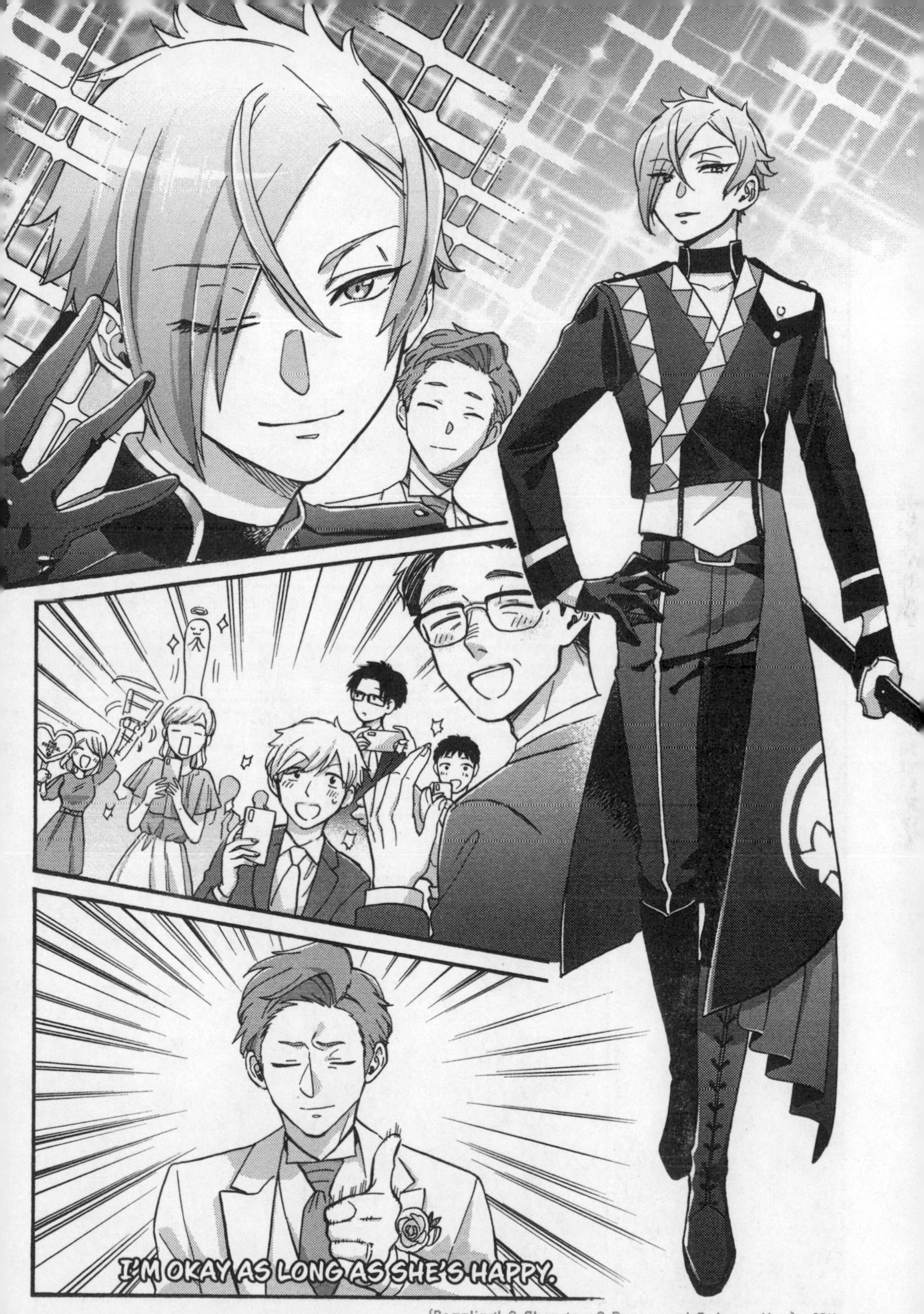
I'M OKAY AS LONG AS SHE'S HAPPY.

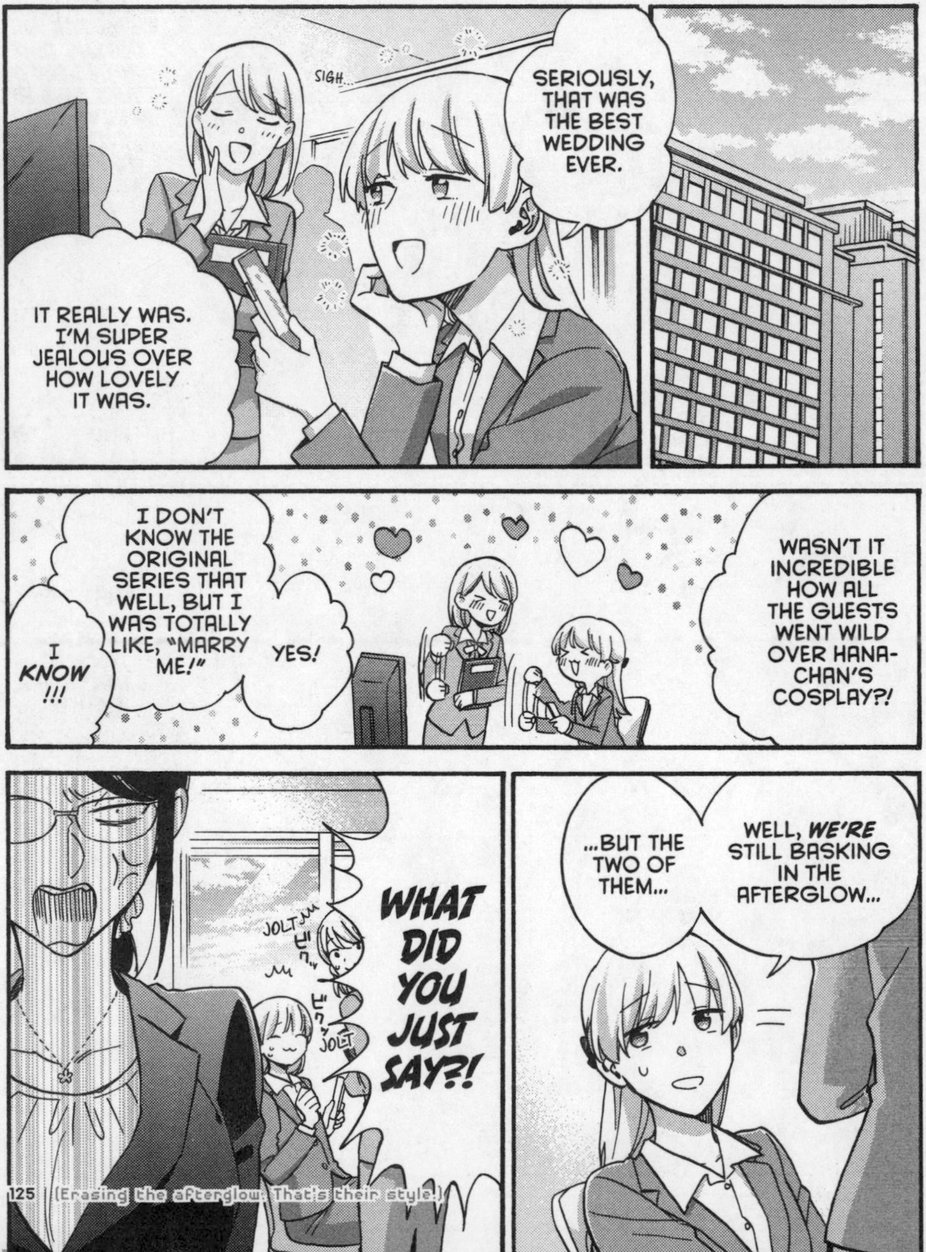
SERIOUSLY, THAT WAS THE BEST WEDDING EVER.
SIGH...
IT REALLY WAS. I'M SUPER JEALOUS OVER HOW LOVELY IT WAS.
WASN'T IT INCREDIBLE HOW ALL THE GUESTS WENT WILD OVER HANA-CHAN'S COSPLAY?!
YES!
I DON'T KNOW THE ORIGINAL SERIES THAT WELL, BUT I WAS TOTALLY LIKE, "MARRY ME!"
I *KNOW* !!!
WELL, *WE'RE* STILL BASKING IN THE AFTERGLOW...
...BUT THE TWO OF THEM...
WHAT DID YOU JUST SAY?!
JOLT
JOLT

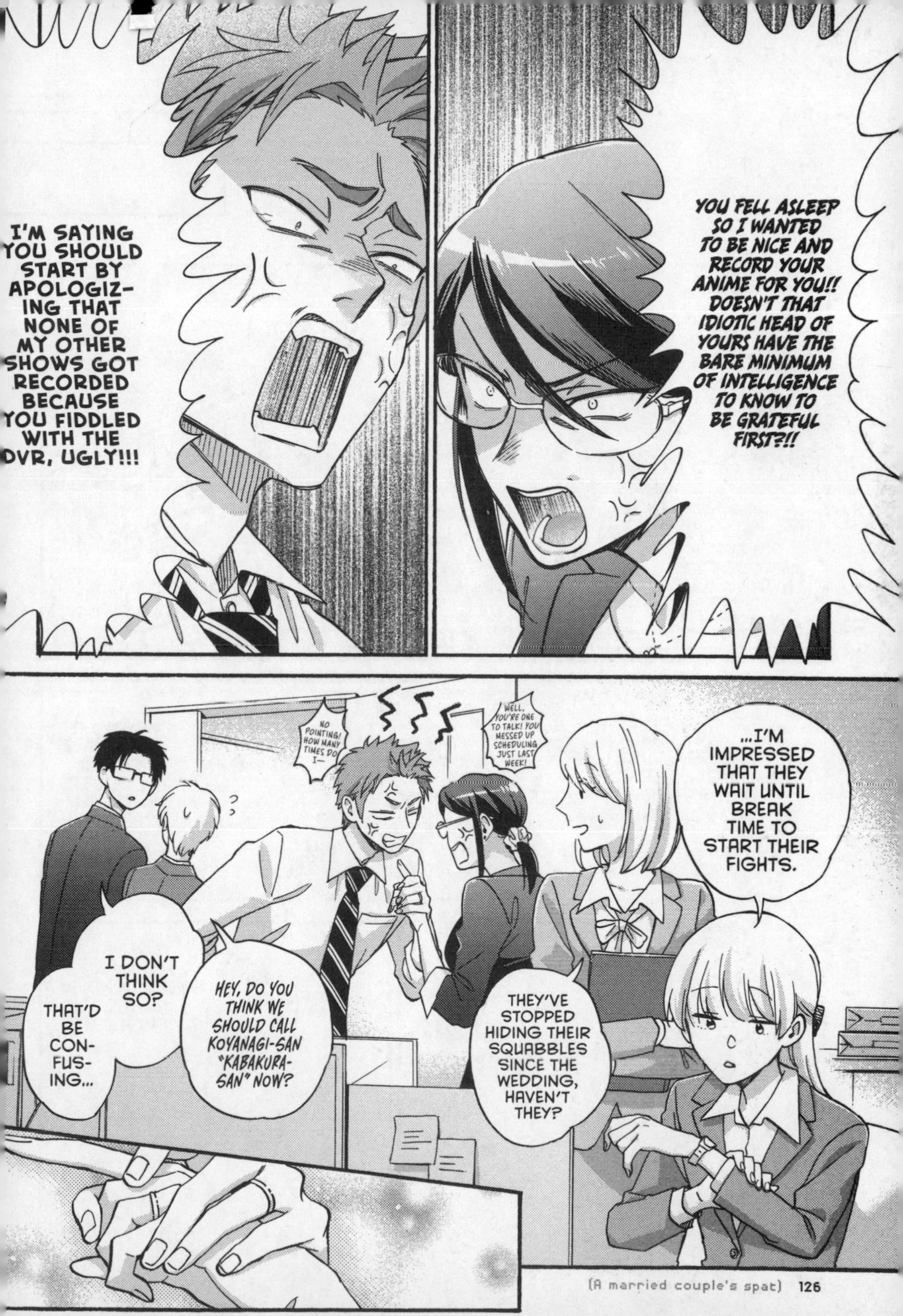
YOU FELL ASLEEP SO I WANTED TO BE NICE AND RECORD YOUR ANIME FOR YOU!! DOESN'T THAT IDIOTIC HEAD OF YOURS HAVE THE BARE MINIMUM OF INTELLIGENCE TO KNOW TO BE GRATEFUL FIRST?!!
I'M SAYING YOU SHOULD START BY APOLOGIZING THAT NONE OF MY OTHER SHOWS GOT RECORDED BECAUSE YOU FIDDLED WITH THE DVR, UGLY!!!
...I'M IMPRESSED THAT THEY WAIT UNTIL BREAK TIME TO START THEIR FIGHTS.
NO POINTING! HOW MANY TIMES DO I—
WELL, YOU'RE ONE TO TALK! YOU MESSED UP SCHEDULING JUST LAST WEEK!
THEY'VE STOPPED HIDING THEIR SQUABBLES SINCE THE WEDDING, HAVEN'T THEY?
HEY, DO YOU THINK WE SHOULD CALL KOYANAGI-SAN "KABAKURA-SAN" NOW?
I DON'T THINK SO?
THAT'D BE CONFUSING...

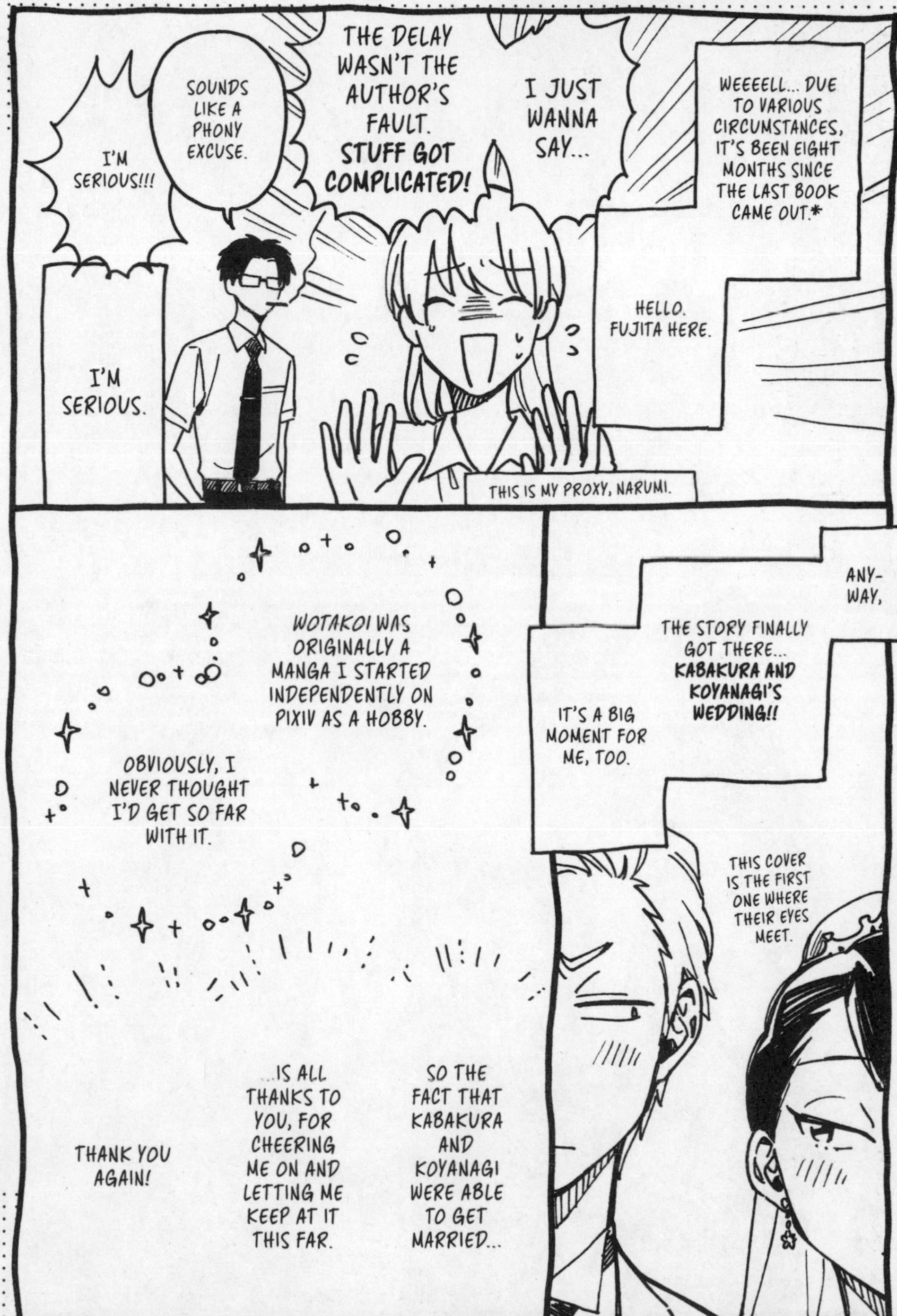
HELLO. FUJITA HERE.
WEEEELL... DUE TO VARIOUS CIRCUMSTANCES, IT'S BEEN EIGHT MONTHS SINCE THE LAST BOOK CAME OUT.*
I JUST WANNA SAY...
THE DELAY WASN'T THE AUTHOR'S FAULT. **STUFF GOT COMPLICATED!**
THIS IS MY PROXY, NARUMI.
SOUNDS LIKE A PHONY EXCUSE.
I'M SERIOUS!!!
I'M SERIOUS.
ANY-WAY,
THE STORY FINALLY GOT THERE... **KABAKURA AND KOYANAGI'S WEDDING!!**
IT'S A BIG MOMENT FOR ME, TOO.
THIS COVER IS THE FIRST ONE WHERE THEIR EYES MEET.
WOTAKOI WAS ORIGINALLY A MANGA I STARTED INDEPENDENTLY ON PIXIV AS A HOBBY.
OBVIOUSLY, I NEVER THOUGHT I'D GET SO FAR WITH IT.
SO THE FACT THAT KABAKURA AND KOYANAGI WERE ABLE TO GET MARRIED...
...IS ALL THANKS TO YOU, FOR CHEERING ME ON AND LETTING ME KEEP AT IT THIS FAR.
THANK YOU AGAIN!

*The gap between vols. 8 and 9 in Japan

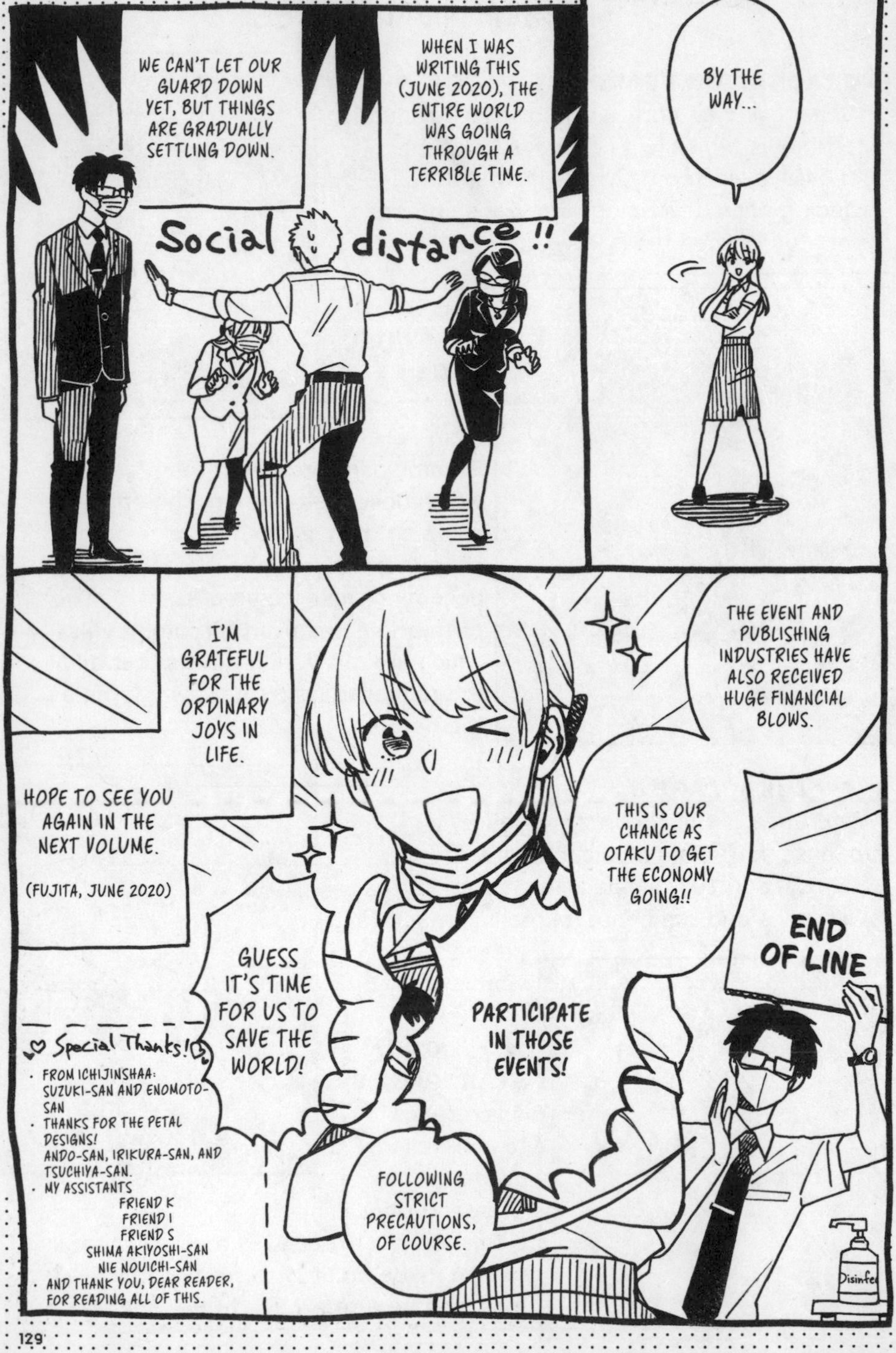
BY THE WAY...
WHEN I WAS WRITING THIS (JUNE 2020), THE ENTIRE WORLD WAS GOING THROUGH A TERRIBLE TIME.
WE CAN'T LET OUR GUARD DOWN YET, BUT THINGS ARE GRADUALLY SETTLING DOWN.
Social distance!!
THE EVENT AND PUBLISHING INDUSTRIES HAVE ALSO RECEIVED HUGE FINANCIAL BLOWS.
THIS IS OUR CHANCE AS OTAKU TO GET THE ECONOMY GOING!!
END OF LINE
PARTICIPATE IN THOSE EVENTS!
FOLLOWING STRICT PRECAUTIONS, OF COURSE.
Disinfec
GUESS IT'S TIME FOR US TO SAVE THE WORLD!
I'M GRATEFUL FOR THE ORDINARY JOYS IN LIFE.
HOPE TO SEE YOU AGAIN IN THE NEXT VOLUME.
(FUJITA, JUNE 2020)
Special Thanks!
· FROM ICHIJINSHAA: SUZUKI-SAN AND ENOMOTO-SAN
· THANKS FOR THE PETAL DESIGNS! ANDO-SAN, IRIKURA-SAN, AND TSUCHIYA-SAN.
· MY ASSISTANTS
FRIEND K
FRIEND I
FRIEND S
SHIMA AKIYOSHI-SAN
NIE NOUICHI-SAN
· AND THANK YOU, DEAR READER, FOR READING ALL OF THIS.

TRANSLATION NOTES

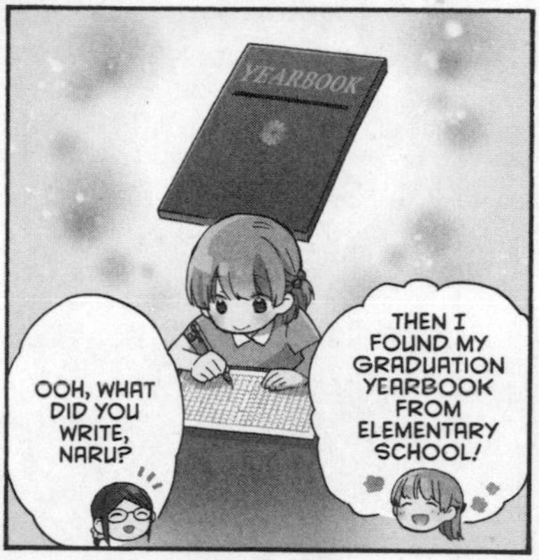
THEN I FOUND MY GRADUATION YEARBOOK FROM ELEMENTARY SCHOOL!
OOH, WHAT DID YOU WRITE, NARU?

▶GRADUATION YEARBOOK, PAGE 4

In Japanese elementary schools, the graduation yearbook is typically a collection of poems and essays written by the students, usually including ones describing what each student wants to be when they grow up.

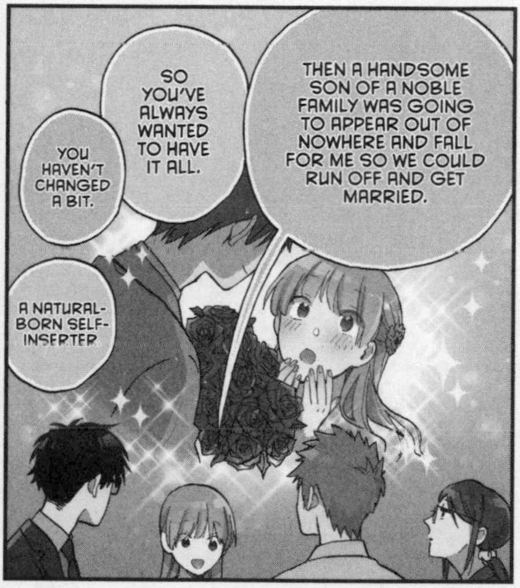
THEN A HANDSOME SON OF A NOBLE FAMILY WAS GOING TO APPEAR OUT OF NOWHERE AND FALL FOR ME SO WE COULD RUN OFF AND GET MARRIED.
SO YOU'VE ALWAYS WANTED TO HAVE IT ALL.
YOU HAVEN'T CHANGED A BIT.
A NATURAL-BORN SELF-INSERTER.

◀ SELF-INSERTER, PAGE 5

The Japanese term here is *yumejoshi*, literally "dream girls," which describes women who enjoy shipping themselves with a certain character, where they fantasize about becoming the heroine of a story. The term originates from "dream novels," which are fan fiction novels that allow the reader to insert her own name as the heroine's.

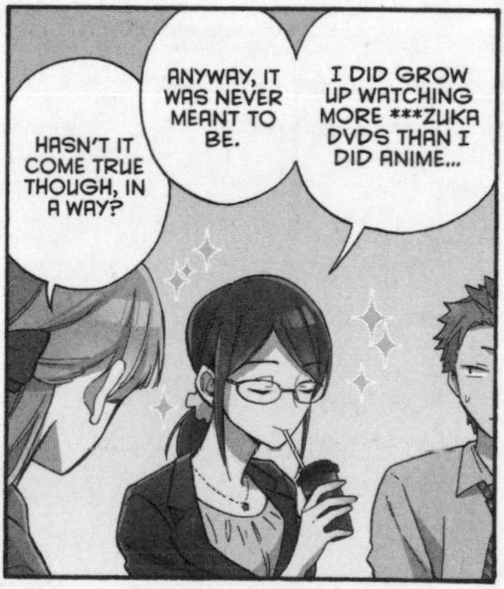
I DID GROW UP WATCHING MORE ***ZUKA DVDS THAN I DID ANIME...
ANYWAY, IT WAS NEVER MEANT TO BE.
HASN'T IT COME TRUE THOUGH, IN A WAY?

▶ ***ZUKA, PAGE 6

A reference to the Takarazuka Revue, a Japanese all-female musical theater troupe established in 1931, especially popular for its lavish style and the beautiful male characters played by women.

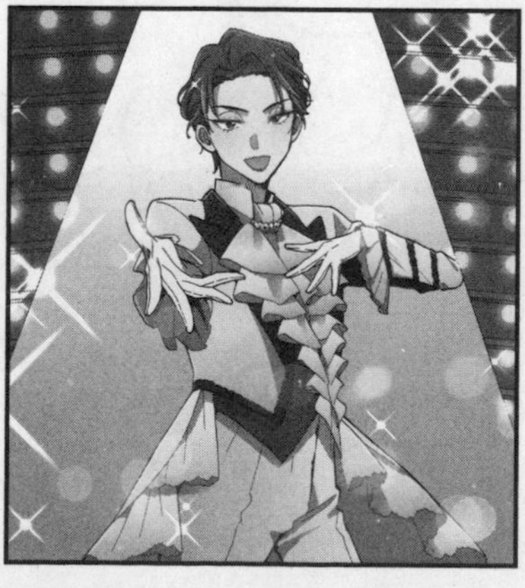

◀ *TEIKOKU* STAR, PAGE 6

A reference to a series of drama track CDs featuring a Taisho-era (1912-1926) musical theater troupe made up of idols from nobility. It may also be a reference to the *Sakura*

Wars video game franchise, which features a Takarazuka-inspired all-female musical troupe called the *Teikoku* (Imperial) Revue that doubles as a government assault force in a fictional Taisho era.

A PLACE FURTHER THAN THE UNIVERSE, PAGE 8

A 2018 anime about a group of high school girls who join an expedition to the Antarctic in search of one of the characters' lost mother.

ACTIVE FOR LIFE, YO., PAGE 9

A meme of unknown origin that depicts a poorly drawn delinquent biker with a brief essay describing what he wants to be when he grows up. The essay is entitled "Active for life, yo," and talks about joining a biker gang to dominate the Greater Tokyo area, graduating school to help his buddy Toru's family welding business, and being a biker for life. The questionable grammar coupled with the odd drawing has spawned various parodies of it.

YOU AND THE END OF SUMMER..., PAGE 12
NATSU NATSU NATSU NATSU COCO-NATSU, PAGE 13
YEAH! SUPER HOLIDAY, PAGE 14
GIVE UP ON SUMMER, PAGE 15
HOT LIMIT, PAGE 16
THOUGHTS ON THE BEACH, ET CETERA, PAGE 17

These are all lyrics from past summer-themed hit songs in Japan. The songs are: "Secret Base (*Kimi ga Kureta Mono*)" by ZONE, "*Futari no Ai-Land*" ("The Two Lovers' Island") by Yuko Ishikawa and Chage, "Yeah! Meccha Holiday" ("Yeah! Super Holiday") by Aya Matsuura, "*Natsu wo Akiramete*" ("Give up on Summer") by Southern All Stars, "HOT LIMIT" by TM Revolution, and "Electric Beach Fever" by Puffy AmiYumi ("Thoughts on the Beach, Et Cetera" being the Japanese title). The lyrics "*Natsu natsu natsu natsu coco-natsu*" is a play on words, as *natsu* means "summer" and sounds like the last syllable of "coconuts."

▶ SWIMSUIT EVENTS, PAGE 14
CHOCOLATE EVENT, PAGE 88

Mobile games have campaigns or "events" that feature characters with outfits or other in-game elements in line with a seasonal theme. On page 88, Hirotaka applies this logic to the possibility of getting chocolates from Narumi on Valentine's Day.

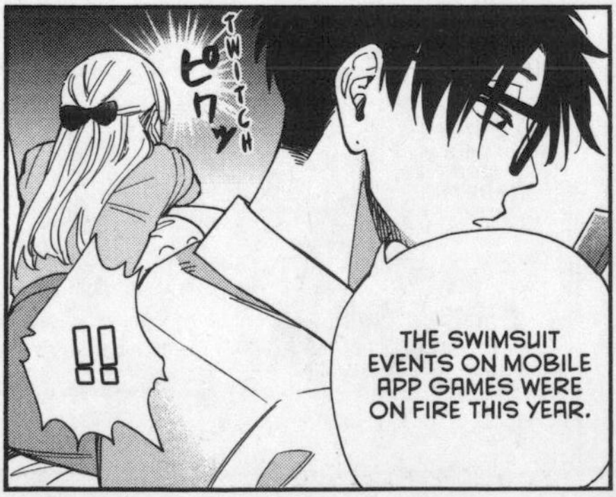
THE SWIMSUIT EVENTS ON MOBILE APP GAMES WERE ON FIRE THIS YEAR.
ピクッ
TWITCH
!!

BOOST THEM UP A BIT—PLAY BACK PLAY BACK, PAGE 18

A reference to Momoe Yamaguchi's song "Play Back Part 2." The actual lyrics are "Hold on a sec—play back play back," but here it alludes to the fact that Narumi's boobs are slightly larger in Hirotaka's imagination.

NUSSHI-SAN, PAGE 24

WE ASKED HOW TO GET SOMEONE STUCK IN A SWAMP, PAGE 25

References to the NHK TV show *Numa ni Hamatte Kiite Mita* (lit. "We Asked People Stuck in a Swamp"). Each episode features a different hobby or fandom, and interviews fans who are stuck in that "swamp." "Nusshi" is the show mascot, a reference to Nessie (the Loch Ness Monster). "Nushi" means "master of the swamp" in this context, a kind of guardian creature of the swamp.

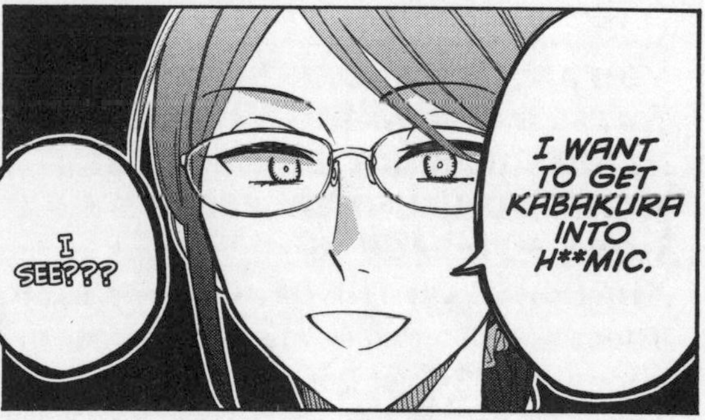
I WANT TO GET KABAKURA INTO H**MIC.
I SEE???

▶ HMIC, PAGE 26**

OTAKU DIVISIONS, PAGE 27

References to the *Hypnosis Mic: Division Rap Battle* franchise about pretty boys from different "divisions" around Tokyo engaging in rap battles. The franchise is primarily geared toward female fans, with attractive men split up into rap battle teams that fans can vote for.

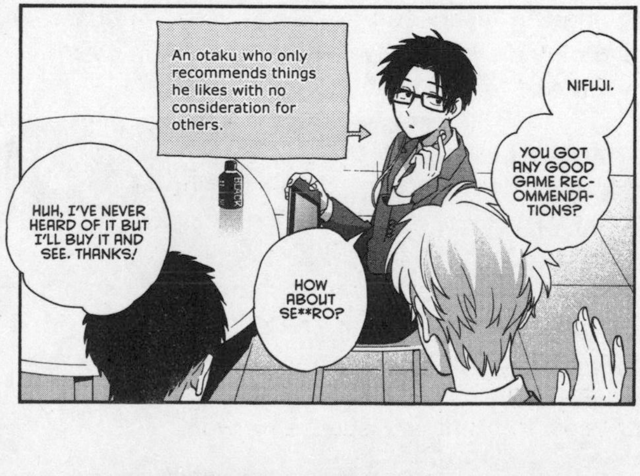
NIFUJI.
YOU GOT ANY GOOD GAME RECOMMENDATIONS?
An otaku who only recommends things he likes with no consideration for others.
HOW ABOUT SE**RO?
HUH, I'VE NEVER HEARD OF IT BUT I'LL BUY IT AND SEE. THANKS!

◀ *SERO,* PAGE 31**

A reference to the solo action adventure game *Sekiro*, which is about a *shinobi* bodyguard in fictional 16th century Japan, and is known for its high level of difficulty. It's a questionable choice to recommend to casual gamers like Aiba and Baba.

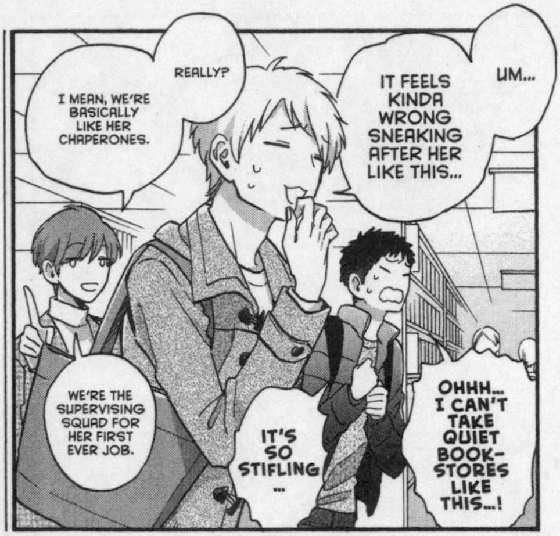
UM...
IT FEELS KINDA WRONG SNEAKING AFTER HER LIKE THIS...
REALLY?
I MEAN, WE'RE BASICALLY LIKE HER CHAPERONES.
OHHH... I CAN'T TAKE QUIET BOOK-STORES LIKE THIS...!
IT'S SO STIFLING...
WE'RE THE SUPERVISING SQUAD FOR HER FIRST EVER JOB.

◀ ***SNEAKING MISSION,* PAGE 51**

A reference to the *Metal Gear* action-adventure game franchise, which pioneered the stealth video game genre. The infiltration missions in the game are referred to as "sneaking missions."

▼ **IT'S NOT MY FAULT!, PAGE 64**

A memorable line from the 2005 RPG *Tales of the Abyss,* uttered by the main protagonist when his teacher manipulates him into unwittingly destroying an entire town.

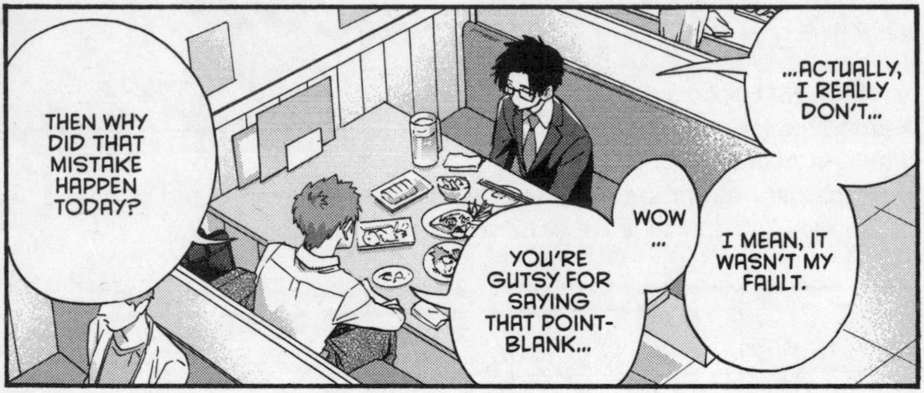
...ACTUALLY, I REALLY DON'T...
I MEAN, IT WASN'T MY FAULT.
WOW...
YOU'RE GUTSY FOR SAYING THAT POINT-BLANK...
THEN WHY DID THAT MISTAKE HAPPEN TODAY?

DON'T MIND IF I DO, PAGE 81
YOU HAVE UNTIL TOMORROW TO THINK ABOUT WHY YOU LOST, PAGE 83

For its Pepsi Japan Cola product, Pepsi Japan launched a campaign in 2019 where people could get a free bottle of the drink by winning a digital rock-paper-scissors challenge against soccer icon Keisuke Honda. But the horrible win rate caused a lot of aggravation, and Honda's patronizing automated response spawned a bunch of memes. In one of the responses, Honda holds up a bottle of Pepsi Japan Cola and says, "I win! You have until tomorrow to think about why you lost. That'll help you see a thing or two. Anyway, don't mind if I do," the last line meaning he will now drink the bottle of Pepsi in his hand because he won.

▶ *EHOMAKI,* SETSUBUN, *MAMEMAKI,* PAGE 90

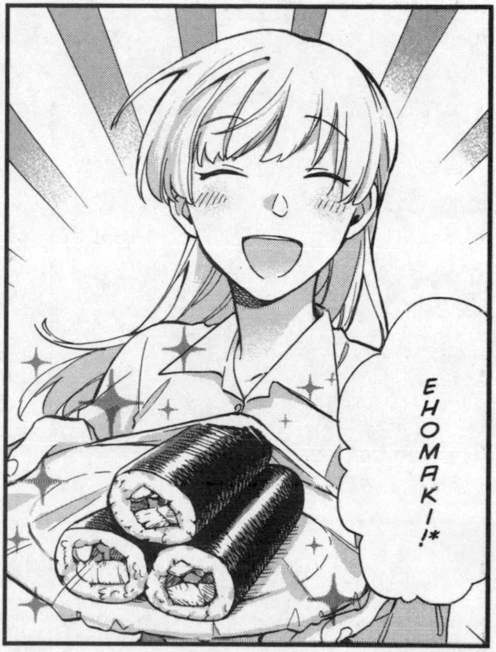
EHOMAKI!*

Setsubun is the day before spring on the Japanese lunar calendar, and a traditional holiday for hailing in good fortune with the coming of the new season. One tradition is to eat a whole roll of thick sushi, called *ehomaki,* in one go while facing that year's lucky direction. Another is *mamemaki,* the tradition of throwing dry soybeans out the door or at someone dressed as a demon to ward off evil, as well as throwing them into the house to bring in good luck.

▼ KOTATSU, PAGE 90

A *kotatsu* is a low table with a built-in heater and blanket skirt that is a winter staple in Japan. They are very warm and cozy and notoriously difficult to leave once you get in.

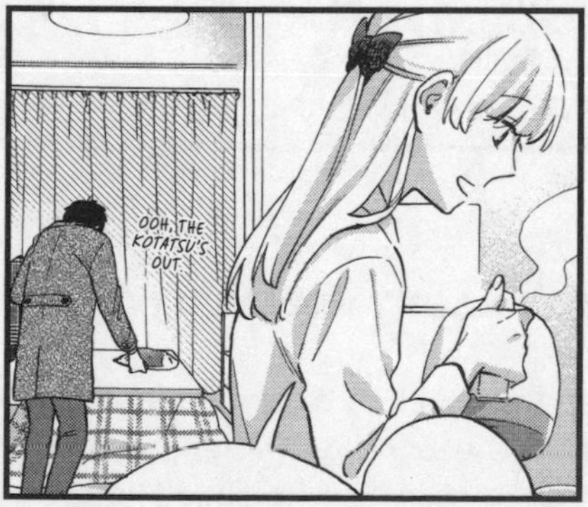
OOH, THE KOTATSU'S OUT.

ME EAT YOU WHOLE, PAGE 92

A reference to the *Shin Megami Tensei* franchise, a series of role-playing games originally based off of a science-fiction novel series called *Digital Devil Story*. Set mainly in modern-day Tokyo with supernatural elements, the franchise also includes the *Persona* sub-series. "ME EAT YOU WHOLE" is a line enemies may say during the negotiation phase of combat, and has appeared in multiple games in the franchise.

SHINKAI FILM, PAGE 100

Best known for the critically acclaimed 2016 film *Your Name,* director Makoto Shinkai's films often have protagonists who miss opportunities to be together due to external circumstances.

ONE MORE CHANCE, PAGE 102

A reference to "One More Time, One More Chance," the ending song from Makoto Shinkai's film *5 Centimeters Per Second,* in which a boy and a girl seemingly fated to be together slowly drift apart over the course of the film.

WINDING ROAD, PAGE 119

A popular 2007 single made in collaboration between Ayaka and the duo Kobukuro, sung about being on a winding road that leads to a promising future.

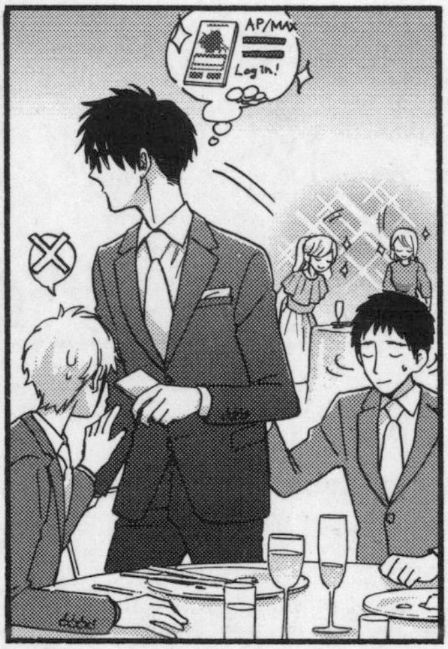

AP/MAX
Log in!

◀ AP/MAX, PAGE 123

AP, or "Action Points" is a stat in the mobile tactical RPG Fate/Grand Order (FGO). AP recharges over time and is required to start quests. Hirotaka notices that his AP is fully charged and intends to slip out to play some FGO, but his colleagues Baba and Aiba are convincing him otherwise.

▼ I'M OKAY AS LONG AS SHE'S HAPPY, PAGE 124

A meme originating from an interview with a university student on the street about Japanese Imperial Princess Mako's engagement to a commoner. The man explained that he was a big fan of Princess Mako and was devastated to hear the news, but finished by giving a thumbs-up and saying that he was okay as long as she was happy. Praised as the "right way to be a fan," a screenshot of the interview with the onscreen caption "I'm okay as long as she's happy" has since been circulated around the web, spawning various parody versions.

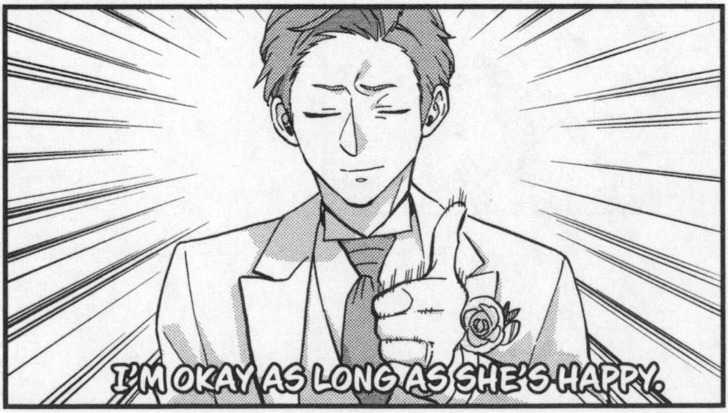

I'M OKAY AS LONG AS SHE'S HAPPY.

▶ GUESS IT'S TIME FOR US TO SAVE THE WORLD!, PAGE 129

A reference to a tweet of unknown origin, thought to be from 2012. It talks about how nice it must be for everyone to be able to joke about how the world is ending (supposedly due to the Mayan calendar's prediction of impending doom), while he has to actually go and rescue the world from peril. He ends the tweet with "Well, guess it's time for me to go save the world," as his "long sword flashes in the moonlight" and he "disappears into the night." The tweet has since been parodied into various iterations.

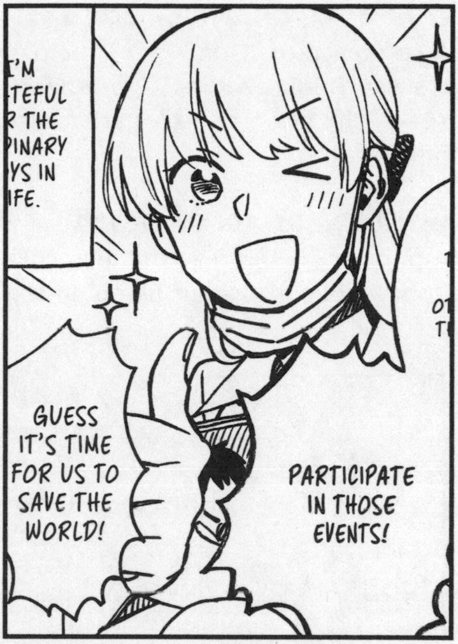
PARTICIPATE IN THOSE EVENTS!
GUESS IT'S TIME FOR US TO SAVE THE WORLD!

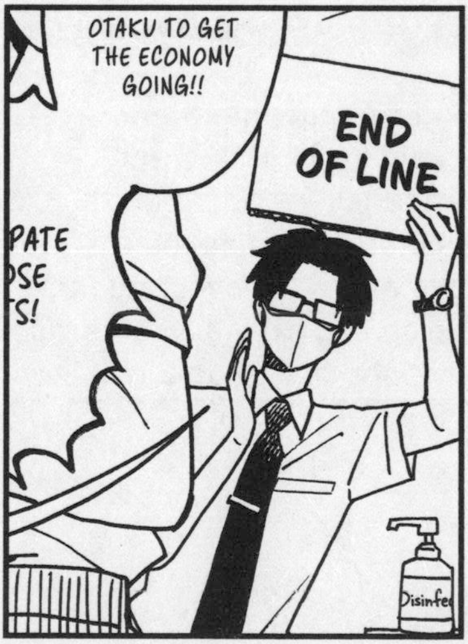
OTAKU TO GET THE ECONOMY GOING!!
END OF LINE

◀ END OF LINE, PAGE 129

To maintain crowd control at *dojinshi* events, the last person in line waiting to buy from a booth holds up a sign that says "End of line" to indicate where the end of the line is. The sign is handed on whenever a new person joins the line.

WOTAKOI:
LOVE IS HARD FOR OTAKU

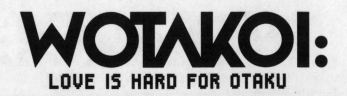

WOTAKOI:
LOVE IS HARD FOR OTAKU

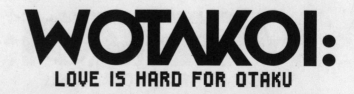

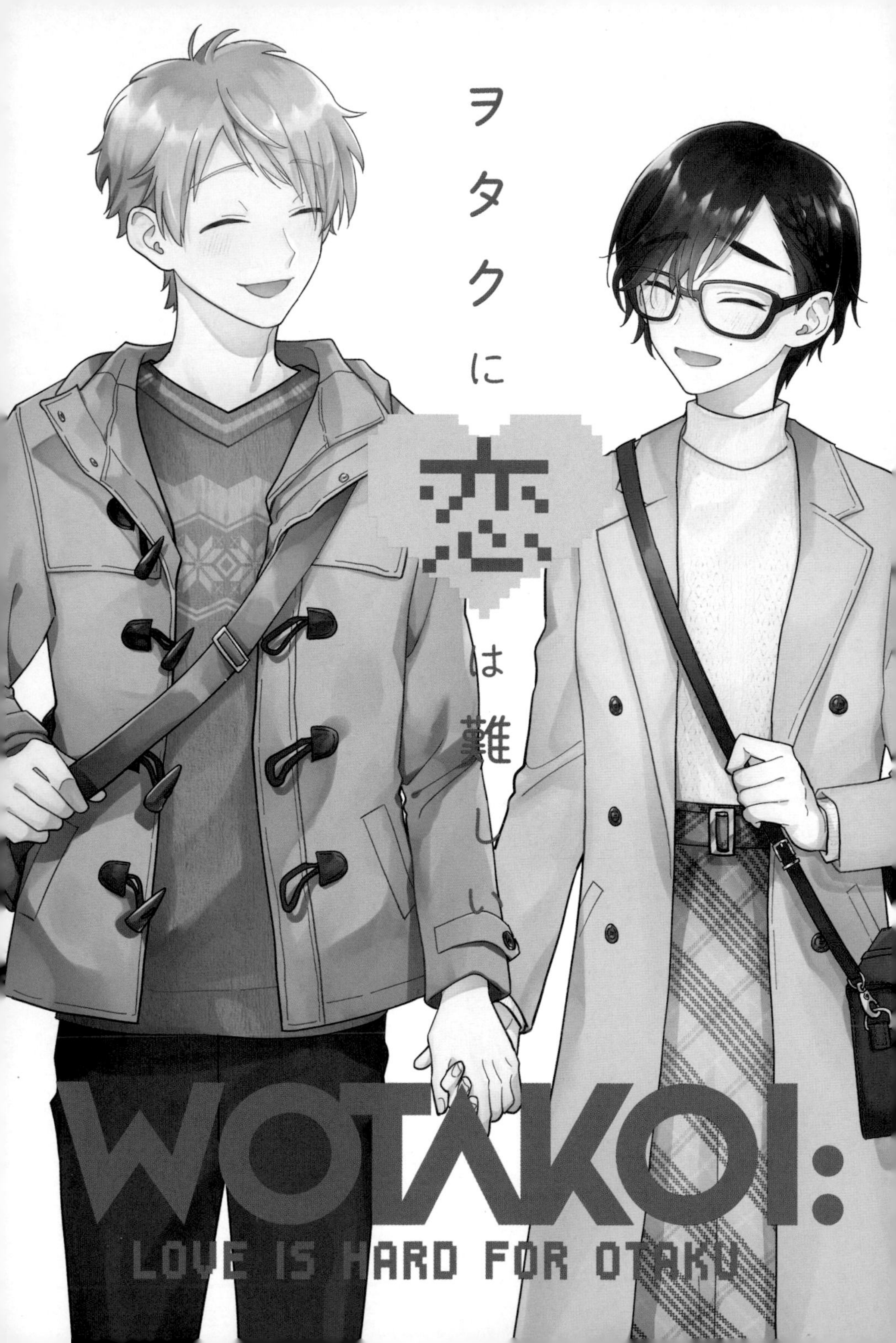
ヲタクに恋は難しい
WOTAKOI:
LOVE IS HARD FOR OTAKU

WOTAKOI:

LOVE IS HARD FOR OTAKU

FUJITA

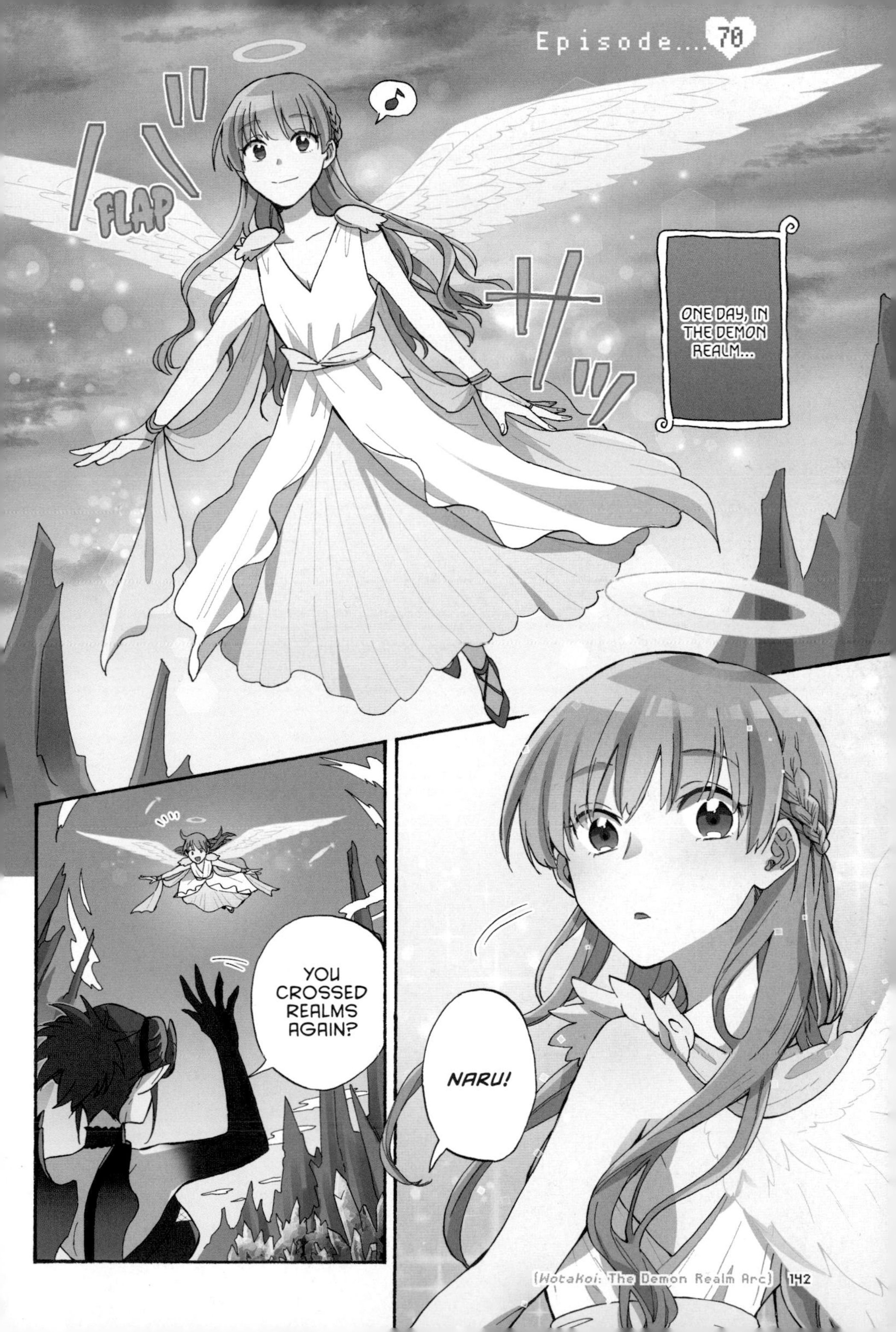
Episode.... 70
FLAP
ONE DAY, IN THE DEMON REALM...
NARU!
YOU CROSSED REALMS AGAIN?

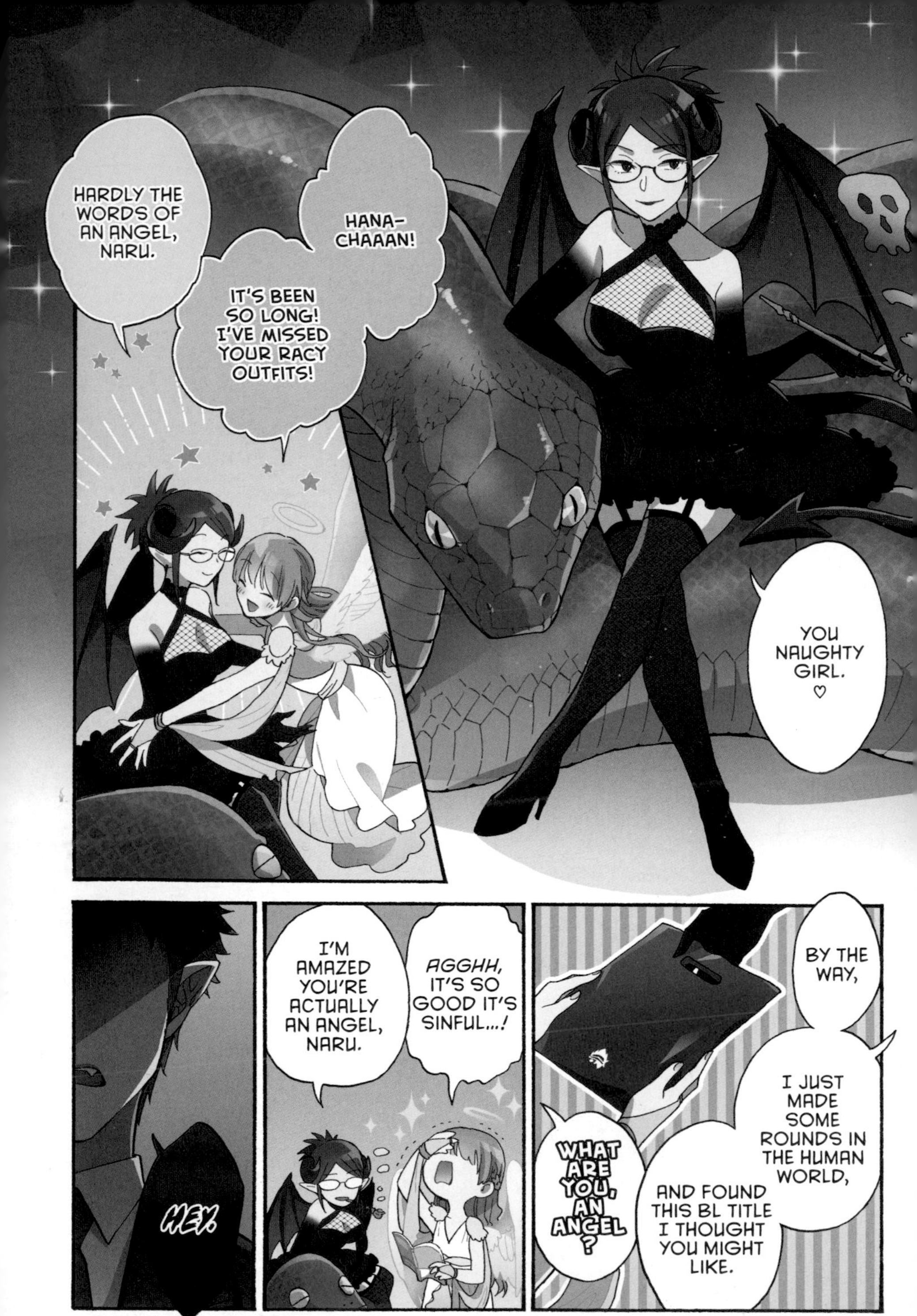
HANA-CHAAAN!
IT'S BEEN SO LONG! I'VE MISSED YOUR RACY OUTFITS!
HARDLY THE WORDS OF AN ANGEL, NARU.
YOU NAUGHTY GIRL. ♡
BY THE WAY,
I JUST MADE SOME ROUNDS IN THE HUMAN WORLD,
AND FOUND THIS BL TITLE I THOUGHT YOU MIGHT LIKE.
WHAT ARE YOU, AN ANGEL?
AGGHH, IT'S SO GOOD IT'S SINFUL...!
I'M AMAZED YOU'RE ACTUALLY AN ANGEL, NARU.
HEY.

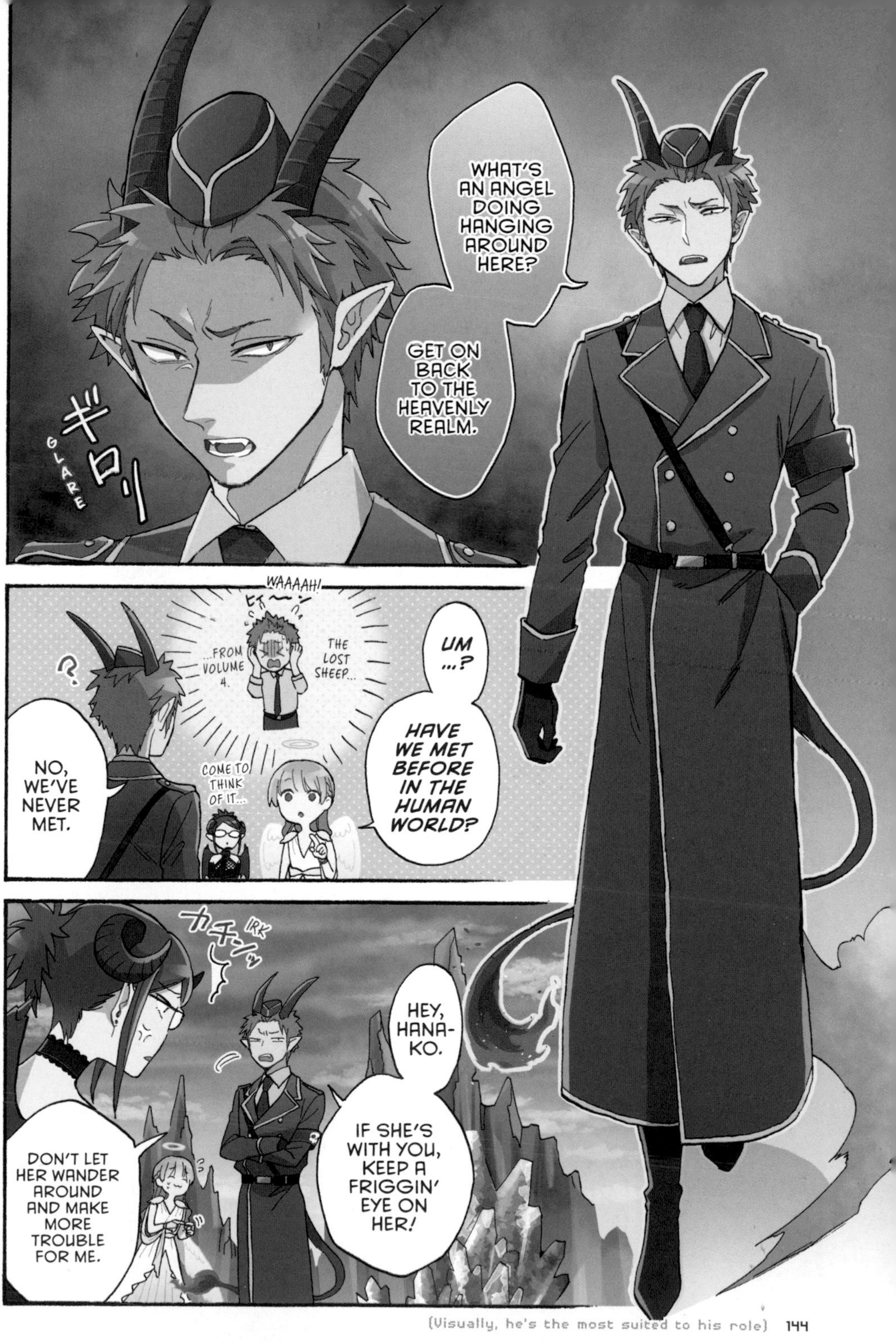
WHAT'S AN ANGEL DOING HANGING AROUND HERE?
GET ON BACK TO THE HEAVENLY REALM.
ギロリ
GLARE
UM ...?
HAVE WE MET BEFORE IN THE HUMAN WORLD?
WAAAAH!
THE LOST SHEEP...
...FROM VOLUME 4.
COME TO THINK OF IT...
NO, WE'VE NEVER MET.
HEY, HANA-KO.
IF SHE'S WITH YOU, KEEP A FRIGGIN' EYE ON HER!
カチンッ
IRK
DON'T LET HER WANDER AROUND AND MAKE MORE TROUBLE FOR ME.

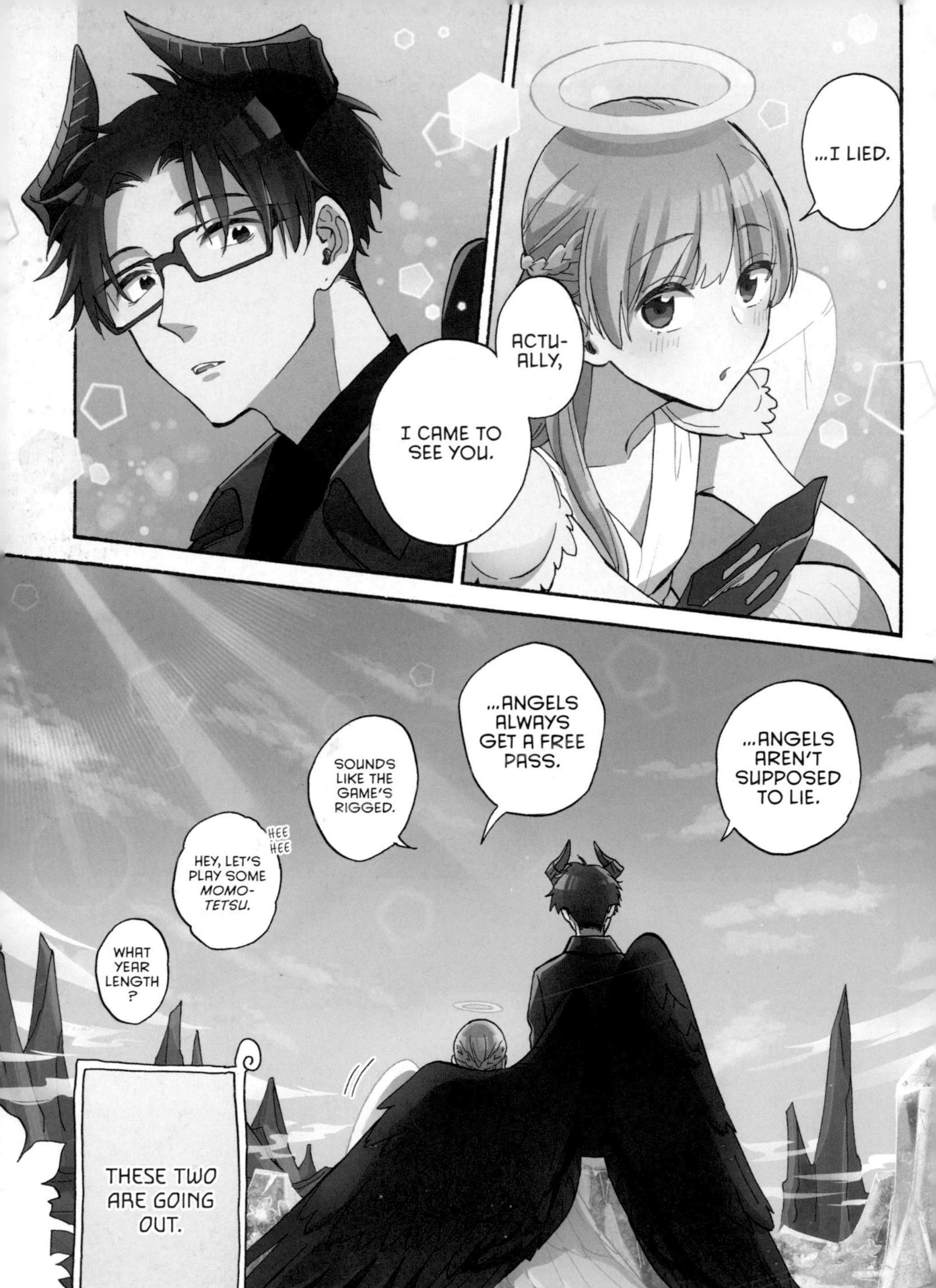
...I LIED.
ACTU-ALLY,
I CAME TO SEE YOU.
...ANGELS AREN'T SUPPOSED TO LIE.
...ANGELS ALWAYS GET A FREE PASS.
SOUNDS LIKE THE GAME'S RIGGED.
HEE HEE
HEY, LET'S PLAY SOME *MOMO-TETSU*.
WHAT YEAR LENGTH?
THESE TWO ARE GOING OUT.

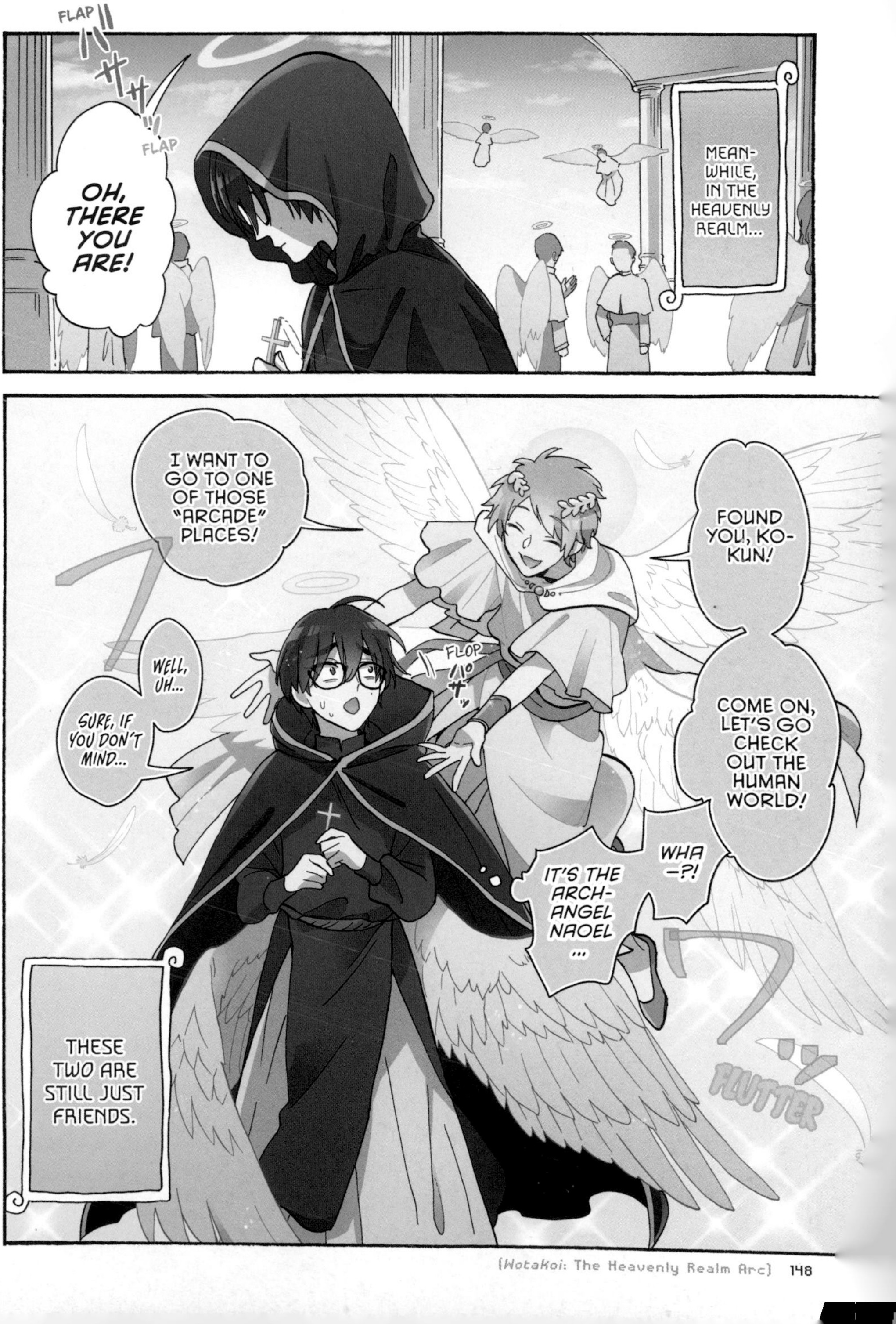
MEANWHILE, IN THE HEAVENLY REALM...
FLAP FLAP
OH, THERE YOU ARE!
FOUND YOU, KO-KUN!
COME ON, LET'S GO CHECK OUT THE HUMAN WORLD!
WHA—?!
IT'S THE ARCHANGEL NAOEL...
FLUTTER
FLOP
I WANT TO GO TO ONE OF THOSE "ARCADE" PLACES!
WELL, UH...
SURE, IF YOU DON'T MIND...
THESE TWO ARE STILL JUST FRIENDS.

Episode....71

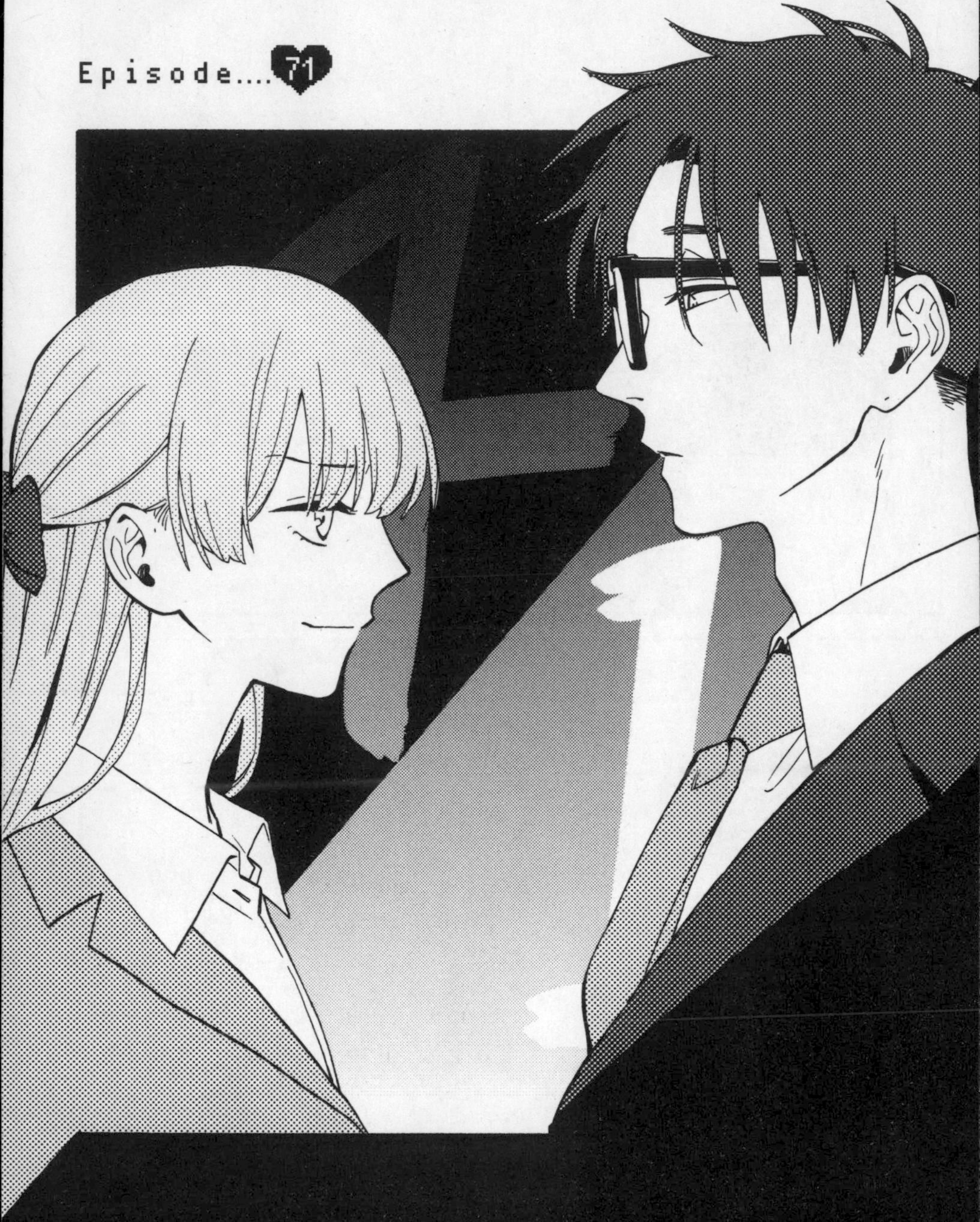

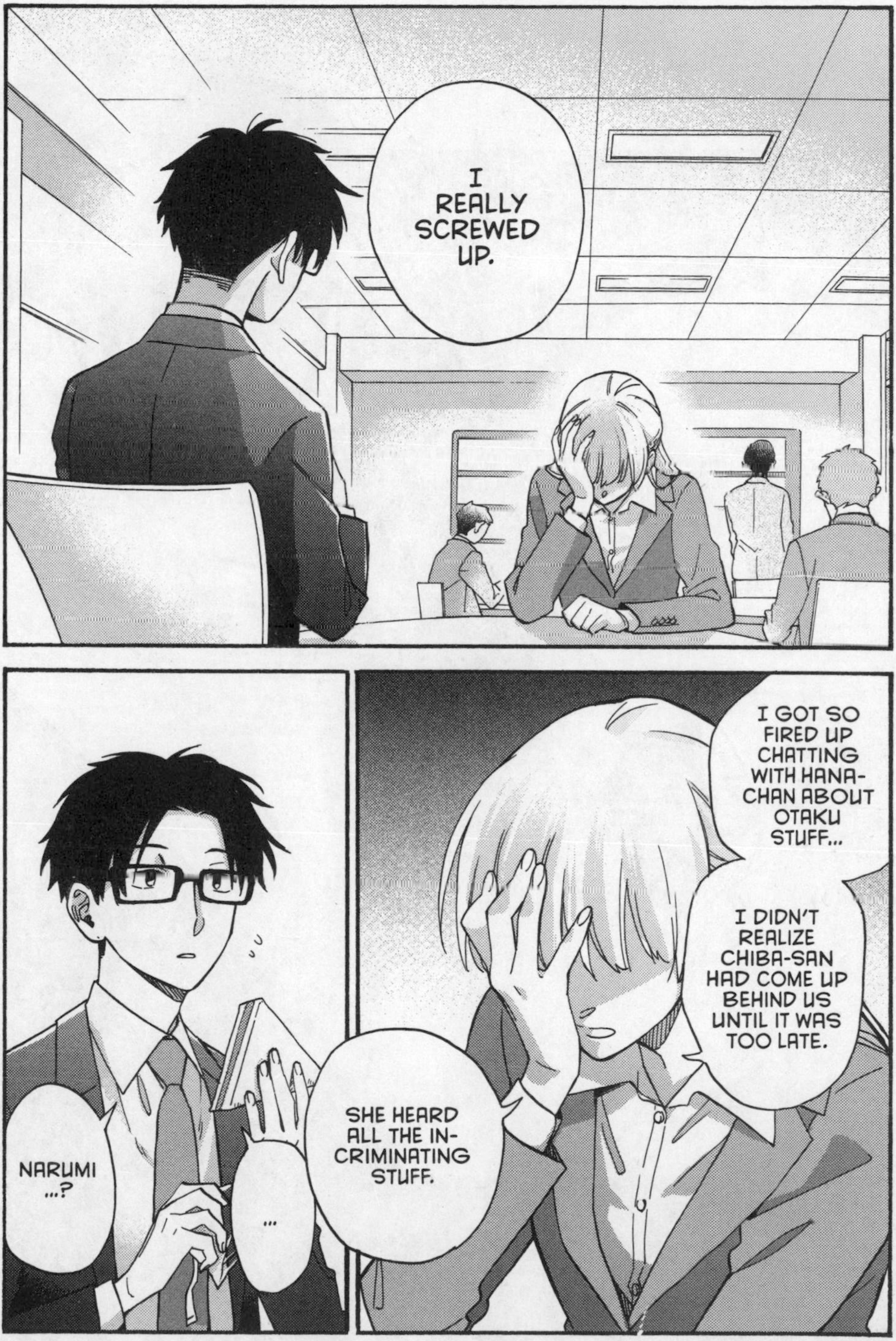
I REALLY SCREWED UP.
I GOT SO FIRED UP CHATTING WITH HANA-CHAN ABOUT OTAKU STUFF...
I DIDN'T REALIZE CHIBA-SAN HAD COME UP BEHIND US UNTIL IT WAS TOO LATE.
SHE HEARD ALL THE IN-CRIMINATING STUFF.
...
NARUMI ...?

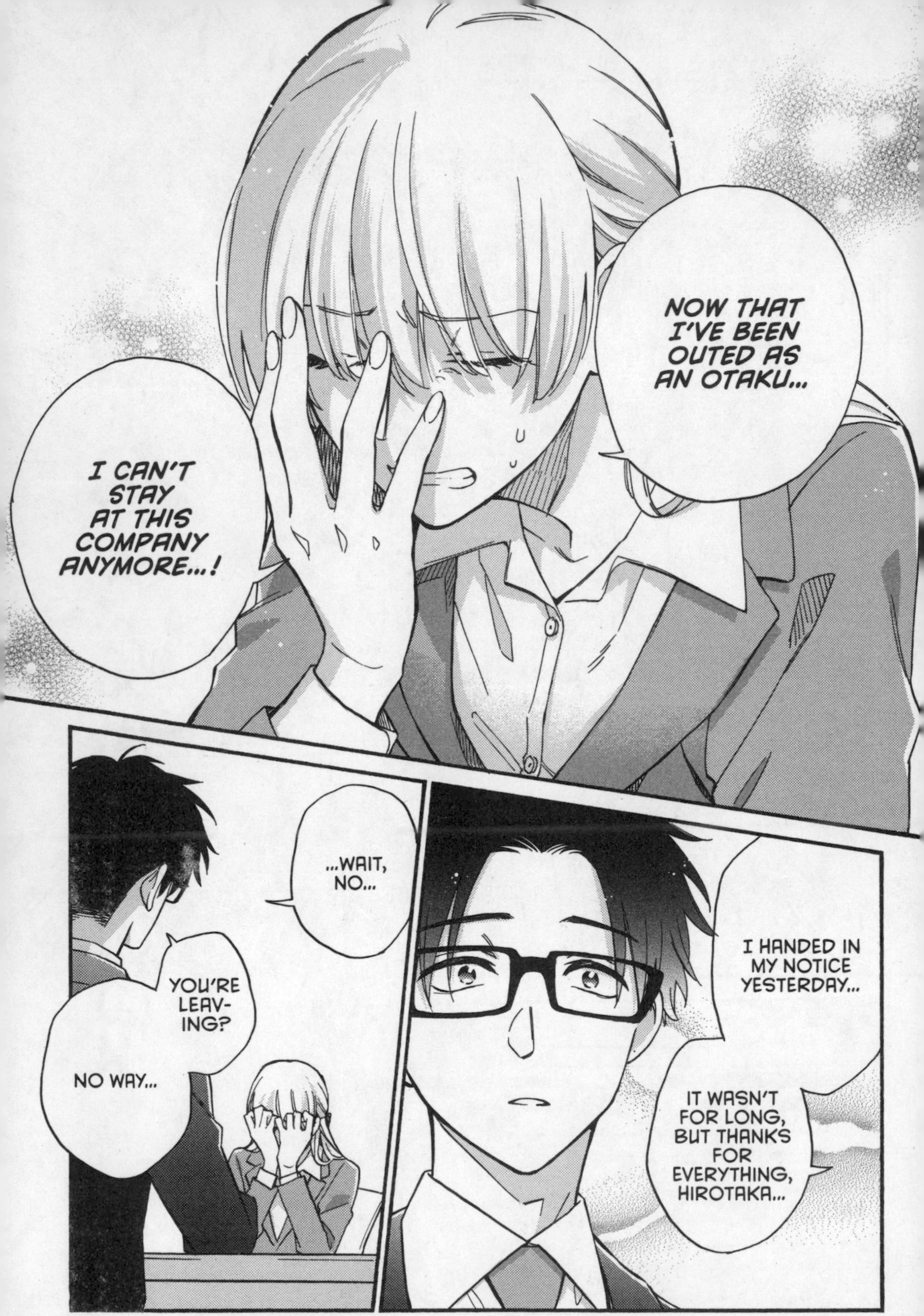
NOW THAT I'VE BEEN OUTED AS AN OTAKU...
I CAN'T STAY AT THIS COMPANY ANYMORE...!
I HANDED IN MY NOTICE YESTERDAY...
IT WASN'T FOR LONG, BUT THANKS FOR EVERYTHING, HIROTAKA...
...WAIT, NO...
YOU'RE LEAVING?
NO WAY...

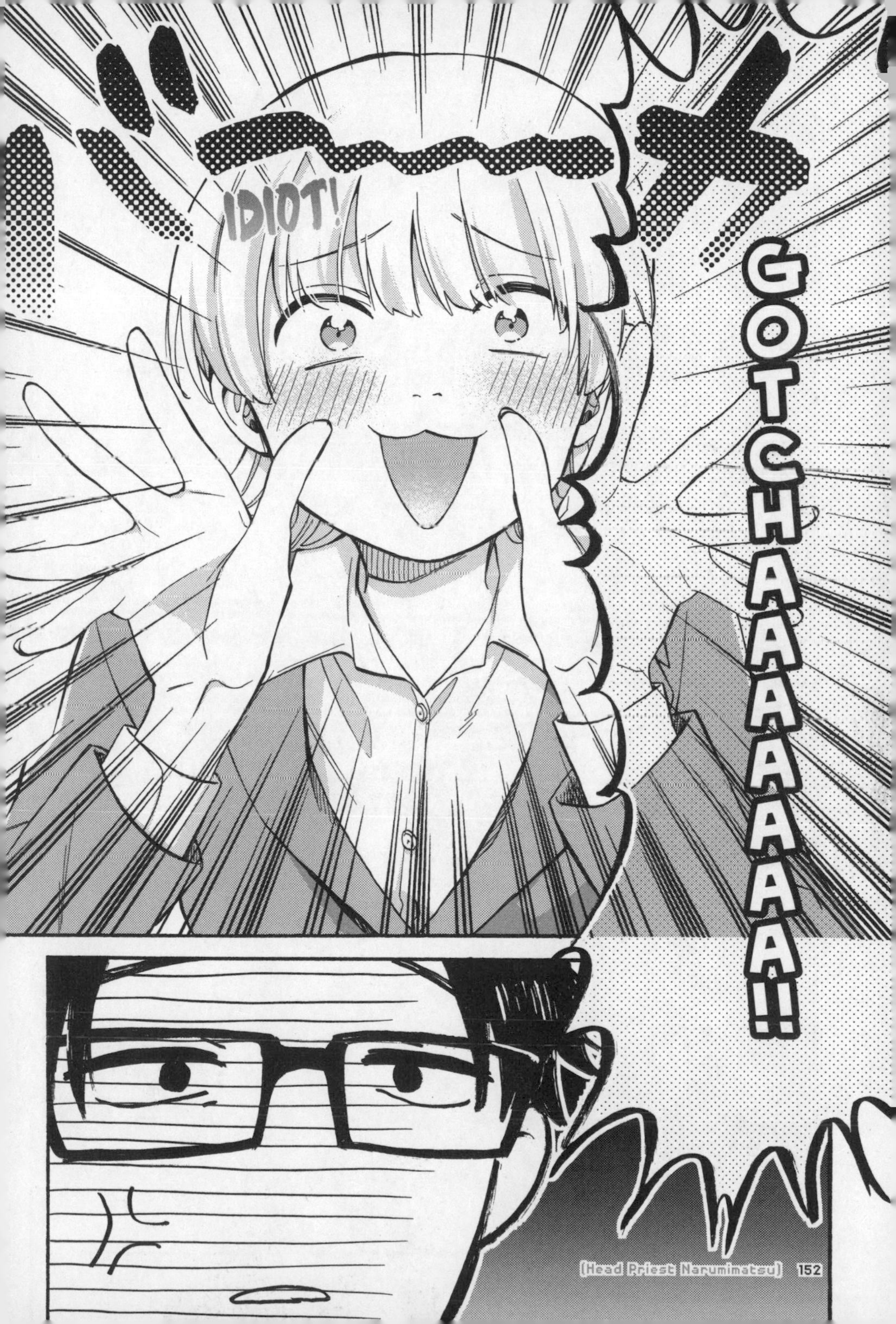
IDIOT!
GOTCHAAAAAAA!!
(Head Priest Narumimatsu)

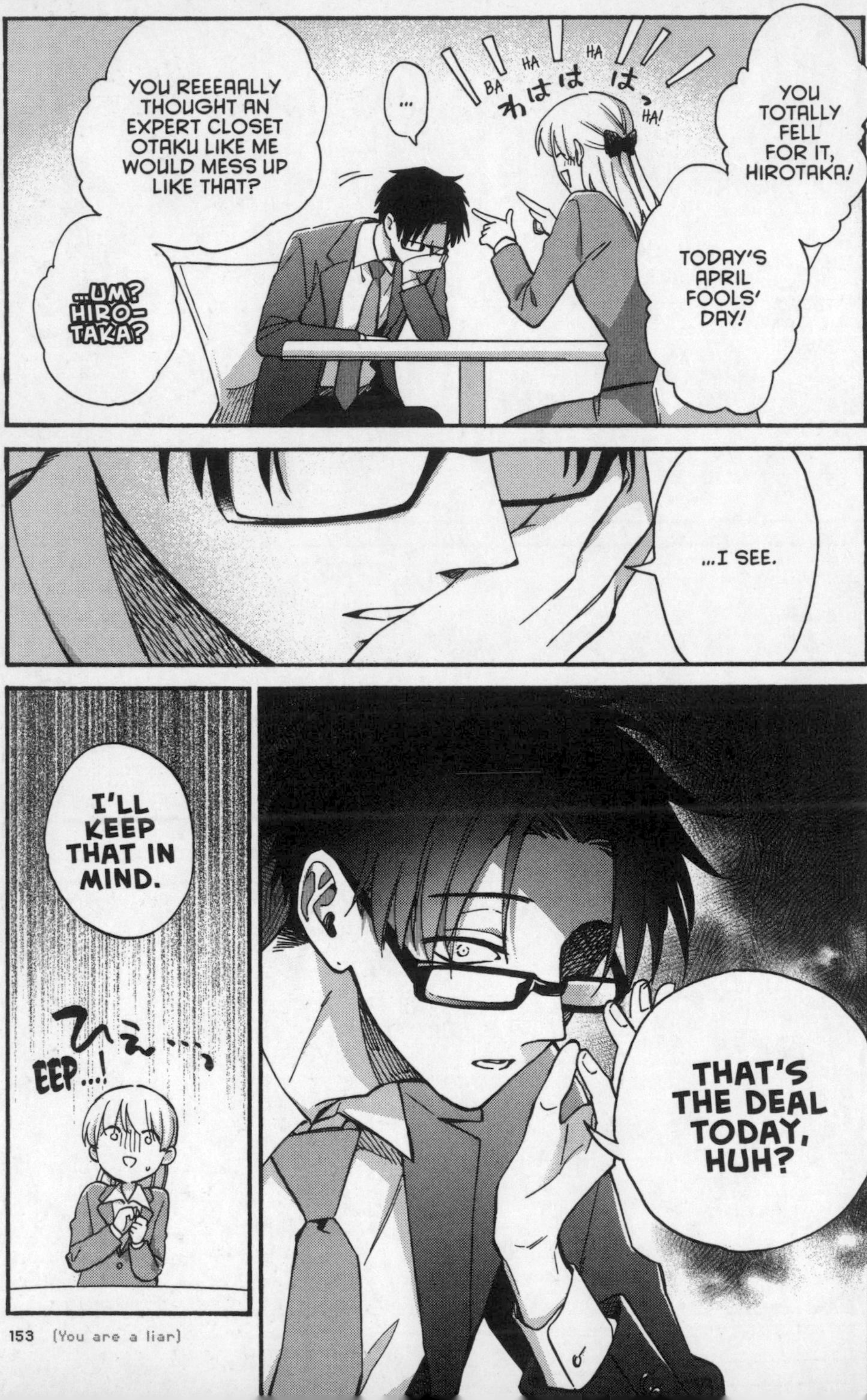
YOU TOTALLY FELL FOR IT, HIROTAKA!
TODAY'S APRIL FOOLS' DAY!
わはは はっ
BA HA HA HA!
...
YOU REEEAALLY THOUGHT AN EXPERT CLOSET OTAKU LIKE ME WOULD MESS UP LIKE THAT?
...UM? HIRO-TAKA?
...I SEE.
THAT'S THE DEAL TODAY, HUH?
I'LL KEEP THAT IN MIND.
ひぇ…っ
EEP...!

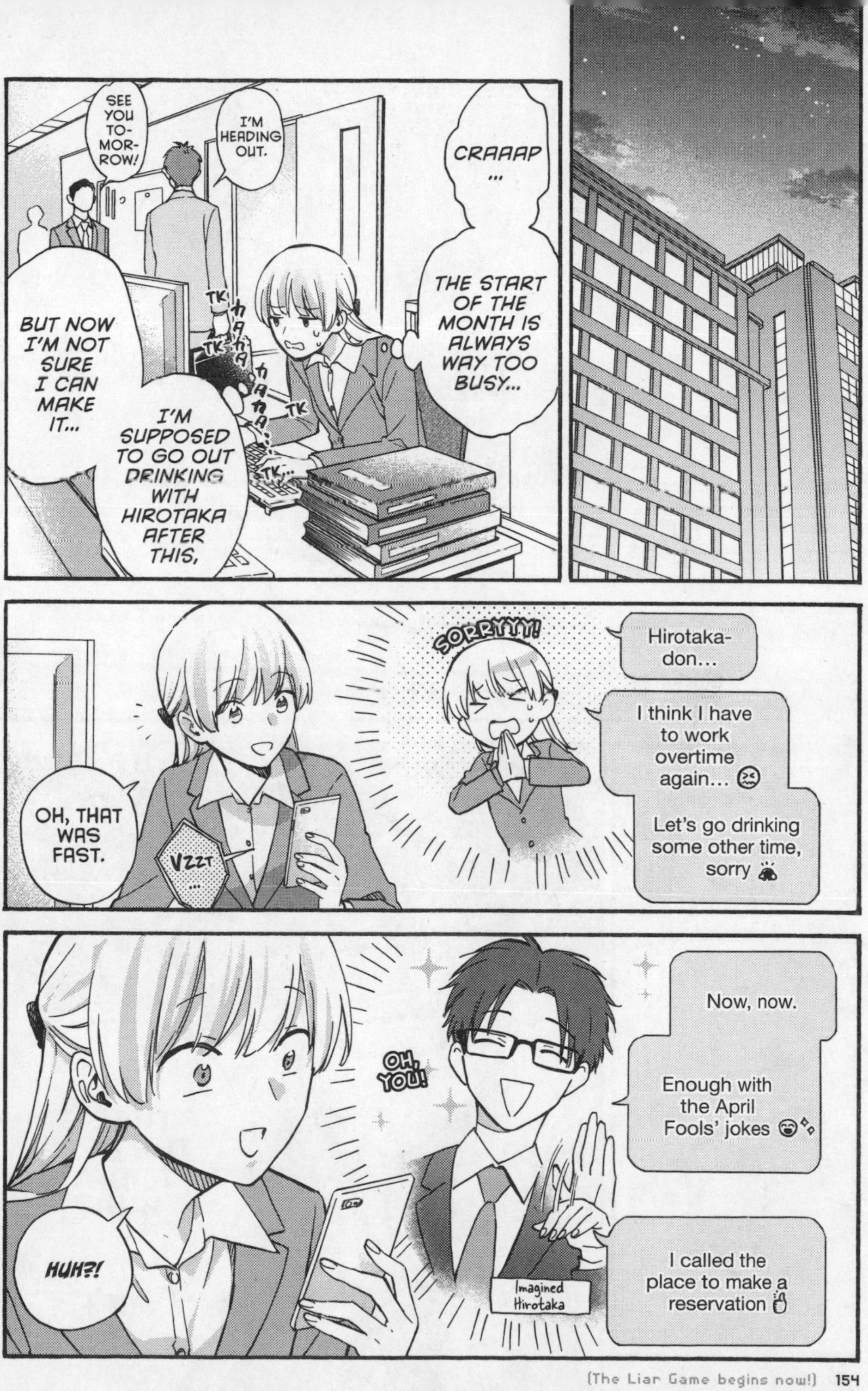
CRAAAP ...
THE START OF THE MONTH IS ALWAYS WAY TOO BUSY...
I'M HEADING OUT.
SEE YOU TO-MOR-ROW!
TK
TK
TK
TK...
I'M SUPPOSED TO GO OUT DRINKING WITH HIROTAKA AFTER THIS,
BUT NOW I'M NOT SURE I CAN MAKE IT...
Hirotaka-don…
I think I have to work overtime again…
Let's go drinking some other time, sorry
SORRYYY!
OH, THAT WAS FAST.
VZZT ...
Now, now.
Enough with the April Fools' jokes
I called the place to make a reservation
OH, YOU!
Imagined Hirotaka
HUH?!

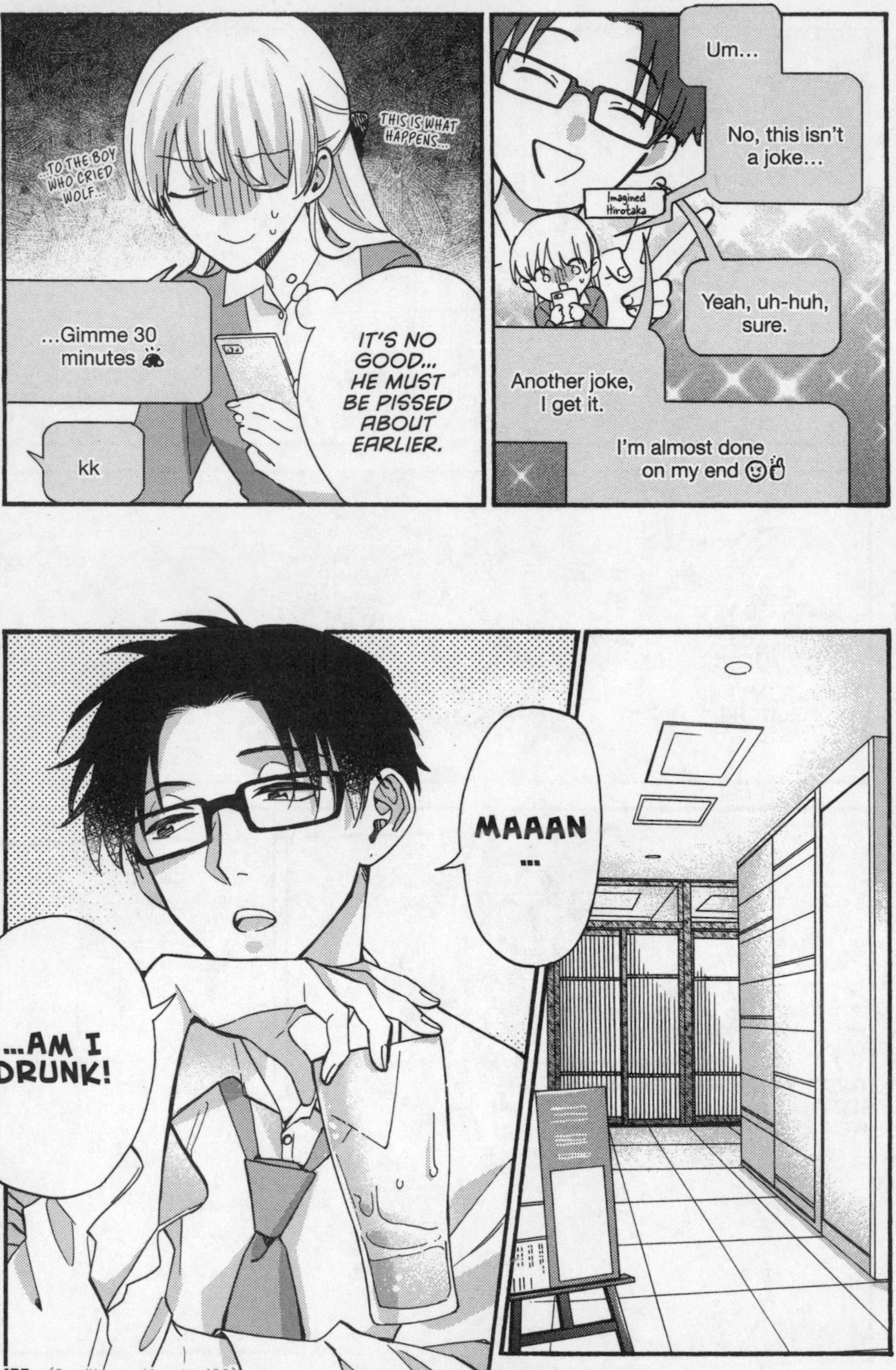
Um…
No, this isn't a joke…
Imagined Hirotaka
Yeah, uh-huh, sure.
Another joke, I get it.
I'm almost done on my end
THIS IS WHAT HAPPENS…
…TO THE BOY WHO CRIED WOLF…
IT'S NO GOOD… HE MUST BE PISSED ABOUT EARLIER.
…Gimme 30 minutes
kk
MAAAN …
…AM I DRUNK!

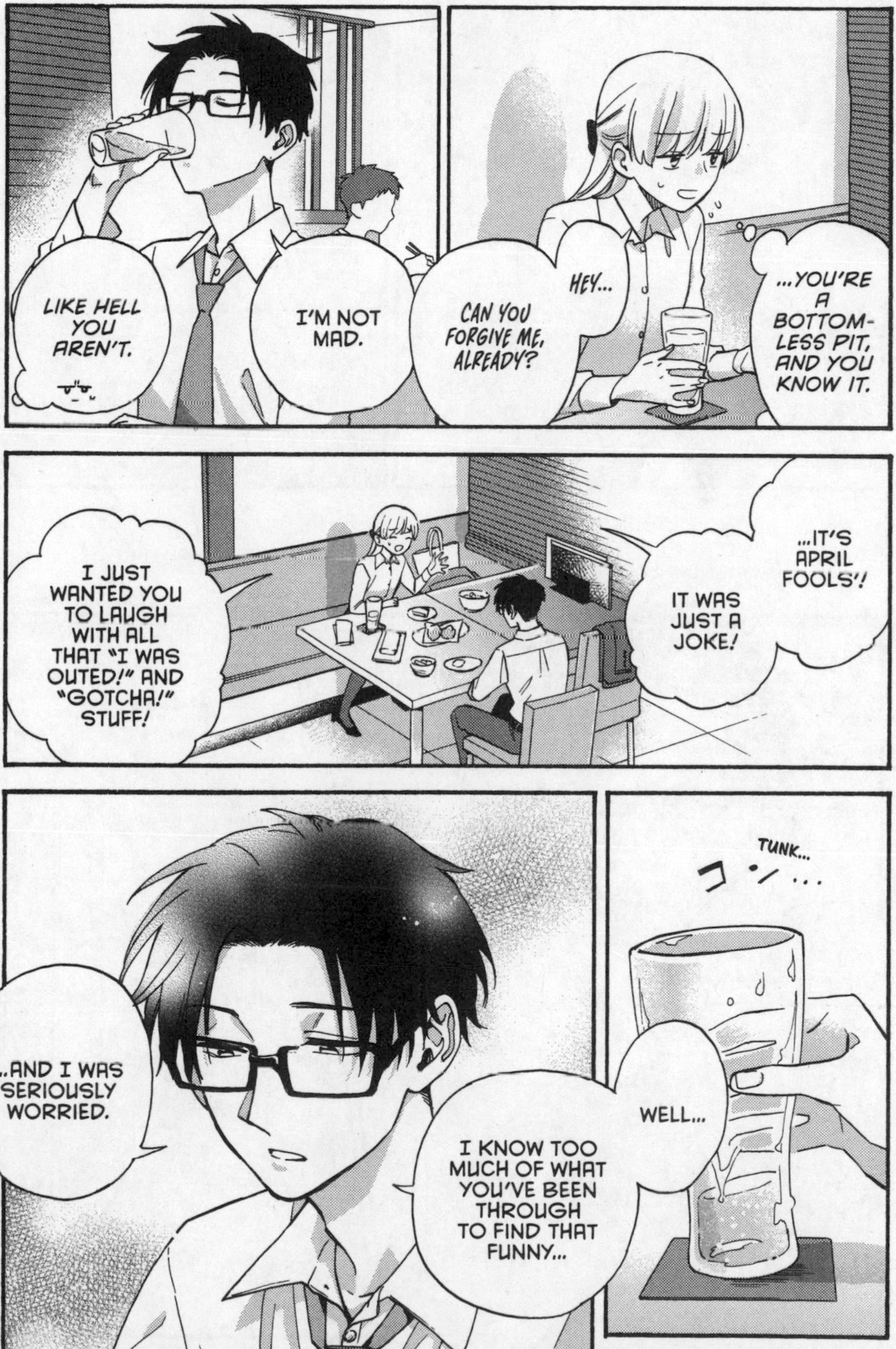

...YOU'RE A BOTTOMLESS PIT, AND YOU KNOW IT.
HEY...
CAN YOU FORGIVE ME, ALREADY?
I'M NOT MAD.
LIKE HELL YOU AREN'T.
...IT'S APRIL FOOLS'!
IT WAS JUST A JOKE!
I JUST WANTED YOU TO LAUGH WITH ALL THAT "I WAS OUTED!" AND "GOTCHA!" STUFF!
TUNK...
コン…
WELL...
I KNOW TOO MUCH OF WHAT YOU'VE BEEN THROUGH TO FIND THAT FUNNY...
...AND I WAS SERIOUSLY WORRIED.

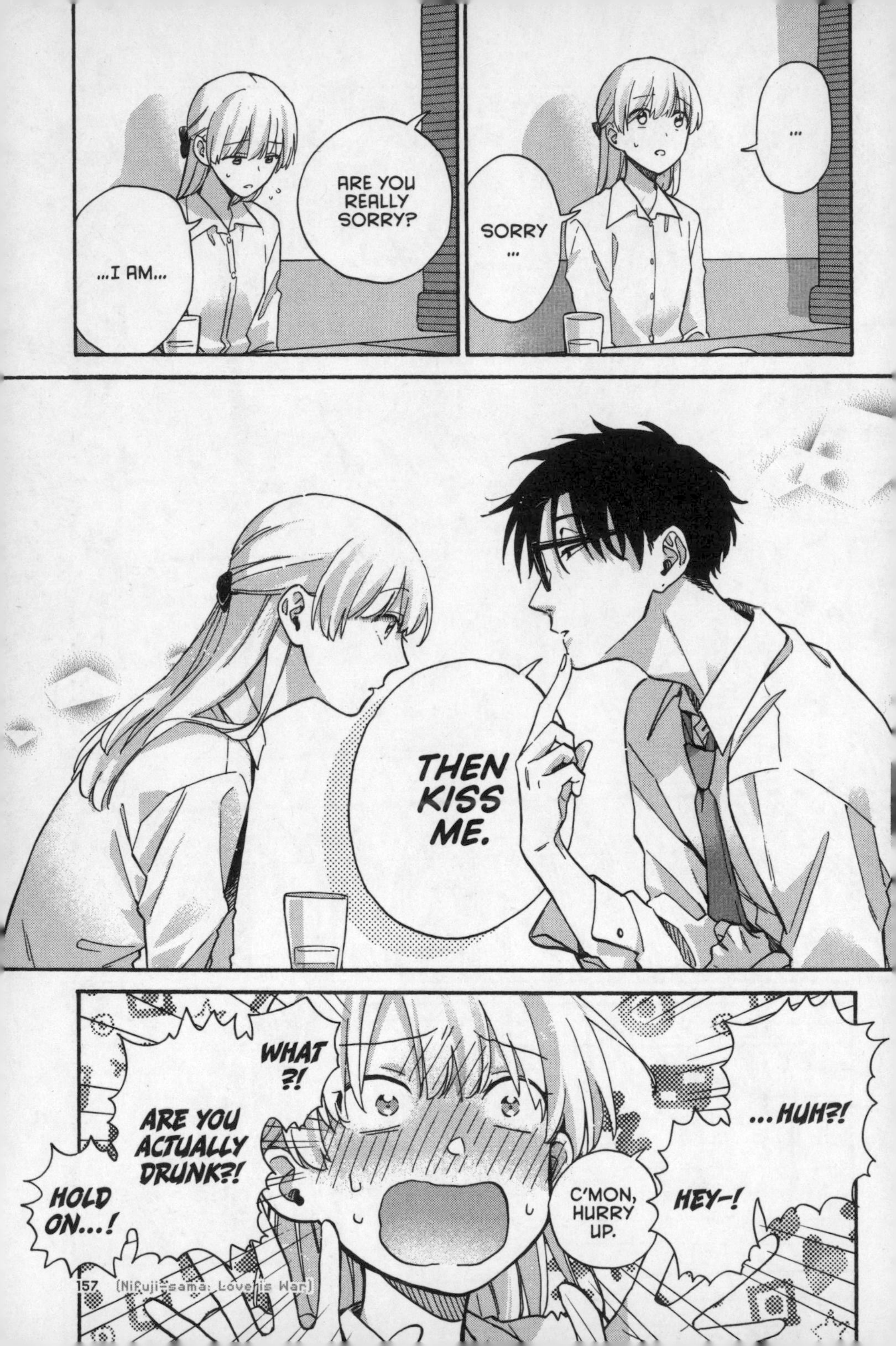
...
SORRY ...
ARE YOU REALLY SORRY?
...I AM...
THEN KISS ME.
...HUH?!
HEY-!
C'MON, HURRY UP.
WHAT ?!
ARE YOU ACTUALLY DRUNK?!
HOLD ON...!

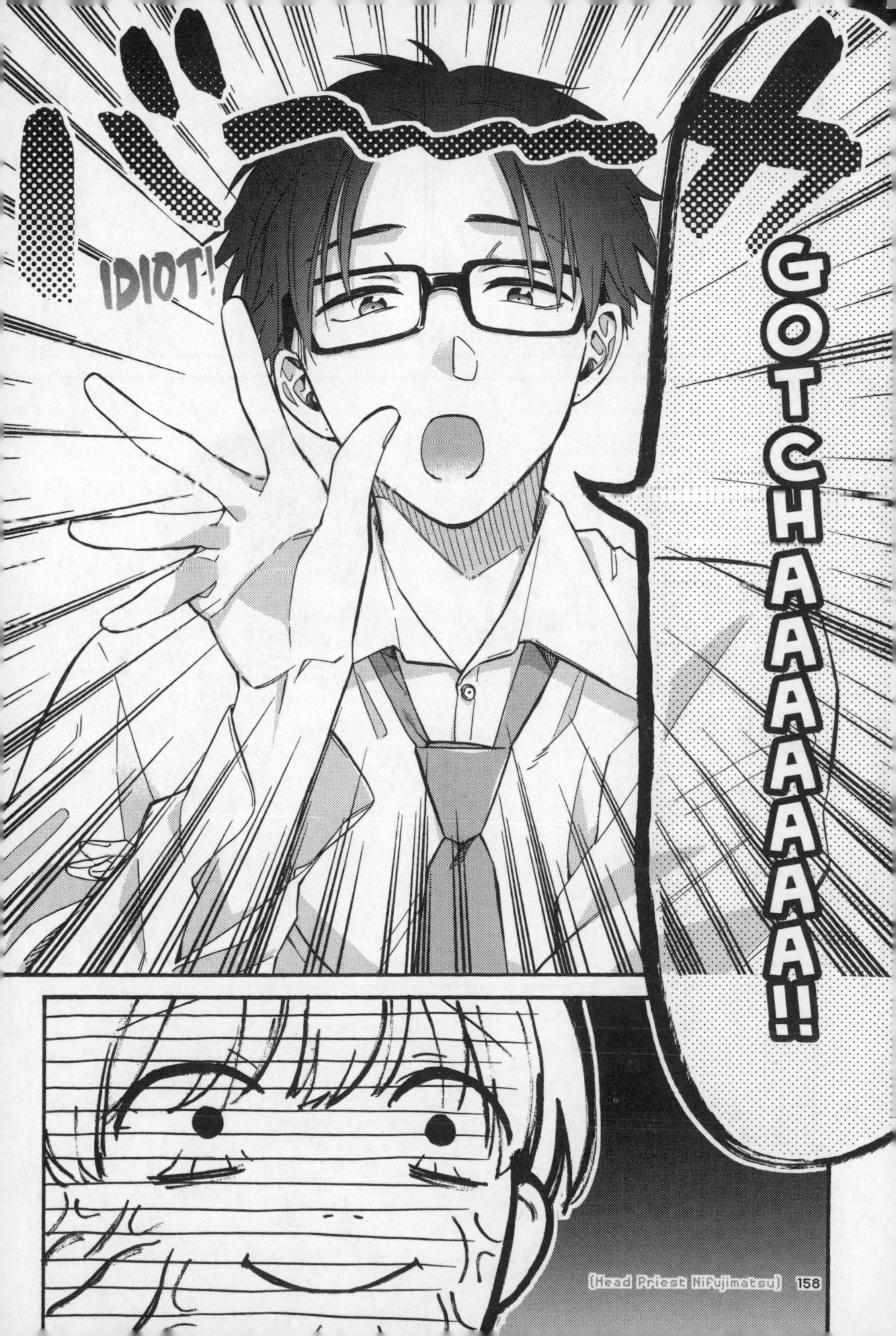
GOTCHAAAAAAA!!
IDIOT!
[Head Priest Nifujimatsu]

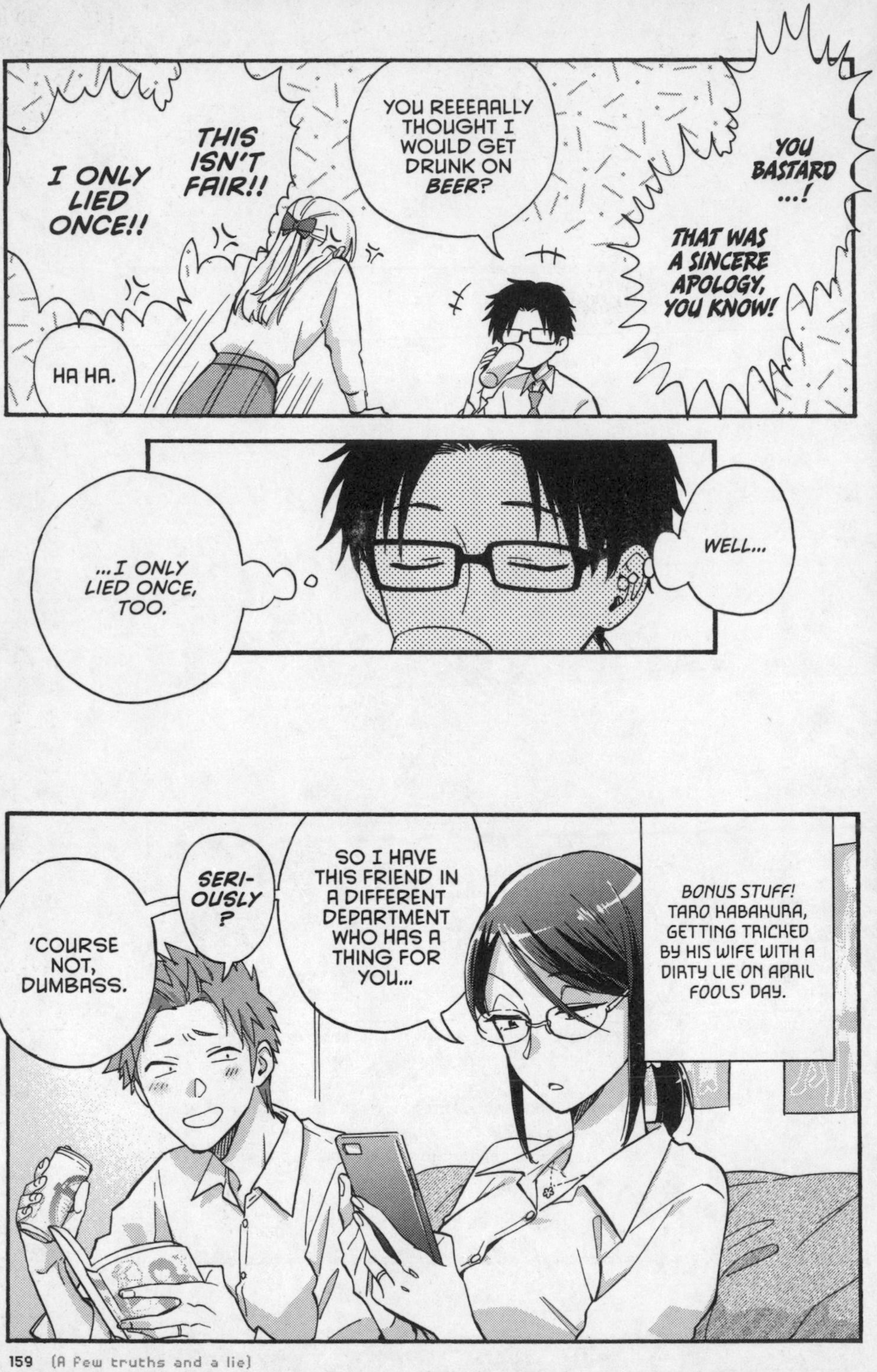
YOU BASTARD ...!
THAT WAS A SINCERE APOLOGY, YOU KNOW!
YOU REEEAALLY THOUGHT I WOULD GET DRUNK ON *BEER*?
THIS ISN'T FAIR!!
I ONLY LIED ONCE!!
HA HA.
WELL...
...I ONLY LIED ONCE, TOO.
BONUS STUFF! TARO KABAKURA, GETTING TRICKED BY HIS WIFE WITH A DIRTY LIE ON APRIL FOOLS' DAY.
SO I HAVE THIS FRIEND IN A DIFFERENT DEPARTMENT WHO HAS A THING FOR YOU...
SERI-OUSLY?
'COURSE NOT, DUMBASS.

CHARACTERS I

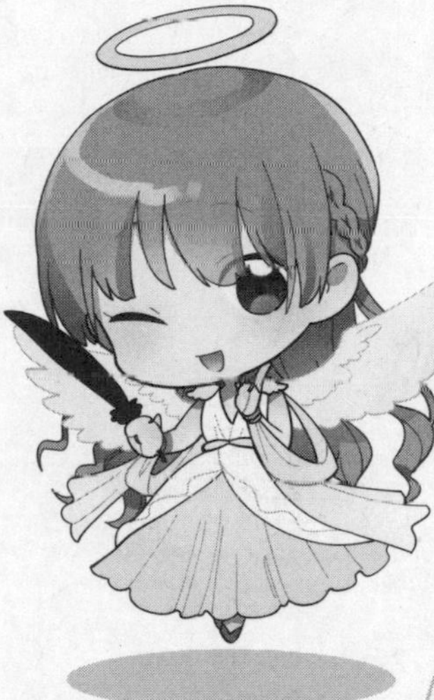

Angel

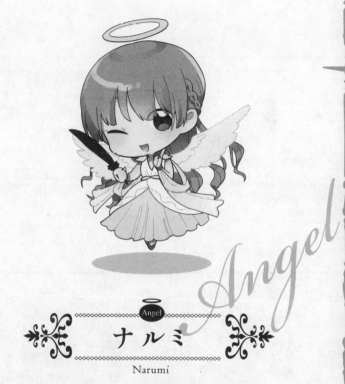

Angel

ナルミ

Narumi

She may look like an angel, but she actually drowns herself in worldly desires.

Her childhood friend Hirotaka was already a devil when they reunited, but they still shared the same interests in gaming, so they started dating.

C H A R A C T E R S II

DEVIL

Devil

ヒロタカ

Hirotaka

A devil who prioritizes video games above all else.

Kids who do nothing but play games all the time may actually be possessed by him.

Rumor has it that his wings were white at some point… or not.

He really loves Narumi.

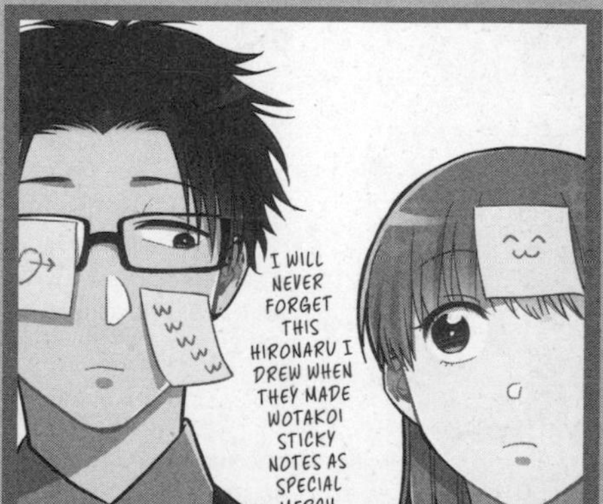
I WILL NEVER FORGET THIS HIRONARU I DREW WHEN THEY MADE WOTAKOI STICKY NOTES AS SPECIAL MERCH.
WWWW

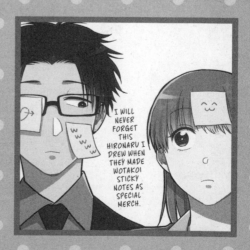

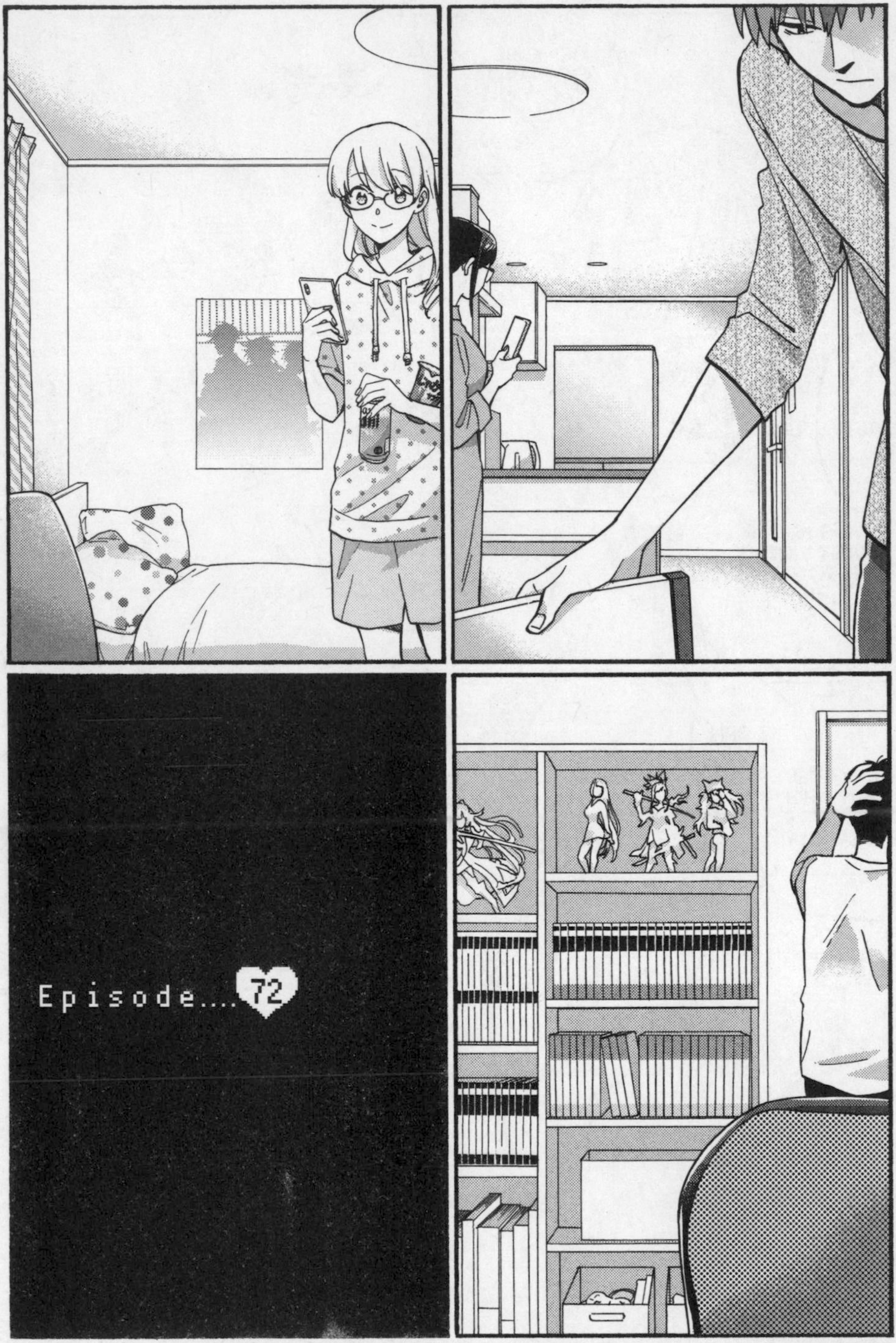
Episode.... 72

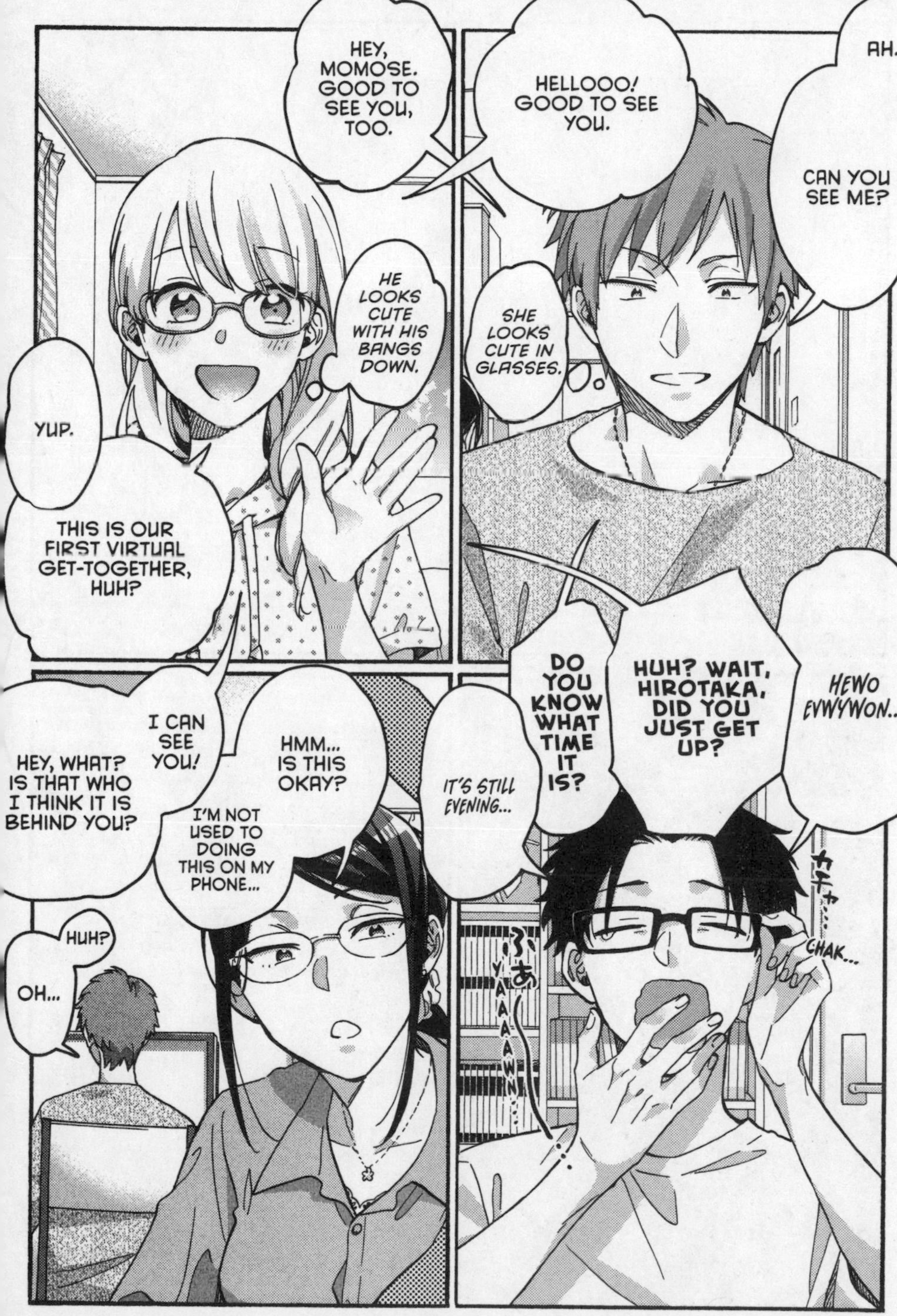
AH.
CAN YOU SEE ME?
HELLOOO! GOOD TO SEE YOU.
SHE LOOKS CUTE IN GLASSES.
HEY, MOMOSE. GOOD TO SEE YOU, TOO.
HE LOOKS CUTE WITH HIS BANGS DOWN.
YUP.
THIS IS OUR FIRST VIRTUAL GET-TOGETHER, HUH?
HEWO EVWYWON...
HUH? WAIT, HIROTAKA, DID YOU JUST GET UP?
DO YOU KNOW WHAT TIME IT IS?
IT'S STILL EVENING...
カチャ... CHAK...
ふあ YAAAAAWN...
HMM... IS THIS OKAY?
I'M NOT USED TO DOING THIS ON MY PHONE...
I CAN SEE YOU!
HEY, WHAT? IS THAT WHO I THINK IT IS BEHIND YOU?
HUH?
OH...

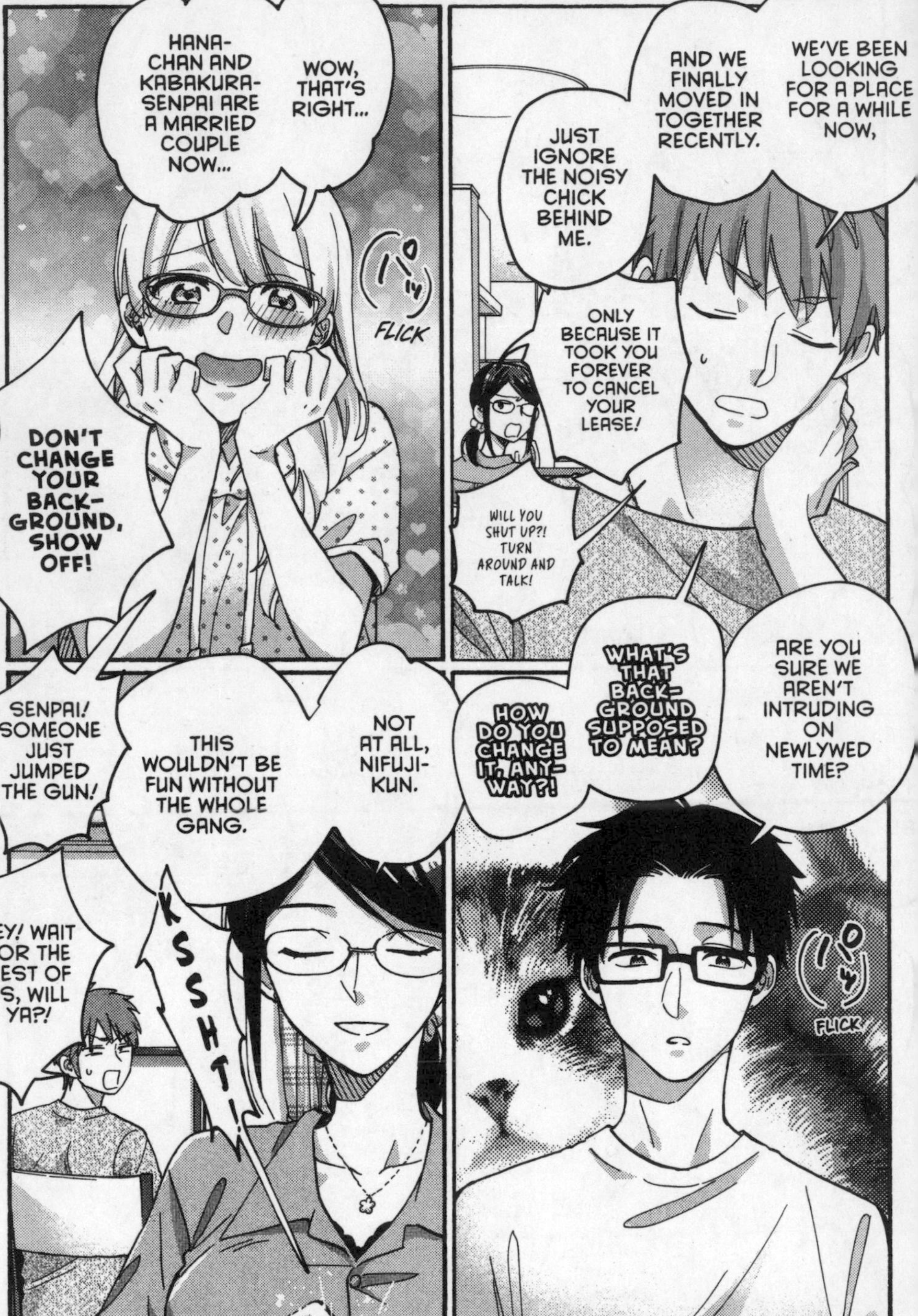
WE'VE BEEN LOOKING FOR A PLACE FOR A WHILE NOW,
AND WE FINALLY MOVED IN TOGETHER RECENTLY.
JUST IGNORE THE NOISY CHICK BEHIND ME.
ONLY BECAUSE IT TOOK YOU FOREVER TO CANCEL YOUR LEASE!
WILL YOU SHUT UP?! TURN AROUND AND TALK!
WOW, THAT'S RIGHT...
HANA-CHAN AND KABAKURA-SENPAI ARE A MARRIED COUPLE NOW...
FLICK
DON'T CHANGE YOUR BACKGROUND, SHOW OFF!
ARE YOU SURE WE AREN'T INTRUDING ON NEWLYWED TIME?
WHAT'S THAT BACKGROUND SUPPOSED TO MEAN?
HOW DO YOU CHANGE IT, ANYWAY?!
FLICK
NOT AT ALL, NIFUJI-KUN.
THIS WOULDN'T BE FUN WITHOUT THE WHOLE GANG.
SENPAI! SOMEONE JUST JUMPED THE GUN!
KSSHT!
HEY! WAIT FOR THE REST OF US, WILL YA?!

 (Video conference enjoyment for dummies)

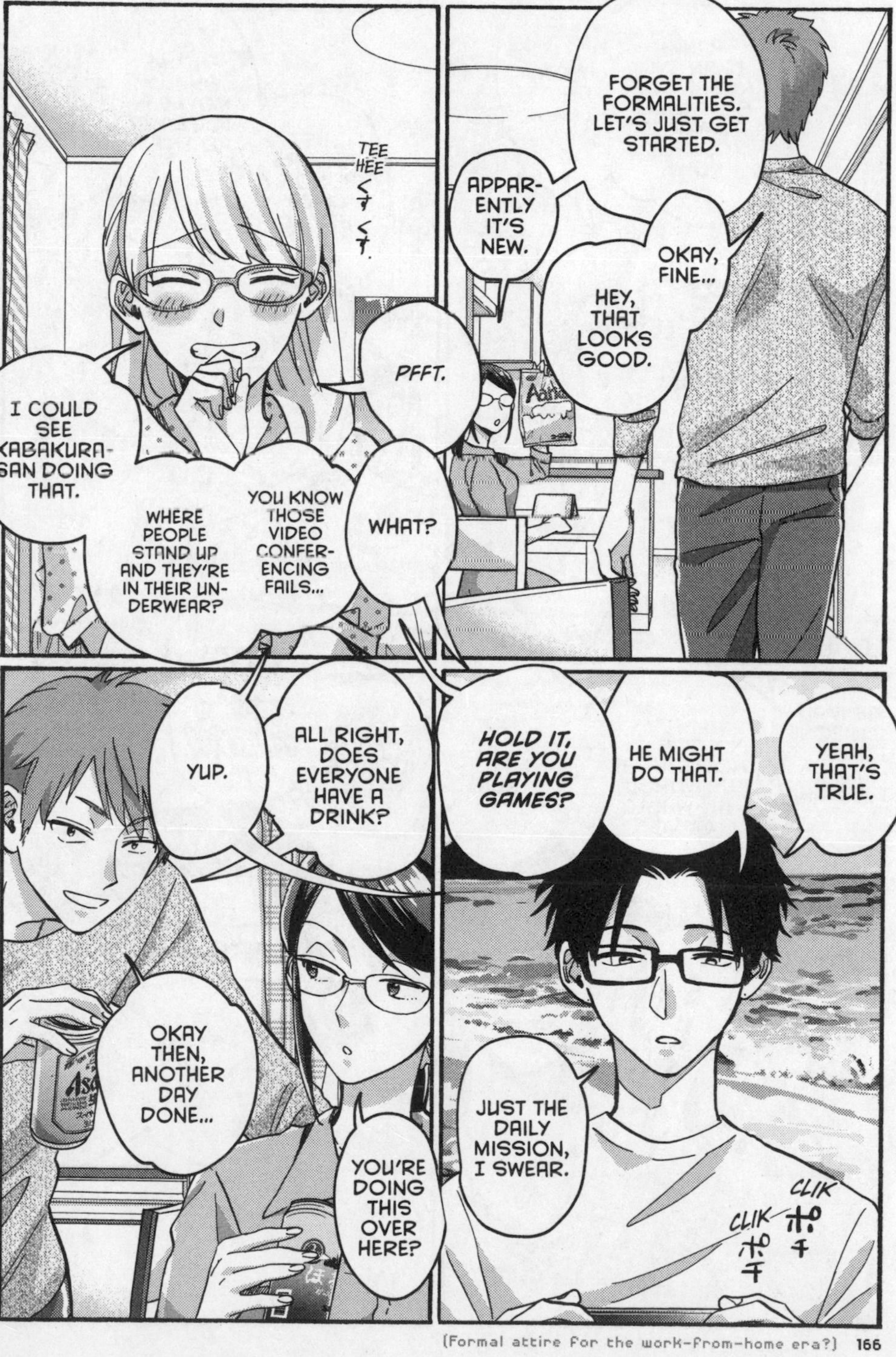

FORGET THE FORMALITIES. LET'S JUST GET STARTED.
OKAY, FINE...
HEY, THAT LOOKS GOOD.
APPARENTLY IT'S NEW.
PFFT.
TEE HEE くす くす
WHAT?
YOU KNOW THOSE VIDEO CONFERENCING FAILS...
WHERE PEOPLE STAND UP AND THEY'RE IN THEIR UNDERWEAR?
I COULD SEE KABAKURA-SAN DOING THAT.
YEAH, THAT'S TRUE.
HE MIGHT DO THAT.
HOLD IT, ARE YOU PLAYING GAMES?
JUST THE DAILY MISSION, I SWEAR.
CLIK ポチ
CLIK ポチ
ALL RIGHT, DOES EVERYONE HAVE A DRINK?
YUP.
OKAY THEN, ANOTHER DAY DONE...
YOU'RE DOING THIS OVER HERE?

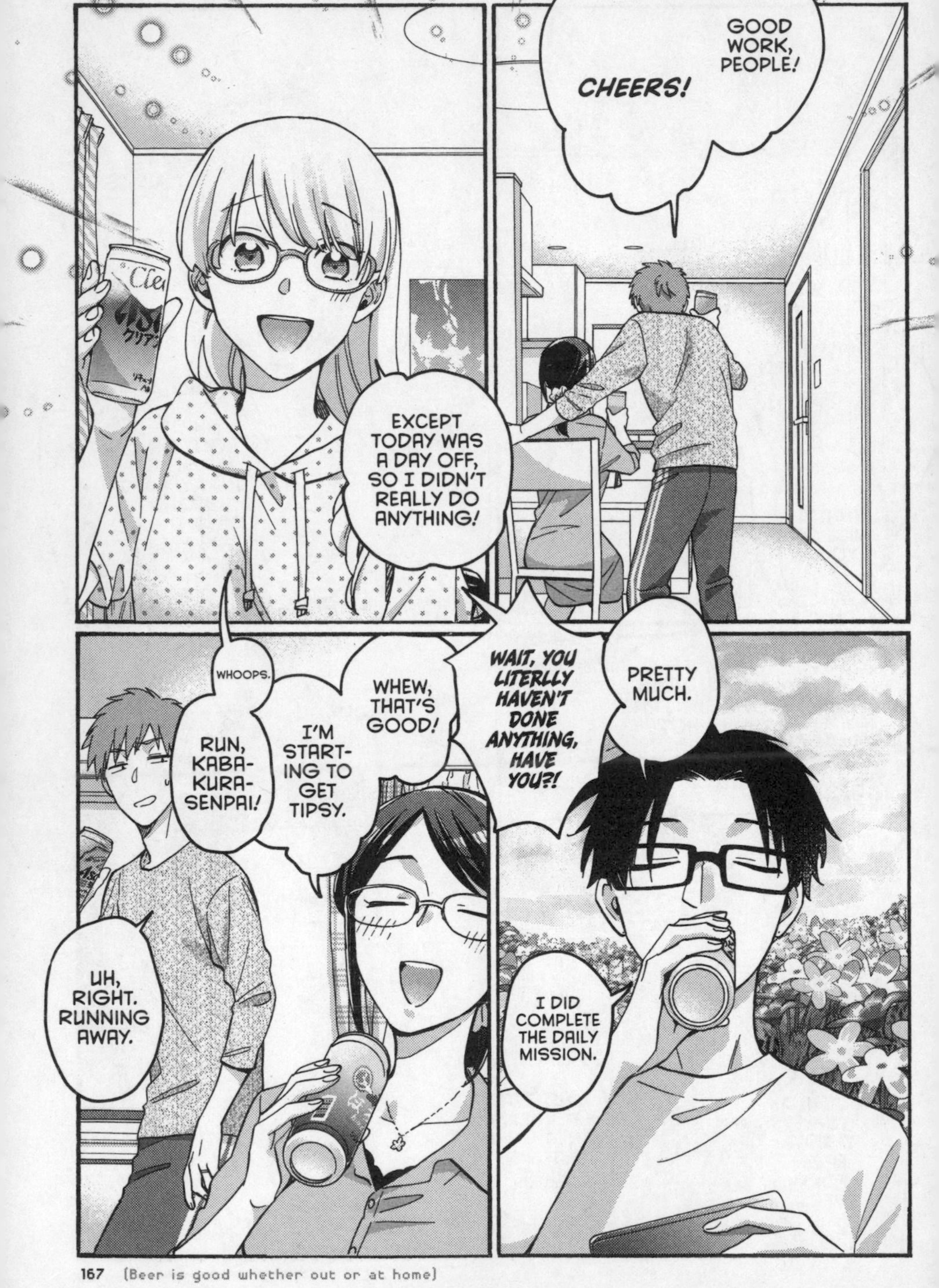
GOOD WORK, PEOPLE!
CHEERS!
EXCEPT TODAY WAS A DAY OFF, SO I DIDN'T REALLY DO ANYTHING!
WAIT, YOU LITERLLY HAVEN'T DONE ANYTHING, HAVE YOU?!
PRETTY MUCH.
I DID COMPLETE THE DAILY MISSION.
WHEW, THAT'S GOOD!
I'M STARTING TO GET TIPSY.
RUN, KABAKURA-SENPAI!
WHOOPS.
UH, RIGHT. RUNNING AWAY.

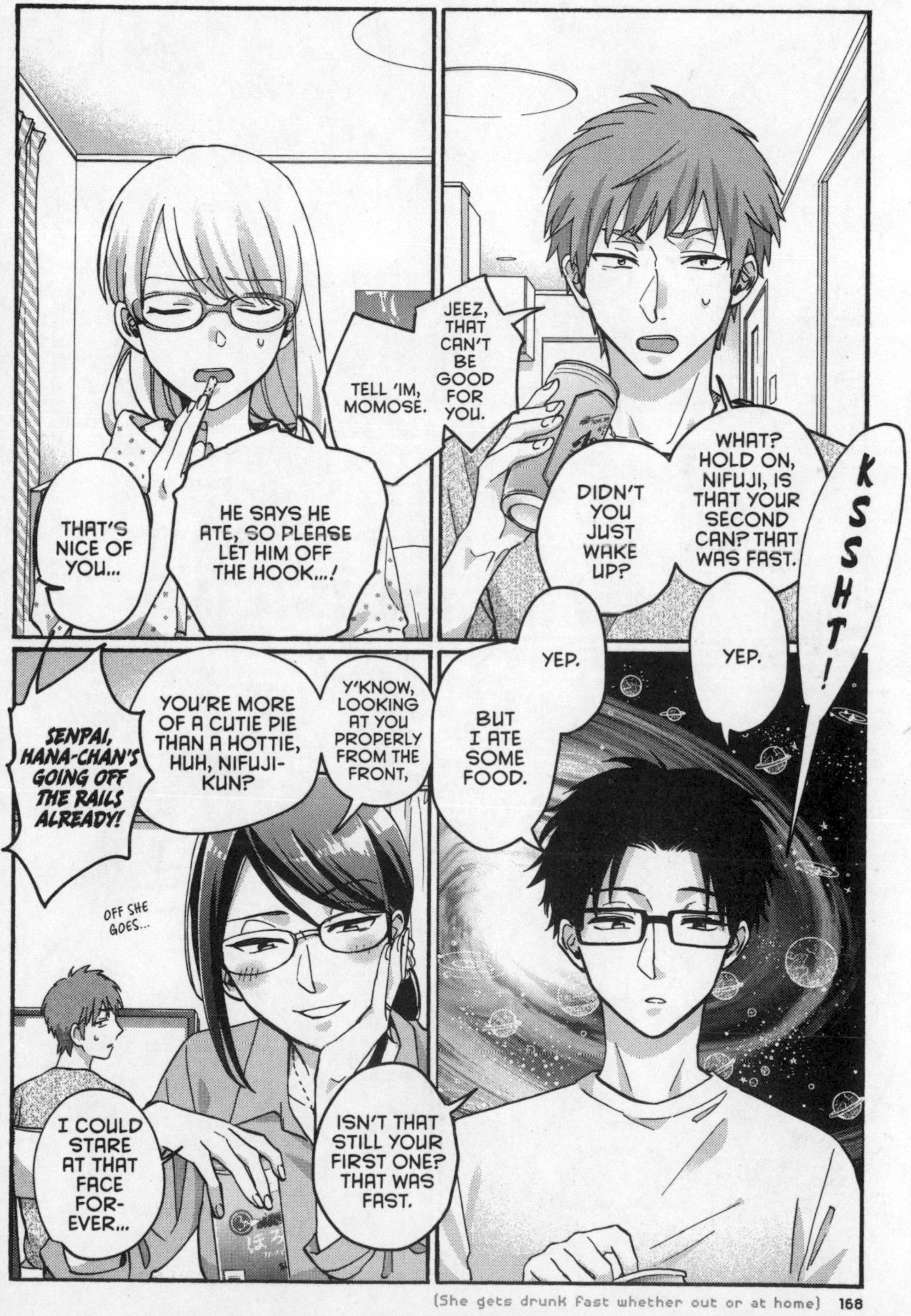
WHAT? HOLD ON, NIFUJI, IS THAT YOUR SECOND CAN? THAT WAS FAST.
DIDN'T YOU JUST WAKE UP?
JEEZ, THAT CAN'T BE GOOD FOR YOU.
TELL 'IM, MOMOSE.
HE SAYS HE ATE, SO PLEASE LET HIM OFF THE HOOK...!
THAT'S NICE OF YOU...
KSSHT!
YEP.
YEP.
BUT I ATE SOME FOOD.
Y'KNOW, LOOKING AT YOU PROPERLY FROM THE FRONT,
YOU'RE MORE OF A CUTIE PIE THAN A HOTTIE, HUH, NIFUJI-KUN?
SENPAI, HANA-CHAN'S GOING OFF THE RAILS ALREADY!
OFF SHE GOES...
ISN'T THAT STILL YOUR FIRST ONE? THAT WAS FAST.
I COULD STARE AT THAT FACE FOR-EVER...

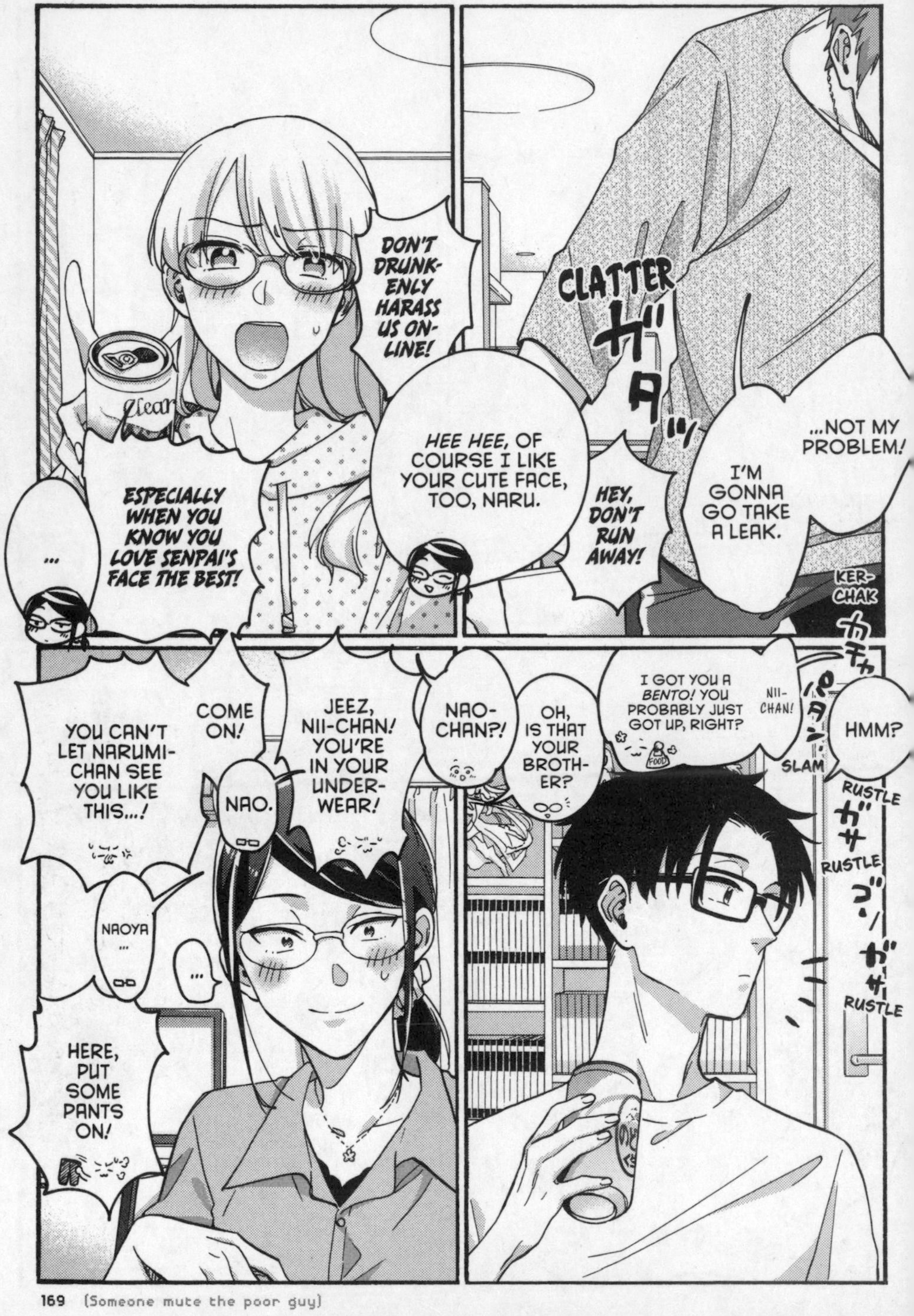
CLATTER
...NOT MY PROBLEM!
I'M GONNA GO TAKE A LEAK.
HEY, DON'T RUN AWAY!
DON'T DRUNK-ENLY HARASS US ON-LINE!
HEE HEE, OF COURSE I LIKE YOUR CUTE FACE, TOO, NARU.
ESPECIALLY WHEN YOU KNOW YOU LOVE SENPAI'S FACE THE BEST!
...
KER-CHAK
SLAM
HMM?
NII-CHAN!
I GOT YOU A BENTO! YOU PROBABLY JUST GOT UP, RIGHT?
OH, IS THAT YOUR BROTHER?
NAO-CHAN?!
RUSTLE
RUSTLE
RUSTLE
JEEZ, NII-CHAN! YOU'RE IN YOUR UNDER-WEAR!
COME ON!
NAO.
YOU CAN'T LET NARUMI-CHAN SEE YOU LIKE THIS...!
NAOYA ...
...
HERE, PUT SOME PANTS ON!

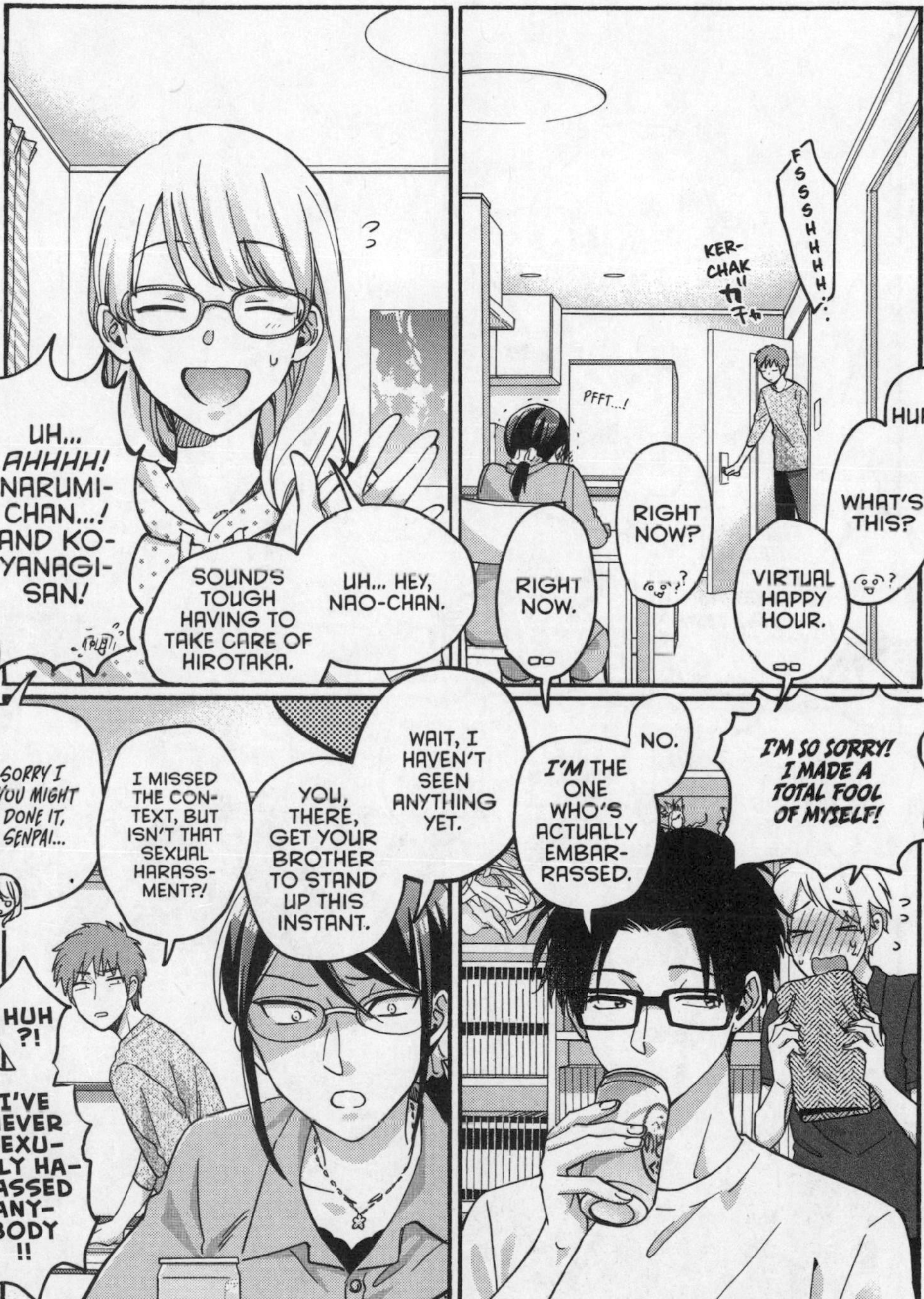
FSSSHHHH...
KER-CHAK
ガチャ
HUH?
WHAT'S THIS?
PFFT...!
VIRTUAL HAPPY HOUR.
RIGHT NOW?
RIGHT NOW.
UH... HEY, NAO-CHAN.
SOUNDS TOUGH HAVING TO TAKE CARE OF HIROTAKA.
UH... AHHHH! NARUMI-CHAN...! AND KO-YANAGI-SAN!
I'M SO SORRY! I MADE A TOTAL FOOL OF MYSELF!
NO.
I'M THE ONE WHO'S ACTUALLY EMBARRASSED.
NO PANTS
WAIT, I HAVEN'T SEEN ANYTHING YET.
YOU, THERE, GET YOUR BROTHER TO STAND UP THIS INSTANT.
I MISSED THE CONTEXT, BUT ISN'T THAT SEXUAL HARASSMENT?!
I'M SORRY I SAID YOU MIGHT HAVE DONE IT, TOO, SENPAI...
NO PANTS...
HUH?!
I'VE NEVER SEXUALLY HARASSED ANYBODY!!

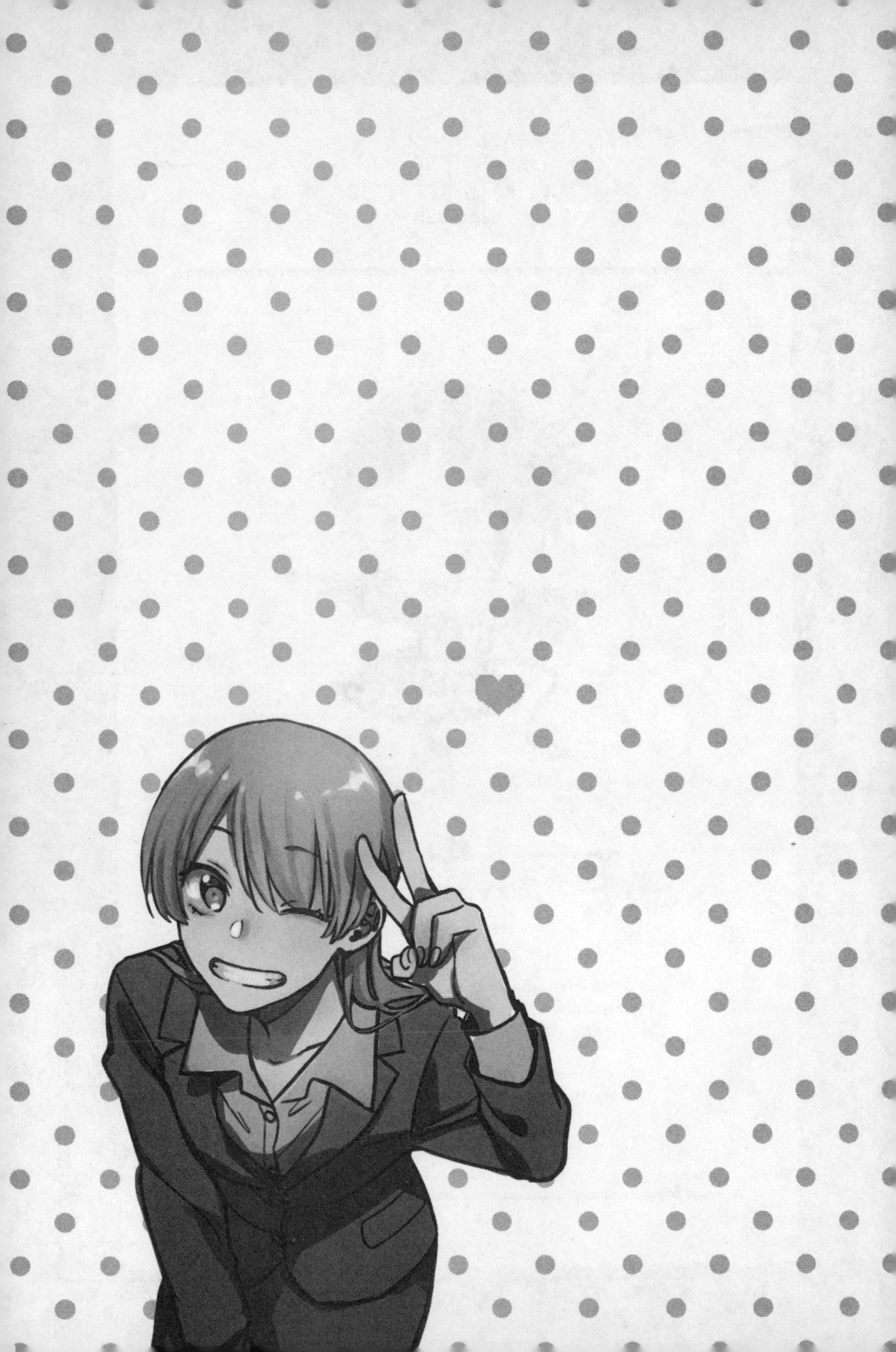

DEVIL

Devil

ハナコ

Hanako

A devil who gives free rein to her desires.
Once she finds a kindred spirit, she'll stop at nothing to
drag that person into the swamp with her.

She fights all the time with Kabakura, but apparently
she finally got him to be her mating partner recently.

C H A R A C T E R S IV

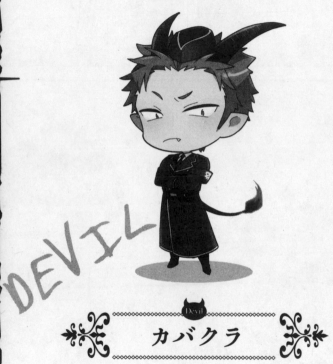

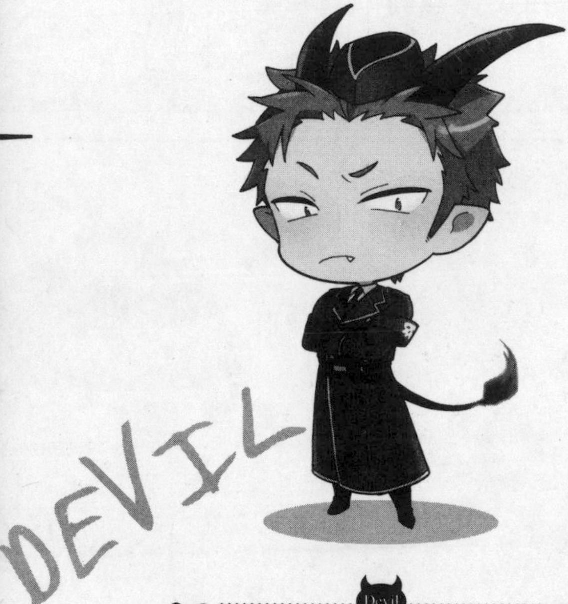
DEVIL

Devil

カバクラ

Kabakura

The conscience of the demon realm.
Valuing order and discipline, he's much more of an angel than a certain other angel we know, but God apparently made him a devil because his face was too scary.

An intense argument with Hanako somehow ended up with him agreeing to be mating partners, but he figures, "Ah, well."

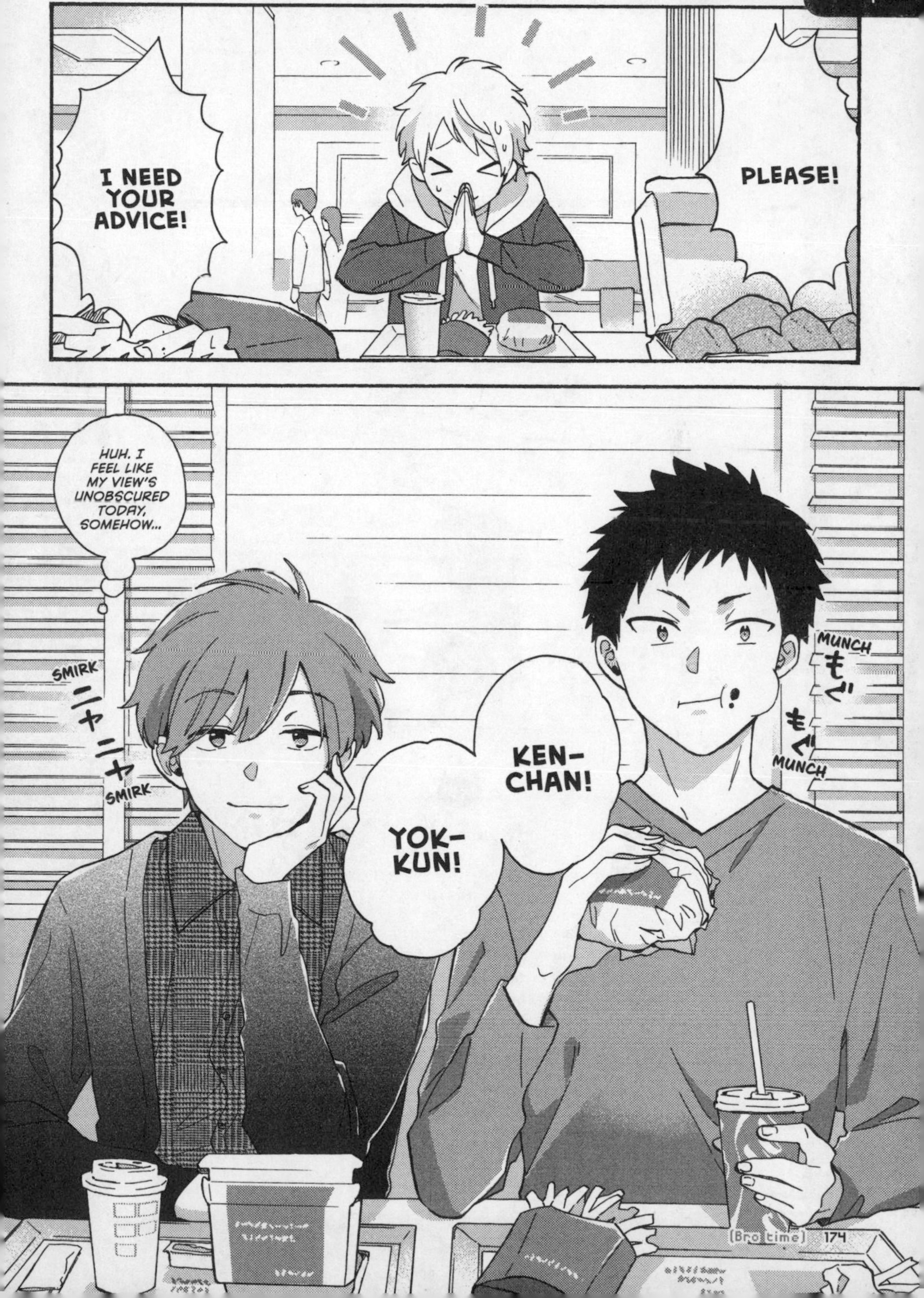
PLEASE!
I NEED YOUR ADVICE!
HUH. I FEEL LIKE MY VIEW'S UNOBSCURED TODAY, SOMEHOW...
MUNCH もぐ
もぐ MUNCH
KEN-CHAN!
SMIRK ニヤ
ニヤ SMIRK
YOK-KUN!

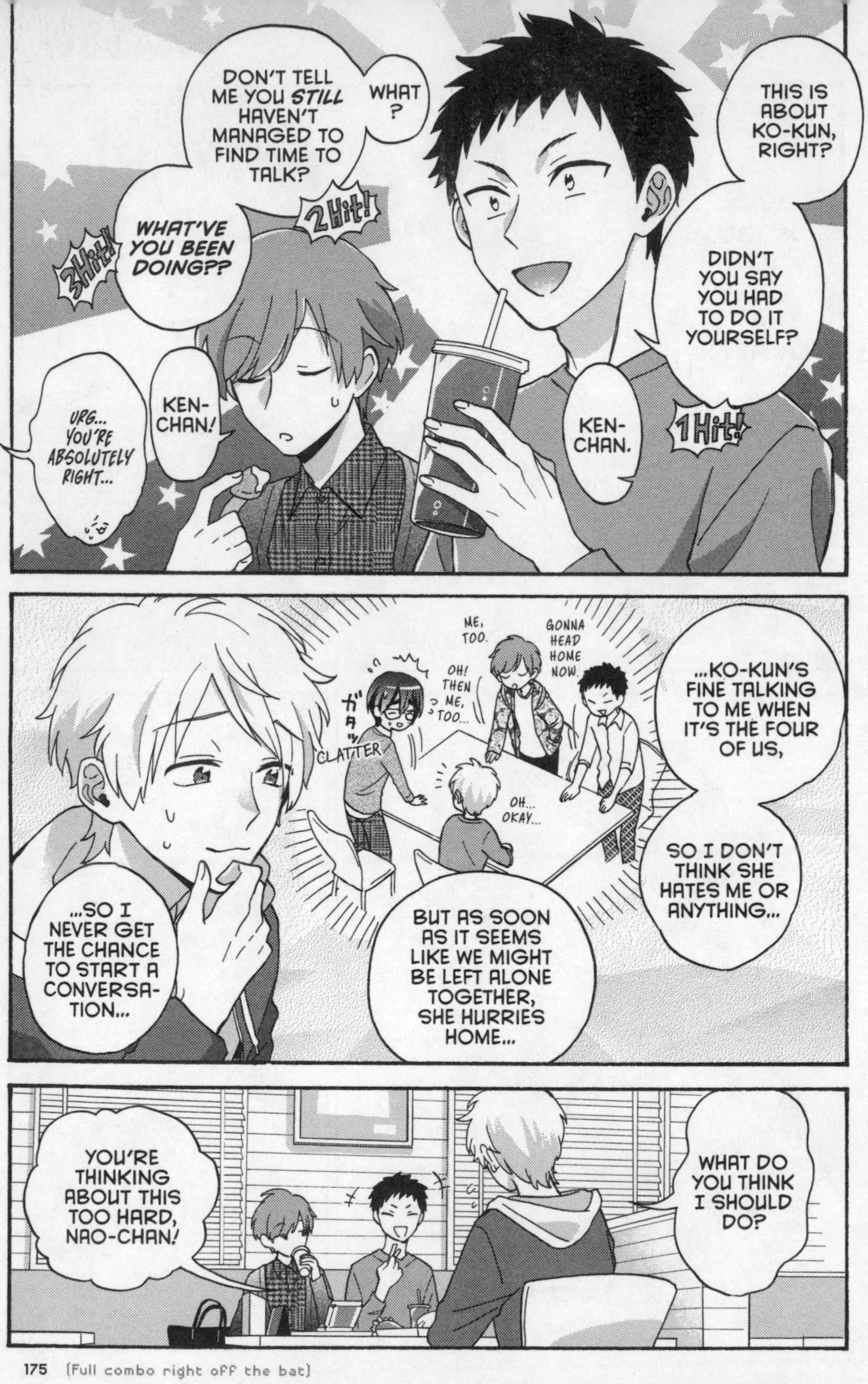
THIS IS ABOUT KO-KUN, RIGHT?
DIDN'T YOU SAY YOU HAD TO DO IT YOURSELF?
KEN-CHAN.
1 Hit!
WHAT?
DON'T TELL ME YOU STILL HAVEN'T MANAGED TO FIND TIME TO TALK?
2 Hit!
WHAT'VE YOU BEEN DOING??
3 Hit!
KEN-CHAN!
URG... YOU'RE ABSOLUTELY RIGHT...
...KO-KUN'S FINE TALKING TO ME WHEN IT'S THE FOUR OF US,
SO I DON'T THINK SHE HATES ME OR ANYTHING...
GONNA HEAD HOME NOW.
ME, TOO.
OH! THEN ME, TOO...
CLATTER
OH... OKAY...
BUT AS SOON AS IT SEEMS LIKE WE MIGHT BE LEFT ALONE TOGETHER, SHE HURRIES HOME...
...SO I NEVER GET THE CHANCE TO START A CONVERSATION...
WHAT DO YOU THINK I SHOULD DO?
YOU'RE THINKING ABOUT THIS TOO HARD, NAO-CHAN!

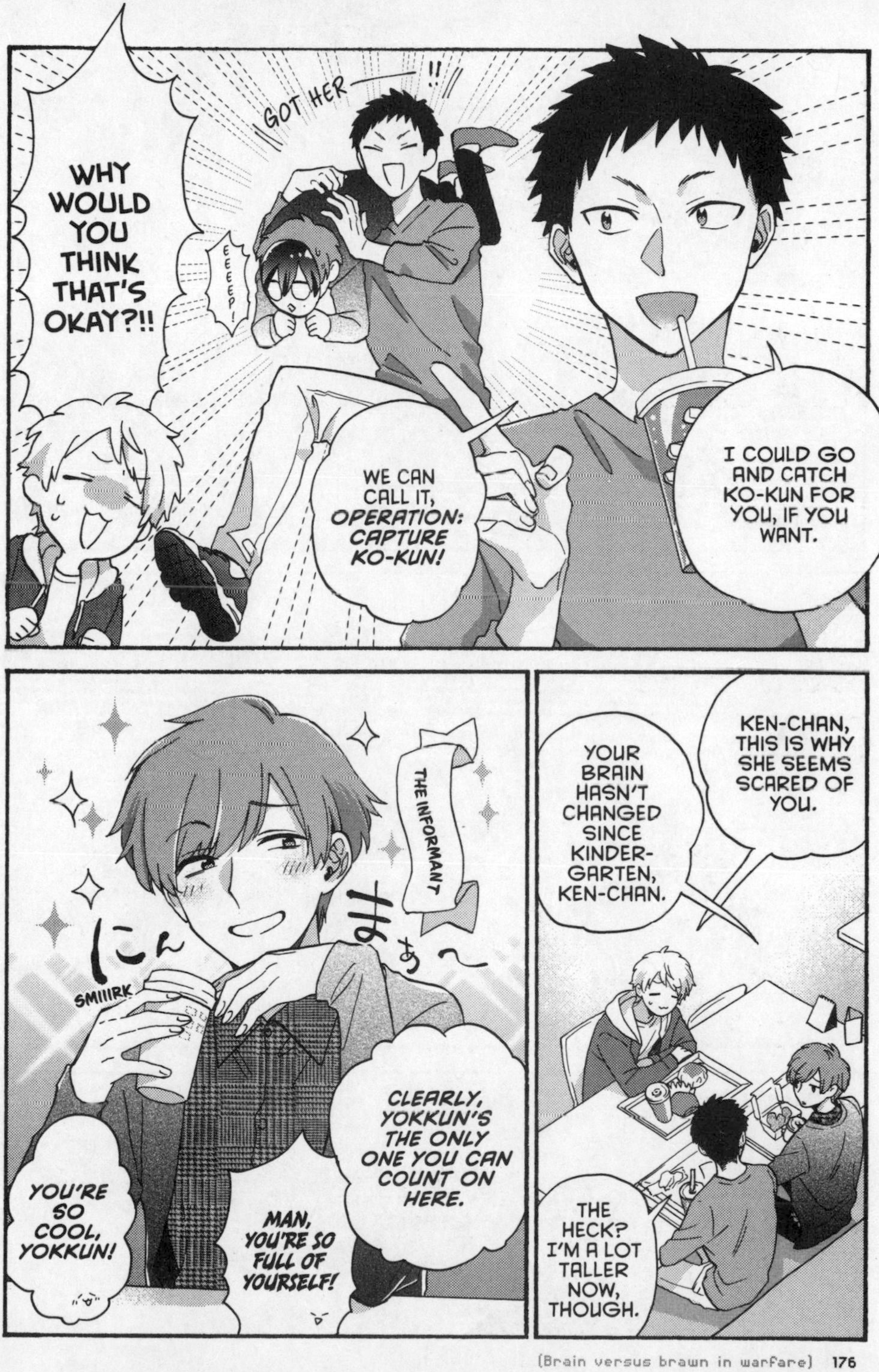

I COULD GO AND CATCH KO-KUN FOR YOU, IF YOU WANT.
WE CAN CALL IT, *OPERATION: CAPTURE KO-KUN!*
GOT HER——!!
EEEEP!
WHY WOULD YOU THINK THAT'S OKAY?!!
KEN-CHAN, THIS IS WHY SHE SEEMS SCARED OF YOU.
YOUR BRAIN HASN'T CHANGED SINCE KINDER-GARTEN, KEN-CHAN.
THE HECK? I'M A LOT TALLER NOW, THOUGH.
THE INFORMANT
まぁ〜
にん
SMIIIRK
CLEARLY, YOKKUN'S THE ONLY ONE YOU CAN COUNT ON HERE.
MAN, YOU'RE SO FULL OF YOURSELF!
YOU'RE SO COOL, YOKKUN!

(Brain versus brawn in warfare)

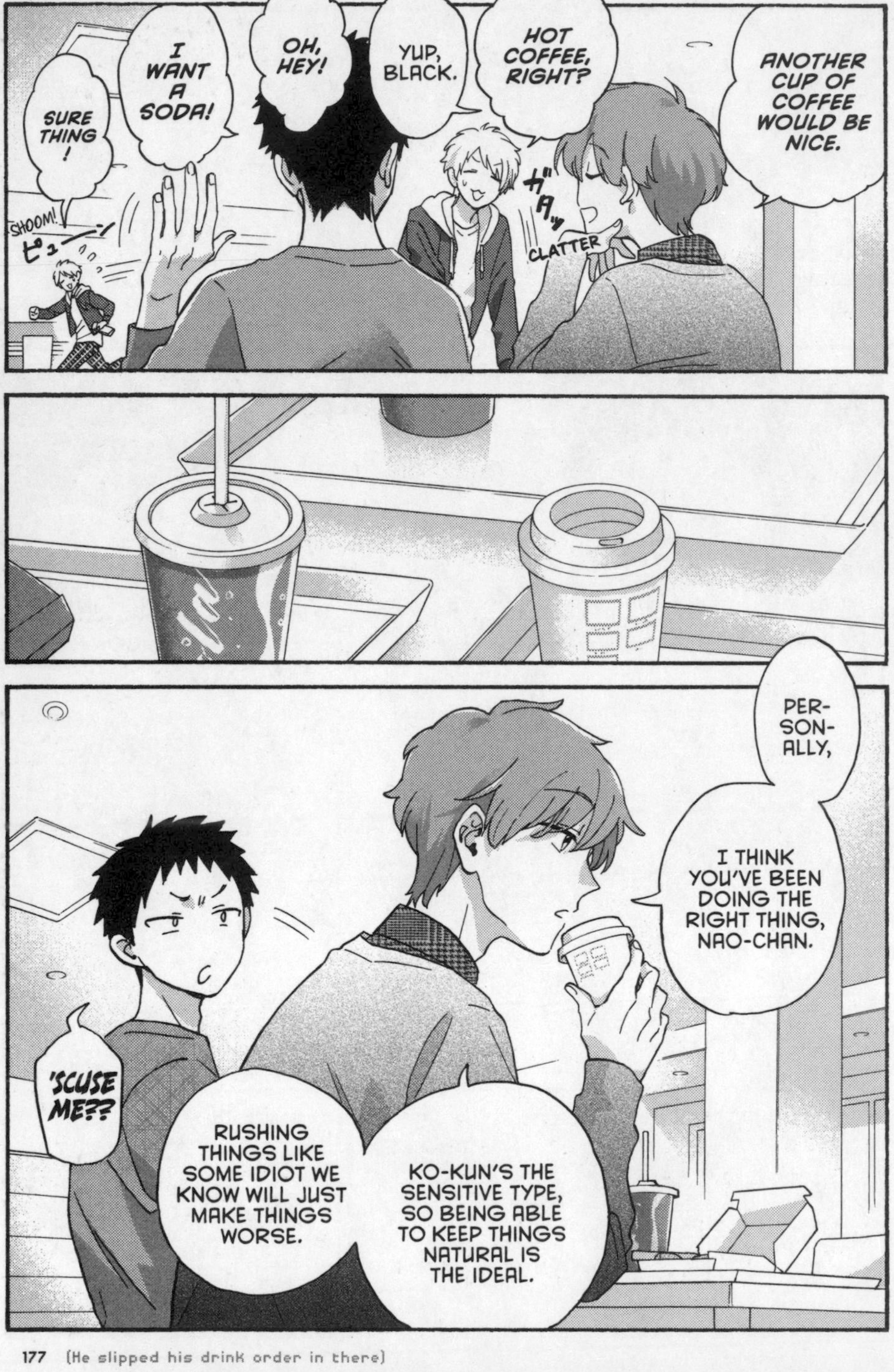
ANOTHER CUP OF COFFEE WOULD BE NICE.
HOT COFFEE, RIGHT?
ガタッ
CLATTER
YUP, BLACK.
OH, HEY!
I WANT A SODA!
SURE THING!
SHOOM!
ピューーッ
PER-SON-ALLY,
I THINK YOU'VE BEEN DOING THE RIGHT THING, NAO-CHAN.
KO-KUN'S THE SENSITIVE TYPE, SO BEING ABLE TO KEEP THINGS NATURAL IS THE IDEAL.
RUSHING THINGS LIKE SOME IDIOT WE KNOW WILL JUST MAKE THINGS WORSE.
'SCUSE ME??

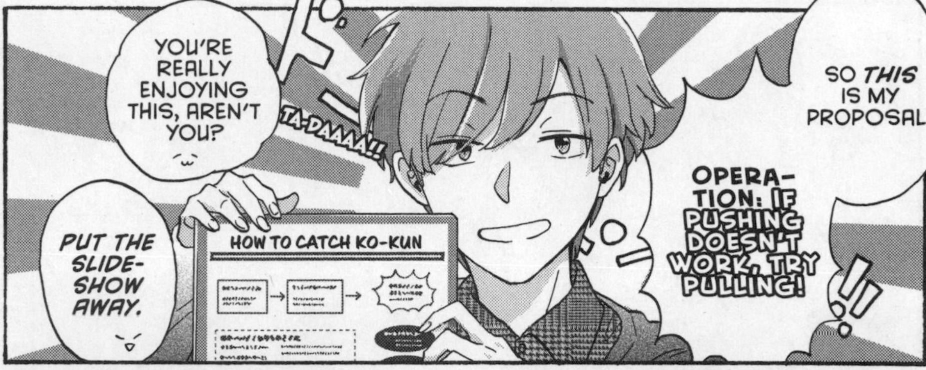
SO THIS IS MY PROPOSAL!
OPERATION: IF PUSHING DOESN'T WORK, TRY PULLING!
TA-DAAAA!!
HOW TO CATCH KO-KUN
YOU'RE REALLY ENJOYING THIS, AREN'T YOU?
PUT THE SLIDE-SHOW AWAY.

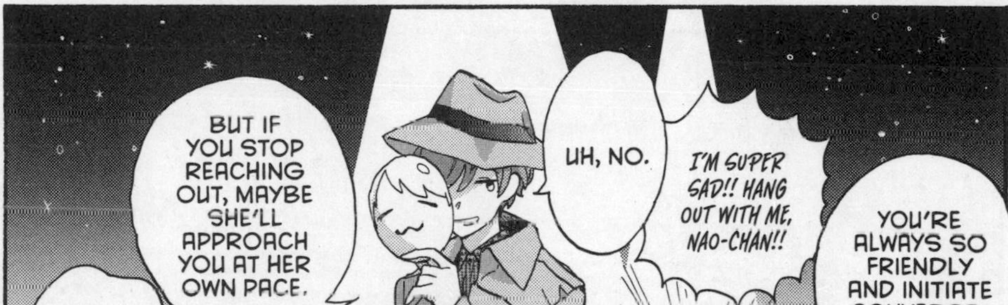
YOU'RE ALWAYS SO FRIENDLY AND INITIATE CONVERSA-TION.
HOW DO YOU THINK KO-KUN WOULD REACT IF YOU SUDDENLY STOPPED?
UH, NO.
I'M SUPER SAD!! HANG OUT WITH ME, NAO-CHAN!!
BUT IF YOU STOP REACHING OUT, MAYBE SHE'LL APPROACH YOU AT HER OWN PACE.
M-MAYBE...?

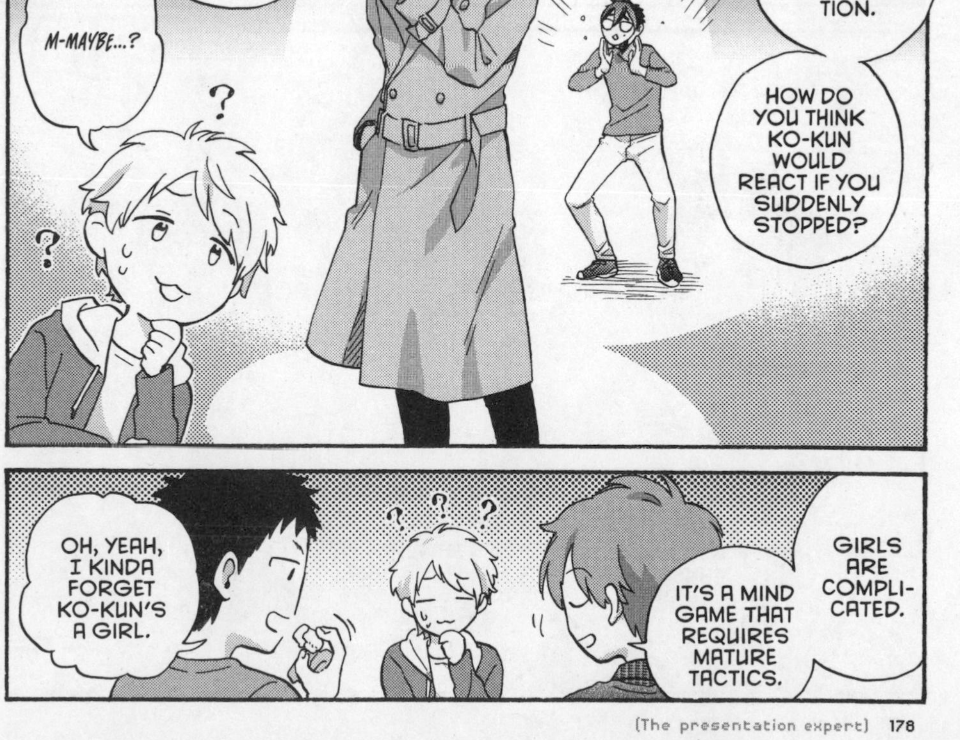
GIRLS ARE COMPLI-CATED.
IT'S A MIND GAME THAT REQUIRES MATURE TACTICS.
OH, YEAH, I KINDA FORGET KO-KUN'S A GIRL.

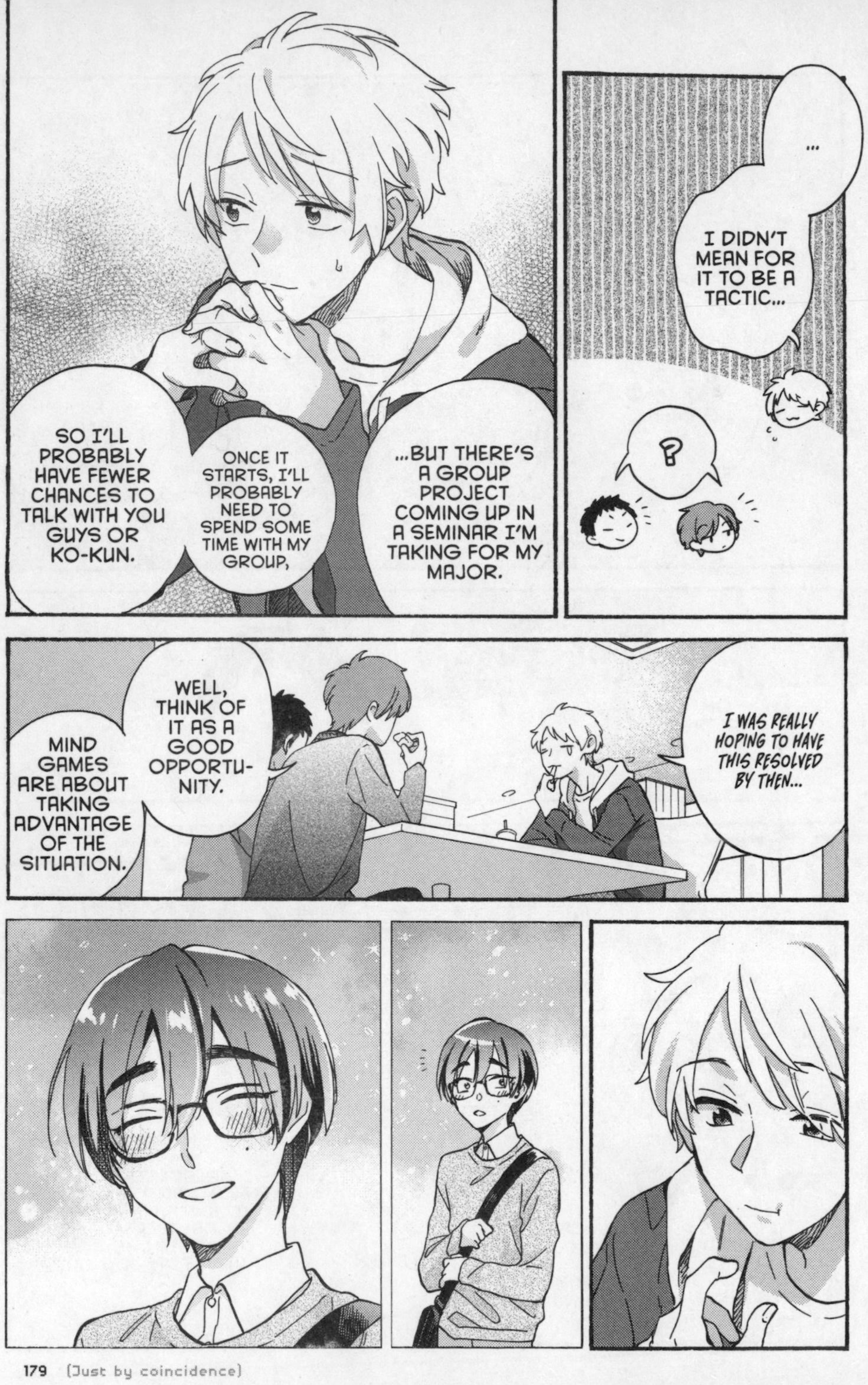
...
I DIDN'T MEAN FOR IT TO BE A TACTIC...
?
...BUT THERE'S A GROUP PROJECT COMING UP IN A SEMINAR I'M TAKING FOR MY MAJOR.
ONCE IT STARTS, I'LL PROBABLY NEED TO SPEND SOME TIME WITH MY GROUP,
SO I'LL PROBABLY HAVE FEWER CHANCES TO TALK WITH YOU GUYS OR KO-KUN.
I WAS REALLY HOPING TO HAVE THIS RESOLVED BY THEN...
WELL, THINK OF IT AS A GOOD OPPORTUNITY.
MIND GAMES ARE ABOUT TAKING ADVANTAGE OF THE SITUATION.

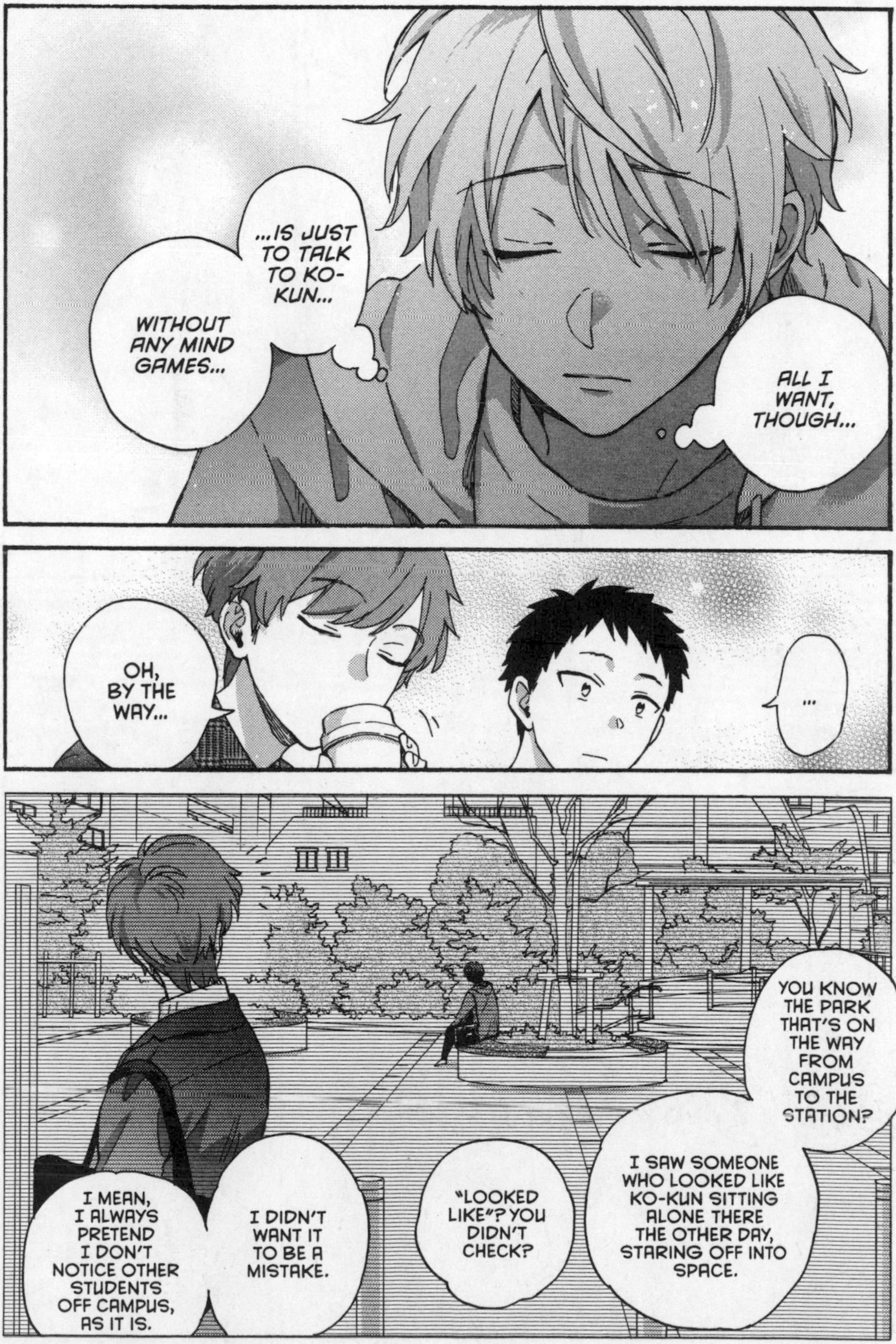
ALL I WANT, THOUGH...
...IS JUST TO TALK TO KO-KUN...
WITHOUT ANY MIND GAMES...
...
OH, BY THE WAY...
YOU KNOW THE PARK THAT'S ON THE WAY FROM CAMPUS TO THE STATION?
I SAW SOMEONE WHO LOOKED LIKE KO-KUN SITTING ALONE THERE THE OTHER DAY, STARING OFF INTO SPACE.
"LOOKED LIKE"? YOU DIDN'T CHECK?
I DIDN'T WANT IT TO BE A MISTAKE.
I MEAN, I ALWAYS PRETEND I DON'T NOTICE OTHER STUDENTS OFF CAMPUS, AS IT IS.

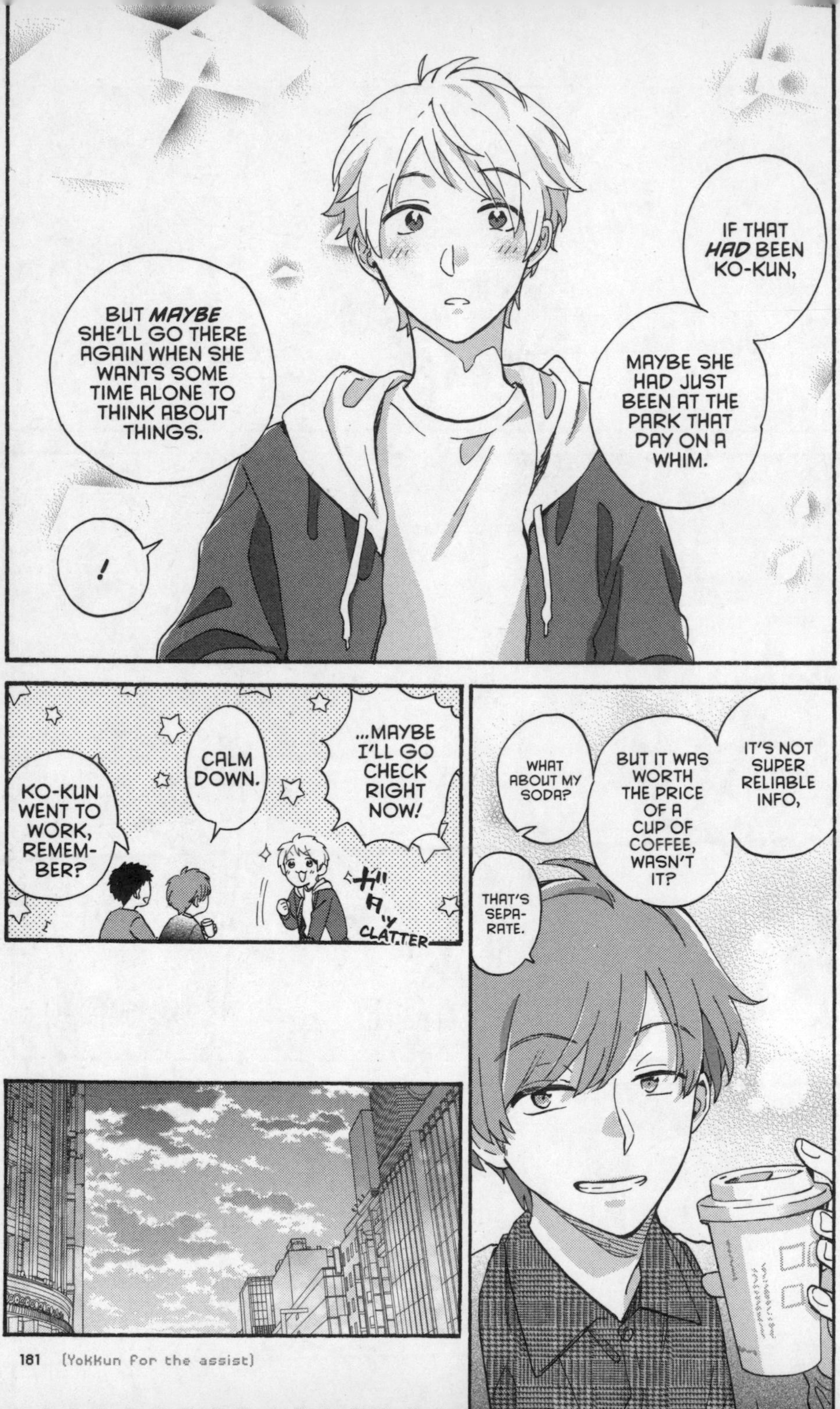
IF THAT *HAD* BEEN KO-KUN,
MAYBE SHE HAD JUST BEEN AT THE PARK THAT DAY ON A WHIM.
BUT *MAYBE* SHE'LL GO THERE AGAIN WHEN SHE WANTS SOME TIME ALONE TO THINK ABOUT THINGS.
!
IT'S NOT SUPER RELIABLE INFO,
BUT IT WAS WORTH THE PRICE OF A CUP OF COFFEE, WASN'T IT?
WHAT ABOUT MY SODA?
THAT'S SEPA-RATE.
...MAYBE I'LL GO CHECK RIGHT NOW!
CALM DOWN.
KO-KUN WENT TO WORK, REMEM-BER?
CLATTER

 (YoKKun for the assist)

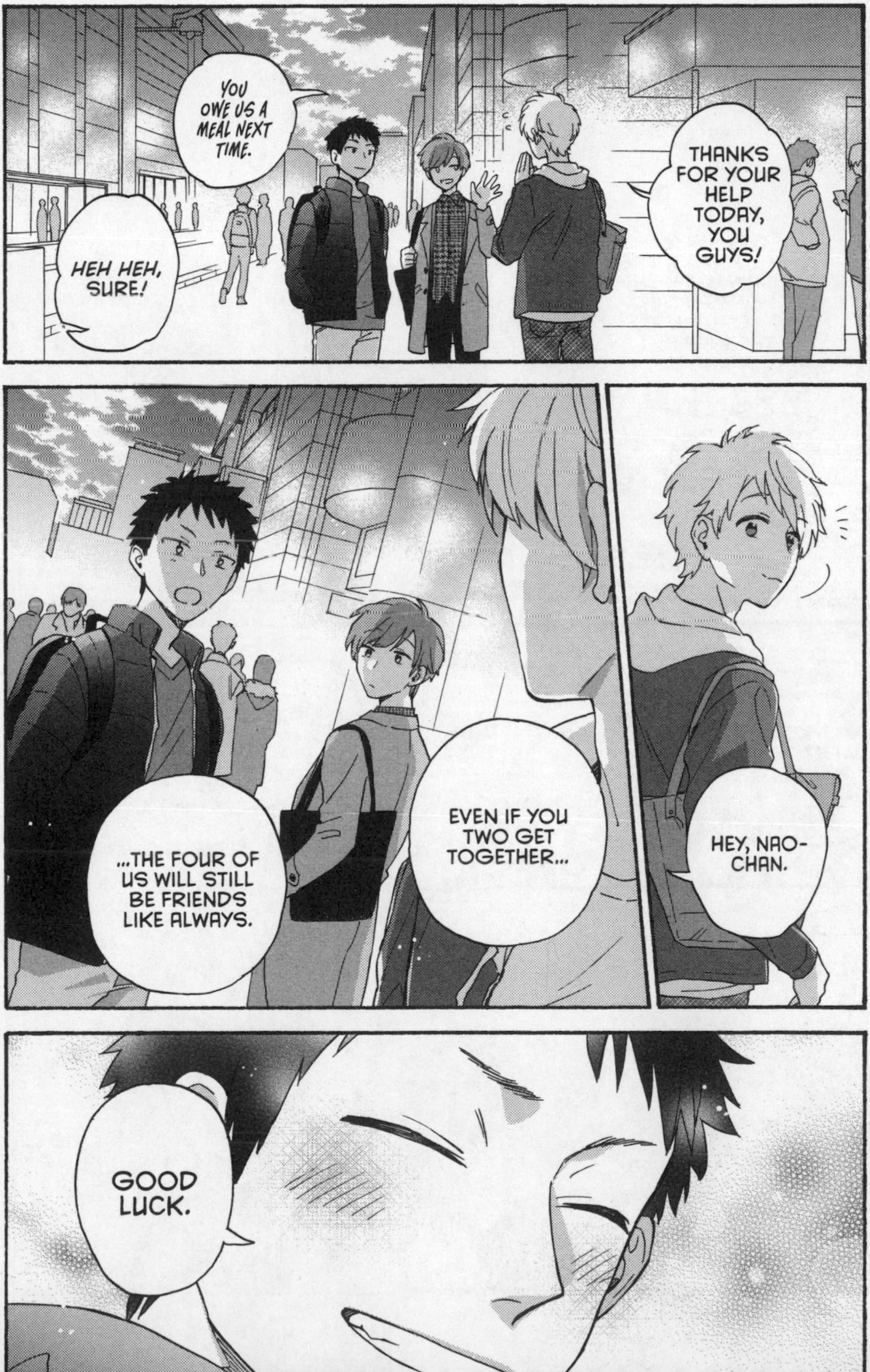
THANKS FOR YOUR HELP TODAY, YOU GUYS!
YOU OWE US A MEAL NEXT TIME.
HEH HEH, SURE!
HEY, NAO-CHAN.
EVEN IF YOU TWO GET TOGETHER...
...THE FOUR OF US WILL STILL BE FRIENDS LIKE ALWAYS.
GOOD LUCK.

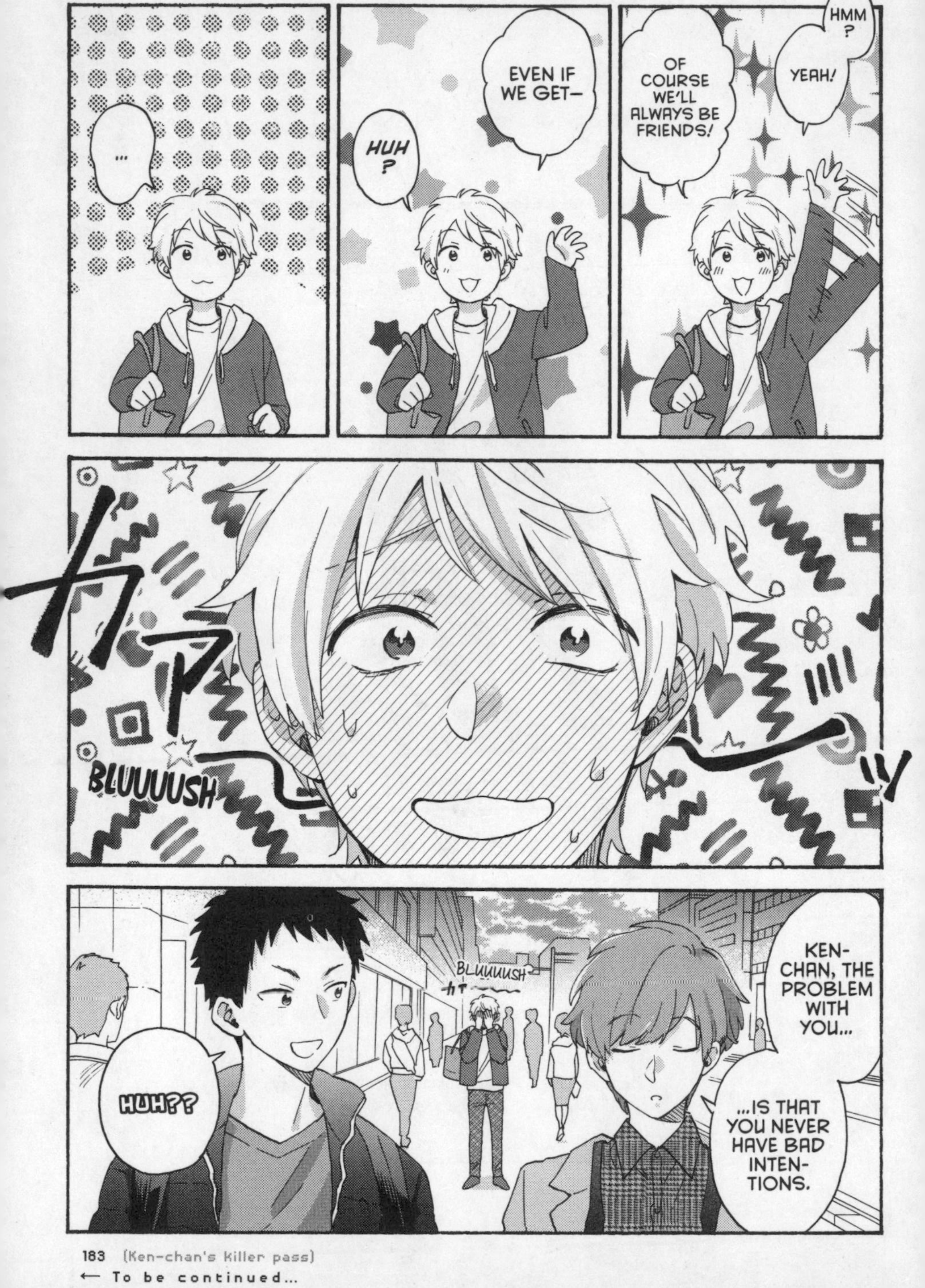
HMM?
YEAH!
OF COURSE WE'LL ALWAYS BE FRIENDS!
EVEN IF WE GET—
HUH?
...
カァーッ
BLUUUUSH
KEN-CHAN, THE PROBLEM WITH YOU...
BLUUUUSH
カァ
...IS THAT YOU NEVER HAVE BAD INTEN-TIONS.
HUH??

183 (Ken-chan's killer pass)

← To be continued...

CHARAVCTERS

コウ

Ko

She feels guilty that she can't control her desire to play
games even though she's an angel.

(Meanwhile, a certain other angel doesn't care at all
about similar urges.)

For some reason, Naoel has taken to her and drags her
off to have fun, but she secretly enjoys it.

CHARACTERS VI

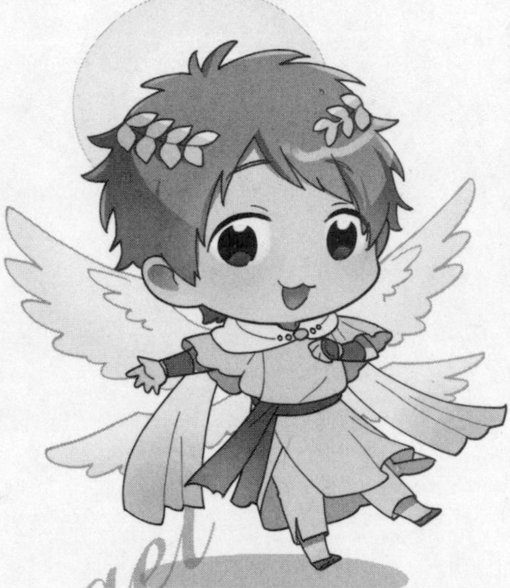

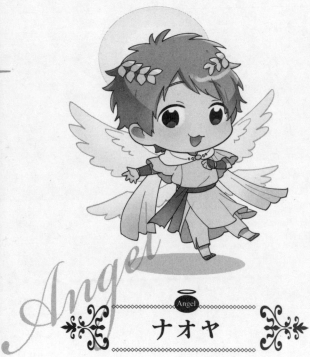

Angel

ナオヤ

Naoya

Somebody dubbed him "the Archangel Naoel."

He's so innocent, it's unbelievable.

Actually, "innocent" might not be the right word. It's entirely possible that he's just an airhead.

He likes playing games against Ko, but he's never going to win in a million years.

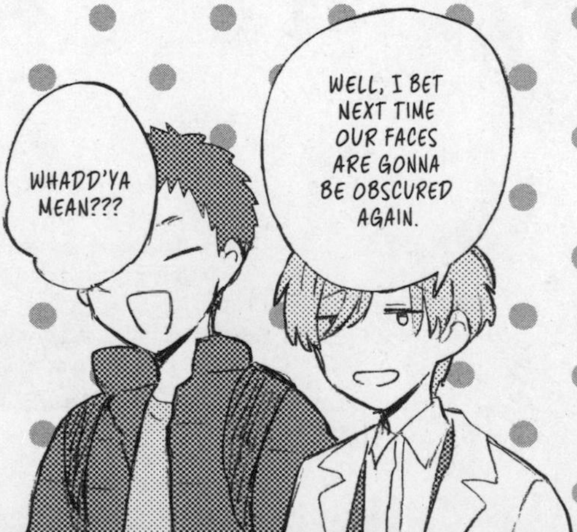
WELL, I BET NEXT TIME OUR FACES ARE GONNA BE OBSCURED AGAIN.
WHADD'YA MEAN???

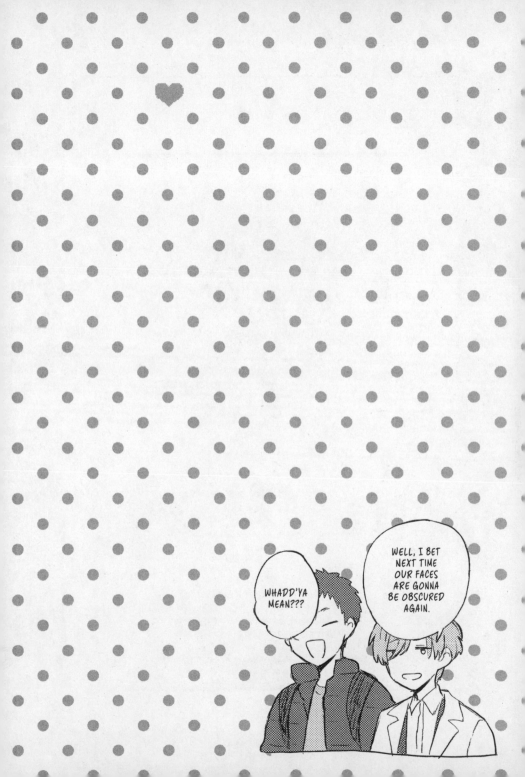

Episode.... 74

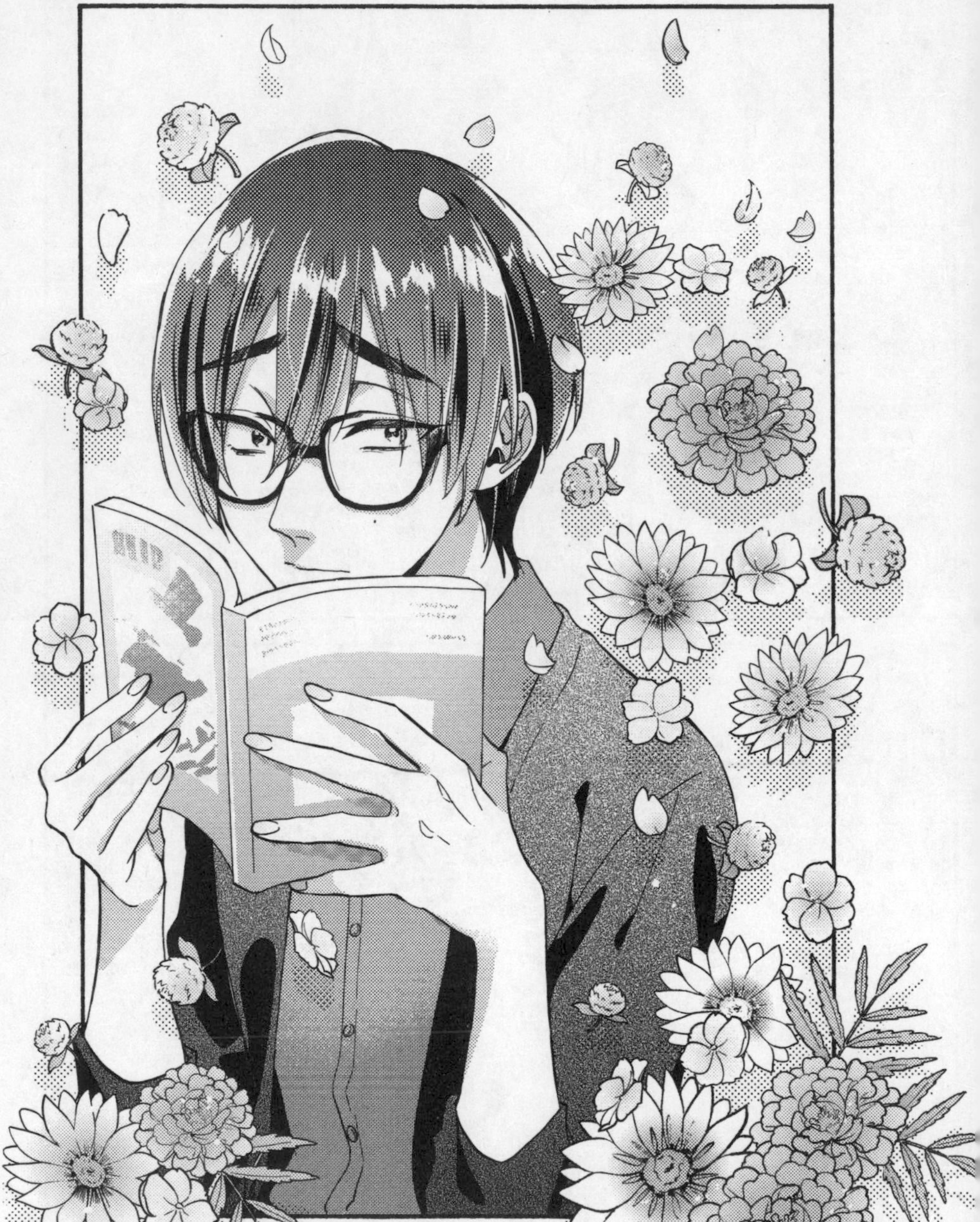

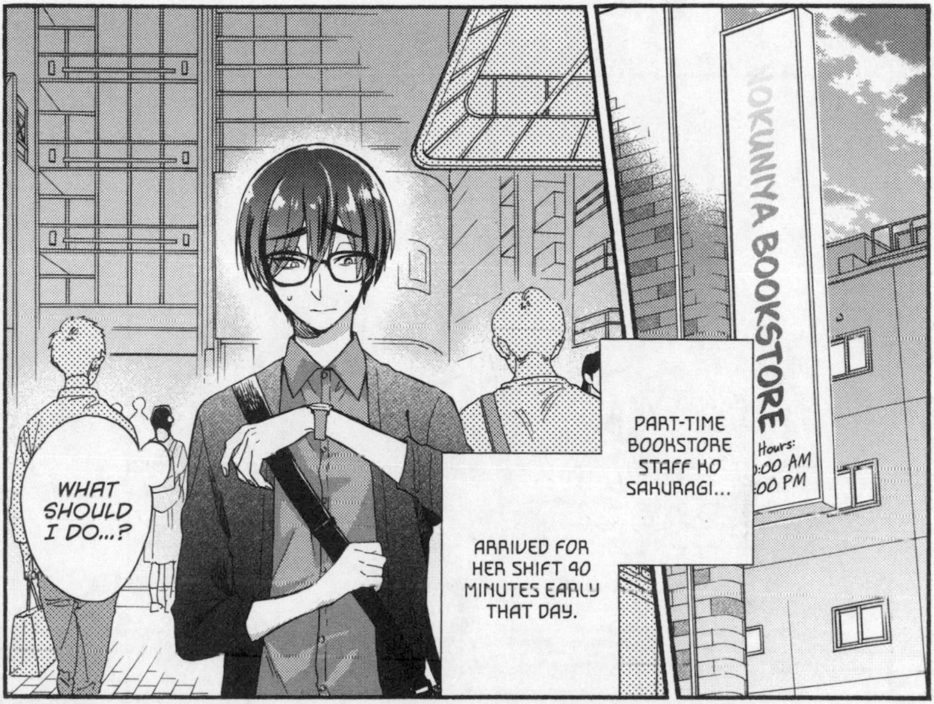
NOKUNIYA BOOKSTORE
PART-TIME BOOKSTORE STAFF KO SAKURAGI...
ARRIVED FOR HER SHIFT 40 MINUTES EARLY THAT DAY.
WHAT SHOULD I DO...?

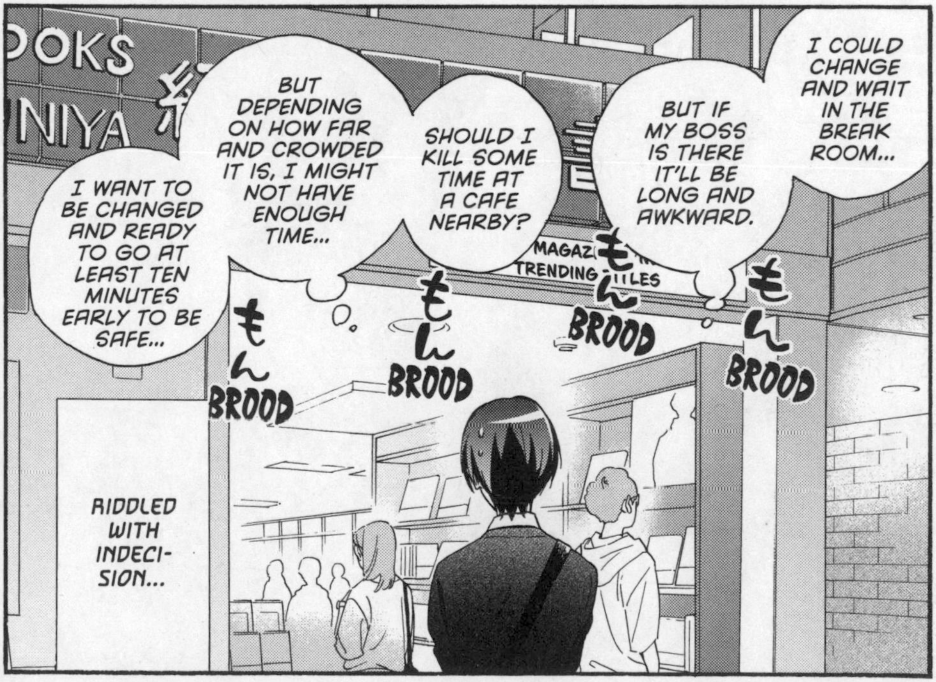
I COULD CHANGE AND WAIT IN THE BREAK ROOM...
BUT IF MY BOSS IS THERE IT'LL BE LONG AND AWKWARD.
SHOULD I KILL SOME TIME AT A CAFE NEARBY?
BUT DEPENDING ON HOW FAR AND CROWDED IT IS, I MIGHT NOT HAVE ENOUGH TIME...
I WANT TO BE CHANGED AND READY TO GO AT LEAST TEN MINUTES EARLY TO BE SAFE...
もん BROOD
もん BROOD
もん BROOD
もん BROOD
RIDDLED WITH INDECISION...

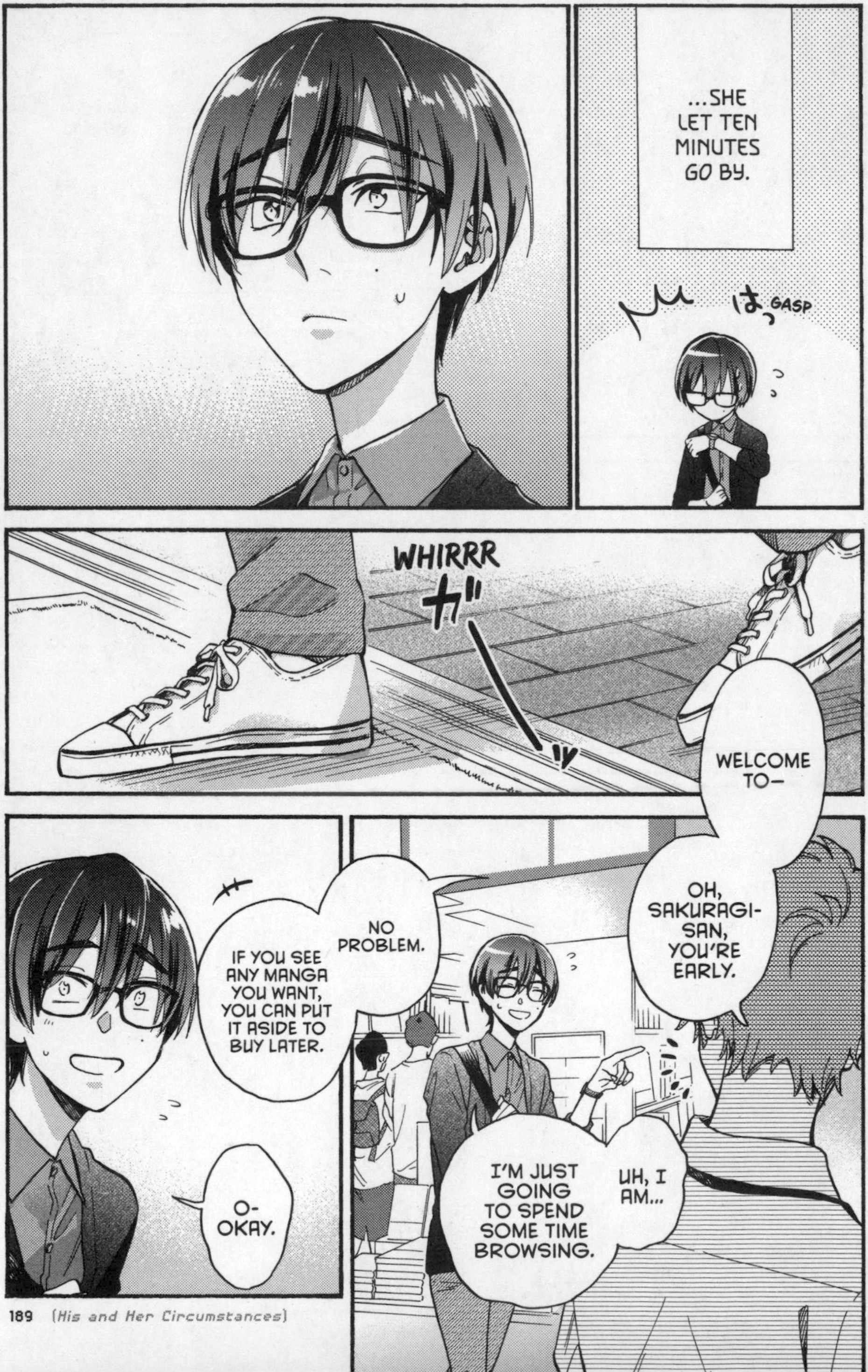
...SHE LET TEN MINUTES GO BY.
は, GASP
WHIRRR
ガ
WELCOME TO—
OH, SAKURAGI-SAN, YOU'RE EARLY.
UH, I AM...
I'M JUST GOING TO SPEND SOME TIME BROWSING.
NO PROBLEM.
IF YOU SEE ANY MANGA YOU WANT, YOU CAN PUT IT ASIDE TO BUY LATER.
O-OKAY.

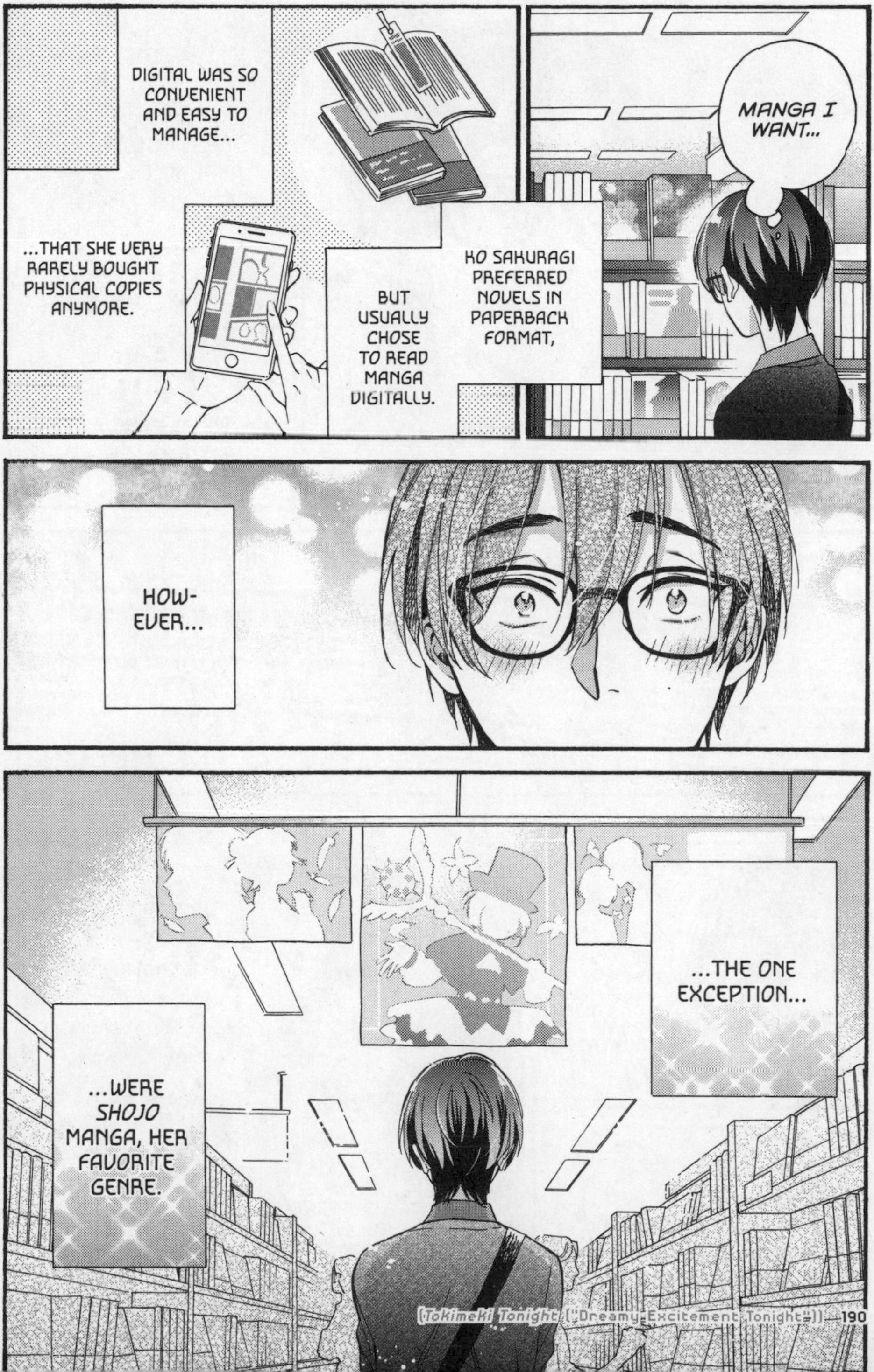
MANGA I WANT...
KO SAKURAGI PREFERRED NOVELS IN PAPERBACK FORMAT,
BUT USUALLY CHOSE TO READ MANGA DIGITALLY.
DIGITAL WAS SO CONVENIENT AND EASY TO MANAGE...
...THAT SHE VERY RARELY BOUGHT PHYSICAL COPIES ANYMORE.
HOW-EVER...
...THE ONE EXCEPTION...
...WERE *SHOJO* MANGA, HER FAVORITE GENRE.
(Tokimeki Tonight ("Dreamy Excitement Tonight"))—190

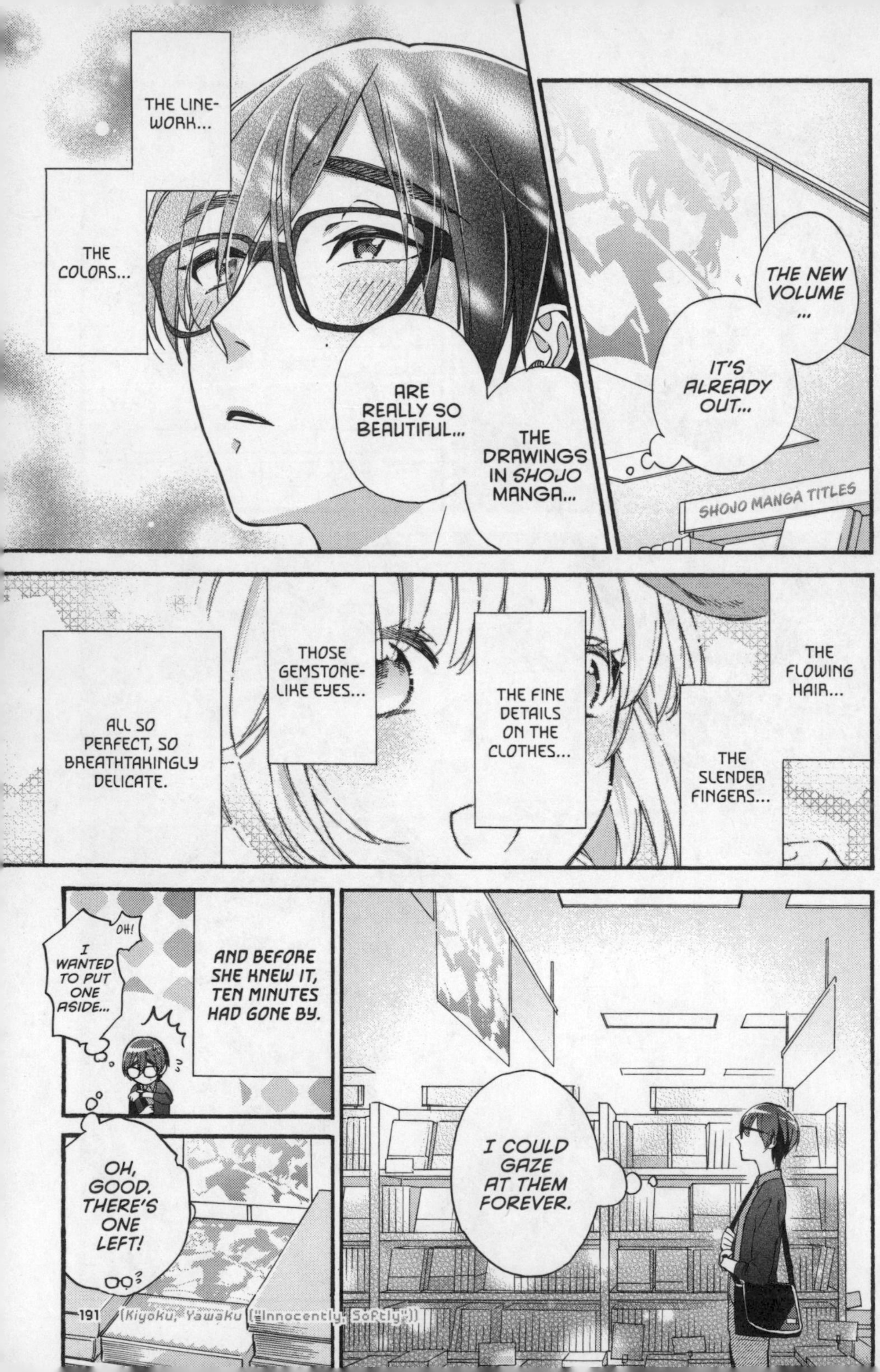
THE NEW VOLUME ...
IT'S ALREADY OUT...
SHOJO MANGA TITLES
THE DRAWINGS IN *SHOJO* MANGA...
ARE REALLY SO BEAUTIFUL...
THE LINE-WORK...
THE COLORS...
THE FLOWING HAIR...
THE SLENDER FINGERS...
THE FINE DETAILS ON THE CLOTHES...
THOSE GEMSTONE-LIKE EYES...
ALL SO PERFECT, SO BREATHTAKINGLY DELICATE.
I COULD GAZE AT THEM FOREVER.
AND BEFORE SHE KNEW IT, TEN MINUTES HAD GONE BY.
OH!
I WANTED TO PUT ONE ASIDE...
OH, GOOD. THERE'S ONE LEFT!

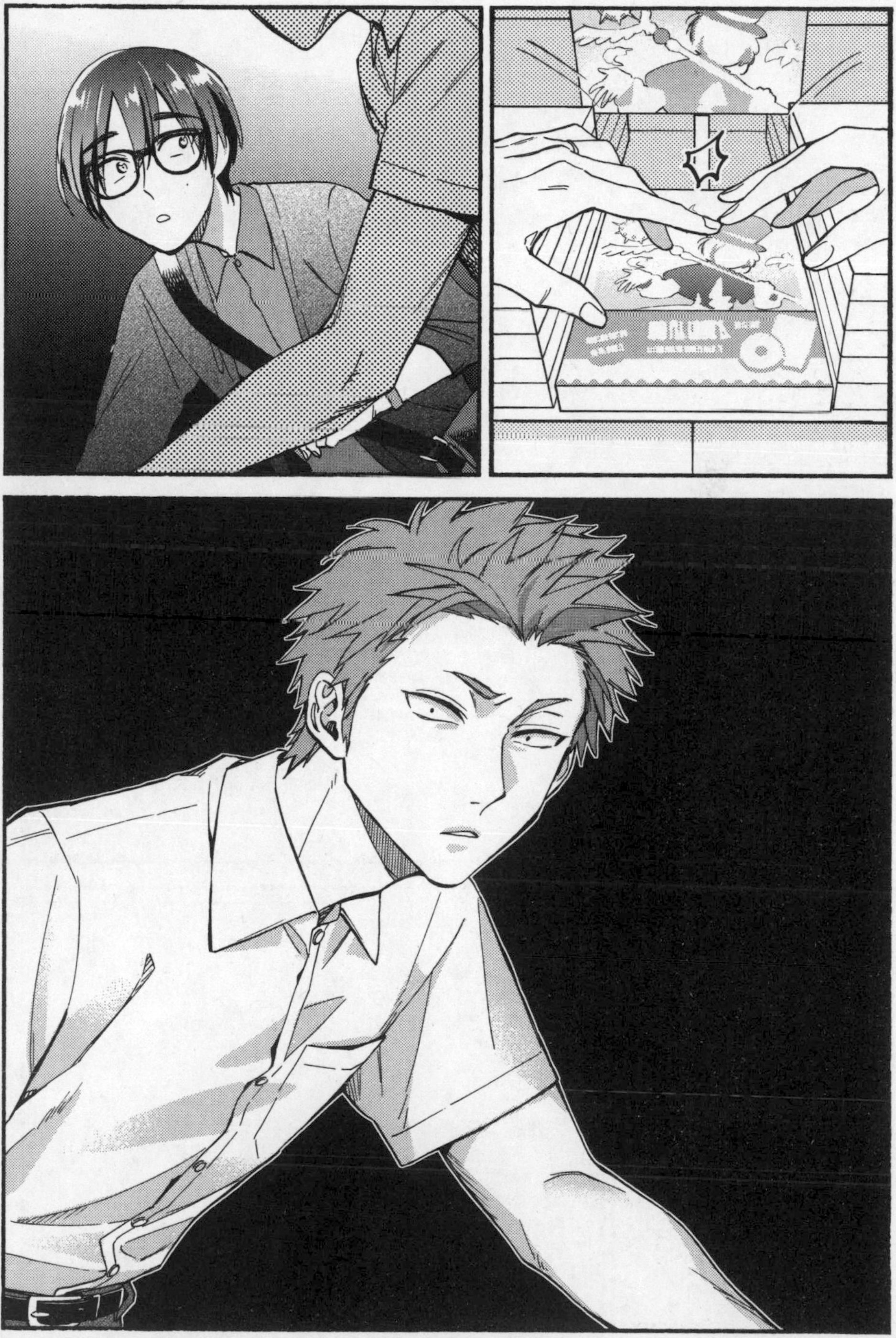

(*Tonari no Kaibutsu-kun* ("The Monster Next to Me"))

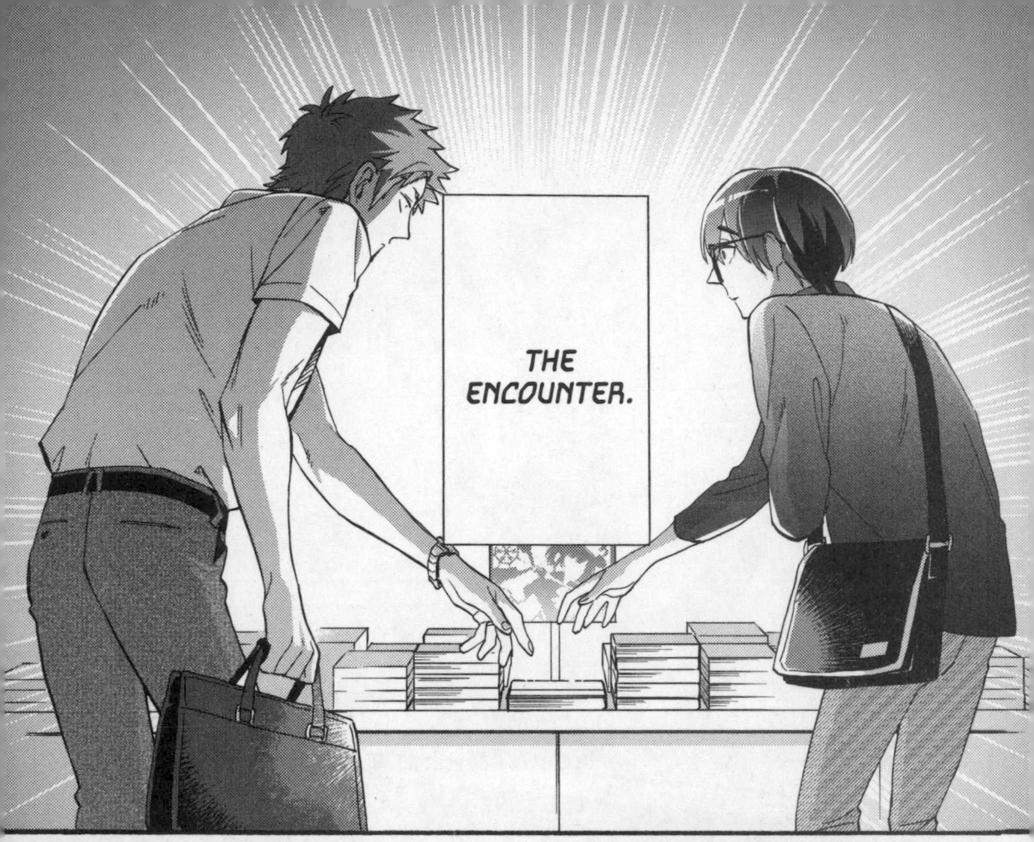
THE ENCOUNTER.

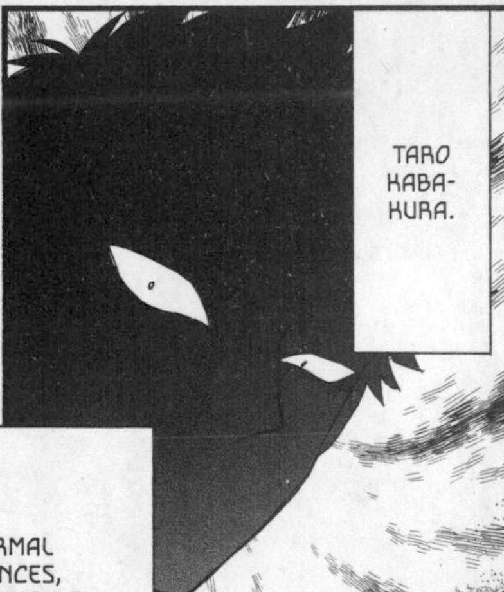
TARO KABAKURA.
UNDER NORMAL CIRCUMSTANCES, KO SAKURAGI WOULD HAVE NEVER CROSSED PATHS WITH HIS TYPE.

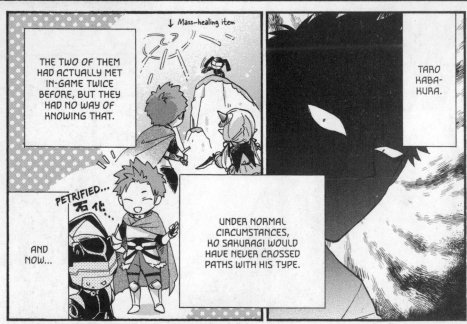

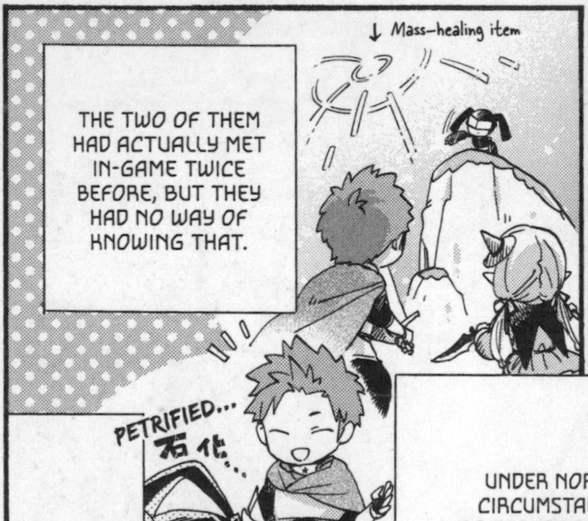
↓ Mass-healing item
THE TWO OF THEM HAD ACTUALLY MET IN-GAME TWICE BEFORE, BUT THEY HAD NO WAY OF KNOWING THAT.
PETRIFIED...
石化...
AND NOW...

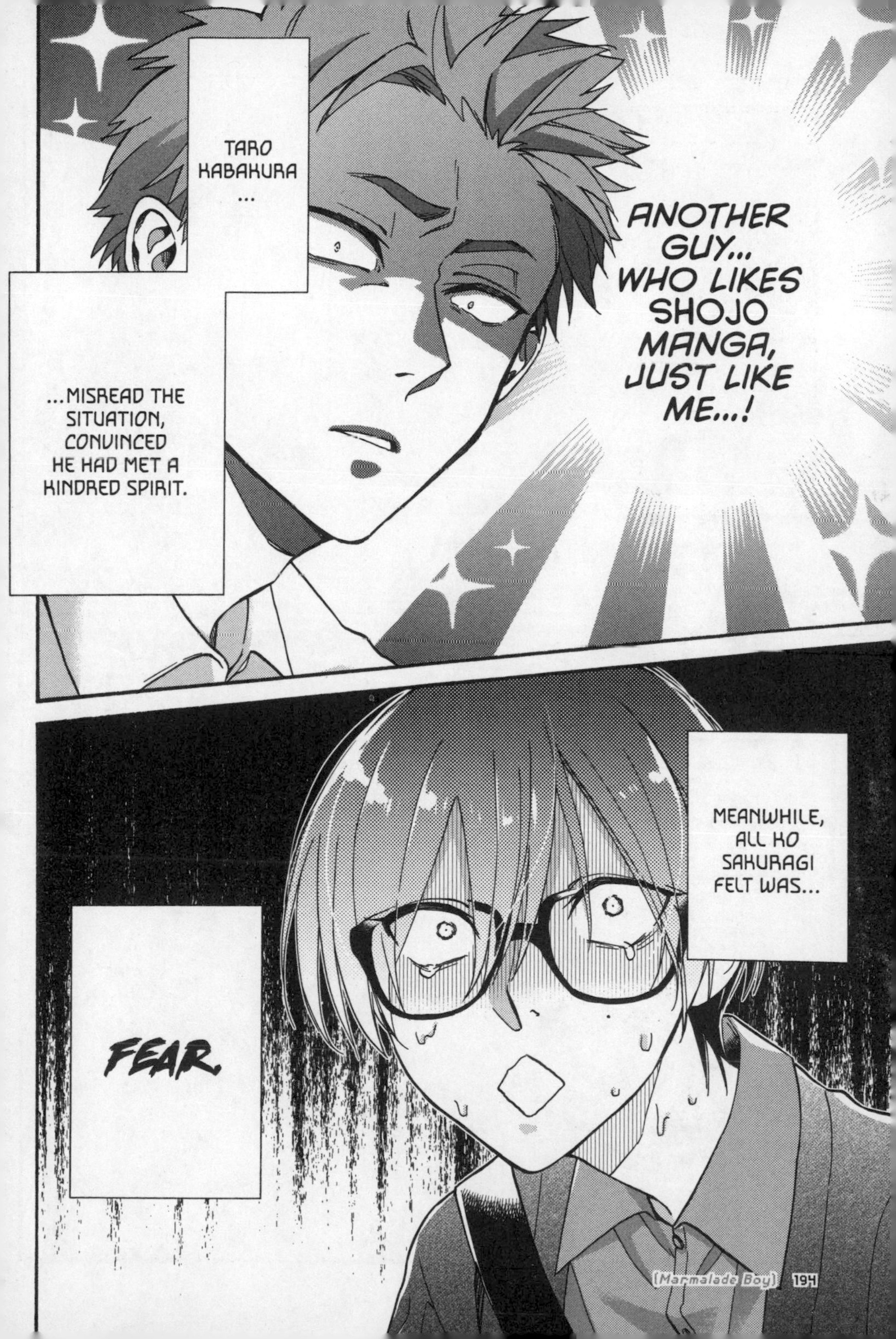
ANOTHER GUY... WHO LIKES SHOJO MANGA, JUST LIKE ME...!
TARO KABAKURA ...
...MISREAD THE SITUATION, CONVINCED HE HAD MET A KINDRED SPIRIT.
MEANWHILE, ALL KO SAKURAGI FELT WAS...
FEAR.
(Marmalade Boy)

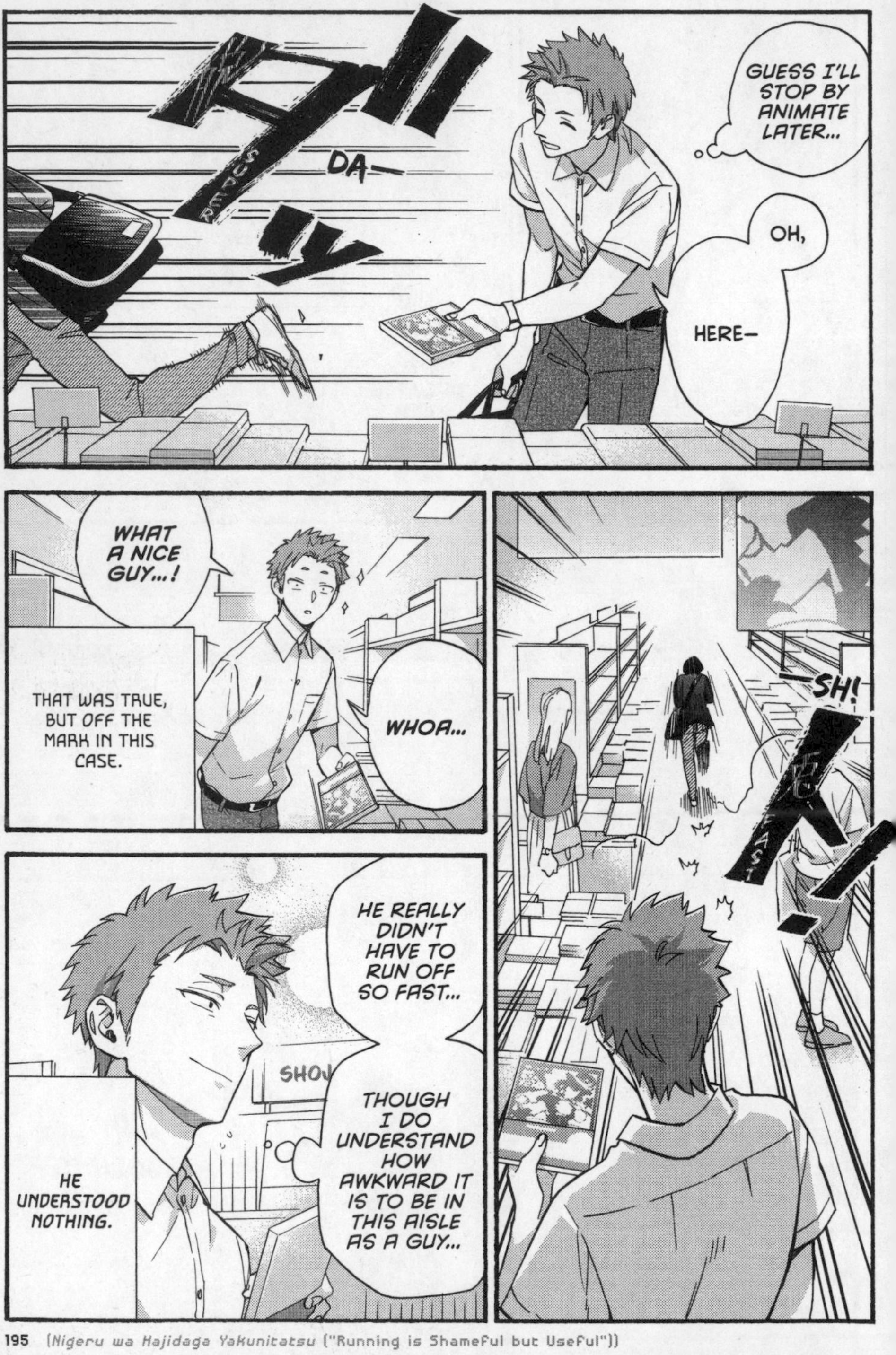
GUESS I'LL STOP BY ANIMATE LATER...
OH,
HERE—
SUPER
DA—
y
—SH!
FAST
WHOA...
WHAT A NICE GUY...!
THAT WAS TRUE, BUT OFF THE MARK IN THIS CASE.
HE REALLY DIDN'T HAVE TO RUN OFF SO FAST...
THOUGH I DO UNDERSTAND HOW AWKWARD IT IS TO BE IN THIS AISLE AS A GUY...
SHOJ
HE UNDERSTOOD NOTHING.

(Nigeru wa Hajidaga Yakunitatsu ("Running is Shameful but Useful"))

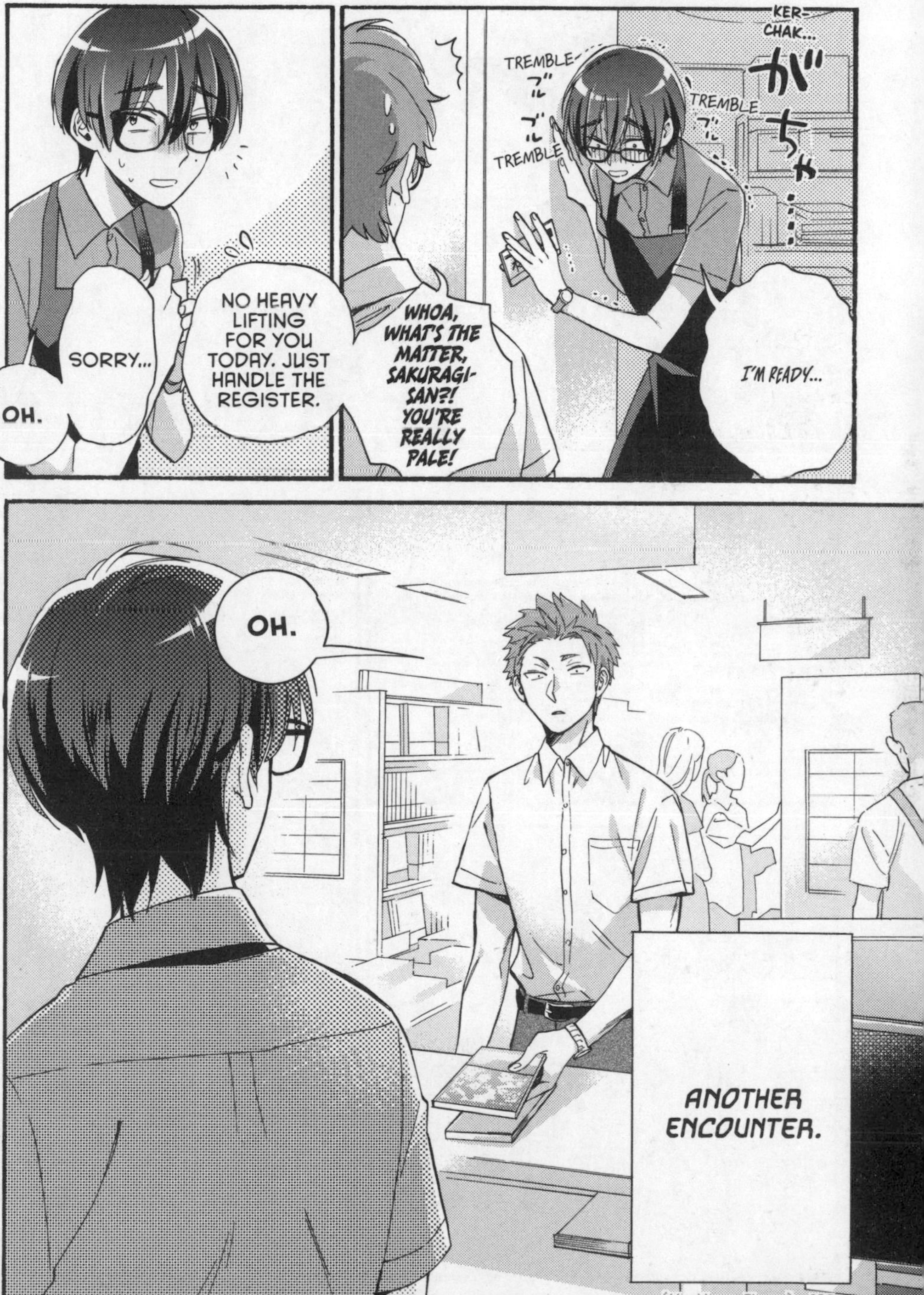
KER-CHAK...
がちゃ...
TREMBLE
ブル
TREMBLE
ブル
TREMBLE
ブル
I'M READY...
WHOA, WHAT'S THE MATTER, SAKURAGI-SAN?! YOU'RE REALLY PALE!
NO HEAVY LIFTING FOR YOU TODAY. JUST HANDLE THE REGISTER.
SORRY...
OH.
OH.
ANOTHER ENCOUNTER.

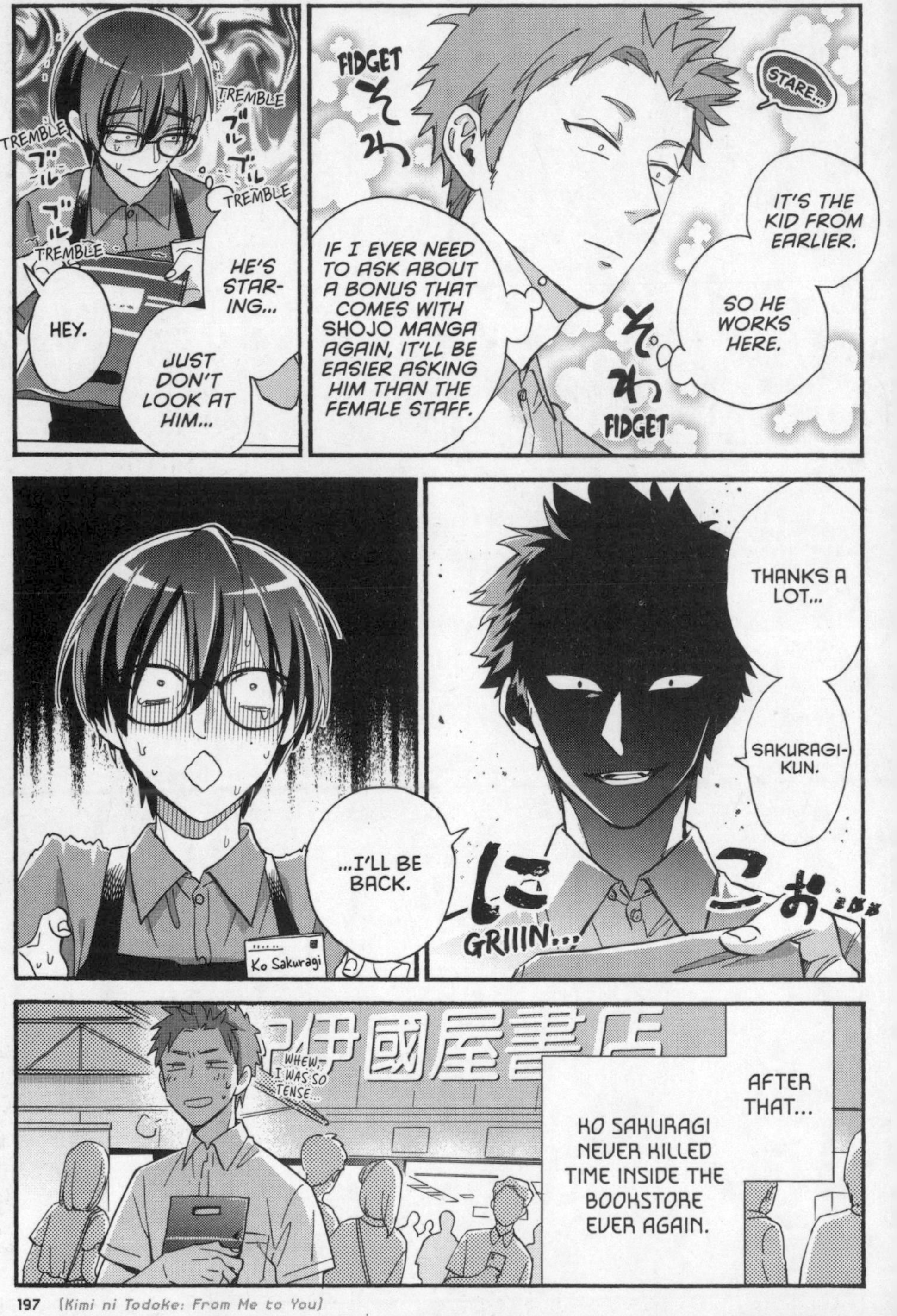
STARE...
FIDGET
そわ
IT'S THE KID FROM EARLIER.
SO HE WORKS HERE.
IF I EVER NEED TO ASK ABOUT A BONUS THAT COMES WITH SHOJO MANGA AGAIN, IT'LL BE EASIER ASKING HIM THAN THE FEMALE STAFF.
そわ
FIDGET
TREMBLE
ブル
TREMBLE
ブル
TREMBLE
ブル
TREMBLE
HE'S STAR-ING...
JUST DON'T LOOK AT HIM...
HEY.
THANKS A LOT...
SAKURAGI-KUN.
にこぉ
GRIIIN...
...I'LL BE BACK.
Ko Sakuragi
AFTER THAT...
KO SAKURAGI NEVER KILLED TIME INSIDE THE BOOKSTORE EVER AGAIN.
伊國屋書店
WHEW, I WAS SO TENSE...

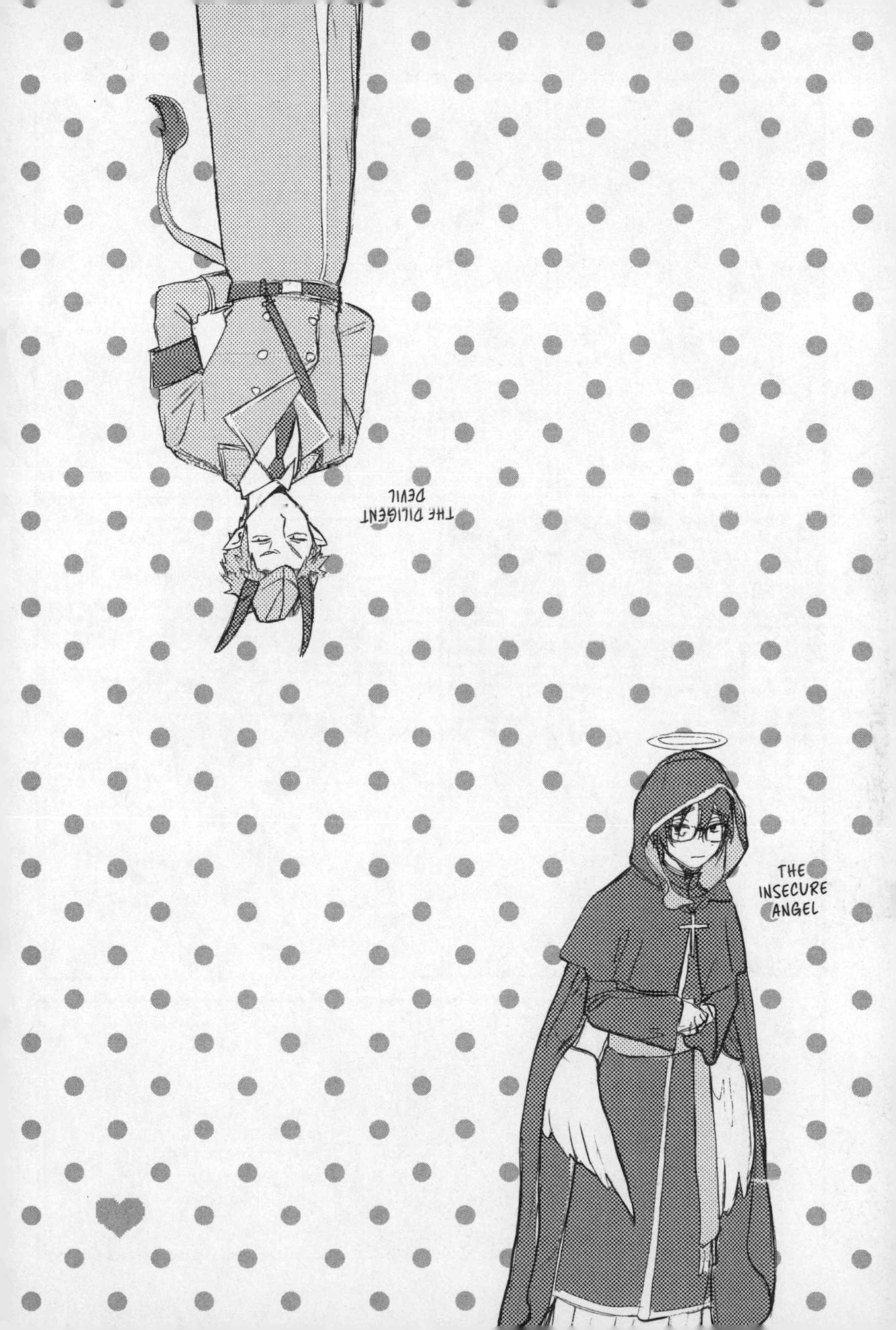
THE DILIGENT DEVIL
THE INSECURE ANGEL

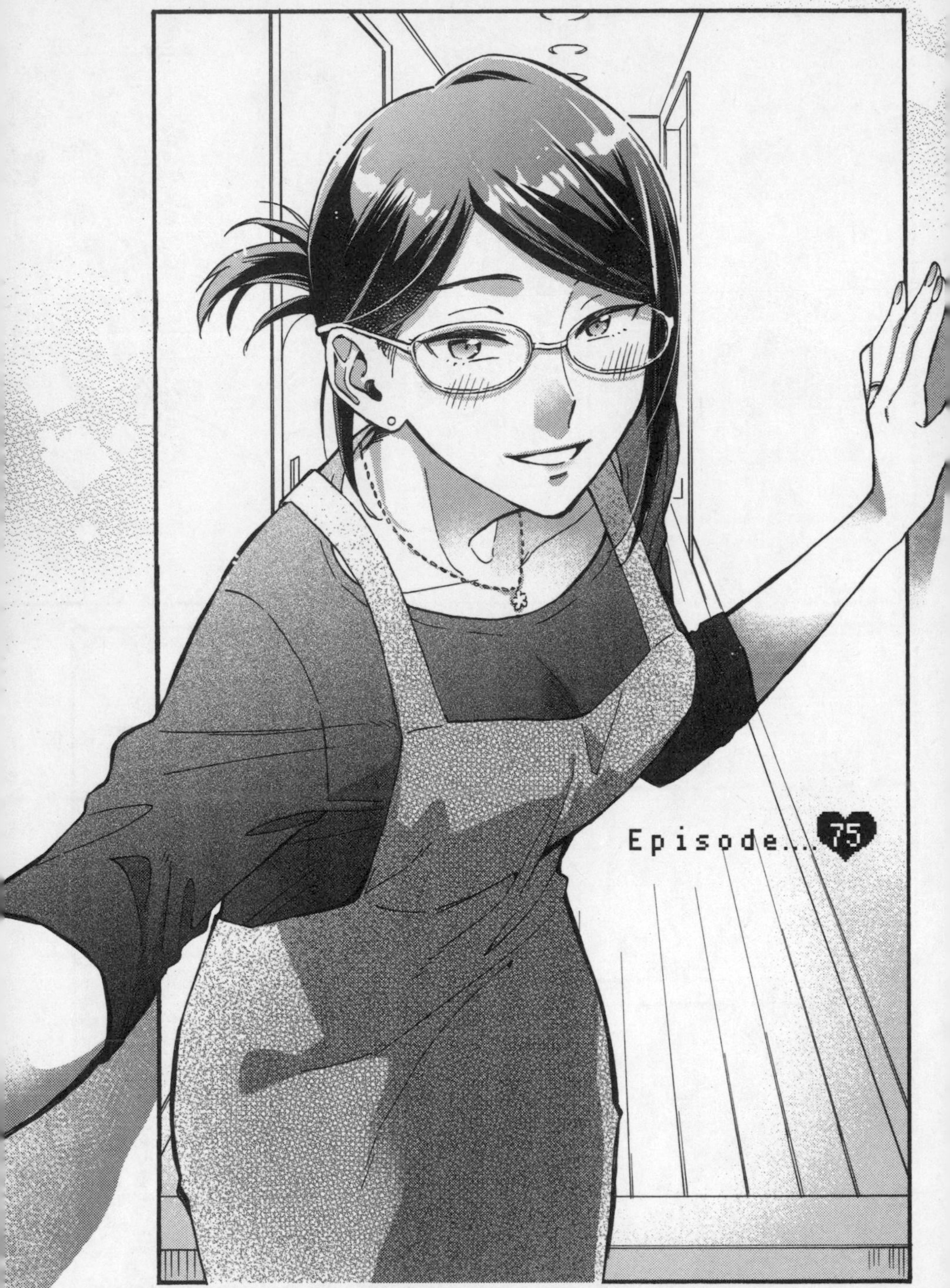
Episode... 75

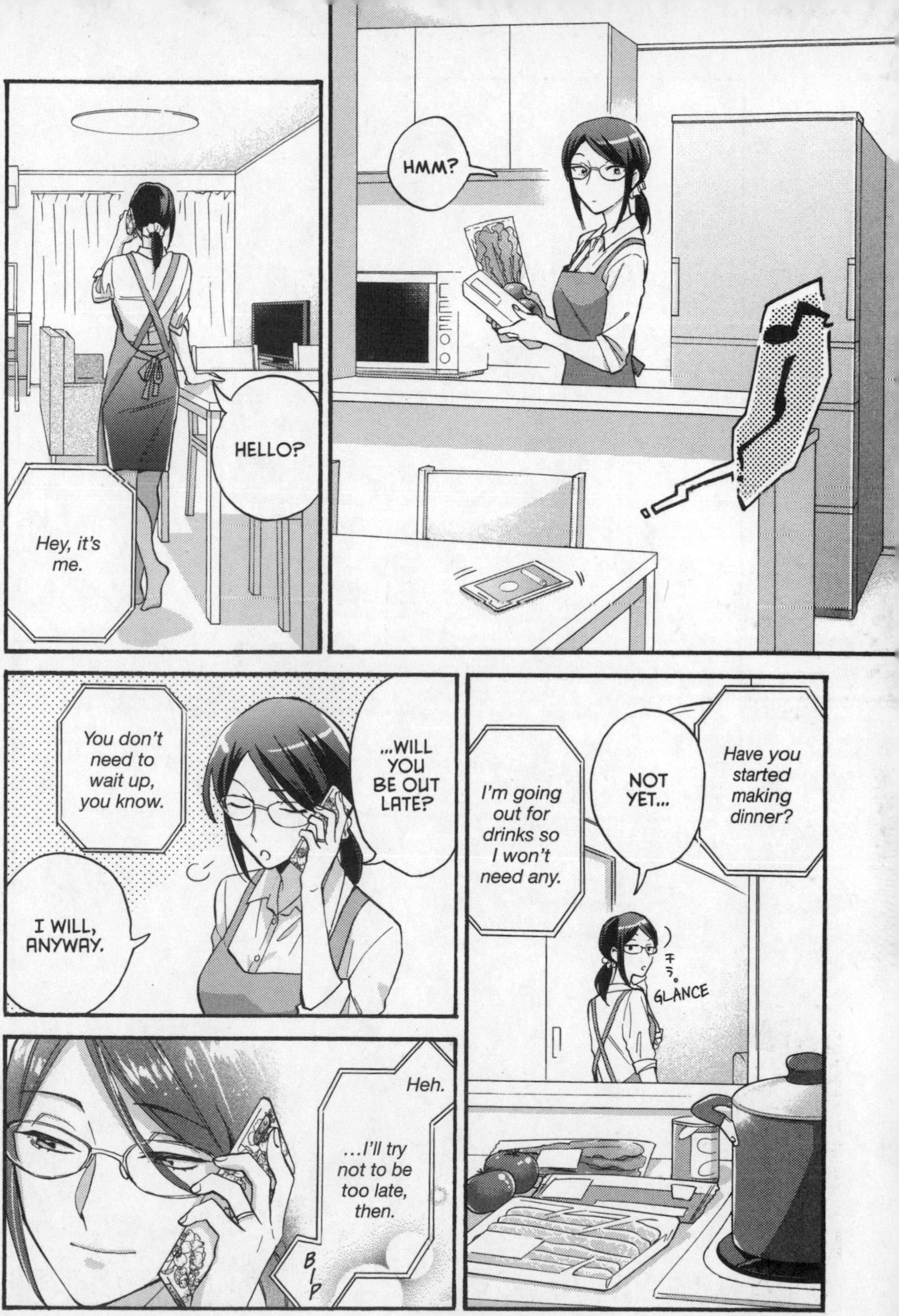
HMM?
HELLO?
Hey, it's me.
Have you started making dinner?
NOT YET...
I'm going out for drinks so I won't need any.
チラ
GLANCE
...WILL YOU BE OUT LATE?
You don't need to wait up, you know.
I WILL, ANYWAY.
Heh.
...I'll try not to be too late, then.
BIP

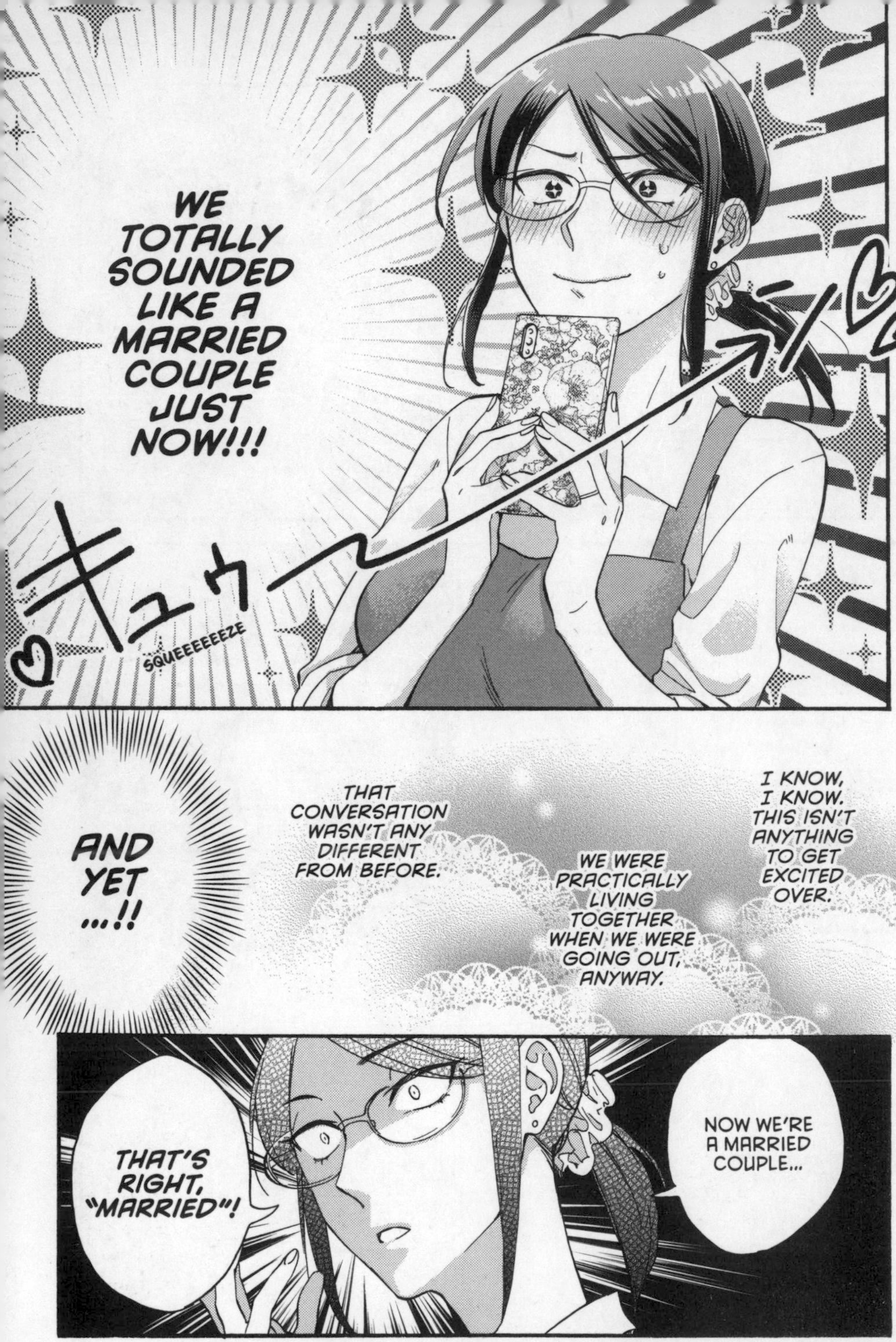
WE TOTALLY SOUNDED LIKE A MARRIED COUPLE JUST NOW!!!
キュウ〜
SQUEEEEEEZE
I KNOW, I KNOW. THIS ISN'T ANYTHING TO GET EXCITED OVER.
WE WERE PRACTICALLY LIVING TOGETHER WHEN WE WERE GOING OUT, ANYWAY.
THAT CONVERSATION WASN'T ANY DIFFERENT FROM BEFORE.
AND YET ...!!
NOW WE'RE A MARRIED COUPLE...
THAT'S RIGHT, "MARRIED"!

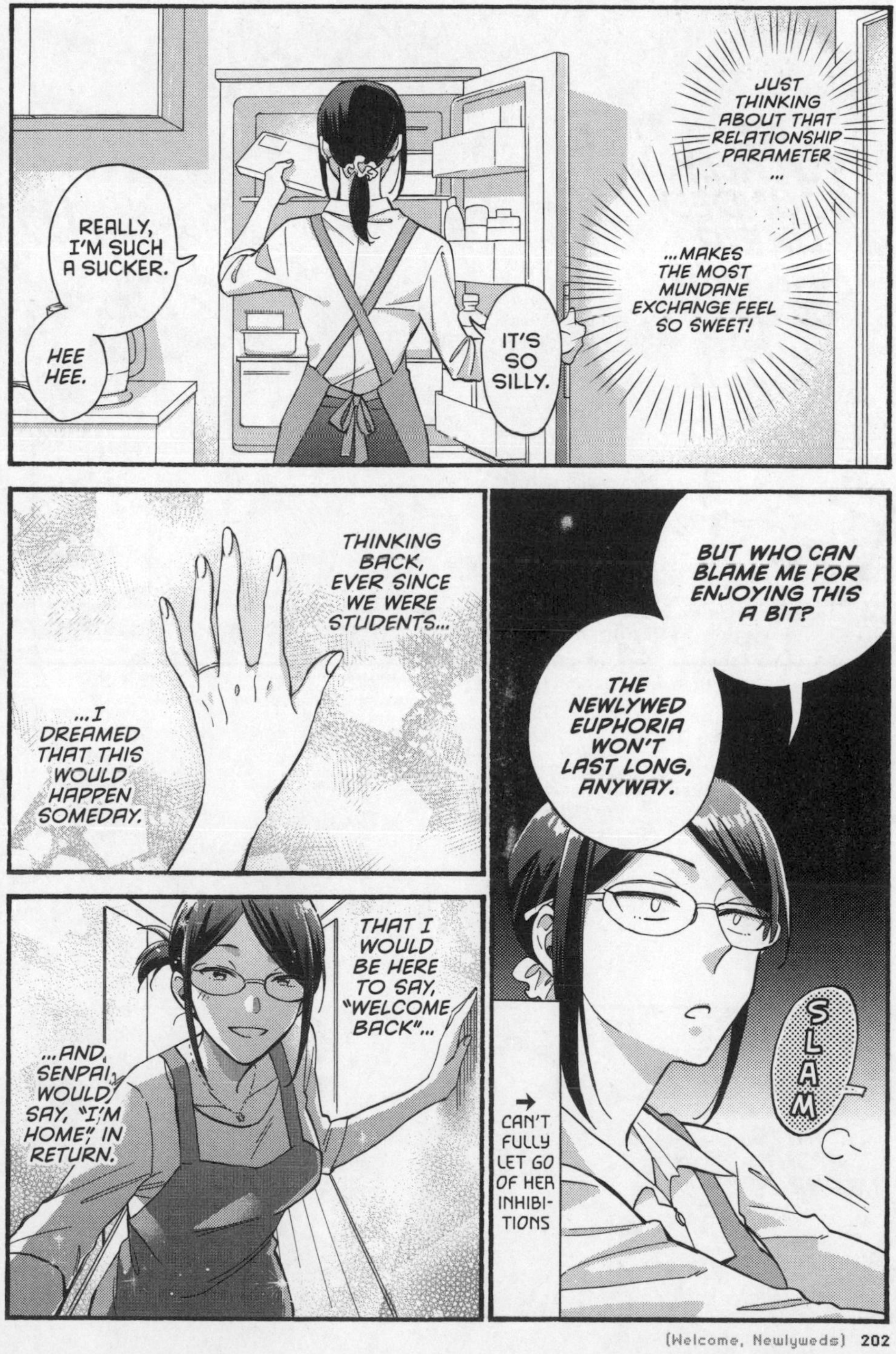
JUST THINKING ABOUT THAT RELATIONSHIP PARAMETER ...
...MAKES THE MOST MUNDANE EXCHANGE FEEL SO SWEET!
IT'S SO SILLY.
REALLY, I'M SUCH A SUCKER.
HEE HEE.
BUT WHO CAN BLAME ME FOR ENJOYING THIS A BIT?
THE NEWLYWED EUPHORIA WON'T LAST LONG, ANYWAY.
SLAM
→ CAN'T FULLY LET GO OF HER INHIBI-TIONS
THINKING BACK, EVER SINCE WE WERE STUDENTS...
...I DREAMED THAT THIS WOULD HAPPEN SOMEDAY.
THAT I WOULD BE HERE TO SAY, "WELCOME BACK"...
...AND, SENPAI, WOULD SAY, "I'M HOME," IN RETURN.

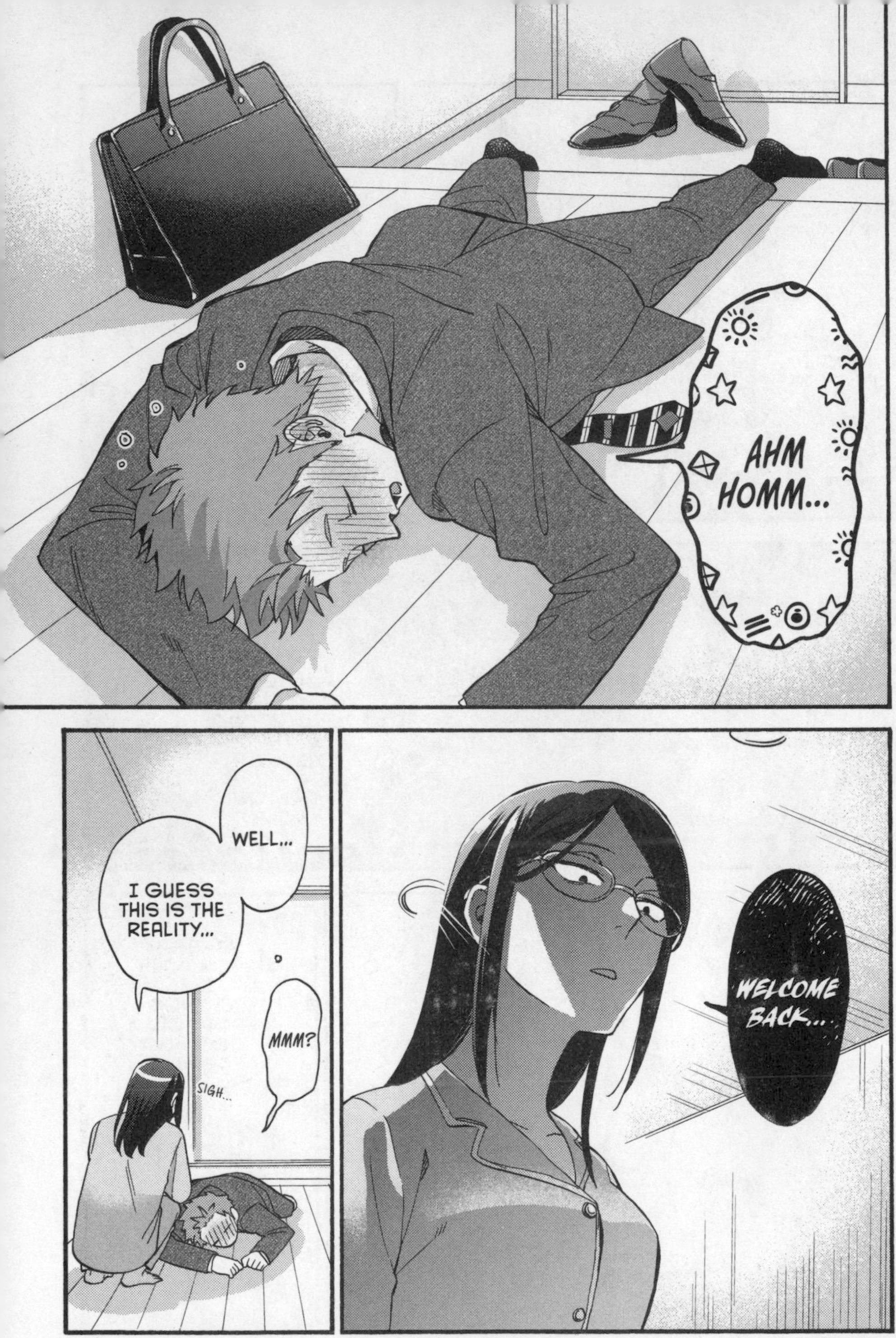
AHM HOMM...
WELCOME BACK...
WELL... I GUESS THIS IS THE REALITY...
MMM?
SIGH...

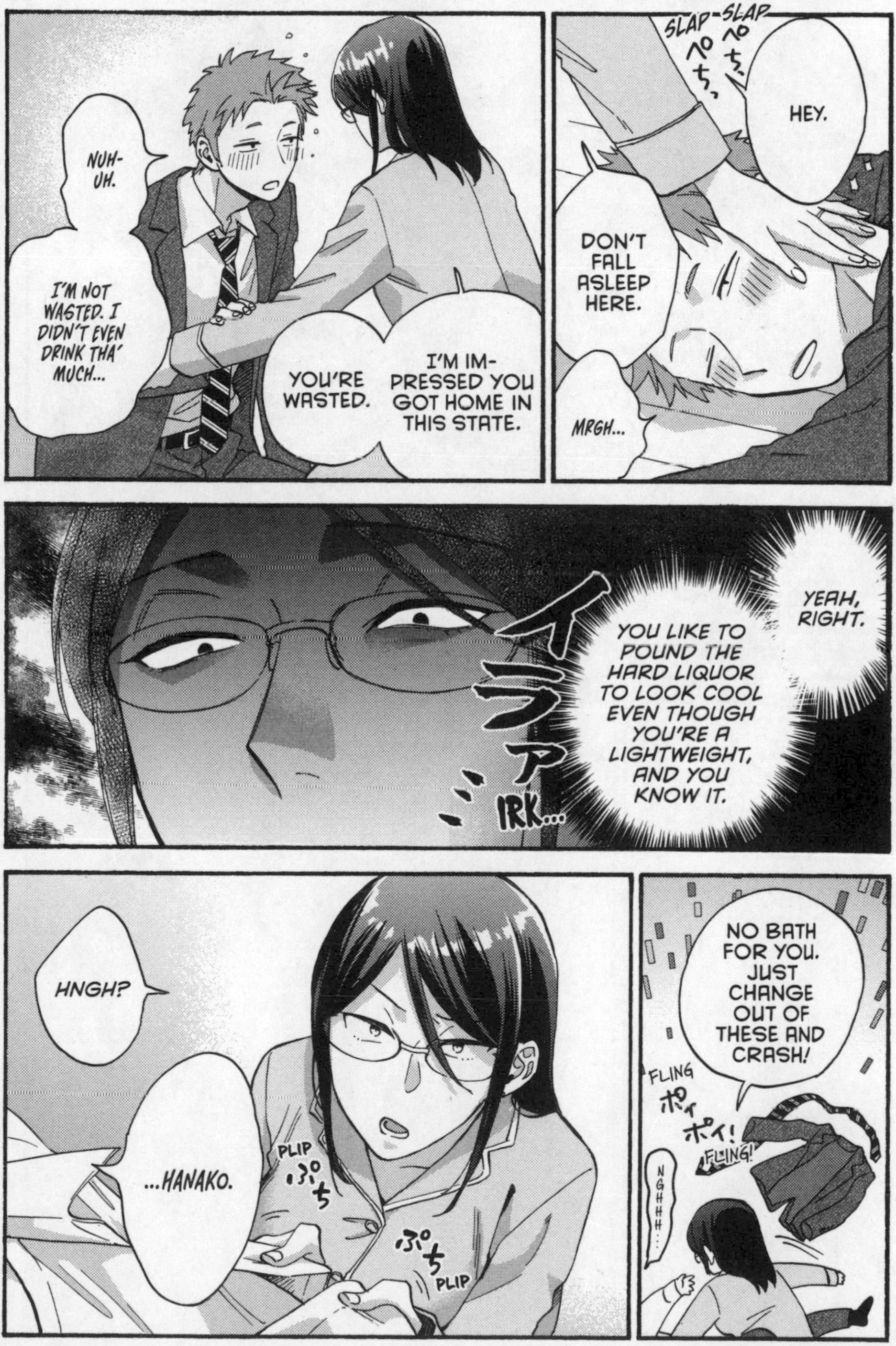
SLAP-SLAP
ぺち ぺち
HEY.
DON'T FALL ASLEEP HERE.
MRGH...
I'M IM-PRESSED YOU GOT HOME IN THIS STATE.
YOU'RE WASTED.
NUH-UH.
I'M NOT WASTED. I DIDN'T EVEN DRINK THA' MUCH...
YEAH, RIGHT.
YOU LIKE TO POUND THE HARD LIQUOR TO LOOK COOL EVEN THOUGH YOU'RE A LIGHTWEIGHT, AND YOU KNOW IT.
イラァ
IRK...
NO BATH FOR YOU. JUST CHANGE OUT OF THESE AND CRASH!
FLING
ポイ
ポイ!
FLING!
NGHHH...
HNGH?
...HANAKO.
PLIP
ぷち
ぷち
PLIP

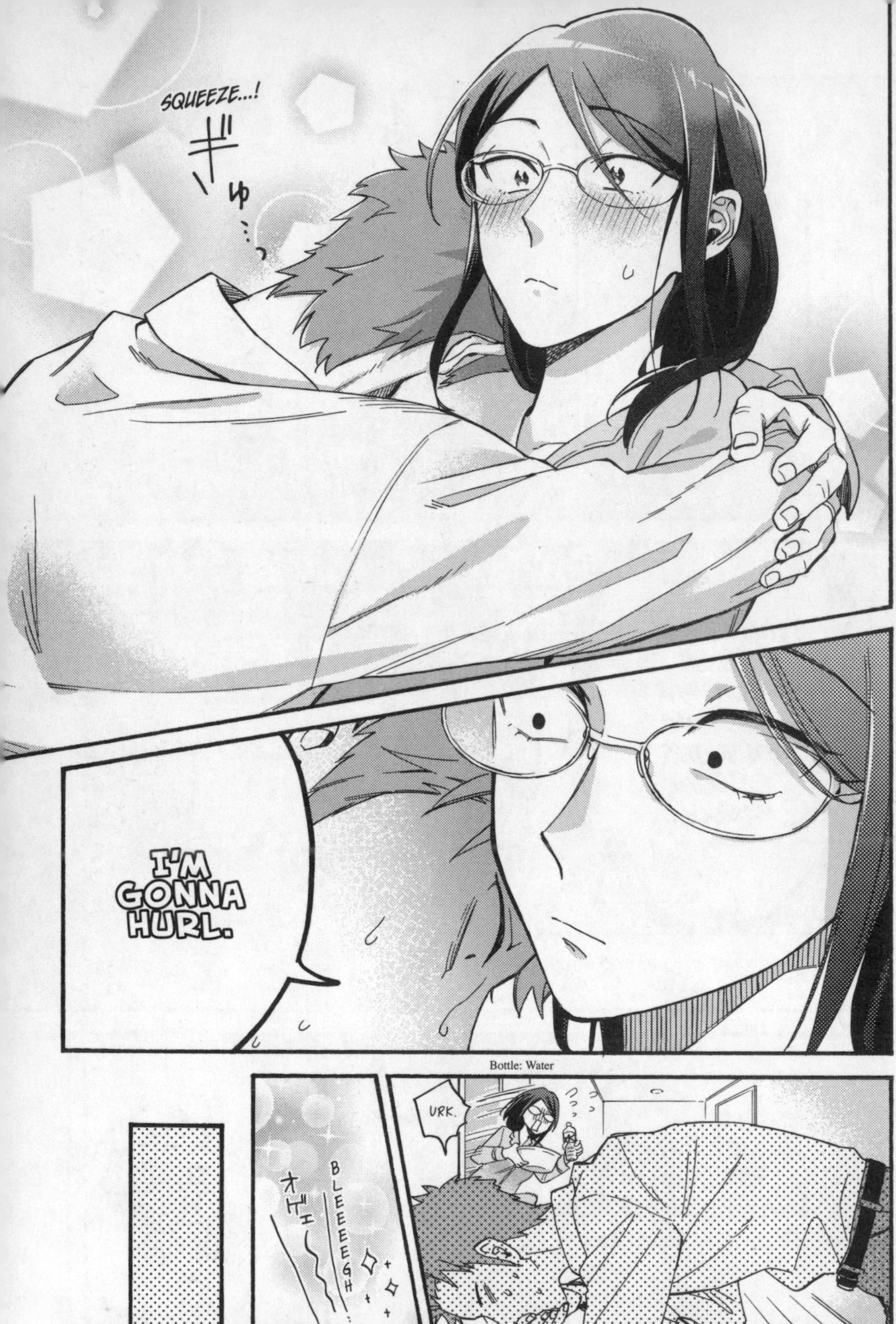
SQUEEZE...!
ギュ…
I'M GONNA HURL.
Bottle: Water
URK.
BLEEEEGH
オゲエ〜

 (There goes the romantic mood with it)

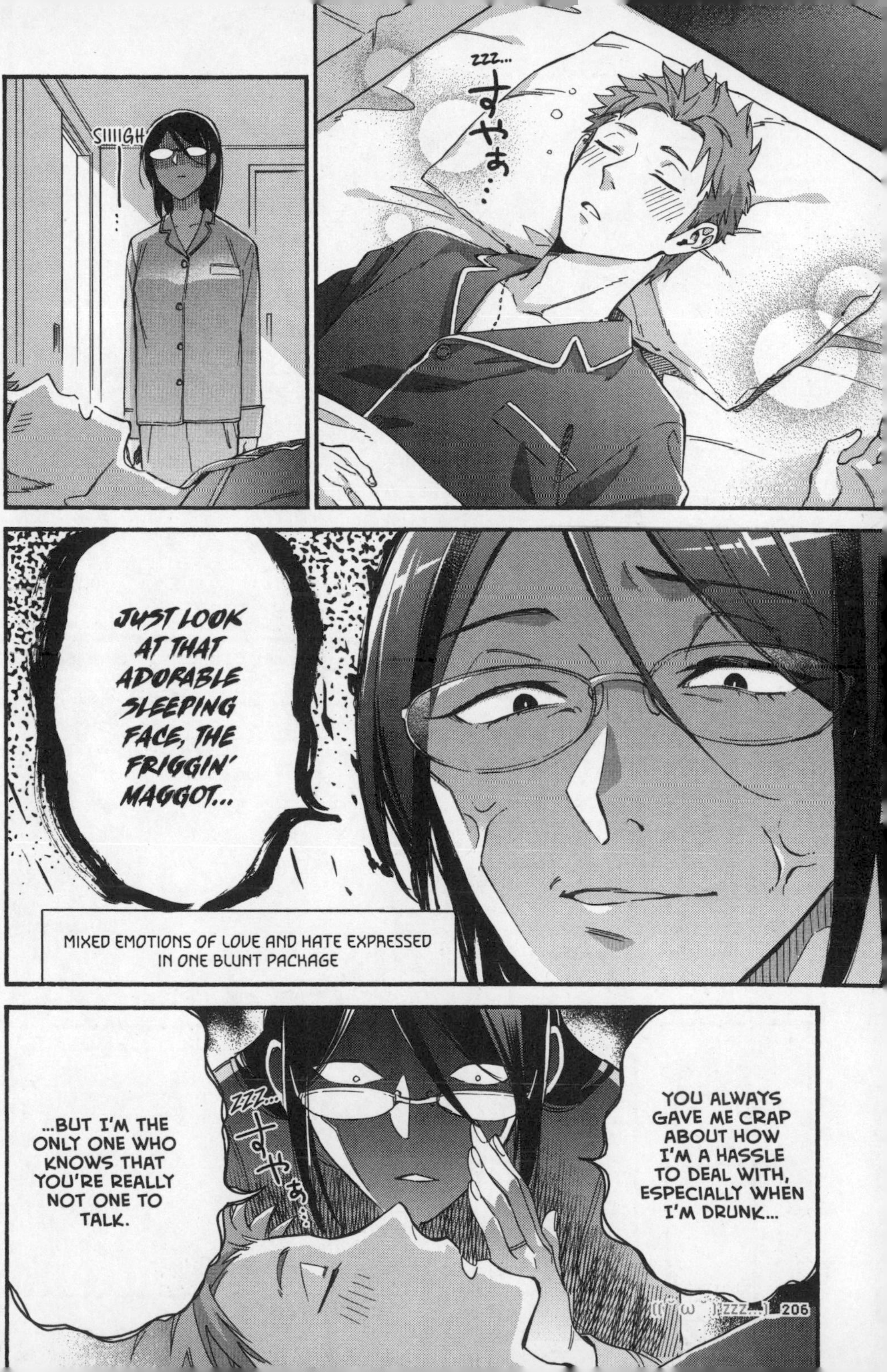
zzz...
すやぁ...
SIIIGH
...
JUST LOOK AT THAT ADORABLE SLEEPING FACE, THE FRIGGIN' MAGGOT...
MIXED EMOTIONS OF LOVE AND HATE EXPRESSED IN ONE BLUNT PACKAGE
YOU ALWAYS GAVE ME CRAP ABOUT HOW I'M A HASSLE TO DEAL WITH, ESPECIALLY WHEN I'M DRUNK...
zzz...
すやぁ...
...BUT I'M THE ONLY ONE WHO KNOWS THAT YOU'RE REALLY NOT ONE TO TALK.

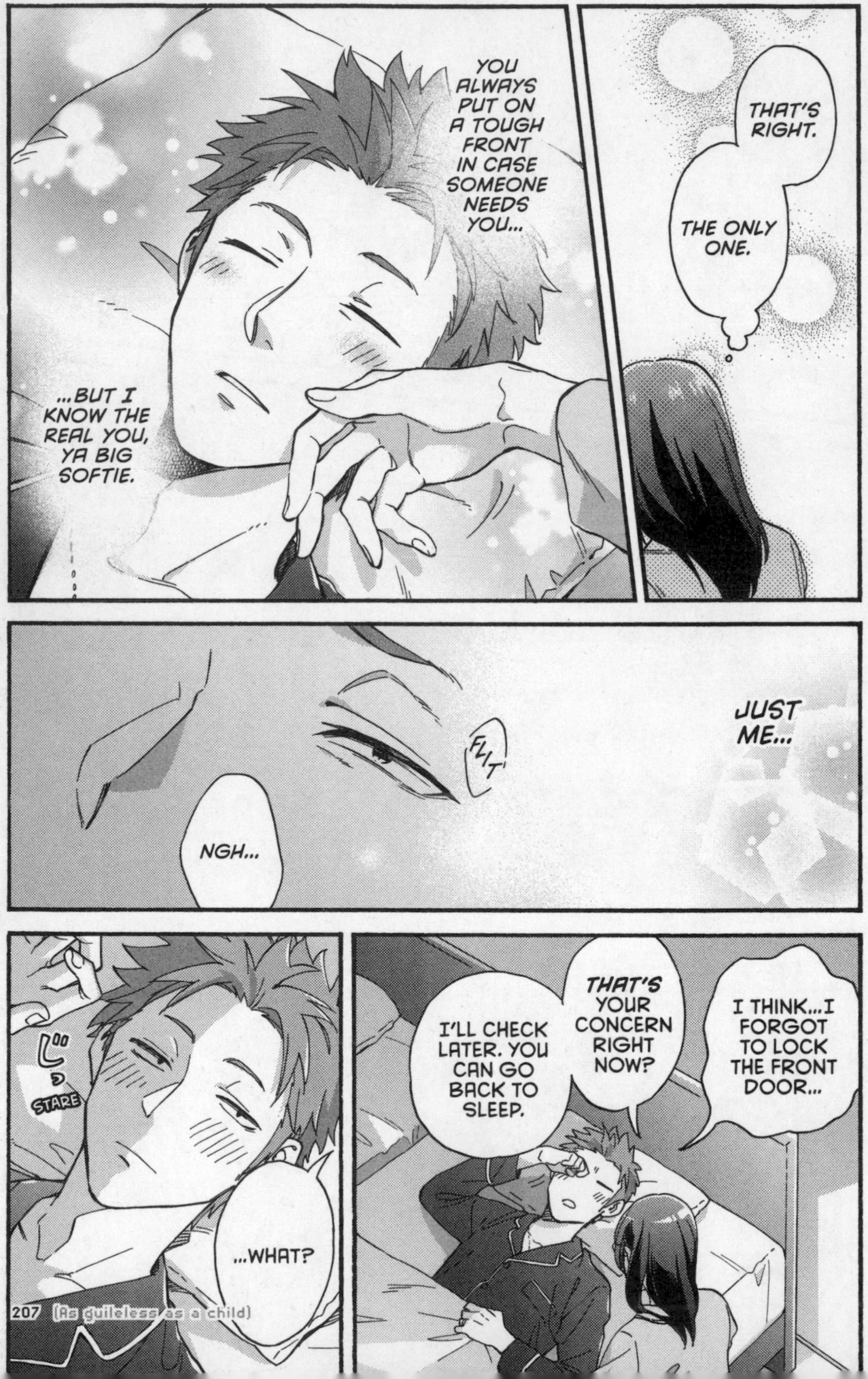
THAT'S RIGHT.
THE ONLY ONE.
YOU ALWAYS PUT ON A TOUGH FRONT IN CASE SOMEONE NEEDS YOU...
...BUT I KNOW THE REAL YOU, YA BIG SOFTIE.
JUST ME...
FLIT
NGH...
I THINK...I FORGOT TO LOCK THE FRONT DOOR...
THAT'S YOUR CONCERN RIGHT NOW?
I'LL CHECK LATER. YOU CAN GO BACK TO SLEEP.
じっ
STARE
...WHAT?

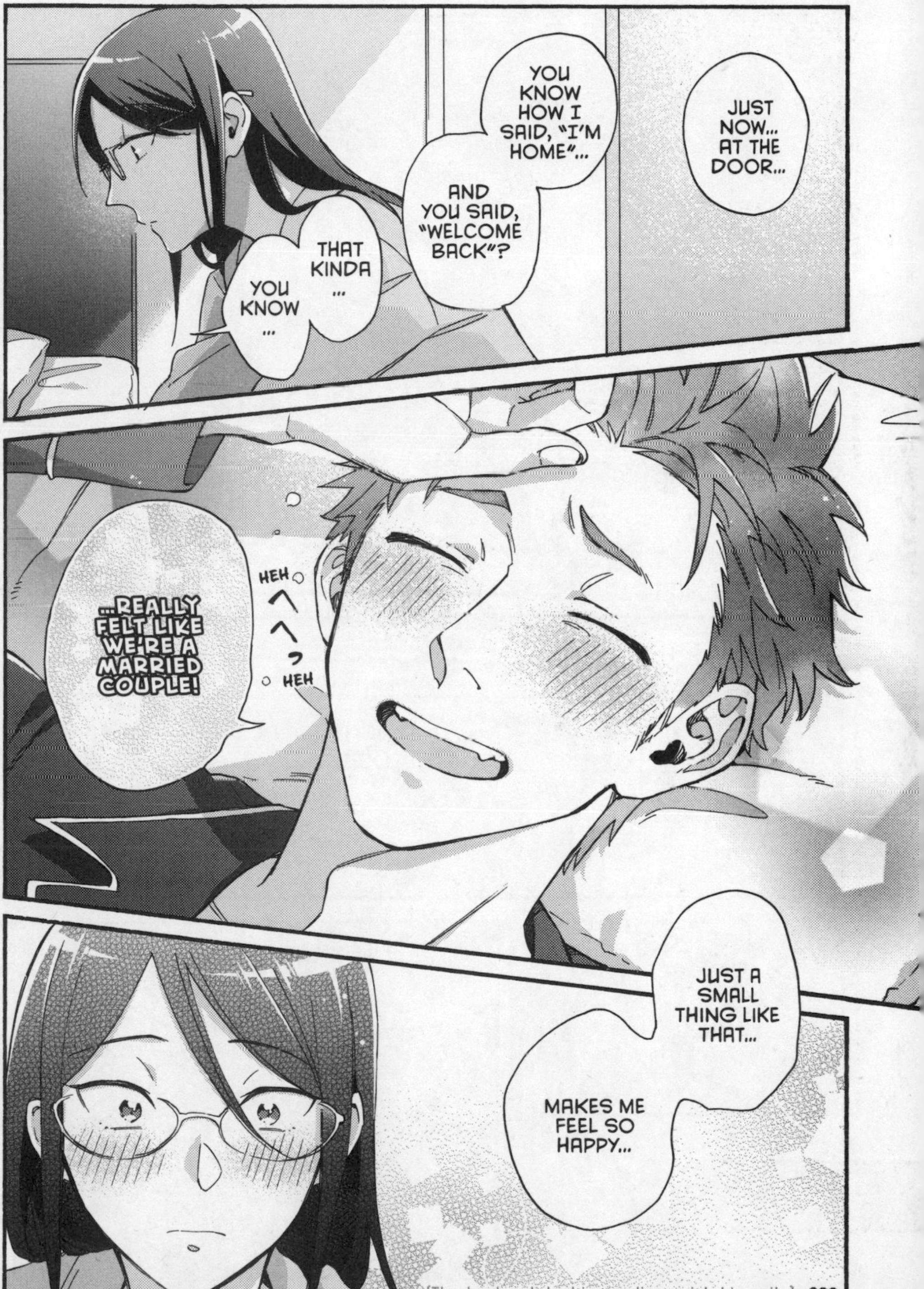
JUST NOW... AT THE DOOR...
YOU KNOW HOW I SAID, "I'M HOME"...
AND YOU SAID, "WELCOME BACK"?
THAT KINDA ...
YOU KNOW ...
HEH へ へっ HEH
...REALLY FELT LIKE WE'RE A MARRIED COUPLE!
JUST A SMALL THING LIKE THAT...
MAKES ME FEEL SO HAPPY...

(The husband, looking radiant with his smile)

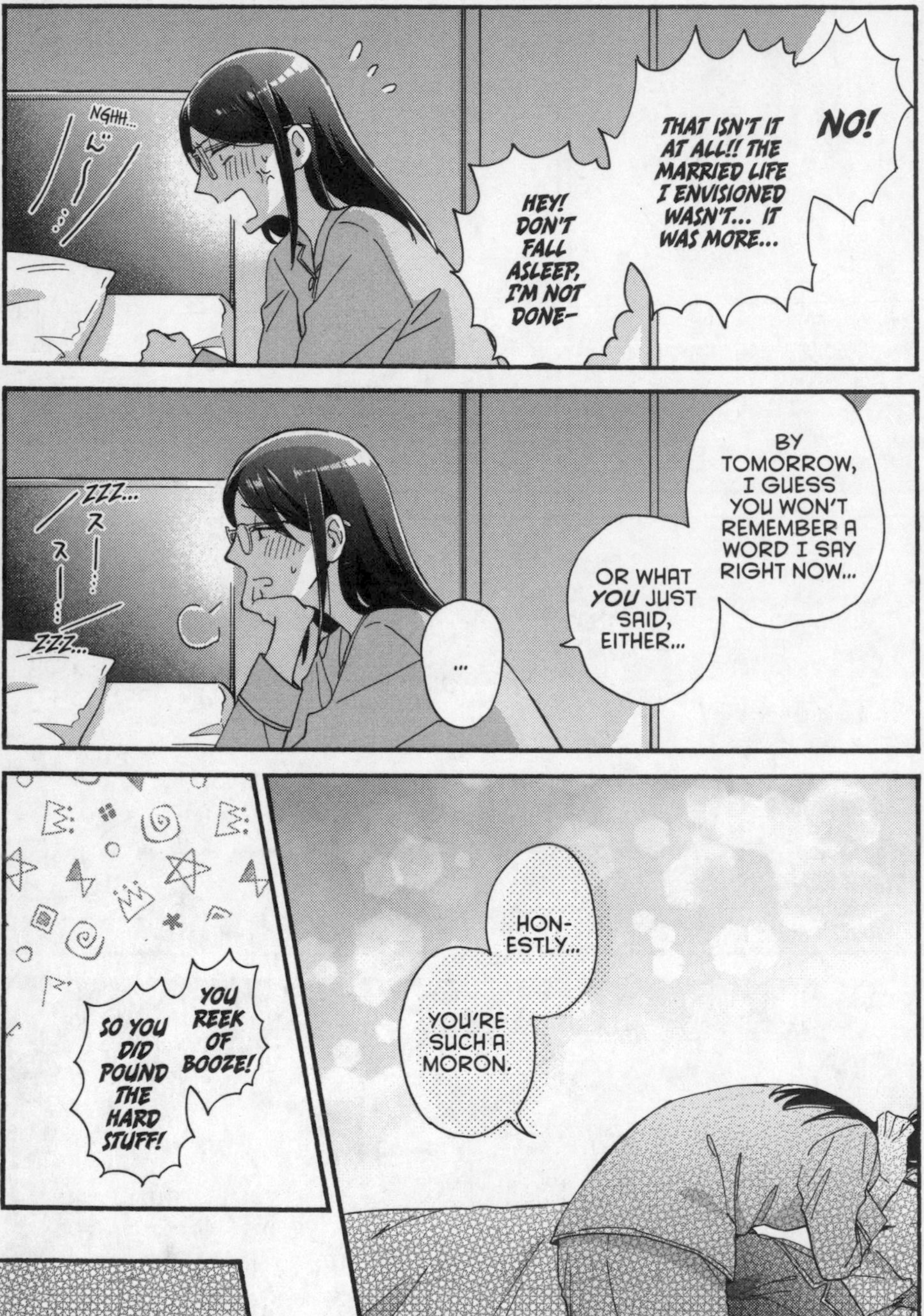
NO!
THAT ISN'T IT AT ALL!! THE MARRIED LIFE I ENVISIONED WASN'T... IT WAS MORE...
HEY! DON'T FALL ASLEEP, I'M NOT DONE-
NGHH...
BY TOMORROW, I GUESS YOU WON'T REMEMBER A WORD I SAY RIGHT NOW...
OR WHAT *YOU* JUST SAID, EITHER...
...
ZZZ...
ZZZ...
HON-ESTLY...
YOU'RE SUCH A MORON.
YOU REEK OF BOOZE!
SO YOU DID POUND THE HARD STUFF!

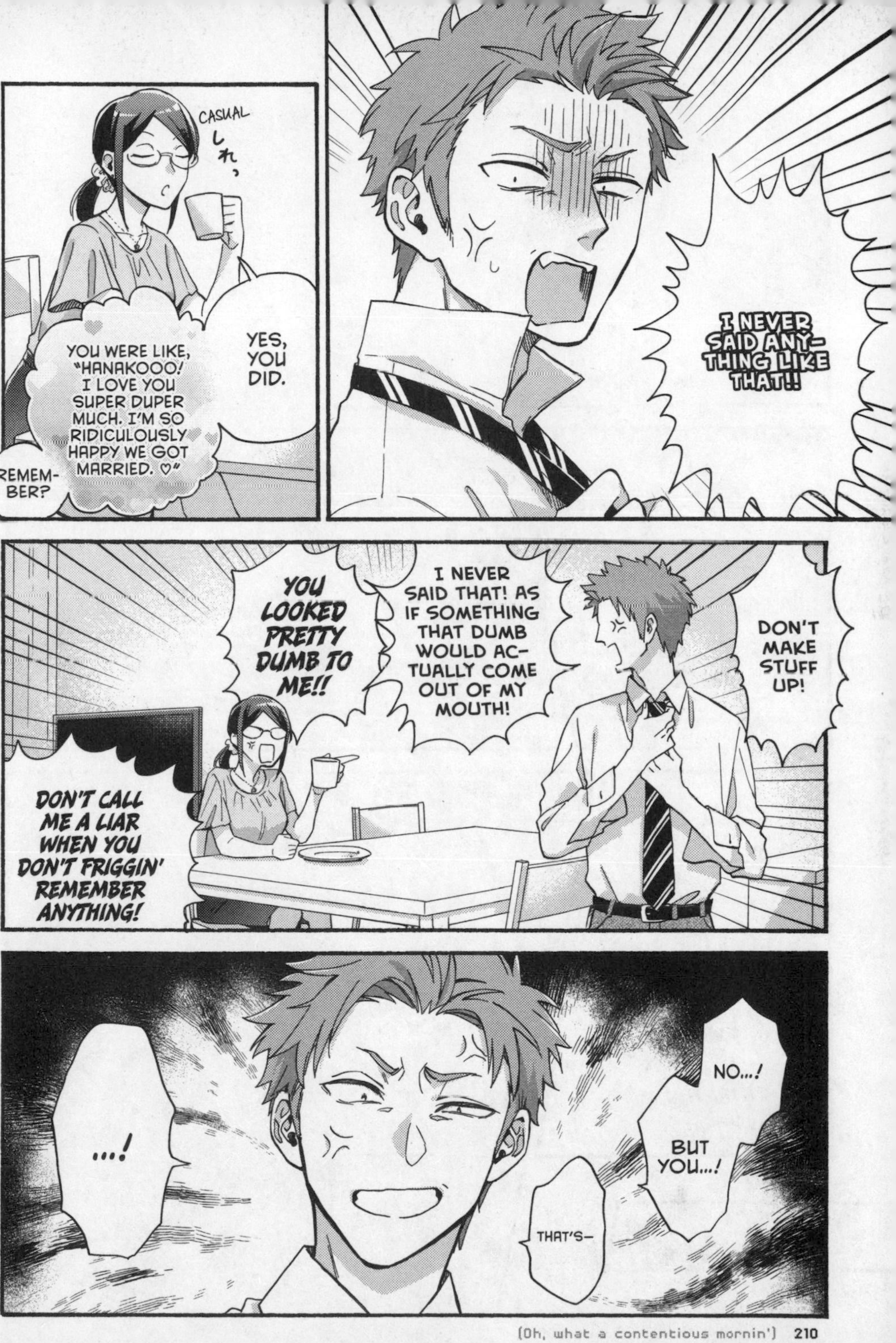
I NEVER SAID ANY-THING LIKE THAT!!
CASUAL
しれっ
YES, YOU DID.
YOU WERE LIKE, "HANAKOOO! I LOVE YOU SUPER DUPER MUCH. I'M SO RIDICULOUSLY HAPPY WE GOT MARRIED. ♡"
REMEM-BER?
DON'T MAKE STUFF UP!
I NEVER SAID THAT! AS IF SOMETHING THAT DUMB WOULD AC-TUALLY COME OUT OF MY MOUTH!
YOU LOOKED PRETTY DUMB TO ME!!
DON'T CALL ME A LIAR WHEN YOU DON'T FRIGGIN' REMEMBER ANYTHING!
NO...!
BUT YOU...!
THAT'S—
...!

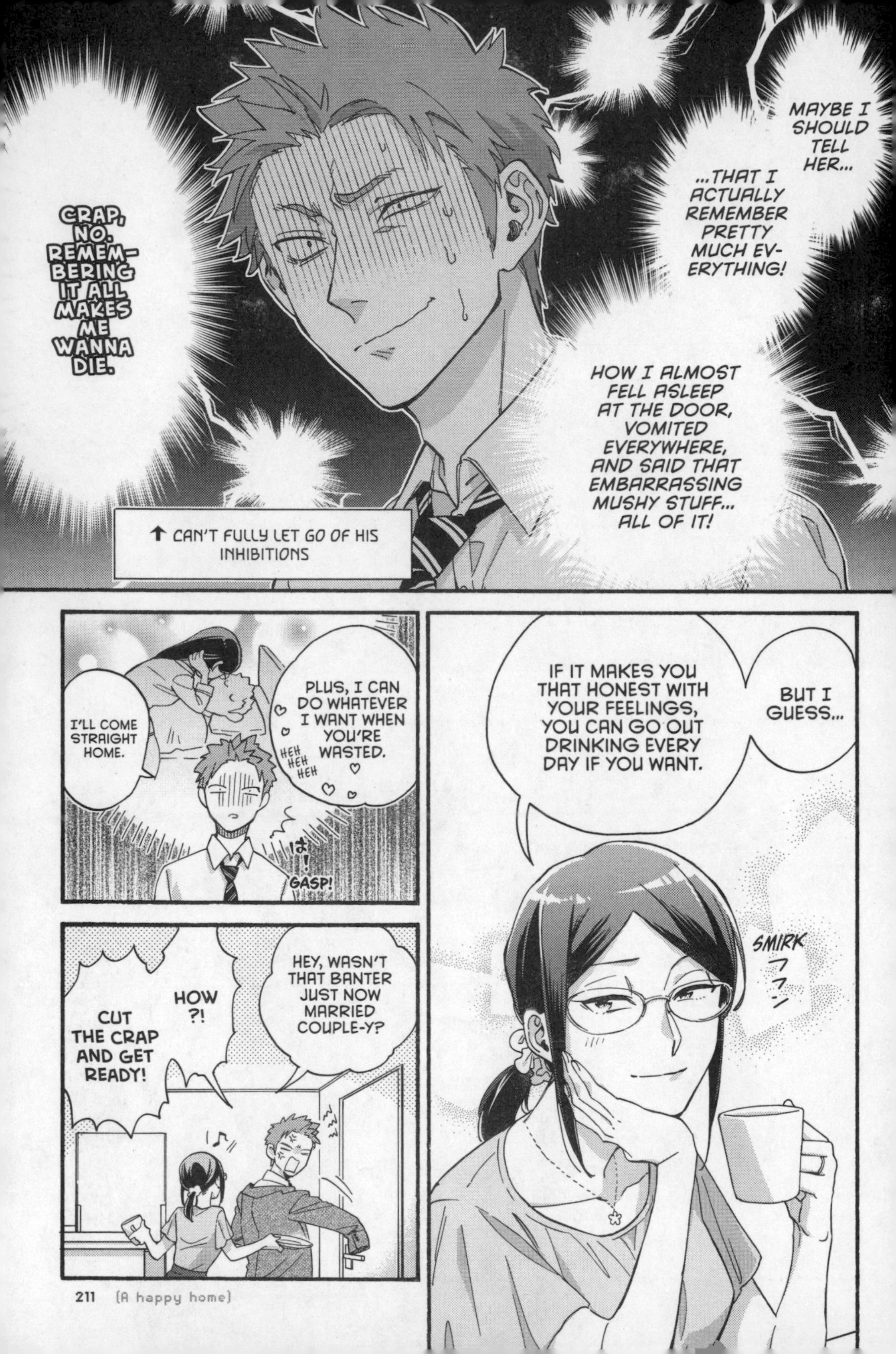
MAYBE I SHOULD TELL HER...
...THAT I ACTUALLY REMEMBER PRETTY MUCH EV-ERYTHING!
HOW I ALMOST FELL ASLEEP AT THE DOOR, VOMITED EVERYWHERE, AND SAID THAT EMBARRASSING MUSHY STUFF... ALL OF IT!
CRAP, NO. REMEM-BERING IT ALL MAKES ME WANNA DIE.
↑ CAN'T FULLY LET GO OF HIS INHIBITIONS
BUT I GUESS...
IF IT MAKES YOU THAT HONEST WITH YOUR FEELINGS, YOU CAN GO OUT DRINKING EVERY DAY IF YOU WANT.
SMIRK
PLUS, I CAN DO WHATEVER I WANT WHEN YOU'RE WASTED.
HEH HEH HEH
I'LL COME STRAIGHT HOME.
は!
GASP!
HEY, WASN'T THAT BANTER JUST NOW MARRIED COUPLE-Y?
HOW ?!
CUT THE CRAP AND GET READY!

Wotakoi: Love is Hard for Otaku

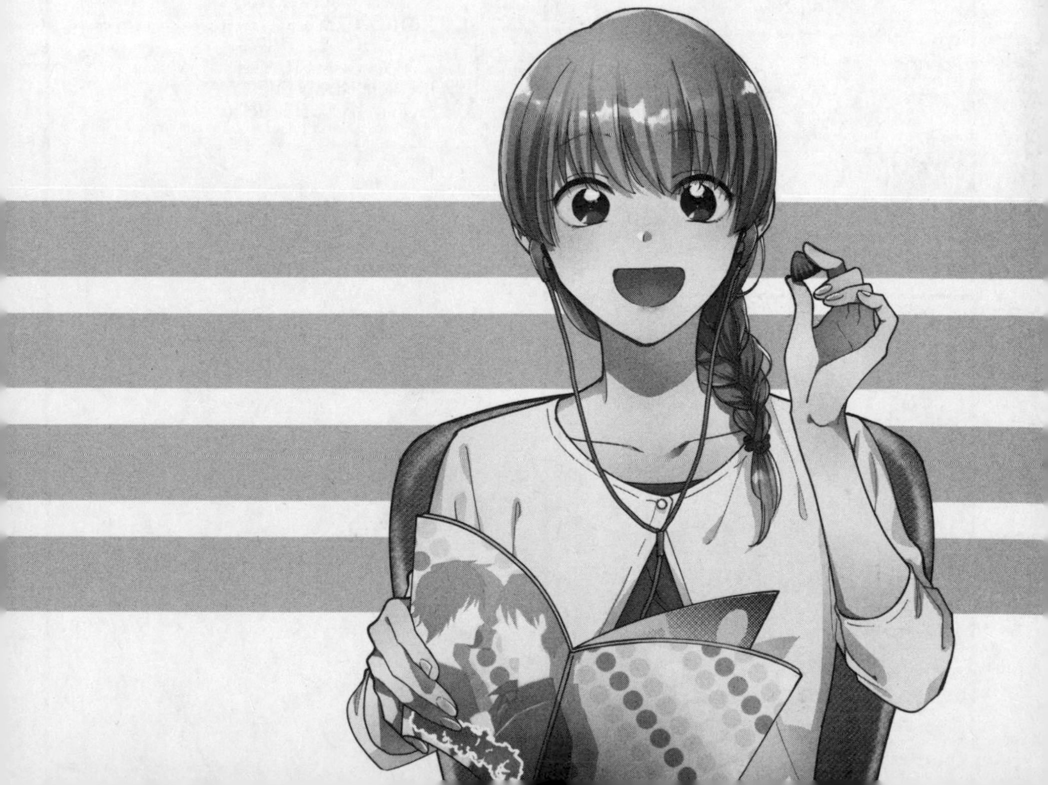

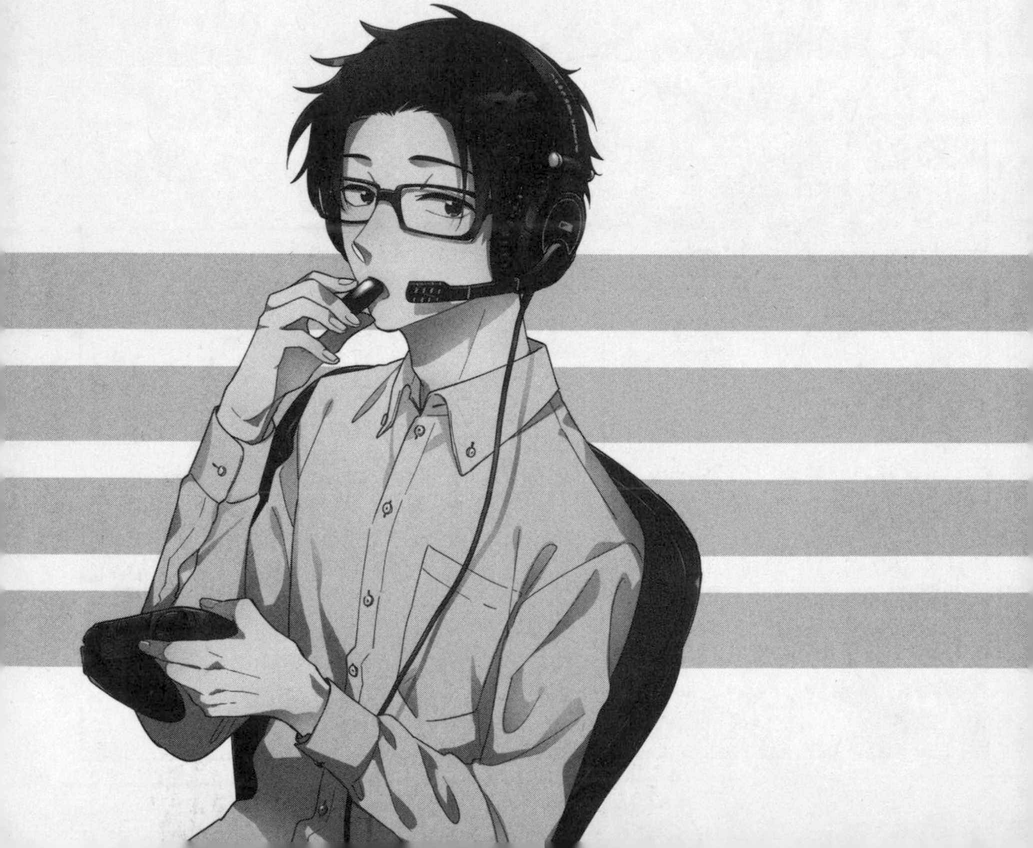

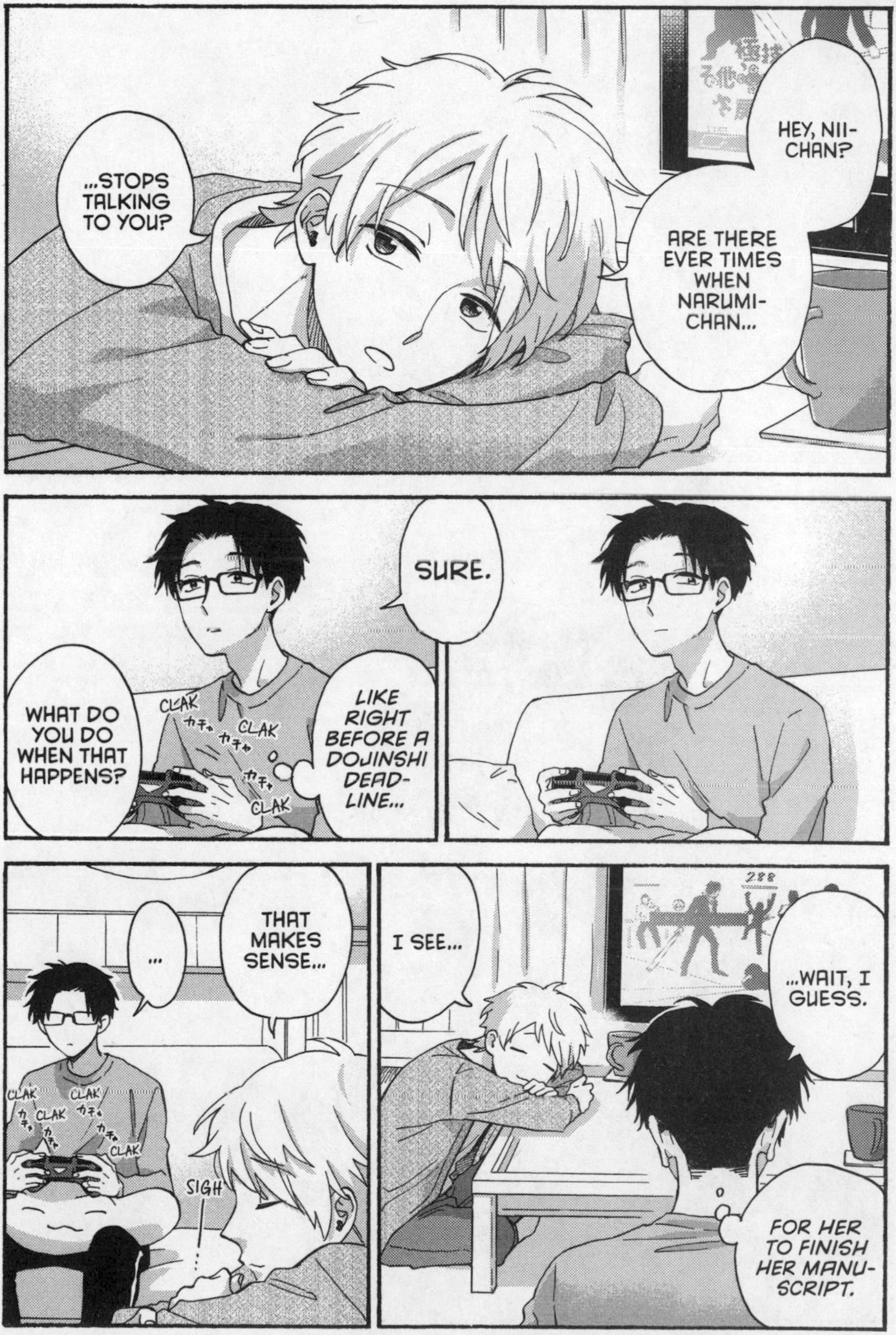
HEY, NII-CHAN?
ARE THERE EVER TIMES WHEN NARUMI-CHAN...
...STOPS TALKING TO YOU?
SURE.
LIKE RIGHT BEFORE A DOJINSHI DEAD-LINE...
CLAK カチャ CLAK カチャ カチャ CLAK
WHAT DO YOU DO WHEN THAT HAPPENS?
...WAIT, I GUESS.
FOR HER TO FINISH HER MANU-SCRIPT.
I SEE...
THAT MAKES SENSE...
...
CLAK CLAK カチャ CLAK カチャ カチャ カチャ CLAK
SIGH

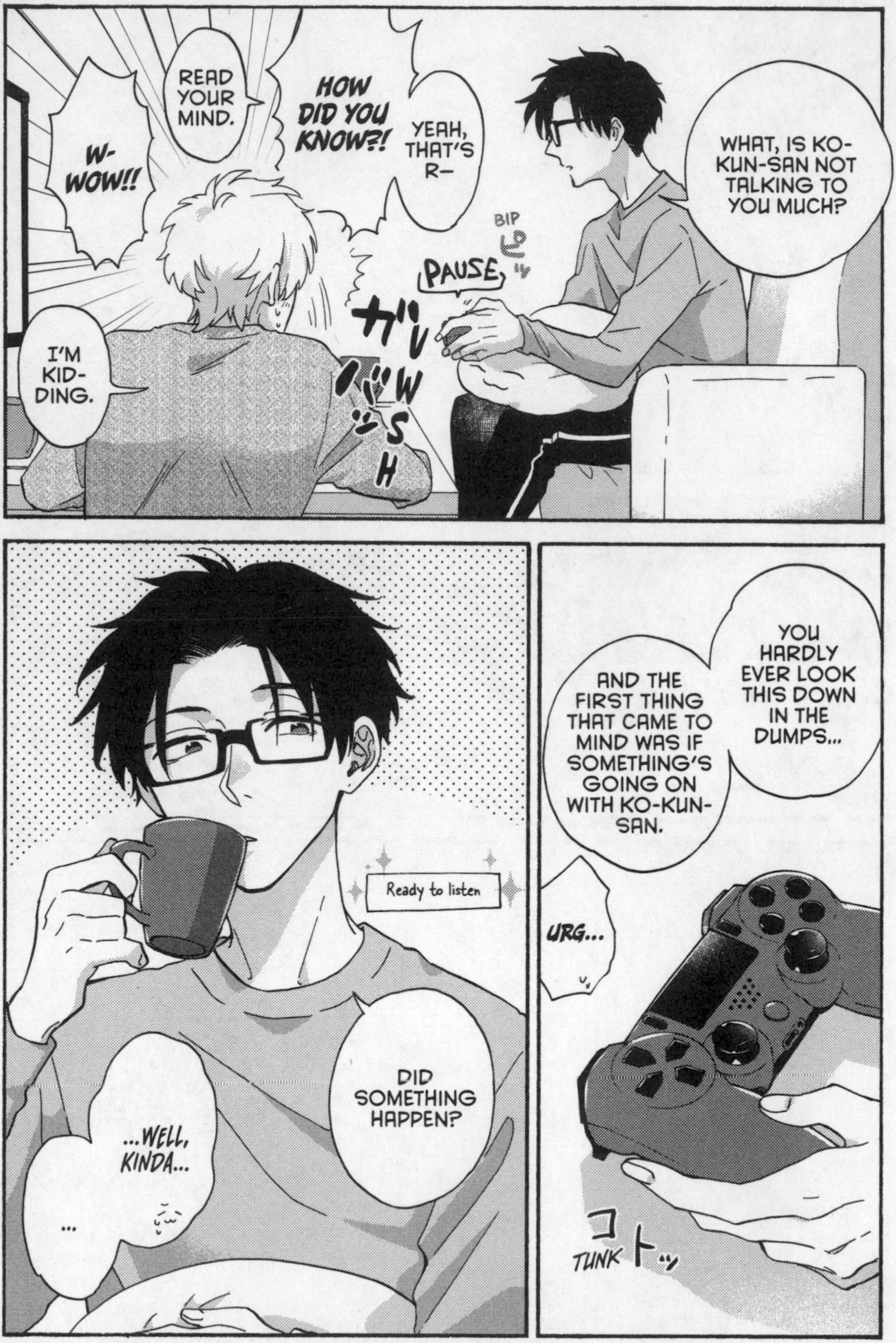
WHAT, IS KO-KUN-SAN NOT TALKING TO YOU MUCH?
BIP ピッ
PAUSE
YEAH, THAT'S R—
HOW DID YOU KNOW?!
READ YOUR MIND.
W-WOW!!
ガバッ WSH
I'M KID-DING.
YOU HARDLY EVER LOOK THIS DOWN IN THE DUMPS...
AND THE FIRST THING THAT CAME TO MIND WAS IF SOMETHING'S GOING ON WITH KO-KUN-SAN.
URG...
コトッ TUNK
Ready to listen
DID SOMETHING HAPPEN?
...WELL, KINDA...
...

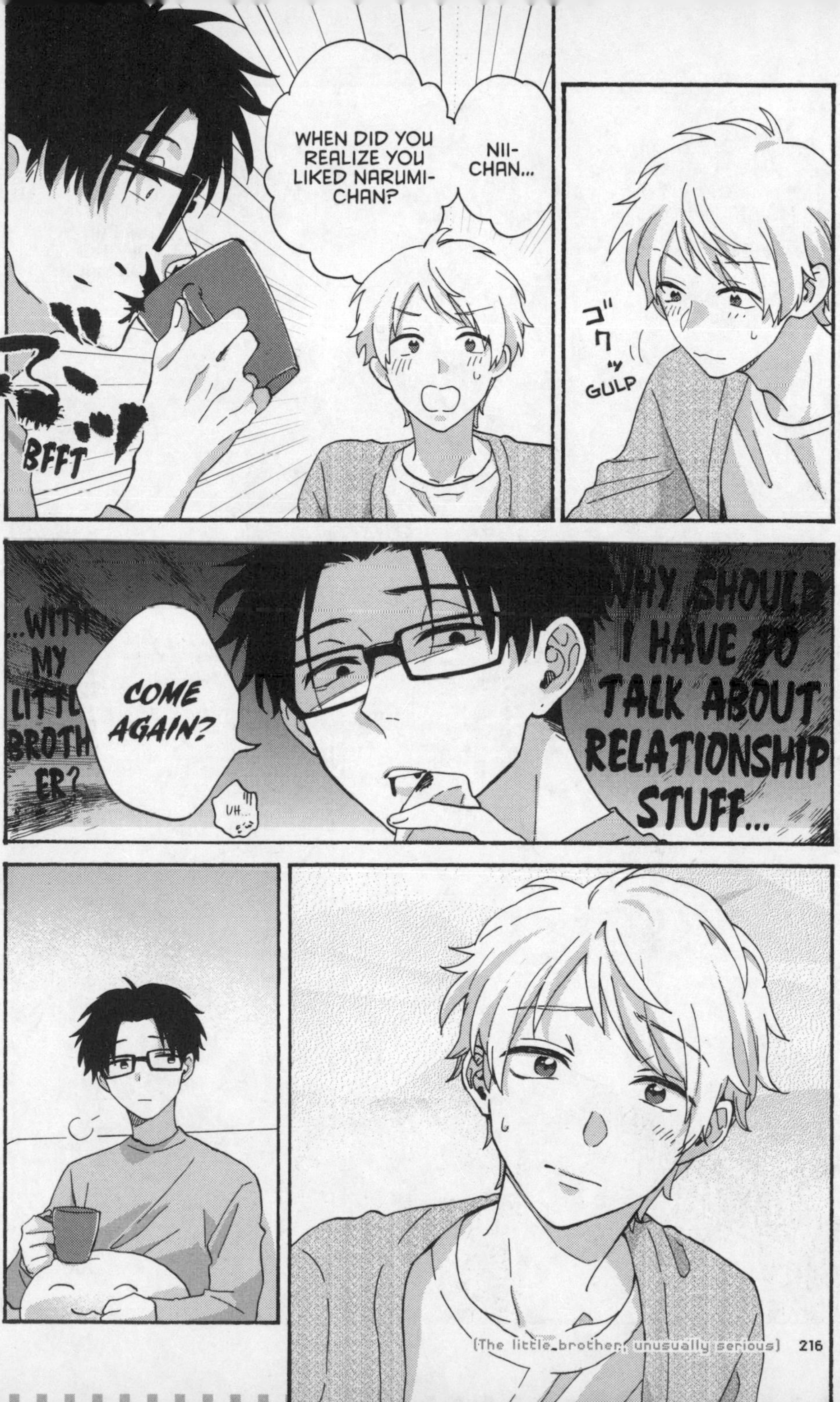
ゴクッ
GULP
NII-CHAN...
WHEN DID YOU REALIZE YOU LIKED NARUMI-CHAN?
BFFT
WHY SHOULD I HAVE TO TALK ABOUT RELATIONSHIP STUFF...
...WITH MY LITTLE BROTHER?
COME AGAIN?
UH...

(The little brother, unusually serious)

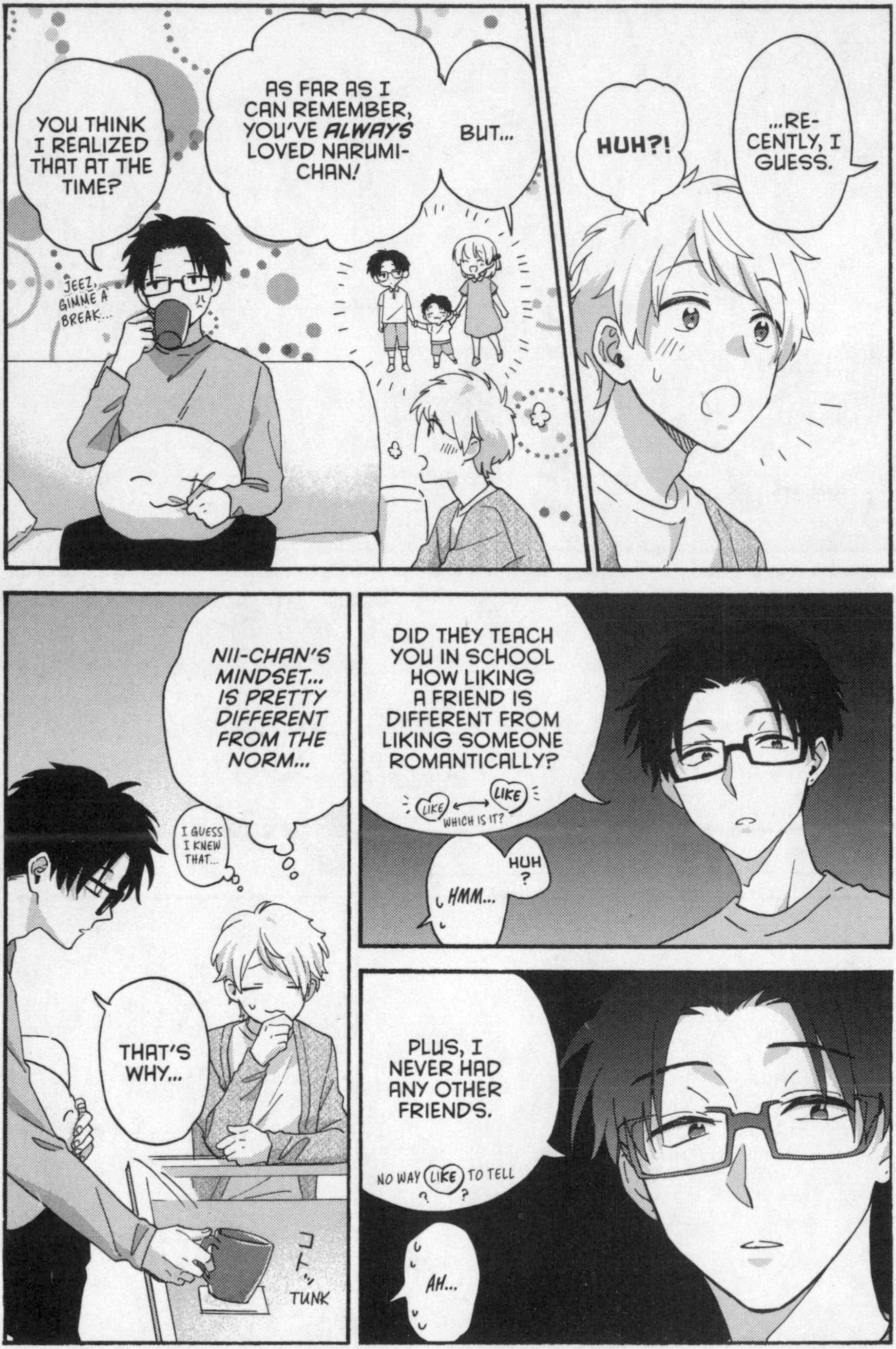
...RE-CENTLY, I GUESS.
HUH?!
BUT...
AS FAR AS I CAN REMEMBER, YOU'VE *ALWAYS* LOVED NARUMI-CHAN!
YOU THINK I REALIZED THAT AT THE TIME?
JEEZ, GIMME A BREAK...
DID THEY TEACH YOU IN SCHOOL HOW LIKING A FRIEND IS DIFFERENT FROM LIKING SOMEONE ROMANTICALLY?
LIKE ↔ LIKE
WHICH IS IT?
HUH?
HMM...
PLUS, I NEVER HAD ANY OTHER FRIENDS.
NO WAY LIKE TO TELL
AH...
NII-CHAN'S MINDSET... IS PRETTY DIFFERENT FROM THE NORM...
I GUESS I KNEW THAT...
THAT'S WHY...
TUNK

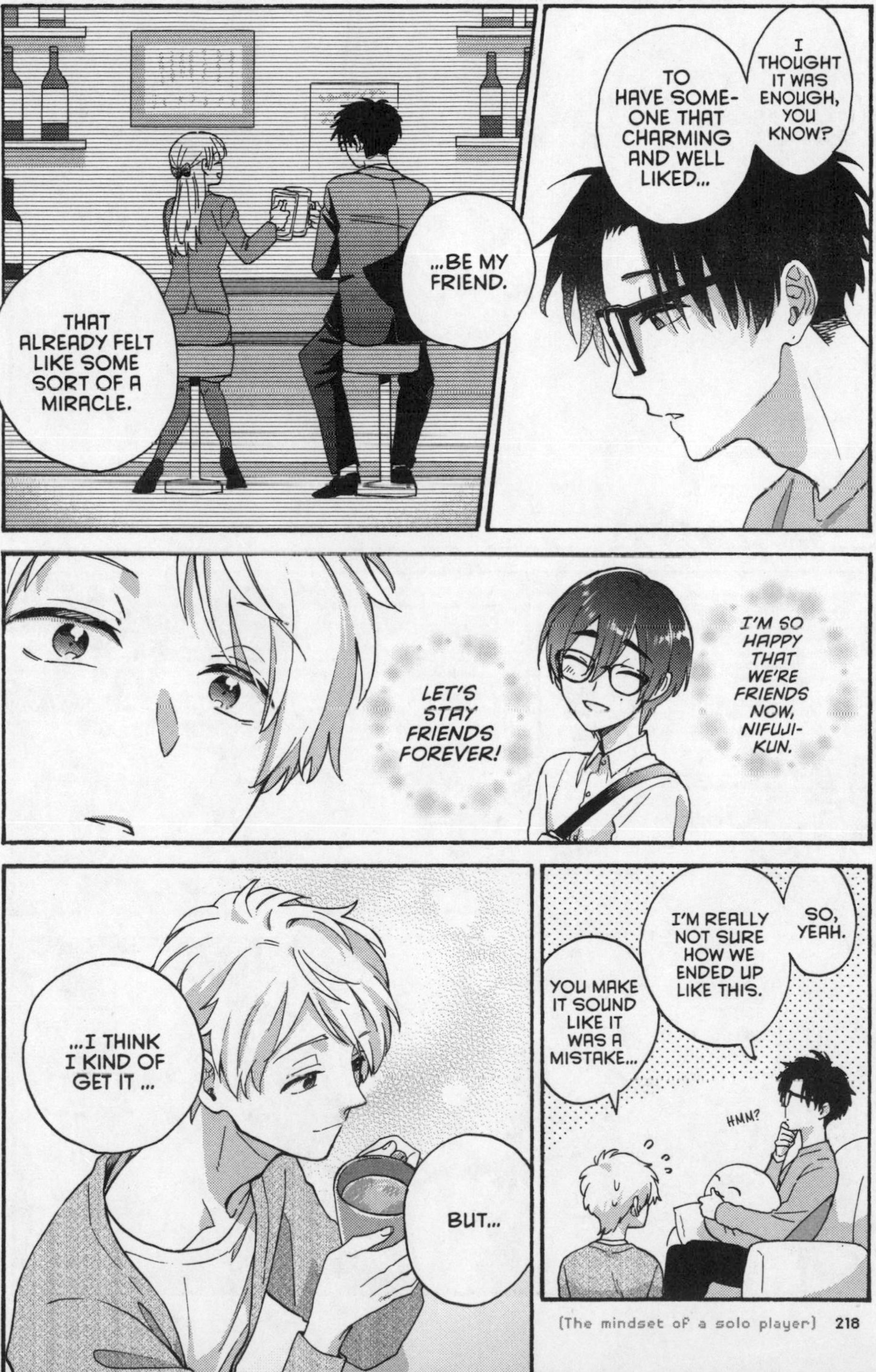
I THOUGHT IT WAS ENOUGH, YOU KNOW?
TO HAVE SOME-ONE THAT CHARMING AND WELL LIKED...
...BE MY FRIEND.
THAT ALREADY FELT LIKE SOME SORT OF A MIRACLE.
I'M SO HAPPY THAT WE'RE FRIENDS NOW, NIFUJI-KUN.
LET'S STAY FRIENDS FOREVER!
SO, YEAH.
I'M REALLY NOT SURE HOW WE ENDED UP LIKE THIS.
YOU MAKE IT SOUND LIKE IT WAS A MISTAKE...
HMM?
...I THINK I KIND OF GET IT ...
BUT...

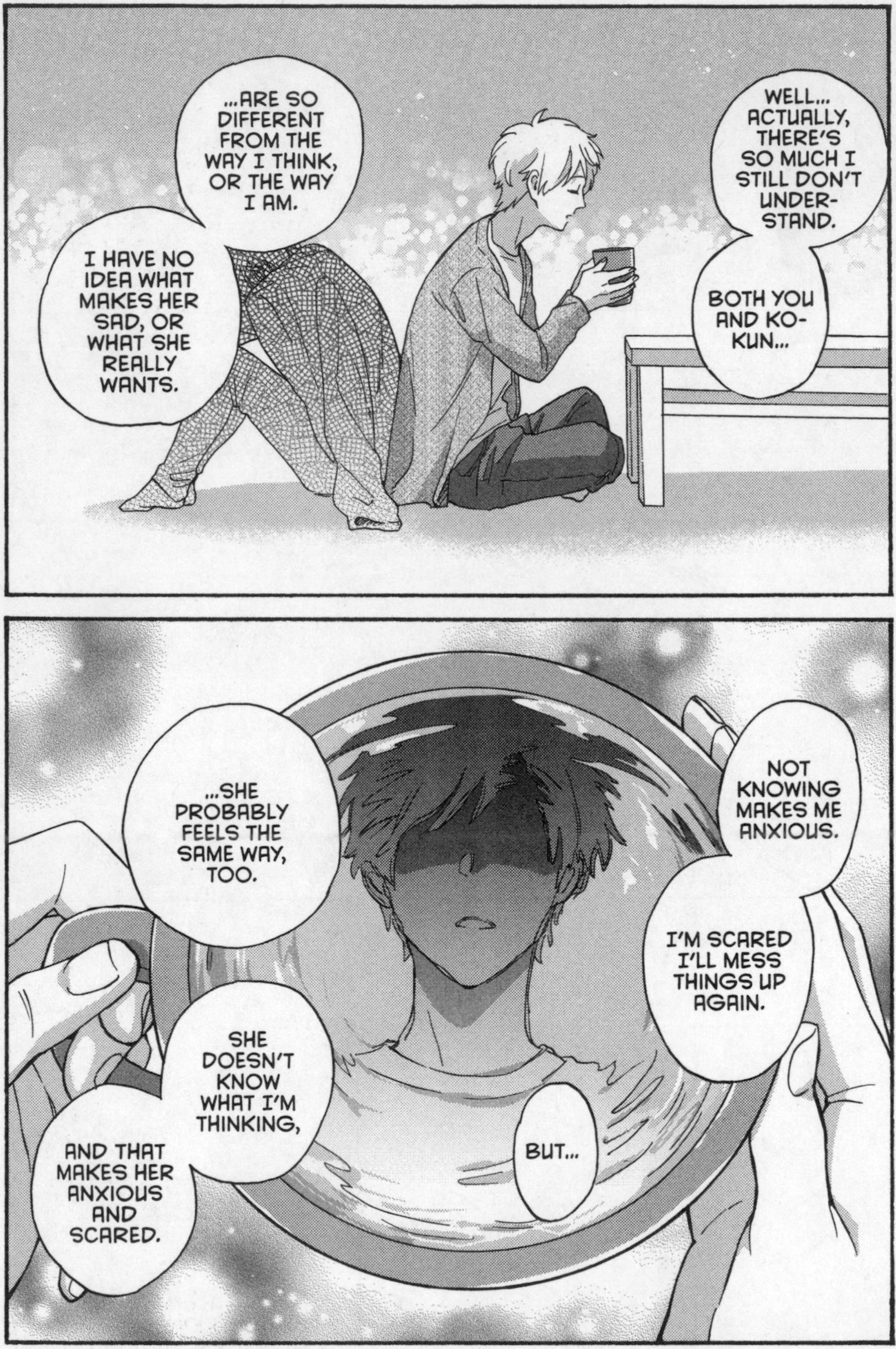
WELL... ACTUALLY, THERE'S SO MUCH I STILL DON'T UNDER-STAND.
BOTH YOU AND KO-KUN...
...ARE SO DIFFERENT FROM THE WAY I THINK, OR THE WAY I AM.
I HAVE NO IDEA WHAT MAKES HER SAD, OR WHAT SHE REALLY WANTS.
NOT KNOWING MAKES ME ANXIOUS.
I'M SCARED I'LL MESS THINGS UP AGAIN.
BUT...
...SHE PROBABLY FEELS THE SAME WAY, TOO.
SHE DOESN'T KNOW WHAT I'M THINKING,
AND THAT MAKES HER ANXIOUS AND SCARED.

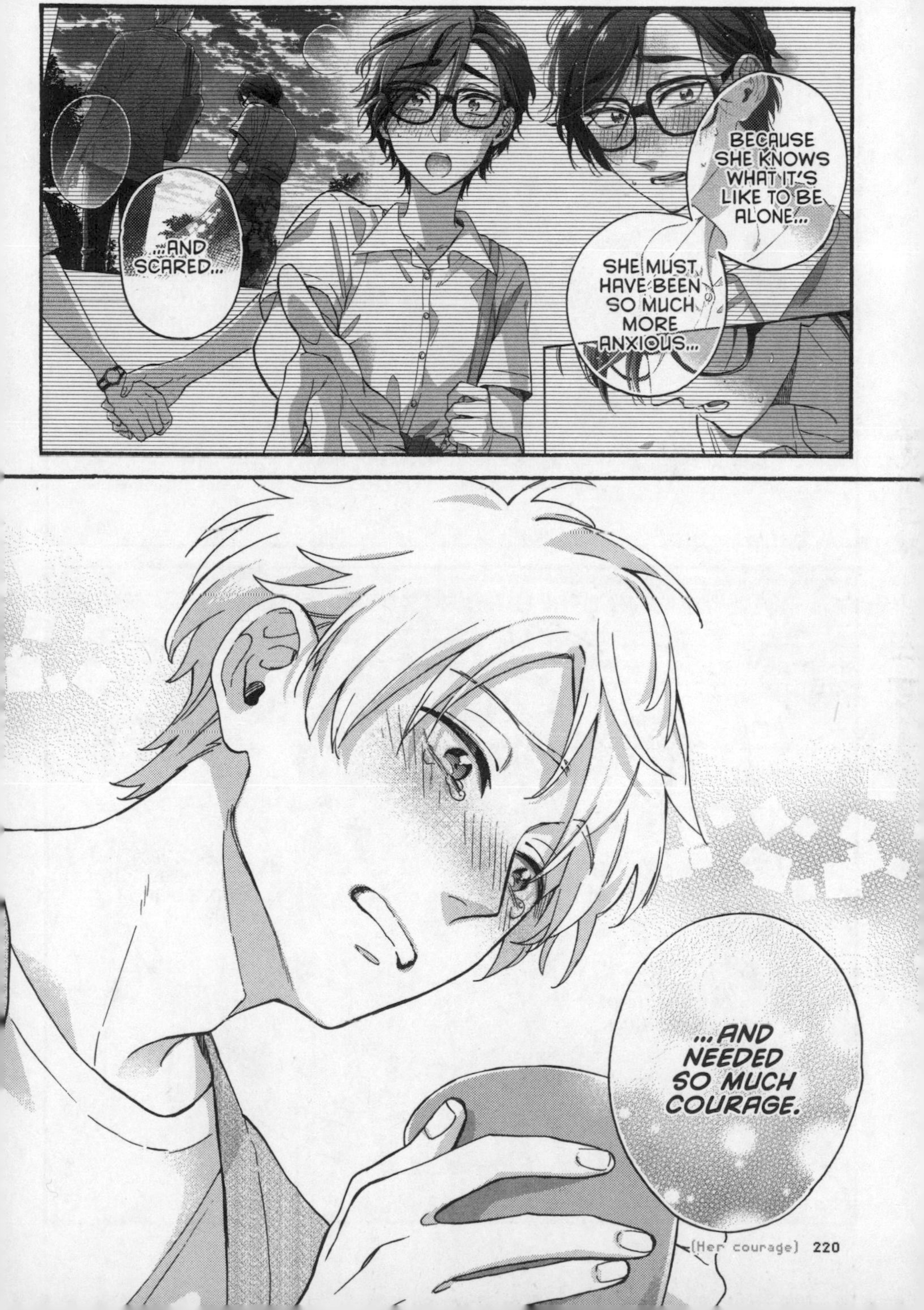
BECAUSE SHE KNOWS WHAT IT'S LIKE TO BE ALONE...
SHE MUST HAVE BEEN SO MUCH MORE ANXIOUS...
...AND SCARED...
...AND NEEDED SO MUCH COURAGE.
(Her courage)

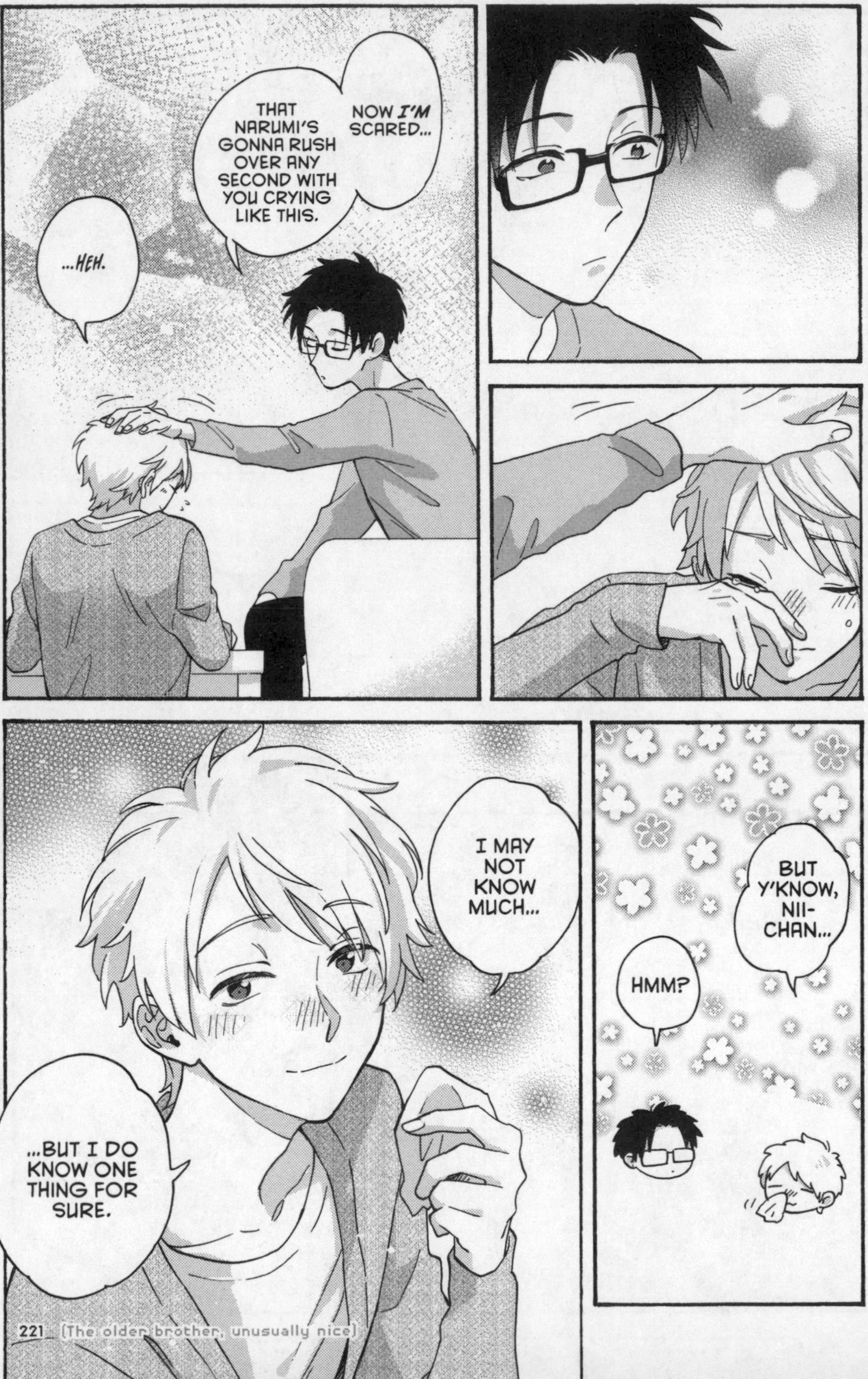
NOW I'M SCARED...
THAT NARUMI'S GONNA RUSH OVER ANY SECOND WITH YOU CRYING LIKE THIS.
...HEH.
BUT Y'KNOW, NII-CHAN...
HMM?
I MAY NOT KNOW MUCH...
...BUT I DO KNOW ONE THING FOR SURE.

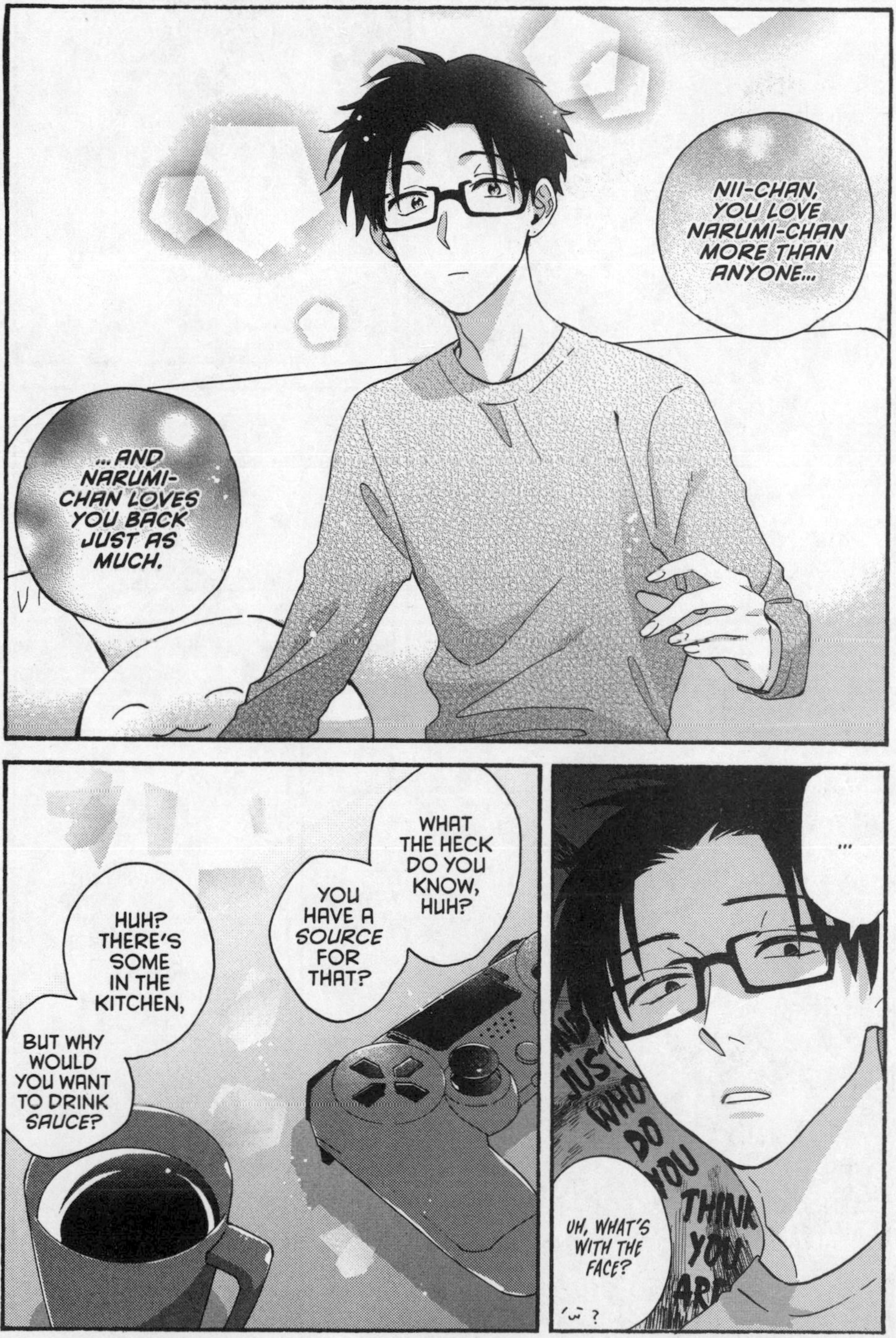
NII-CHAN, YOU LOVE NARUMI-CHAN MORE THAN ANYONE...
...AND NARUMI-CHAN LOVES YOU BACK JUST AS MUCH.
...
JUST WHO DO YOU THINK YOU
UH, WHAT'S WITH THE FACE?
WHAT THE HECK DO YOU KNOW, HUH?
YOU HAVE A SOURCE FOR THAT?
HUH? THERE'S SOME IN THE KITCHEN,
BUT WHY WOULD YOU WANT TO DRINK SAUCE?

← To be continued...

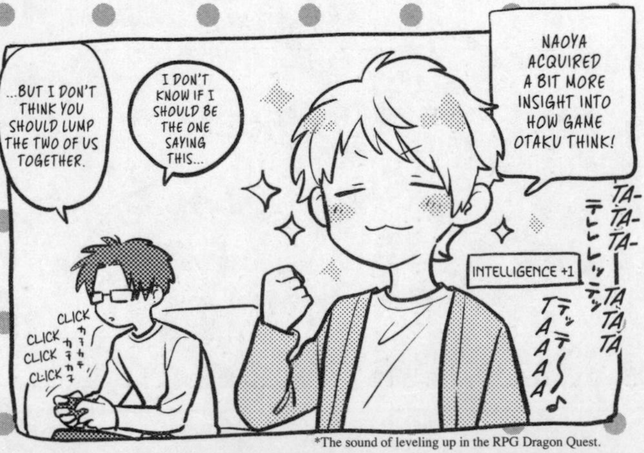
NAOYA ACQUIRED A BIT MORE INSIGHT INTO HOW GAME OTAKU THINK!
TA-TA-TA-TA TA TA TA
TA-AAAA-A♪
INTELLIGENCE +1
I DON'T KNOW IF I SHOULD BE THE ONE SAYING THIS...
...BUT I DON'T THINK YOU SHOULD LUMP THE TWO OF US TOGETHER.
CLICK CLICK CLICK CLICK

*The sound of leveling up in the RPG Dragon Quest.

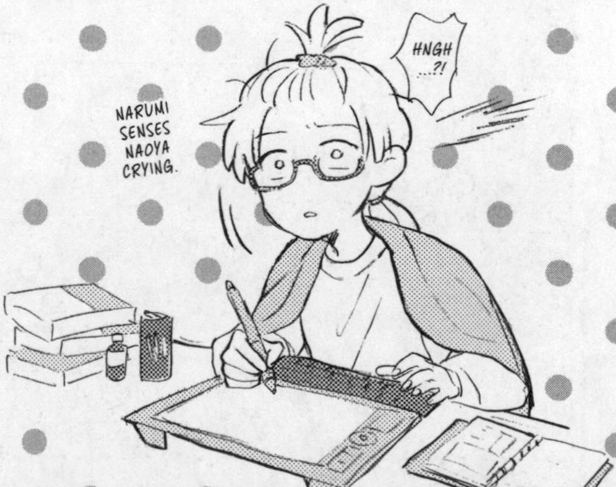
HNGH ...?!
NARUMI SENSES NAOYA CRYING.

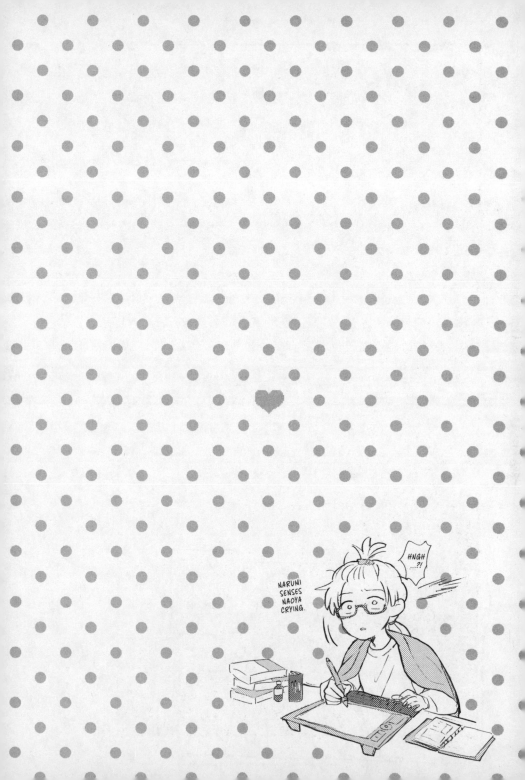

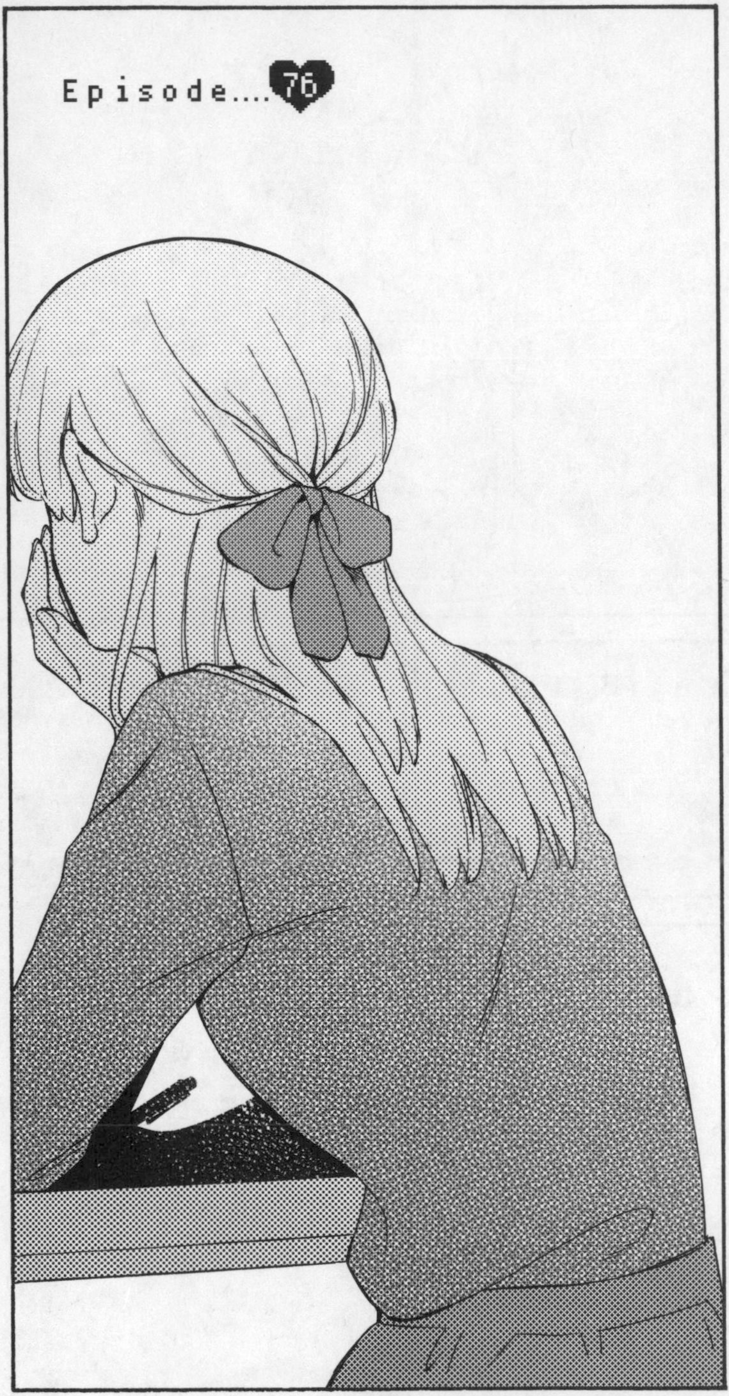
Episode.... 76

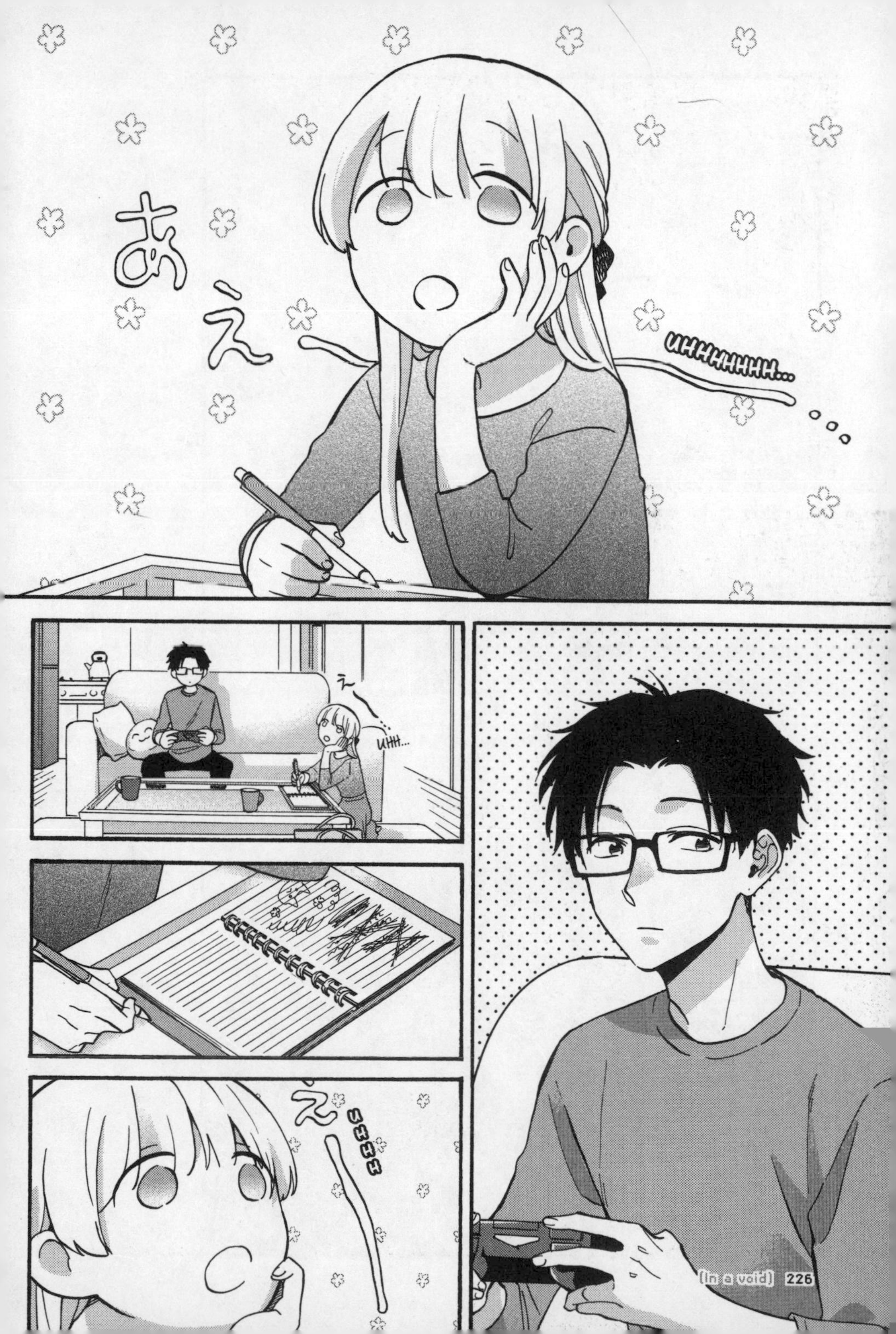
あえ～
UHHHHHHHH...
え～
UHH...
え
UHHH

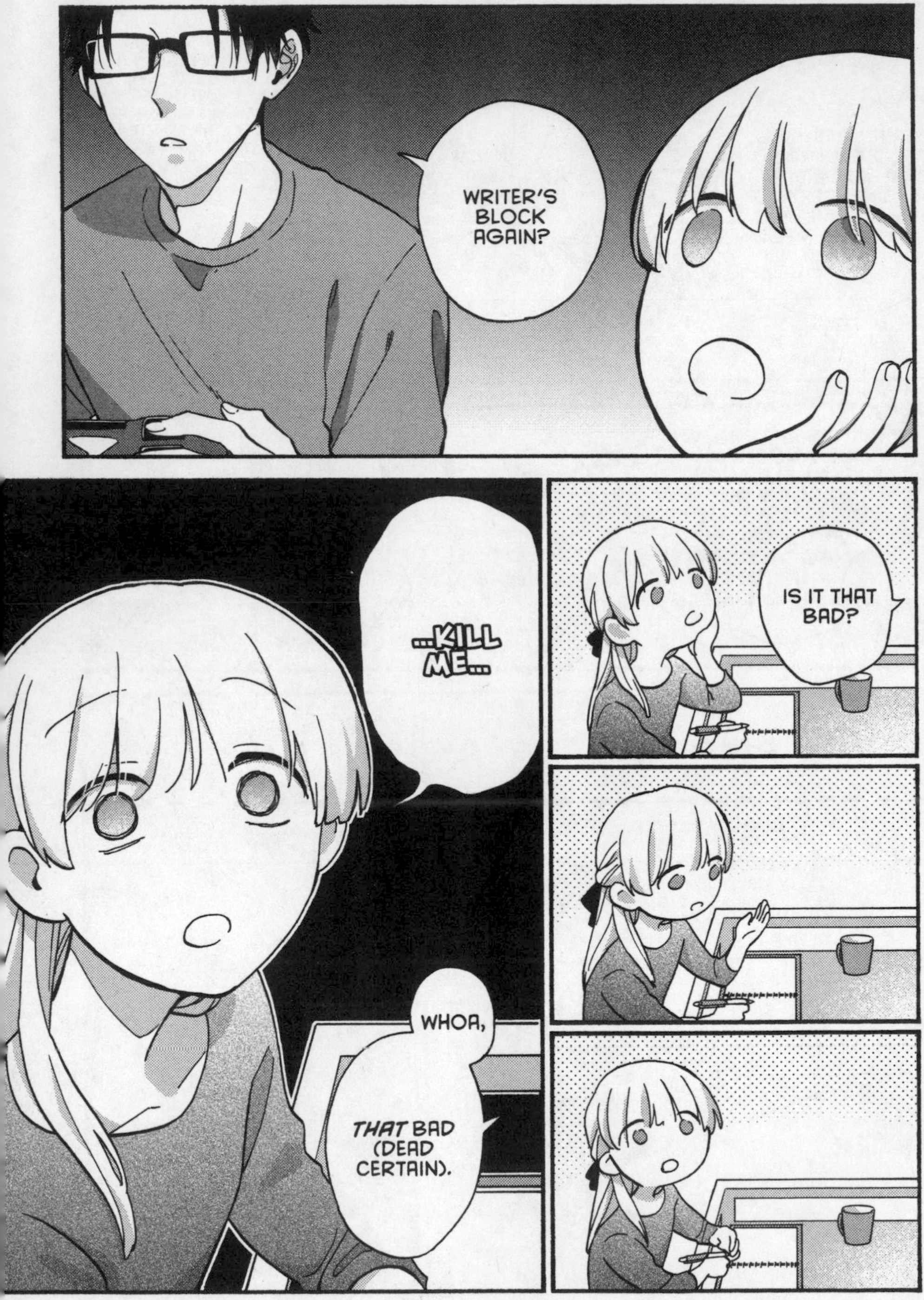
WRITER'S BLOCK AGAIN?
IS IT THAT BAD?
...KILL ME...
WHOA,
THAT BAD (DEAD CERTAIN).

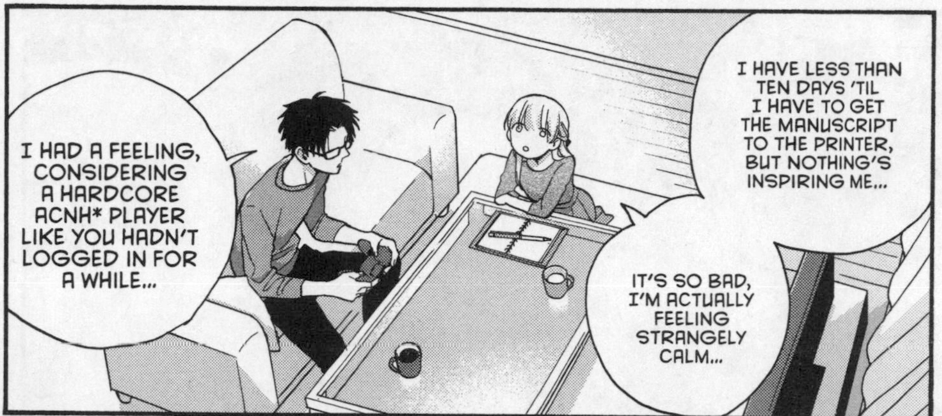
I HAVE LESS THAN TEN DAYS 'TIL I HAVE TO GET THE MANUSCRIPT TO THE PRINTER, BUT NOTHING'S INSPIRING ME...
IT'S SO BAD, I'M ACTUALLY FEELING STRANGELY CALM...
I HAD A FEELING, CONSIDERING A HARDCORE ACNH* PLAYER LIKE YOU HADN'T LOGGED IN FOR A WHILE...

*Reference to the 2020 simulation game *Animal Crossing: New Horizons*

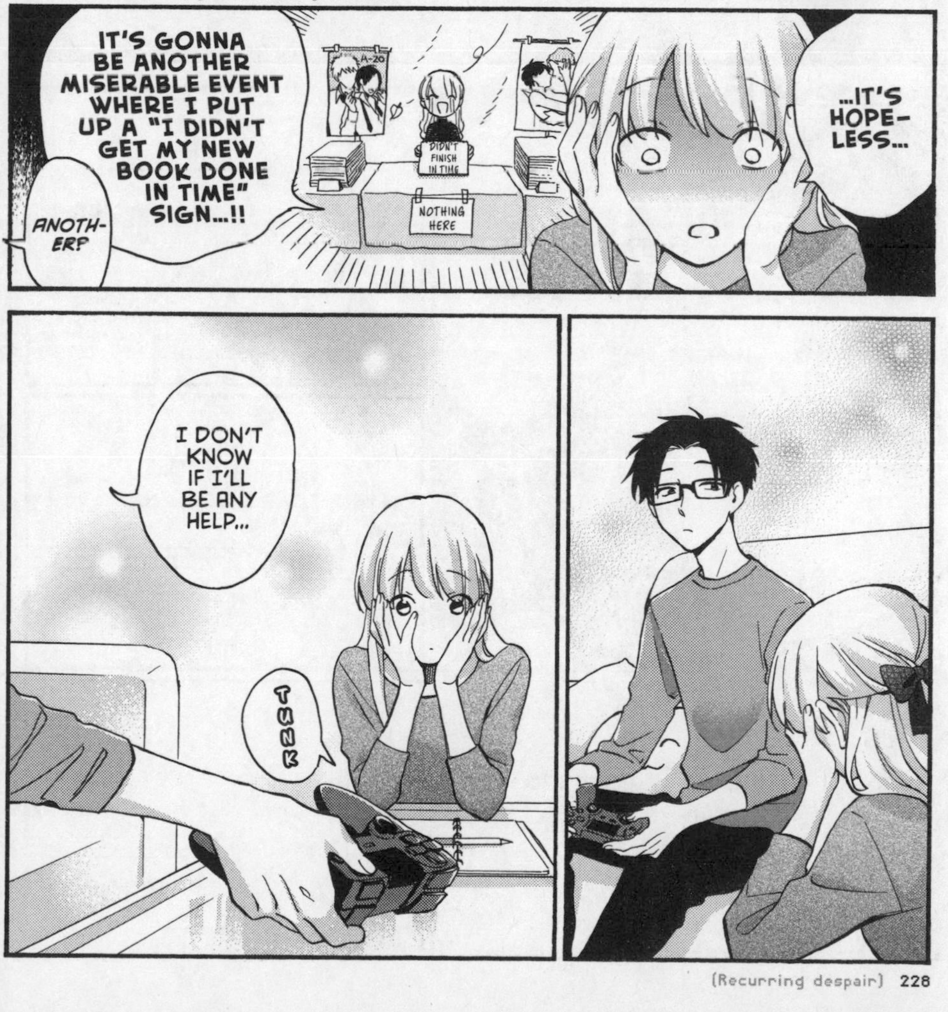
...IT'S HOPE-LESS...
IT'S GONNA BE ANOTHER MISERABLE EVENT WHERE I PUT UP A "I DIDN'T GET MY NEW BOOK DONE IN TIME" SIGN...!!
A-20
DIDN'T FINISH IN TIME
NOTHING HERE
ANOTH-ER?
I DON'T KNOW IF I'LL BE ANY HELP...
TUNK

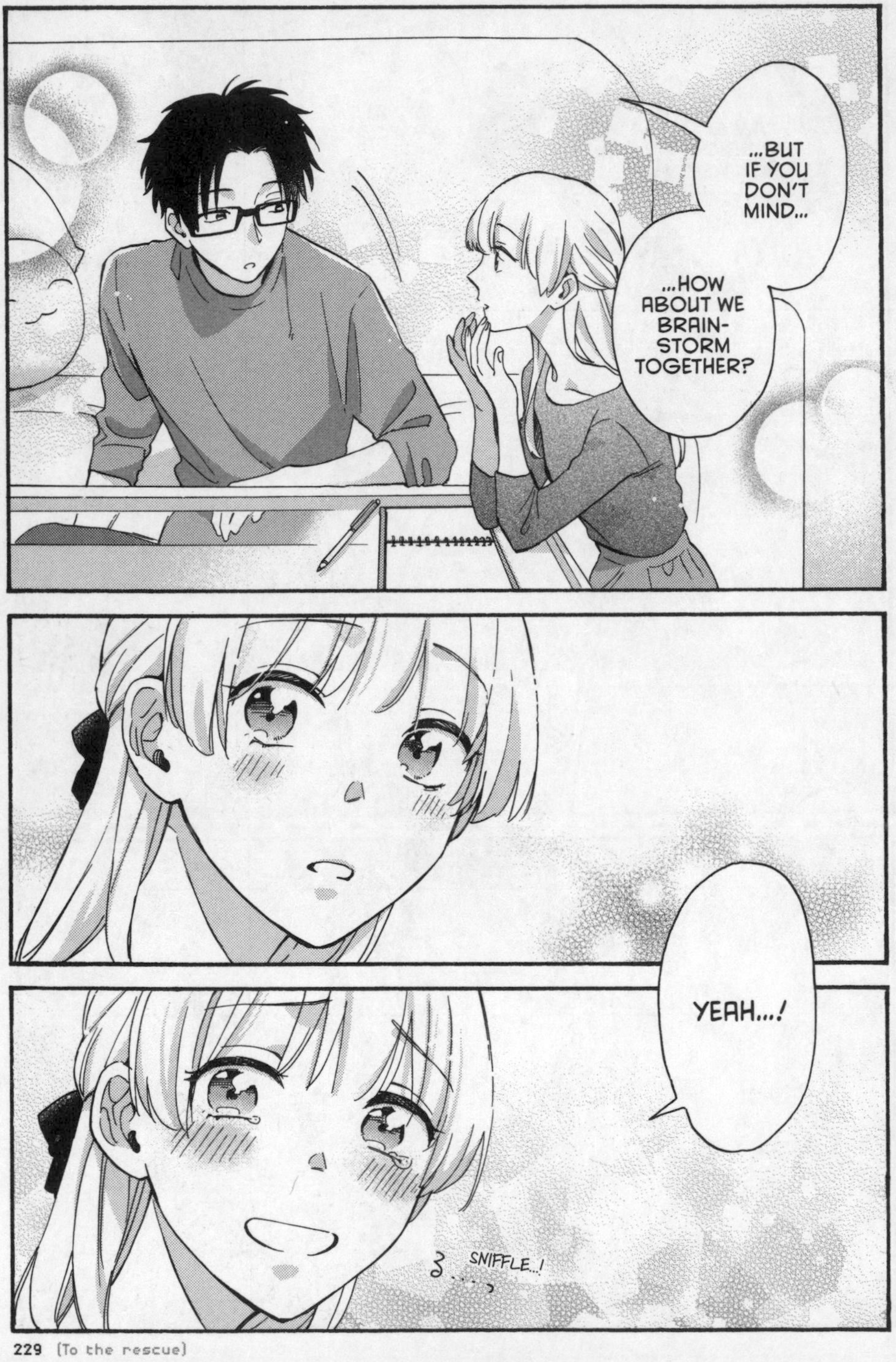
...BUT IF YOU DON'T MIND...
...HOW ABOUT WE BRAIN-STORM TOGETHER?
YEAH...!
SNIFFLE...!

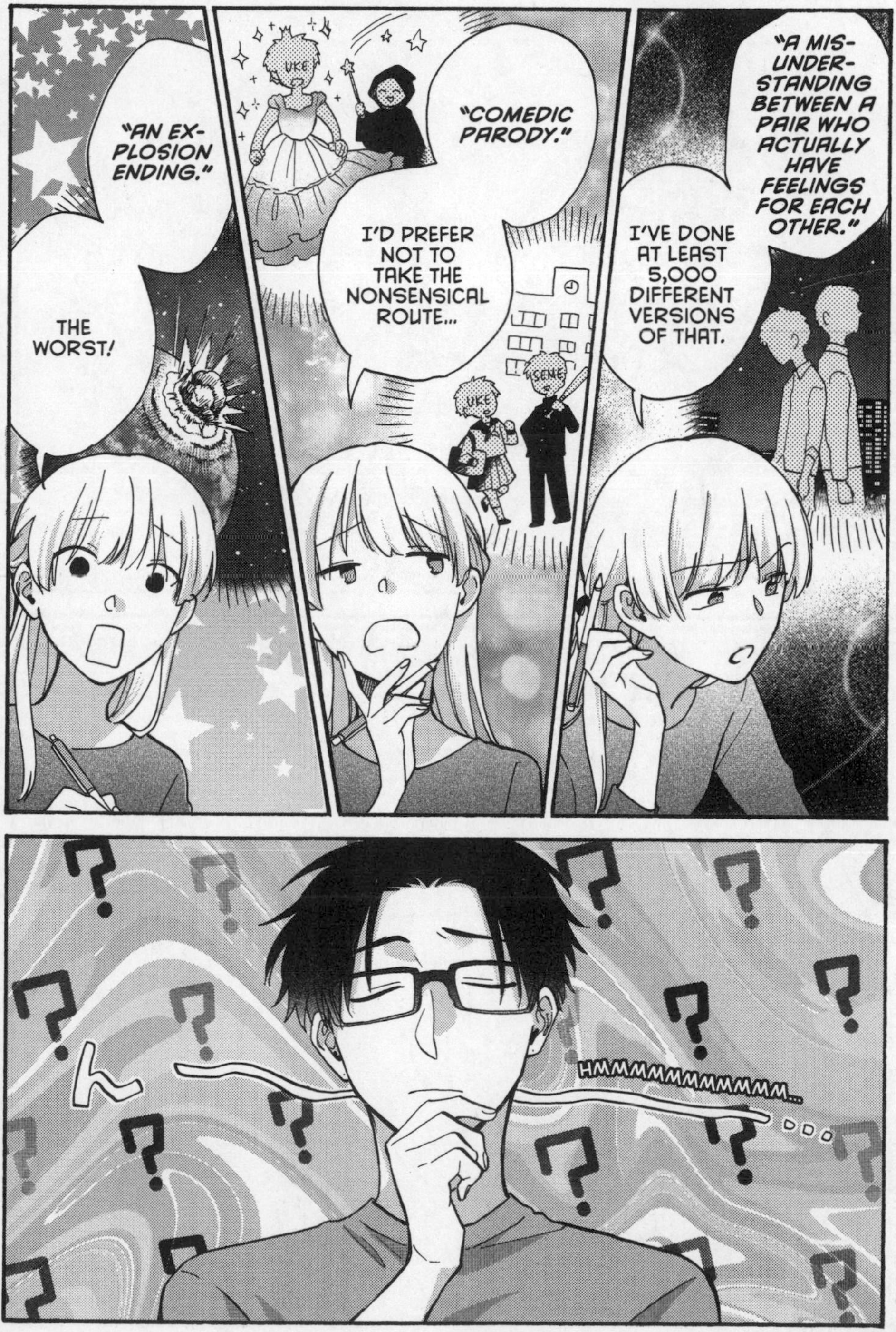
"A MIS-UNDER-STANDING BETWEEN A PAIR WHO ACTUALLY HAVE FEELINGS FOR EACH OTHER."
I'VE DONE AT LEAST 5,000 DIFFERENT VERSIONS OF THAT.
"COMEDIC PARODY."
UKE
I'D PREFER NOT TO TAKE THE NONSENSICAL ROUTE...
UKE
SEME
"AN EX-PLOSION ENDING."
THE WORST!
ん〜
HMMMMMMMMMMM...

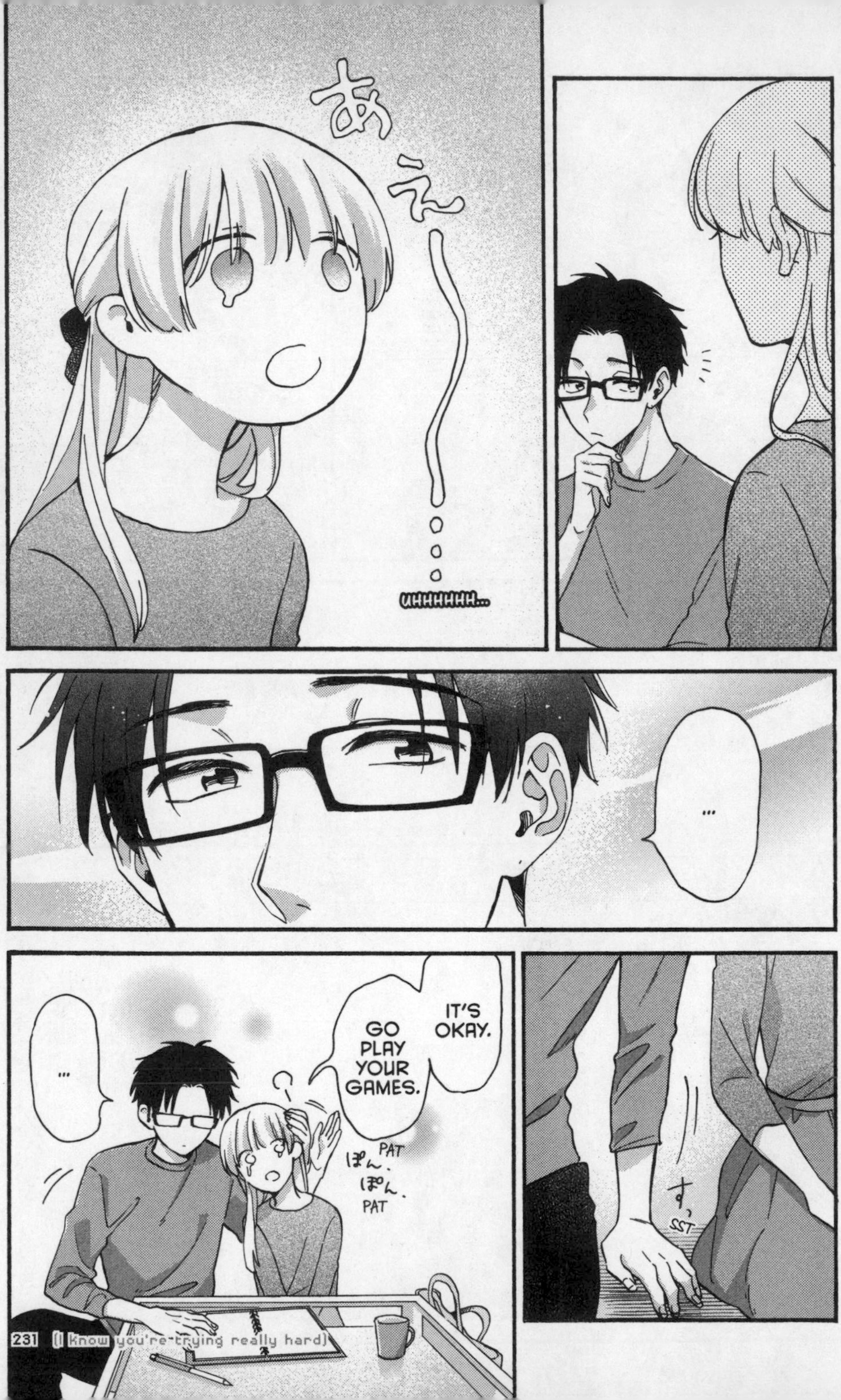
あえ～…
UHHHHHHH...
…
すっ
SST
IT'S OKAY.
GO PLAY YOUR GAMES.
ぽん。ぽん。
PAT PAT
…

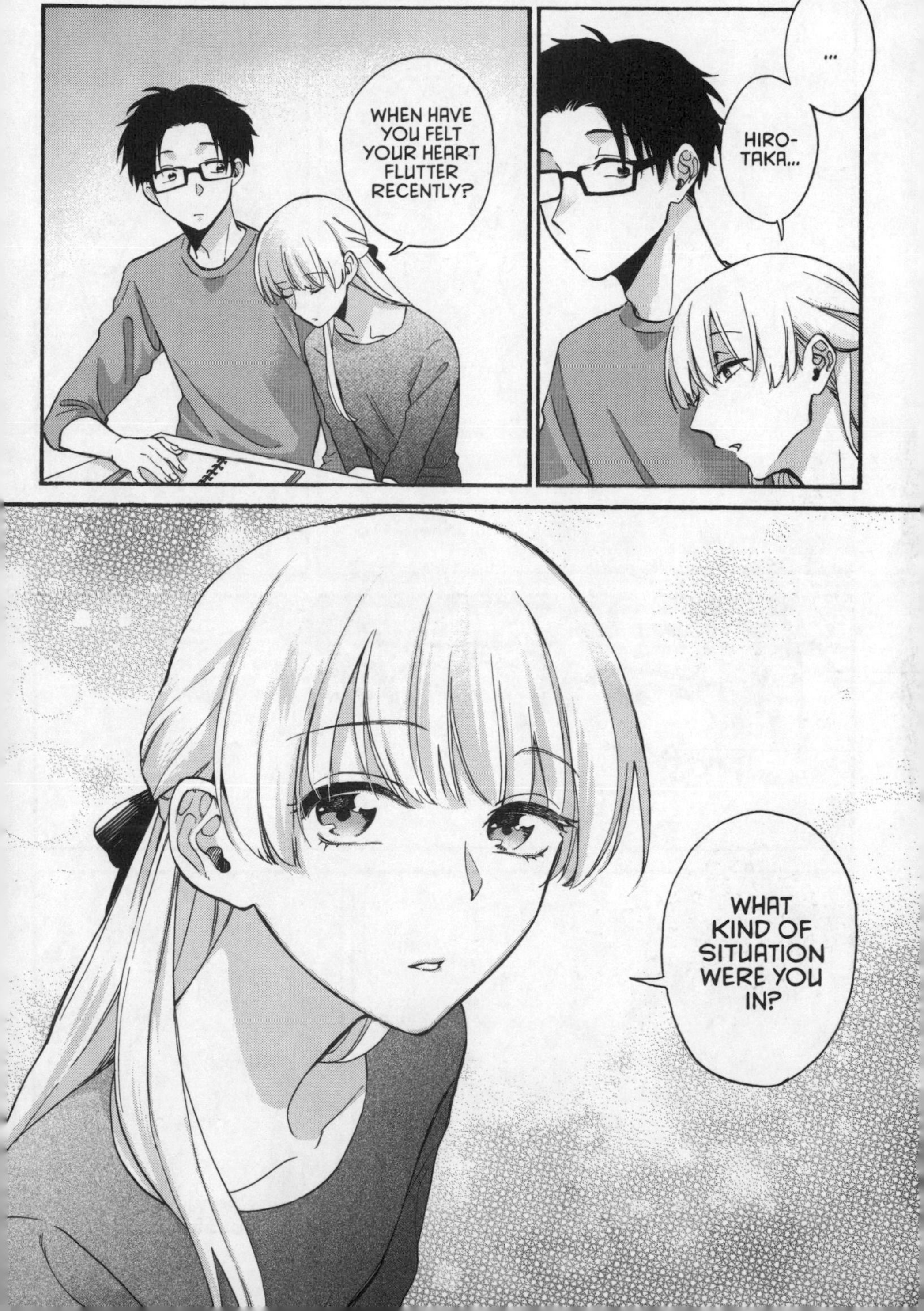
...
HIRO-TAKA...
WHEN HAVE YOU FELT YOUR HEART FLUTTER RECENTLY?
WHAT KIND OF SITUATION WERE YOU IN?

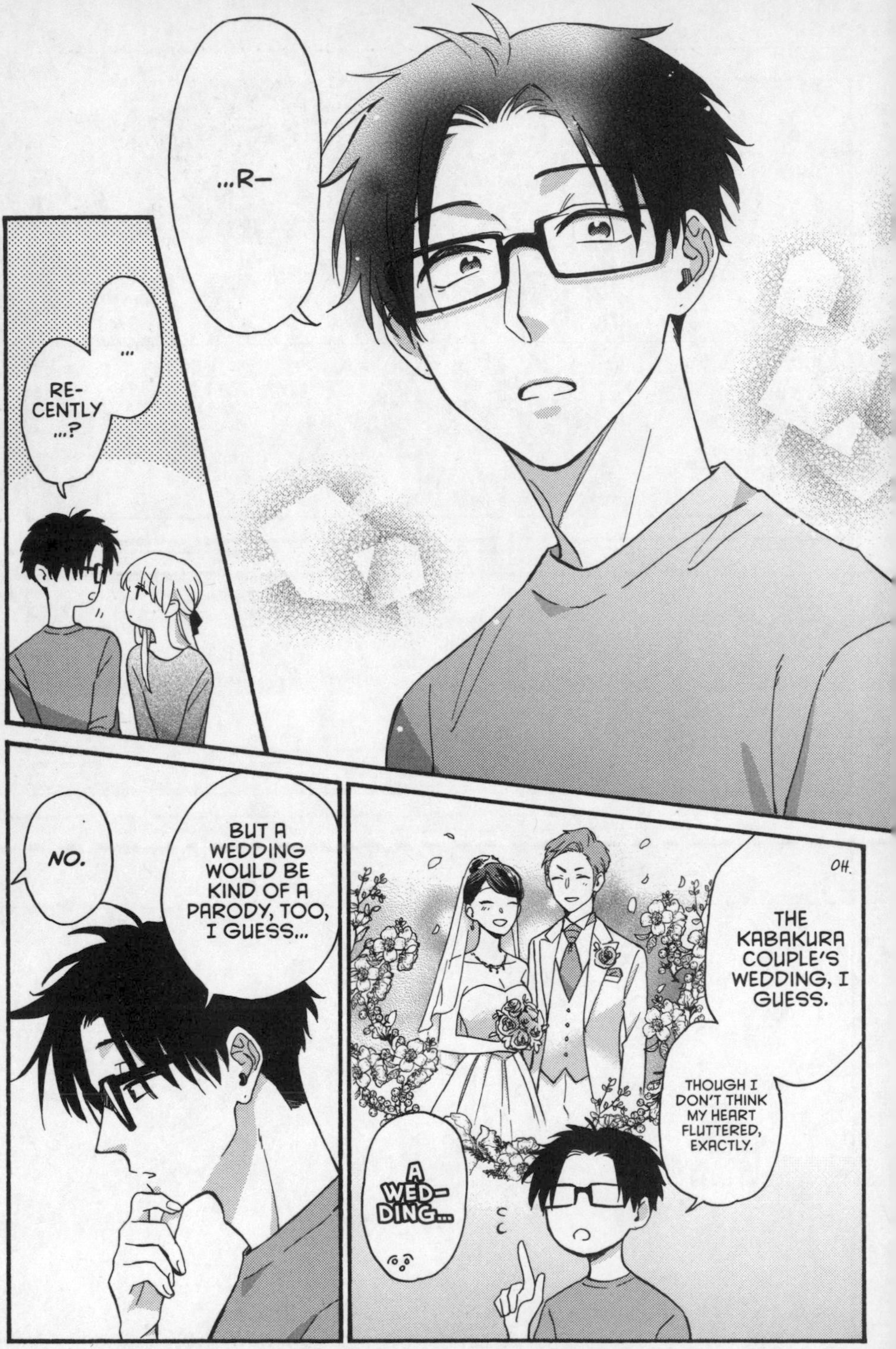
...R-
... RE-CENTLY ...?
OH.
THE KABAKURA COUPLE'S WEDDING, I GUESS.
THOUGH I DON'T THINK MY HEART FLUTTERED, EXACTLY.
A WED-DING...
BUT A WEDDING WOULD BE KIND OF A PARODY, TOO, I GUESS...
NO.

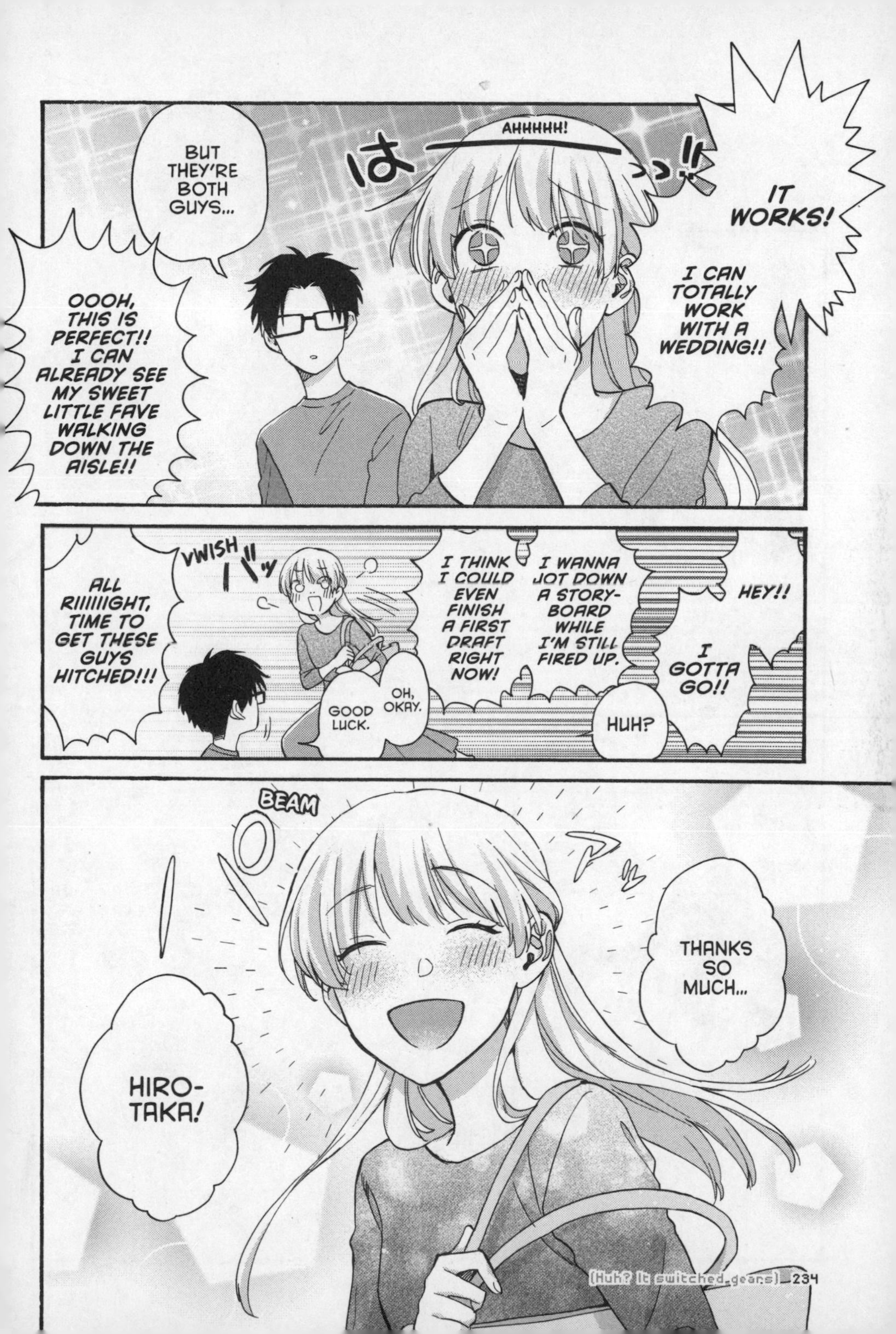
IT WORKS!
I CAN TOTALLY WORK WITH A WEDDING!!
AHHHHH!
はーーっ!!
BUT THEY'RE BOTH GUYS...
OOOH, THIS IS PERFECT!! I CAN ALREADY SEE MY SWEET LITTLE FAVE WALKING DOWN THE AISLE!!
HEY!!
I GOTTA GO!!
HUH?
I WANNA JOT DOWN A STORY-BOARD WHILE I'M STILL FIRED UP.
I THINK I COULD EVEN FINISH A FIRST DRAFT RIGHT NOW!
VWISH
バッ
OH, OKAY.
GOOD LUCK.
ALL RIIIIIIGHT, TIME TO GET THESE GUYS HITCHED!!!
BEAM
THANKS SO MUCH...
HIRO-TAKA!
(Huh? It switched gears)

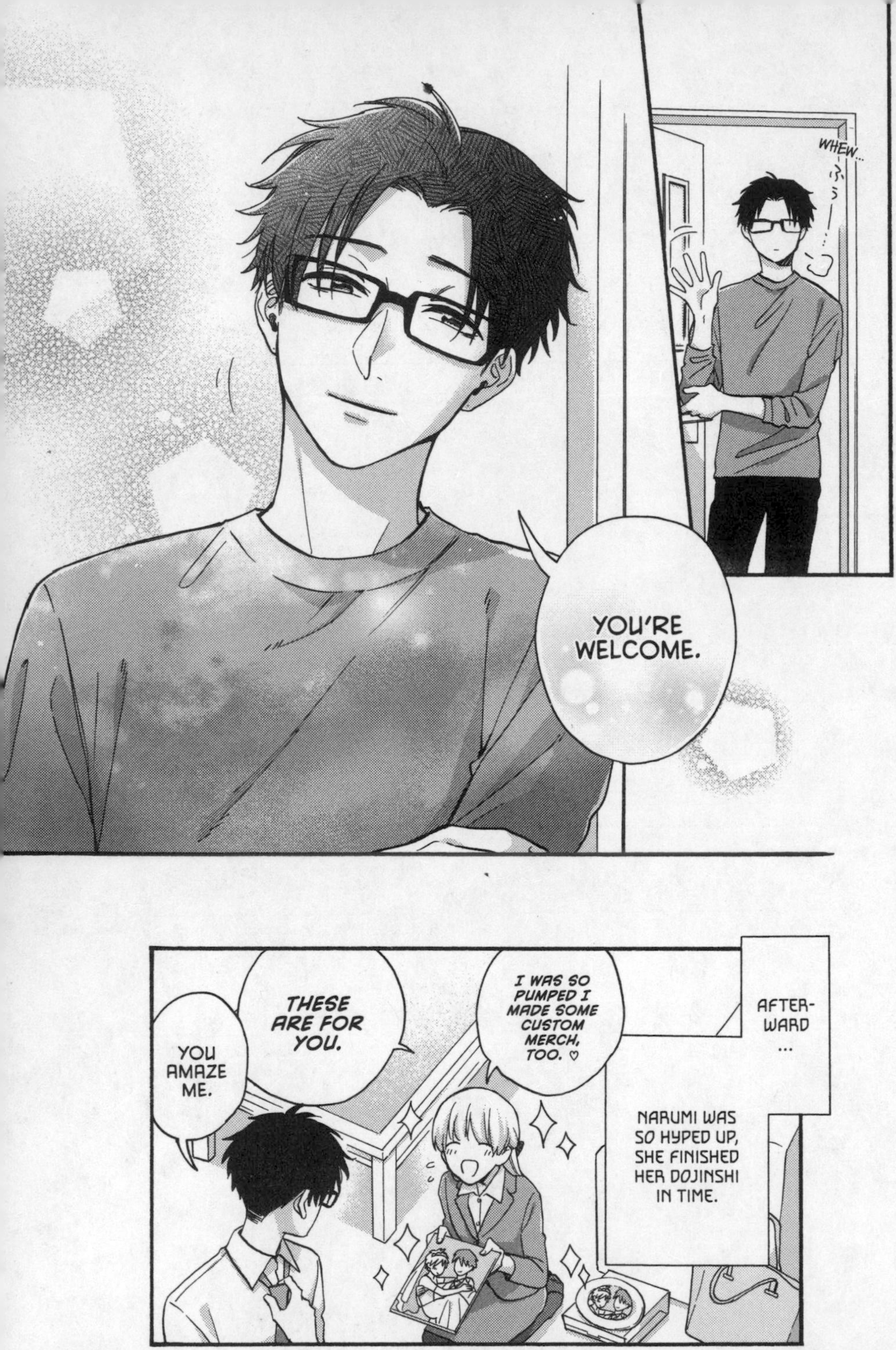
WHEW...
ふぅー…
YOU'RE WELCOME.
AFTERWARD...
NARUMI WAS SO HYPED UP, SHE FINISHED HER DOJINSHI IN TIME.
I WAS SO PUMPED I MADE SOME CUSTOM MERCH, TOO. ♡
THESE ARE FOR YOU.
YOU AMAZE ME.

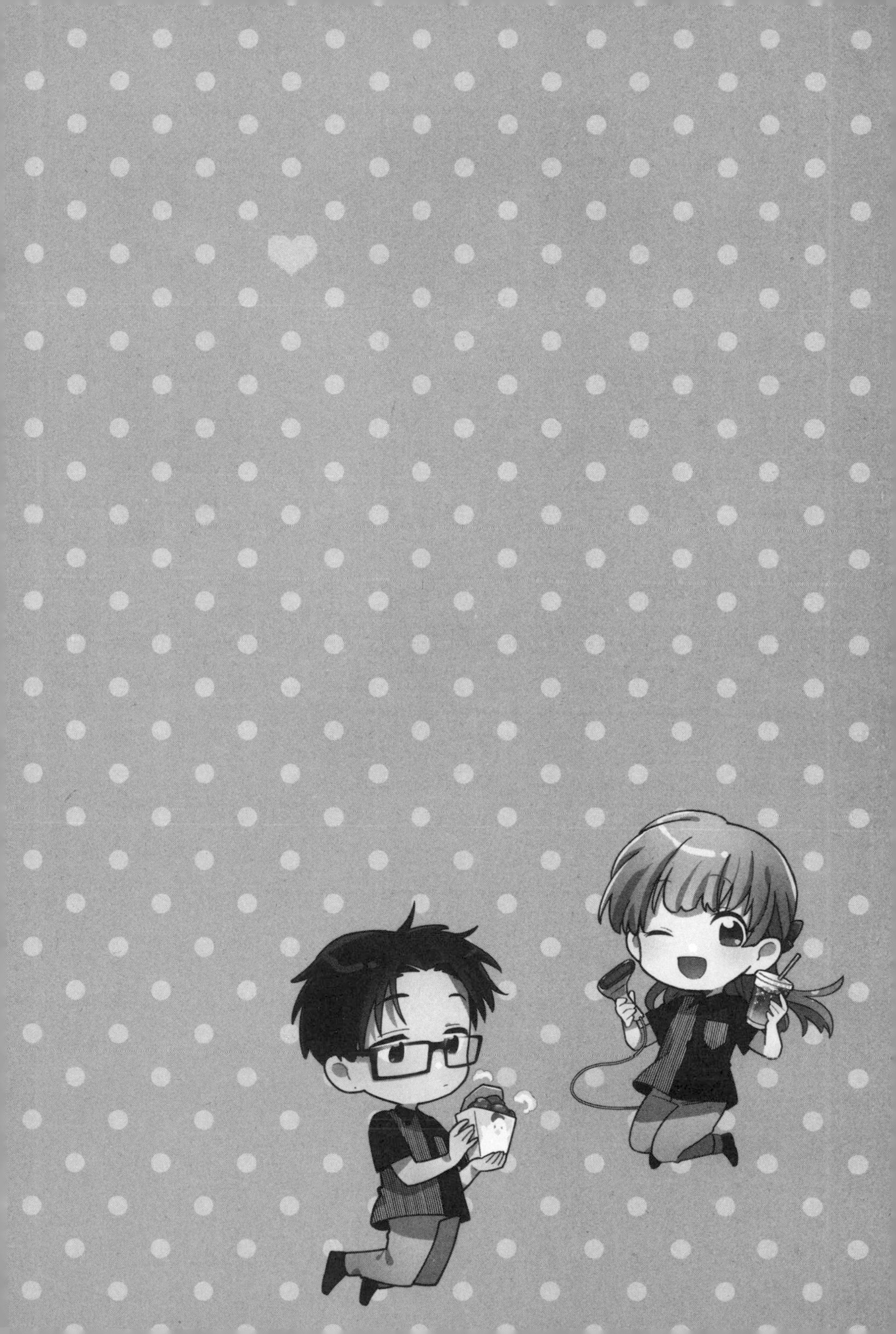

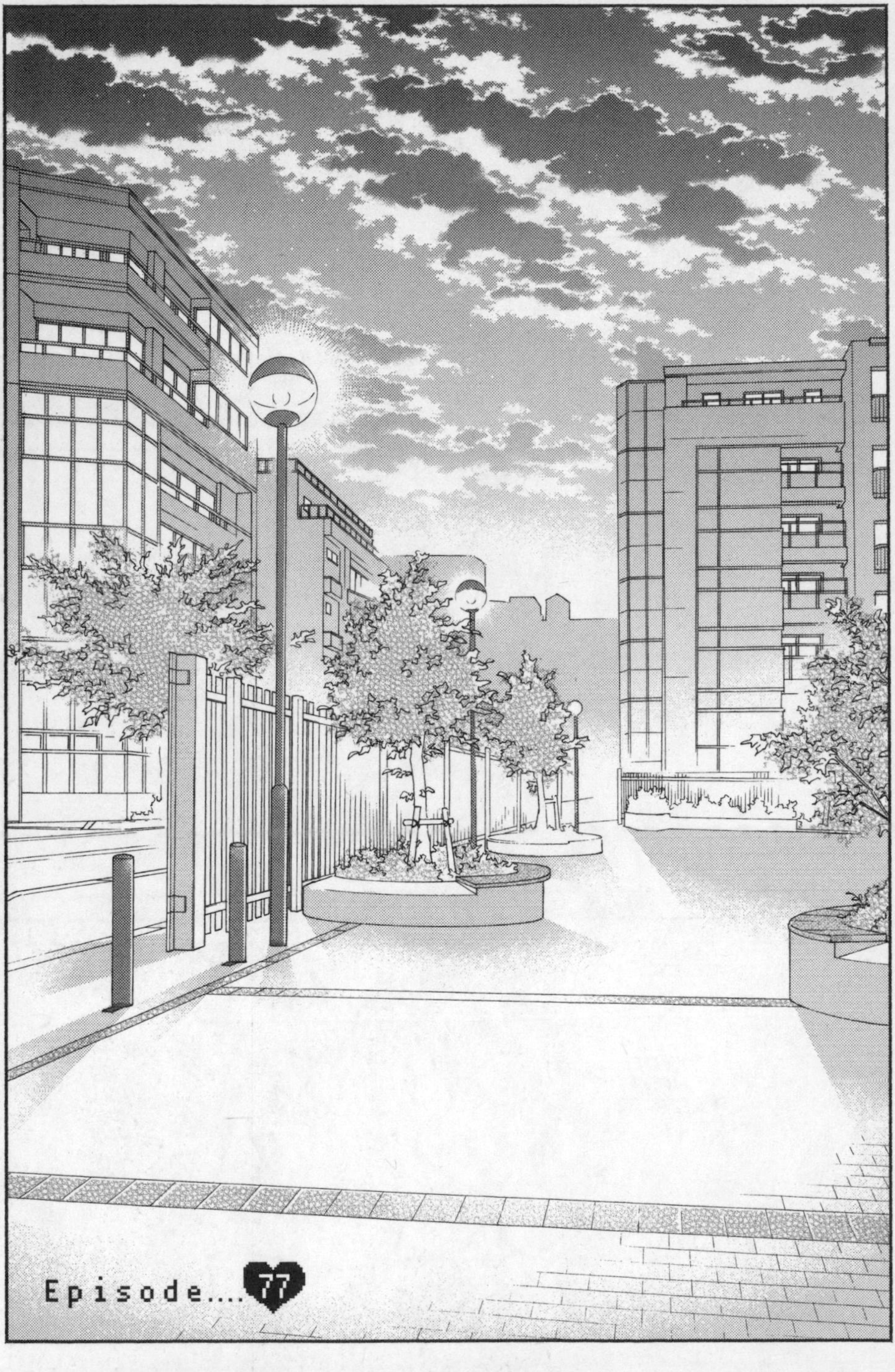
Episode.... 77

WHO THE HELL DOES SHE THINK SHE IS?!
GAHHHHH!
WHOA!
ビクッ
JOLT
WHAT?
THAT MAN-STEALER!!
NGGGGH!

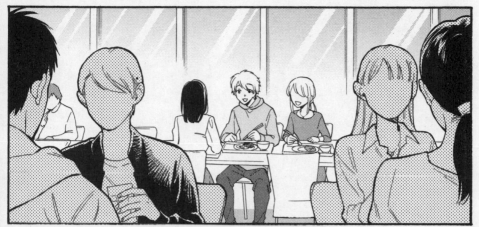

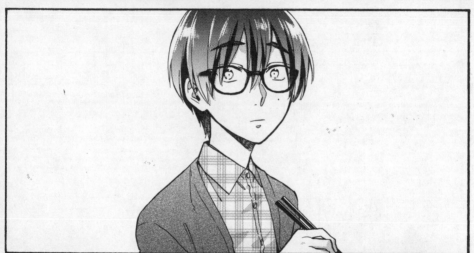

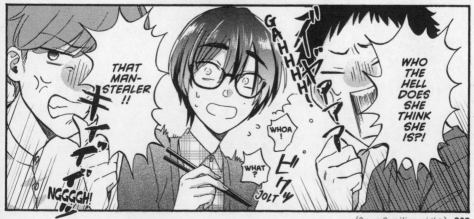

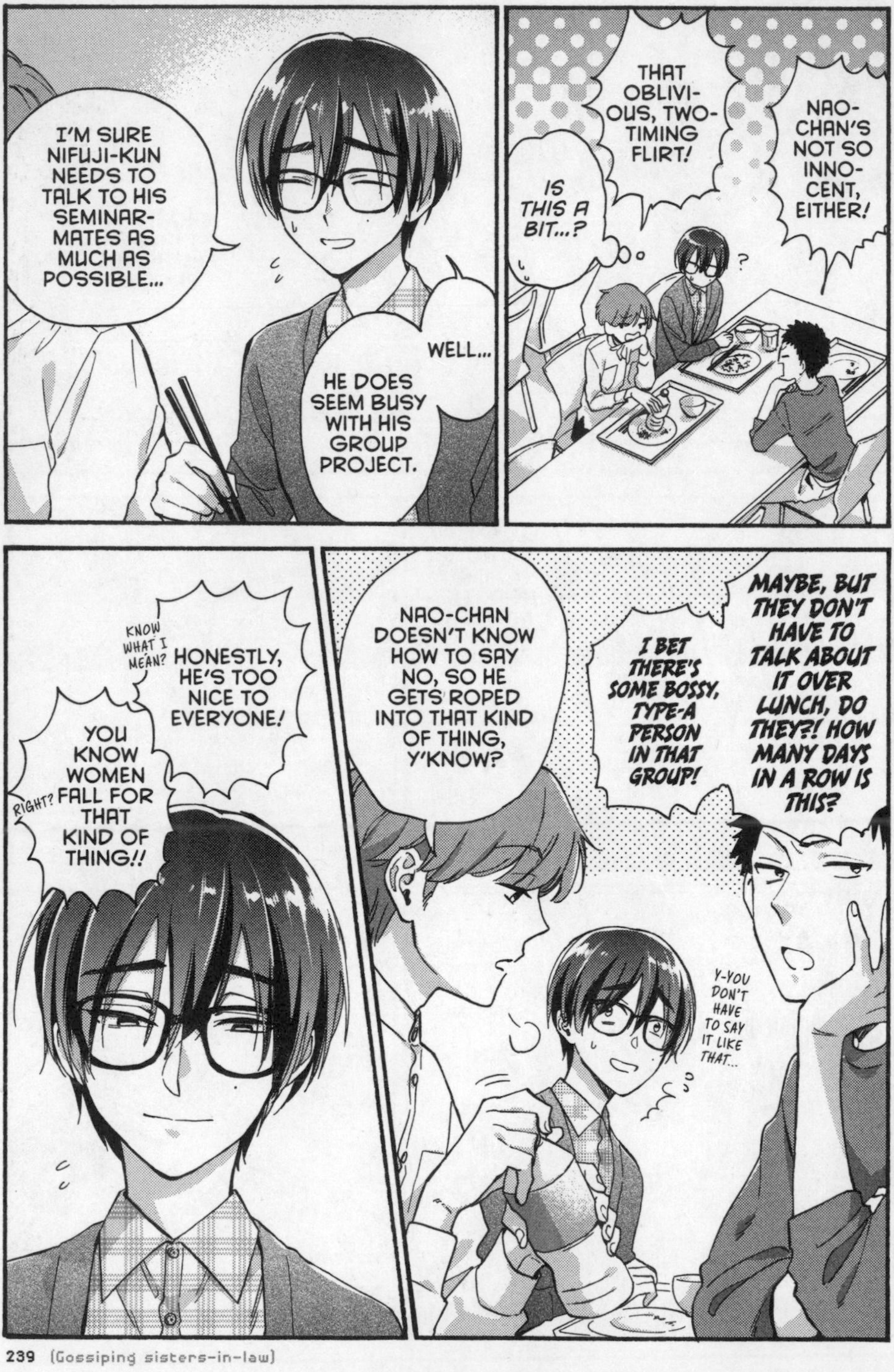
NAO-CHAN'S NOT SO INNOCENT, EITHER!
THAT OBLIVIOUS, TWO-TIMING FLIRT!
IS THIS A BIT...?
WELL...
HE DOES SEEM BUSY WITH HIS GROUP PROJECT.
I'M SURE NIFUJI-KUN NEEDS TO TALK TO HIS SEMINAR-MATES AS MUCH AS POSSIBLE...
MAYBE, BUT THEY DON'T HAVE TO TALK ABOUT IT OVER LUNCH, DO THEY?! HOW MANY DAYS IN A ROW IS THIS?
I BET THERE'S SOME BOSSY, TYPE-A PERSON IN THAT GROUP!
NAO-CHAN DOESN'T KNOW HOW TO SAY NO, SO HE GETS ROPED INTO THAT KIND OF THING, Y'KNOW?
Y-YOU DON'T HAVE TO SAY IT LIKE THAT...
HONESTLY, HE'S TOO NICE TO EVERYONE!
KNOW WHAT I MEAN?
YOU KNOW WOMEN FALL FOR THAT KIND OF THING!!
RIGHT?

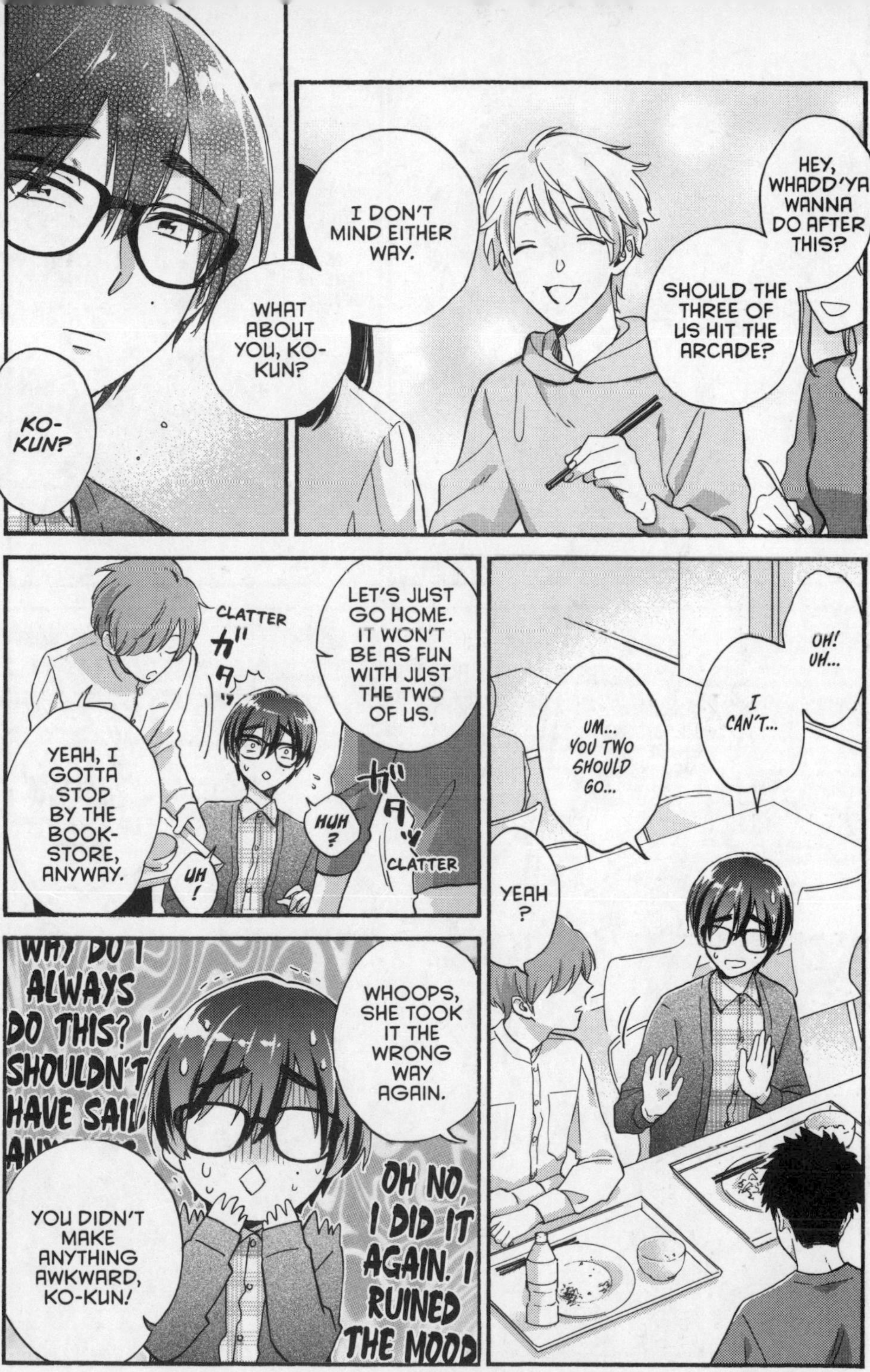
HEY, WHADD'YA WANNA DO AFTER THIS?
SHOULD THE THREE OF US HIT THE ARCADE?
I DON'T MIND EITHER WAY.
WHAT ABOUT YOU, KO-KUN?
KO-KUN?
OH! UH...
I CAN'T...
UM... YOU TWO SHOULD GO...
YEAH?
LET'S JUST GO HOME. IT WON'T BE AS FUN WITH JUST THE TWO OF US.
CLATTER
ガタッ
HUH?
CLATTER
ガタッ
YEAH, I GOTTA STOP BY THE BOOKSTORE, ANYWAY.
UH!
WHOOPS, SHE TOOK IT THE WRONG WAY AGAIN.
OH NO, I DID IT AGAIN. I RUINED THE MOOD
WHY DO I ALWAYS DO THIS? I SHOULDN'T HAVE SAI
YOU DIDN'T MAKE ANYTHING AWKWARD, KO-KUN!

SOMETIMES YOU JUST DON'T FEEL LIKE HANGING OUT, Y'KNOW?

THEN THE FOUR OF US CAN HANG OUT AGAIN.

BESIDES, NAO-CHAN'LL BE BACK AS SOON AS HIS PROJECT'S DONE.

YEP.

...WOW.

SIGH...

IF ONLY I COULD THINK THAT WAY, TOO...

BYE.

SEE YA!

(The trust that comes from being friends forever)

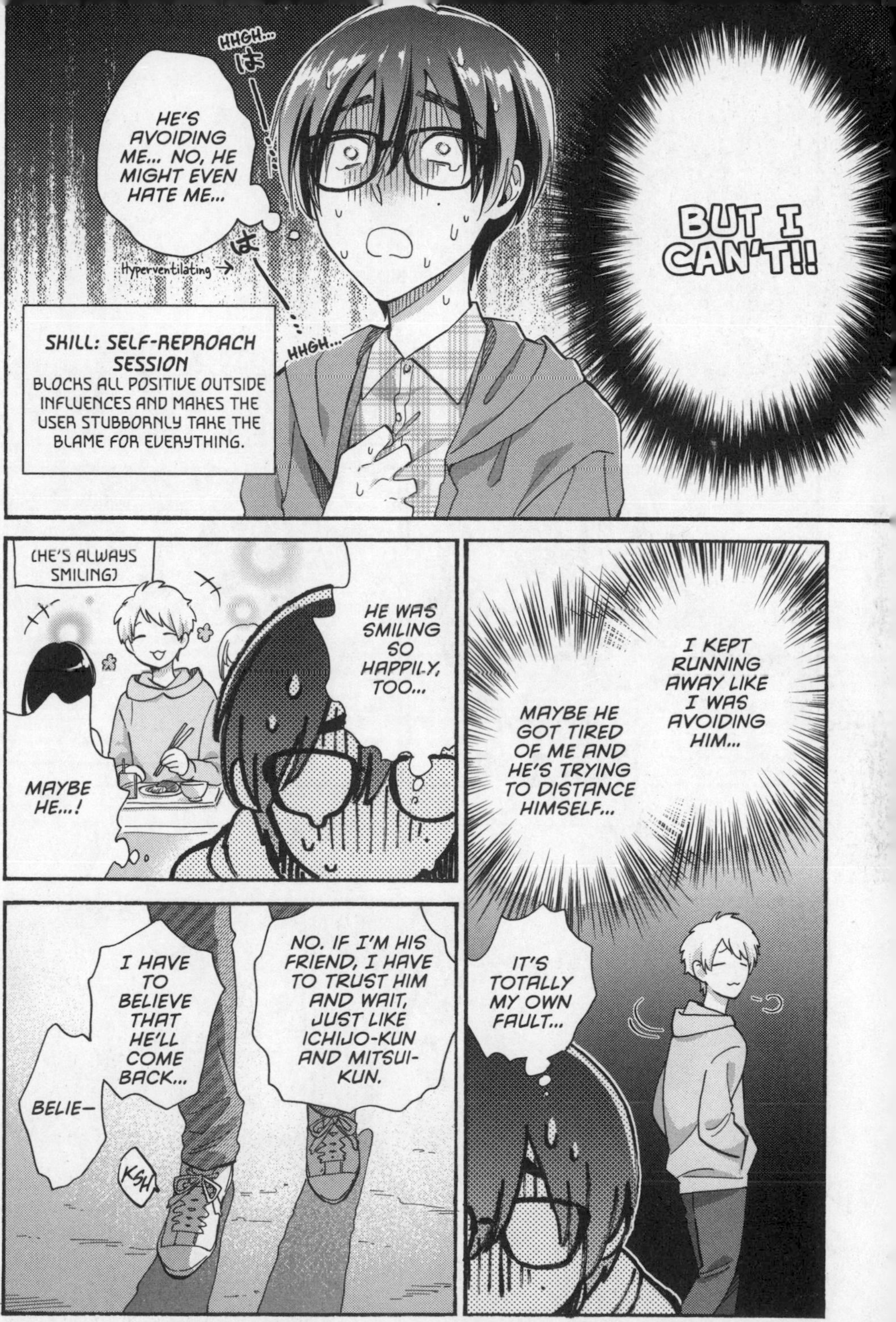
BUT I CAN'T!!
HHGH... は
HE'S AVOIDING ME... NO, HE MIGHT EVEN HATE ME...
は
Hyperventilating →
HHGH...
SKILL: SELF-REPROACH SESSION
BLOCKS ALL POSITIVE OUTSIDE INFLUENCES AND MAKES THE USER STUBBORNLY TAKE THE BLAME FOR EVERYTHING.
I KEPT RUNNING AWAY LIKE I WAS AVOIDING HIM...
MAYBE HE GOT TIRED OF ME AND HE'S TRYING TO DISTANCE HIMSELF...
IT'S TOTALLY MY OWN FAULT...
(HE'S ALWAYS SMILING)
HE WAS SMILING SO HAPPILY, TOO...
MAYBE HE...!
NO. IF I'M HIS FRIEND, I HAVE TO TRUST HIM AND WAIT, JUST LIKE ICHIJO-KUN AND MITSUI-KUN.
I HAVE TO BELIEVE THAT HE'LL COME BACK...
BELIE—
KSH

(By now, being full of doubt is second nature)

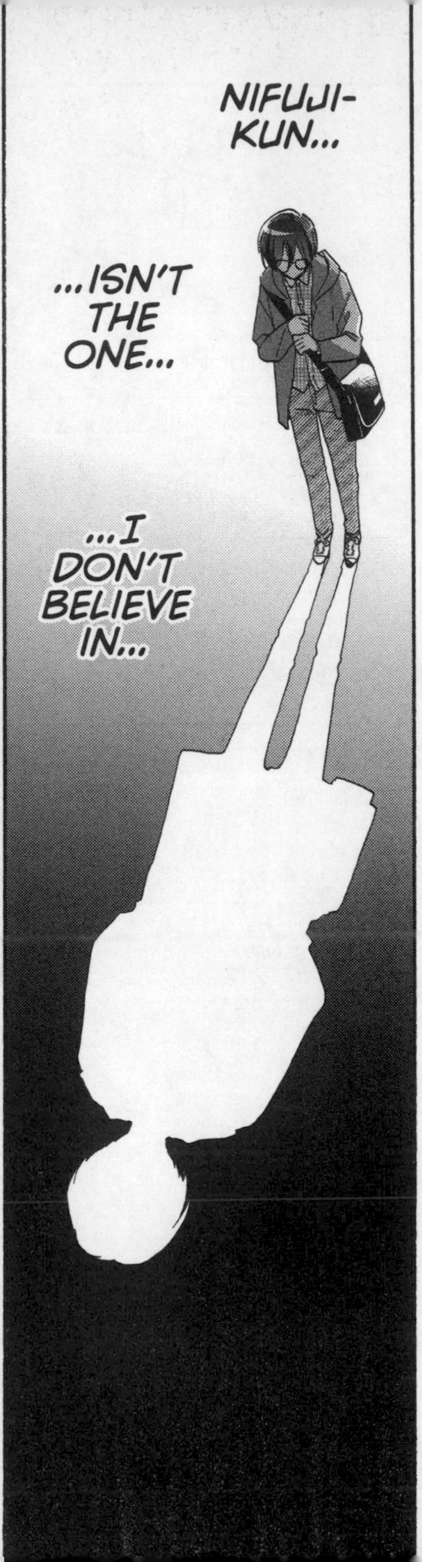
NIFUJI-KUN...
...ISN'T THE ONE...
...I DON'T BELIEVE IN...

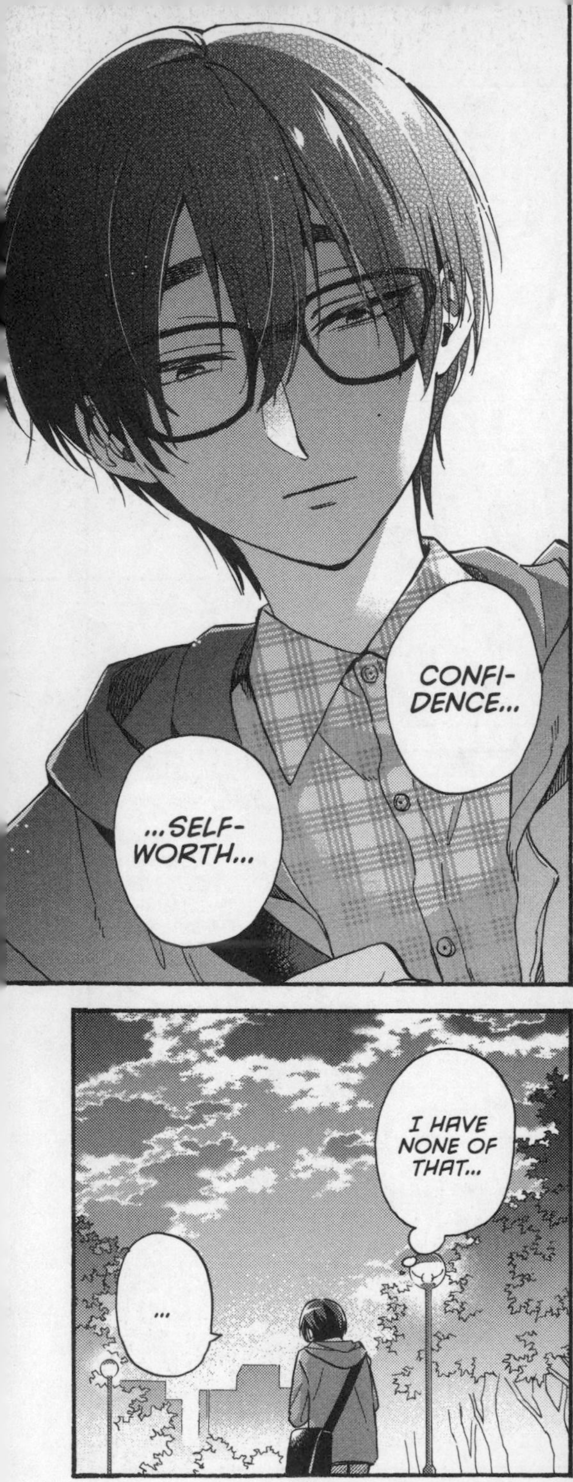
CONFI-DENCE...
...SELF-WORTH...
I HAVE NONE OF THAT...
...

 (Now, whooo's acting pathetic around here?)

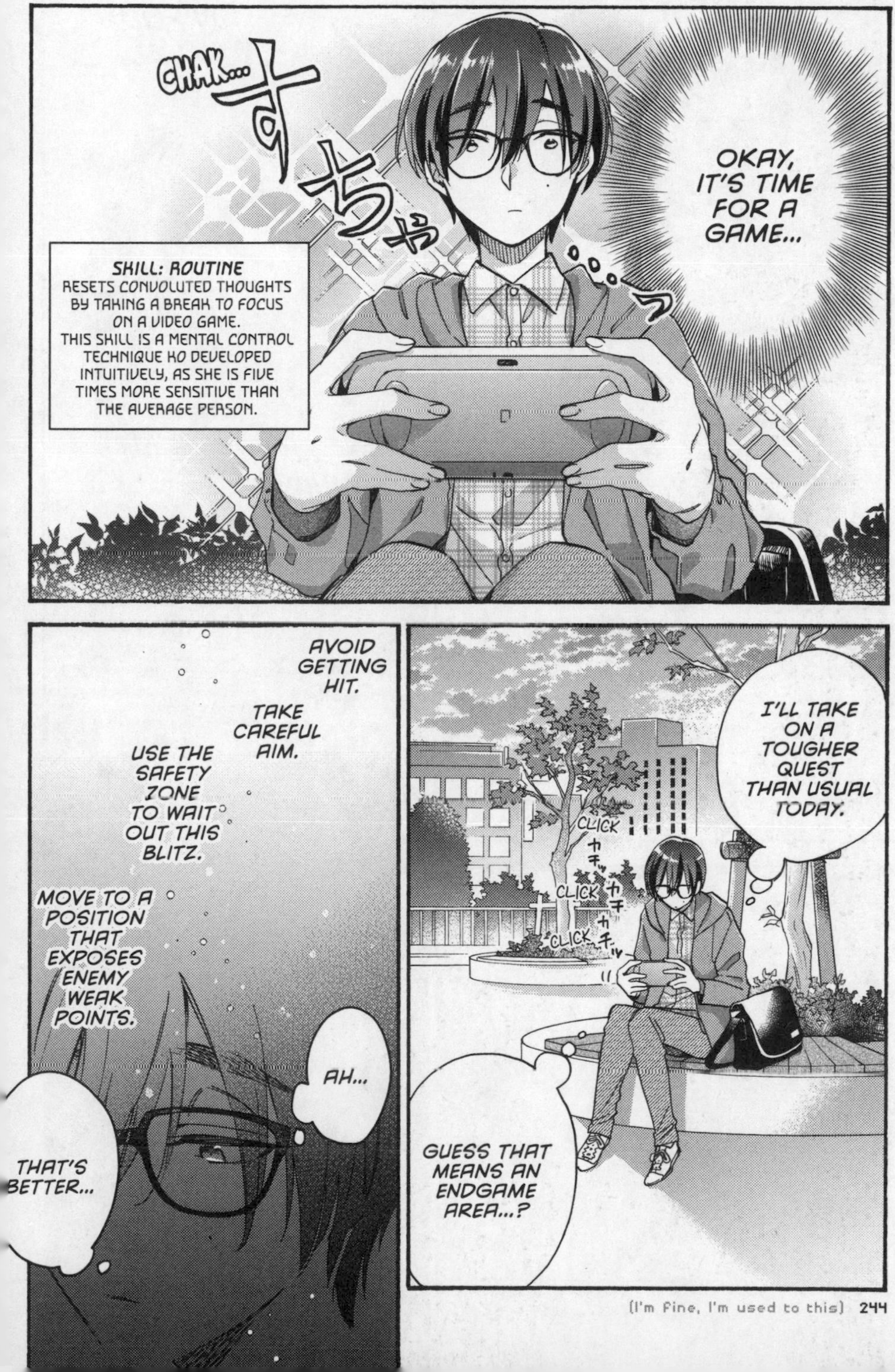
OKAY, IT'S TIME FOR A GAME...
CHAK...
SKILL: ROUTINE
RESETS CONVOLUTED THOUGHTS BY TAKING A BREAK TO FOCUS ON A VIDEO GAME. THIS SKILL IS A MENTAL CONTROL TECHNIQUE KO DEVELOPED INTUITIVELY, AS SHE IS FIVE TIMES MORE SENSITIVE THAN THE AVERAGE PERSON.
I'LL TAKE ON A TOUGHER QUEST THAN USUAL TODAY.
CLICK
CLICK
CLICK
GUESS THAT MEANS AN ENDGAME AREA...?
AVOID GETTING HIT.
TAKE CAREFUL AIM.
USE THE SAFETY ZONE TO WAIT OUT THIS BLITZ.
MOVE TO A POSITION THAT EXPOSES ENEMY WEAK POINTS.
AH...
THAT'S BETTER...

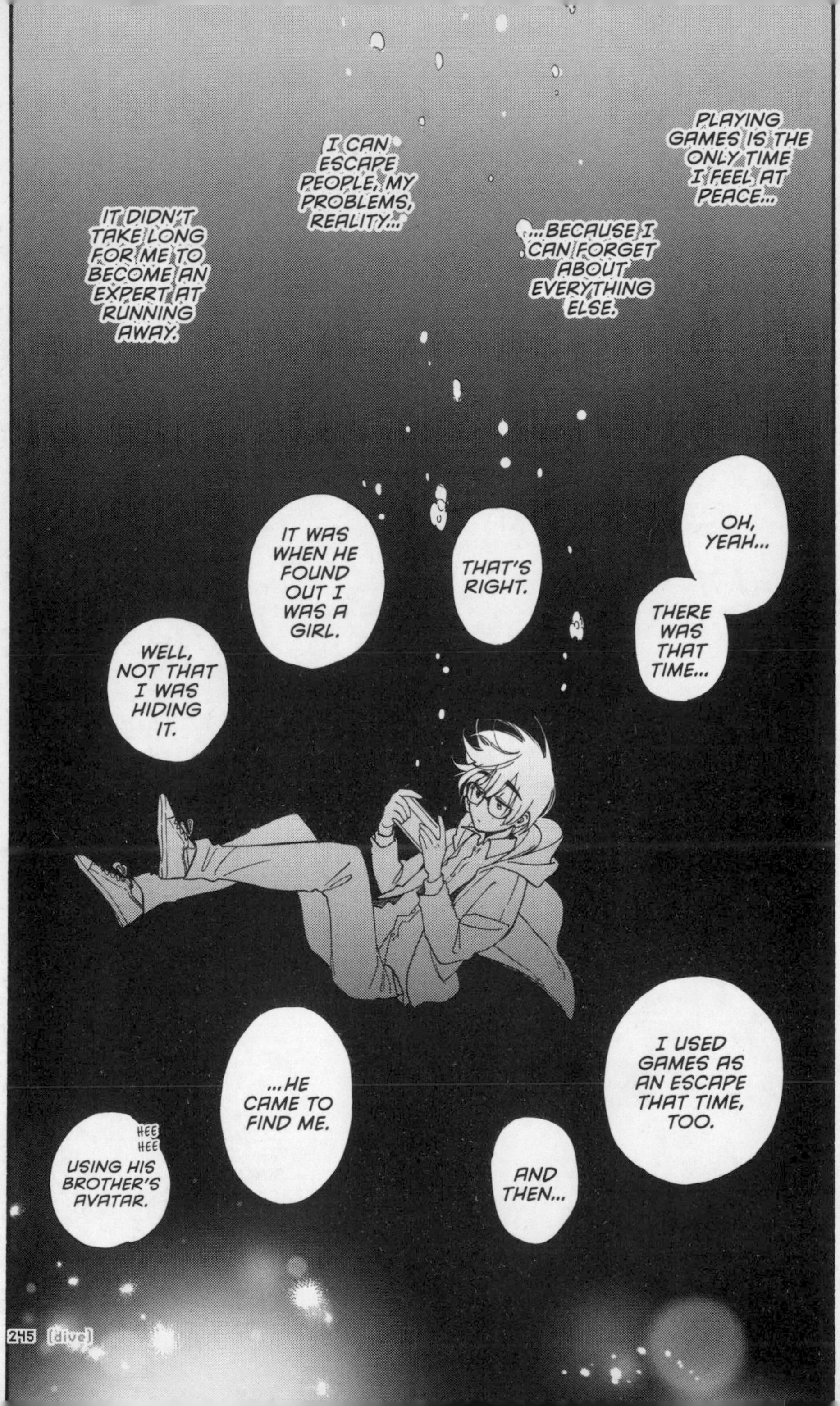
PLAYING GAMES IS THE ONLY TIME I FEEL AT PEACE...
...BECAUSE I CAN FORGET ABOUT EVERYTHING ELSE.
I CAN ESCAPE PEOPLE, MY PROBLEMS, REALITY...
IT DIDN'T TAKE LONG FOR ME TO BECOME AN EXPERT AT RUNNING AWAY.
OH, YEAH...
THERE WAS THAT TIME...
THAT'S RIGHT.
IT WAS WHEN HE FOUND OUT I WAS A GIRL.
WELL, NOT THAT I WAS HIDING IT.
I USED GAMES AS AN ESCAPE THAT TIME, TOO.
AND THEN...
...HE CAME TO FIND ME.
HEE HEE
USING HIS BROTHER'S AVATAR.

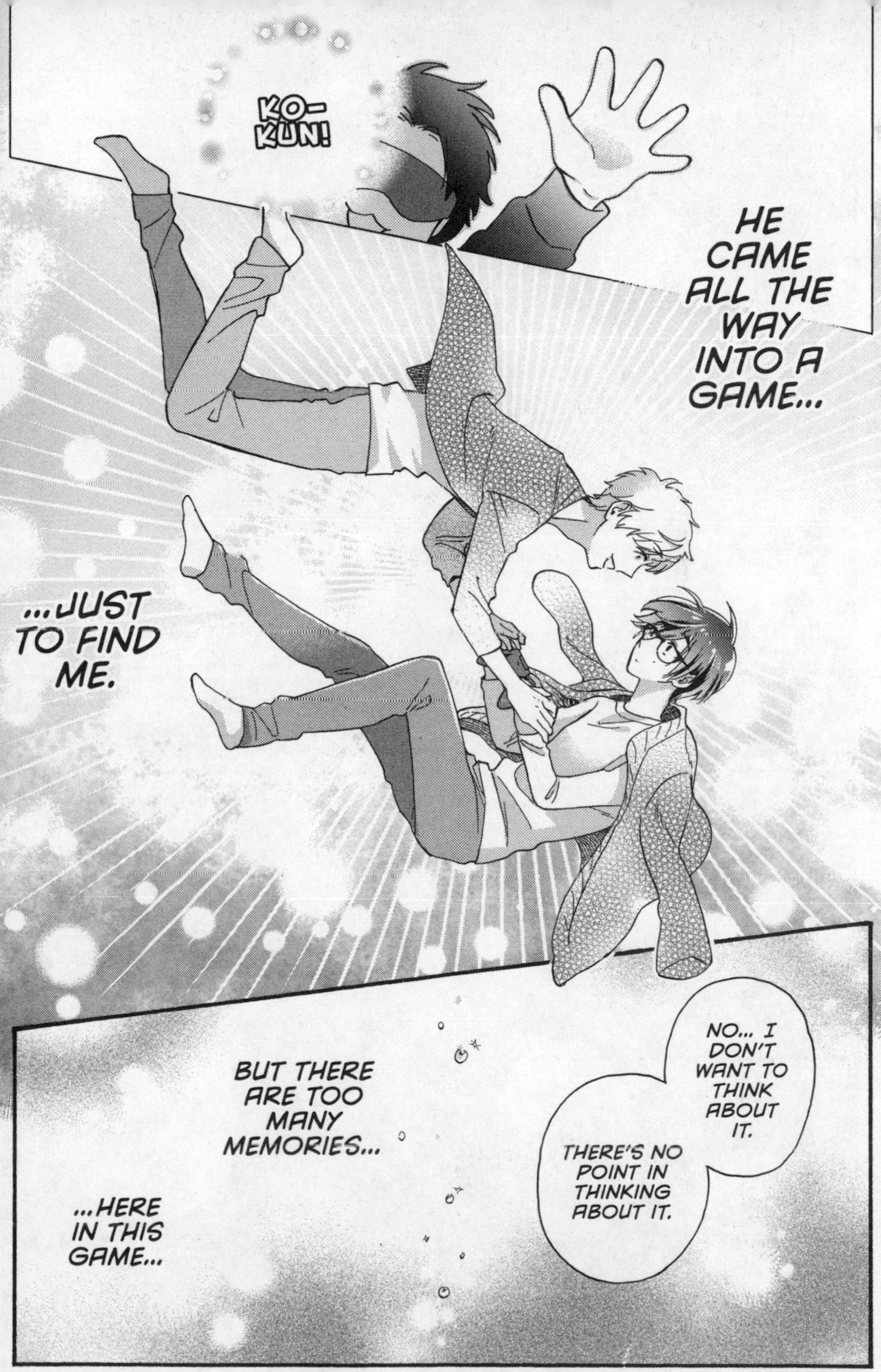
KO-KUN!
HE CAME ALL THE WAY INTO A GAME...
...JUST TO FIND ME.
NO... I DON'T WANT TO THINK ABOUT IT.
THERE'S NO POINT IN THINKING ABOUT IT.
BUT THERE ARE TOO MANY MEMORIES...
...HERE IN THIS GAME...

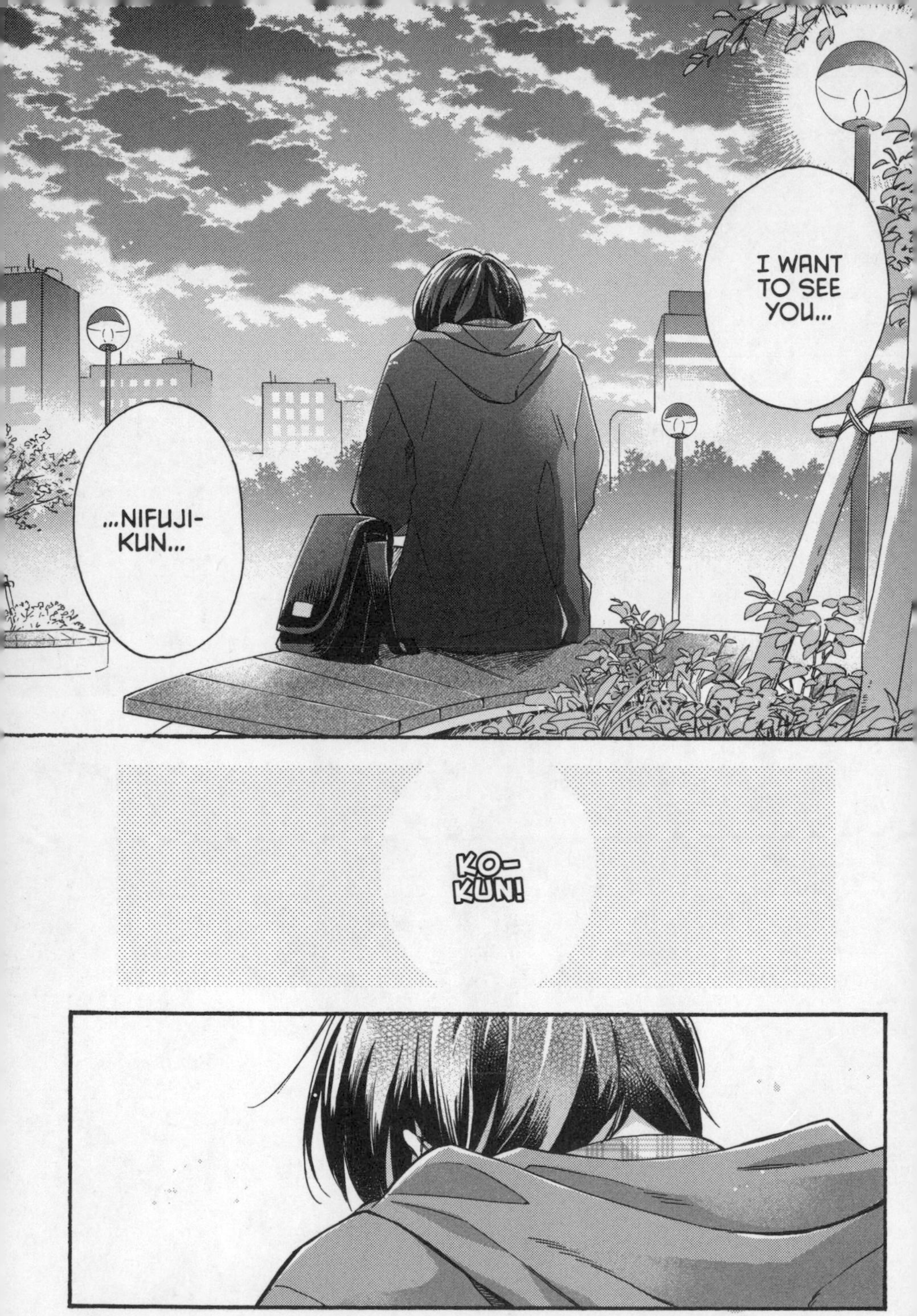
I WANT TO SEE YOU...
...NIFUJI-KUN...
KO-KUN!

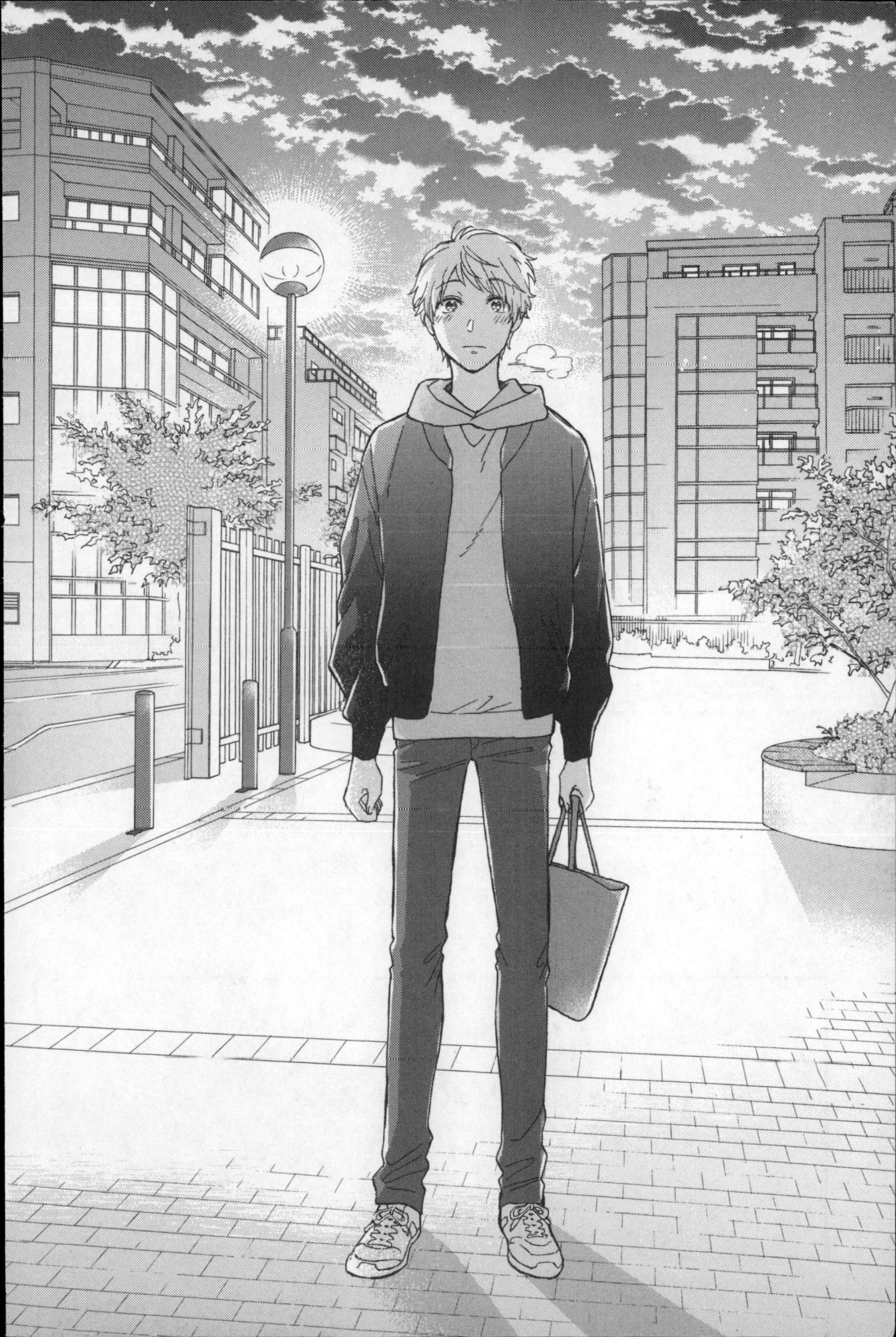

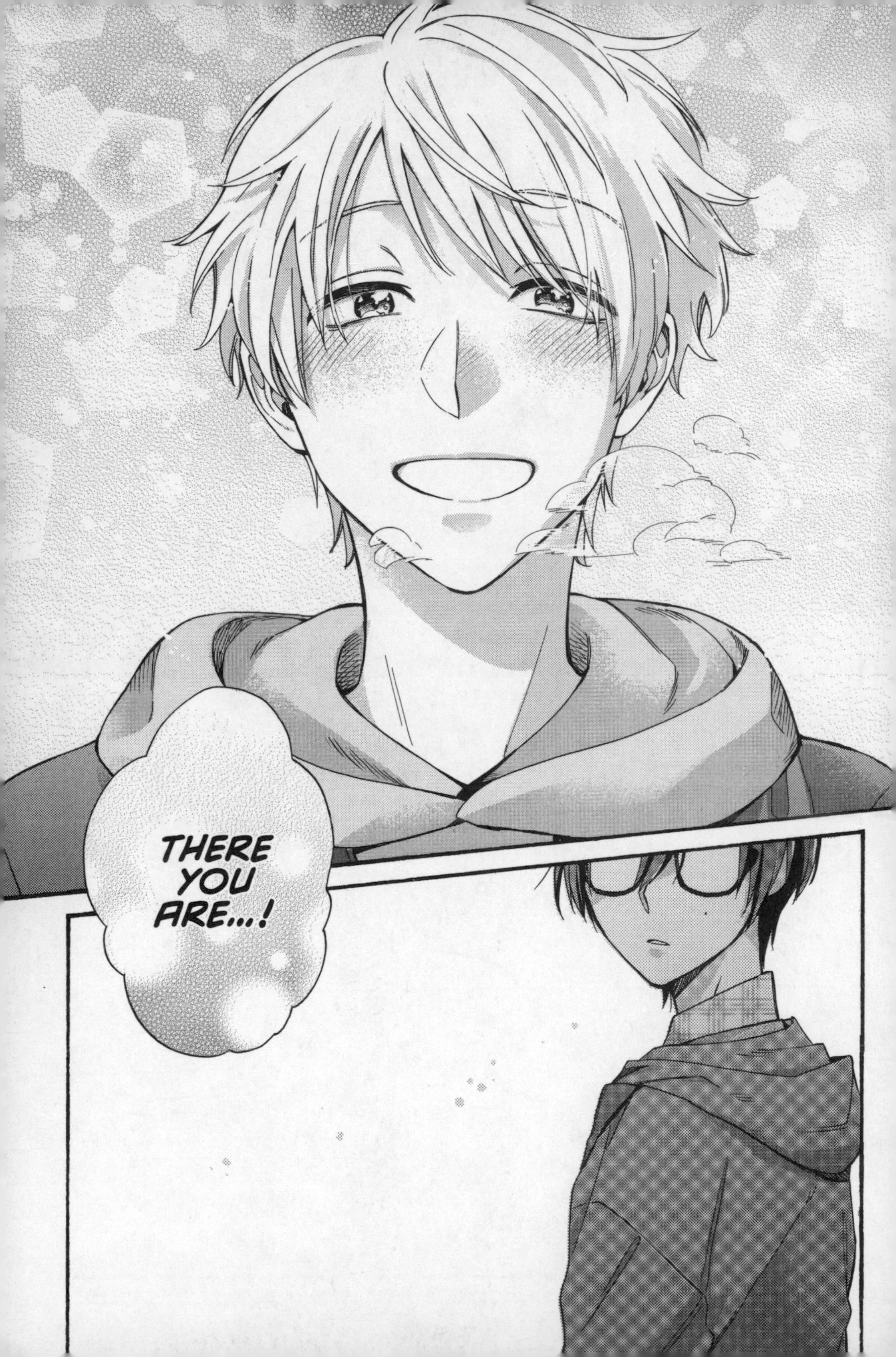
THERE YOU ARE...!

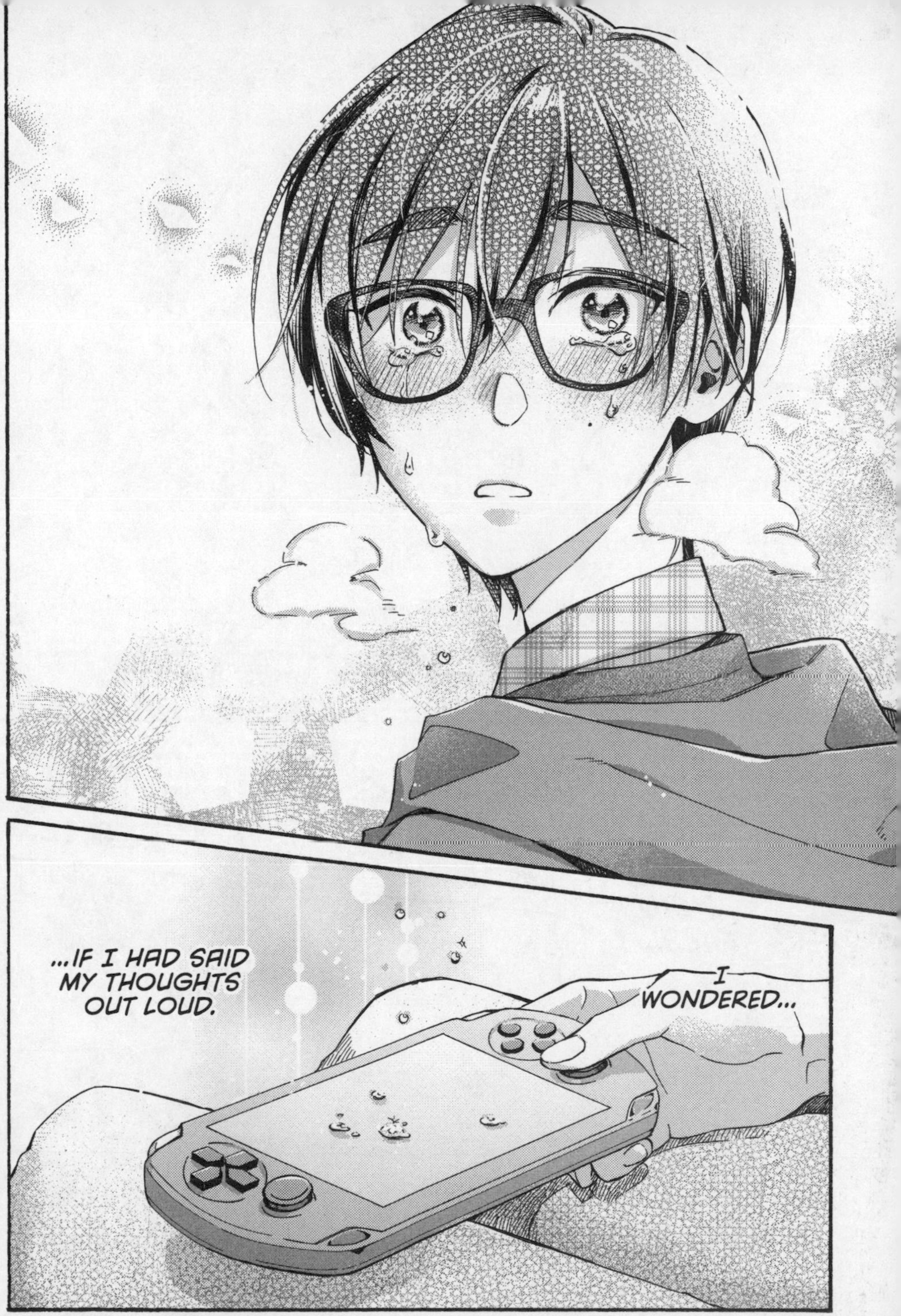
I WONDERED...
...IF I HAD SAID MY THOUGHTS OUT LOUD.

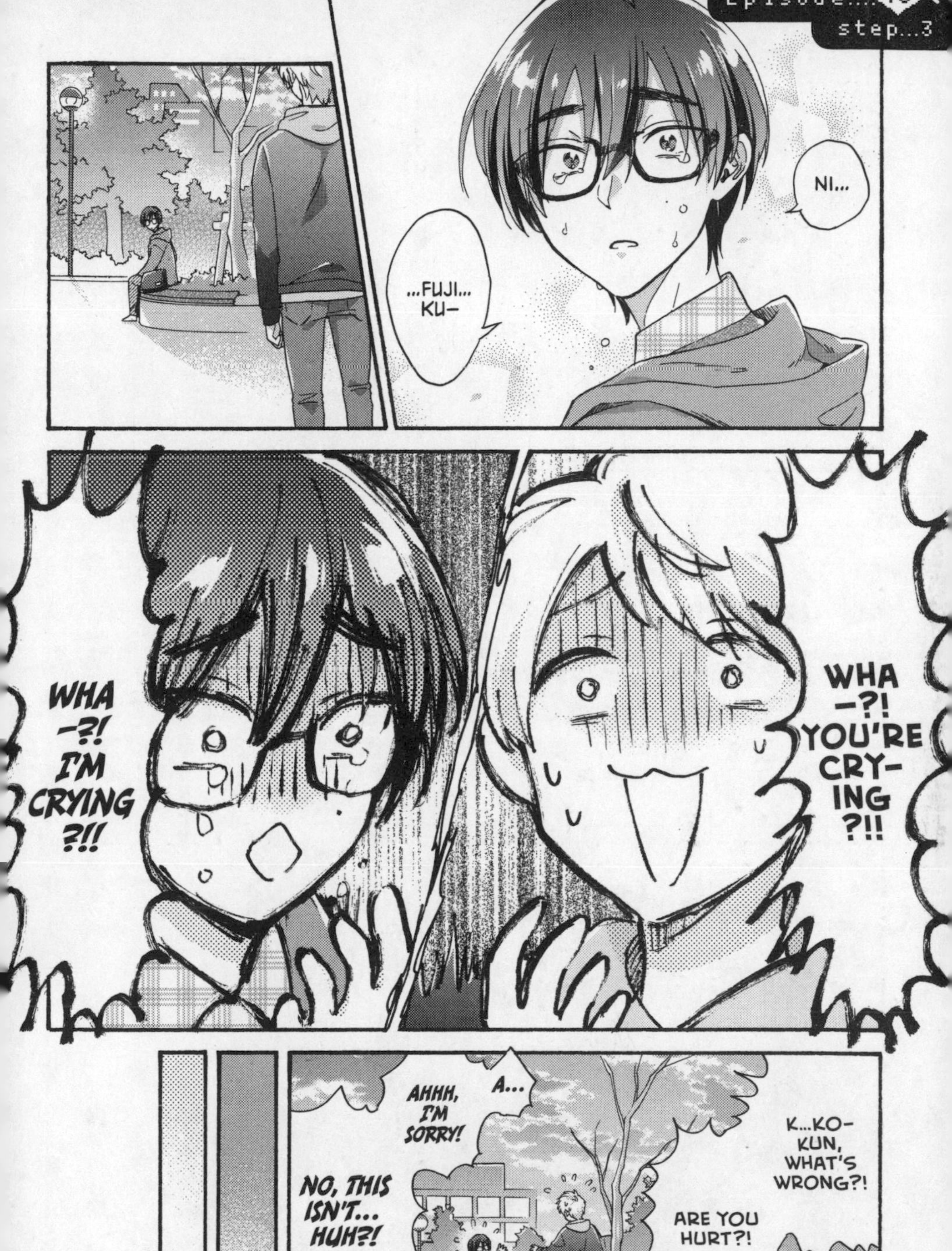
NI...
...FUJI... KU—
WHA —?! YOU'RE CRY-ING ?!!
WHA —?! I'M CRYING ?!!
K...KO-KUN, WHAT'S WRONG?!
ARE YOU HURT?!
A...
AHHH, I'M SORRY!
NO, THIS ISN'T... HUH?!

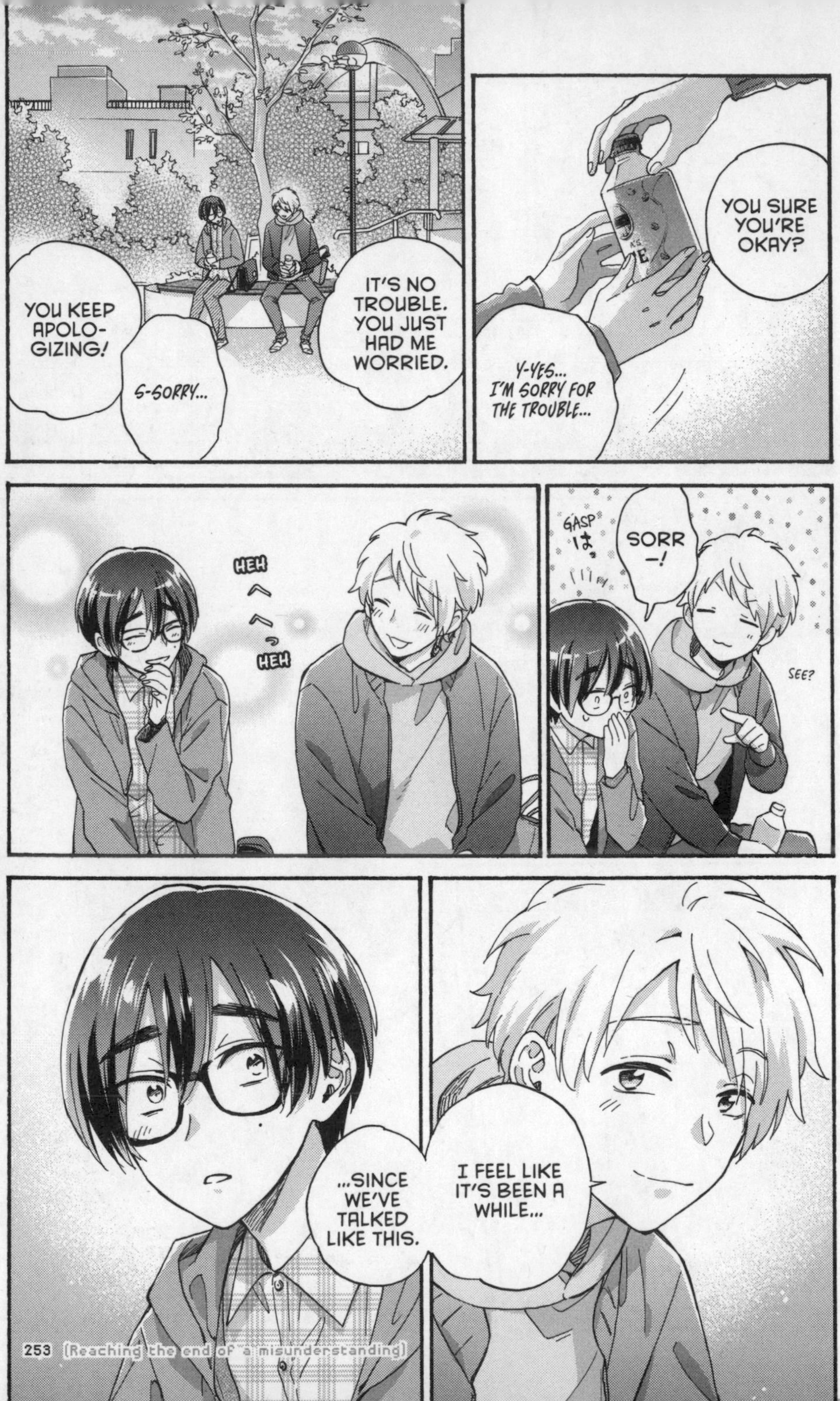
YOU SURE YOU'RE OKAY?
Y-YES... I'M SORRY FOR THE TROUBLE...
IT'S NO TROUBLE. YOU JUST HAD ME WORRIED.
S-SORRY...
YOU KEEP APOLOGIZING!
GASP
は
SORR—!
SEE?
HEH
へへっ
HEH
I FEEL LIKE IT'S BEEN A WHILE...
...SINCE WE'VE TALKED LIKE THIS.

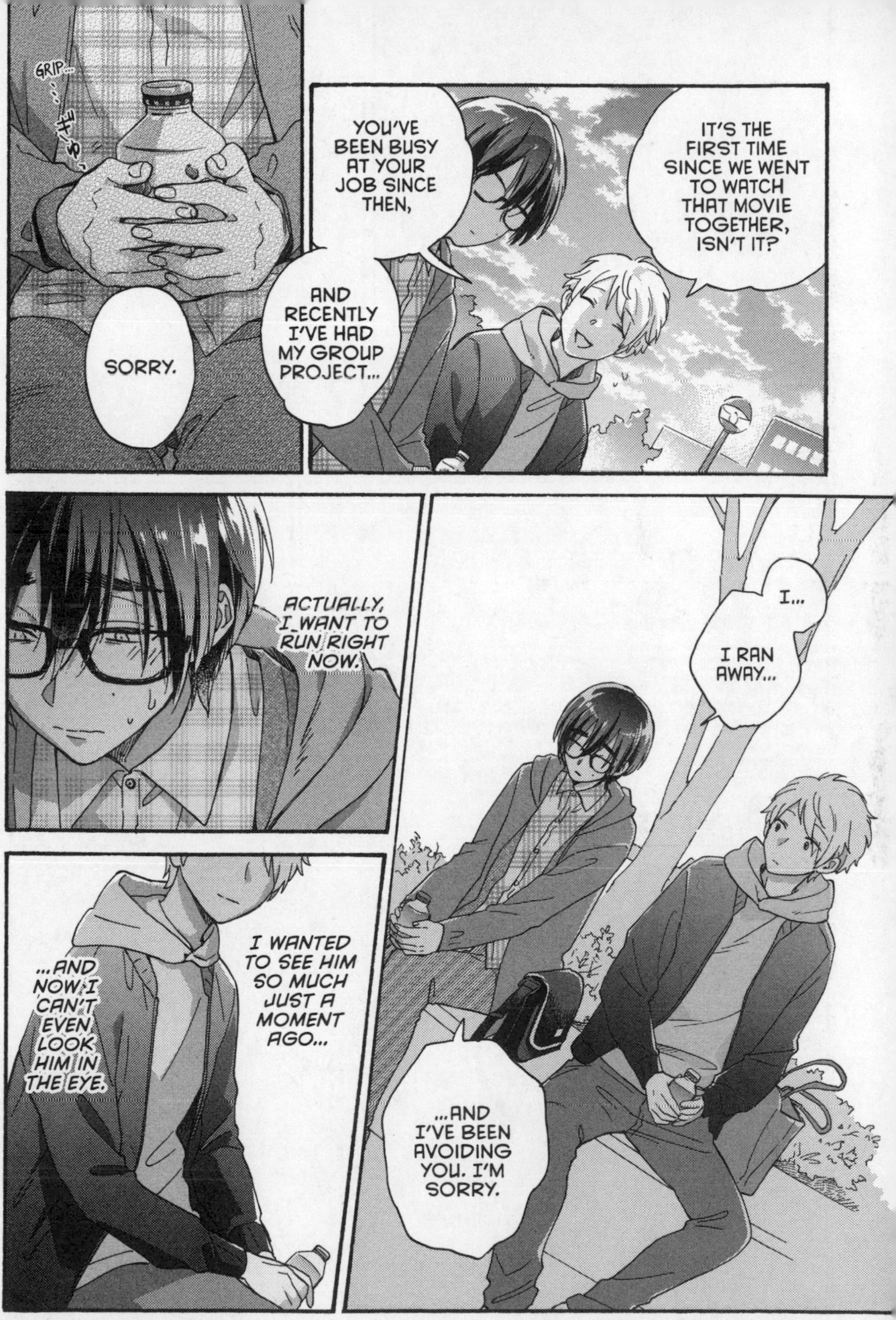
IT'S THE FIRST TIME SINCE WE WENT TO WATCH THAT MOVIE TOGETHER, ISN'T IT?
YOU'VE BEEN BUSY AT YOUR JOB SINCE THEN,
AND RECENTLY I'VE HAD MY GROUP PROJECT...
GRIP...
SORRY.
I...
I RAN AWAY...
...AND I'VE BEEN AVOIDING YOU. I'M SORRY.
ACTUALLY, I WANT TO RUN RIGHT NOW.
I WANTED TO SEE HIM SO MUCH JUST A MOMENT AGO...
...AND NOW I CAN'T EVEN LOOK HIM IN THE EYE.

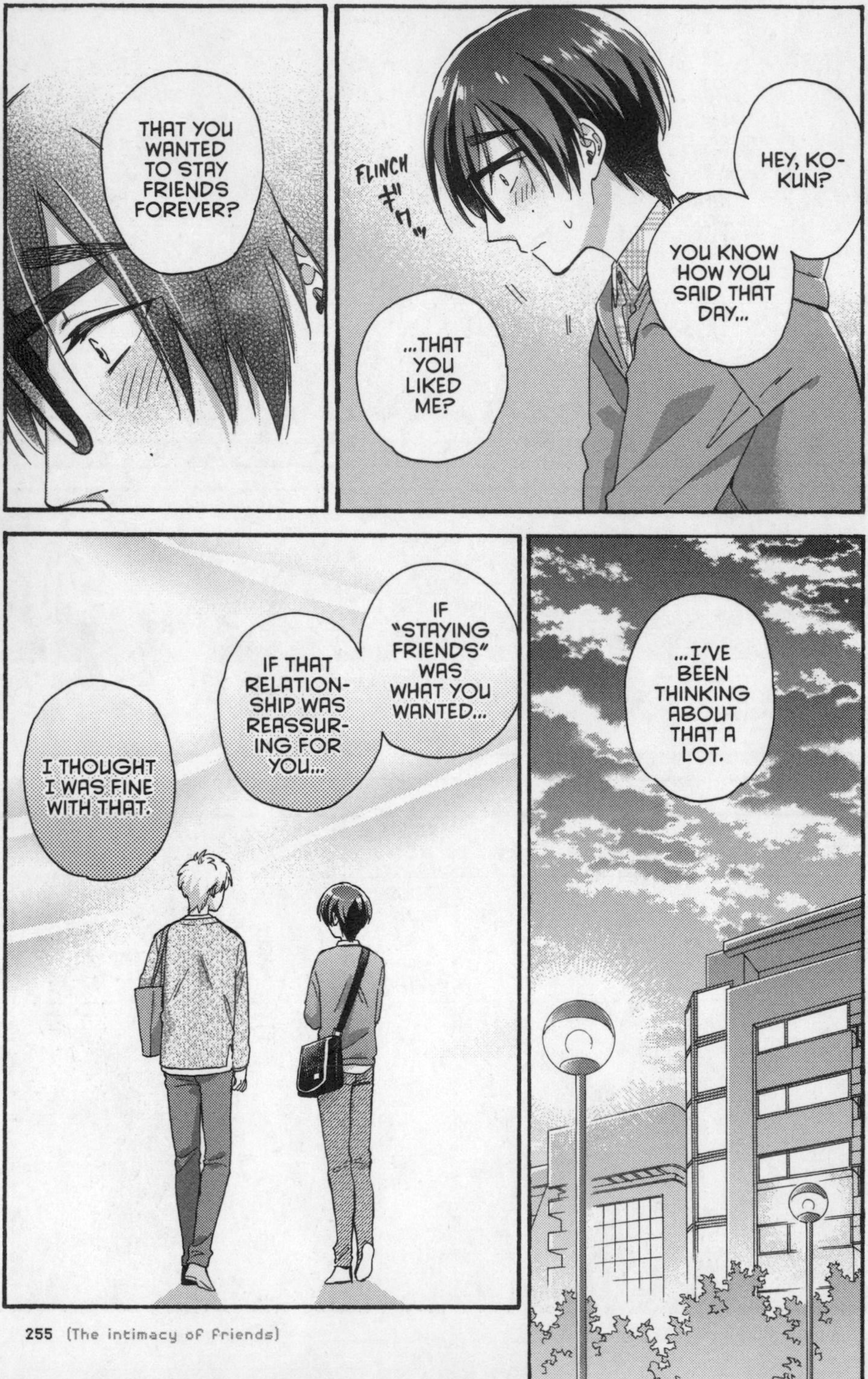
HEY, KO-KUN?
YOU KNOW HOW YOU SAID THAT DAY...
FLINCH
...THAT YOU LIKED ME?
THAT YOU WANTED TO STAY FRIENDS FOREVER?
...I'VE BEEN THINKING ABOUT THAT A LOT.
IF "STAYING FRIENDS" WAS WHAT YOU WANTED...
IF THAT RELATIONSHIP WAS REASSURING FOR YOU...
I THOUGHT I WAS FINE WITH THAT.

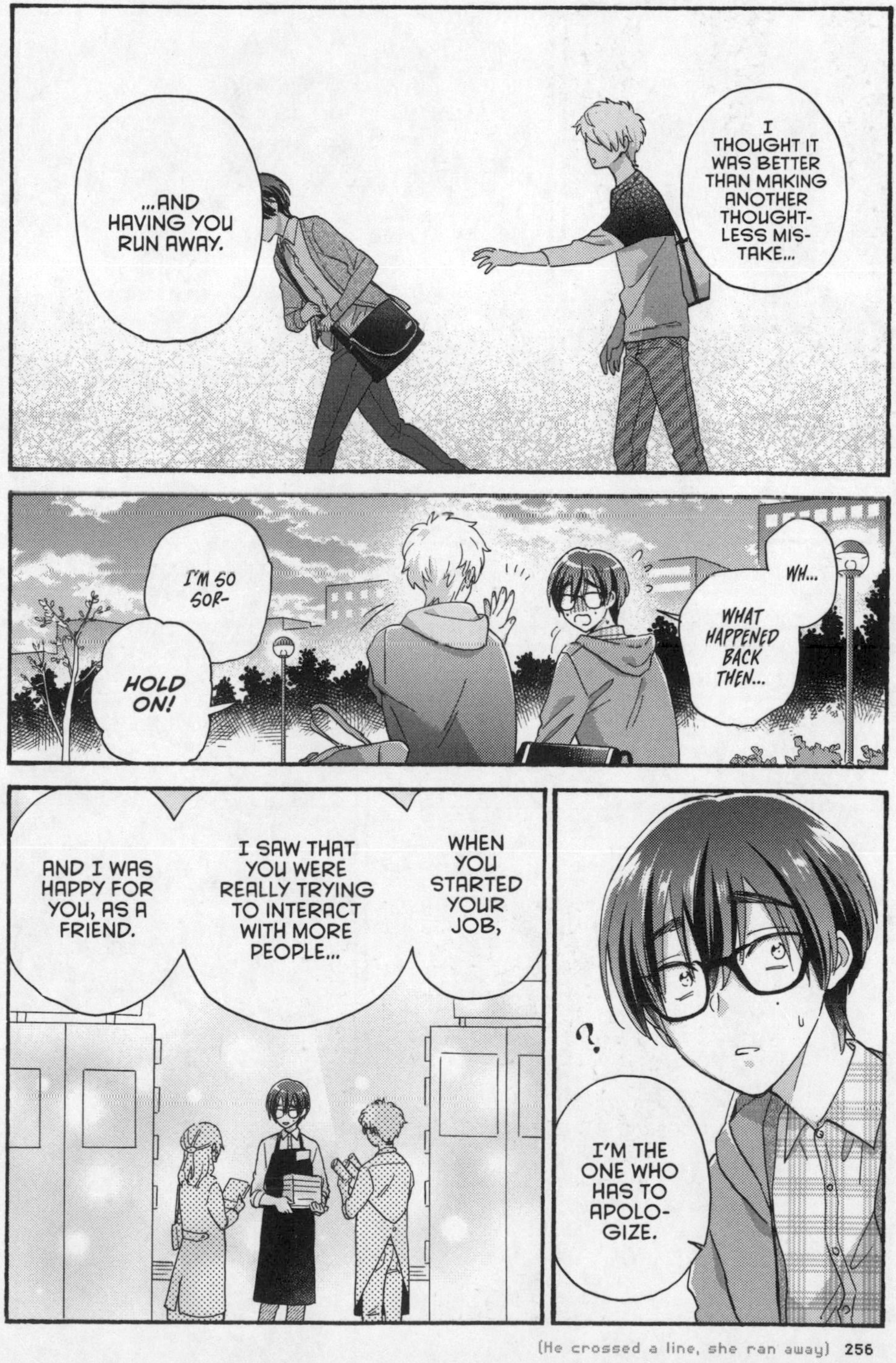
I THOUGHT IT WAS BETTER THAN MAKING ANOTHER THOUGHT-LESS MIS-TAKE...
...AND HAVING YOU RUN AWAY.
WH...
WHAT HAPPENED BACK THEN...
I'M SO SOR-
HOLD ON!
I'M THE ONE WHO HAS TO APOLO-GIZE.
WHEN YOU STARTED YOUR JOB,
I SAW THAT YOU WERE REALLY TRYING TO INTERACT WITH MORE PEOPLE...
AND I WAS HAPPY FOR YOU, AS A FRIEND.

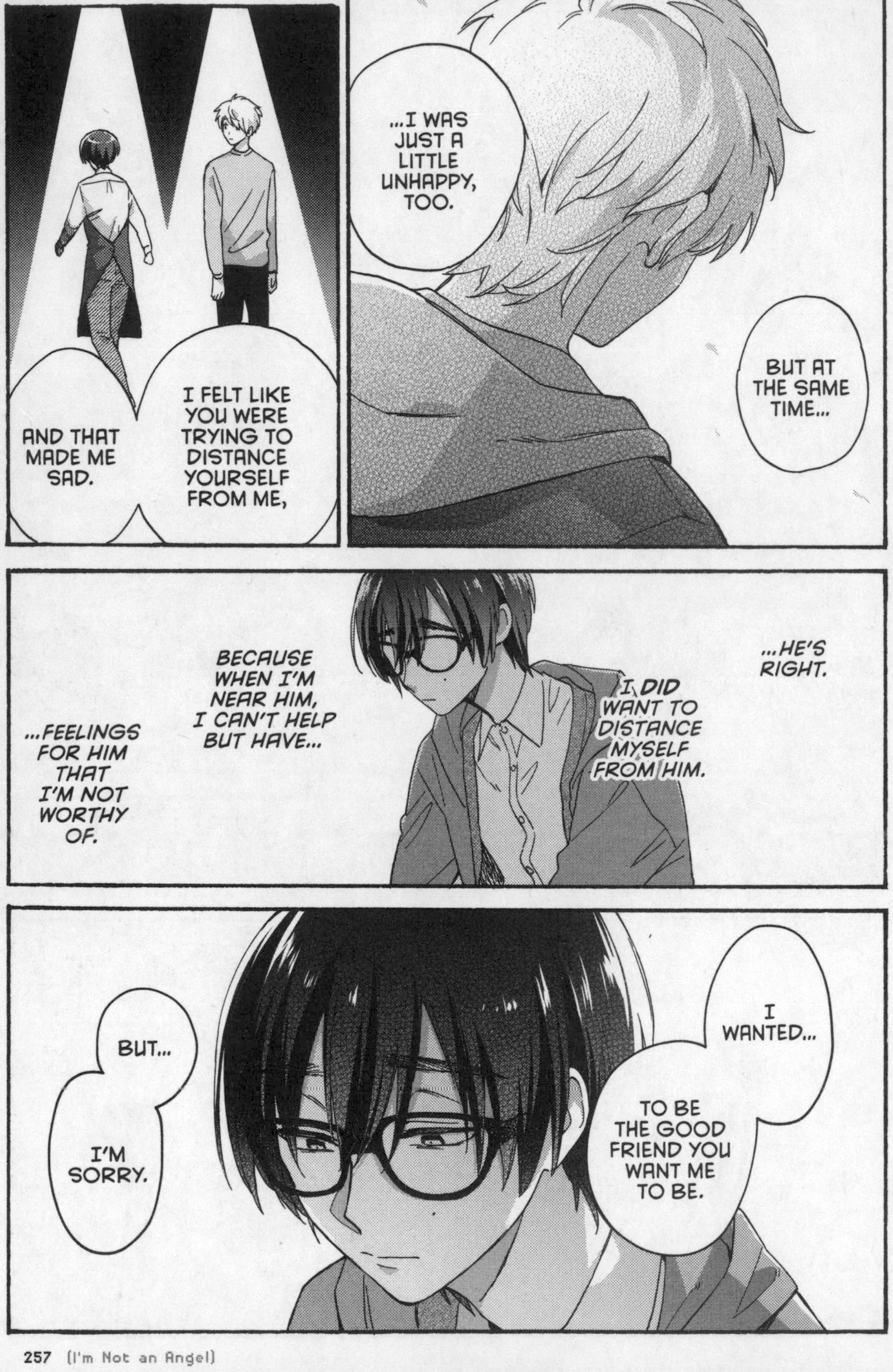
...I WAS JUST A LITTLE UNHAPPY, TOO.
BUT AT THE SAME TIME...
I FELT LIKE YOU WERE TRYING TO DISTANCE YOURSELF FROM ME,
AND THAT MADE ME SAD.
...HE'S RIGHT.
I **DID** WANT TO DISTANCE MYSELF FROM HIM.
BECAUSE WHEN I'M NEAR HIM, I CAN'T HELP BUT HAVE...
...FEELINGS FOR HIM THAT I'M NOT WORTHY OF.
I WANTED...
TO BE THE GOOD FRIEND YOU WANT ME TO BE.
BUT...
I'M SORRY.

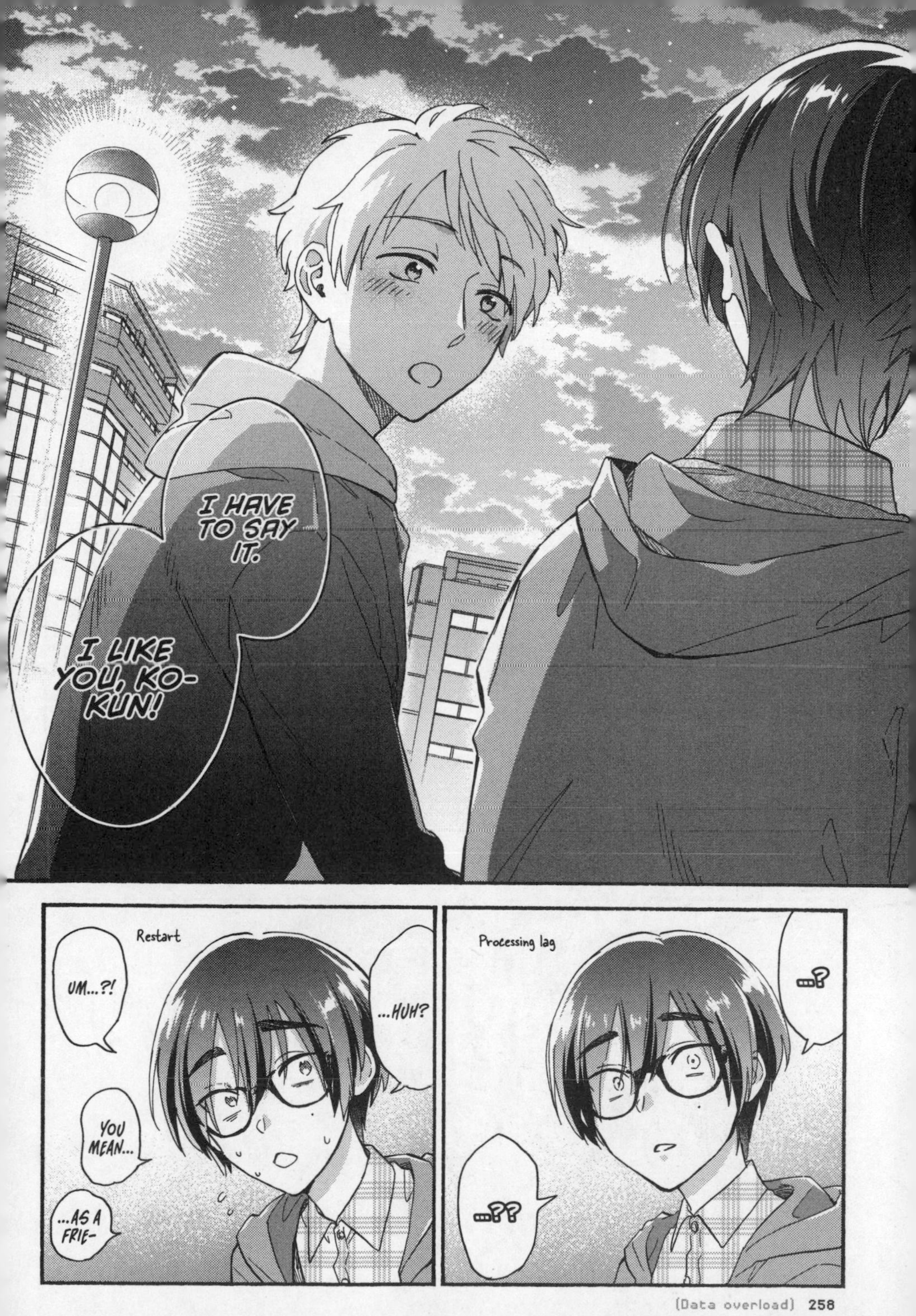
I HAVE TO SAY IT.
I LIKE YOU, KO-KUN!
Processing lag
...?
...??
Restart
...HUH?
UM...?!
YOU MEAN...
...AS A FRIE-

(Data overload)

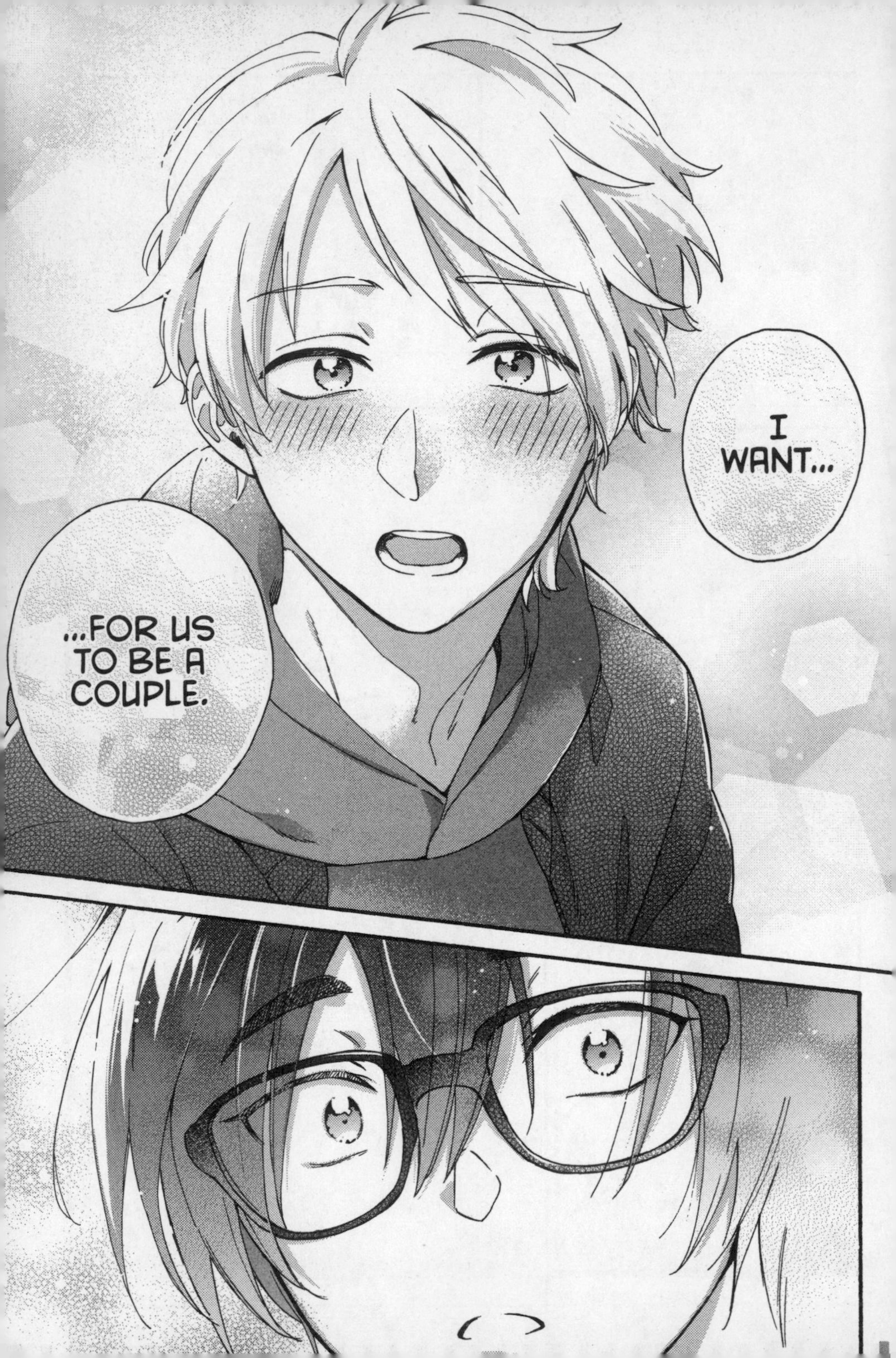
I WANT...
...FOR US TO BE A COUPLE.

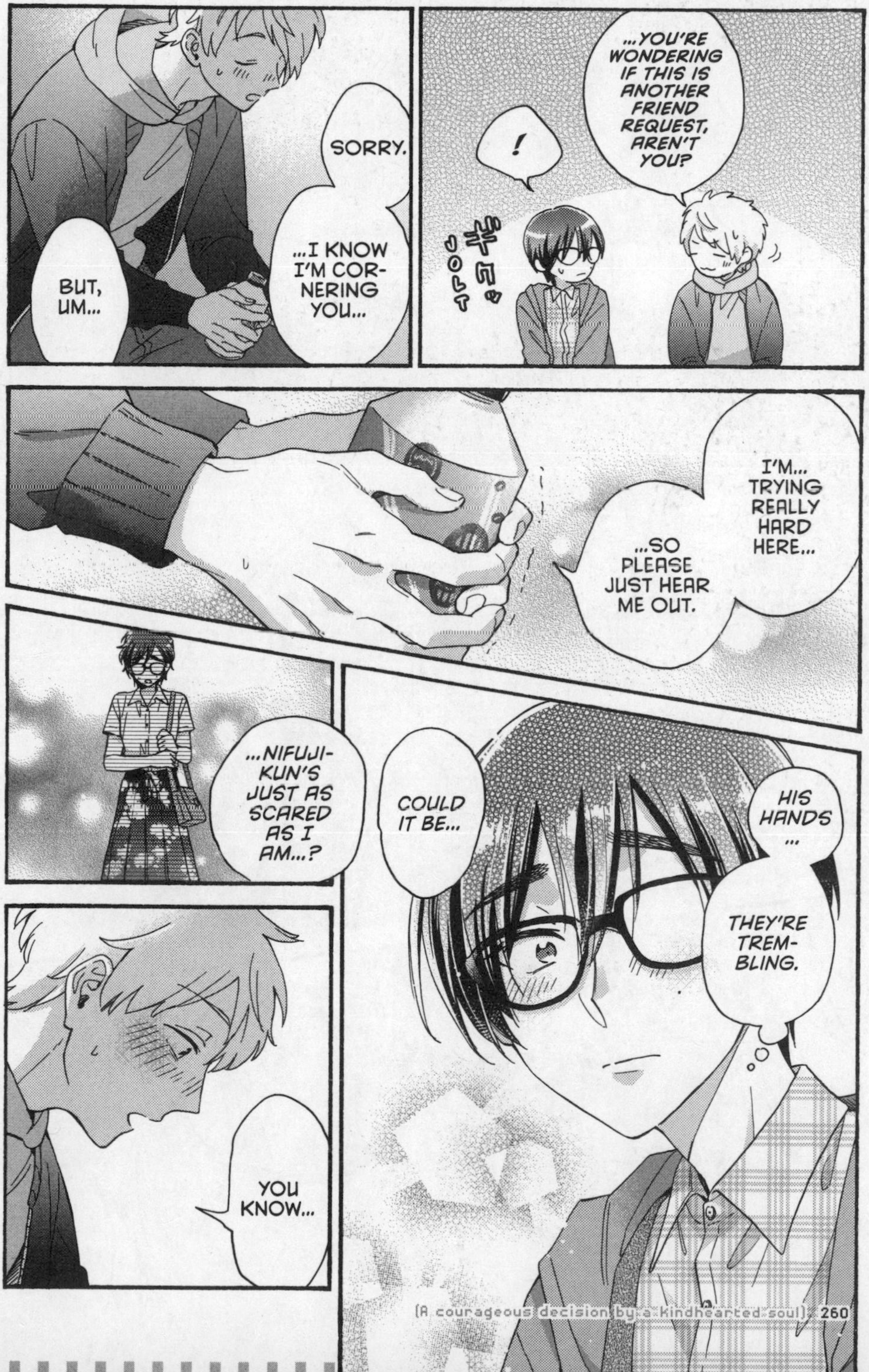
...YOU'RE WONDERING IF THIS IS ANOTHER FRIEND REQUEST, AREN'T YOU?
!
ギクッ
JOLT
SORRY.
...I KNOW I'M CORNERING YOU...
BUT, UM...
I'M... TRYING REALLY HARD HERE...
...SO PLEASE JUST HEAR ME OUT.
HIS HANDS...
THEY'RE TREMBLING.
COULD IT BE...
...NIFUJI-KUN'S JUST AS SCARED AS I AM...?
YOU KNOW...

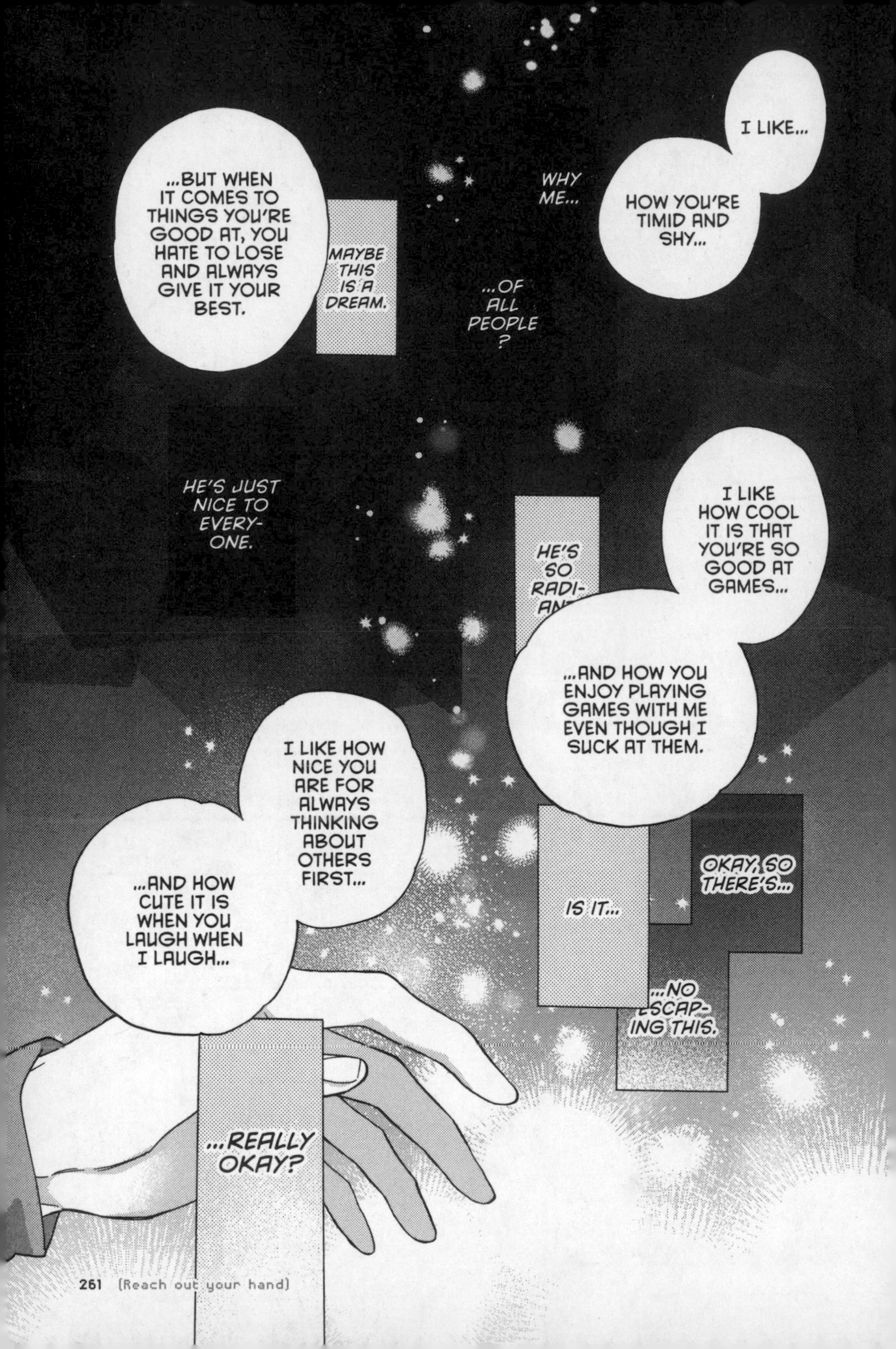
I LIKE...
HOW YOU'RE TIMID AND SHY...
...BUT WHEN IT COMES TO THINGS YOU'RE GOOD AT, YOU HATE TO LOSE AND ALWAYS GIVE IT YOUR BEST.
WHY ME...
...OF ALL PEOPLE?
MAYBE THIS IS A DREAM.
I LIKE HOW COOL IT IS THAT YOU'RE SO GOOD AT GAMES...
...AND HOW YOU ENJOY PLAYING GAMES WITH ME EVEN THOUGH I SUCK AT THEM.
HE'S SO RADI-
HE'S JUST NICE TO EVERY-ONE.
OKAY, SO THERE'S...
...NO
ING THIS.
IS IT...
I LIKE HOW NICE YOU ARE FOR ALWAYS THINKING ABOUT OTHERS FIRST...
...AND HOW CUTE IT IS WHEN YOU LAUGH WHEN I LAUGH...
...REALLY OKAY?

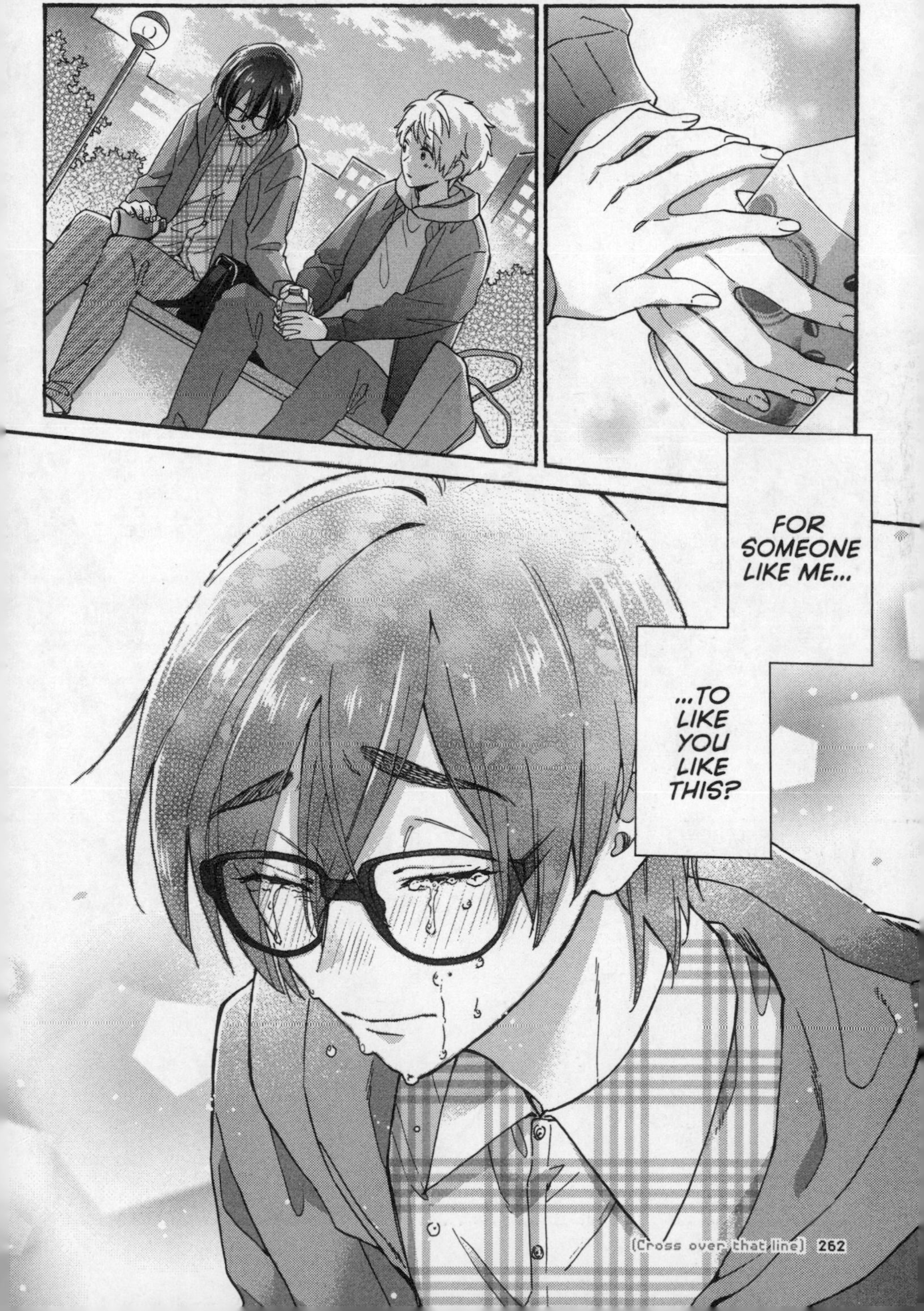
FOR SOMEONE LIKE ME...
...TO LIKE YOU LIKE THIS?

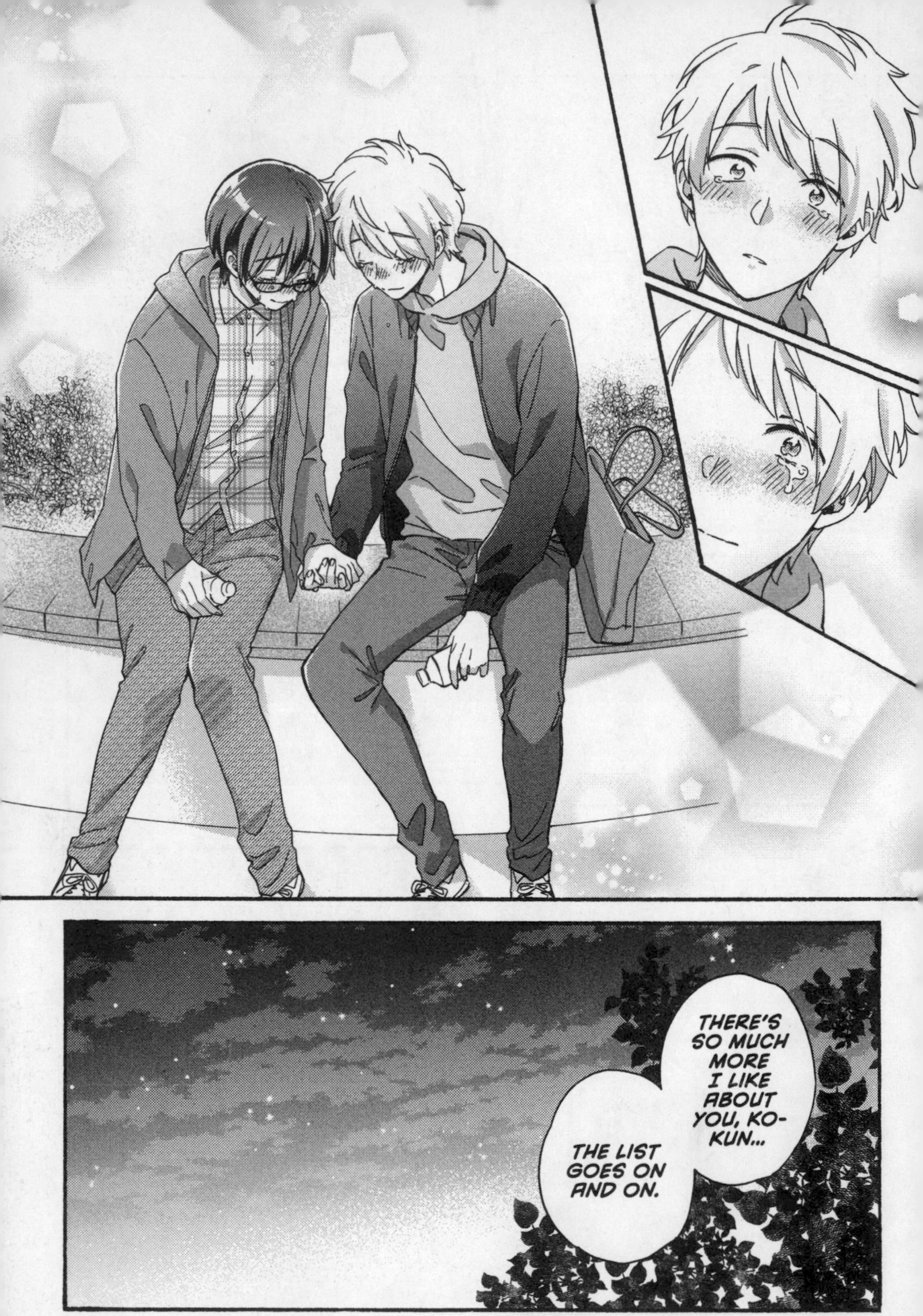
THERE'S SO MUCH MORE I LIKE ABOUT YOU, KO-KUN...
THE LIST GOES ON AND ON.

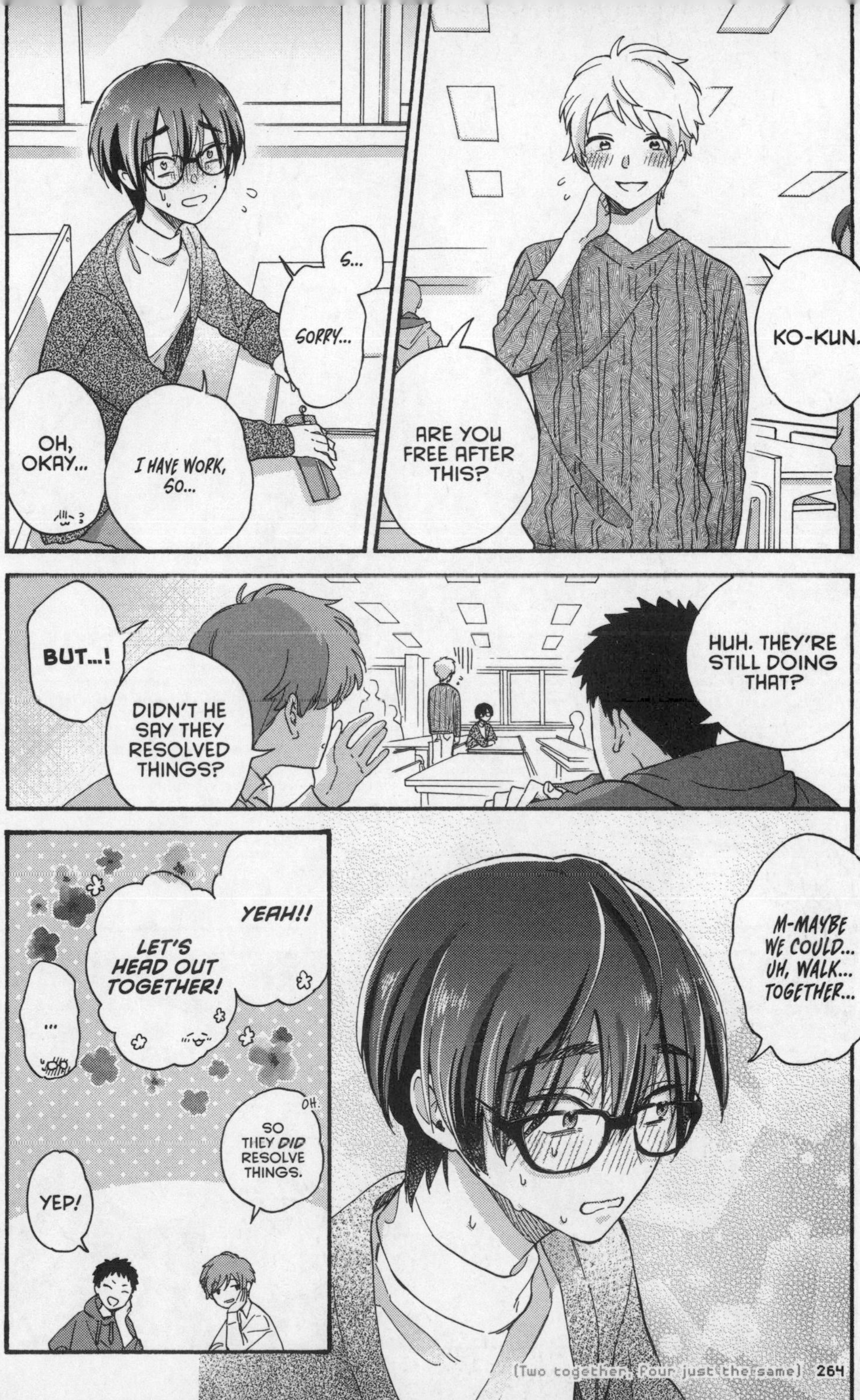
KO-KUN.
ARE YOU FREE AFTER THIS?
S...
SORRY...
I HAVE WORK, SO...
OH, OKAY...
HUH. THEY'RE STILL DOING THAT?
DIDN'T HE SAY THEY RESOLVED THINGS?
BUT...!
M-MAYBE WE COULD... UH, WALK... TOGETHER...
YEAH!!
LET'S HEAD OUT TOGETHER!
...
OH.
SO THEY *DID* RESOLVE THINGS.
YEP!

▶CONTINUE

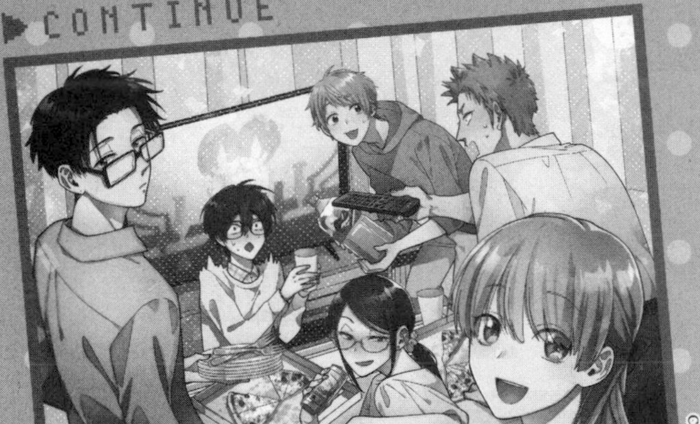
祝1000万部

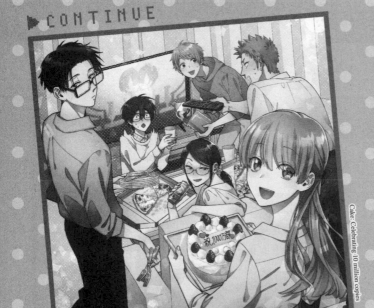

Cake: Celebrating 10 million copies

Banner: Yes! Thank you for Volume 10!

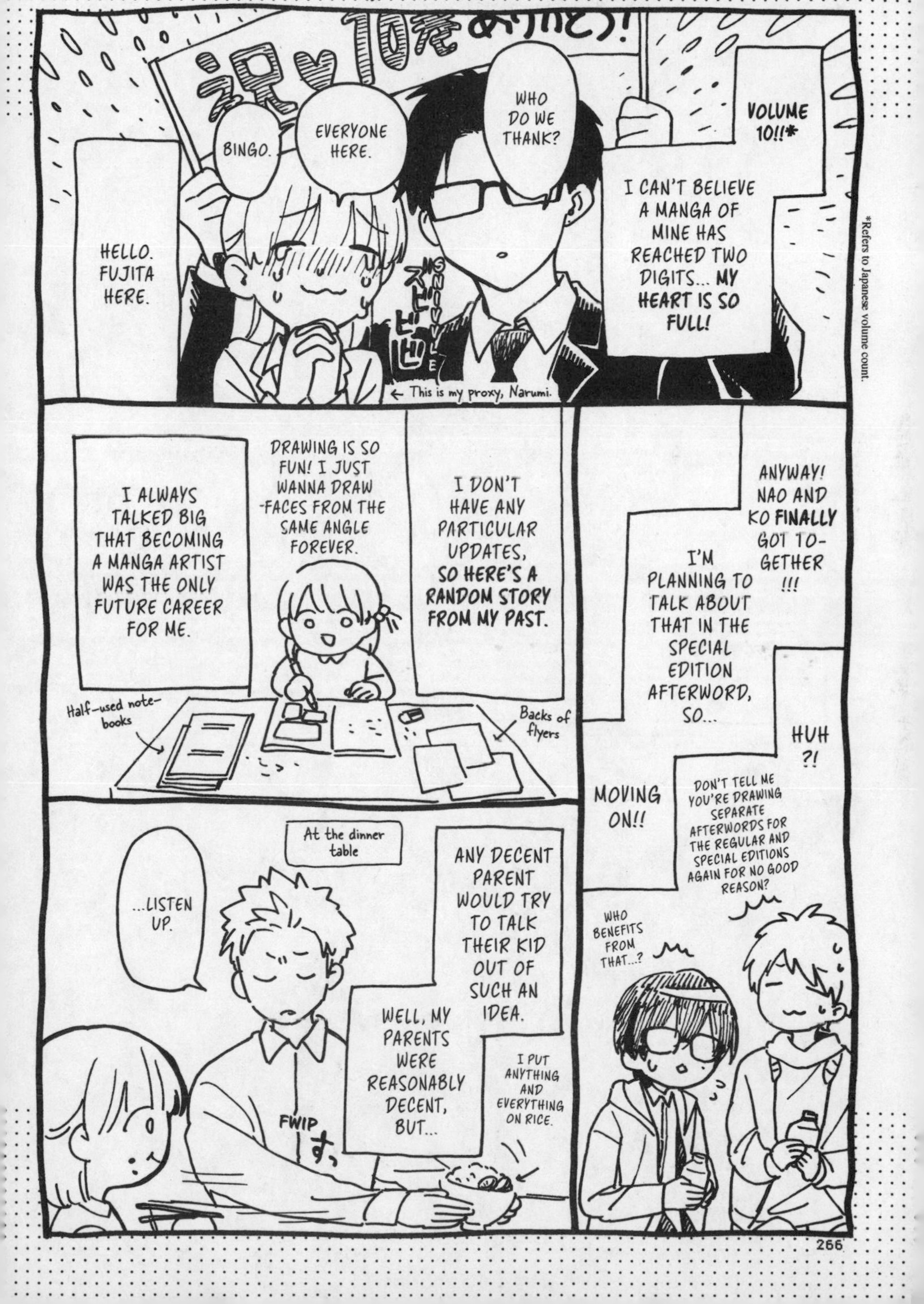
祝♥10巻ありがとう!
VOLUME 10!!*
I CAN'T BELIEVE A MANGA OF MINE HAS REACHED TWO DIGITS... MY HEART IS SO FULL!
WHO DO WE THANK?
EVERYONE HERE.
BINGO.
HELLO. FUJITA HERE.
SNIVVLE
← This is my proxy, Narumi.
ANYWAY! NAO AND KO FINALLY GOT TOGETHER!!!
I'M PLANNING TO TALK ABOUT THAT IN THE SPECIAL EDITION AFTERWORD, SO...
HUH?!
MOVING ON!!
DON'T TELL ME YOU'RE DRAWING SEPARATE AFTERWORDS FOR THE REGULAR AND SPECIAL EDITIONS AGAIN FOR NO GOOD REASON?
WHO BENEFITS FROM THAT...?
I DON'T HAVE ANY PARTICULAR UPDATES, SO HERE'S A RANDOM STORY FROM MY PAST.
DRAWING IS SO FUN! I JUST WANNA DRAW FACES FROM THE SAME ANGLE FOREVER.
I ALWAYS TALKED BIG THAT BECOMING A MANGA ARTIST WAS THE ONLY FUTURE CAREER FOR ME.
Backs of flyers
Half-used notebooks
At the dinner table
ANY DECENT PARENT WOULD TRY TO TALK THEIR KID OUT OF SUCH AN IDEA.
...LISTEN UP.
WELL, MY PARENTS WERE REASONABLY DECENT, BUT...
I PUT ANYTHING AND EVERYTHING ON RICE.
FWIP
すっ

*Refers to Japanese volume count.

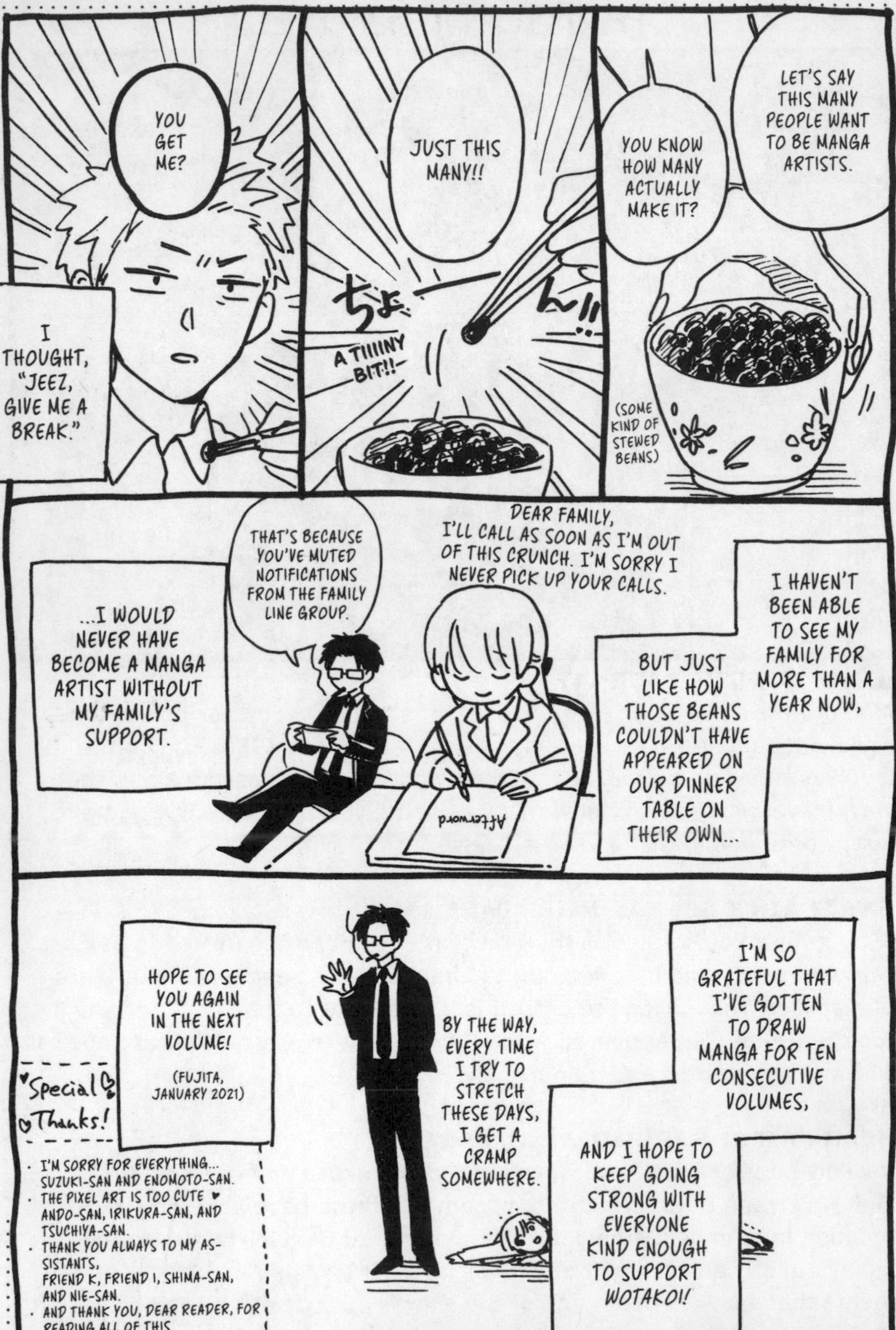
LET'S SAY THIS MANY PEOPLE WANT TO BE MANGA ARTISTS.
YOU KNOW HOW MANY ACTUALLY MAKE IT?
(SOME KIND OF STEWED BEANS)
JUST THIS MANY!!
ちょ—ん!!
A TIIIINY BIT!!
YOU GET ME?
I THOUGHT, "JEEZ, GIVE ME A BREAK."
I HAVEN'T BEEN ABLE TO SEE MY FAMILY FOR MORE THAN A YEAR NOW,
BUT JUST LIKE HOW THOSE BEANS COULDN'T HAVE APPEARED ON OUR DINNER TABLE ON THEIR OWN...
DEAR FAMILY, I'LL CALL AS SOON AS I'M OUT OF THIS CRUNCH. I'M SORRY I NEVER PICK UP YOUR CALLS.
Afterword
THAT'S BECAUSE YOU'VE MUTED NOTIFICATIONS FROM THE FAMILY LINE GROUP.
...I WOULD NEVER HAVE BECOME A MANGA ARTIST WITHOUT MY FAMILY'S SUPPORT.
I'M SO GRATEFUL THAT I'VE GOTTEN TO DRAW MANGA FOR TEN CONSECUTIVE VOLUMES,
AND I HOPE TO KEEP GOING STRONG WITH EVERYONE KIND ENOUGH TO SUPPORT WOTAKOI!
BY THE WAY, EVERY TIME I TRY TO STRETCH THESE DAYS, I GET A CRAMP SOMEWHERE.
HOPE TO SEE YOU AGAIN IN THE NEXT VOLUME!
(FUJITA, JANUARY 2021)
Special Thanks!
· I'M SORRY FOR EVERYTHING... SUZUKI-SAN AND ENOMOTO-SAN.
· THE PIXEL ART IS TOO CUTE ANDO-SAN, IRIKURA-SAN, AND TSUCHIYA-SAN.
· THANK YOU ALWAYS TO MY ASSISTANTS, FRIEND K, FRIEND I, SHIMA-SAN, AND NIE-SAN.
· AND THANK YOU, DEAR READER, FOR READING ALL OF THIS.

TRANSLATION NOTES

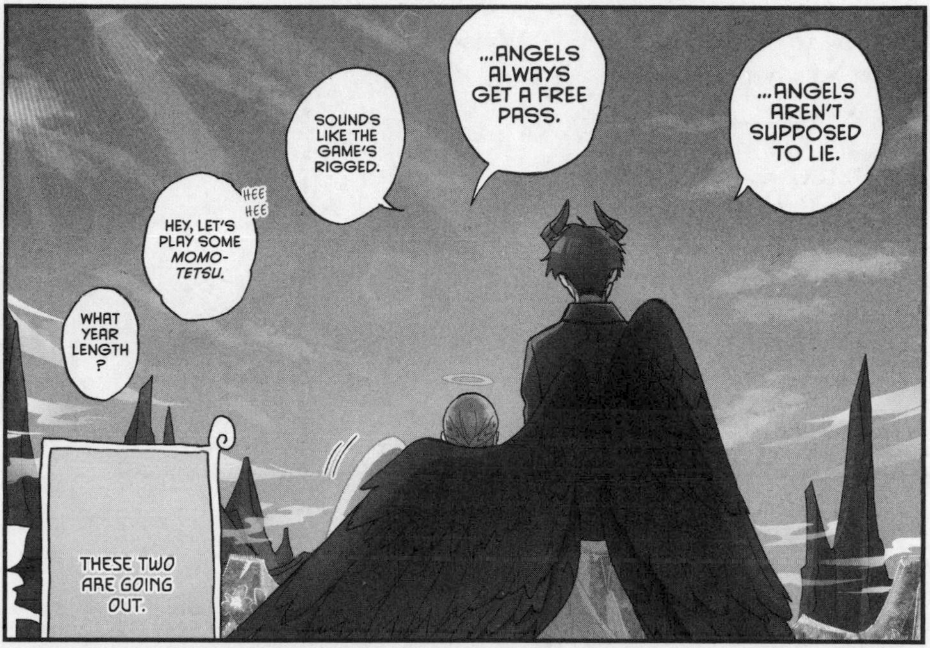
...ANGELS AREN'T SUPPOSED TO LIE.
...ANGELS ALWAYS GET A FREE PASS.
SOUNDS LIKE THE GAME'S RIGGED.
HEE HEE
HEY, LET'S PLAY SOME MOMO-TETSU.
WHAT YEAR LENGTH?
THESE TWO ARE GOING OUT.

▲ *MOMOTESTU,* PAGE 147

Momotaro Dentestu, or *"Momotestu"* for short, is a popular boardgame-style video game series that has been around since 1988. The game involves traveling by rail, sea, and air while acquiring assets along the way. Players can specify how many in-game years they want a game to last, where one in-game year is twelve turns each.

SAY IT AIN'T SO, NARUMIE!, PAGE 151

"Say it Ain't So, Bernie!" is the title of the fifth episode in *Mobile Suit Gundam 0080,* and has since turned into a meme used as an expression of disbelief. The episode title itself is a reference to the headline "Say it Ain't So, Joe!" that appeared when Chicago White Sox outfielder Shoeless Joe Jackson was disgraced in a scandal.

HEAD PRIEST NARUMIMATSU, PAGE 152

A wildly popular variety show called *Gaki no Tsukaiya Arahende!!* (lit. "we ain't no errand boys") featured a segment where people weren't allowed to laugh in funny situations, or else they would be punished. Narumi's use of "Idiot!" and the way she holds up her hands is reminiscent of a meme that spawned from one of the show's episodes that took place in a Buddhist temple.

YOU ARE A LIAR, PAGE 153

The catchphrase of notorious gambler Baku Madarame in the manga series *Usogui* (lit. "Lie Eater"). Madarame has an uncanny knack for knowing when opponents are lying, earning him the eponymous moniker "Lie Eater."

LIAR GAME, PAGE 154

A fictional tournament in the manga series *Liar Game* that pits contestants against each other in games of deception to win money to pay off their debts.

ARE YOU A WEREWOLF?, PAGE 155

A reference to a deception party game in which a group of villagers must find out who among them are the werewolves that are eating them during the night, similar to the game *Mafia*. This type of deception game was not widespread in Japan before the introduction of *Werewolf,* after which its popularity exploded in the early 2010s.

NIFUJI-SAMA: LOVE IS WAR, PAGE 157

A reference to *Kaguya-sama: Love is War,* a romantic comedy anime/manga about two otherwise very intelligent students who stubbornly try to manipulate the other into making the first move in their relationship.

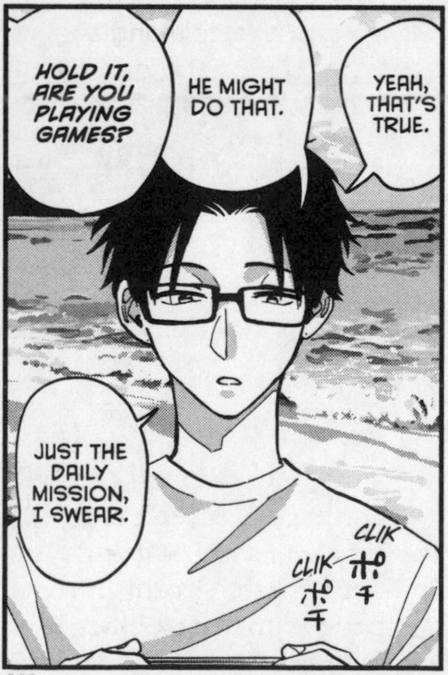
YEAH, THAT'S TRUE.
HE MIGHT DO THAT.
HOLD IT, ARE YOU PLAYING GAMES?
CLIK ポチ
CLIK ポチ
JUST THE DAILY MISSION, I SWEAR.

◀ DAILY MISSION, PAGE 166

A lot of online games have a "daily mission" that gives a player in-game bonuses. These bonuses are often essential to gameplay and encourage the player to play at least once every day.

RED SUPER CHAT, PAGE 170

A Super Chat is a feature on YouTube that allows viewers to send money to their favorite creators during live streams. In return, the viewer gets their comment pinned on the live chat stream, highlighted in the color that corresponds to their contribution amount. Red indicates that the contribution is in the highest range possible.

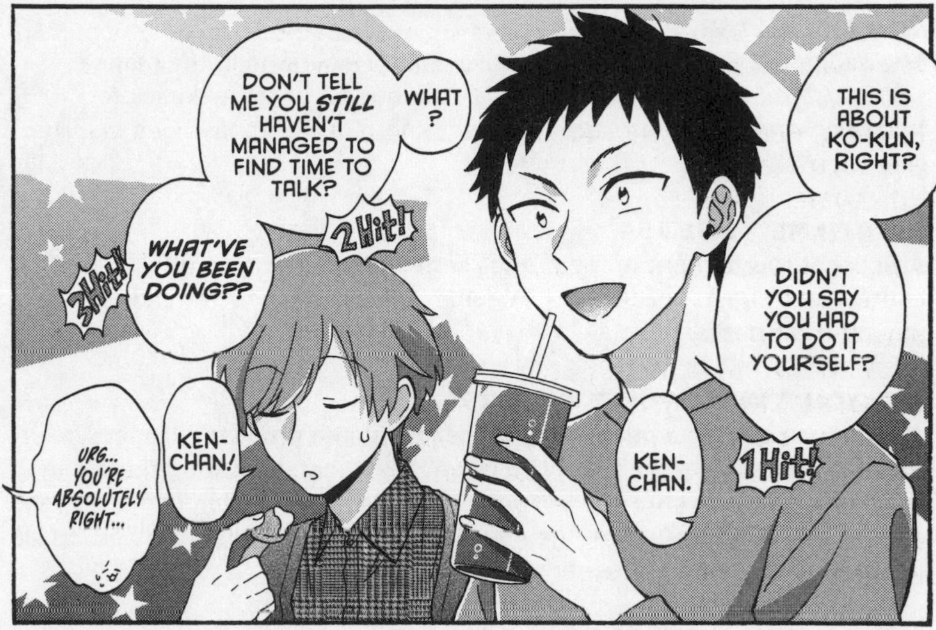
THIS IS ABOUT KO-KUN, RIGHT?
DIDN'T YOU SAY YOU HAD TO DO IT YOURSELF?
1 Hit!
KEN-CHAN.
WHAT?
DON'T TELL ME YOU *STILL* HAVEN'T MANAGED TO FIND TIME TO TALK?
2 Hit!
WHAT'VE YOU BEEN DOING??
3 Hit!
KEN-CHAN!
URG... YOU'RE ABSOLUTELY RIGHT...

▲ FULL COMBO, PAGE 175

A fighting game term that involves successfully executing a sequence of special attacks. Each part of the sequence lands a "hit." In this case, Kensuke's cutting remarks land three consecutive hits on Naoya, achieving a full combo on Naoya's distress.

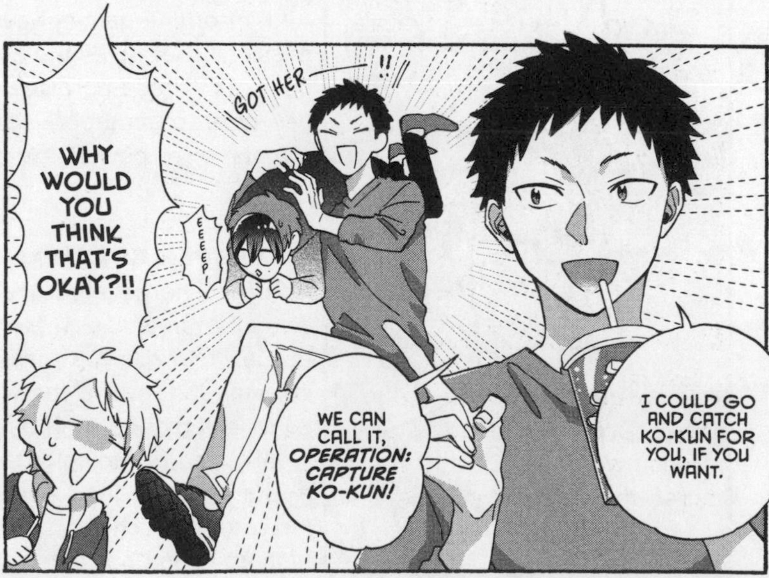
I COULD GO AND CATCH KO-KUN FOR YOU, IF YOU WANT.
WE CAN CALL IT, *OPERATION: CAPTURE KO-KUN!*
GOT HER—!!
EEEEP!
WHY WOULD YOU THINK THAT'S OKAY?!!

▶ GOT HER!, PAGE 176

The term *tottado* (lit. "caught it") is a meme originating from a *Survivor*-like TV show hosted by the comedy

duo Cocorico. Comedian Masaru Hamaguchi was known to yell the phrase when he caught fish or successfully attained something on the show.

POISON BERRY IN MY BRAIN,
HIS AND HER CIRCUMSTANCES,
TOKIMEKI TONIGHT,
KIYOKU, YAWAKU,
TONARI NO KAIBUTSU-KUN,
CHIHAYAFURU,
MARMALADE BOY,
NIGERU WA HAJIDAGA YAKUNITATSU,
WE WERE THERE,
***KIMI NI TODOKE: FROM ME TO YOU,* PAGES 188-197**

These are all popular *shojo* manga titles, fitting in with Ko's unexpected love for the genre. Literal translations were provided for series that either don't have an official English title at the time of writing, or have an official title that didn't quite match the scene.

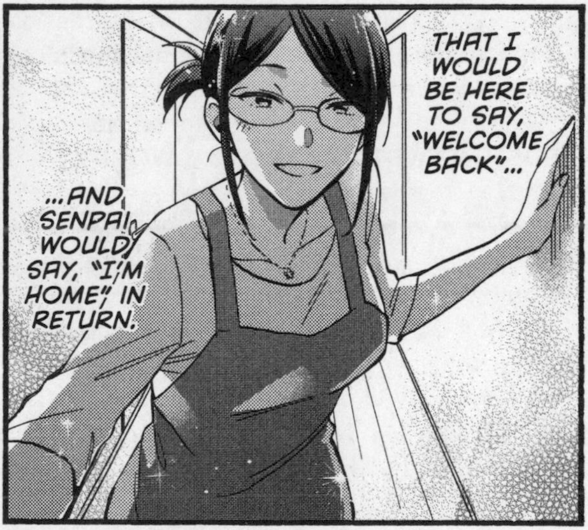
THAT I WOULD BE HERE TO SAY, "WELCOME BACK"...
...AND SENPAI WOULD SAY, "I'M HOME," IN RETURN.

◀ *WELCOME, NEWLYWEDS,* PAGE 202

A reference to a long-running weekly talk show that features interviews with newlywed couples. It first began airing in 1971.

I SEE RIGHT THROUGH YOU, UTTERLY AND COMPLETELY!, PAGE 215

A reference to *Trick,* a popular TV series from the early 2000s that featured the unlikely duo of struggling stage magician Yamada and physics professor Ueda who go around debunking phony spiritualists. Yamada would say this line or some variant of it when she solved the secret behind the con artist's supposed "powers."

▶ (DEAD CERTAIN), PAGE 227
HUH? IT SWITCHED GEARS, PAGE 234

References to trolling jargon and inside jokes used by a 2ch community connected to *A Midsummer Night's Lewd Dream,* a Japanese adult video from the early 2000s known for its terrible acting and production quality. The first reference alludes to the community's frequent use of qualifiers in parentheses, while the second is a comment frequently used to address abrupt transitions in videos.

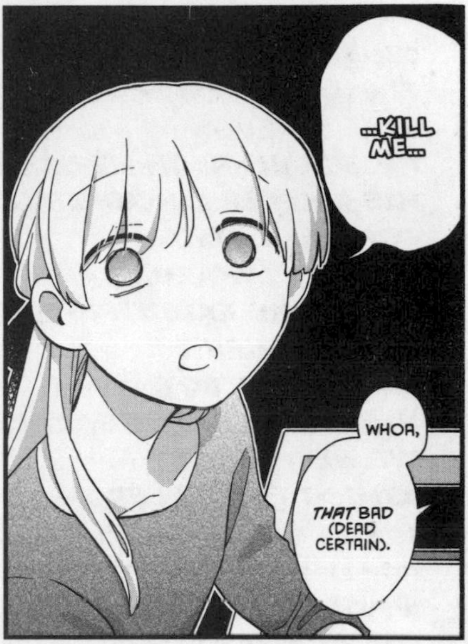

...KILL ME...
WHOA, THAT BAD (DEAD CERTAIN).

FORGET "WAH," IT'S "KILL ME", PAGE 227

This is a reference to slang used by high school girls in Japan, where the Japanese word for "wah" was originally used in situations when one felt a bit like crying. This later evolved into an expression roughly translated as "Forget 'wah,' it's 'bwahh'" for situations that warranted more crying.

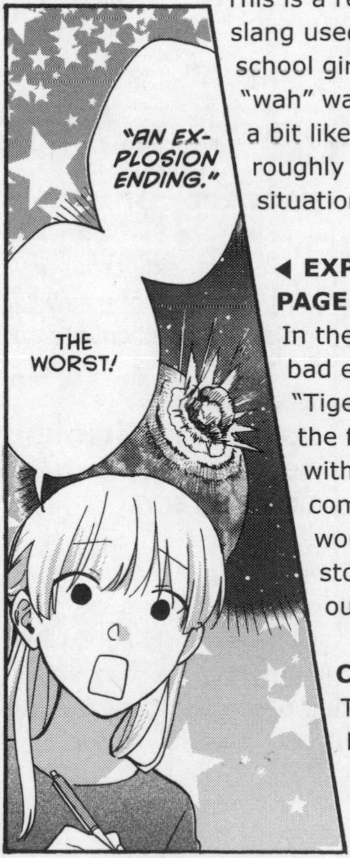

"AN EXPLOSION ENDING."
THE WORST!

◀ EXPLOSION ENDINGS ARE THE WORST, PAGE 230

In the visual novel game *Fate/stay night*, each bad ending is followed by an optional clip called "Tiger Dojo," which offers tips on the game in the form of a comedic skit. One of the skits ends with a nonsensical explosion, with a character commenting that "explosion endings are the worst." This phrase is often used to criticize stories that end with explosions as an easy way out.

COMPROMISE IS DEATH, PAGE 230

The company motto of Kamikaze Douga Co. Ltd., the animation company probably best known for the 2018 animated parody show *Pop Team Epic.*

GOSSIPING SISTERS-IN-LAW, PAGE 239
One stereotypical Japanese image of a sister-in-law is a busybody who loves commenting on her sibling's marriage. In poking fun at Naoya, Kensuke and Yoshiki are acting like his sisters and Ko's sisters-in-law.

I'M NOT AN ANGEL, PAGE 257
A *shojo* manga from the early '90s by Ai Yazawa, the creator of *NANA*. It features a main character likened to an angel, who at some point exclaims, "I'm not actually an angel at all, but I can be an angel for your sake" as she thinks of her love interest who has disappeared abroad. Here, it's a reference to how Naoya was called Ko's "guardian angel," but he exclaimed that he wasn't an angel after all when he realizes his true feelings for Ko earlier in this volume.

▶ SPECIAL EDITION AFTERWORD, PAGE 266
Japanese volume 10 had a special edition that came with a Blu-ray OVA. The manga volume itself has a number of differences between the regular and special versions, including the cover art (featured on page 139) and the afterword.

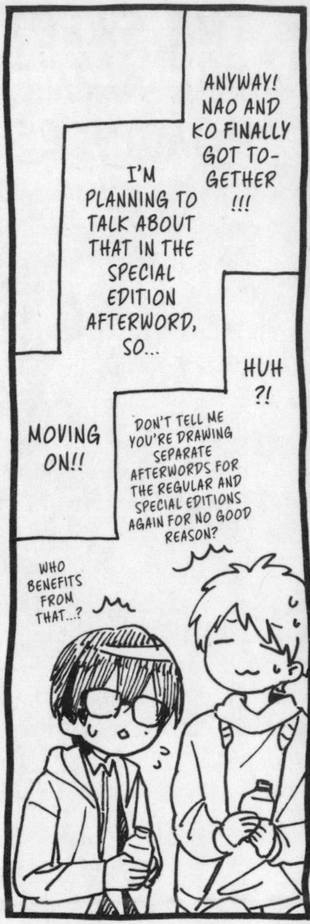
ANYWAY! NAO AND KO FINALLY GOT TO-GETHER !!!
I'M PLANNING TO TALK ABOUT THAT IN THE SPECIAL EDITION AFTERWORD, SO...
HUH ?!
MOVING ON!!
DON'T TELL ME YOU'RE DRAWING SEPARATE AFTERWORDS FOR THE REGULAR AND SPECIAL EDITIONS AGAIN FOR NO GOOD REASON?
WHO BENEFITS FROM THAT...?

▼ LINE, PAGE 267
LINE is the most popular free messaging app in Japan—basically the Japanese equivalent of Whatsapp or KaKaoTalk. Many people use the service to make free calls, and Fujita's family seems to be no exception.

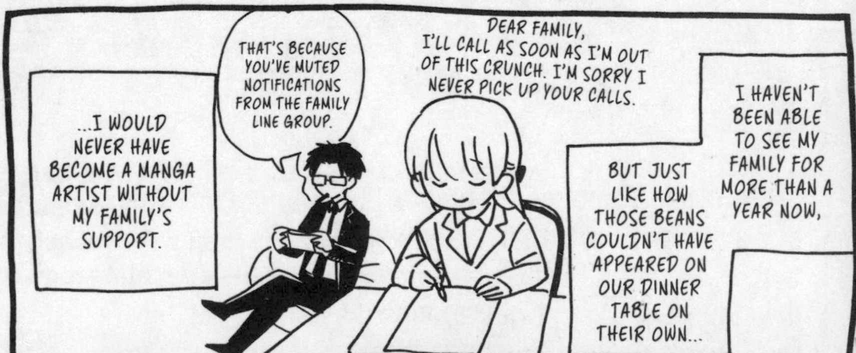
I HAVEN'T BEEN ABLE TO SEE MY FAMILY FOR MORE THAN A YEAR NOW,
BUT JUST LIKE HOW THOSE BEANS COULDN'T HAVE APPEARED ON OUR DINNER TABLE ON THEIR OWN...
DEAR FAMILY, I'LL CALL AS SOON AS I'M OUT OF THIS CRUNCH. I'M SORRY I NEVER PICK UP YOUR CALLS.
THAT'S BECAUSE YOU'VE MUTED NOTIFICATIONS FROM THE FAMILY LINE GROUP.
...I WOULD NEVER HAVE BECOME A MANGA ARTIST WITHOUT MY FAMILY'S SUPPORT.

THE SWEET SCENT OF LOVE IS IN THE AIR! FOR FANS OF OFFBEAT ROMANCES LIKE *WOTAKOI*

Sweat and Soap © Kintetsu Yamada / Kodansha Ltd.

In an office romance, there's a fine line between sexy and awkward... and that line is where Asako — a woman who sweats copiously — meets Koutarou — a perfume developer who can't get enough of Asako's, er, scent. Don't miss a romcom manga like no other!

A SMART, NEW ROMANTIC COMEDY FOR FANS OF *SHORTCAKE CAKE* AND *TERRACE HOUSE*!

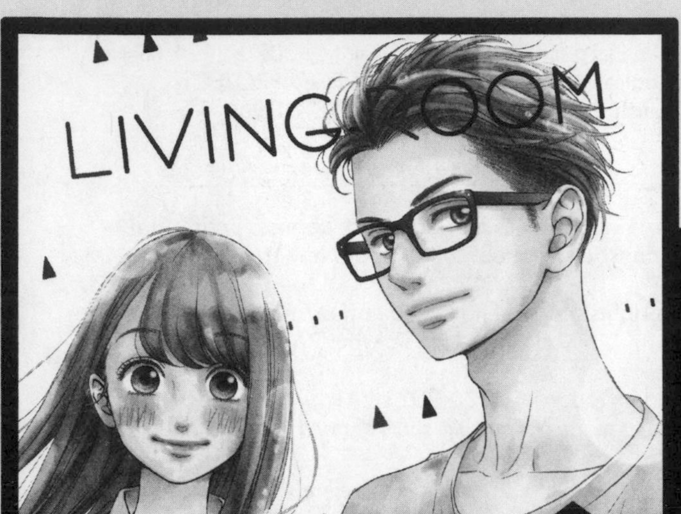
LIVING-ROOM
MATSUNAGA-SAN
1
Keiko Iwashita

KC KODANSHA COMICS

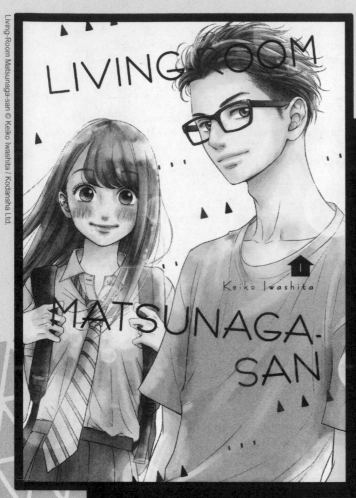

A romance manga starring high school girl Meeko, who learns to live on her own in a boarding house whose living room is home to the odd (but handsome) Matsunaga-san. She begins to adjust to her new life away from her parents, but Meeko soon learns that no matter how far away from home she is, she's still a young girl at heart — especially when she finds herself falling for Matsunaga-san.

Wotakoi: Love is Hard for Otaku 5 is a work of fiction. Names, characters, places, and incidents are the products of the author's imagination or are used fictitiously. Any resemblance to actual events, locales, or persons, living or dead, is entirely coincidental.

A Kodansha Comics Trade Paperback Original

Published in the United States by Kodansha Comics, an imprint of Kodansha USA Publishing, LLC, New York.

Publication rights for this English edition arranged through Kodansha Ltd., Tokyo.

First published in Japan in 2020-2021 by Ichijinsha Inc., Tokyo as *Wotaku ni koi ha muzukashi*, volumes 9 and 10.

ISBN 978-1-64651-363-5

Printed in the United States of America.

www.kodansha.us

2nd Printing
Translation: Sawa Matsueda Savage
Lettering: AndWorld Design
Editing: Vanessa Tenazas
Kodansha Comics edition cover design by Phil Balsman

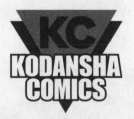

Publisher: Kiichiro Sugawara

Director of publishing services: Ben Applegate
Associate director of operations: Stephen Pakula
Publishing services managing editors: Alanna Ruse, Madison Salters
Production managers: Emi Lotto, Angela Zurlo